W9-CNP-100

THE COLLECTOR'S GUIDE TO

Antique THIRD EDITION

Radios

Identification & Values

— Marty & Sue Bunis —

COLLECTOR BOOKS

A Division of Schroeder Publishing Co., Inc.

The current values of this book should be used only as a guide. They are not intended to set prices, which vary from one section of the country to another. Auction prices as well as dealer prices vary and are affected by condition as well as demand. Neither the Authors nor the Publisher assumes responsibility for any losses that might be incurred as a result of consulting this guide.

Searching for a Publisher?

We are always looking for knowledgeable people considered to be experts within their fields. If you feel that there is a real need for a book on your collectible subject and have a large comprehensive collection, contact us.

Collector Books
P.O. Box 3009
Paducah, KY 42002-3009

On the Cover:

Ace Radio Repair by Bill Bell, © 1987, used with permission.

Cover design by Sherry Kraus
Book design by Terri Stalions

Additional copies of this book may be ordered from:

Collector Books
P.O. Box 3009
Paducah, Kentucky 42002-3009

or

Marty and Sue Bunis
RR 1, Box 36
Bradford, NH 03221
(603) 938-5051

@$18.95. Add $2.00 for postage and handling.
Copyright: Marty and Sue Bunis, 1995

This book or any part thereof may not be reproduced without the written consent of the Authors and Publisher.

Printed by IMAGE GRAPHICS, INC., Paducah, Kentucky

Dedication

This book is dedicated to our special friends, Mazzie & Brozie.

Acknowledgments

Once again, we extend our most sincere thanks to the following people, who provided the radios, photographs, and some of the facts and figures that made this book possible. We couldn't have done this without your help and generosity and we thank you.

Len Arzoomanian, Frank Atwood/Nostalgia Radio, Merrill Bancroft, John Bayusik, Dick and Kay Botzum, Ron Boucher, Rain Buttignol, Peter Burton, Warren Chamberland, Robert Crawford, Dave Crocker, Bob Davidson, Al DeCristofano, John DeLoria, Jean-Bpte. Desautels, Karl Doerflinger, Ward Eaton, Paul Eisenman, John Ellsworth, Richard Foster, Charlie Fox, Ernie Gilford, Bob Goad, Lionel Haid, John Hayes, George Kaczowka, George and Julia Kay, Steve Lange, David Lent, Ray and Rose Lumb, Dick Mackiewicz and Alice Villard, Joe Milano, Tom Mooningham, Al Monroe, Michael Morin, Herb Parsons, Jeff Peterson, Bruce Phillips, Scott and Sue Phillips, Sr., Frances Pond, Dave Pope, Harry Poster, Doyle and Doris Roberts, Steve and Yvonne Slabe, David Smith, Glenn Smith, John Terrey, Ron Trench, Jr., Conrad Trautmann, Rusty Wallace, Cliff Watts, Ralph Williams, Chet Wisner, Wally Worth.

Special thanks to the Leandre Poisson Collection for the following photos: Emerson 400, Emerson 511, Philco 37-610, Philco 42-321, RCA 65X1, Silvertone 4500A, Sylvania 5T13, Telechron 8H67, Teletone 135, and Westinghouse H-474T5.

Sincere thanks also to all those who loaned radio-related paper goods, catalogs, photos, encouragement and constructive suggestions. We appreciate your help and support.

Introduction

Once again, welcome to the wonderful world of Antique Radios!

This third edition of *The Collector's Guide to Antique Radios* features nearly all of the information from the first and second books along with hundreds of new model numbers, updated pricing and all new photographs. Whether you're a newcomer to the fascinating hobby of vintage radio collecting or an "old timer" who has been building a radio collection for many years, we hope you find this book informative and helpful.

You may notice several changes from the previous editions. First, because many radio collectors, especially newcomers to the hobby, are interested in the newer, more affordable plastic radios from the 1960's, we have expanded our listings of those sets. Second, you will no longer find any transistor radios listed here with the tube sets. Because transistors are fast becoming important collectibles in their own right, we have written *The Collector's Guide To Transistor Radios,* in which you will find over 2,000 models listed along with over 400 full color photos — all exclusively on transistor radios.

Be sure to check the back of this book for current information on antique radio clubs throughout the country. Radio collecting is growing at a rapid pace and there are new clubs forming all the time. We recommend joining a club near you — it's a great way to meet others with the same interests.

Explanation of Pricing Section

Many of the prices listed in this book are the same as or lower than they have been in previous editions, due entirely to the state of the economy in the last few years. Cathedral prices are among those hardest hit, with many formerly high priced sets decreasing considerably in value. However, despite bad economic conditions, some radio prices have held the line or even increased, especially those of the ever popular Deco, streamlined, novelty and hard-to-find sets.

A special note to Catalin collectors:

Catalin radios are still the most avidly sought after and hardest to find in good condition radios around and, despite the predictions (usually made by battery set collectors who are shocked that a 1940's radio can be worth thousands of dollars) that the bottom has to fall out of the Catalin market any day now, many of them still continue to command high prices. Because there are so many factors that affect the price of Catalin sets — color, the smallest stress cracks, heat discoloration, the part of the country you're in — it is impossible to establish firm prices and we have chosen to generalize the pricing in this book. You will find most Catalin prices followed by a "+," which means you should expect to pay at least this much for a set in good condition, depending on the above variables.

The pricing information in this book is provided for the potential buyer and has been gathered from many different sources: regional and national radio meets, flea markets, auctions, private collectors, various antique radio classified magazines, etc. Our method is to gather as many prices as possible on each set and take an average to arrive at a fairly current figure. Keep in mind there is no "suggested retail price" for old radios and pricing is extremely variable and depends on many factors.

The primary factor when considering whether an old radio is "worth it" is CONDITION. We have tried to provide pricing that reflects sets in "good" condition, using the following guidelines:

1. **Electronically complete.** Although the set may not be working, all the electrical components, including tubes, are there and a minimal amount of repair would bring it to operating condition.

2. **Cabinet in good condition.** All knobs and other removable parts are in place. There are no cracks, chips or other highly visible damage to the case.

These prices in no way reflect sets in "MINT" condition — very few old radios fall into that category. There may be an occasional set that was very seldom or never used that may be close to or even mint, but most radios were a vital and functional part of the household and they will usually bear a few nicks and scratches and show some signs of wear.

A secondary factor in determining a fair price for an old set is where you happen to be at the time. Prices generally tend to be higher on the West Coast than the East Coast, auctions are usually more expensive than yard sales, etc.

Naturally if you have a radio for sale, you want to receive the best possible price. Keep in mind that radio prices are very volatile and are more dependent on condition than age. For example, we receive many phone calls and letters from people who have sets for sale, and we *always* ask very specifically about the condition. We have learned this the hard way — too many times we have been told that a radio has been "in storage" for years and is in "good" condition only to arrive and find a dirty set that has been sitting in a damp basement or hot attic for years, with a grill cloth full of cat scratches, peeling veneer, missing knobs, no tubes and the sellers expect to get top dollar because the set is OLD! Remember, "OLD" does not necessarily mean "GOOD!" To avoid disappointment, the best policy is to be realistic about your radio's condition when you contact a potential buyer.

Basic Radio Terms and Descriptive Information

1. **Addresses** – We have included addresses for as many companies as possible, along with brief histories of a few of the well-known companies. This is not necessarily complete information; many radio companies, especially during the 1920's, went in and out of business so fast, or merged with one another so often, or moved so frequently that it is sometimes impossible to pinpoint exact addresses and historical background.

2. **Model Numbers** – Model numbers are tricky critters! There seems to be no consistency to them sometimes; even within a given company's advertising, model numbers can be written several different ways. For example: A model #AR36-809 might be written AR-36-809 or AR36809 or even AR-36809! The best plan is to use a little creativity when searching for model numbers in this price guide. We have tried to list them in a logical numerical sequence, so try different combinations until you find the right one.

3. **Style** – There are many different types or styles of radios available. We have used various common descriptive terms in this price guide. The following is a basic description of each:

Breadboard – An early radio with the tubes and other component parts attached to a rectangular board that usually has "breadboard" ends. Breadboard radios have no cases or covers, all parts and tubes are exposed.

Cathedral – Sometimes referred to as "beehives," cathedrals are taller than wide with a top that is usually rounded or sometimes comes to a rounded peak, generally thought to resemble a cathedral window in shape. The cathedral is the "classic" radio shape.

Chairside – A console radio with a low shape made to sit beside an armchair, usually with the controls on the top within easy reach.

Console – The console is also called a floor model. It can consist of a cabinet on legs or just a rectangular (higher than wide) case that sits directly on the floor.

Portable – A radio made to be used in the home as well as outdoors or in a location with no electricity. Most portables run on battery power, although a great many are three-way sets, using electricity or batteries.

Table – A general term used to describe many shapes and sizes of radios that are table-top sets.

Tombstone – These are sets that are rectangular in shape, higher than they are wide and are flat on top; generally they resemble the shape of a tombstone. They are sometimes called "upright table" models.

C – Clock.

N – Novelty. This is a very broad term and covers all radios that are highly collectible due to their unusual case, whether they sport a Mickey Mouse, a Charlie McCarthy, a built-in camera, look like a baseball, a bar, a bottle or any other design where one would not expect to find a radio.

R/P – Radio/phono combination.

R/P/Rec – Radio/phono/recorder combination.

R/P/Rec/PA - Radio/phono/recorder/public address system combination.

4. **Year** – We have tried to list the correct year for most of the sets listed; however, there is some flexibility here as many manufacturers overlapped models from one year to the next and many popular models were made for a number of years.

5. **Description** – We have included, wherever possible, the material of which the case is made, a general description of the set's shape, placement of the dial, grill and knobs, power source(s), bands, and any other information important to identifying each set. The following terms are frequently used in the descriptions:

AC – Alternating Current

Airplane Dial – A dial which moves in a 360 degree circle.

BC – Broadcast

DC – Direct Current

Highboy – A floor model radio whose legs can be as much as half the total height of the case.

Lowboy – A floor model radio whose legs are considerably lower than a highboy's; generally, less than half the height of the case.

LW – Long Wave.

Midget – A small table set, usually less than seven inches in its longest measurement.

Movie Dial – A dial which features a projected image from a circular film rotating around a bulb.

Plastic – We have used the word "plastic" as a generic term to cover most, but not all, plastics. In the case of Catalin plastics, we have used the word "Catalin" specifically rather than the generic word "plastic," because of the much higher pricing structure of Catalin sets.

Repwood – A type of pressed wood popular in the 1930's and used to make various decorative items, including ornate radio cases that have a beautiful "carved" appearance.

Robot Dial – A feature of some Zenith radios, the robot dial is really three dials in one — standard broadcast, shortwave and police/amateur. Only one dial is visible at any time and can be changed by the turn of a lever.

Slide Rule Dial – A rectangular dial, usually horizontal, which features a thin sliding indicator.

SW – Short Wave.

6. **Pictures** – We have tried, to the best of our ability, to photograph only sets that are as close to original as possible. There may be a few pictures included here that show radios with replacement knobs or grill cloths, but in most cases the replacements blend well with the sets and should not be considered a detriment.

Keep in mind that this is a GUIDE only and it is was written to do just that — guide you with identification information and current pricing. Because there are so many variables to consider and radio prices are changing so rapidly, we make no guarantees that these prices are hard and fast but we do recommend that you use your judgement when considering the purchase of an old radio — if it is in good condition, the price seems fair according to the book and you like it — buy it!

A-C DAYTON
The A-C Electrical Mfg. Co., Dayton, Ohio
The A-C Dayton Company, Dayton, Ohio

The A-C Electrical Manufacturing Company began business in Dayton, Ohio, in 1901 as a manufacturer of electric motors. By 1922 they were manufacturing and selling radios and radio parts. The company was out of business by 1930.

AC-63, table, 1928, wood, low rectangular case, center front dial w/large escutcheon, lift top, 6 tubes, AC $100.00

AC-65, table, 1928, wood, low rectangular case, center front dial w/large escutcheon, lift top, AC $100.00

AC-98 "Navigator," table, 1929, wood, low rectangular case, center front window dial w/escutcheon, lift top, battery........$100.00

AC-9960 "Navigator," console, 1929, wood, lowboy, upper front window dial, metal escutcheon, lower round grill, 3 knobs, battery.....$115.00

AC-9970 "Navigator," console, 1929, wood, lowboy, inner window dial, metal escutcheon, lower round grill w/cut-outs, double sliding doors, battery $130.00

AC-9980 "Navigator," console, 1929, wood, lowboy, upper front window dial, metal escutcheon, lower grill w/vertical bars, battery $115.00

AC-9990 "Navigator," console, 1929, wood, highboy, inner window dial, metal escutcheon, lower cloth grill w/cut-outs, 3 knobs, double doors, battery $145.00

R-12, table, 1924, mahogany finish, low rectangular case, 3 dial front panel, 4 tubes, battery....................................$125.00

XL-5, table-glass, 1925, plate glass, low see-through rectangular case, 3 dial front panel, 5 tubes, battery $250.00

XL-5, table, 1925, wood, low rectangular case, 3 dial front panel, lift top, 5 tubes, battery $110.00

XL-10, table, 1924, wood, low rectangular case, 3 dial front panel, lift top, 5 tubes, battery $135.00

XL-15, console, 1923, wood, highboy, 3 dial front panel, storage, 5 tubes, battery $165.00

XL-20, table, 1926, wood, high rectangular case, slanted 3 dial front panel, lift top, battery.......................................$135.00

XL-25, table, 1926, wood, low rectangular case, 2 dial front panel, lift top, 5 tubes, battery $175.00

XL-30, table, 1925, wood, low rectangular case, 2 dial front panel w/escutcheons, meter, fluted columns, battery $130.00

XL-50, table, 1927, walnut, low rectangular case, 1 front dial w/metal escutcheon, 2 knobs, 6 tubes, AC $85.00

XL-60, console, 1927, wood, lowboy, inner dial & knobs, fold-down front, battery storage, 6 tubes, battery..............$250.00

XL-61, table, 1928, wood, low rectangular case, center front dial w/ large escutcheon, 6 tubes, battery.........................$80.00

XL-71 "Navigator," table, 1929, wood, low rectangular case, center front window dial w/metal escutcheon, battery........$85.00

ABBOTWARES
Los Angeles, California

Z477, table-N, metal horse w/saddle stands on radio base, 2 knobs, horizontal grill bars, BC..................................$285.00

ACE
The Precision Equipment Co., Inc., Peebles Corner, Cincinnati, Ohio

In 1922, Crosley bought Precision Equipment but continued to use the old Precision "Ace" trademark on this line until 1924.

Type 3B, table, 1923, wood, low rectangular case, 1 dial black front panel, lift top, battery..$160.00

Type V, table, 1923, wood, low rectangular case, 1 dial black front panel, lift top, 1 tube, battery $190.00

ACRATONE
Federated Purchasers, Inc.
25 Park Place, New York, New York

87, console-R/P, 1934, wood, upper front dial, lower cloth grill w/cut-outs, lift top, inner phono, feet $150.00

ADDISON
Addison Industries, Ltd.
Toronto, Ontario, Canada

5F, table, 1940, Catalin, shouldered, upper front slide rule dial, lower cloth grill w/5 vertical bars, 3 "pinwheel" knobs, AM/SW, AC ....$1,000.00+

A2A, table (Catalin), 1940, Catalin, Deco, right front dial, left vertical wrap-over grill bars, 2 "pinwheel" knobs, AC ....$1,000.00+

A2A, table (plastic), 1940, plastic, Deco, right front dial, left vertical wrap-over grill bars, 2 "pinwheel" knobs, AC $350.00

B2E, table, plastic, Deco, right front dial, left vertical wrap-over grill bars, 2 "pinwheel" knobs, AC..............................$350.00

ADLER
Adler Manufacturing Co.
881 Broadway, New York, New York

199 "Royal," table, 1924, wood, low rectangular case, 3 dial front panel, 5 tubes, battery...$150.00

201-A "Royal," table, 1924, walnut or mahogany, low rectangular case, 3 dial front panel, 5 tubes, battery $125.00

324, console, 1930, wood, highboy, inner dial, cloth grill w/cut-outs, double front doors, stretcher base.....................$150.00

325, console, 1930, wood, highboy, inner dial, cloth grill w/cut-outs, double front doors, stretcher base $150.00

ADMIRAL
Continental Radio & Television Corporation
3800 W. Cortland Street, Chicago, Illinois
Admiral Corporation, 3800 W. Cortland St., Chicago, Illinois

Admiral was founded as the Continental Radio & Television Corporation in 1934 by a group of four investors, some of whom literally sold their belongings to raise the initial capital. Growing rapidly due to the production of good products at affordable prices, the company ranked #5 in sales volume by 1939. Because of quality control problems and competition from Japanese TV manufacturers, the company was forced to close its last plant in 1979.

4A4, table, plastic, lower right front dial knob & lower left front on/off/volume knob over large textured grill area, feet, AC/DC **$10.00**

4D11, portable, 1948, plastic, right side dial, front vertical wrap-over grill bars, stand-up handle, 2 knobs, BC, 4 tubes, battery ....:..**$45.00**

4L21, table, 1958, ebony plastic, upper right front dial overlaps vertical grill bars, 2 knobs, BC, 4 tubes, AC/DC **$15.00**

4L24, table, 1958, pink plastic, upper right front dial overlaps vertical grill bars, 2 knobs, BC, 4 tubes, AC/DC..................**$15.00**

4L26, table, 1958, yellow plastic, upper right front dial overlaps vertical grill bars, 2 knobs, BC, 4 tubes, AC/DC **$15.00**

4L27B, table, 1958, plastic, upper right front dial overlaps vertical grill bars, 2 knobs, BC, 4 tubes, AC/DC $15.00

4L28, table, 1958, turquoise plastic, upper right front dial overlaps vertical grill bars, 2 knobs, BC, 4 tubes, AC/DC $15.00

4V18, portable, 1952, plastic, upper front half-round dial, lower lattice grill area, top thumbwheel on/off knob, flex handle, BC, AC/DC **$35.00**

4W19, portable, 1951, plastic, front raised dial, lower lattice grill, flex handle, top right button, BC, AC/DC/battery **$40.00**

4Z12, portable, 1954, maroon plastic, top dial, front metal perforated grill with center emblem, handle, BC, AC/DC/battery...**$40.00**

4Z14, portable, 1954, beige plastic, top dial, front metal perforated grill with center emblem, handle, BC, AC/DC/battery....**$40.00**

4Z18, portable, 1954, green plastic, top dial, front metal perforated grill with center emblem, handle, BC, AC/DC/battery **$40.00**

4Z19, portable, 1954, light gray plastic, top dial, front metal perforated grill with center emblem, handle, BC, AC/DC/battery **$40.00**

5A32/16, table-C, 1953, plastic, metal front panel, right round dial, left round alarm clock, 4 knobs, BC, 5 tubes, AC.........**$30.00**

5A33, table-C, 1952, plastic, round clock & round dial faces, gold front, AC **$30.00**

5E22, table, 1951, plastic, center front round dial with inner perforated grill, handle, 2 knobs, BC, AC/DC **$25.00**

5F11, portable, 1949, plastic, inner right dial, center lattice grill, flip-up front, handle, BC, AC/DC/battery **$35.00**

5G22, table-C, 1951, plastic, right front square dial & left square alarm clock over vertical bars, 4 knobs, BC, AC **$30.00**

5G32N, table, plastic, raised top, upper front slide rule dial, lower horizontal bars, 2 knobs, BC **$30.00**

5J21, table, 1951, plastic, right trapezoid dial, left horizontal grill openings, 2 knobs, BC, AC/DC **$30.00**

5J23, table, 1951, painted plastic, right trapezoid dial, left horizontal grill openings, 2 knobs, BC............................$30.00

5K32, portable, 1954, maroon plastic, top dial, front metal perforated grill with emblem, handle, 2 knobs, BC, AC/DC/battery **$40.00**

5K34, portable, 1954, beige plastic, top dial, front metal perforated grill with emblem, handle, 2 knobs, BC, AC/DC/battery **$40.00**

5K38, portable, 1954, green plastic, top dial, front metal perforated grill with emblem, handle, 2 knobs, BC, AC/DC/battery **$40.00**

5K39, portable, 1954, light gray plastic, top dial, front metal perforated grill with emblem, handle, 2 knobs, BC, AC/DC/battery **$40.00**

5L21, table-C, 1952, plastic, right front square dial w/inner perforations & left square alarm clock over vertical bars, BC, AC **$30.00**

5M21, table-R/P, 1952, plastic, front round dial w/inner concentric circular louvers, 2 knobs, 3/4 lift top, inner phono, BC, AC **$45.00**

5R11, table, 1949, plastic, right front square dial, left square checkerboard grill, 2 knobs, BC, AC/DC **$30.00**

5R11UL, table, 1949, plastic, right front square dial, left square checkerboard grill, 2 knobs, BC, AC/DC **$30.00**

5R12-N, table, 1949, plastic, right front square dial, left square checkerboard grill, 2 knobs, BC, AC/DC **$30.00**

5R35N, table, plastic, upper right front dial knob over horizontal bars, left lattice grill area, feet, BC **$15.00**

5S22AN, table, 1953, plastic, right front curved dial, off-center concentric circular louvers, 2 knobs, BC, AC **$35.00**

5T12, table-R/P, 1949, plastic, upper front slide rule dial, lower criss-cross grill, 3 knobs, lift top, inner phono, BC, AC...**$45.00**

5W12, table-R/P, 1949, plastic, center front round dial w/inner concentric circular louvers, 2 knobs, 3/4 lift top, inner phono, BC, AC **$50.00**

5X12, table, 1949, plastic, right front round dial over horizontal grill bars, 2 knobs, BC, AC/DC **$30.00**

5X12N, table, 1949, plastic, right front round dial over horizontal grill bars, 2 knobs, BC, AC/DC **$30.00**

5X13, table, 1949, plastic, right front round dial over horizontal grill bars, 2 knobs, BC, AC/DC **$30.00**

5X22, table-C, 1953, plastic, lower front slide rule dial, large upper alarm clock, side grill, 4 knobs, BC, AC **$35.00**

5X23, table-C, 1953, plastic, lower front slide rule dial, large upper alarm clock, side grill, 4 knobs, BC, AC **$35.00**

5Y22, table-R/P, 1952, plastic, center front round dial w/inner concentric circular louvers, 2 knobs, 3/4 lift top, inner phono, BC, 5 tubes, AC...**$45.00**

5Z, table, 1937, plastic & chrome, can be used horizontally or vertically, 2 grill bars, BC, 5 tubes, AC **$85.00**

5Z22, table, 1952, plastic, large center front metal dial with inner perforated grill area, 2 knobs, BC, AC.............$30.00

6A22, table, 1950, plastic, right front round dial w/center crest over horizontal grill bars, 2 knobs, BC, AC/DC **$30.00**

6C11, portable, 1949, plastic, inner right dial, center lattice grill, flip-up front, molded handle, BC, 5 tubes, AC/DC/battery **$35.00**

6C22, table, 1954, plastic, large center front gold metal dial over cloth grill, feet, center knob, AC/DC **$45.00**

6C22AN, table, 1954, plastic, large center front gold metal dial over cloth grill, feet, center knob **$45.00**

6C71, console-R/P, 1946, wood, upper front slide rule dial, 4 knobs, 6 pushbuttons, center pull-out phono w/doors, lower grill, BC, 3SW, AC **$90.00**

6J21, table-R/P, 1949, plastic, front round dial w/inner concentric circular louvers, 2 knobs, 3/4 lift top, inner phono, BC, AC...**$55.00**

6J21N, table-R/P, 1950, plastic, front round dial w/inner concentric circular louvers, 2 knobs, 3/4 lift top, inner phono, BC, AC **$55.00**

6N26, console-R/P, 1952, wood, inner pull-out radio/phono, slide rule dial, 3 knobs, double doors, lower grill, BC, AC **$50.00**

6P32, portable, 1946, simulated alligator, inner right dial, left palm tree grill, 2 knobs, fold down front, double handle, BC, AC/DC/battery **$75.00**

6Q12, table, 1949, plastic, right front round dial over horizontal louvers, 2 knobs, AM, FM, AC/DC **$30.00**

6R11, table-R/P, 1949, plastic, upper front slide rule dial, lower criss-cross grill, 3 knobs, lift top, inner phono, BC, FM, AC.......**$45.00**

6RT42A, table-R/P, 1947, wood, lower front slide rule dial, upper grill w/3 horizontal bars, 2 knobs, lift top, inner phono, BC, AC **$35.00**

6RT43-5BL, table-R/P, 1946, wood, lower front slide rule dial, upper horizontal louvers, 3/4 lift top, inner phono, 2 knobs, BC, AC **$35.00**

6RT44, table-R/P, 1947, wood, lower front dial, upper horizontal grill bars, 4 knobs, 3/4 lift top, inner phono, BC, SW, AC **$35.00**

6RT44A-7B1, table-R/P, 1947, wood, lower front slide rule dial, upper horizontal louvers, 4 knobs, lift top, inner phono, AC **$35.00**

6S12, table-R/P, 1950, plastic, front round dial w/inner concentric circular louvers, 2 knobs, 3/4 lift top, inner phono, BC, AC...**$55.00**

6T01, table, 1946, plastic, lower front slide rule dial, upper horizontal louvers, 2 knobs, BC, 6 tubes, AC/DC...............**$30.00**

6T02, table, 1946, plastic, lower front slide rule dial, upper horizontal louvers, 2 knobs, BC, AC/DC **$35.00**

6T02-5B1-MA, table, plastic, lower front slide rule dial, upper horizontal louvers, 2 knobs $35.00

6T06, table, 1946, two-tone wood, lower front slide rule dial, upper cloth grill w/circular cut-outs, 2 knobs, BC, battery........**$45.00**

6V12, table-R/P, 1949, plastic, upper front slide rule dial, lower criss-cross grill, 3 knobs, lift top, inner phono, BC, AC...**$45.00**

6W12, table-R/P, 1949, plastic, upper front slide rule dial, lower criss-cross grill, 3 knobs, lift top, inner phono, BC, FM, AC **$45.00**

6Y18, portable, 1949, leatherette, inner right dial, center lattice grill, fold-down front, handle, BC, AC/DC/battery **$35.00**

7C60M, console-R/P, 1948, wood, inner slide rule dial/4 knobs/phono, lift top, lower record storage, BC, AC **$60.00**

7C62, console-R/P, 1947, wood, upper front dial w/large escutcheon, 4 knobs, center fold-down phono door, lower grill, BC, AC **$60.00**

7C63-UL, console-R/P, 1947, wood, upper front dial w/large escutcheon, 4 knobs, center fold-down phono door, lower grill, BC, SW, AC **$60.00**

7C65W, console-R/P, 1948, wood, inner right dial & 4 knobs, door, left pull-down phono door, lower 2 section grill, BC, AC **$60.00**

7G14, console-R/P, 1949, wood, inner right dial & 3 knobs, door, left fold-down phono door, lower grill & storage, BC, AC........**$65.00**

7P33, portable, 1947, briefcase-style, inner slide rule dial, checkered grill, 2 knobs, fold-down front, handle, BC, AC/DC/battery **$30.00**

7P33-4, portable, 1947, briefcase-style, inner slide rule dial, checkered grill, 2 knobs, fold-down front, handle, BC, AC/DC/battery **$30.00**

7RT41-N, table-R/P, plastic, upper front slide rule dial, lower cloth grill w/metal cut-outs, 4 knobs, lift top, inner phono, AC ..**$45.00**

7RT42, table-R/P, 1947, wood, upper front slide rule dial, lower cloth grill w/metal cut-outs, 4 knobs, lift top, inner phono, BC, AC **$30.00**

7RT42N, table-R/P, 1947, wood, upper front slide rule dial, lower cloth grill w/metal cut-outs, 4 knobs, lift top, inner phono, BC, AC $30.00

7T01C-N, table, 1948, plastic, lower front slide rule dial, upper horizontal louvers, 2 "A" knobs, BC....................................$35.00

7T01M-UL, table, 1948, plastic, lower front slide rule dial, upper horizontal louvers, 2 knobs, BC......................................$35.00

7T04-UL, table, 1948, two-tone, lower front slide rule dial, upper cloth grill, 2 knobs, BC, AC/DC $35.00

7T10, table, 1947, plastic, right front square dial, left horizontal louvers, 2 "A" knobs, BC, AC/DC $35.00

7T10E-N, table, 1947, plastic, right front square dial, left horizontal louvers, 2 "A" knobs, BC, AC/DC $35.00

7T12, table, 1947, plastic, upper front slanted slide rule dial, large lower grill area, 2 knobs, BC, battery $30.00

8D15, console-R/P, 1949, wood, right front tilt-out black dial, 3 knobs, left fold-down phono door, BC, FM, AC $80.00

9B14, console-R/P, 1948, wood, right front tilt-out black dial, 4 knobs, left fold-down phono door, BC, FM, AC $80.00

9E15, console-R/P, 1949, wood, right front tilt-out black dial, 4 knobs, left fold-down phono door, BC, FM, AC $80.00

12-B5, table, 1940, ebony plastic, right front dial, left horizontal louvers, 2 knobs, 2 bands, 5 tubes, AC/DC $35.00

13-C5, table, 1940, mahogany plastic, right front dial, left horizontal louvers, handle, 2 knobs, 5 tubes, AC/DC................$40.00

14-B5, table, 1940, ivory plastic, right front dial, left horizontal louvers, handle, 2 knobs, 2 bands, 5 tubes, AC/DC $40.00

14-C5, table, 1940, ivory plastic, right front dial, left horizontal louvers, handle, 2 knobs, 5 tubes, AC/DC $40.00

15-B5, table, 1940, walnut plastic, streamline, right front dial, left horizontal wrap-around louvers, 2 knobs, 2 bands, 5 tubes, AC/DC $80.00

15-D5, table, 1940, mahogany plastic, streamline, right front dial, left horizontal wrap-around louvers, 2 knobs, BC, 5 tubes, AC/DC $80.00

16-B5, table, 1940, chartreuse/ivory plastic, streamline, right front dial, left horizontal wrap-around louvers, 2 knobs, 2 bands, 5 tubes, AC/DC $80.00

16-D5, table, 1940, ivory plastic, streamline, right front dial, left horizontal wrap-around louvers, 2 knobs, BC, 5 tubes, AC/DC $80.00

17-B5, table, 1940, walnut wood, right front dial, left horizontal louvers, handle, 2 bands, 5 tubes, AC/DC $40.00

18-B5, table, 1940, walnut wood, right front dial, left horizontal louvers, 2 knobs, 2 bands, 5 tubes, AC/DC $35.00

20-A6, table, 1940, walnut plastic, streamline, right front dial, rounded left w/horizontal wrap-around louvers, 2 knobs, 2 bands, 6 tubes, AC/DC...$80.00

21-A6, table, 1940, ivory plastic, streamline, right front dial, rounded left w/horizontal wrap-around louvers, 2 knobs, 2 bands, 6 tubes, AC/DC $80.00

22-A6, table, 1940, walnut wood, right front dial, left vertical grill bars, 2 knobs, 2 bands, 6 tubes, AC/DC $40.00

23-A6, table, 1940, walnut wood, right front dial, left vertical grill bars, 2 knobs, 2 bands, 6 tubes, AC/DC $40.00

25-Q5, table, 1940, walnut wood, right front dial, left horizontal louvers, 4 pushbuttons, 5 tubes, AC/DC $45.00

28-G5, portable, 1942, inner dial, horizontal louvers, fold-open front door, handle, AC/DC/battery $50.00

29-G5 "Bantam," portable, 1941, plastic/leatherette, inner dial/grill/2 knobs, AC/DC/battery switch, fold-open front door, handle, BC, AC/DC/battery $50.00

33-F5, portable, 1940, upper front slide rule dial, lower square grill area, 2 knobs, handle, 5 tubes, AC/DC/battery.............$20.00

34-F5, portable, 1940, leatherette, upper front slide rule dial, lower horizontal louvers, 2 knobs, handle, 5 tubes, AC/DC/battery $25.00

35-G6, portable, 1940, brown leatherette, inner slide rule dial, horizontal louvers, detachable cover, handle, 6 tubes, AC/DC/battery $25.00

37-G6, portable, 1940, upper front slide rule dial, lower horizontal louvers, 2 knobs, handle, 6 tubes, AC/DC/battery $25.00

43-B4, table, 1940, wood, upper right front dial, left grill w/2 vertical bars, 2 knobs, BC, 4 tubes, battery $35.00

44-J5, table, 1940, ebony plastic, right front dial, left horizontal louvers, 3 bullet knobs, BC, SW, 5 tubes, AC/DC.........$40.00

45-J5, table, 1940, ivory plastic, right front dial, left horizontal louvers, 3 bullet knobs, BC, SW, 5 tubes, AC/DC.............$40.00

47-J55, table, 1940, walnut wood, right front dial, left horizontal louvers, 3 knobs, 2 bands, 5 tubes, AC/DC $35.00

48-J6, table, 1940, mahogany plastic, right front dial, left horizontal louvers, pushbuttons, 3 knobs, 2 bands, AC/DC $50.00

49-J6, table, 1940, ivory plastic, right front dial, left horizontal louvers, pushbuttons, 3 knobs, 2 bands, AC/DC $50.00

50-J6, table, 1940, walnut wood, right front dial, left horizontal wrap-around grill bars, 4 pushbuttons, 3 knobs, 6 tubes, AC/DC $50.00

51-J55, table, 1940, mahogany plastic, right front dial, left horizontal louvers, 3 knobs, 2 bands, AC/DC, 5 tubes........$40.00

51-K6, table, 1940, mahogany plastic, right front dial, left horizontal wrap-around louvers, 3 knobs, 2 bands, 6 tubes, AC $40.00

52-J55, table, 1940, ivory plastic, right front dial, left horizontal louvers, 3 knobs, 2 bands, AC/DC, 5 tubes $40.00

52-K6, table, 1940, ivory plastic, right front dial, left horizontal wrap-around louvers, 3 knobs, 2 bands, 6 tubes, AC ...$40.00

53-K6, table, 1940, walnut wood, right front dial, left horizontal wrap-around grill bars, 3 knobs, 2 bands, 6 tubes, AC $40.00

54-XJ55, table-R/P, 1940, wood, right front dial, left horizontal louvers, lift top, inner phono, 2 band, 5 tubes, AC $35.00

55-A7, table, 1940, walnut wood, right front dial, left grill w/bars, pushbuttons, 3 knobs, 2 bands, 7 tubes, AC $45.00

56-A77, console, 1940, walnut, upper front slanted dial, lower vertical grill bars, pushbuttons, 3 knobs, 2 bands, 7 tubes, AC $100.00

57-B7, console-R/P, 1940, wood, inner dial & pushbuttons, phono, front vertical bars, BC, SW, 7 tubes, AC $100.00

58-A11, console-R/P, 1940, wood, lift top, front grill w/3 vertical bars, tuning eye, pushbuttons, 5 bands, 11 tubes, AC ..$135.00

59-A11, console-R/P, 1940, wood, inner dial, pushbuttons, tuning eye, phono, lift top, front grill, 5 bands, 11 tubes, AC $150.00

61-K7, table-R/P/Rec, 1940, walnut, inner dial/phono/recorder, lift top, right & left front wrap-around louvers, BC, 6 tubes, AC $40.00

62-B7, console-R/P, 1940, walnut, upper front dial, lower horizontal grill bars, doors, inner phono, pushbuttons, 3 knobs, BC, SW, 7 tubes, AC..$100.00

63-A11, console, 1940, walnut, upper front slanted dial, tuning eye, lower vertical grill bars, 5 bands, 11 tubes, AC ...$125.00

64-K5, table-R/P, 1940, walnut, inner dial/phono, lift top, right & left front wrap-around louvers, BC, 5 tubes, AC...........$40.00

69-M5, table-R/P, 1941, walnut, right front dial, left grill w/horizontal bars, lift top, inner phono, BC, 5 tubes, AC/DC $35.00

70-K5, table-R/P, 1941, wood, inner right dial, left phono, lift top, right & left front horizontal wrap-around bars, 5 tubes, AC $35.00

70-N6, table-R/P, 1941, walnut, inner right dial, left phono, lift top, right & left front horizontal wrap-around bars, BC, 6 tubes, AC $40.00

71-M6, console-R/P, 1941, walnut, upper front dial, center pull-out phono behind double doors, lower grill w/horizontal bars, 2 bands, 6 tubes, AC..$100.00

74-M5, console-R/P, 1942, walnut, double front doors, horizontal grill bars, lower storage, BC, 5 tubes, AC $100.00

76-P5, portable, 1941, mahogany plastic, right front dial, left horizontal grill bars, 2 knobs, handle, 5 tubes, AC/DC/battery $30.00

77-P5, portable, 1941, cloth-covered, right front dial, left patterned grill, 2 knobs, handle, BC, 5 tubes, AC/DC/battery $25.00

78-P6, portable, 1941, leatherette, inner right dial, left patterned grill, fold-down front, handle, BC, 6 tubes, AC/DC/battery $25.00

79-P6, portable, 1941, leatherette, inner right dial, left patterned grill, fold-down front, handle, BC, 6 tubes, AC/DC/battery........$25.00

81-F4, table, 1942, walnut, right front slide rule dial, left grill w/horizontal bars, 2 knobs, BC, 4 tubes, battery....................$30.00

102-6B, table, 1938, walnut, right front slide rule dial, left cloth grill w/cut-outs, 6 pushbuttons, 4 knobs, 6 tubes $45.00

103-6B, table, 1938, wood, right front slide rule dial, left cloth grill w/cut-outs, 6 pushbuttons, 4 knobs, BC, SW, 6 tubes, AC...$45.00

113-5A, table, 1938, black plastic, right front magnifying lens dial, left vertical grill bars, pushbuttons, 5 tubes, AC $100.00

114-5A, table, 1938, walnut plastic, right front magnifying lens dial, left vertical grill bars, pushbuttons, 5 tubes, AC **$100.00**

115-5A, table, 1938, ivory plastic, right front magnifying lens dial, left vertical grill bars, pushbuttons, 5 tubes, AC $100.00

123-5E, table, 1938, black plastic, midget, right front round dial knob, vertical wrap-over grill bars, AC.....................$75.00

124-5E, table, 1938, walnut plastic, midget, right front round dial knob, vertical wrap-over grill bars, AC.........................$75.00

125-5E, table, 1938, ivory plastic, midget, right front round dial knob, left vertical wrap-over grill bars, AC....................$75.00

126-5E, table, 1938, red plastic, midget, right front round dial knob, left vertical wrap-over grill bars, AC.....................$95.00

129-5F, table, 1938, two-tone walnut, right front dial, left cloth grill w/vertical bars, 2 knobs, BC, 5 tubes, AC $40.00

139-11A, console, 1939, wood, upper front slide rule dial, pushbuttons, lower cloth grill w/vertical bars, 3 bands, AC........$100.00

141-4A, table, 1939, two-tone wood, right front slide rule dial, left cloth grill w/2 horizontal bars, 2 knobs, 4 tubes, battery ..$35.00

142-8A, console-R/P, 1938, wood, inner slide rule dial, pushbuttons, Deco front grill w/horizontal bars & discs, 3 bands, 8 tubes, AC...$150.00

144-16S, console-R/P, 1938, wood, upper right front dial, left phono, lower grill w/center vertical divider, 13 pushbuttons, 3 bands, 16 tubes, AC...$250.00

148-6K, table, 1939, walnut, right front slide rule dial, left horizontal grill bars, 4 pushbuttons, thumbwheel knobs, BC $45.00

153-5L "The Gypsy," portable-R/P, 1939, fold-down front, inner right dial, 2 knobs, left grill, lift top, inner phono, handle, AC $30.00

156-5J, table, 1939, walnut plastic, right front dial, left vertical wrap-over grill bars, 2 knobs, BC, 5 tubes $45.00

157-5J, table, 1939, ivory plastic, right front dial, left vertical wrap-over grill bars, 2 knobs, BC, 5 tubes $45.00

158-5J, table, 1939, onyx plastic, right front dial, left vertical wrap-over grill bars, 2 knobs, BC, 5 tubes $45.00

159-5L, table-R/P, 1939, wood, right front dial, left horizontal wrap-around louvers, lift top, inner phono, AC $40.00

162-5L, table, 1939, plastic, right front dial, left horizontal wrap-around louvers, AC/DC.................................$40.00

164-4D, portable, 1939, right front dial, left grill area, 2 knobs, handle, BC, 4 tubes, battery....................................$25.00

166-5D, table, 1939, walnut plastic, streamline, right front dial, rounded left w/horizontal wrap-around louvers, 4 pushbuttons, 6 tubes, AC/DC..$100.00

167-5D, table, 1939, ivory plastic, streamline, right front dial, rounded left w/horizontal wrap-around louvers, 4 pushbuttons, 6 tubes, AC/DC..$100.00

168-5D, table, 1939, onyx plastic, streamline, right front dial, rounded left w/horizontal wrap-around louvers, 4 pushbuttons, 6 tubes, AC/DC..$100.00

169-5D, table, 1939, wood, right front dial, left horizontal wrap-around louvers, pushbuttons $45.00

202, portable, 1958, leatherette, right front half-round dial, perforated grill, 2 knobs, handle, BC, 4 tubes, AC/DC/battery $40.00

218, portable, 1958, leatherette, right front half-round dial, metal perforated grill w/logo, handle, 2 knobs $40.00

242, table, 1958, maroon plastic, right round dial over horizontal front bars, "Admiral" logo, BC, 5 tubes, AC/DC.............$20.00

244, table, 1958, pink/white plastic, right round dial over horizontal front bars, "Admiral" logo, BC, 5 tubes, AC/DC.............$20.00

245, table, 1958, red/white plastic, right round dial over horizontal front bars, "Admiral" logo, BC, 5 tubes, AC/DC.............$20.00

248, table, 1958, turquoise/white plastic, right round dial over horizontal front bars, "Admiral" logo, BC, 5 tubes, AC/DC....$20.00

284, table-C, 1958, plastic, lower right front dial over horizontal louvers, left alarm clock, feet, BC, 5 tubes, AC $20.00

292, table-C, 1958, plastic, lower left front dial, upper alarm clock, right horizontal louvers, BC, 5 tubes, AC $20.00

303, table, 1959, wood, lower front slide rule dial, large upper grill, 2 knobs, AM, FM, 6 tubes, AC/DC.............................$20.00

331-4F, portable, 1939, striped fabric, upper front dial, lower square grill, 2 flat knobs, handle, battery.....................$25.00

361-5Q, table, 1939, plastic, right front dial, left horizontal wrap-around louvers, 2 knobs, AC $45.00

384-5S, table, 1939, walnut, right front dial, left horizontal grill bars, handle, BC, 5 tubes, AC/DC.............................$45.00

396-6M, table, 1940, walnut plastic, streamline, right front dial, rounded left w/horizontal wrap-around louvers, 4 pushbuttons, 6 tubes, AC/DC..$95.00

397-6M, table, 1940, ivory plastic, streamline, right front dial, rounded left w/horizontal wrap-around louvers, 4 pushbuttons, 6 tubes, AC/DC..$95.00

398-6M, table, 1940, onyx plastic, streamline, right front dial, rounded left w/horizontal wrap-around louvers, 4 pushbuttons, 6 tubes, AC/DC..$95.00

399-6M, table, 1940, walnut, right front dial, left horizontal louvers, 4 pushbuttons, 2 bands, 6 tubes, AC/DC $45.00

512-6D, table, 1938, two-tone wood, right front slide rule dial, left cloth grill w/Deco cut-outs, 4 knobs, 2 bands, 6 tubes, DC...$50.00

516-5C, table, 1938, plastic, right front dial, raised left w/vertical grill bars, 2 knobs, 2 bands, 5 tubes, AC/DC $45.00

521-5C, table-R/P, 1938, two-tone wood, right front dial, left cloth grill w/3 horizontal bars, lift top, inner phono, 5 tubes, AC $35.00

521-5F, table-R/P, 1938, two-tone wood, right front dial, left cloth grill w/horizontal bars, lift top, inner phono, 5 tubes, AC ..$35.00

549-6G, console-R/P, 1939, walnut, inner slide rule dial, 8 pushbuttons, phono, large front grill, 2 band, 6 tubes, AC $85.00

920-6Q, tombstone, 1937, wood, center front dial, upper horizontal grill bars, 4 knobs, BC, SW, battery.........................$65.00

930-16R, console, 1937, wood, upper front slanted slide rule dial, lower cloth grill w/vertical divider, BC, SW, 16 tubes, AC $150.00

935-11S, console, 1937, walnut, upper front slide rule dial, lower cloth grill w/3 vertical bars, BC, SW, 11 tubes, AC $110.00

940-11S, console, 1937, walnut, rounded sides, upper front slide rule dial, lower cloth grill w/3 vertical bars, BC, SW, 11 tubes, AC $125.00

945-8K, console, 1937, walnut, upper front round dial, lower cloth grill w/center vertical bar, BC, SW, 8 tubes, AC $115.00

945-8T, console, 1937, walnut, upper front round dial, lower cloth grill w/center vertical bar, BC, SW, 8 tubes, AC $115.00

950-6P, console, 1937, wood, upper front dial, lower cloth grill w/center vertical bar, 4 knobs, BC, SW, 6 tubes, battery $80.00

955-8K, chairside, 1937, walnut, Deco, top dial, streamline semi-circular front w/ashtray, BC, SW, 8 tubes, AC............$180.00

955-8T, chairside, 1937, walnut, Deco, top dial, streamline semi-circular front w/ashtray, BC, SW, 8 tubes, AC/DC $180.00

960-8K, table, 1937, wood, right front round dial, left horizontal louvers, pushbuttons, 4 knobs, feet, BC, SW, 8 tubes, AC $60.00

960-8T, table, 1937, wood, right front round dial, left horizontal louvers, pushbuttons, 4 knobs, feet, BC, SW, 8 tubes, AC/DC $60.00

965-6P, table, 1937, wood, right front dial, left grill w/3 horizontal bars, 4 knobs, BC, SW, 6 tubes, battery $45.00

965-7M, table, 1937, wood, right front dial, left grill w/3 horizontal bars, 4 knobs, BC, SW, 7 tubes, AC $55.00

975-6W, table, 1937, wood, right front dial, left cloth grill w/3 horizontal bars, 3 knobs, BC, SW, 6 tubes, AC...................$55.00

980-5X, table, 1937, wood, right front dial, left cloth grill w/Deco cut-outs, 3 knobs, BC, SW, 5 tubes, AC $55.00

985-5Z, table, 1937, ivory & gold plastic, can be used horizontally or vertically, 2 grill bars, BC, 5 tubes, AC $70.00

985-6Y, table, 1937, ivory & gold plastic, can be used horizontally or vertically, 2 grill bars, BC, SW, 6 tubes, AC $70.00

990-5Z, table, 1937, ebony plastic & chrome, can be used horizontally or vertically, 2 grill bars, BC, 5 tubes, AC................$85.00

990-6Y, table, 1937, ebony plastic & chrome, can be used horizontally or vertically, 2 grill bars, BC, SW, 6 tubes, AC $85.00

4202-B6, table, 1941, plastic, upper front slide rule dial, lower horizontal grill bars, 2 knobs, BC, 6 tubes, AC/DC.............$40.00

4204-B6, table, 1941, two-tone wood, upper front slide rule dial, cloth grill w/lyre cut-out, 2 knobs, BC, SW $60.00

4207-A10, console-R/P, 1941, walnut, upper front dial, pushbuttons, 4 knobs, inner pull-out phono, doors, BC, SW, 10 tubes, AC $125.00

4207-B10, console-R/P, 1941, walnut, upper front dial, pushbuttons, 4 knobs, inner pull-out phono, doors, 3 bands, 10 tubes, AC $125.00

4214-L5, table-R/P, 1942, two-tone wood, upper front slide rule dial, lower horizontal grill bars, 2 knobs, lift top, inner phono, AC $30.00

A126, table, 1936, wood, large center front round airplane dial, top grill cut-outs, 4 knobs, 3 bands, 5 tubes, AC...........$95.00

AM6, console, 1936, wood, rounded upper front w/oval 4 band dial area, lower cloth grill w/vertical bars, 4 knobs, AC $135.00

AM488, console, 1936, rounded upper front w/oval 4 band dial area, lower cloth grill w/vertical bars, 4 knobs, 12 tubes, AC...$135.00

AM786, console, 1936, wood, upper front dial area w/oval escutcheon, lower cloth grill w/3 vertical bars, 4 knobs, BC, LW, SW, 11 tubes, AC $110.00

AM787, console, 1936, wood, rounded upper front w/oval dial area, lower cloth grill w/4 vertical bars, 4 knobs, BC, SW, 11 tubes, AC...$135.00

AM889, console, 1936, walnut, rounded upper front w/oval dial area, lower cloth grill w/vertical bars, 4 knobs, 4 bands, 17 tubes, AC..$185.00

AZ593, console, 1936, wood, upper front round dial, lower cloth grill w/center vertical divider, 4 knobs, 6 tubes, battery $70.00

B125, table, 1936, walnut, right front round airplane dial, left round grill w/cut-outs, 3 knobs, 3 bands, 5 tubes, AC ...$50.00

B225, table, 1936, walnut, right front round airplane dial, left round grill w/cut-outs, 3 knobs, 3 bands, 6 tubes, AC/DC..$50.00

CL-684, console, 1936, wood, upper front round airplane dial, lower cloth grill w/cut-outs, 4 knobs, 3 bands, 8 tubes $110.00

L767, tombstone, 1936, wood, lower front round airplane dial, upper cloth grill w/cut-outs, 4 knobs, 7 tubes, battery $50.00

L783, console, 1936, wood, upper front round airplane dial, lower cloth grill w/3 vertical bars, 4 knobs, 7 tubes, battery $70.00

M169, table, 1936, wood, left front round airplane dial, right round cloth grill w/cut-outs, 3 bands, 6 tubes, AC $65.00

R58-B11, console-R/P/Rec, 1940, wood, front grill w/3 vertical bars, tuning eye, pushbuttons, recorder, BC, SW, 11 tubes, AC $135.00

R59-B11, console-R/P/Rec, 1940, wood, inner dial & pushbuttons, phono, wire recorder, front grill, BC, SW, 11 tubes, AC $150.00

Y2993 "Avalon," table, 1961, dove white plastic, upper right front dial knob, left horizontal grill bars, feet, AM, 4 tubes, AC/DC $10.00

Y2996 "Avalon," table, 1961, harvest yellow plastic, upper right front dial knob, left horizontal grill bars, feet, AM, 4 tubes, AC/DC..........$10.00

Y2998 "Avalon," table, 1961, turquoise plastic, upper right front dial knob, left horizontal grill bars, feet, AM, 4 tubes, AC/DC $10.00

Y2999 "Avalon," table, 1961, charcoal gray plastic, upper right front dial knob, left horizontal grill bars, feet, AM, 4 tubes, AC/DC $10.00

Y3004 "Ashley," table, 1961, shell pink plastic, right front half-round dial, vertical grill bars w/lower left Admiral logo, AM, 5 tubes, AC/DC $10.00

Y3006 "Ashley," table, 1961, harvest yellow plastic, right front half-round dial, vertical grill bars w/lower left Admiral logo, AM, 5 tubes, AC/DC $10.00

Y3008 "Ashley," table, 1961, turquoise plastic, right front half-round dial, vertical grill bars w/lower left Admiral logo, AM, 5 tubes, AC/DC $10.00

Y3012 "Argyle," table, 1962, reef coral/white plastic, right front dial over vertical grill bars, feet, AM, 5 tubes, AC/DC ...$10.00

Y3016 "Argyle," table, 1962, harvest yellow/white plastic, right front dial over vertical grill bars, feet, AM, 5 tubes, AC/DC $10.00

Y3019 "Argyle," table, 1962, charcoal gray/white plastic, right front dial over vertical grill bars, feet, AM, 5 tubes, AC/DC $10.00

Y3021 "Winston," table, 1961, starlight black/white plastic, right front dial knob/left volume knob overlap center oval grill area, feet, AM, 5 tubes, AC/DC $15.00

Y3027 "Winston," table, 1961, walnut grained finish/white plastic, right front dial knob/left volume knob overlap center oval grill area, feet, AM, 5 tubes, AC/DC $15.00

Y3037 "Sinclair," table-C, 1962, desert beige/white plastic, upper right front dial knob, left alarm clock, center vertical grill bars, AM, 4 tubes, AC $15.00

Y3046 "Welborne," table-C, 1962, harvest yellow/white plastic, left front half-round dial and clock face, right horizontal grill bars, feet, AM, 5 tubes, AC $15.00

Y3048 "Welborne," table-C, 1962, turquoise/white plastic, left front half-round dial and clock face, right horizontal grill bars, feet, AM, 5 tubes, AC $15.00

Y3049 "Welborne," table-C, 1962, charcoal gray/white plastic, left front half-round dial and clock face, right horizontal grill bars, feet, AM, 5 tubes, AC $15.00

Y3051 "Duncan," table-C, 1962, starlight black plastic, left front panel w/quarter round dial/volume windows and alarm clock, right vertical grill bars, top pushbuttons, feet, AM, 5 tubes, AC $15.00

Y3053 "Duncan," table-C, 1962, dove white plastic, left front panel w/quarter round dial/volume windows and alarm clock, right vertical grill bars, top pushbuttons, feet, AM, 5 tubes, AC $15.00

Y3058 "Duncan," table-C, 1962, Nassau green plastic, left front panel w/quarter round dial/volume windows and alarm clock, right vertical grill bars, top pushbuttons, feet, AM, 5 tubes, AC $15.00

Y3061 "Walton," table, 1962, starlight black/white plastic, right front dial knob/left volume knob overlap center oval grill area, feet, FM, AC/DC $15.00

Y3067 "Walton," table, 1962, walnut grained finish/white plastic, right front dial knob/left volume knob overlap center oval grill area, feet, FM, AC/DC..$15.00

Y3071 "Dexter," table, 1961, starlight black/white plastic, right vertical slide rule dial, left oval grill w/horizontal bars, 2 knobs, AM, FM, AC/DC...$15.00

Y3077 "Dexter," table, 1961, walnut grained finish/white plastic, right vertical slide rule dial, left oval grill w/horizontal bars, 2 knobs, AM, FM, AC/DC..$15.00

Y3079 "Dexter," table, 1961, cherry grained finish/white plastic, right vertical slide rule dial, left oval grill w/horizontal bars, 2 knobs, AM, FM, AC/DC..$15.00

Y3083 "Stanton," table, 1962, desert beige/white plastic, right front window dial over horizontal grill bars, 2 knobs, feet, FM, 5 tubes, AC/DC $10.00

Y3083A "Stanton," table, 1962, desert beige/white plastic, right front window dial over horizontal grill bars, 2 knobs, feet, FM, 5 tubes, AC/DC $10.00

Y3100 "Sonnet," table, 1963, granite gray plastic, lower right front dial knob/lower left volume knob over vertical grill bars, feet, AM, AC/DC $10.00

Y3100A "Sonnet," table, 1963, magna gray plastic, lower right front dial knob/lower left volume knob over vertical grill bars, feet, AM, AC/DC $10.00

Y3104 "Sonnet," table, 1963, fiesta pink plastic, lower right front dial knob/lower left volume knob over vertical grill bars, feet, AM, AC/DC $10.00

Y3104A "Sonnet," table, 1963, cameo pink plastic, lower right front dial knob/lower left volume knob over vertical grill bars, feet, AM, AC/DC $10.00

Y3107 "Sonnet," table, 1963, boulder beige plastic, lower right front dial knob/lower left volume knob over vertical grill bars, feet, AM, AC/DC $10.00

Y3107A "Sonnet," table, 1963, Brighton beige plastic, lower right front dial knob/lower left volume knob over vertical grill bars, feet, AM, AC/DC $10.00

Y3109 "Sonnet," table, 1963, strata blue plastic, lower right front dial knob/lower left volume knob over vertical grill bars, feet, AM, AC/DC $10.00

Y3109A "Sonnet," table, 1963, beryl blue plastic, lower right front dial knob/lower left volume knob over vertical grill bars, feet, AM, AC/DC $10.00

Y3137 "Chaperone," table-C, 1962, boulder beige plastic, left front oval alarm clock face and dial knob over vertical grill bars, feet, AM, 4 tubes, AC $15.00

Y3146 "Celebrity," table-C, 1962, sun gold plastic, left front clock face and dial knob over vertical grill bars, feet, AM, AC $15.00

Y3147 "Celebrity," table-C, 1962, boulder beige plastic, left front clock face and dial knob over vertical grill bars, feet, AM, AC $15.00

Y3149 "Celebrity," table-C, 1962, strata blue plastic, left front clock face and dial knob over vertical grill bars, feet, AM, AC $15.00

Y3153 "Capri," table-C, 1963, slate white plastic, left front clock face and dial knob over vertical grill bars, feet, AM, AC $15.00

Y3154 "Capri," table-C, 1963, fiesta pink plastic, left front clock face and dial knob over vertical grill bars, feet, AM, AC $15.00

Y3158 "Capri," table-C, 1963, reseda green plastic, left front clock face and dial knob over vertical grill bars, feet, AM, AC $15.00

Y3203 "Waverly," table, 1962, mist green/white plastic, right front window dial over horizontal grill bars, 2 knobs, feet, AM, FM, 5 tubes, AC/DC $10.00

Y3221 "Citadel," table, 1962, starlight black/white plastic, right vertical slide rule dial, left oval grill w/horizontal bars, 3 knobs, AM, FM, AC/DC $15.00

Y3227 "Citadel," table, 1962, walnut grained finish/white plastic, right vertical slide rule dial, left oval grill w/horizontal bars, 3 knobs, AM, FM, AC/DC $15.00

Y3229 "Citadel," table, 1962, fruitwood finish/white plastic, right vertical slide rule dial, left oval grill w/horizontal bars, 3 knobs, AM, FM, AC/DC $15.00

Y3303 "Minuet," table, 1963, ermine white plastic, lower front dial knob overlaps left vertical grill bars, feet, AM, AC/DC...$10.00

Y3308 "Minuet," table, 1963, tempra turquoise plastic, lower front dial knob overlaps left vertical grill bars, feet, AM, AC/DC $10.00

Y3309 "Minuet," table, 1963, magna gray plastic, lower front dial knob overlaps left vertical grill bars, feet, AM, AC/DC...$10.00

Y3313 "Melody," table, 1963, ermine white plastic, right front oval dial over vertical grill bars, feet, AM, AC/DC.........$10.00

Y3318 "Melody," table, 1963, tempra turquoise plastic, right front oval dial over vertical grill bars, feet, AM, AC/DC.........$10.00

Y3321 "Overture," table 1963, Baltic black plastic, center round dial, right and left grill bars, dual speakers, feet, AM, AC/DC $10.00

Y3323 "Overture," table 1963, ermine white plastic, center round dial, right and left grill bars, dual speakers, feet, AM, AC/DC $10.00

Y3337 "Serenade," table-C, 1963, Brighton beige plastic, right clock face with lower dial knob over lattice patterned front panel, feet, AM, AC $15.00

Y3343 "Lyric," table-C, 1963, ermine white plastic, left oval clock face and dial knob over patterned front panel, feet, AM, AC $15.00

Y3346 "Lyric," table-C, 1963, Ming yellow plastic, left oval clock face and dial knob over patterned front panel, feet, AM, AC $15.00

Y3353 "Duet," table-C, 1963, ermine white plastic, left oval clock face and dial knob over patterned front panel, feet, AM, AC $15.00

Y3354 "Duet," table-C, 1963, cameo pink plastic, left oval clock face and dial knob over patterned front panel, feet, AM, AC $15.00

Y3359 "Duet," table-C, 1963, beryl blue plastic, left oval clock face and dial knob over patterned front panel, feet, AM, AC $15.00

Y3363 "Tempo," table-C, ermine white plastic, left front clock face and dial knob over vertical grill bars, feet, AM, AC $15.00

Y3364 "Tempo," table-C, cameo pink plastic, left front clock face and dial knob over vertical grill bars, feet, AM, AC........$15.00

Y3368 "Tempo," table-C, grotto green plastic, left front clock face and dial knob over vertical grill bars, feet, AM, AC........$15.00

Y3376 "Fiesta," table-C, 1963, Ming yellow plastic, left front clock face and dial knob over vertical grill bars, top pushbuttons, feet, AM, AC $15.00

Y3377 "Fiesta," table-C, 1963, Brighton beige plastic, left front clock face and dial knob over vertical grill bars, top pushbuttons, feet, AM, AC $15.00

Y3379 "Fiesta," table-C, 1963, beryl blue plastic, left front clock face and dial knob over vertical grill bars, top pushbuttons, feet, AM, AC $15.00

Y3381 "Marquis," table-C, 1963, Baltic black plastic, lower front dial, upper round clock face, top pushbuttons, feet, dual speakers, AM, AC $15.00

Y3383 "Marquis," table-C, 1963, ermine white plastic, lower front dial, upper round clock face, top pushbuttons, feet, dual speakers, AM, AC $15.00

Y3399 "Fanfare," table, 1962, beryl blue/white plastic, right round dial over patterned front panel, feet, FM, 6 tubes, AC/DC $10.00

Y3408 "Lark," table, 1962, grotto green/white plastic, right round dial over patterned front panel, feet, FM, AC/DC...$10.00

Y3411 "Balladier," table-C, 1963, Baltic black/white plastic, right round dial and round clock face, left patterned panel, feet, AM, FM, AC/DC $15.00

Y3412 "Balladier," table-C, 1963, sea coral/white plastic, right round dial and round clock face, left patterned panel, feet, AM, FM, AC/DC $15.00

Y3421 "Minstrel," table, 1963, Baltic black/white plastic, right vertical slide rule dial, left vertical grill bars, feet, AM, FM, AC/DC $10.00

Y3426 "Minstrel," table, 1963, Ming yellow/white plastic, right vertical slide rule dial, left vertical grill bars, feet, AM, FM, AC/DC $10.00

Y3431 "Maestro," table-C, 1963, Baltic black/white, right vertical slide rule dial, left clock face, center vertical bars, AM, FM, AC/DC $15.00

Y3436 "Maestro," table-C, 1963, Ming yellow/white, right vertical slide rule dial, left clock face, center vertical bars, AM, FM, AC/DC $15.00

Y3443 "Skylark," table-C, 1963, ivory white plastic, right clock face and dial knob over pattern front panel, feet, AM, AC $10.00

YR503, table, plastic, lower right front dial knob & lower left front on/off/volume knob over vertical grill bars, feet, BC $10.00

ADVANCE ELECTRIC
Advance Electric Company
1260 West Second Street, Los Angeles, California

Advance Electric was founded in 1924 by Fritz Falck. He had previously manufactured battery chargers, transformers and did repair work and rewinding of electric motors. By 1924, the company was producing radios and continued to do so until 1933, when it dropped the radio line and continued in business with the production of electrical relays and electronic parts.

4, table, 1924, wood, high rectangular case, 2 dial slant front panel, 3 exposed tubes, lift top $150.00
4 Junior, table, C1924, wood, high rectangular case, 2 dial slant front panel, 2 exposed tubes, lift top $150.00
69, cathedral, 1930, two-tone wood, center front window dial, upper scalloped cloth grill w/cut-outs, 3 knobs, AC $200.00
88, cathedral, 1930, wood, center front window dial, upper scalloped cloth grill w/ cut-outs, 3 knobs, AC $200.00
89, cathedral, 1930, two-tone wood, center window dial, scalloped grill w/cut-outs, 3 knobs, AC $200.00
F, cathedral, 1932, wood, lower front half-round dial w/escutcheon, upper round cloth grill w/cut-outs, 3 knobs $175.00

AERMOTIVE
Aermotive Equipment Corp.
1632-8 Central Street, Kansas City, Missouri

181-AD, table, 1947, wood, right front black dial w/airplane, left round grill area w/horizontal bars, 2 knobs, BC, AC/DC**$45.00**

AERODYN
Aerodyn Co.,
1780 Broadway, New York, New York

Special, table, 1925, wood, rectangular case, slanted three dial black front panel, 5 tubes $125.00

AETNA

19A66W, tombstone, wood, center front dial, upper grill w/cut-outs, 4 knobs, BC, SW, AC $100.00

255, table, 1937, upper front dial, large lower grill area w/horizontal bars & Aetna logo, 4 knobs.............................$60.00

M-253, table, wood, large front oval three-colored dial with Aetna logo, top grill area with cut-outs, 3 knobs $75.00

AIR CASTLE
Spiegel, Inc., 1061- 1101 West 35th Street, Chicago, Illinois

7B, console-R/P, 1948, wood, inner right slide rule dial, 4 knobs, left pull-out phono drawer, BC, FM, AC.........................$80.00
9, table, 1948, plastic, upper slanted slide rule dial, lower horizontal louvers, 3 knobs, BC, FM, AC/DC $35.00
102B, portable, 1950, plastic, lower slide rule dial, upper curved horizontal louvers, handle, 2 knobs, BC, AC/DC/battery.........$30.00

106B, table, 1947, plastic, streamline, right square dial, left horizontal louvers, 2 knobs, BC, AC/DC $100.00

121, console, wood, upper front dial, pushbuttons, tuning eye, lower grill w/vertical bars, BC, SW, AC $125.00

153, console-R/P, 1951, wood, inner slide rule dial, 4 knobs, center pull-out phono, double doors, BC, 7 tubes, AC........$50.00

171, table, 1950, plastic, lower front slide rule dial, upper horizontal grill bars, 2 knobs, BC, AC/DC $40.00

179, portable, 1948, upper front slide rule dial, lattice grill, handle, 2 knobs, BC, battery $35.00

180, portable, 1948, upper front slide rule dial, lattice grill, handle, 2 knobs, BC, AC/DC/battery $35.00

198, table, 1950, wood, lower slide rule dial, upper recessed grill, feet, 2 knobs, AM, FM, AC $30.00

201, table, 1950, plastic, lower slide rule dial, recessed checkerboard grill, 2 knobs, BC, AC/DC $45.00

211, table, 1949, plastic, right round dial over front lattice grill, 2 knobs, BC, AC/DC..$30.00

212, table, 1949, plastic, lower slide rule dial, upper vertical grill bars, 2 knobs, BC, FM, AC...................................$35.00

213, portable, 1949, plastic, lower slide rule dial, upper lattice grill, handle, 2 knobs, BC, AC/DC/battery.............................$35.00

227I, table, 1950, plastic, right square dial, left horizontal wraparound louvers, 2 knobs, BC $60.00

350, console-R/P, 1951, wood, inner slide rule dial, 4 knobs, pull-out phono, double doors, BC, FM, 8 tubes, AC............$50.00

472-053VM, console-R/P, 1952, wood, pull-out front drawer contains right dial, 3 knobs, left phono, BC, 5 tubes, AC $45.00

472.254, console-R/P, 1953, wood, inner right slide rule dial, 4 knobs, pull-out phono, double doors, BC, 7 tubes, AC...$50.00

568, table, 1947, upper right front slide rule dial, left round grill, 3 recessed knobs, BC, SW, AC/DC $35.00

572, console-R/P, 1949, wood, inner right dial, 4 knobs, left phono, lift top, front grill, BC, AC $50.00

603.880, table-R/Rec, 1954, leatherette, inner left dial, disc recorder, lift top, outer grill, handle, BC, 6 tubes, AC $25.00

603-PR-8.1, table-R/P/Rec, 1951, leatherette, inner left dial, phono, recorder, mike, lift top, handle, BC, 6 tubes, AC $25.00

606-400WB, table, 1951, wood, right rectangular dial, left cloth grill w/cut-outs, 2 knobs, BC, 4 tubes, battery $35.00

607.299, table, 1952, plastic, right half-round dial, left horizontal grill bars, 2 knobs, BC, AC/DC $40.00

607-314, table, 1951, plastic, large front dial w/horizontal decorative lines, 2 knobs, BC, 6 tubes, AC/DC........................$35.00

607-316-1, table, 1951, plastic, right front round dial, diagonally divided grill area, 2 knobs, BC, AC/DC $30.00

611-1, tombstone, wood, lower front cylindrical dial, upper cloth grill, 6 pushbuttons, 4 knobs....................................$85.00

629, table, 1937, wood, right slide rule dial, 6 pushbuttons, tuning eye, left grill w/cut-outs, 4 knobs $100.00

651, table, 1947, plastic, upper slide rule dial, lower horizontal louvers, 2 knobs, BC, AC/DC $35.00

652.505, table-R/P, 1952, leatherette, inner right round dial, left phono, lift top, handle, BC, 5 tubes, AC $20.00

652.5X5, table-R/P, 1955, wood, right side dial knob, large front grill, 3/4 lift top, inner phono, BC, 6 tubes, AC $30.00

659.511, table-C, 1952, plastic, center front round dial, right checkered grill, left alarm clock, BC, AC $30.00

659.520E, table-C/N, 1952, plastic, clock/radio/lamp, center round dial knob, left alarm clock, BC, AC $75.00

751, table, wood, right front black slide rule dial, left grill w/diagonal bars, 3 knobs, black top.....................................$50.00

782.FM-99-AC, table, 1955, plastic, lower front slide rule dial, 2 knobs, large upper grill, AM, FM, 9 tubes, AC..............$35.00

935, table-C, 1951, plastic, right round dial, horizontal center bars, left clock, 4 knobs, BC, AC....................................$30.00

1200, table, two-tone wood, right dial, 4 pushbuttons, left grill w/cut-outs, 5 knobs, battery $50.00

5000, table, 1947, plastic, right front dial, left grill w/3 horizontal bars, step-down top, 2 knobs, BC, AC/DC $50.00

5001, table, 1947, plastic, right front square dial, left cloth grill, 2 knobs, BC, AC/DC...$35.00

5002, table, 1947, plastic, right front square dial, left vertical wrapover louvers, 2 knobs, BC, AC/DC $50.00

5003, table, 1947, plastic, upper front slide rule dial, lower wraparound louvers, 2 knobs on top of case, BC, AC/DC $40.00

5008, table, 1948, two-tone wood, upper slanted slide rule dial, lower grill area, 3 knobs, BC, AC/DC $45.00

5011, table, 1947, two-tone wood, upper slanted slide rule dial, lower cloth grill, 4 knobs, BC, SW, AC/DC $50.00

5015.1, table, 1950, plastic, raised top, upper slanted slide rule dial, lower horizontal louvers, 2 knobs, BC, AC/DC $45.00

5020, portable, 1947, luggage-style, right square dial, left cloth grill, 3 knobs, handle, BC, AC/DC/battery $25.00

5022, portable, 1951, "snakeskin" w/plastic front panel, right dial, handle, 3 knobs, BC, AC/DC/battery $45.00

5024, table, 1948, wood, upper slanted slide rule dial, lower cloth grill, top burl veneer, 3 knobs, BC, AC/DC/battery $45.00

5025, portable, 1947, "snakeskin," top dial, front horizontal louvers, 3 knobs, handle, BC, AC/DC/battery $35.00

5027, portable, 1948, leatherette, top slide rule dial, front horizontal louvers, handle, 3 knobs, BC, AC/DC/battery $30.00

5028, portable, 1948, "alligator," right front dial, left horizontal louvers, handle, 3 knobs, BC, AC/DC/battery $35.00

5029, portable, 1948, "alligator," right front square dial, left horizontal louvers, handle, 2 knobs, BC, battery.................$30.00

5035, table-R/P, 1948, leatherette, outer "horse-shoe" dial, horizontal louvers, 3 knobs, lift top, inner phono, BC, AC ...$25.00

5036, table-R/P, 1949, wood, outer front slide rule dial, 3 knobs, lift top, inner phono, BC, AC....................................$30.00

5044, table-R/P, 1951, wood, outer front slide rule dial, 3 knobs, lift top, inner phono, BC, AC....................................$30.00

5050, table, 1948, right front dial, left large square cloth grill, 2 knobs, BC, AC/DC...$30.00

5052, table, 1948, plastic, right front dial, left horizontal grill bars, step-down top, 2 knobs, BC, AC/DC $50.00

5056-A, table, 1951, small case, right front dial, left checkered grill, 2 knobs, BC, AC/DC $35.00

6042, table-R/P, 1949, wood, outer front slanted slide rule dial, 4 knobs, lift top, inner phono, BC, AC $35.00

6050, table-R/P, 1949, wood, outer front slanted slide rule dial, 4 knobs, lift top, inner phono, BC, AC $35.00

6053, table-R/P, 1950, wood, outer front slanted slide rule dial, 4 knobs, lift top, inner phono, BC, 5 tubes, AC $35.00

6514, table, 1947, wood, upper slanted slide rule dial, lower cloth grill w/ 5 horizontal bars, 2 knobs, BC, 5 tubes, AC/DC $40.00

6541, table-R/P, 1947, wood, outer slide rule dial, horizontal louvers, 4 knobs, lift top, inner phono, BC, AC $35.00

6547, table-R/P, 1947, wood, outer slide rule dial, horizontal louvers, 4 knobs, lift top, inner phono, BC, AC $35.00

6634, table-R/P, 1947, leatherette, slide rule dial w/small cover, 4 knobs, lift top, inner phono, handle, BC, SW, AC.........$35.00

7553, table, 1948, plastic, upper front slide rule dial, lower wraparound horizontal louvers w/"x", 2 knobs, BC, AC/DC ..$55.00

9008W, table, 1950, plastic, right front dial, left vertical wrap-over grill bars, 2 knobs, BC, AC/DC $45.00

9009W, table, 1950, plastic, streamline, right front dial, horizontal wrap-around louvers, 2 knobs, BC, AC/DC $65.00

9012W, table, 1950, plastic, Deco, right front dial, left wrap-around horizontal louvers, 2 knobs, BC, AC/DC $65.00

9151-W, table-C, 1951, plastic, right half-round dial, left alarm clock, perforated center grill, BC, AC $30.00

9904, tombstone, 1934, wood, lower round dial, upper grill w/cut-outs, 4 knobs, BC, SW, 7 tubes, AC $140.00

10002, table, 1949, plastic, upper slide rule dial, lower horizontal wrap-around louvers, 3 knobs, BC, AC/DC..................$40.00

10003-I, table, 1949, plastic, streamline, right front square dial, left horizontal wrap-around louvers, 4 knobs, BC, AC/DC $65.00

10005, table, 1949, plastic, upper front slide rule dial, lower horizontal wrap-around louvers, 4 knobs, AM, FM, AC/DC $40.00

10023, table-R/P, 1949, outer right front round dial, 3 knobs, handle, lift top, inner phono, BC, AC $25.00

108014, table, 1949, plastic, upper slanted slide rule dial, lower horizontal grill bars, 4 knobs, BC, 6 tubes, AC $35.00

121104, console-R/P, 1949, wood, right tilt-out dial, 4 knobs, left pull-out phono drawer, BC, FM, AC $70.00

121124, console-R/P, 1949, wood, outer right slide rule dial, 4 knobs, left lift top, inner phono, BC, FM, AC $60.00

127084, console-R/P, 1949, wood, outer front dial, 4 knobs, lower grill, lift top, inner phono, BC, AC $50.00

131504, table, 1949, plastic, upper slanted slide rule dial, lower horizontal grill bars, 4 knobs, BC, FM, AC/DC $35.00

132564, table, 1949, wood, right square dial, left cloth grill w/crossed bars, 2 knobs, BC, battery............................$30.00

138104, console-R/P, 1949, wood, outer right front slide rule dial, 5 knobs, left lift top, inner phono, BC, AC $60.00

138124, console-R/P, 1949, wood, right tilt-out slide rule dial, 5 knobs, left pull-out phono drawer, BC, AC $75.00

147114, portable, 1949, inner right dial, lattice grill, 2 knobs, flip-up front, handle, BC, AC/DC/battery $40.00

149654, table, 1949, plastic, upper slanted slide rule dial, lower horizontal grill bars, 4 knobs, BC, FM, AC $35.00

150084, console-R/P, 1949, wood, slide rule dial, 4 knobs, lift top, inner phono, criss-cross grill, BC, FM, 8 tubes, AC......$50.00

A-2000, table, wood, center cylindrical dial, pushbuttons, tuning eye, upper cloth grill, 4 knobs.....................................$95.00

G-516, table-R/P, 1948, wood, outer slanted slide rule dial, lower grill, 4 knobs, lift top, inner phono, AC.........................$35.00

G-521, portable, 1949, leatherette, slide rule dial, tambour top, checkered grill area, telescope antenna, BC, SW, AC/DC/battery $45.00

G-722, console-R/P, 1948, wood, inner right dial, pushbuttons, door, left pull-out phono drawer, AC $80.00

G-724, table, 1948, wood, upper slanted slide rule dial, large criss-cross grill, 4 knobs, BC, FM, AC/DC $35.00

G-725, console-R/P, 1948, wood, inner right dial, 4 knobs, door, left pull-out phono drawer, BC, FM, AC/DC $75.00

L-6, tombstone, 1936, wood, large lower front round airplane dial, upper cloth grill w/cut-outs, 4 knobs, BC, SW, 8 tubes, AC..$135.00

PX, table, 1947, wood, upper slanted slide rule dial, lower cloth grill w/side cut-outs, 2 knobs, BC, battery $30.00

REV248, table, 1951, plastic, upper curved slide rule dial, lower horizontal louvers w/center divider, 3 knobs, BC, AC/DC $50.00

WEU-262, table, 1950, plastic, right front dial, left cloth grill, decorative case lines, 4 knobs, BC, FM, AC/DC..................$45.00

AIR KING
Air King Products Co., Inc., 1523 63rd Street, Brooklyn, New York

5H110, table, 1946, plastic, right front round dial w/gold pointer, left lattice grill, 2 knobs, AC $45.00

47, table, 1937, wood, rounded sides, lower front round dial, upper cloth grill w/3 vertical bars, 2 knobs, 5 tubes.......$80.00

52, tombstone, 1933, plastic, Deco, center window dial, upper insert w/Egyptian figures, 3 knobs, AC..................$4,000.00+

66, tombstone, 1935, plastic, Deco, center front round dial, upper insert w/globes, 3 knobs, 2 band, AC....................$3,000.00+

222, table, 1938, plastic, midget, right front dial, left grill, 2 knobs, BC, 4 tubes, AC/DC $60.00

770, tombstone, C1935, plastic, Deco, center front square dial, upper cloth grill w/vertical bars, 4 knobs .... **$1,000.00+**
800, console-R/P, 1949, wood, right tilt-out slide rule dial, 4 knobs, pull-out phono drawer, BC, FM, AC **$70.00**

815 "Comet," table, 1938, wood, right front dial, left cloth grill w/3 vertical wrap-over bars, 3 knobs **$60.00**
911, table, 1938, wood, right front dial, left horizontal louvers, 6 pushbuttons, 3 knobs, BC, 6 tubes, AC/DC **$45.00**
4129, table-R/P, 1941, wood, lower front slide rule dial, upper grill, 2 knobs, lift top, inner phono, AC **$30.00**

4603, table, 1946, wood, upper slanted slide rule dial, lower horizontal grill bars, 2 knobs, BC, AC/DC **$30.00**
4604, table, 1946, wood, upper slanted slide rule dial, lower criss-cross grill, 4 knobs, BC, SW, AC **$30.00**
4604-D, table, 1946, wood, upper slanted slide rule dial, lower grill area, 4 knobs, BC, SW **$35.00**
4608, table, 1946, plastic, right vertical slide rule dial, left perforated grill, 2 knobs, BC, AC/DC **$45.00**
4609, table, 1947, wood, right vertical slide rule dial, left horizontal louvers, 2 knobs, BC, AC/DC **$35.00**
4610, table, 1947, plastic, right vertical slide rule dial, left horizontal louvers, 2 knobs, BC, AC/DC **$35.00**
4700, console-R/P/Rec, 1948, wood, inner right slide rule dial, left phono, lift top, criss-cross grill, BC, AC **$55.00**
4704, table-R/P, 1947, wood, outer top slide rule dial, 4 knobs, louvers, lift top, inner phono, BC, AC **$40.00**
4705, table, 1946, plastic, right round dial w/gold pointer, left lattice grill, 2 knobs, BC, AC/DC **$45.00**

4706, table, 1946, painted plastic, right round dial w/gold pointer, left lattice grill, 2 knobs, AC **$45.00**
A-400, table, 1947, plastic, right half-moon dial, left checkered grill, 2 knobs, BC, AC/DC **$50.00**
A-403 "Court Jester," table-R/P, 1947, wood, outer right front dial, left cloth grill w/3 horizontal bars, 3 knobs, open top phono, BC, AC **$30.00**
A-410, portable/Camera, 1948, "alligator," lower front dial, perforated grill, 2 knobs, inner camera, strap, BC, battery .. **$125.00**
A-426, portable, 1948, inner metal grill, louvers, 2 thumbwheel knobs, flip-open door, handle, BC, battery **$45.00**
A-450, table, plastic, midget, raised top, right half-round dial, left checkered grill, 2 knobs, AC **$60.00**
A-502, table, 1948, plastic, right front dial, left lattice grill, 3 knobs, BC, 2SW, AC/DC **$45.00**
A-510, portable, 1947, leatherette, right front dial, horizontal grill bars, 2 knobs, handle, BC, AC/DC/battery **$25.00**
A-511, table, 1947, plastic, right front dial, left lattice grill, 2 knobs, BC, AC/DC **$45.00**
A-520, portable, 1948, plastic, recessed lower right dial, vertical grill bars, handle, BC, AC/DC/battery **$35.00**
A-600 "Duchess," table, 1947, two-tone Catalin, lower slide rule dial, recessed lattice grill, 2 knobs, BC, AC/DC .... **$900.00+**
A-604, table, 1950, wood, upper slanted slide rule dial, lower horizontal louvers, 4 knobs, BC, SW, AC **$30.00**
A-625, table, 1948, two-tone plastic, lower slanted slide rule dial, upper horizontal louvers, 2 knobs, BC, AC/DC **$50.00**
A-650, table, 1948, two-tone plastic, lower slide rule dial, upper horizontal louvers, 2 knobs, BC, FM, AC/DC **$50.00**

AIR KNIGHT
Butler Brothers,
Randolph & Canal Streets,
Chicago, Illinois

CA-500, table, 1947, wood, right square dial, left cloth wrap-around grill, 2 knobs, BC, AC/DC **$35.00**
N5-RD291, table-R/P, 1947, wood, outer front square dial, right/left cloth grills, 2 knobs, lift top, inner phono, BC, AC **$35.00**

AIR-WAY
Air-Way Electric Appliance Corp,
Toledo, Ohio

The Air-Way Company began business in 1920 as a manufacturer of vacuum cleaners and electrical parts. They made radios and radio parts briefly during the mid twenties but by 1926 they had ceased radio production.

41, table, 1924, wood, low rectangular case, 2 dial front panel, lift top, 4 tubes, battery **$140.00**
51, table, 1924, wood, low rectangular case, 3 dial front panel, lift top, 5 tubes, battery **$175.00**
61, table, 1925, walnut, low rectangular case, 2 front window dials, fluted columns, 6 tubes, battery **$150.00**
62, table, 1925, walnut, high rectangular case, 2 front window dials, built-in loud speaker, battery **$165.00**
B, table, 1922, wood, high rectangular case, detector & 1 stage amp, 2 dial front panel, battery **$250.00**
C, table, 1922, wood, high rectangular case, detector & 2 stage amp, 3 dial front panel, battery **$275.00**
F, table, 1923, wood, high rectangular case, 2 dial front panel, 4 tubes, battery **$225.00**
G, table, 1923, wood, high rectangular case, 3 dial front panel, 5 tubes, battery **$275.00**

AIRADIO
Airradio, Inc., Stamford, Connecticut

3049, table-R/P, wood, outer slide rule dial, horizontal grill bars, 4 knobs, lift top, inner phono, BC, AC $40.00
3100, table, 1948, wood, upper front slide rule dial, lower cloth grill area, 4 knobs, FM only, AC/DC $25.00

AIRITE

3000, table-N, 1936, desk set radio, center radio w/top grill bars, right pen/inkwell, left clock face $385.00

AIRLINE
Montgomery Ward & Co.,
619 Chicago Avenue, Chicago, Illinois

Airline was the brand name used for Montgomery Ward's radio line. Airlines were second only to Sear's Silvertones in mail order radio sales. In the 1930's, Airline sets were made for Montgomery Ward by several companies: Wells-Gardner & Co., Davidson-Hayes Mfg. Co., and US Radio & Television Corp.

04BR-397A, table, wood, large center front multi-band dial w/escutcheon, side grill bars, 4 knobs $55.00

04BR-513A, table, plastic, Deco, right slide rule dial, 5 pushbuttons, left horizontal louvers, 2 knobs, BC $90.00
04BR-566A, portable, cloth covered, inner right slide rule dial, left cloth grill, 2 knobs, fold-in front, handle $30.00
04BR-609A, table, wood w/inlay, right slide rule dial, 6 pushbuttons, left grill w/horizontal bars, 4 knobs $60.00
04WG-754C, table, wood, center front cylindrical dial, 6 pushbuttons, upper grill w/cut-outs, battery $50.00
05B-A, table, 1934, right front dial, center shield-shaped grill w/cut-outs, flared base, handle $75.00
05GAA-992A, table-R/P, 1951, outer front round dial, 4 knobs, 3/4 lift top, inner phono, BC, AC....................................$25.00
05GCB-1541 "Lone Ranger," table-N, 1951, plastic, Lone Ranger & Silver on rounded left front, right round dial knob $750.00
05GCB-1541A "Lone Ranger," table-N, 1951, plastic, Lone Ranger & Silver on rounded left front, right dial knob, BC, AC/DC $750.00
05GHM-1061A, portable, 1951, leather case, right front round dial knob over grill, handle, BC, AC/DC/battery $25.00
05WG-1813A, table, 1951, wood, right front rectangular dial over large cloth grill, 4 knobs, AM, FM, AC $30.00

05WG-2748F, console-R/P, 1951, wood, inner right slide rule dial, 4 knobs, pull-out phono, double doors, BC, FM, 9 tubes, AC $65.00
05WG-2749D, console-R/P, 1951, wood, inner right slide rule dial, 4 knobs, left pull-out phono drawer, BC, FM, 9 tubes, AC $80.00
05WG-2752, console-R/P, 1950, wood, inner right slide rule dial, 4 knobs, left pull-out phono drawer, BC, FM, 7 tubes, AC $65.00
4BR-511A, table, 1946, plastic, lower slide rule dial, upper horizontal louvers, rounded top, 2 knobs, BC $50.00
5D8-1, table, plastic, right front dial, left horizontal louvers, 2 knobs, handle, AC/DC..$40.00
14BR-514B, table, 1946, painted plastic, Deco, right slide rule dial, pushbuttons, left horizontal louvers, 2 knobs, BC..$90.00
14BR-521A, table, 1941, plastic, small case, lower front dial, upper horizontal grill bars, 2 knobs, BC $70.00
14BR-522A, table, 1941, plastic, lower front slide rule dial, upper horizontal louvers, rounded top, 2 knobs, BC $70.00
14BR-525A, table, plastic, large center front dial, right & left side horizontal wrap-around grill bars, 5 pushbuttons, 2 knobs, BC, AC/DC $50.00
14BR-736A, table, wood, center front dial, right & left horizontal wrap-around grill bars, pushbuttons, 4 knobs $65.00

14WG-680A, portable, 1941, inner right slide rule dial, left grill, 3 knobs, fold-down cover, handle....................$25.00
14WG-806A, table, 1941, wood, right slide rule dial, curved left w/vertical grill bars, pushbuttons, 4 knobs....................$70.00
15BR-1535B, table, plastic, lower front slide rule dial, upper quarter-round louvers, 4 knobs, BC, FM $50.00
15BR-1536B, table, 1951, plastic, right slide rule dial, left lattice grill, 6 pushbuttons, 2 knobs, BC, AC/DC $45.00
15BR-1544A, table, 1951, plastic, lower front slide rule dial, upper lattice grill, 2 knobs, BC, AC/DC..................................$35.00
15BR-1547A, table, 1951, plastic, lower front curved slide rule dial, upper lattice grill, 4 knobs, BC, AC/DC $40.00
15GAA-995A, table-R/P, 1952, leatherette, outer front dial, 3 knobs, switch, 3/4 lift top, inner phono, BC, AC $25.00
15GHM-934A, table-R/P, 1952, suitcase-style, inner right dial, left phono, lift top, handle, BC, 5 tubes, AC $25.00
15GHM-1070A, portable, 1952, suitcase-style, right front round dial over grill, handle, 3 knobs, BC, AC/DC/battery $35.00
15GSE-2764A, console-R/P, 1952, wood, right front dial, 4 knobs, left pull-out phono drawer, storage, BC, 6 tubes, AC $65.00
15WG-1545A, table, 1952, plastic, top curved slide rule dial, lower horizontal wrap-around louvers, 4 knobs, BC, FM, AC....$55.00

15WG-2745C, console-R/P, 1951, wood, inner right slide rule dial, pull-out phono, storage, double doors, BC, FM, 10 tubes, AC $60.00

15WG-2758A, console-R/P, 1951, wood, inner right slide rule dial, 4 knobs, pull-out phono, double doors, BC, FM, 8 tubes, AC $50.00

17A80, console-R/P, 1941, wood, upper front slide rule dial, 4 knobs, lower cloth grill w/vertical bars, inner phono $90.00

20, cathedral, 1931, wood, small case, left front half-round dial, cloth grill w/cut-outs, scalloped top, 4 tubes $195.00

25BR-1542A, table, 1953, plastic, lower front slide rule dial, upper lattice grill, 4 knobs, BC, AC/DC...................................$45.00

25BR-1549B, table-C, 1953, plastic, perforated front panel, right dial, left clock, center horizontal lines, BC, AC.............$30.00

25GAA-996A, table-R/P, 1952, outer center front round dial & knobs, 3/4 lift top, inner phono, handle, AC $30.00

25GSE-1555A, table, 1952, plastic, right front round dial over large woven grill area, lower left "Airline" logo, 2 knobs...........$30.00

25GSG-2016A, table-R/P, 1953, wood, right front dial over large grill, 3 knobs, 3/4 lift top, inner phono, BC, AC.............$30.00

25GSL-1560A, table-C, 1952, plastic, right side dial, large front rectangular alarm clock, 4 knobs, BC, AC....................$30.00

25GSL-1814A, table, 1953, wood, front half-round dial over criss-cross grill, 2 knobs, BC, AC/DC $30.00

25GSL-2000A, table-R/P, 1953, plastic, outer right front round dial, left vertical grill bars, open top phono, BC, AC $30.00

25WG-1573A, table, 1953, plastic, right front vertical slide rule dial, left perforated grill, 4 knobs, BC, SW, AC.............$40.00

35GAA-3969A, table-R/Rec, 1954, leatherette, inner left dial, disc recorder, lift top, outer grill, handle, BC, 6 tubes, AC $20.00

35GSE-1555D, table, 1952, plastic, right front round dial over large woven grill area, lower left "Airline" logo, 2 knobs...........$30.00

35GSL-2770A, end table-R/P, 1954, wood, step-down top, slide rule dial, 4 knobs, front pull-out phono drawer, BC, 6 tubes, AC $100.00

35WG-1573B "Global," table, 1954, plastic, right front vertical slide rule dial, left perforated grill, 4 knobs, BC, SW, AC $40.00

54BR-1501A, table, 1946, plastic, lower slide rule dial, upper horizontal louvers, 2 knobs, BC, AC/DC $45.00

54BR-1503A, table, 1946, plastic, upper slide rule dial, lower horizontal wrap-around louvers, 2 bullet knobs, BC, AC/DC $45.00

54BR-1503B, table, 1946, plastic, curved slide rule dial, horizontal louvers, bullet knobs..$35.00

54BR-1505B, table, 1946, plastic, large center dial, horizontal side louvers, 2 knobs, 5 pushbuttons, BC, AC/DC........$45.00

54BR-1506A, table, 1946, plastic, large center front dial, horizontal side louvers, 5 pushbuttons, 2 knobs $45.00

54KP-1209B, table, 1946, two-tone wood, upper slide rule dial, lower cloth grill, 2 knobs, BC, battery $30.00

54WG-2500A, console-R/P, 1946, wood, upper front slanted slide rule dial, lower cloth grill w/vertical bars, 4 knobs, BC, SW, AC $65.00

54WG-2700A, console-R/P, 1946, wood, upper front slanted slide rule dial, lower tilt out phono unit, 4 knobs, BC, SW, AC ..$75.00

62-77, cathedral, 1933, wood, center front window dial, upper cloth grill w/cut-outs, 3 knobs, battery $115.00

62-84, console, wood, lowboy, upper half-round dial, lower cloth grill w/cut-outs, 6 legs, 3 knobs $150.00

62-114, tombstone, wood, shouldered, lower front round dial, upper grill w/3 vertical bars, 3 knobs $85.00

62-123, console, two-tone wood, upper round dial, lower cloth grill w/cut-outs, 4 knobs, fluted front & side panels............$150.00

62-131, tombstone, 1935, wood, shouldered, lower airplane dial, upper grill w/3 vertical bars, 4 knobs $85.00

62-148, tombstone, wood, rounded shoulders, lower round dial, upper cloth grill w/cut-outs, 2 knobs $100.00

62-177, tombstone, wood, lower round dial, upper cloth grill w/black cut-outs, 4 knobs, horizontal fluting on base ..$110.00

62-288 "Miracle," table, plastic, right front dial, 6 pushbuttons, finished all sides, tuning eye, right side knob $125.00

62-306, table, C1938, wood, right front round "telephone" dial, tuning eye, left horizontal wrap-around louvers, AC $75.00

62-316, table, wood, off-center oval dial, tuning eye, left cloth grill w/Deco cut-outs, 3 knobs $95.00

62-318, table, 1935, wood, off-center "movie dial," tuning eye, left grill w/cut-outs, 4 knobs, BC, 2SW, 8 tubes $90.00

62-336, table, C1939, wood, center front oval dial, left grill w/horizontal bars, right horizontal lines, 3 knobs $50.00

62-370, console, 1938, wood, upper front slide rule dial, tuning eye, lower grill w/vertical divider, pushbuttons, BC, SW $100.00

62-376, table, 1939, wood, right oval dial, tuning eye, left wrap-around grill bars, 4 knobs, BC, SW, battery $50.00

62-403, console, 1939, wood, upper front "movie dial," pushbuttons, lower grill w/vertical divider, 13 tubes $135.00

62-416, table, wood, right front oval dial, left cloth grill w/vertical bars, tuning eye, 3 knobs, BC, SW, AC.............$60.00

62-425, table, 1936, wood, right front round dial, left cloth grill w/free-form cut-outs, 2 knobs **$60.00**

62-437, table, 1936, wood, off-center "movie dial," left cloth grill w/Deco cut-outs, 4 knobs **$80.00**

62-455, table, plastic, rounded right w/"telephone" dial, left grill w/vertical wrap-over bars, 2 knobs, BC, AC/DC$95.00

62-476, table, 1941, plastic, right front "telephone" dial, tuning eye, left vertical grill bars, 2 knobs **$85.00**

62-553, table, wood, right front slide rule dial, 6 pushbuttons, left round grill w/Deco cut-outs, 2 knobs **$125.00**

62-606, table, 1938, right front "telephone" dial, tuning eye, left vertical wrap-over grill bars, 2 knobs **$85.00**

64BR-1051A, portable, 1946, luggage style, small upper slide rule dial, lower grill area, handle, 2 knobs, BC, AC/DC/battery ..**$25.00**

64BR-1205A, table, 1946, plastic, center front dial, right & left side horizontal wrap-around louvers, 2 knobs, BC, battery **$30.00**

64BR-1208A, table, 1947, wood, right slide rule dial, left wrap-around grill, 4 knobs, 6 pushbuttons, BC, SW, battery ..**$35.00**

64BR-1501A, table, 1946, plastic, lower slide rule dial, upper horizontal grill bars, 2 knobs, rounded top **$50.00**

64BR-1514A, table, painted plastic, lower slide rule dial, 6 pushbuttons, upper metal grill, 4 knobs, BC, SW **$45.00**

64BR-1808, table, 1947, wood, left front slide rule dial, right criss-cross grill, pushbuttons, 3 knobs, BC, 2SW **$45.00**

64BR-1808A, table, 1947, wood, left front slide rule dial, criss-cross grill, 3 knobs, 8 pushbuttons, BC, 4SW, AC **$45.00**

64WG-1050A, portable, 1946, inner right half-round dial, center square grill, left volume knob, flip-up lid, BC, AC/DC/battery **$40.00**

64WG-1052A, portable, 1946, inner right slide rule dial, 3 knobs, left grill, fold-down front, handle, BC, AC/DC/battery **$35.00**

64WG-1207B, table, 1947, wood, upper front slide rule dial, large center cloth grill, 2 knobs, BC, battery....................**$25.00**

64WG-1511A, table, 1946, plastic, lower recessed slide rule dial, recessed cloth grill, 2 knobs, BC, AC/DC.....................**$35.00**

64WG-1801C, table, 1946, wood, right square dial over criss-cross grill area, round sides, 3 knobs, BC, AC/DC.......**$35.00**

64WG-1804B, table, 1946, wood, lower recessed slide rule dial, recessed cloth grill, 2 knobs, BC, AC/DC **$40.00**

64WG-1807A, table, 1946, wood, lower recessed slide rule dial, recessed cloth grill, 4 knobs, BC, SW, AC **$35.00**

64WG-1809A, table, 1946, wood, lower recessed slide rule dial, upper recessed cloth grill, 2 knobs, base **$35.00**

64WG-2007B, table-R/P, 1946, wood, outer right dial, 2 knobs, criss-cross grill, lift top, inner phono, BC, AC **$30.00**

64WG-2009A, table-R/P, 1946, wood, outer slide rule dial, 3 knobs, cloth grill, lift top, inner phono, BC, AC **$30.00**

74BR-1053A, portable, 1948, upper slide rule dial, lower horizontal louvers, handle, 2 knobs, BC, AC/DC/battery **$30.00**

74BR-1055A, portable, 1948, upper slide rule dial, lower lattice grill, handle, 2 knobs, BC, AC/DC/battery **$30.00**

74BR-1501B, table, 1946, walnut plastic, lower slide rule dial, upper horizontal louvers, metal back, 2 knobs **$70.00**

74BR-1502B, table, 1946, ivory plastic, lower slide rule dial, upper horizontal louvers, metal back, 2 knobs $70.00

74BR-1514B, table, 1947, plastic, lower slide rule dial, large upper grill, 4 knobs, 6 pushbuttons, BC, SW, AC/DC ...**$45.00**

74BR-1812B, table, 1947, wood, lower slanted slide rule dial, upper recessed cloth grill, 4 knobs, BC, FM, AC...........**$45.00**

74BR-2001A, table-R/P, 1947, right front slanted slide rule dial, left wrap-around grill, 3 knobs, open top phono, BC, AC.......**$40.00**

74BR-2001B, table-R/P, 1947, right front slanted slide rule dial, left wrap-around grill, 3 knobs, open top phono, BC, AC.......**$40.00**

74BR-2701A, console-R/P, 1947, wood, inner right slide rule dial, pushbuttons, left pull-out phono drawer, BC, 4SW, AC...**$85.00**

74BR-2702B, console-R/P, 1947, wood, inner right slide rule dial, 4 knobs, phono, lift top, vertical grill bars, BC, FM, AC.......**$65.00**

74KR-1210A, table, 1948, wood, lower slide rule dial, upper cloth grill, rounded sides, 2 knobs, BC, AC/DC/battery **$35.00**

74KR-2706B, console-R/P, 1948, wood, see-through slide rule dial in front of grill, pull-out phono drawer, 3 knobs, BC, AC ...**$50.00**

74KR-2713A, console-R/P, 1948, wood, inner right slide rule dial, 3 knobs, left pull-out phono drawer, BC, AC **$70.00**

74WG-1054A, portable, 1947, leatherette, right front half-round dial, center perforated grill, handle, 2 knobs, BC, AC/DC/battery **$30.00**

74WG-1056A, portable, 1947, cloth covered, inner right dial, left grill, 3 knobs, fold-down front, handle, BC, AC/DC/battery.......**$25.00**

74WG-1057A, portable, 1948, leatherette & plastic, inner right dial, center perforated grill, flip-up front, BC, AC/DC/battery **$35.00**

74WG-1510A, table, 1947, plastic, lower slide rule dial, upper recessed cloth grill, 2 knobs, BC, AC/DC.....................**$35.00**

74WG-1802A, table, 1947, wood, right round dial over large woven grill area, rounded corners, 2 knobs, BC, AC/DC **$25.00**

74WG-2002A, table-R/P, 1947, wood, outer front slide rule dial, cloth grill, 3 knobs, lift top, inner phono, BC, AC **$30.00**

74WG-2004A, table-R/P, 1947, wood, outer front round dial, 2 knobs, lift top, inner phono, BC, AC **$30.00**

74WG-2010B, table-R/P, 1947, wood, inner right slide rule dial, 4 knobs, left phono, lift top, criss-cross grill, BC, SW, AC...**$35.00**

74WG-2504A, console, 1947, wood, upper front slide rule dial, 4 knobs, lower cloth grill w/3 horizontal bars, BC, SW, AC.....**$65.00**

74WG-2505A, console, 1947, wood, upper slanted slide rule dial, 4 knobs, 6 pushbuttons, tuning eye, lower grill w/2 horizontal bars, BC, SW, FM, AC **$75.00**

74WG-2704A, console-R/P, 1947, wood, upper slide rule dial, 4 knobs, tilt-out phono, cloth grill w/vertical bars, BC, SW, AC **$70.00**

74WG-2709A, console-R/P, 1947, wood, upper slide rule dial, 4 knobs, tilt-out phono, vertical grill bars, BC, SW, AC **$70.00**

83BR-351A, table, 1938, plastic, Deco, rounded right side w/knob, pushbuttons, left vertical wrap-over grill bars, AC **$95.00**

84BR-1065A, portable, 1949, inner slide rule dial, horizontal louvers, plays when front is opened, handle, AC/DC/battery..........**$35.00**

84BR-1065B, portable, 1949, inner slide rule dial, horizontal louvers, plays when front is opened, handle, battery **$35.00**

84BR-1502B, table, 1946, plastic, lower front slide rule dial, upper horizontal louvers, rounded top, 2 knobs **$70.00**

84BR-1815B, table, 1949, wood, large plastic recessed half-round dial/circular louvers, 2 knobs, BC, AC/DC....................**$45.00**

84GCB-1062A, portable, 1948, leatherette & plastic, inner round dial, flip-up front, side handle, BC, battery **$45.00**

84GSE-2731A, console-R/P, 1949, wood, top dial, 4 knobs, lift cover, inner phono, lower storage, BC, AC **$50.00**

84HA-1529A, table, 1950, plastic, slanted slide rule dial, upper recessed grill, 4 knobs, BC, FM $35.00

84HA-1810, table, 1949, wood, slanted slide rule dial, large metal perforated grill/front, 4 knobs, BC, FM **$30.00**

84HA-1810A, table, 1949, wood, slanted slide rule dial, large perforated grill/front, 4 knobs, BC, FM, AC/DC **$30.00**

84HA-1810C, table, 1949, wood, slanted slide rule dial, large perforated grill/front, 4 knobs, BC, FM, AC/DC **$30.00**

84KR-1520A, table, 1949, metal, right vertical slide rule dial, left horizontal louvers, 2 knobs, BC, AC/DC.............$60.00

84KR-2510A, end table, 1949, wood, "2 drawer" end table, tilt-out front w/inner slide rule dial, 2 knobs, AC **$85.00**

84KR-2511A, end table, 1949, wood, "2 drawer" end-table, tilt-out front w/slide rule dial, 2 knobs, BC, AC/DC **$85.00**

84WG-1056B, portable, 1949, cloth covered, inner right slide rule dial, 3 knobs, fold-down front, handle, BC, AC/DC/battery **$30.00**

84WG-1060A, portable, 1948, inner right dial, center perforated grill, 2 knobs, flip-up front, handle, BC, AC/DC/battery **$30.00**

84WG-1060C, portable, 1948, inner right dial, center perforated grill, 2 knobs, flip-up front, handle, BC, AC/DC/battery **$30.00**

84WG-2015A, table-R/P, 1948, wood, top slide rule dial, criss-cross grill, 4 knobs, 3/4 lift top, inner phono, BC, FM, AC **$30.00**

84WG-2506B, console, 1949, two-tone wood, upper slide rule dial, 4 knobs, lower cloth grill w/bars, BC, FM, AC........**$75.00**

84WG-2712A, console-R/P, 1948, wood, inner right slide rule dial, 6 knobs, 6 pushbuttons, tuning eye, left pull-out phono drawer, BC, SW, FM, AC **$90.00**

84WG-2714A, console-R/P, 1948, wood, upper slide rule dial, 4 knobs, front tilt-out phono, BC, FM, AC....................**$80.00**

84WG-2714F, console-R/P, 1949, wood, upper slide rule dial, 4 knobs, front tilt-out phono door, BC, FM, AC **$80.00**

84WG-2720A, console-R/P, 1948, wood, inner right slide rule dial, 4 knobs, 6 pushbuttons, tuning eye, left pull-out phono drawer, BC, SW, FM, AC **$85.00**

84WG-2721A, console-R/P, 1948, wood, inner right slide rule dial, 4 knobs, left pull-out phono drawer, BC, FM, AC **$80.00**

93BR-420B, table, plastic, midget, lower front slide rule dial, upper horizontal wrap-around louvers, 2 knobs **$85.00**

93BR-421B, table, 1938, plastic, midget, lower front slide rule dial, upper horizontal wrap-around louvers, 2 knobs.....**$85.00**

93BR-460A, table, 1940, wood, lower front slide rule dial, upper horizontal grill bars, 2 knobs, battery...........................**$45.00**

93BR-563A, table, wood, right cylindrical dial, left herringbone grill, 6 pushbuttons, 2 knobs, battery $45.00

93WG-604A, table, 1946, plastic, right dial, 2 thumbwheel knobs, 6 pushbuttons, left wrap-around louvers **$115.00**

94BR-1525A, table, 1950, plastic, upper curved slide rule dial, lower horizontal wrap-around louvers, 2 bullet knobs ...**$40.00**

94BR-1533A, table, 1950, plastic, lower slide rule dial, upper quarter-round louvers, 4 knobs, BC, FM, AC/DC **$50.00**

94BR-1535A, table, plastic, lower front slide rule dial, upper quarter-round louvers, 4 knobs, crest...................................**$50.00**

94BR-2740A, console-R/P, 1950, wood, inner right slide rule dial, 4 knobs, left pull-out phono drawer, BC, FM, AC **$80.00**

94BR-2741A, console-R/P, 1950, wood, inner right slide rule dial, 4 knobs, left pull-out phono drawer, BC, FM, 7 tubes ...**$80.00**

94GCB-1064A, portable, 1950, leatherette & plastic, inner dial, perforated grill, fold-open front, handle, BC, battery **$40.00**

94GSE-2735A, console-R/P, 1949, wood, top slide rule dial, 4 knobs, lift top, inner phono, storage, BC, FM, AC **$50.00**

94HA-1528C, table, 1949, plastic, right half-round dial over large woven grill/front area, 2 knobs, BC, AC/DC **$25.00**

94HA-1529A, table, 1950, plastic, lower slanted slide rule dial, upper recessed grill, 4 knobs, BC, FM, AC/DC **$40.00**

94HA-1562, table, 1945, plastic, right front round metal dial over large plastic woven grill, 2 knobs, AC...........................**$25.00**

94WG-1059A, portable, 1949, leatherette, inner right slide rule dial, 3 knobs, left perforated grill, lift-open lid, handle, BC, AC/DC/battery **$40.00**

94WG-1804D, table, 1950, wood, lower recessed slide rule dial, upper recessed cloth grill, 2 knobs, BC, 6 tubes, AC/DC ...**$40.00**

94WG-1811A, table, 1950, wood, right round dial over woven grill, mitered corners, 4 knobs, AM, FM, AC **$35.00**

94WG-2742A, console-R/P, 1949, wood, inner right slide rule dial, 4 knobs, left pull-out phono drawer, BC, FM, AC **$75.00**

94WG-2745A, console-R/P, 1949, wood, inner right slide rule dial, 4 knobs, pull-out phono, criss-cross grill, AM, FM, AC..**$65.00**

94WG-2748A, console-R/P, 1950, wood, inner right dial, 4 knobs, pull-out phono, criss-cross grill, BC, FM, AC................**$65.00**

345, table, C1941, wood, right "telephone" dial, tuning eye, left cloth grill w/Deco cut-outs, battery **$65.00**

GAA-990A, table-R/P, 1956, leatherette, right side dial & knobs, front grill, 3/4 lift-top, inner phono, BC, AC...................**$25.00**

GEN-1090A, portable, 1957, leather case, right round dial overlaps upper grill, side thumbwheel knob, handle, BC, 4 tubes, battery **$25.00**

GSL-1079-A, portable, 1955, leatherette, right front slide rule dial, left grill, map, telescope antenna, BC, SW, 5 tubes, AC/DC/battery $65.00

GTM-1639B, table, 1958, plastic, lower front slide rule dial, upper vertical grill bars, 2 knobs, BC, AC/DC.......................**$20.00**

GTM-1720A, table, plastic, upper right front half-round dial, lower horizontal grill bars, feet, BC **$15.00**

Rudolph, table-N, 1951, plastic, right round dial knob, Rudolph on rounded left, side louvers, AC **$750.00**

WG-1637, table, 1957, plastic, front recessed slide rule dial, upper grill w/crest, twin speakers, 3 knobs, BC, 6 tubes, AC/DC **$25.00**

WG-1637A, table, 1957, plastic, front recessed slide rule dial, upper grill w/crest, twin speakers, 3 knobs, BC, 6 tubes, AC/DC **$25.00**

ALADDIN

Big 4, table, wood, low rectangular case, 2 dial front panel, battery **$140.00**

ALDEN
Alden, Inc.

1818, portable, 1949, inner slide rule dial, 2 knobs, fold-down front, handle, BC, AC/DC/battery **$35.00**

ALGENE
Algene Radio Corp.,
305 Throop Avenue, Brooklyn, New York

AR5U, portable, 1947, "cosmetic case," inner right dial, left horizontal grill bars, 2 square knobs, mirror in lid, BC, AC/DC **$85.00**

AR6M, portable, 1948, "cosmetic case," inner right dial, left horizontal grill bars, 2 square knobs, mirror in lid **$85.00**

AR-6U, portable, 1947, "cosmetic case," inner right square dial, left horizontal grill bars, 3 square knobs, mirror in lid, BC, AC/DC/battery **$85.00**

AR-404 "Jr.," portable, 1948, "cosmetic case," inner dial and knobs, front grill, fold-open lid, carrying strap................**$55.00**

AR-406 "Middie," portable, 1948, "cosmetic case," "alligator," inner right dial, 2 square knobs, fold-open lid, battery...**$60.00**

ALL-STAR
Warwick Manufacturing Co.

613, table, 1938, wood, right front dial w/tuning eye, left cloth grill w/vertical wrap-over cut-outs and 2 vertical brass bars, 4 knobs, 5 tubes, AC **$65.00**

ALLEN
The Premier Radio Corp.

5 "Rectaflex," table, wood, low rectangular case, metal 2 dial front panel, lift top, 5 tubes, battery $125.00

AMBER
Amber Sales, Inc.,
112 Chambers St., New York, New York

512-C "Marv-o-dyne," table, 1924, low rectangular case, 3 dial front panel, Weston meter, 5 tubes, battery **$225.00**

AMC
Associated Merchants Corp., 1440 Broadway, New York, New York

13N48-09, table, 1962, plastic, lower left front slide rule dial, large upper grill area with upper left logo, 3 knobs, feet, AC...**$15.00**

31N29-09, table, 1962, plastic, lower right front dial over large patterned grill area, 3 knobs, feet, AM, FM, AC/DC..........**$15.00**

32N43-09, table, 1962, mahogany, right front dial, left grill area with upper left logo, AM, FM, AC/DC **$15.00**

32N48-09, table, 1962, walnut, right front dial, left grill area with upper left logo, AM, FM, AC/DC.............................**$15.00**

42N43-09, table-C, 1963, mahogany, right front dial, center alarm clock face, left grill, AM, FM, AC/DC **$15.00**

42N48-09, table-C, 1963, walnut, right front dial, center alarm clock face, left grill, AM, FM, AC/DC **$15.00**

125-P, table, 1946, plastic, upper front slide rule dial, lower horizontal wrap-around louvers, 2 knobs, BC, AC/DC **$45.00**

126, table, 1947, Catalin, upper front slide rule dial, lower grill w/3 overlapping circular cut-outs, handle, 2 knobs, BC, AC/DC ....**$2,000.00+**

AMERICAN BOSCH
American Bosch Magneto Corporation, Springfield, Massachusetts
United American Bosch Corporation, Springfield, Massachusetts

The American Bosch Magneto Corporation was formed in 1919 selling magnetos and automobile parts. Radio sales began in 1925. In addition to their own models, American Bosch produced radios for other companies such as Sonora and Eveready. By the mid 1930's radio production had ceased.

04, table, 1935, wood, center round dial w/surrounding 4-section circular grill, 2 knobs, AC/DC **$60.00**

05, table, 1935, wood, lower round dial, large upper grill with cut-outs, 2 knobs, BC, SW, AC/DC **$75.00**

5A, table, 1931, wood, right window dial, center round grill w/cut-outs, gold pinstriping, 2 knobs, AC **$75.00**

5C, console, 1931, wood, upper front dial, lower criss-cross grill, bowed front legs **$125.00**

10, tombstone, C1935, two-tone wood, small case, lower round dial, cloth grill w/cut-outs, 3 knobs **$70.00**

16 "Amborola," table, 1925, wood, 2 dial Bakelite panel w/escutcheon, lift top, feet, burl front, 6 tubes, battery **$250.00**

18, console, 1929, wood, decorative case, inner dial, 3 knobs, grill with urn cut-out, sliding doors **$225.00**

20-L, console, 1931, wood, ornate case, upper window dial, lower grill w/cut-outs, stretcher base..............................**$200.00**

27 "Amborada," console, 1926, wood, plain cabinet looks like dresser, inner 2 dials & knobs, feet, battery **$210.00**

28, table, 1928, wood, low rectangular case, center front window dial w/escutcheon, 3 knobs, AC **$135.00**

35 "Cruiser," table, 1926, wood, upper front window dial, lift top, 3 knobs, feet, battery **$135.00**

35 "Imperial Cruiser," console, 1926, walnut, low cabinet, inner front dial, 3 knobs, double front doors, feet, battery **$165.00**

35 "Royal Cruiser," table, 1926, walnut, upper front window dial, lift top, 3 knobs, feet, 5 tubes, battery **$135.00**

46 "Little Six," table, 1927, walnut, high rectangular case, right thumbwheel window dial, 2 lower knobs, 6 tubes, battery **$140.00**

57, console, 1927, wood, lowboy, inner dial, fold-down front, lower double doors, inner grill, battery **$145.00**

58A, console, 1930, wood, upper front dial, lower cloth grill w/cut-outs, AC..**$140.00**

60, console, wood, inner window dial, cloth grill w/cut-outs, 5 knobs, sliding doors, decorative case moldings ...**$150.00**

66 "Cruiser," table, 1927, wood, front window dial w/escutcheon, 3 knobs, lift top, horizontal moldings, battery **$140.00**

66AC, table, 1927, wood, front window dial w/escutcheon, 3 knobs, lift top, horizontal moldings, separate A & B power unit, AC **$135.00**

76 "Cruiser," console, 1927, wood, lowboy, inner window dial w/escutcheon, fold-down front door, lower grill, battery... **$125.00**

87 "Cruiser," table, 1927, wood, low rectangular case, center front window dial w/escutcheon, battery.......................**$110.00**

96, console, 1927, wood, lowboy, inner front window dial w/escutcheon, fold-down front, lower grill, AC **$115.00**

107, console, 1927, wood, lowboy, inner dial, 3 knobs, fold-down front, lower fancy grill w/double doors, AC **$165.00**

116, table, 1927, wood, front window dial w/escutcheon, 3 knobs, right & left front panels, feet, AC **$100.00**

126, table, 1927, wood, right front thumbwheel window dial, 2 lower knobs, lift top, A/C...**$110.00**

200-A "Treasure Chest," table, 1932, wood, chest-style, inner dial & grill, lift top, fancy "carved" front, 2 knobs, AC **$250.00**

205-A, table, 1932, mahogany finish, right front window dial, center round grill w/cut-outs, 2 knobs, 5 tubes, AC............**$75.00**

226-F "Fireside," console, 1932, wood, upper front window dial, lower grill w/cut-outs, 3 knobs, 8 tubes, battery **$100.00**

236-A, table, 1932, mahogany w/inlay, upper front dial, lower grill w/cut-outs, 2 knobs, 6 tubes, AC..................................**$75.00**

242 "Empire," console, 1932, wood, lowboy, upper front dial, lower square grill w/cut-outs, 3 knobs, 8 tubes **$150.00**

250-M "Mansion," console, 1932, wood, upper front dial, lower square grill w/cut-outs, 3 knobs, stretcher base, 10 tubes, AC **$150.00**

260-C "World Cruiser," console, 1932, wood, upper front dial, lower grill w/cut-outs, 4 knobs, feet, BC, SW, 10 tubes, AC..**$160.00**

260-R "World Rover," console, 1932, wood, upper front dial, lower 2-section grill, 4 knobs, stretcher base, BC, SW, 10 tubes, AC..**$160.00**

312-C "Grand Concert," console, 1932, wood, upper front dial, lower grill w/cut-outs, 3 knobs, feet, BC, SW, 12 tubes, AC **$175.00**

350, table, 1933, mahogany w/inlay, right front window dial, center grill w/scrolled cut-outs, 4 knobs, 5 tubes, AC..............**$65.00**

355, table, 1933, mahogany w/inlay, right front window dial, center grill/w scrolled cut-outs, 4 knobs, 5 tubes, AC/DC **$65.00**

360T, tombstone, 1933, wood, center front dial, upper cloth grill w/cut-outs, 4 knobs, BC, SW, 7 tubes, AC **$100.00**

370S, console, 1933, wood, lowboy, upper front dial, lower grill w/cut-outs, 4 knobs, stretcher base, AC......................**$135.00**

370T, tombstone, 1933, wood, center front dial, upper cloth grill w/cut-outs, 4 knobs, BC, SW, AC................................**$100.00**

402, table, 1934, wood, right front window dial, center round cloth grill w/star cut-out, 5 tubes, AC/DC **$60.00**

420, table, 1934, wood, right front window dial, center 3-section cloth grill, 4 knobs, 5 tubes, AC..................................**$70.00**

440-C, console, 1934, wood, upper front round compass dial, lower grill w/cut-outs, 4 knobs, BC, SW, 6 tubes, AC **$135.00**

440-T, tombstone, 1934, wood, center front round compass dial, upper cloth grill w/cut-outs, rounded top, BC, SW, 6 tubes, AC...**$295.00**

460-A, tombstone, 1934, wood, center front rectangular dial, upper grill w/circular cut-outs, 4 knobs, BC, SW, 7 tubes, AC..**$100.00**

460-B, tombstone, 1934, wood, center front rectangular dial, upper square grill w/cut-outs, 4 knobs, BC, SW, 7 tubes, AC..**$110.00**

460-R, console, 1934, wood, inner slanted dial, fold-back top, "horseshoe" grill w/splayed bars, BC, SW, 7 tubes, AC..**$145.00**

470-G, console, 1935, wood, upper front slanted dial w/escutcheon, lower grill w/scroll cut-outs, AC..........**$120.00**

470-U, tombstone, 1935, wood, lower front dial, upper grill w/cut-outs, right & left fluted columns, AC **$115.00**

480-D, console, 1934, wood, inner slanted dial, fold-back top, lower cloth grill w/cut-outs, BC, SW, 10 tubes, AC......**$175.00**

500, table, 1933, wood w/inlay, right front window dial, center grill w/cut-outs, 2 knobs, 5 tubes, AC/DC **$65.00**

501, table, 1933, wood w/inlay, right front window dial, center grill w/cut-outs, 2 knobs, 5 tubes, AC/DC **$70.00**

505, table, 1935, wood, right front square black dial, left square cloth grill, center star, 3 knobs, AC...............................**$75.00**

510, tombstone, 1935, wood, small case, lower round airplane dial, cloth grill w/cut-outs, 3 knobs, BC, SW, 5 tubes, AC.........**$75.00**

510-E, console, 1935, wood, upper front round dial, lower grill w/scroll cut-outs, 3 knobs, BC, SW, 5 tubes, AC **$100.00**

565-W, tombstone, 1935, wood, center front round dial, upper cloth grill w/intersecting cut-outs, AC **$85.00**

575-F, tombstone, 1935, wood, lower front round airplane dial, upper grill w/vertical bars, 4 knobs, BC, SW, 7 tubes, AC..........**$85.00**

575-Q, console, 1935, wood, upper round airplane dial, lower cloth grill w/vertical bars, 4 knobs, BC, SW, 7 tubes, AC........**$110.00**

585-Y, tombstone, 1935, wood, lower front round airplane dial, upper grill w/scroll cut-outs, 4 knobs, BC, SW, 8 tubes, AC $110.00

585-Z, console, 1935, wood, upper front round airplane dial, lower cloth grill w/cut-outs, 4 knobs, BC, SW, 8 tubes, AC...$110.00

595-P, console, 1935, wood, upper front round dial, lower cloth grill w/cut-outs, 4 knobs, BC, SW, 10 tubes, AC $120.00

604, table, 1935, wood, right front dial, left cloth grill w/horizontal bars, 3 knobs, BC, SW, AC $40.00

604A2, table, 1935, wood, right front dial, left grill area, 3 knobs, 5 tubes..$40.00

610A2, table, wood, right front square airplane dial, left grill w/horizontal bars, 3 knobs $40.00

625, console, 1936, wood, upper front round dial, lower cloth grill w/center vertical bar, BC, SW, AC $95.00

650, console, 1936, wood, upper front round dial, lower grill w/center vertical bars, 4 knobs, BC, SW, AC $95.00

660T, table, 1936, wood, right round dial, left & right grills w/horizontal bars, 4 knobs, BC, SW, AC $55.00

670C, console, 1936, wood, front recessed black dial, lower grill w/vertical bars, 4 knobs, BC, SW, AC $115.00

680, console, 1934, two-tone wood, upper front black dial, lower cloth grill w/vertical bars, 5 knobs..............................$150.00

805, table, wood, right front window dial, center grill w/cut-outs, two shield-shaped escutcheons, gold pin-striping........$70.00

AMERICAN RADIO
American Radio Corp.,
6116 Euclid Ave., Cleveland, Ohio

3-A "Arc-Lininger," table, 1925, wood, low rectangular case, 2 dial front panel, 3 tubes, battery $110.00

4 "Arc-Lininger," table, 1925, wood, low rectangular case, 2 dial front panel, 4 tubes, battery $120.00

Super 5 "Arc-Lininger," table, 1925, wood, low rectangular case, 2 dial front panel, 5 tubes, battery $130.00

AMERICAN SPECIALTY
American Specialty Co.
Bridgeport, Connecticut

Standard "Electrola," table, 1925, wood, high rectangular case w/arched top, 3 dial front panel, upper built-in speaker w/cut-outs, 5 tubes, battery..$175.00

AMPLEX

C "Lectrosonic," table, metal, low rectangular case, center window dial, lift-off top, 2 knobs, switch............................$115.00

De Exer, table, C1925, wood, low rectangular case, brown Bakelite 3 dial front panel w/gold trim..............................$150.00

AMRAD
The Amrad Corporation,
Medford Hillside, Massachusetts
American Radio & Research Corporation,
Medford Hillside, Massachusetts

The name Amrad is short for American Radio & Research Corporation. The company began business manufacturing transmitters and receivers for the government during WW I and produced its first crystal set in 1921. By 1925 Amrad was in serious financial trouble and was bought out by Crosley although their radios still retained the Amrad label. A victim of the Depression, Amrad closed in 1930.

70 "Concerto," console, 1928, walnut, highboy, inner dial & escutcheon, double doors w/brass hardware, stretcher base, AC $150.00

70 "Nocturne," console, 1928, walnut, highboy, inner dial & escutcheon, double doors, stretcher base, AC $125.00

70 "Sonata," console, 1928, walnut, highboy, inner dial w/escutcheon, double doors, stretcher base, AC........$140.00

81 "Aria," console, 1929, walnut, inner front window dial, 3 knobs, lower grill, double doors, stretcher base, AC $145.00

81 "Duet," console-R/P, 1929, wood w/inlay, lowboy, inner dial & escutcheon, large double doors, stretcher base, AC ..$120.00

81 "Serenata," console, 1929, wood, highboy, inner front dial, double doors, stretcher base, AC...............................$125.00

81 "Symphony," console, 1929, wood, Art Moderne, highboy, inner front dial, double doors, stretcher base, AC $120.00

2575, table, 1922, wood, square case, crystal receiver, black Bakelite front panel with 1 center dial..................$450.00

2575/2776, table, 1922, wood, 2 units – crystal receiver and 2 stage amp, black front panels $725.00

2596/2634, table, 1921, "double-decker," detector/two-stage amp & shortwave tuner, Bakelite panels $1,000.00

3366, table, 1923, wood, low rectangular case, crystal set, 2 dial Bakelite panel, top screen, 1 tube $650.00

3500-1 (3475/2634), table, 1923, two unit double-decker, receiver & tuner, front Bakelite panels, top screens, battery..$1,000.00

3500-3 "Inductrole," table, 1925, wood, high rectangular case, upper 2 dial panel, lower storage, doors, 4 tubes, battery...$500.00

3500-4 "Cabinette," table, 1925, wood, high rectangular case, 2 dial black front panel, 4 tubes, battery......................$325.00

3500-6 "Jewel," table, 1925, wood, chest-type case, inner 2 dial panel, double front doors w/carvings, battery...........$375.00

AC-5, table, 1926, wood, low rectangular case, 3 front window dials, front columns, 4 knobs, AC...........................$225.00

AC-5-C, console, 1926, mahogany, lowboy, 3 inner window dials, 4 knobs, fold-down front door, AC..........................$250.00

AC-6 "The Warwick," table, 1927, walnut, low rectangular case, center front dial w/escutcheon, 3 knobs, AC..............$130.00

AC-6-C "The Berwick," console, 1927, walnut, lowboy, inner dial w/escutcheon, 3 knobs, fold-down front, AC..............$160.00

AC-7 "The Windsor," table, 1927, wood, low rectangular case, center dial w/escutcheon, 3 knobs, AC $130.00

AC-7-C "The Hastings," console, 1927, wood, lowboy, inner dial, large double doors, stretcher base, AC......................$160.00

AC-9, table, 1926, mahogany, low rectangular case, 2 window dials, 5 knobs, front columns, AC..................................$140.00

AC-9-C, console, 1926, wood, lowboy, 2 inner front dials, 7 tubes, AC $170.00

Neutrodyne, table, 1923, wood, low rectangular case, 2 dial front panel, lift top, 5 tube, battery $140.00

S-522, table, 1926, wood, low rectangular case, 3 window dials, 4 knobs, lift top, front columns, 5 tubes, battery $145.00

S-522-C, console, 1926, two-tone mahogany, lowboy, inner front panel w/3 window dials, fold-down front door, 5 tubes, battery $175.00

S-733, table, 1926, two-tone mahogany, low rectangular case, 2 front window dials, lift top, battery $125.00

S-733-C, console, 1927, wood, lowboy, 2 inner front window dials, fold-down front door, 7 tubes, battery.........................$150.00

ANDREA
Andrea Radio Corporation,
27-01 Bridge Plaza North,
Long Island City, New York

The Andrea Radio Corporation was begun by Frank D'Andrea in 1934 after the sale of his previous radio company — F. A. D. Andrea, Inc.

2-D-5, table, 1937, walnut, right front lighted dial, left grill w/diagonal bars, 3 knobs, BC, SW, 5 tubes, AC $55.00

2-D-8, table, 1937, wood, slanted front, right dial, left cloth grill w/wrap-over bars, 8 tubes $50.00

2-E-6, table, 1938, wood, upper front slanted slide rule dial, lower horizontal grill bars w/center vertical divider of 6 pushbuttons, 4 knobs, 3 bands, 6 tubes, AC $95.00

2-E-8, table, 1938, wood, right front slide rule dial, rounded left with vertical grill bars, 8 pushbuttons, 4 knobs, 8 tubes, AC $100.00

5-E-11, console, 1939, wood, upper front dial, 4 knobs, pushbuttons, lower grill w/horizontal bars, BC, SW, AC $90.00

6-E-6, console-R/P, 1938, wood, upper front slanted slide rule dial, lower horizontal grill bars, pushbuttons, 4 knobs, lift top, inner phono, AC $110.00

6G63, portable, 1940, brown striped cloth, inner right dial, left grill, fold-up front, handle, 3 bands, AC/DC/battery $25.00

6G63A, portable, 1940, "alligator" leatherette, inner right dial, left grill, fold-up front, handle, 3 bands, AC/DC/battery $30.00

6H44, table, 1941, two-tone walnut w/black trim, right front dial, left grill, 4 knobs, 3 bands, 6 tubes $45.00

8-E-11, console-R/P, 1938, wood, upper front slide rule dial, center pull-out phono drawer, lower horizontal grill bars, pushbuttons, 4 knobs $115.00

14-E-6, table, 1938, walnut/rosewood, right front vertical slide rule dial, left horizontal wrap-around louvers, pushbuttons, 4 knobs, BC, SW, 6 tubes, AC $45.00

826, upright table, 1940, wood, lower front rectangular dial, upper grill w/horizontal bars, 5 knobs $65.00

CO-UI5, table-R/P, 1947, wood, outer slanted slide rule dial, 5 knobs, lift top, inner phono, BC, SW, AC $30.00

P-I63, portable, 1947, luggage-type, inner right black dial, 3 knobs, fold-up door, handle, BC, 2SW, AC/DC/battery $30.00

T-16, table, 1947, two-tone wood, upper slanted slide rule dial, lower U-shaped cloth grill w/2 vertical bars, 4 knobs, BC, 2SW, AC...$50.00

T-U15, table, 1947, plastic, upper slanted slide rule dial, lower lattice grill, 4 knobs, BC, SW, 5 tubes, AC/DC.................$40.00

T-U16, table, 1947, two-tone wood, upper slanted slide rule dial, lower U-shaped grill w/2 vertical bars, 4 knobs, BC, 2SW, AC/DC $50.00

W69P "Spacemaster Deluxe," portable, 1957, leatherette, flip-up front w/map, telescope antenna, handle, 9 bands, 6 tubes, AC/DC/battery $80.00

ANDREWS

**Andrews Radio Co.,
327 S. LaSalle St.
Chicago, Illinois**

De Luxe "Deresnadyne," table, 1925, wood, low rectangular case, 3 dial front panel, 5 tubes, battery $120.00

ANSLEY

**Ansley Radio Corp.,
41 St. Joes Avenue
Trenton, New York**

53, console-R/P, 1947, wood, modern, inner right dial, 5 knobs, 8 pushbuttons, left phono, lift top, storage, BC, SW, FM, AC $95.00

105, piano console-R/P, 1948, upright piano-style, unusual piano/radio/record player combination $1,500.00

D-4, table-R/P, 1933, wood, outer front grill w/vertical bars, lift top inner phono, AC $30.00

D-10 "Dynaphone," table-R/P, 1935, wood, outer front dial & grill, 4 knobs, lift top, inner phono, BC, SW, 7 tubes, AC $30.00

D-10-A "Dynaphone," table-R/P, 1941, wood, right front slide rule dial, front/right/left grills, lift top, inner phono, AC...$30.00

D-17 "Dynaphone," console-R/P, 1936, wood, front tilt-out radio unit, lower grill, lift top, inner phono, BC, SW, 7 tubes, AC.........$90.00

D-23 "Dynaphone," chairside-R/P, 1937, wood, inner dial & phono, "glider top" slides sideways, front grill, BC, SW, 7 tubes, AC...$85.00

APEX

**Apex Electric Manufacturing Company,
1410 West 59th Street, Chicago, Illinois
Apex Radio & Television Corp.
United States Radio & Television Corporation,
Chicago, Illinois**

The Apex Electric Manufacturing Company began business selling parts for automobiles. By 1925 they were producing radios. Financial difficulties forced a merger with Case to form the United States Radio & Television Corporation in 1928.

5, table, 1926, wood, low rectangular case, single front window dial, feet, 3 knobs $100.00

6, table, 1926, wood, low rectangular case, inner window dial, fold-down front, 3 knobs $120.00

8A, cathedral, 1931, wood, center front dial, upper scalloped grill w/cut-outs, fluted columns, 3 knobs, 2 right side toggle switches, AC..$200.00

10B, console, 1931, wood, lowboy, inner quarter-round dial, lower grill w/cut-outs, doors, stretcher base, AC.................$150.00

11, console, 1930, wood, lowboy, upper front dial, lower scalloped grill w/cut-outs $150.00

12B, console, 1932, wood, upper front curved dial, lower grill w/gothic cut-outs, 6 legs, stretcher base, AC $150.00

60, console, 1928, walnut, upper front dial, 2 knobs, lower grill w/cut-outs, stretcher base, 7 tubes, AC $125.00

70, console, 1928, walnut, highboy, upper front dial, 2 knobs, lower cloth grill w/cut-outs, stretcher base, 9 tubes, AC $160.00

89, table, 1929, metal, low rectangular case, center front window dial w/escutcheon, 2 knobs, 9 tubes, AC $70.00

106, console, 1926, wood, highboy, inner window dial, fold-down front, lower storage, 3 knobs $145.00

116, console, 1926, wood, highboy, inner window dial, upper speaker grill, double doors, storage $160.00

120B, console, 1932, wood, lowboy, ornate cabinet, double front doors, 6 legs, stretcher base, 12 tubes, AC **$160.00**
160, console, 1930, wood, highboy, lower window dial, upper grill w/cut-outs, stretcher base **$140.00**
Baby Grand, console, 1925, wood, spinet piano-style, inner 3 dial panel, fold-down front door, battery..........................**$225.00**
Corsair, table, 1927, wood, low rectangular case, center front dial w/escutcheon, fluted columns **$90.00**
Deluxe, table, 1925, wood, high rectangular case, lower 3 dial front panel, upper built-in speaker, battery.................**$145.00**
Lyric, table, 1927, wood, low rectangular case, inner window dial, fold-down front......................**$110.00**
Milan Electric, console, 1927, wood, lowboy, inner front dial, 2 knobs, lower gothic grill, double doors, 6 tubes, AC ...**$120.00**
Minstrel, console, 1927, wood, inner dial, 2 knobs, lower gothic grill, double doors, stretcher base, AC **$125.00**
Music Chest, table, 1928, wood, low rectangular case, center front dial & escutcheon, 2 knobs, 6 tubes **$85.00**
Neutrodyne, table, 1930, walnut finish metal rectangular case, front illuminated dial, 2 knobs, AC.............................**$70.00**
Super Five, table, 1925, wood, low rectangular case, 3 dial front panel, lift top, feet, battery **$125.00**
Troubadour, console, 1927, wood, inner front dial, grill w/gothic cut-outs, double doors, stretcher base, storage, AC ...**$225.00**

APEX INDUSTRIES
Apex Industries,
192 Lexington Avenue, New York, New York

4B5, table, 1948, plastic, right square dial, left horizontal louvers, 2 knobs, BC, AC/DC **$35.00**

APPLEBY
Appleby Mfg. Co.,
250 N. Juniper St., Philadelphia, Pennsylvania

60, table, wood, low rectangular case, 2 dial metal front panel, meter, lift top.................................**$165.00**

ARBORPHONE

27, table, 1927, wood, low rectangular case w/rounded front corners, metal 2 dial panel, battery **$150.00**

ARC
ARC Radio Corp.,
523 Myrtle Avenue, Brooklyn, New York

601, portable, 1947, shoulder bag-style, "alligator," 2 top thumbwheel knobs, front grill, strap, BC, battery....................**$55.00**

ARCADIA
Whitney & Co.,
933 5th Avenue, San Diego, California

7D14-600, table, 1946, wood, upper slanted slide rule dial, lower criss-cross grill, 3 knobs, BC, SW, 7 tubes, AC/DC **$45.00**

ARGUS

TR-320, (top right) portable w/base & lamp, plastic, small portable radio can be used either with or without matching base/lamp, made in Japan, BC, 4 tubes, AC/battery ..**$70.00**

ARIA
International Detrola Co.,
Detroit, Michigan

554-1-61A, table-R/P, 1946, wood, outer top right dial, 3 knobs, inner phono, lift top, BC, AC..................................**$40.00**
571, table, plastic, right front slide rule dial, left horizontal louvers, 2 knobs, AC.....................................**$45.00**
572-10, table, wood, right front slide rule dial, left & right metal perforated grills, feet, 3 knobs, AC **$45.00**
572-21, table, wood, right front slide rule dial, cloth grill with chrome molding, 3 knobs **$55.00**
593, table, wood, right front dial, left curved grill w/vertical bars, 3 knobs (1 on grill), AC/DC..**$95.00**

ARKAY

421, table, 1934, wood, right front dial, center grill w/cut-outs, 2 knobs...**$75.00**
633, console, 1934, wood, upper front round dial, lower cloth grill w/vertical bars, fluting.................................**$125.00**

ARLINGTON

AH, table, plastic, right front dial, left horizontal wrap-around grill bars, 2 knobs, BC, AC/DC...**$60.00**

ARTHUR ANSLEY
Arthur Ansley Mfg. Co.,
Doylestown, Pennsylvania

R-1, table, 1953, wood, inner right vertical slide rule dial, left grill, 4 knobs, fold-up front, AM, FM, AC **$50.00**

ARTONE
Affiliated Retailers, Inc.,
Empire State Building, New York, New York

524, table-C, 1949, upper front slide rule dial, center alarm clock, 2 knobs, grill bars on case top, BC, AC.........................**$40.00**

ARVIN

Noblitt-Sparks Industries, Inc.,
13th Street & Big Four R. R., Columbus, Indiana
Arvin Industries, Inc., Columbus, Indiana

The Arvin line was produced by Noblitt-Sparks Industries which was founded in 1927 for the manufacture of automobile parts. The company began making automobile radios in 1933 and by 1934 was producing radios for the home. They also made radios for Sears which were sold under the Silvertone brand name.

10R16, table, 1961, ice green plastic, lower front dial and volume knobs over vertical bars, feet, AM, 5 tubes, AC $10.00

10R17, table, 1961, white plastic, lower front dial and volume knobs over vertical bars, feet, AM, 5 tubes, AC $10.00

10R18, table, 1961, beige plastic, lower front dial and volume knobs over vertical bars, feet, AM, 5 tubes, AC $10.00

10R32, table, 1961, persimmon plastic, upper center front dial window, right and left vertical bars, feet, dual speakers, AM, 5 tubes, AC..$15.00

10R38, table, 1961, sandstone plastic, upper center front dial window, right and left vertical bars, feet, dual speakers, AM, 5 tubes, AC..$15.00

10R39, table, 1961, gray plastic, upper center front dial window, right and left vertical bars, feet, dual speakers, AM, 5 tubes, AC $15.00

12R23, table, 1963, sunset plastic, large right front dial overlaps horizontal grill bars, feet, AM, 5 tubes, AC $10.00

12R25, table, 1963, blue plastic, large right front dial overlaps horizontal grill bars, feet, AM, 5 tubes, AC $10.00

12R27, table, 1963, white plastic, large right front dial overlaps horizontal grill bars, feet, AM, 5 tubes, AC $10.00

12R29, table, 1963, charcoal plastic, large right front dial overlaps horizontal grill bars, feet, AM, 5 tubes, AC $10.00

30R12, table 1961, persimmon plastic, right front slide rule dial, left checkered grill area, FM, 5 tubes, AC $15.00

30R18, table 1961, sandstone plastic, right front slide rule dial, left checkered grill area, FM, 5 tubes, AC $15.00

31R25, table, 1962, moonstone plastic, large right front dial, left vertical grill bars, feet, AM, FM, 7 tubes, AC/DC...........$15.00

31R26, table, 1962, mint green plastic, large right front dial, left vertical grill bars, feet, AM, FM, 7 tubes, AC/DC...........$15.00

32R89 "Stereophonic," table, 1962, front slide rule dial, step-back raised top with speaker grill, pushbuttons, 4 knobs, 2 speakers, AM, FM, 8 tubes, AC $45.00

33R28, table, 1963, beige plastic, large right front dial, left vertical grill bars, feet, AM, FM, 6 tubes, AC/DC $15.00

33R29, table, 1963, charcoal plastic, large right front dial, left vertical grill bars, feet, AM, FM, 6 tubes, AC/DC................$15.00

40 "Mighty Mite," table, 1938, metal, midget, right front dial, left horizontal louvers, rounded top, 2 knobs, AC/DC $80.00

52R35, table-C, 1962, moonstone plastic, center front dial, right alarm clock face, left lattice grill area, AM, 5 tubes, AC...$15.00

52R37, table-C, 1962, white plastic, center front dial, right alarm clock face, left lattice grill area, AM, 5 tubes, AC $15.00

58, table, 1939, black plastic, right front dial, left round grill w/horizontal bars, 2 knobs, 5 tubes, AC/DC $60.00

58A, table, 1939, ivory plastic, right front dial, left round grill w/horizontal bars, 2 knobs, 5 tubes, AC/DC................$60.00

68, table, 1938, brown plastic, right pushbutton tuning, left round grill w/horizontal bars, 3 knobs, 5 tubes, AC $75.00

78, table, 1938, wood, right front dial, left grill w/horizontal bars, 4 pushbuttons, 3 knobs, BC, SW, AC $55.00

88, table-R/P, 1938, wood, outer right dial, left grill w/vertical bars, 2 knobs, lift top, inner phono, BC, SW, AC $35.00

89, table, 1939, wood, right front dial, left grill w/vertical bars, pushbuttons, tuning eye, 4 knobs, 6 tubes, AC $60.00

91, console, 1939, walnut, slanted front rectangular dial, pushbuttons, tuning eye, 4 knobs, BC, SW, 6 tubes $120.00

140-P, portable, 1947, two-tone, upper slide rule dial, 2 knobs on top, lattice grill, handle, BC, AC/DC/battery $35.00

150TC, table-R/P, 1948, mahogany veneer, outer slide rule dial, horizontal grill bars, 4 knobs, 3/4 lift top, BC, AC $35.00

151TC, table-R/P, 1948, walnut veneer, outer slide rule dial, horizontal grill bars, 4 knobs, 3/4 lift top, BC, 5 tubes, AC ..$35.00

152T, table, 1948, plastic, left half-round dial, horizontal wrap-around bars, 2 knobs, BC, AC/DC $35.00

160T, table, 1948, plastic, upper slide rule dial, lower metal perforated grill, case top is ribbed, 3 knobs $35.00

182TFM, table, 1948, wood, upper slide rule dial w/clear escutcheon, lower perforated grill, 4 knobs, BC, FM, AC/DC $40.00

240-P, portable, 1948, plastic, center vertical slide rule dial, checkered grill, 2 knobs, handle, BC, battery $40.00

241P, portable, 1949, plastic, center vertical slide rule dial, checkered grill, handle, 2 knobs, AC/DC/battery $40.00

242T, table, 1948, metal, small case, right front dial, vertical grill bars w/oblong cut-outs, 2 knobs, BC, AC/DC $85.00

243T, table, 1948, metal, small case, right front dial, vertical grill bars w/oblong cut-outs, 2 knobs, BC, AC/DC ...$85.00

250-P, portable, 1948, metal, upper slide rule dial, vertical lattice louvers, handle, 2 knobs, BC, AC/DC/battery $50.00

253T, table, 1949, right front round dial over vertical grill bars, lower left volume knob $40.00

255T, table, 1949, right round dial knob over vertical grill bars, lower left volume knob, BC, AC/DC $40.00

264T, table, 1949, wood, lucite covered slide rule dial on top of case, large lower grill, 4 knobs, BC, AC/DC.................$40.00

280TFM, table, 1948, wood, lucite covered slide rule dial on top of case, large lower grill, 4 knobs, BC, FM, AC/DC...........$40.00

302A, table-R/P, 1939, metal, rounded front w/left dial and center vertical grill bars, 2 knobs, open top phono, BC, AC.....$75.00

341T, table, 1950, metal, midget, right round dial knob, left horizontal louvers, rounded top, BC, AC/DC $75.00

350P, portable, 1949, plastic, right dial part of circular grill bars, handle, 2 knobs, BC, 5 tubes, AC/DC/battery $40.00

350PL, portable, 1950, plastic, right dial part of circular grill bars, handle, 2 knobs, BC, AC/DC/battery $40.00

356T, table, 1949, plastic, right round dial knob over vertical grill bars, lower left volume knob, BC, AC/DC $40.00

358T, table, 1948, plastic, left raised half-round dial over horizontal wrap-around louvers, 2 knobs $45.00

360TFM, table, 1949, plastic, raised top with curved slide rule dial, large lower grill, 3 knobs, BC, FM, 6 tubes, AC/DC **$40.00**

440T, table, 1950, metal, midget, right front round dial knob, left round checkered grill, BC, AC/DC..............................**$75.00**
441-T "Hopalong Cassidy," table-N, 1950, metal, aluminum front Hopalong Cassidy, right dial, rear "lariatenna," BC, AC/DC, Black **$350.00**
Red **$475.00**

402, table, 1939, **walnut metal, midget, right front dial, left horizontal louvers, 2 knobs, BC, 3 tubes, AC/DC.....$80.00**
402-A, table, 1939, ivory metal, midget, right front dial, left wrap-around louvers, 2 knobs, feet, BC, 3 tubes, AC/DC **$80.00**

442, table, 1948, **metal, midget, right front dial, left horizontal louvers, rounded top, 2 knobs, BC, 4 tubes, AC/DC ..$70.00**
444, table, 1946, metal, midget, right front dial, rounded corners, horizontal louvers, 2 knobs, BC, 4 tubes, AC/DC..........**$80.00**
444A, table, 1946, metal, midget, right front dial, horizontal louvers, raised top, 2 knobs, BC, 4 tubes **$80.00**

444AM, table, 1947, **metal, midget, right front dial, horizontal louvers, raised top, 2 knobs, BC, 4 tubes, AC/DC....$80.00**
446P, portable, 1950, plastic, right side dial knob, center front vertical louvers, handle, BC, 4 tubes, battery **$35.00**
450T, table, 1950, plastic, center round dial w/inner metal perforated grill, 2 knobs, BC, AC/DC..................................**$50.00**
451T, table, 1950, plastic, center round dial w/inner metal perforated grill, 2 knobs, BC, AC/DC..................................**$50.00**
451-TL, table, 1950, plastic, center round dial w/inner metal perforated grill, 2 knobs, BC, AC/DC..................................**$50.00**
460T, table, 1950, plastic, right see-through dial, left horizontal grill bars, 3 knobs, BC, AC/DC **$30.00**
462-CM, console-R/P, 1950, wood, upper front dial, 3 knobs, center front pull-out phono drawer, lower grill, BC, 6 tubes, AC..**$50.00**

17 "Rhythm Baby," tombstone, 1936, **wood, lower round dial, upper oval grill w/3 splayed bars, 2 knobs, BC, SW, 4 tubes, AC**...**$175.00**
22, table, 1941, brown, midget, right front dial, left wrap-around louvers, 2 knobs, BC, 4 tubes, AC/DC **$85.00**
22-A, table, 1941, ivory, midget, right front dial, left wrap-around louvers, 2 knobs, BC, 4 tubes, AC/DC **$85.00**

467 "Rhythm Belle," table, 1936, wood, left front round dial, right round grill, 3 knobs, BC, SW, 4 tubes, AC $70.00

480TFM, table, 1950, plastic, right see-through dial, left horizontal grill bars, 3 knobs, AM, FM, AC..........................$35.00

502, table, 1939, metal, midget, right front square dial, left wrap-around louvers, 2 knobs, AM, 5 tubes, AC/DC..............$85.00

502A, table, 1939, metal, midget, right front square dial, left wrap-around louvers, 2 knobs, AM, 5 tubes, AC/DC..............$85.00

517 "Rhythm Junior," tombstone, 1936, wood, center front round dial, oval grill w/3 splayed bars, 4 knobs, BC, SW, 5 tubes, AC $150.00

518 "Phantom Baby," table, 1937, wood, lower front round dial, upper cloth grill w/horizontal bars, BC, SW, AC $70.00

518DW "Phantom Pal," table, 1937, ivory/mahogany wood, lower front round dial, upper cloth grill w/horizontal bars, 5 tubes..................$110.00

522, table, 1941, brown metal, midget, right front square dial, left horizontal louvers, raised top, 2 knobs, 5 tubes, AC $85.00

522A, table, 1940, ivory metal, midget, right front square dial, left horizontal louvers, raised top, 2 knobs, 5 tubes, AC $85.00

524, table, 1940, brown, right front square dial, left horizontal louvers, raised top, 2 knobs, 5 tubes, AC/DC $70.00

524A, table, 1940, ivory, right front square dial, left horizontal louvers, raised top, 2 knobs, 5 tubes, AC/DC $70.00

527 "Rhythm Senior," console, 1936, wood, upper front round dial, lower oval grill w/3 splayed bars, 4 knobs, BC, SW, 5 tubes, AC..................$140.00

528CS "Phantom Mate," chairside, 1938, wood, top round dial and knobs, side grill w/horizontal bars, storage, BC, SW, 5 tubes, AC..................$125.00

532, table, 1941, two-tone Catalin, left front dial, raised right w/vertical wrap-over grill bars, 2 knobs, AC/DC .....$1,000.00+

532A, table, 1941, two-tone Catalin, left front dial, raised right w/vertical wrap-over grill bars, 2 knobs, 5 tubes, AC/DC .... $1,000.00+

540T, table, 1951, painted metal, large right round dial knob over lattice grill, BC, AC/DC..................$80.00

541TL, table, 1950, plastic, large center front round dial w/stars & inner perforated grill, 2 knobs $50.00

542J, table, 1947, metal, right front round dial knob, horizontal grill bars, lower left knob..................$65.00

544, table, 1946, plastic, left front dial, right wrap-over vertical grill bars, 2 knobs, rounded corners $60.00

544A, table, 1946, plastic, left front dial, right wrap-over vertical grill bars, rounded corners, 2 knobs, BC, AC/DC..........$60.00

547, table, 1948, plastic, left front dial, right vertical wrap-over grill bars, 2 knobs, BC, AC/DC..................$60.00

555, table, 1947, walnut plastic, upper slide rule dial, lower vertical grill bars, 2 knobs, BC, 5 tubes, AC/DC..................$45.00

555A, table, 1947, ivory plastic, upper slide rule dial, vertical grill bars, 2 knobs, BC, 5 tubes, AC/DC..................$45.00

558, table-R/P, 1946, wood, lower front slide rule dial, 4 knobs, upper cloth grill, lift top, inner phono, BC, AC/DC........$30.00

568A "Phantom Blonde," table, 1938, lower round dial, upper wrap-over vertical grill bars, 4 knobs..................$65.00

568DW "Phantom Ace," table, 1937, ivory/mahogany, lower round dial, upper wrap-over vertical grill bars, 4 knobs, 5 tubes..................$65.00

580TFM, table, 1951, plastic, right front see-through dial, left horizontal bars, 3 knobs, AM, FM, AC..................$35.00

581TFM, table, 1953, plastic, right front dial, left cloth grill, 3 knobs, feet, AM, FM $35.00

602, table, 1939, walnut plastic, right front dial, left round grill w/horizontal bars, handle, 3 knobs, 6 tubes, AC/DC.....$60.00

602A, table, 1939, ivory plastic, right front dial, left round grill w/horizontal bars, handle, 3 knobs, 6 tubes, AC/DC.....$60.00

616, table, 1941, walnut plastic, left front dial, right vertical wrap-over grill bars, 2 knobs, 6 tubes, AC/DC $50.00

616-A, table, 1941, ivory plastic, left front dial, right vertical wrap-over grill bars, 2 knobs, 6 tubes, AC/DC $50.00

617 "Rhythm Maid," tombstone, 1936, wood, center front round dial, upper oval grill w/3 splayed bars, BC, SW, 6 tubes, AC..................$235.00

618, table, 1937, two-tone wood, off-center round dial, left side grill w/horizontal bars, tuning eye, 4 knobs, BC, SW, AC..................$70.00

622, table, 1941, walnut plastic, midget, right front dial, horizontal wrap-around grill bars, rounded top, 2 knobs, 5 tubes, AC/DC..................$75.00

622-A, table, 1941, ivory plastic, midget, right front dial, horizontal wrap-around grill bars, rounded top, 2 knobs, 5 tubes, AC/DC..................$75.00

627 "Rhythm Master," console, 1936, wood, upper front round dial, lower oval grill w/3 splayed bars, BC, SW, 6 tubes, AC..................$155.00

628CS "Phantom Bachelor," chairside, 1937, two-tone wood, Deco, top dial, rounded front w/vertical bars, BC, SW, AC..................$200.00

632, table, 1941, walnut, right front rectangular dial, left cloth grill w/vertical bars, 2 knobs, 5 tubes, AC/DC..................$45.00

638 "Phantom Fawn," console, 1938, wood, upper front dial, lower grill w/vertical bars, 4 knobs, BC, SW, 5 tubes, AC..................$120.00

638CS "Phantom Grad," chairside, 1938, wood, top round dial, step-down front w/horizontal louvers, lower storage, BC, SW, 6 tubes, AC..................$150.00

650-P, portable, 1952, large center front round dial, right & left side knobs, flex handle, BC, AC/DC/battery $30.00

655SWT, table, 1952, plastic, right see-through dial, left horizontal grill bars, 3 knobs, BC, SW, AC/DC..................$35.00

657-T, table-C, 1952, plastic, lower right front slide rule dial, left square alarm clock, 2 side knobs, BC, AC..................$25.00

664, table, 1947, plastic, right front square dial, left vertical grill bars, handle, 3 knobs, BC, 6 tubes, AC/DC..................$50.00

665, console-R/P, 1947, wood, inner right slide rule dial, 4 knobs, left phono, lift top, legs, BC, AC $50.00

669, table-R/P, walnut, lower front dial, pushbuttons, 4 knobs, horizontal grill bars, lift top, inner phono, 6 tubes, AC........$35.00

702, table, 1940, walnut, right front dial, left louvers, step-down top w/pushbuttons, 3 knobs, 6 tubes, AC/DC $75.00

722, table, 1941, walnut plastic, right front square dial, left vertical grill bars, handle, 3 knobs, 6 tubes, AC..................$45.00

722-A, table, 1941, ivory plastic, right front square dial, left vertical grill bars, handle, 3 knobs, 6 tubes, AC..................$45.00

732, table, 1941, walnut, right front dial, left horizontal louvers, 3 knobs, AC..................$40.00

741T, table, 1953, plastic, right front round dial, left criss-cross grill, BC, AC/DC..................$30.00

746P, portable, 1953, plastic, top dial and volume knobs, large front metal lattice grill w/logo, handle $75.00

753T, table, 1953, plastic, right front see-through round dial over oblong cloth grill, 2 knobs, BC, AC/DC..................$35.00

758T, table-C, 1953, plastic, right vertical slide rule dial, left clock face, woven grill, 5 knobs, BC, AC..................$25.00

760T, table, 1953, plastic, right front dial, left cloth grill, 3 knobs on lower right strip, feet, BC, 6 tubes, AC/DC..............$30.00

802, portable, 1939, cloth w/lower stripe, right front dial, left grill, knobs, handle, AC/DC/battery..................$25.00

822, portable, 1940, inner right dial, left grill, 3 knobs, fold-down front, handle, BC, 5 tubes, AC/DC/battery $25.00

828AT "Phantom President," console, 1937, two-tone wood, upper front dial, lower cloth grill w/2 vertical bars, 5 knobs, tubes..................$150.00

838AT "Phantom Princess," console, 1938, wood, upper front dial, lower cloth grill w/2 vertical bars, 5 knobs, tubes..................$150.00

838CS "Phantom Deb," chairside, 1938, wood, inner dial and controls, fold-over top, side grill area, storage, 8 tubes, AC ...$150.00

840T, table, 1954, metal, right round plastic dial knob over vertical bars, lower left plastic knob, 4 tubes, BC $65.00

842J, table, metal, right front round dial knob over horizontal grill bars, left volume knob $65.00

848CS "Phantom Vogue," chairside-R/P, 1938, wood, top round dial and knobs, lift top, inner phono, side grill w/horizontal bars, storage, 8 tubes, AC...$175.00

850T, table, 1955, plastic, large right round dial over oval metal perforated grill, BC, AC/DC..$35.00

857T, table-C, 1955, plastic, modern, lower slide rule dial, center front alarm clock, 5 knobs, BC, 5 tubes, AC.................$25.00

927 "Rhythm Queen," console, 1936, wood, large upper front round dial, lower oval grill w/3 splayed bars, BC, SW, 9 tubes, AC $250.00

950T, table, 1955, plastic, upper right front round dial over horizontal grill bars, BC, 5 tubes, AC/DC.................................$30.00

950T2, table, 1958, plastic, upper right front round dial over checkered grill, BC, AC/DC..$30.00

951T, table, 1955, plastic, upper right front round dial over horizontal grill bars, BC, 5 tubes, AC/DC.................................$30.00

952P, portable, 1955, plastic, large right front round dial over checkered grill area, top right thumbwheel knob, handle, 4 tubes, AC/battery... $35.00

952P1, portable, 1956, plastic, large right front round dial over checkered grill area, top right thumbwheel knob, handle $35.00

954P, portable, 1955, plastic, large right front round dial over checkered grill area, top right thumbwheel knob, handle, 4 tubes, AC/battery...$35.00

957T, table-C, 1956, plastic, lower right front slide rule dial, large left alarm clock face, side knobs, feet, 5 tubes, AC...........$25.00

958T, table-C, 1956, plastic, lower slide rule dial, center alarm clock w/day-date, 5 knobs, BC, 5 tubes, AC $30.00

1127 "Rhythm King," console, 1936, wood, large upper front round dial, lower oval grill w/3 vertical bars, BC, SW, 11 tubes, AC $265.00

1237 "Phantom Prince," console, 1937, wood, upper front round telephone dial, lower horseshoe-shaped grill w/3 vertical bars, 12 tubes, AC..$265.00

1247 "Phantom Queen," bookcase, 1937, wood, upper front round dial, right & left bookcases, BC, SW, 12 tubes, AC $295.00

1247D, bookcase, 1938, wood, center front round dial, pushbuttons, right & left 3 shelf bookcases, 12 tubes $295.00

1427 "Phantom King," console, 1937, walnut, upper round front dial, pushbuttons, tuning eye, 2 speakers, BC, SW, 14 tubes, AC..$300.00

1581, table, 1958, plastic, right side dial knob, left side on/off/volume knob, front lattice grill, BC, 4 tubes, AC/DC $25.00

2410P, portable, 1948, plastic, center front vertical slide rule dial, checkerboard grill, handle, 2 knobs, BC, 4 tubes, AC/DC/battery $40.00

2563, table, 1957, plastic, right front vertical slide rule dial, left lattice grill, 2 knobs, BC, 5 tubes, AC/DC...........................$20.00

2572, table, 1958, plastic, lower right front dial knob, upper vertical grill bars, feet, BC, 5 tubes, AC/DC $20.00

2581, table, 1959, plastic, right side dial knob, left side on/off/volume knob, front lattice grill, BC, 5 tubes, AC/DC $30.00

2584, table, 1959, plastic, large center round dial w/"steering wheel" pointer, horizontal front bars, twin speakers, feet, BC, 5 tubes, AC/DC $25.00

3561, table, 1957, plastic, center vertical slide rule dial & tone control, right/left lattice grills, twin speakers, 2 knobs, BC, 6 tubes, AC/DC $35.00

3582, table, 1959, plastic, lower front slide rule dial, raised upper grill area w/hi/fi logo, 4 knobs, BC, 7 tubes, AC/DC $40.00

3586, table, 1959, plastic, lower front slide rule dial, raised upper grill area, 4 knobs, pushbuttons, AM, FM, 9 tubes, AC $45.00

4561, table-C, 1957, pink plastic, lower left dial w/alarm clock face, right front checkered grill, BC, 5 tubes, AC $25.00

4571, table-C, 1958, plastic, right round dial knob over horizontal bars, left alarm clock face, feet, BC, 5 tubes, AC.........$20.00

5572, table-C, 1958, plastic, right round dial knob, left alarm clock face, feet, BC, 5 tubes, AC..$20.00

5581, table-C, 1957, green plastic, lower left dial w/alarm clock face, right front checkered grill, BC, 5 tubes, AC $25.00

5591, table-C, 1960, plastic, lower right thumbwheel dial, lower left thumbwheel on/off/volume, center front alarm clock face, BC, 5 tubes, AC...$30.00

6640, table, 1948, walnut, right front square dial, left cloth grill w/Deco cut-outs, 3 knobs, BC, AC/DC............................$50.00

8565, portable, 1957, British tan leatherette, right front round dial, left grill area w/lattice cut-outs, top right thumbwheel knob, handle, BC, 4 tubes, battery......................................$20.00

8572, portable, 1958, leather, right side dial knob, left side on/off/volume knob, front perforated grill w/random lines, handle, BC, AC/DC/battery $35.00

8583 "Velvet Voice," portable, 1959, leatherette/aluminum, upper right front thumbwheel dial knob, upper left thumbwheel on/off/volume knob, front horizontal bars, rotatable handle, BC, 4 tubes, AC/DC/battery..........$40.00

RE-200, table, 1946, metal, midget, raised top, right front dial, horizontal louvers, 2 knobs...$75.00

ATKINS

Atkins Concert Hall
Frederick Wholesale Corp.
New York, New York

12N27-11, table, 1963, plastic, large right front dial knob overlaps grill area, left on/off/volume knob, AM, 5 tubes, AC/DC $10.00

13N49-11, table, 1964, plastic, lower left front slide rule dial, large upper grill area, 3 knobs, feet, AM, 6 tubes, AC/DC $15.00

31N28-11, table, 1963, plastic, lower right panel w/dial & knobs over large patterned grill area, feet, AM, FM, 6 tubes, AC/DC $15.00

32N43-11, table, 1963, wood, lower right panel w/half-round dial and knobs over large grill area, AM, FM, 6 tubes, AC/DC $15.00

42N25-11, table-C, 1963, plastic, lower right front dial, center round alarm clock face, left vertical grill bars, AM, FM, 6 tubes, AC..$15.00

51N28-11, table-C, 1963, plastic, right round dial over horizontal grill bars, left alarm clock face, feet, AM, 5 tubes, AC...$15.00

ATLANTIC
Atlantic Radio Corp., Brooklyn, New York

31AC, grandfather clock, 1931, wood, Colonial-style grandfather clock, front dial, knobs and grill, AC **$350.00**
AC, cathedral, wood, center front quarter-round dial w/brass escutcheon, upper cloth grill w/cut-outs, 3 knobs, AC **$350.00**

ATLAS
Atomic Heater & Radio Co., 102-104 Park Row, New York, New York

AB-45, table, 1947, wood, right front square dial, left cloth grill w/ vertical bars, 3 knobs, BC, SW, AC/DC **$40.00**

ATWATER KENT
Atwater Kent Manufacturing Company, 4703 Wissahickon Avenue, Philadelphia, Pennsylvania

Atwater Kent began business manufacturing electrical items and parts for automobiles. In 1922 the Atwater Kent Manufacturing Company began to market component parts for radios and the first of their large line of breadboards. By 1924 the company produced the first of their cabinet sets. Both the Pooley Company and the Red Lion Cabinet Company were among several furniture manufacturers who made radio cabinets for Atwater Kent. From 1925 to 1927, the company sponsored the Atwater Kent Radio Hour, a popular Sunday night show of radio music. A victim of the Depression, Atwater Kent was out of business by 1936.

1, breadboard, 1922, small rectangular wooden board, 1 left & one center dial, 2 right side tubes, battery **$825.00**

2, breadboard, 1922, small rectangular wooden board, 1 left & one center dial, 3 right side tubes, battery $800.00

5, breadboard, 1923, small rectangular wooden board, 1 left side dial, 5 right side tubes, battery $5,000.00

9, breadboard, 1923, rectangular wooden board, one left & one center dial, 4 tubes, battery **$1,200.00**
9A, breadboard, 1923, rectangular wooden board, one left and one center dial, 4 tubes, battery **$1,200.00**
9C, breadboard, 1923, rectangular wooden board, one left & one center dial, 4 tubes, battery **$1,100.00**
10, breadboard, 1923, rectangular wooden board, one left & 2 centered dials, 5 tubes, battery **$1,000.00**
10, console, 1923, model 10 breadboard unit built into large, ornate "Valley Tone" cabinet, battery **$1,400.00**
10A, breadboard, 1923, rectangular wooden board, one left & 2 centered dials, 5 tubes, battery **$900.00**
10B, breadboard, 1924, rectangular wooden board, one left & two centered dials, 5 tubes, battery **$900.00**
10C, breadboard, 1924, rectangular wooden board, one left and two centered dials, 5 tubes, battery...........................**$950.00**
12, breadboard, 1924, rectangular wooden board, one left & two centered dials, 6 tubes, battery **$1,300.00**
19, table, 1924, wood, low rectangular case, black 2 dial front panel w/AK logo, lift top, battery **$350.00**
20 "Big Box," table, 1924, wood, low rectangular case, 3 dial black front panel w/ AK logo, lift top, battery **$100.00**
20C, table, 1925, wood, low rectangular case, 3 dial front panel w/center AK logo, lift top, 5 tubes, battery **$100.00**

21, table, 1925, wood, low rectangular case, 3 dial black front panel w/AK logo, lift top, battery............................$200.00
24, table, 1925, wood, low rectangular case w/overhanging lid, 3 dial front panel, button feet, battery **$300.00**
30, console, 1926, 1 dial front panel w/center AK logo, battery, built into various console cabinets...............................**$175.00**
30, table, 1926, wood, low rectangular case, 1 dial front panel w/center AK logo, lift top, 6 tubes, battery **$130.00**
32, table, 1926, wood, low rectangular case, 1 dial front panel w/center AK logo, lift top, 7 tubes, battery..................**$110.00**
33, console, 1927, 1 dial front panel w/center AK logo, battery, built into various console cabinets.............................**$150.00**
33, table, 1927, wood, low rectangular case, 1 dial metal panel w/center AK logo, lift top, battery................................**$90.00**

35, table, 1926, metal, low rectangular case, right front dial top gold AK logo, 6 tubes, battery $65.00
36, console, 1927, model 36 built into various console cabinets left front dial, center AK logo, AC **$150.00**

36, table, 1927, metal, low rectangular case, left front dial, center AK logo, AC $125.00

37, table, 1927, metal, low rectangular case, left front dial, top gold ship logo, lift-off top, AC $80.00

38, table, 1927, metal, low rectangular case, left front dial, lift-off top with AK ship logo, AC $60.00

40, console, 1928, model 40 built into various console cabinets, left front dial, AC $150.00

40, table, 1928, metal, low rectangular case, left front dial, lift-off top with gold AK logo, AC $65.00

41, table, 1928, metal, low rectangular case, left front dial, lift-off top, feet $75.00

42, table, 1928, metal, low rectangular case, left front dial, lift-off top w/gold AK logo, AC $50.00

42F, table, 1928, metal, low rectangular case, left front dial, lift-off top, feet $50.00

43, table, 1928, metal, low rectangular case, left front dial, lift-off top, feet, AC $85.00

44, console/bar, 1928, model 44 built into Pooley bar cabinet, lift top, inner bar supplies, 8 tubes, AC $975.00

44, table, 1928, metal, low rectangular case, left front dial, lift-off top w/AK logo, feet, AC $75.00

44F, table, 1928, metal, low rectangular case, left front dial, lift-off top w/gold AK logo, feet $75.00

45, table, 1929, metal, low rectangular case, left front dial, lift-off top w/AK logo, AC $75.00

46, console, 1929, model 46 built into various console cabinets, left front dial, AC $165.00

46, table, 1929, metal, low rectangular case, left front dial, lift-off top w/AK logo, AC $85.00

47, console, 1929, model 47 built into various console cabinets, left front dial, AC $175.00

47, table, 1929, metal, low rectangular case, left front dial, center gold AK logo, lift-off top, AC $70.00

48, table, 1928, wood, low rectangular case, front panel w/left dial & center AK logo, lift top, battery $75.00

49, table, 1928, metal, low rectangular case, metal front panel w/left dial, lift top, 6 tubes, AC $85.00

50, table, 1928, wood, low rectangular case, front panel w/left dial, shielded interior, battery $900.00

52, console, 1928, metal, upper left front dial, lower large center round "caned" grill, legs, AC............................$120.00

53, console, 1929, metal, upper left front dial, lower round "caned" grill, center AK logo, legs, AC............................$120.00

55, table, 1929, metal, low rectangular case, center front window dial w/escutcheon, 3 knobs, AC $75.00

55, Kiel table, 1929, wooden 6 legged table, inner front window dial w/escutcheon, 3 knobs, fold-down door, lift-top, AC $225.00

55, console, 1929, center front window dial w/escutcheon, 3 knobs, AC, various console cabinets......................$125.00

55-C, Kiel table, 1929, wooden 6 legged table, inner front window dial w/escutcheon, 3 knobs, fold-down door, lift-top....$225.00

55-C, console, 1929, model 55-C built into various console cabinets, window dial w/escutcheon, AC $150.00

56, console, 1929, metal, upper left front dial, lower round grill w/7 circular cut-outs, legs, AC $100.00

57, console, 1929, metal, upper left front dial, lower round grill w/7 circular cut-outs, legs, AC $100.00

60, console, 1929, model 60 built into various console cabinets, window dial w/escutcheon, AC...................................$200.00

60, Kiel table, 1929, wooden 6 legged table, inner front window dial w/escutcheon, 3 knobs, fold-down door, lift-top, AC $300.00

60, table, 1929, metal, low rectangular case, center front window dial w/escutcheon, 3 knobs, AC $70.00

60C, Kiel table, 1929, wooden 6 legged table, inner front window dial w/escutcheon, 3 knobs, fold-down door, lift-top, AC $300.00

61, table, 1929, metal, low rectangular case, center front window dial w/escutcheon, 3 knobs, lift-off top, DC $65.00

66, console, 1929, wood, inner window dial, 3 knobs, upper cloth grill w/cut-outs, sliding doors, AC $175.00

67, table, 1930, metal painted to look like wood, center front window dial, lift-off top, 3 knobs, battery $75.00

70, console, 1930, wood, lowboy, upper front quarter-round dial, lower cloth grill, 3 knobs, available as AC, DC or battery $115.00

72, console, 1930, wood, highboy, upper front quarter-round dial, 3 knobs, lower cloth grill, stretcher base, AC $160.00

74, console, 1930, wood, lowboy, upper front quarter-round dial, lower cloth grill, 3 knobs, available as AC or DC........$160.00

75, console-R/P, 1930, wood, lowboy, front quarter-round dial, lower cloth grill, 3 knobs, lift top, inner phono, AC $195.00

76, console, 1930, wood, highboy, inner dial and knobs, lower grill, double front doors, available as AC, DC or battery $150.00

80, cathedral, 1931, wood, front half-round dial, upper cloth grill w/cut-outs, twisted columns, 3 knobs, AC...................$350.00

81, console, 1932, wood, lowboy, inner quarter-round dial, double doors, stretcher base, 6 legs, AC $165.00

82, cathedral, 1931, wood, front half-round dial, upper grill w/gothic cut-outs, 3 knobs, twisted columns, AC...................$375.00

82D, cathedral, 1931, wood, front half-round dial, upper grill w/gothic cut-outs, 3 knobs, twisted columns, DC $375.00

82Q, cathedral, 1931, wood, front half-round dial, upper grill w/gothic cut-outs, 3 knobs, twisted columns, 7 tubes, battery $300.00

83, console, 1931, walnut, lowboy, upper front half-round dial, lower grill w/cut-outs, AC $140.00

84, cathedral, 1931, wood, center front half-round dial, upper cloth grill w/gothic cut-outs, 3 knobs, AC $400.00

84, grandfather clock, 1931, wood, center front half-round dial, lower grill, upper clock face, 3 knobs $650.00

84B, cathedral, 1931, wood, center front half-round dial w/escutcheon, upper grill w/cut-outs, 3 knobs.............$400.00

84D, cathedral, 1931, wood, center front half-round dial, upper cloth grill w/gothic cut-outs, 3 knobs, DC $400.00

85, console, 1931, wood, lowboy, upper front quarter-round dial, lower cloth grill w/cut-outs, AC $140.00

85Q, console, 1931, wood, lowboy, upper front quarter-round dial, lower cloth grill w/cut-outs, battery $135.00

87D, console, 1931, wood, available as highboy or lowboy, quarter-round dial, grill cut-outs, DC $135.00

89, console, 1931, wood, highboy, inner quarter round dial, 3 knobs, double sliding front doors, AC..........................$150.00

90, cathedral, 1931, wood, front half-round dial, upper cloth grill w/cut-outs, twisted columns, 3 knobs, 7 tubes, AC $400.00

92, cathedral, 1931, wood, center front half-round dial, upper cloth grill w/cut-outs, twisted columns, 3 knobs, AC $400.00

94, console, 1931, wood, available as highboy or lowboy, upper front quarter-round dial, lower grill cut-outs, 7 tubes, AC $135.00

96, console, 1931, wood, available as highboy or lowboy, upper front quarter-round dial, lower grill cut-outs, 8 tubes, AC $165.00

99, console, 1932, wood, available as highboy or lowboy, upper front quarter-round dial, lower grill cut-outs, 10 tubes, AC $165.00

112N, console, 1934, wood, upper front quarter-round dial, lower cloth grill w/scrolled cut-outs, BC, SW, 12 tubes, AC ...$200.00

112S, console, 1934, wood, upper front quarter round dial, lower cloth grill w/scrolled cut-outs, BC, SW, 12 tubes, AC ...$175.00

145, tombstone, 1934, wood, lower front round dial, upper cloth grill w/cut-outs, fluting, 4 knobs, BC, SW, 5 tubes, AC.........$145.00

155, table, 1933, wood, right front window dial, large center cloth grill w/cut-outs, 2 knobs, AC...$80.00

165, cathedral, 1933, wood, right front window dial, cloth grill w/scrolled cut-outs, 3 knobs, BC, 5 tubes, AC $225.00

165Q, cathedral, 1933, wood, right front window dial, cloth grill w/scrolled cut-outs, 3 knobs, BC, battery $225.00

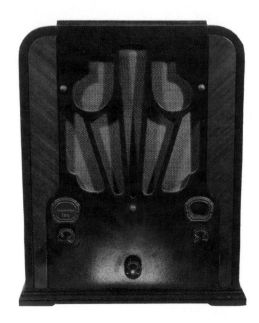

184, tombstone, 1935, two-tone wood, lower right front window dial, upper cloth grill w/cut-outs, 3 knobs, 4 tubes, AC $175.00

185, tombstone, 1934, wood, Deco, lower right front window dial, center cloth grill with right & left cut-outs, 3 knobs, AC **$150.00**

185A, tombstone, 1934, wood, Deco, lower right front window dial, center cloth grill with right & left cut-outs, 3 knobs **$150.00**

188, console, 1932, wood, lowboy, upper front quarter-round dial, lower cloth grill w/cut-outs, 8 tubes, AC **$145.00**

206, cathedral, 1934, wood, lower front round dial, upper grill w/cut-outs, 4 knobs, fluted columns, BC, SW, 6 tubes, AC.....**$300.00**

217, table, 1933, wood, right front window dial, center grill w/cut-outs, round top, 4 knobs, BC, SW, 7 tubes, AC **$350.00**

225, tombstone, 1932, wood, lower front round airplane dial, upper cloth grill w/cut-outs, 3 knobs, AC **$160.00**

228, cathedral, 1932, wood, center front half-round dial, upper cloth grill w/gothic cut-outs, 3 knobs, 8 tubes, AC...$350.00

246, table, 1933, two-tone wood, right front window dial, center grill w/cut-outs, rounded top, 3 knobs, AC........$275.00

260, console, 1932, wood, lowboy, upper quarter-round dial, lower cloth grill w/cut-outs, 4 knobs, 6 legs, 10 tubes, AC....**$155.00**

266, console, 1933, wood, small upper right window dial, lower cloth grill w/cut-outs, 3 knobs, 6 legs, AC **$135.00**

275, table, 1933, wood, right front window dial, center cloth grill w/Deco cut-outs, 4 knobs, BC, SW, 5 tubes, AC/DC ..**$195.00**

305, tombstone, 1935, wood, lower front round airplane dial, upper cloth grill w/cut-outs, 4 knobs, DC **$135.00**

310, console, 1933, wood, upper front quarter-round dial, lower grill w/scrolled cut-outs, 5 knobs, 6 legs, BC, SW, 10 tubes **$235.00**

317, console, 1935, wood, upper front round dial, lower cloth grill w/vertical bars, 4 knobs, BC, SW, 7 tubes, AC **$160.00**

318, console, 1934, wood, upper front quarter-round dial, lower grill w/cut-outs, 5 knobs, BC, SW, AC **$200.00**

318K, console, 1934, wood, upper front quarter-round dial, lower grill w/cut-outs, 6 legs, BC, SW, 8 tubes, AC **$200.00**

325E, console, 1934, wood, lowboy, upper front round dial, lower grill w/cut-outs, 6 legs, 4 knobs, BC, SW, 5 tubes, AC ..**$175.00**

328, console, 1935, wood, upper front quarter-round dial, lower cloth grill w/cut-outs, 5 knobs, BC, SW, AC **$175.00**

337, tombstone, 1935, wood, lower front round airplane dial, upper grill w/cut-outs, fluted columns, 4 knobs, BC, SW, 7 tubes, AC...**$250.00**

356, tombstone, 1935, wood, lower front round airplane dial, upper grill w/cut-outs, 4 knobs, fluting, AC **$225.00**

387, cathedral, 1934, wood, center front half-round dial, upper cloth grill w/cut-outs, 3 knobs $275.00

427, console, 1933, wood, lowboy, small right front window dial, lower cloth grill w/cut-outs, 4 knobs, 6 legs, BC, SW, 7 tubes, AC **$135.00**

427D, console, 1933, wood, lowboy, small right front window dial, lower cloth grill w/cut-outs, 4 knobs, 6 legs, BC, SW, 7 tubes, DC **$135.00**

435, console, 1935, wood, upper front round airplane dial, lower cloth grill w/cut-outs, 3 knobs, BC, SW, 5 tubes, AC...**$160.00**

447, tombstone, 1934, wood, rounded shoulders, lower quarter-round dial, upper grill cut-outs, 5 knobs, BC, SW, AC ...**$225.00**

448, console, 1933, wood, lowboy, upper front quarter-round dial, lower cloth grill w/cut-outs, 4 knobs, 6 legs, AC **$235.00**

456, tombstone, 1936, wood, lower front round dial, upper cloth grill w/cut-outs, 4 knobs, AC **$250.00**

465Q, tombstone, 1934, wood, rounded top, lower round airplane dial, upper grill cut-outs, 4 knobs, battery...................**$235.00**

469, console, 1932, walnut, lowboy, upper front quarter-round dial, lower grill cut-outs, 4 knobs, available AC, DC or battery ...**$155.00**

509, console, 1935, wood, center front quarter-round dial, upper "tune-o-matic" clock, 5 knobs, BC, SW, AC **$250.00**

509-W, console, 1935, wood, center front quarter-round dial, upper "tune-o-matic" clock, 5 knobs, BC, SW, 9 tubes, AC **$250.00**

510, console, 1933, wood, modern, upper front quarter-round dial, lower grill w/cut-outs, 5 knobs, BC, SW, 10 tubes, AC ..**$250.00**

511W, console, 1934, wood, center front quarter-round dial, upper "tune-o-matic" clock, 5 knobs, BC, SW, 11 tubes, AC ...**$250.00**

521N, console, 1930, metal, upper left front dial, large lower center "caned" grill, legs.....................................**$125.00**

535, console, 1936, wood, upper front round dial, lower cloth grill w/center vertical bars, 3 knobs, 5 tubes, AC **$150.00**

545, tombstone, 1935, wood, lower round airplane dial, upper grill w/cut-outs, 3 knobs, BC, SW, AC.....................**$125.00**

555, table, 1933, inlaid walnut, chest-style, lift top, inner metal panel, front grill w/cut-outs, AC **$375.00**

558, cathedral, 1932, wood, center front half-round dial, upper cloth grill w/cut-outs, 4 knobs, available as AC, DC or battery **$350.00**

559N, console, 1934, wood, upper front quarter-round dial, lower cloth grill w/cut-outs, BC, SW, 9 tubes, AC **$150.00**

567, cathedral, 1932, wood, center front half-round dial, upper grill w/gothic cut-outs, front carved columns, 3 knobs, AC ...**$350.00**

612, console, 1932, wood, lowboy, upper front quarter-round dial, lower cloth grill w/cut-outs, 4 knobs, 2 speakers, 12 tubes, AC...**$200.00**

627, cathedral, 1932, wood, center front half-round dial, upper grill w/cut-outs, front columns, 3 knobs, 7 tubes, AC **$375.00**

637, tombstone, 1932, wood, lower front round multi-colored dial, upper cloth grill w/cut-outs, 4 knobs **$175.00**

649, console, 1935, wood, upper quarter-round dial, lower cloth grill w/cut-outs, 5 knobs, BC, SW, AC **$160.00**

667, console, 1933, wood, modern, upper front window dial, lower grill w/cut-outs, 4 knobs, BC, SW, 7 tubes, AC **$225.00**

676, console, 1936, wood, upper round "rainbow" dial, lower cloth grill w/vertical bars, 4 knobs, 6 tubes, AC **$150.00**

708, table, 1933, wood, right front dial, cloth grill w/cut-outs, 4 knobs, rounded top, BC, SW, 8 tubes, AC **$275.00**

711, console, 1933, wood, lowboy, inner quarter-round dial, double doors, 6 legs, 5 knobs, BC, SW, 11 tubes, AC.....**$260.00**

725, tombstone, 1936, wood, lower front round dial w/globes, upper grill w/cut-outs, 3 knobs, BC, SW, 5 tubes **$165.00**

735, cathedral, 1935, wood, lower front round airplane dial, upper cloth grill w/cut-outs, fluted columns, 4 knobs, AC **$250.00**

808, console, 1933, wood, upper front dial, lower cloth grill w/cut-outs, 6 legs, BC, SW, AC **$225.00**

810, console, 1935, wood, upper front quarter-round dial, lower cloth grill w/cut-outs, 5 knobs, BC, SW, AC **$200.00**

812, console, 1932, wood, lowboy, inner quarter-round dial, cloth grill w/cut-outs, double sliding doors, 6 legs, 12 tubes, AC...**$250.00**

854, tombstone, 1935, wood, small right front window dial, upper cloth grill w/cut-outs, 3 knobs, AC **$175.00**

856, tombstone, 1935, wood, lower round airplane dial, upper grill w/cut-outs, 4 knobs, BC, SW, AC..............................**$130.00**

944, cathedral, 1934, two-tone wood, right front window dial, upper cloth grill w/cut-outs, 2 knobs, 4 tubes, AC **$250.00**

976, console, 1935, wood, upper front round airplane dial, lower grill w/cut-outs, 4 knobs, 6 tubes, AC **$140.00**

AUDAR
Audar, Inc., Argos, Indiana

AV-7T, table-R/P, 1952, wood, inner dial & 5 knobs, fold-down front door, lift top, inner phono **$40.00**

PR-6, table-R/P, 1947, inner dial, phono & knobs, lift top, outer grill, handle, BC, AC **$20.00**

PR-6A, table-R/P, 1947, inner dial, phono & knobs, lift top, outer grill, handle, BC, AC **$20.00**

RER-9 "Telvar," console-R/P/Rec, 1949, wood, vertical dial & 4 knobs on top of case, left inner phono, sliding door, storage, BC, AC **$45.00**

AUDIOLA
Audiola Radio Co.
Chicago, Illinois

5W, table, 1933, wood, front dial, center grill w/cut-outs, 2 knobs, 5 tubes, AC/DC **$75.00**

517, cathedral, 1932, wood, ornate scrolled front, lower half-round dial, upper grill w/cut-outs, BC, SW, 5 tubes **$250.00**

610, cathedral, 1931, wood, center front quarter-round dial, upper grill w/scrolled cut-outs, 3 knobs **$200.00**

612, console, 1931, wood, lowboy, upper front quarter-round dial, lower grill w/scrolled cut-outs **$125.00**

811, cathedral, 1932, wood, center front quarter-round dial, upper cloth grill, fluted columns, 3 knobs, 8 tubes..............**$165.00**

814, console, 1931, wood, lowboy, upper front quarter-round dial, lower cloth grill w/scrolled cut-outs, stretcher base **$140.00**

1168, console, 1932, wood, lowboy, upper front half-round dial, lower cloth grill w/cut-outs, 6 legs, 11 tubes, AC........**$140.00**

10300D, console, 1933, wood, lowboy, upper front half-round dial, lower cloth grill w/cut-outs, 6 legs.............................**$150.00**

AUTOCRAT
Autocrat Radio Co.,
3855 N. Hamilton Ave.
Chicago, Illinois

101, table, 1938, plastic, right front dial panel over horizontal grill bars, decorative case lines, BC, 4 tubes, AC/DC **$60.00**

AUTOMATIC
Automatic Radio Mfg. Co., Inc.,
122 Brookline Avenue
Boston, Massachusetts

The Automatic Radio Manufacturing Company began in 1920. The company is well-known for its line of car radios and farm tractor sets as well as for their "Tom Thumb" line of home radios. The company is still in business as manufacturers of solid state products and test equipment.

8-15, table, 1937, plastic, Deco, right front square dial, left grill w/Deco design, 2 knobs **$75.00**

141, table-R/P, 1941, wood, outer right front dial, left grill w/diagonal bars, 3 knobs, lift top, inner phono, AC **$35.00**

145, table-R/P, 1941, walnut, outer right front dial, left grill, 3 knobs, lift top, inner phono, 6 tubes, AC **$35.00**

152, table-R/P, 1941, wood, right front dial, left grill w/Deco bands, 2 knobs, open top phono, 4 tubes, AC **$35.00**

434-A, table-R/P, 1940, walnut, center front square dial, right & left vertical grill bars, lift top, inner phono, 5 tubes, AC **$35.00**

458, table, 1939, wood, upper front rectangular dial, lower horizontal louvers, tapered cylindrical sides, 3 knobs **$100.00**

601, table, 1947, plastic, right front square dial, left vertical louvers, 2 knobs, curved sides, BC, 5 tubes, AC/DC........**$60.00**

602, table, 1947, plastic, right front square dial, left vertical louvers, curved sides, 2 knobs, AC **$60.00**

612X, table, 1946, wood, right front round convex dial, "S" curve on top of case, 2 knobs, BC, AC/DC **$95.00**

614X, table, 1946, plastic, right round starburst dial, left grill w/concentric squares, 2 knobs, BC, AC/DC **$60.00**

620, table, 1947, two-tone wood, upper front slanted slide rule dial, lower criss-cross grill, 2 knobs, BC, AC/DC..........**$50.00**
640, table-R/P, 1946, wood, outer right square dial, 3 knobs, criss-cross grill, lift top, inner phono, BC, AC **$30.00**
662, table, 1947, wood, upper front slanted slide rule dial, lower horizontal grill bars, 3 knobs, BC, SW, AC/DC.............**$45.00**
677, table-R/P, 1947, wood, inner right dial, 4 knobs, phono, lift top, wooden grill, BC, AC **$30.00**
720, table, 1947, wood, right front black dial, left criss-cross grill, rounded sides, 2 knobs, BC, AC/DC **$45.00**
933 "Tom Thumb," table, 1939, Catalin, small case, right front dial, left grill w/Deco cut-outs, 2 knobs, AC...........**$2,000.00+**
986, table, 1939, wood, right front dial, left cloth grill w/vertical bars, 6 pushbuttons, 3 knobs, BC, SW **$70.00**
1975, table, 1935, wood, right front slide rule dial, left horizontal wrap-around louvers, 3 knobs, AC **$50.00**
ATTP "Tom Thumb," portable, 1947, leatherette & plastic, inner half-moon dial & grill, door, handle, BC, 4 tubes, AC/DC/battery **$95.00**

B-44 "Tom Thumb," portable-bike, 1949, bike radio, left front vertical slide rule dial, right horizontal louvers, bottom mounting brackets, telescope antenna, handle, BC, battery..**$100.00**
Bluebird, table, 1926, leatherette, low rectangular case, 2 dial black Bakelite front panel w/bluebird decal, 1 tube **$500.00**
C-51, portable, 1952, leatherette, center front round dial w/inner perforations, handle, 2 knobs, BC, AC/DC/battery.......**$30.00**
C-60, portable, 1946, luggage style, right front dial, left horizontal louvers, 3 knobs, handle, BC, AC/DC/battery **$35.00**
C-60X, portable, 1947, two-tone leatherette, right front dial, left horizontal louvers, handle, BC, AC/DC/battery **$40.00**
C-65, portable, 1942, leatherette, right front dial, left horizontal louvers, handle, AC/DC/battery....................................**$35.00**

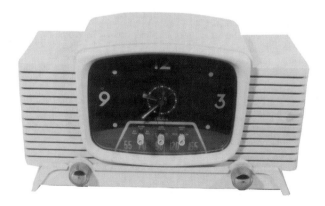

CL-61, table-C, plastic, raised top, lower slide rule dial, large center front clock face, right/left horizontal wrap-around bars, 5 knobs, feet, BC..**$50.00**
CL-100, table-C, 1959, plastic, right front square dial, left alarm clock, center vertical wrap-over bars, BC, 5 tubes, AC ..**$35.00**

CL-152B, table-C, 1953, plastic, right front square dial, center horizontal grill bars, left alarm clock, BC, AC **$30.00**

CL-175, table-C, wood, right front dial, left alarm clock, center lattice grill panel, 2 knobs, AC **$40.00**
F-790, console-R/P, 1947, wood, modern, inner right half-round dial, 4 knobs, left pull-out phono drawer, BC, AC........**$100.00**
P-64, portable, leatherette, front plastic panel, center round dial w/inner perforations, handle, 2 knobs **$40.00**
P-72, portable, 1939, cloth covered, upper front dial, lower grill, handle, 2 knobs, 5 tubes, AC/DC/battery **$30.00**
Tom Boy, portable, 1947, two-tone leatherette, right front dial, left criss-cross grill, handle, 2 knobs, BC, battery **$35.00**
Tom Thumb Buddy, portable, 1949, leatherette & plastic, inner slide rule dial, vertical grill bars, flip-open front, handle, BC, AC/DC/battery **$60.00**
Tom Thumb Camera, portable-camera, 1948, leatherette, top reflex camera, lower horizontal grill bars, top rear slide rule dial, strap, 2 knobs, BC, battery **$175.00**
Tom Thumb Jr., table, 1933, black Bakelite w/chrome trim, Deco, left front dial, center grill, chrome ball feet, AC...........**$160.00**
Tom Thumb Jr., portable, 1947, "snakeskin," right front square dial, left horizontal grill bars, 2 knobs, handle, BC, battery **$35.00**
Tom Thumb Portable, portable, 1929, leather case, inner engraved metal one dial panel, hinged front cover, handle, battery **$300.00**
TT528, portable, 1957, plastic, right front dial, left lattice grill, top right thumbwheel knob, handle **$150.00**
TT600, portable, 1957, plastic, tubes & transistors, right front dial, left checkered grill, handle, battery **$200.00**

AVIOLA
Aviola Radio Corp., Phoenix, Arizona

509, table-R/P, 1946, wood, right front dial, 3 knobs, left octagonal grill, feet, lift top, inner phono, BC, AC **$35.00**
601, table, 1947, plastic, upper slanted slide rule dial, lower checkerboard grill, 2 knobs, BC, AC/DC **$40.00**
608, table-R/P, 1947, wood, inner right slide rule dial, 3 knobs, phono, lift top, criss-cross grill, BC, AC **$40.00**
612, table, 1947, wood, upper slanted slide rule dial, lower horizontal louvers, 2 knobs, BC, AC/DC **$40.00**

B. F. GOODRICH
B. F. Goodrich Co., Akron, Ohio

92-523, table, 1951, plastic, right front round dial over rectangular grill bars, 2 knobs, BC, AC/DC **$35.00**

BALDWIN
Nathaniel Baldwin, Inc.

50 "Baldwinette," tombstone, 1930, wood, arched top, left front window dial, upper scalloped grill w/cut-outs, AC **$150.00**

BALKEIT
Balkeit Radio Corporation,
Clinton & Randolph Streets, Chicago, Illinois

The Balkeit Radio Company was formed as subsidiary of the Pfanstiehl Radio Company in 1929.

44, table, 1933, two-tone case, center front grill w/vertical cut-outs, 4 tubes......................**$65.00**

A-3, table, 1928, metal, low rectangular case, center front slanted thumbwheel dial, AC......................**$130.00**

A-5, table, 1928, wood, low rectangular case, center front slanted thumbwheel dial, AC......................**$140.00**

A-7, console, 1928, wood, highboy, inner slanted thumbwheel dial, lower grill, double front doors, 7 tubes, AC.........**$175.00**

B-7, console, 1928, wood, inner slanted thumbwheel dial, upper speaker grill w/cut-outs, double front doors, AC.........**$225.00**

B-9, console-R/P, 1928, wood, inner front thumbwheel dial, speaker grill w/cut-outs, double doors, lift top, inner phono, AC..**$200.00**

C, console, 1929, wood, inner front window dial, upper cloth grill w/scalloped cut-outs, double doors, AC......................**$200.00**

BARBAROSSA

Beer Bottle, table-N, 1934, Bakelite, looks like large Barbarossa beer bottle, base with switch, AC **$350.00**

BELLTONE
Jewel Radio Corp.,
583 Sixth Avenue, New York, New York

500, table, 1946, wood, upper slanted slide rule dial, lower horizontal grill bars, 2 knobs, BC, AC/DC **$40.00**

BELMONT
Belmont Radio Corp.,
5921 West Dickens Avenue
Chicago, Illinois

4B17, table, 1946, wood, lower front slide rule dial, upper vertical grill openings, 2 knobs, BC, battery................................**$30.00**

4B112, table, 1946, plastic, right front dial, left horizontal wrap-around louvers, 2 knobs, BC, battery **$40.00**

4B115, table, 1948, plastic, rounded top, front half-round dial curves over checkered grill, 2 knobs, BC, battery **$100.00**

5D110, table-R/P, 1947, wood, lower front slide rule dial, upper cloth grill, 2 knobs, 3/4 lift top, inner phono, BC, AC **$30.00**

5D118, table, 1948, plastic, center front airplane dial inside concentric circular grill, 2 knobs, AC **$95.00**

5D128, table, 1946, plastic, streamline, right front slide rule dial, left horizontal bars, right side knob, 5 pushbuttons, BC, AC/DC **$150.00**

5D137, table, 1947, plastic, Deco, right front dial, left round grill w/lower horizontal bars, 4 pushbuttons, right side knob, 5 tubes..**$150.00**

5P19, portable, 1946, luggage-style, upper front slide rule dial, lower grill area, 2 knobs on top of case, handle, BC, AC/DC/battery **$30.00**

5P113 "**Boulevard**," portable, 1947, very small case, dial & 2 knobs on top of case, earphone only, BC, 5 tubes, battery **$200.00**

6D111, table, 1946, plastic, streamlined, right front half-round dial, left horizontal grill bars, 6 pushbuttons, right side knob, AC..**$175.00**

6D120, table, 1947, plastic, streamline, right front half-round dial, left horizontal wrap-around louvers, 6 pushbuttons, right side knob, BC, AC/DC **$150.00**

8A59, console-R/P, 1946, wood, inner right slide rule dial, 4 knobs, pushbuttons, left pull-out phono drawer, BC, 4SW, AC..**$75.00**

401, cathedral, two-tone wood, lower front round airplane dial, upper grill w/cut-outs, 3 knobs....................................**$195.00**

407, portable, 1939, striped cloth, luggage-style, top dial & knobs, front grill, handle, battery..**$30.00**

507, portable, cloth covered, right front dial, left grill area, handle, 2 knobs, BC, AC/DC/battery..........................**$25.00**

509, table, 1940, wood, lower front slide rule dial, upper grill w/vertical bars, pushbuttons **$70.00**

510, table, 1938, plastic, streamline, right front dial, left horizontal wrap-around louvers, 2 knobs, AC **$75.00**

519, table, 1939, plastic, streamline, right front dial, left circular grill w/horizontal bars, 6 pushbuttons, 5 tubes **$175.00**

522, table, 1936, right front round dial, left cloth grill w/Deco cut-outs, 2 knobs, 5 tubes, battery **$45.00**

525, table, 1933, wood, Deco case lines, right front dial, center cloth grill w/cut-outs, 2 knobs **$75.00**

526, table, 1938, plastic, Deco, right front "Bel-Monitor" tuning system, left vertical grill bars, 5 tubes **$95.00**

533-D, table-R/P, 1941, wood, right front square dial, left grill, 2 knobs, lift top, inner phono, AC **$30.00**

534, table, 1940, plastic, streamline, right front slide rule dial, left horizontal louvers, right side knob, pushbuttons, AC ..**$150.00**

571, table-C, 1940, walnut, lower front slide rule dial, upper electric clock face, ribbed sides, 2 knobs, 5 tubes, AC........**$55.00**

575, tombstone, 1934, wood, shouldered, center front round dial, upper cloth grill w/cut-outs, AC....................................**$110.00**

602 "Scotty," table, 1937, plastic, raised right top, right front dial, left vertical wrap-over grill bars, AC/DC....................**$85.00**

636, table, 1939, plastic, right front dial, left wrap-around louvers, 5 pushbuttons, right side knob **$100.00**

675, tombstone, 1934, wood, center front round dial, upper cloth grill w/cut-outs, BC, SW, AC....................................**$115.00**

675E, console, 1934, two-tone wood, upper front round dial, lower cloth grill w/cut-outs, BC, SW, AC **$115.00**

686, table, 1936, wood, right front oval dial, left/right cloth grill areas, 3 knobs, BC, SW, AC $55.00

770, console, 1936, wood, upper front oval dial, lower cloth grill w/vertical bars, 4 knob, 7 tubes $125.00

777, tombstone, wood, lower front round airplane dial, upper cloth grill w/cut-outs, 4 knobs, 7 tubes $110.00

778A, table, 1936, wood, right front oval dial, left cloth grill w/cut-outs, 4 knobs, BC, SW, 7 tubes, AC $65.00

792, console, 1939, wood, upper front rectangular dial, lower grill area, pushbuttons, 4 knobs, AC $100.00

797, console-R/P/Rec, 1940, wood, inner right rectangular dial, pushbuttons, left phono, lift top, BC, SW, AC.............$100.00

840, console, 1937, wood, upper front oval dial, tuning eye, lower grill w/vertical bars, 4 knobs, BC, 2SW, AC $135.00

1070, console, 1935, wood, upper front oval dial, lower cloth grill w/vertical bars, 4 knobs, BC, SW, 10 tubes, AC $140.00

1170, console, 1936, wood, upper front oval dial, tuning eye, lower cloth grill w/vertical bars, 4 knobs $145.00

A-6D110, table, 1947, plastic, right front slide rule dial, left vertical grill bars, 2 knobs, 6 pushbuttons, BC, AC/DC $95.00

C640, table, 1946, plastic, streamlined, right front half-round dial, left horizontal grill bars, 6 pushbuttons, right side knob, AC $175.00

BENDIX

Bendix Radio/Bendix Aviation, Baltimore, Maryland

The company began in 1937 as a division of Bendix Aviation. During World War II, Bendix was a major supplier of radio-related aircraft equipment for the British and American governments.

0516A, table, 1946, plastic, Deco case, upper front slide rule dial, lower vertical louvers, 2 knobs, BC, AC/DC $65.00

0526A, table, 1946, plastic, Deco case, upper front slide rule dial, lower vertical louvers, 2 knobs, BC, AC/DC $65.00

0526B, table, 1946, plastic, Deco case, upper front slide rule dial, lower vertical louvers, 2 knobs, BC, AC/DC $65.00

0526E, table, 1946, wood, upper front slanted slide rule dial, lower vertical grill bars, rounded sides, 2 knobs, BC, AC/DC $50.00

55L2, table, 1949, ivory plastic, upper front slide rule dial, lower vertical grill bars, rear hand-hold, 2 knobs, BC, AC/DC $40.00

55L3, table, 1949, ivory plastic, upper front slide rule dial, lower wood-grained grill, rear hand-hold, 2 knobs, AC/DC $45.00

55P2, table, 1949, walnut plastic, upper front slide rule dial, lower vertical grill bars, rear hand-hold, 2 knobs, BC, AC/DC..$40.00

55P3, table, 1949, walnut plastic, upper front slide rule dial, lower wood-grained grill, rear hand-hold, 2 knobs, AC/DC $45.00

55P3U, table, 1949, walnut plastic, upper front slide rule dial, lower wood-grained grill, rear hand-hold, 2 knobs, AC/DC $45.00

55X4, portable, 1949, plastic, inner slide rule dial, horizontal louvers, 2 knobs, flip-up front, BC, AC/DC/battery.............$40.00

65P4, table, 1949, plastic, upper front slide rule dial, lower metal grill, rear hand-hold, 3 knobs, BC, AC/DC....................$40.00

65P4U, table, 1949, plastic, upper front slide rule dial, lower metal grill, rear hand hold, 3 knobs, BC, AC/DC $40.00

69B8, console-R/P, 1949, blonde wood, inner right radio/phono, left storage, double front doors, BC, FM, AC $75.00

69M8, console-R/P, 1949, mahogany, inner right radio/phono, left storage, double front doors, BC, FM, AC $75.00

69M9, console-R/P, 1949, wood, inner right slide rule dial, 3 knobs, pull-out phono, door, BC, FM, AC...................$75.00

75B5 "Fairfax," console-R/P, 1949, blonde wood, top left dial & knobs, right front pull-out phono drawer, storage, BC, FM, AC $100.00

75M8 "Heritage," console-R/P, 1949, mahogany, upper front dial and knobs, inner pull-out phono drawer & storage, door, BC, FM, AC $100.00

75P6, table, 1949, walnut plastic, upper front slide rule dial, lower wood-grained grill, rear hand-hold, AM, FM, AC/DC.....$45.00

75P6U, table, 1949, walnut plastic, upper front slide rule dial, lower wood-grained grill, rear hand-hold, AM, FM, AC/DC $45.00

75W5 "York," console-R/P, 1949, walnut wood, top left dial & knobs, right front pull-out phono drawer, BC, FM, AC..$100.00

79M7, console-R/P, 1949, wood, inner right slide rule dial, 3 knobs, lower pull-out phono, door, BC, FM, AC $80.00

95B3 "Boulevard," console-R/P, 1949, blonde wood, right tilt-out radio, 3 knobs, left pull-out phono drawer, BC, FM, AC...$95.00

95M3 "Wiltondale," console-R/P, 1949, mahogany, right tilt-out radio, 3 knobs, left pull-out phono drawer, BC, FM, AC...$95.00

95M9 "Wayne," console-R/P, 1949, mahogany, right tilt-out radio, 3 knobs, left pull-out phono drawer, BC, FM, AC $95.00

110, table, 1948, walnut plastic, upper front slide rule dial, lower vertical grill bars, rear hand-hold, 2 knobs, BC, AC/DC...$50.00

110W, table, 1948, ivory plastic, upper front slide rule dial, lower vertical grill bars, rear hand-hold, 2 knobs, BC, AC/DC...$50.00

111, table, 1949, walnut plastic, upper front slide rule dial, lower vertical grill bars, rear hand-hold, 2 knobs, BC, AC/DC...$50.00

111W, table, 1949, ivory plastic, upper front slide rule dial, lower vertical grill bars, rear hand-hold, 2 knobs, BC, AC/DC...$50.00

112, table, 1948, walnut, upper front slide rule dial, large lower perforated grill area, 2 knobs, BC, AC/DC $40.00

114, table, 1948, tan & brown plastic, upper front slide rule dial, lower horizontal wrap-around grill bars, 2 knobs, BC, AC/DC $275.00

115, table, 1948, ivory & burgundy plastic, upper front slide rule dial, lower horizontal wrap-around grill bars, 2 knobs, AC/DC ..$275.00

300, table, 1948, brown plastic, upper front slanted slide rule dial, lower vertical grill bars, 3 knobs, BC, AC/DC $40.00

300W, table, 1948, ivory plastic, upper front slanted slide rule dial, lower vertical grill bars, 3 knobs, BC, AC/DC $40.00

301, table, 1948, wood, upper front slanted slide rule dial, lower horizontal grill bars, 3 knobs, BC, AC/DC $35.00

302, table, 1948, wood, upper front slanted slide rule dial, lower horizontal grill bars, 3 knobs, BC, AC/DC $35.00

416A, table, 1948, wood, upper front slide rule dial, lower horizontal louvers, small base, 2 knobs, BC, battery $35.00

526C, table, 1946, Catalin, green & black, upper front slide rule dial, lower horizontal louvers, 2 knobs, BC, AC/DC $625.00

526MB, table, 1947, plastic, Deco case, upper front slide rule dial, lower vertical grill bars, 2 knobs, BC, AC/DC $65.00

613, table-R/P, 1948, wood, outer slide rule dial over large grill area, 4 knobs, lift top, inner phono, BC, AC $30.00

626-A, table, 1947, plastic, upper front slanted slide rule dial, lower vertical louvers, 3 knobs, rear hand-hold, BC, SW, AC/DC $50.00

626-C, table, 1947, plastic, upper front slanted slide rule dial, lower vertical louvers, 3 knobs, rear hand-hold, BC, SW, AC/DC $50.00

636A, table, 1947, plastic, upper front slanted slide rule dial, lower vertical louvers, 3 knobs, BC, AC/DC............$40.00

636B, table, 1947, wood, upper front slanted slide rule dial, lower woven grill, 3 knobs, BC, AC/DC............$65.00

636C, table, 1947, wood, upper front slanted slide rule dial, lower woven grill, 3 knobs, BC, AC/DC............$65.00

636D, table, 1947, wood, upper front slanted slide rule dial, lower woven metal grill, 3 knobs, AC $65.00

646A, end table, 1946, wood, drop leaf end table, dial lights up across lower panel, 4 knobs, BC, AC/DC............$125.00

656A, table-R/P, 1946, wood, inner right dial, 3 knobs, left phono, lift top, outer louvers, BC, AC $35.00

676D, console-R/P, 1946, wood, inner right vertical slide rule dial, 4 knobs, left phono, lift top, front grill, BC, SW, AC $65.00

687A, portable, 1949, leatherette, inner slide rule dial, vertical grill bars, fold-down front, handle, BC, AC/DC/battery $35.00

697A, end table-R/P, 1947, wood, step-down end table, radio in top, phono in base with sliding door, BC, AC $125.00

736-B, console-R/P, 1946, wood, inner right vertical dial, 4 knobs, left phono, lift top, BC, 2SW, AC $100.00

753F, table-C, 1953, wood, lower slide rule dial, large front alarm clock, side louvers, handle, feet, AC $65.00

753M, table-C, 1953, wood, lower slide rule dial, large front alarm clock face, handle, feet, BC, 5 knobs, AC $65.00

847-B, console-R/P, 1947, wood, inner right dial, 4 knobs, pushbuttons, left phono, lift top, BC, FM, AC $75.00

1217B, console-R/P, 1947, wood, inner right dial, pushbuttons, lift top, front pull-out phono drawer, BC, SW, FM, AC $70.00

1217D, console-R/P, 1948, wood, inner right slide rule dial, lift top, left front pull-out phono, oval grill, BC, SW, FM, AC $75.00

1518, console-R/P, 1948, mahogany, inner dial, pushbuttons, lift-up lid, left pull-out phono, BC, FM, AC $70.00

1519, console-R/P, 1948, walnut, inner dial, pushbuttons, lift-up lid, left pull-out phono, BC, FM, AC $70.00

1521, console-R/P, 1948, wood, inner right slide rule dial, 4 knobs, door, lift top, inner phono, BC, FM, AC $75.00

1524, console-R/P, 1948, mahogany, inner right dial, pushbuttons, lift-up lid, left pull-out phono, BC, FM, AC $70.00

1525, console-R/P, 1948, walnut, inner dial, pushbuttons, lift-up lid, left pull-out phono, BC, FM, AC $70.00

PAR-80, portable, 1948, luggage style, inner slide rule dial, vertical grill bars, fold-down front, handle, BC, SW, LW, AC/DC/battery $35.00

PAR-80A, portable, 1948, luggage style, inner slide rule dial, vertical grill bars, fold-down front, handle, BC, SW, LW, AC/DC/battery $35.00

BENRUS
Benrus Watch Co., Inc.,
50 West 44th Street
New York, New York

10B01B15B, table-C, 1955, metal, right side dial knob, left side on/off/volume knob, large front clock face, BC, AC $50.00

BEST

221, table, 1936, wood, rounded right side, right front oval dial, left grill w/chrome wrap-around bars, 3 knobs $110.00

BETTS & BETTS
Betts & Betts Corp.,
643 W. 43rd St., New York, New York

T8 "Trans-Continental," table, 1925, wood, high rectangular case, 2 dial front panel, 8 tubes, battery $200.00

BOSWORTH
The Bosworth Mfg. Co., Cinncinati, Ohio

B-2, table, 1926, wood, rectangular case, 2 dial fancy slanted metal panel, lift top, 5 tubes, battery $150.00

BOWMAN
A. W. Bowman & Co.,
Cambridge, Massachusetts

Airophone, table, 1923, wood, low rectangular case, 2 dial black bakelite front panel, battery $210.00

BRADFORD

96628, table-C, 1963, plastic, top right dial knob, front off-center alarm clock face, left random-patterned grill area, AM, 5 tubes, AC...$20.00

96636, table-C, 1962, plastic, right front dial over horizontal bars, left alarm clock face, AM, 5 tubes, AC $15.00

96651, table, 1962, plastic, lower right front dial panel over large patterned grill area, 3 knobs, feet, AM, FM, 6 tubes, AC/DC $15.00

BRANDES

**J. F. Brandes Corp.,
35 1/2 Oxford St., Newark, New Jersey**

B10, table, 1929, wood, low rectangular case, center front window dial w/escutcheon, 3 knobs, 7 tubes $135.00

B15, console, 1929, wood, upper front window dial w/escutcheon, lower cloth grill w/cut-outs, 3 knobs, AC.....................$150.00

Brandola, table, 1925, wood, low rectangular case, one center front dial, storage, battery...$185.00

BREMER-TULLY

**Bremer-Tully Manufacturing Company,
520 South Canal Street, Chicago, Illinois**

Bremer-Tully was begun in 1922 by John Tully and Harry Bremer. The company started in business manufacturing radio parts and kits and by 1925 they were selling fully assembled radios. The company was sold to Brunswick in 1928.

6-22 "Counterphase," table, 1927, two-tone wood, rectangular case, center front dial w/escutcheon, battery $125.00

6-35 "Counterphase," table, 1927, wood, rectangular case w/slant front, 2 center front dials w/escutcheon, battery $135.00

6-37 "Counterphase," console, 1927, wood, lowboy, 2 inner front dials w/escutcheon, 4 knobs, fold-down front, battery $150.00

6-40C, console, 1928, wood, lowboy, upper front dial w/escutcheon, lower cloth grill w/cut-outs, AC $150.00

6-40R, table, 1928, wood, low rectangular case, center front dial w/escutcheon, right & left decorative emblems $130.00

6-40S, table, 1928, wood, low rectangular case, center front dial w/escutcheon, right & left decorative emblems $130.00

7-70, table, 1928, wood, low rectangular case, recessed center front dial w/escutcheon, AC.......................................$135.00

7-71, console, 1928, wood, highboy, center front dial w/escutcheon, upper grill w/cut-outs, AC $175.00

8 "Counterphase," table, 1926, wood, rectangular case w/slant front, center dial w/escutcheon, lift top, battery $135.00

8-12 "Counterphase," table, 1927, wood, rectangular case w/slant front, center dial w/escutcheon, lift top, battery.............$135.00

8-20, table, 1928, wood, low rectangular case, recessed center front dial w/escutcheon, lift top, AC $130.00

8-21, console, 1928, wood, upper front dial, lower cloth grill w/cut-outs, AC...$135.00

81, console, 1929, wood, highboy, center front dial, upper grill w/oval cut-out, stretcher base, 3 knobs, AC $150.00

82, console, 1929, walnut, highboy, center front dial, upper grill w/cut-outs, double doors, 3 knobs, AC........................$185.00

BREWSTER

**Meissner Mfg. Div.,
Maguire Industries, Inc., Mt Carmel, Illinois**

9-1084, table, 1946, plastic, recessed right, slide rule dial, left horizontal bars, step-down top, 3 knobs..................$55.00

9-1086, table, 1946, plastic, recessed right, slide rule dial, left horizontal bars, step-down top, 3 knobs, BC, SW, AC/DC...$55.00

BROWNING-DRAKE

**Browning-Drake Corporation,
353 Washington Street
Brighton, Massachusetts**

Frederick Drake and Glenn Browning created the Browning-Drake circuit in 1924. In 1925 their Browning-Drake Company was selling fully-assembled radios. Their business slowly decreased until the partners went their separate ways in 1937.

4-R, table, wood, low rectangular case, 2 dial black front panel, lift top, 4 tubes $140.00

5-R, table, 1926, wood, low rectangular case, 2 dial black front panel, lift top, 5 tubes, battery $150.00

6-A, table, 1927, wood, low rectangular case, inner front dial, 5 knobs, double front doors, lift top, battery $110.00

7-A, table, 1927, walnut, low rectangular case, inner dial & knobs, double front doors, lift top, battery $115.00

30, table, 1928, wood, low rectangular case, center front dial, 3 knobs, AC $130.00

32, console, 1928, wood, lowboy, upper front dial, lower cloth grill w/gothic cut-outs, 3 knobs, AC $180.00

34, table, 1928, wood, low rectangular case, center front window dial w/escutcheon, 3 knobs, AC $125.00

53, table, 1929, wood, low rectangular case, center window dial with escutcheon, 3 knobs, AC $115.00

54, console, 1929, wood, lowboy, upper front window dial w/escutcheon, lower round grill w/cut-outs, 3 knobs, AC....$150.00

57, console, 1929, wood, upper front window dial w/escutcheon, lower scalloped grill w/cut-outs, 3 knobs, AC $150.00

84, console, 1929, wood, lowboy, upper front window dial, lower round grill w/cut-outs, battery $135.00

B-D Junior, table, 1925, wood, low rectangular case, 2 dial front panel, lift top, 5 tubes, battery $120.00

B-D Senior, table, 1925, wood, lower radio w/2 dial front panel, upper speaker w/scroll grill, 6 tubes, battery $200.00

B-D Standard, table, 1925, mahogany, low rectangular case, 2 dial front panel, lift top, 5 tubes, battery $140.00

BRUNSWICK

5KR, table, 1928, wood, low rectangular case, center front dial w/escutcheon, lift top, 7 tubes, 2 knobs, AC $110.00

5-WO, table, 1928, wood, low rectangular case, center window dial w/escutcheon, lift top, 9 tubes $125.00

11, tombstone, 1931, wood, shouldered case, center front window dial, upper grill w/cut-outs, AC..................................$165.00

14, console, 1929, wood, upper front dial, lower grill w/cut-outs, 3 knobs, stretcher base, AC $145.00

15, console, 1930, wood, upper front window dial, lower scalloped grill, 2 knobs, stretcher base, AC $145.00

16, console, 1931, wood, lowboy, upper front window dial, lower cloth grill w/cut-outs, AC...$125.00

21, console, 1929, wood, highboy, inner front dial & knobs, double doors, stretcher base, AC..$150.00

22, console, 1930, wood, inner front dial & knobs, double doors, stretcher base, AC..$150.00

31, console-R/P, 1929, wood, inner front dial & knobs, double doors, phono, arched stretcher base, AC....................$150.00

33, console-R/P, 1931, wood, upper front dial, lower grill w/cut-outs, lift top, inner phono, AC $135.00

50, console, wood, upper front window dial, lower tapestry grill w/cut-outs, right & left medallions, 2 knobs $145.00

1559, side table, 1939, wood, French Provincial styling, inner right dial/left grill, double front doors, 5 tubes, AC/DC $135.00

1580, table, wood, rectangular case, inner right dial, 2 knobs, left grill w/cut-outs, double doors..$100.00

1669, side table, 1939, wood, Hepplewhite styling, inner right dial/left grill/pushbuttons, double front doors, 6 tubes, AC $150.00

2559, side table, 1939, wood, Early American styling, inner right dial/ left grill, double front doors, 5 tubes, AC/DC $110.00

2689, side table, 1939, wood, Duncan Phyfe styling, inner dial/tuning eye/pushbuttons, double doors, 6 tubes, AC $175.00

3689, side table, 1938, wood, French styling, half-round table, front dial, pushbuttons, BC, SW, LW, 6 tubes, AC $150.00

4689, console, 1939, wood, Queen Anne styling, inner dial/tuning eye/pushbuttons, double doors, 6 tubes, AC $200.00

5000, console-R/P, 1948, wood, inner right front slide rule dial, 4 knobs, fold-back door, BC, FM, AC...........................$100.00

8109, console-R/P, 1939, wood, Queen Anne styling, inner dial/grill/tuning eye/pushbuttons, lift top, inner phono, 8 tubes, AC $225.00

A-2700, console-R/P, 1939, wood, inner right front slide rule dial, pushbuttons & 3 knobs, "tambour" doors, lift top, inner phono, BC, SW, AC $150.00

BJ-6836 "Tuscany," end table-R/P, 1947, wood, step-down end table, dial & 5 knobs in top, doors, phono in base, BC, AC..........$125.00

D-1000, console-R/P, 1949, wood, inner right slide rule dial, 4 knobs, left pull-out phono drawer, double doors, BC, FM, AC $100.00

T-2580, table, 1939, wood, inner right dial, left cloth grill w/cut-outs, 2 knobs, double doors, AC..................$100.00

BUCKINGHAM

80, table, metal, low rectangular case, large front escutcheon w/window dial, lift top, 3 knobs................................$150.00

BULOVA
Electronics Guild, Inc.,
Sunrise Highway, Valley Stream,
Long Island, New York

100, table-C, 1957, plastic, left front dial & clock, right metal grill, side knobs, step-down top, BC, 5 tubes, AC................$40.00
110, table-C, 1957, plastic, left front dial & clock, right grill, step-down top, side knobs, feet, BC, AC........................$40.00
120, table-C, plastic, left front dial & clock, right grill w/center logo, step-down top, side knobs, feet, BC, AC....................$40.00
170, table-C, plastic, lower right front half-round dial & left on/off/volume knob over horizontal bars, center clock face, feet, BC, AC $25.00
300, table-C, plastic, center front square dial in middle of concentric square louvers, feet, 2 knobs, AC/DC....................$40.00

400 Series, table-C, plastic, lower right front dial knob, large left clock face, lattice grill area, feet, BC, AC $20.00
A, table-C, plastic, left front dial & clock, right grill, step-down top, side knobs, feet, BC, AC $40.00
M-701, cathedral-C, 1932, wood, center front half-round "rainbow" dial, upper grill w/round clock & cut-outs, 7 tubes $375.00

BUSH & LANE
Bush and Lane Piano Company,
Holland Michigan

11K, console, 1930, wood, lowboy, Deco, shouldered, upper front dial, lower square grill w/cut-outs, varigated veneers..$195.00
34, console, 1929, wood, upper front dial, lower scalloped grill w/cut-outs, stretcher base, AC $145.00
40, console, 1929, wood, inner front dial & knobs, double doors, stretcher base, AC..$165.00

CAMEO
Cameo
Columbus, OH

14N18-03, table, 1964, beige/wood grain, center front panel with dial and knobs, right and left twin speakers, 5 tubes, AC/DC $10.00
52N17-03, table-C, 1960, plastic, lower right front thumbwheel tuning and volume knobs, upper lattice grill area, left alarm clock face, AM, 5 tubes, AC $15.00
52N18-03, table-C, 1960, plastic, lower right front thumbwheel tuning and volume knobs, upper lattice grill area, left alarm clock face, AM, 5 tubes, AC $15.00

CAPEHART
Farnsworth Television & Radio Corp.,
Fort Wayne, Indiana

1P55, portable, 1955, plastic, center front round dial over horizontal grill bars, top thumbwheel knob, handle, BC, 4 tubes, AC/DC/battery $35.00
2P56, portable, 1956, center front round dial over grill, top thumbwheel knob, handle, BC, 4 tubes, AC/DC/battery $30.00
3T55E, table, 1954, plastic, right front round dial over large woven grill area, feet, BC, 5 tubes, AC/DC $25.00
10, portable, 1952, plastic, upper front half-round dial over lattice grill, top left thumbwheel knob, fold-down handle $30.00
17RPQ155F, console-R/P/Rec, 1955, wood, inner center slide rule dial, right phono, left recorder, lift top, BC, FM, 11 tubes, AC $65.00
29P4, console-R/P, 1949, wood, inner right black dial, 5 knobs, left pull-out phono, double doors, BC, FM, AC.............$90.00
33P9, console-R/P, 1949, wood, inner dial, 4 knobs, phono, lift top, lower front grill w/cut-outs, storage, BC, FM, AC ...$80.00
75C56, table-C, 1956, right side dial knob, center front square alarm clock face over recessed grill, BC, 5 tubes, AC ..$25.00
88P66BNL, portable, 1956, leatherette, flip-up front w/map, inner multi-band slide rule dial, telescope antenna, handle, 8 band, 5 tubes, AC/DC/battery $75.00
115P2, console-R/P, 1949, wood, inner right dial, left lift top, inner phono, woven front grill, BC, SW, FM, 25 tubes, AC ..$275.00
413P, console-R/P, 1949, wood, inner right dial, door, left lift top, inner phono, BC, SW, FM, 28 tubes, AC....................$300.00
1002F, console-R/P, 1951, wood, inner right slide rule dial, 4 knobs, inner left pull-out phono, doors, BC, FM, AC $90.00
1006-M, console-R/P, 1951, wood, inner right slide rule dial, 4 knobs, left pull-out phono drawer, BC, 8 tubes, AC $70.00
1007AM, console-R/P, 1951, wood, inner right slide rule dial, 4 knobs, left pull-out phono drawer, BC, FM, 11 tubes, AC ..$75.00
C14, table-C, plastic, lower slide rule dial, large upper alarm clock face, step-down top, feet, 4 knobs $35.00
P-213, portable, 1954, plastic & metal, top dial & 2 knobs, front V-shaped plaid grill, handle, BC, 4 tubes, AC/DC/battery.$45.00
RP-152, console-R/P, 1953, wood, inner front slide rule dial, 4 knobs, lower phono, large double doors, BC, 7 tubes, AC............$50.00
T-30, table, 1951, plastic, right front half-round dial, center raised patterned grill, 2 knobs, feet, BC, AC/DC....................$40.00
T-522, table, 1953, plastic, large front dial w/inner perforations, 2 knobs, slanted feet, BC, AC/DC $40.00

TC-20, table-C, 1951, plastic, right side dial knob, left front alarm clock, step-down top, BC, AC......................................$30.00
TC-62, table-C, 1953, plastic, right side dial knob, left front alarm clock, step-down top, BC, AC......................................$30.00

CAPITOL
Capitol Radio Corp.

UN-61 "Music Master," table, 1948, upper slanted slide rule dial, lower horizontal louvers, 2 knobs, BC, AC/DC..............$40.00
UN-72, table, 1949, two-tone wood, upper slanted slide rule dial, lower horizontal louvers, 4 knobs.................................$45.00
UN-72P "High Fidelity Symphonic," table-R/P, 1948, wood, outer slanted slide rule dial, horizontal louvers, lift top, inner phono, BC, SW..$35.00

CARDINAL
Cardinal Radio Manufacturing Co.,
2812 South Main St., Los Angeles, California

60, cathedral, 1931, wood, center front quarter-round dial, upper 4-section grill, 3 knobs $275.00
60, tombstone, 1931, wood, arched top, center quarter-round dial, upper grill w/cut-outs, 3 knobs...................................$150.00

CARLOYD
Carloyd Electric & Radio Co.,
342 Madison Ave., New York, New York

Mark II "Malone-Lemmon," table, 1925, wood, high rectangular case, 3 dial slanted front panel, lift top, 5 tubes, battery $250.00

CASE
Indiana Mfg. & Elec. Co.,
570 Case Avenue, Marion, Indiana

60A, table, 1926, mahogany, low rectangular case, 2 dial front panel, lift top, feet, 6 tubes, battery $95.00
61C, console, 1926, two-tone walnut, center front dial, upper speaker grill w/cut-outs, battery....................................$150.00
62C, console, 1927, wood, center front dial w/escutcheon, upper speaker grill w/cut-outs, 6 tubes, AC...........................$150.00
66A, table, 1928, wood, low rectangular case, center illuminated window dial w/escutcheon, 6 tubes, AC......................$115.00
73B, console, 1928, wood, highboy, upper window dial w/escutcheon, lower grill w/cut-outs, 3 knobs $135.00
73C, console, 1928, wood, lowboy, inner dial & knobs, double front doors, stretcher base, AC $165.00
90A, table, 1927, walnut, low rectangular case, center front dial, left side loop antenna, feet, battery $175.00
90C, console, 1927, wood, lowboy, large case, inner dial & knobs, front doors, battery..$175.00
500, table, 1925, mahogany, low rectangular case, slanted 3 dial front panel, lift top, 5 tubes, battery $95.00
503, table, 1926, wood, low rectangular case, front panel w/3 pointer dials, 6 tubes, battery $100.00
510, tombstone, 1935, wood, center front "Tell-Time Jumbo Dial," upper cloth grill with cut-outs, 5 tubes $135.00
701, console, 1926, walnut, inner left 3 dial panel, right grill, fold-down front, fold-up top, battery...............................$215.00
710, tombstone, 1935, wood, center front "Tell-Time Jumbo Dial," upper cloth grill with cut-outs, 7 tubes $135.00
1015, console, 1935, wood, upper front round dial, lower cloth grill w/cut-outs, 10 tubes $150.00

1017, console, 1935, wood, upper front round "Tell-Time Jumbo Dial," lower cloth grill w/cut-outs $150.00

CAVALCADE
Cavalcade Radio Company
2341 Wolfram St.
Chicago, Illinois

361, table, 1935, walnut, center front round airplane dial over cloth grill w/cut-outs, 2 knobs, 5 tubes, AC $75.00
3651, console, 1935, two-tone wood, upper front airplane dial, lower cloth grill w/cut-outs, 4 knobs, 3 bands, 6 tubes, AC...$125.00

CAVALIER

4CL4, table-C, 1955, plastic, right side dial knob, center front clock over checkered grill, BC, 4 tubes, AC $30.00
5C1, table-C, 1954, plastic, right side dial knob, center front clock over checkered grill, BC, 5 tubes, AC $30.00
603, table, 1957, plastic, right side dial knob, large front perforated grill w/crown logo & "V," BC, 6 tubes, AC/DC..........$40.00
LK-447, cathedral, 1933, two-tone wood, center front half-round dial, upper cloth grill w/cut-outs......................$150.00
SF-547, cathedral, 1933, two-tone wood, center front half-round dial, upper cloth grill w/cut-outs $150.00

CBS-COLUMBIA
CBS-Columbia Inc.,
3400 47th Avenue,
Long Island City, New York

515A, table, 1953, plastic, large right front round dial, diagonally divided lattice grill, lower left knob $35.00
525, portable, 1953, plastic, lower right front dial knob, upper right thumbwheel knob, left patterned grill area, handle........$35.00
541, table-C, 1953, plastic, right round dial, left alarm clock face, center checkered panel, BC, AC $30.00
5165, table, plastic, large half-round metal dial w/inner horizontal lines, large dial pointer, feet, 5 tubes $40.00
5220, portable, 1954, plastic, right side dial knob, upper front horizontal bars, fold-down handle, BC, AC/DC/battery $25.00
5440, table-C, 1956, plastic, right round dial, left round alarm clock face, center panel, BC, 5 tubes, AC $30.00
T202, table, 1956, plastic, recessed front panel with right "steering wheel" dial over horizontal bars, BC, 5 tubes, AC........$45.00

CHANCELLOR
Radionic Equipment Co.,
170 Nassau Street, New York, New York

35P, portable, 1947, leatherette, plastic front panel w/right dial over horizontal bars, 2 knobs, handle, BC, AC/DC/battery..$25.00

CHANNEL MASTER
Channel Master Corp.,
Ellenville, New York

6532, table, 1960, two-tone plastic, center front dial, right & left twin speakers, 2 knobs, tubes, AM $20.00
6533, table-C, 1960, two-tone plastic, center alarm clock & dial, right & left twin speakers, snooze bar, tubes, AM $25.00

6535, table, 1960, walnut, two right front slide rule dials, left lattice grill, 4 knobs, tubes, AM, FM.........................$25.00
6536, table-C, 1960, walnut, right front clock & slide rule dial, left lattice grill, 4 knobs, tubes, AM, FM $25.00

CHELSEA
Chelsea Radio Co.,
150 Fifth Street, Chelsea, Massachusetts

102, table, 1923, wood, high rectangular case, 2 dial black front panel, 3 tubes, battery.........................$120.00
107 "Regenodyne," table, 1925, wood, low rectangular case, 2 dial front panel, 4 tubes, battery $110.00
122, table, 1925, wood, high rectangular case, slant front 2 dial black Bakelite panel, lift top, battery.........................$110.00
Super Five, table, 1925, wood, slant front, 3 oval window dials, 5 Bakelite knobs, curved sides, battery.........................$110.00

Super Five, table, 1925, wood, three dial slant front wooden panel, lift top, battery $110.00

Super Five, table, 1925, wood, metal front panel, three window dials w/brass escutcheons, 5 knobs, battery .$120.00
Super Six, table, 1925, wood, high rectangular case, slant front, three window dials, curved sides, battery..................$115.00

CHEROKEE

571-X50-2A, table, wood, upper right front rectangular dial over large plastic horizontal louvers, 2 knobs $40.00

CISCO
Cities Service Oil Co., New York, New York

1A5, table, 1948, wood, right front square dial, left horizontal louvers, 2 knobs, BC, AC/DC.........................$40.00
9A5, table, 1947, plastic, right front square dial, left horizontal louvers, 2 knobs, handle, BC, AC/DC $75.00

CLAPP-EASTHAM
Clapp-Eastham Company,
136 Main Street, Cambridge, Massachusetts

The Clapp-Eastham Company was formed in 1908 to manufacture X-ray and wireless parts and eventually produced complete radio sets. The company declined during the early 1920s and was out of business by 1929.

Baby Emerson, table, 1927, small case, 1 dial front panel, Emerson Multivalve, battery.........................$475.00
DD Radak, table, 1925, leatherette or wood, low rectangular case, 2 dial black front panel, 3 tubes, battery $225.00
Gold Star, table, wood, low rectangular case, black front panel w/3 pointer dials and gold trim.........................$250.00

HR, table, 1922, wood, high rectangular case, 2 dial black Bakelite front panel, 1 tube, battery $375.00
HR/HZ, table, 1922, wood, 2 units w/black Bakelite front panels, battery $725.00
R-3 Radak, table, 1923, wood, high rectangular case, black Bakelite front panel, battery.........................$250.00
R-4 Radak, table, 1924, wood, high rectangular case, black Bakelite front panel, 1 tube, battery..................$300.00
RZ Radak, table, 1922, wood, rectangular case, black Bakelite front panel, 3 tubes, battery.........................$500.00

CLARION
Warwick Mfg. Corp.,
4640 West Harrison Street
Chicago, Illinois

61, cathedral, 1931, wood, off-center front window dial, upper scalloped grill w/cut-outs, 6 tubes, AC $175.00

80, tombstone, 1931, wood, shouldered top, front half-round dial, upper grill w/cut-outs, 3 knobs, 8 tubes $175.00

81, console, 1931, wood, lowboy, upper front half-round dial, lower cloth grill w/cut-outs, 7 tubes $135.00

85, cathedral, 1931, wood, center front half-round dial, upper cloth grill w/cut-outs, 3 knobs......................$275.00

90, tombstone, 1931, wood, shouldered top, front half-round dial, upper grill w/cut-outs, 3 knobs, 8 tubes......................$160.00

91, console, 1931, wood, lowboy, upper front half-round dial, lower cloth grill w/cut-outs, 8 tubes $150.00

280, console, wood, lowboy, upper front half-round dial, lower cloth grill w/cut-outs, 6 legs $150.00

300, console, wood, inner half-round dial, double doors, lower criss-cross grill area, decorative columns, 2 speakers......................$200.00

320 Clarion Jr., tombstone, wood, center front window dial w/escutcheon, upper cloth grill w/cut-outs, 3 knobs $90.00

321, tombstone, wood, center front window dial w/escutcheon, upper cloth grill w/cut-outs, 3 knobs, 5 tubes $90.00

322, console, wood, lowboy, upper front window dial, lower cloth grill w/cut-outs, 3 knobs......................$125.00

340, tombstone, wood, center front window dial, upper cloth grill w/cut-outs, 3 knobs $100.00

400, table, 1937, wood, step-down top, right front dial, center grill w/cut-outs, 2 knobs, AC/DC $90.00

422, table, 1933, wood, rounded top, right front dial, center grill w/cut-outs, 5 tubes, AC/DC $75.00

450, table, 1933, wood, right front dial, center grill w/cut-outs, ribbed sides, 6 tubes, AC/DC $90.00

470, cathedral, 1933, wood, small case, center front window dial, upper grill w/cut-outs, 4 knobs, AC......................$175.00

691, table, 1937, two-tone wood, right front round telephone dial, left horizontal louvers, 4 knobs $75.00

770, table, 1937, wood, large right front dial, left cloth grill w/2 horizontal bars, 3 knobs, BC, SW......................$45.00

11011, portable, 1947, leatherette, slide rule dial, horizontal louvers, 2 knobs, handle, BC, AC/DC/battery $25.00

11305, table-R/P, 1947, wood, outer front dial, 2 knobs, criss-cross grill, lift top, inner phono, BC, AC......................$30.00

11411-N, portable, 1947, inner right dial, lattice grill, 2 knobs, switch, flip-up cover, BC, AC/DC/battery......................$35.00

11801, table, 1947, plastic, lower slanted slide rule dial, upper horizontal louvers, 2 knobs, BC, AC/DC $50.00

12110M, console-R/P, 1949, wood, right tilt-out dial, 4 knobs, left pull-out phono drawer, BC, FM, AC $70.00

12310W, console-R/P, 1948, wood, upper slanted slide rule dial, 5 knobs, center pull-out phono drawer, BC, SW, AC $90.00

12708, console-R/P, 1948, wood, upper front slide rule dial, lower criss-cross grill, 4 knobs, lift top, inner phono, BC, AC......................$50.00

12801, table, 1949, plastic, right front square dial, left lattice grill, ridged base, 2 knobs, BC, AC/DC......................$50.00

13101, table, 1948, plastic, upper slanted slide rule dial, horizontal grill bars, 4 knobs, AM, FM, AC/DC $40.00

13201, table, 1949, plastic, right square dial, left horizontal wrap-around louvers, 2 knobs, BC, battery $30.00

14601, table, 1949, plastic, right square dial, left checkerboard grill, ridged base, 2 knobs, BC, AC/DC $50.00

14965, table, 1949, plastic, upper slanted slide rule dial, lower horizontal grill bars, 4 knobs, BC, FM, AC $40.00

AC-51, console, 1929, wood, lowboy, upper front window dial, lower scalloped grill, stretcher base, 3 knobs..............$125.00

AC-53, console, 1929, wood, lowboy, upper front window dial, lower scalloped grill, stretcher base, 3 knobs..............$125.00

AC-60 "Junior," cathedral, 1932, walnut, off-center window dial, upper scalloped cloth grill w/cut-outs, 3 knobs...........$200.00

AC-85, (top right) cathedral, wood, center front half-round dial, upper cloth grill w/cut-outs, 3 knobs, AC $275.00

C100, table, 1946, plastic, right front square dial, left horizontal wrap-around louvers, 2 knobs, BC, AC/DC...................$45.00

C101, table-R/P, 1946, wood, right front square dial, 3 knobs, left horizontal louvers, lift top, inner phono, BC, AC...........$35.00

C102, table, 1946, plastic, upper front slide rule dial, lower horizontal wrap-around grill bars, 2 knobs, BC, AC/DC $40.00

C103, table, 1946, plastic, upper front slide rule dial, lower cloth grill w/horizontal bars, 4 knobs, BC, AC $40.00

C104, table, 1946, wood, upper front curved dial, lower cloth grill w/horizontal louvers, 4 knobs, BC, AC/DC...................$45.00

C105-A, console-R/P, 1946, wood, upper front slide rule dial, lower horizontal louvers, 4 knobs, doors, lift top, inner phono, BC, 6 tubes, AC......................$65.00

C108, table, 1946, wood, upper slanted slide rule dial, lower cloth grill w/harp cut-out, 2 knobs, BC, battery $50.00

TC-2, console, 1934, wood, Deco, upper front quarter-round dial, lower grill w/geometric cut-outs, 3 knobs $130.00

CLARK'S
Clark's,
30 Boylston St., Boston, Massachusetts

Acme Reflex, table, wood, low rectangular case, 2 dial black front panel, lift top, battery $130.00

CLEARSONIC
U. S. Television Mfg. Co.,
3 West 61st Street, New York, New York

5C66, table, 1947, wood, right front square dial, left cloth grill w/horizontal bars, 2 knobs, BC, AC/DC $35.00

5D66, table-R/P, 1947, wood, right front dial, 2 knobs, criss-cross grill, lift top, inner phono, BC, AC/DC $35.00

CLEARTONE
Cleartone Radio Company,
2427 Gilbert Avenue, Cincinnati, Ohio

60 "Goldcrest," table, 1925, wood, low rectangular case, front panel w/3 pointer dials, 4 tubes, battery $100.00

70 "Clear-O-Dyne," table, 1925, wood, low rectangular case, front panel w/2 pointer dials, 4 tubes, battery $100.00

72 "Clear-O-Dyne," console, 1925, wood, inner panel w/2 pointer dials, drop front, built-in speaker, 4 tubes, battery $200.00

80 "Super Clear-O-Dyne," table, 1925, wood, low rectangular case, front panel w/3 pointer dials, 5 tubes, battery $115.00

82, console, 1925, wood, inner panel w/3 pointer dials, drop front, built-in speaker, 5 tubes, battery $200.00

100, table, 1926, wood, high rectangular case, slant front panel, lift top, 5 tubes, battery $125.00

Mayflower, console, 1926, wood, upper front dial w/escutcheon, lower built-in speaker w/scrolled grill, 5 tubes, AC $175.00

CLEVELAND
Cleveland Products Co., 714 Huron Rd., Cleveland, Ohio

A-5, table, 1925, wood, low rectangular case, 3 dial front panel, 5 tubes, battery...$125.00

CLIMAX
Climax Radio & Tel. Co., Inc., 513 South Sangamon Street Chicago, Illinois

35 "Ruby," table, 1937, walnut veneer, ultra streamlined, teardrop shaped, right oval dial, left horizontal grill bars, tuning eye, BC, SW, 7 tubes, AC/DC.......................$300.00

Emerald, table, 1937, walnut veneer, streamlined, right oval convex dial, left wrap-around grill bars $115.00

CLINTON
Clinton Mfg. Co., 1217 West Washington Boulevard, Chicago, Illinois

216, table, wood, rounded sides, right front dial, left grill w/Deco cut-outs, 3 knobs, BC, SW, 5 tubes, AC/DC $100.00

254, portable, 1937, leatherette, inner right front dial, left round grill, fold-open front door, handle $65.00

620XP, table, wood, right front airplane dial, left cloth grill w/2 horizontal bars, 6 pushbuttons, feet, 3 knobs, BC, SW AC...$65.00

1102, console, 1937, wood, large upper front round dial, tuning eye, lower cloth grill w/vertical bars $135.00

CO-OP
National Cooperatives Inc., 343 South Dearborn, Chicago, Illinois

6A47WT, table, 1949, wood, lower front slide rule dial, large upper recessed grill, 4 knobs, BC, SW, AC...................$35.00

COCA COLA
Point of Purchase Displays, Inc.

Coke Bottle, (left) table-N, Bakelite, large bottle-shaped set complete with "Drink Coca-Cola" slogan, small front window dial, 2 knobs $2,500.00

Coke Cooler, table-N, 1949, red plastic, looks like Coca Cola cooler, upper front slide rule dial, 2 knobs............$650.00

COLBLISS
The Colbliss Radio Company, 827 South Hoover St., Los Angeles, California

500 "Petite," cathedral, 1931, wood, lower front window dial, upper scalloped grill w/cut-outs, 3 knobs $225.00

COLONIAL
Colonial Radio Corporation,
Buffalo, New York

16, table, 1925, wood, low rectangular case, 3 dial front panel, 5 tubes, battery..$125.00

17, table, 1925, wood, low rectangular case, 2 dial front panel, 4 tubes, battery..$125.00

20-6, table, 1925, wood, low rectangular case, 3 dial front panel, 6 tubes, battery..$125.00

39, cathedral, 1931, wood, lower front window dial, upper scalloped grill w/cut-outs, AC....................................$175.00

41C, grandfather clock, 1931, wood, front window dial, lower grill w/cut-outs, rectangular clock face $350.00

250, table, 1933, walnut w/inlay, right front dial, center cloth grill w/cut-outs, AC $90.00

279, table, 1933, walnut w/inlay, arched top, right front dial, center 3-section cloth grill w/cut-outs $90.00

300, table, 1933, plastic, Deco, right front dial, center circular chrome cut-outs, ribbed sides, feet, 5 tubes, AC/DC ..$275.00

301, table, 1933, wood, Deco, right front dial, center cloth grill w/chrome cut-outs, 5 tubes, AC $225.00

315EV, tombstone, wood, lower front dial, upper cloth grill w/cut-outs, 5 knobs, BC, SW, 8 tubes, AC $100.00

600A, console, 1934, wood, upper front window dial, lower cloth grill w/2 vertical bars, 6 tubes, AC $120.00

601, console, 1934, wood w/metal inlay, upper front window dial, lower cloth grill w/4 vertical columns, 5 knobs, 10 tubes, AC $150.00

603, console, 1934, wood, upper front round airplane dial, lower cloth grill w/cut-outs, 5 knobs, feet, BC, SW, 6 tubes, AC.........$125.00

604, console, 1934, wood, upper front round airplane dial, lower cloth grill w/3 vertical bars, 5 knobs, BC, SW, 8 tubes, AC $125.00

605, console, 1934, wood, inner front airplane dial, door, lower front cloth grill w/cut-outs, BC, SW, 7 tubes, AC $145.00

651, table, 1934, wood, raised top, right and left front knobs, center cloth grill w/cut-outs, BC, SW, 5 tubes, AC $75.00

652, tombstone, 1934, wood, lower front round airplane dial, upper cloth grill w/cut-outs, 3 knobs, BC, SW, 5 tubes, AC $100.00

653, tombstone, 1934, wood w/metal inlay, arched top, lower front dial, upper cloth grill w/cut-outs, 3 knobs, BC, 5 tubes, AC.........$175.00

654, table, 1934, wood w/inlay, right and left front knobs, center cloth grill w/cut-outs, BC, 5 tubes, AC $70.00

655, table, 1934, wood, raised top, right and left front knobs, center cloth grill w/oblong cut-outs, BC, SW, 6 tubes, AC $70.00

656, tombstone, 1934, wood, lower front round airplane dial, upper cloth grill w/cut-outs, 3 knobs, BC, SW, 6 tubes, AC $150.00

658, table, 1934, wood, right and left front knobs, center cloth grill with cut-outs, BC, SW, 6 tubes, AC $85.00

New World, (left) table-N, 1933, plastic, world globe on stand, front window dial, side knobs, top vents, 5 tubes, AC/DC.........$775.00

T345, cathedral, wood, lower front quarter-round dial, upper cloth grill w/cut-outs, 3 knobs...............................$175.00

COLUMBIA PHONOGRAPH
Columbia Phonograph Company, Inc.,
55 Fifth Avenue, New York, New York

C-1, table, 1928, wood, center front window dial w/escutcheon, lift top, 3 knobs, switch, 7 tubes, AC $130.00

C-81, upright table, 1932, two-tone walnut, center front window dial, upper grill w/cut-outs & "notes," 3 knobs, 8 tubes, AC $185.00

C-83, console, 1932, walnut, lowboy, upper front window dial, lower grill w/cut-outs & "notes," 6 legs, 8 tubes, AC....$140.00

C-84, console, 1932, walnut, highboy, upper front window dial, lower twin grills w/cut-outs, 6 legs, 8 tubes, AC $150.00

C-85, console-R/P, 1932, walnut, center front dial, lower grill w/cut-outs & "notes," lift top, inner phono, 8 tubes, AC $150.00

C-93, console, 1932, walnut, lowboy, upper front dial, lower grill w/cut-outs & "notes," 6 legs, 11 tubes, AC $175.00

C-95, console, 1932, walnut, upper front window dial, lower twin grills w/cut-outs, 6 legs, 3 knobs, AC $150.00

C-103, console, 1932, walnut, upper front dial, lower grill w/scalloped cut-outs & "notes," 3 knobs, AC........................$130.00

C-150, table, wood, right front dial, center cloth grill w/cut-outs, left volume, 2 knobs $65.00

COLUMBIA RECORDS
Columbia Records,
799 Seventh Avenue
New York, New York

530, console-R/P, 1957, wood, inner right dial & knobs, left phono, lift top, front grill, legs, BC, FM, 11 tubes, AC ...$40.00

COMMONWEALTH

170, cathedral, 1933, wood, center front quarter-round dial, upper cloth grill w/cut-outs, 7 tubes $225.00

CONCERT
Concert Radiophone Co.,
626 Huron Rd., Cleveland, Ohio

Concert Grand, table, 1925, wood, low rectangular case, 3 dial front panel, 4 tubes, battery $110.00

Concert Sr., portable, 1925, leatherette, inner 2 dial panel, built-in loop antenna, handle, 2 tubes, battery $200.00

CONCORD
Concord Radio Company,
901 West Jackson Boulevard, Chicago, Illinois

1-403, table, 1948, plastic, streamline, right front dial, left horizontal wrap-around louvers, 2 knobs, BC, AC/DC $65.00

1-411, table, 1948, plastic, streamline, right front half-round dial, left horizontal wrap-around louvers, 2 knobs, BC, AC/DC.....$50.00

1-504, table, 1949, plastic, upper slanted slide rule dial, lower horizontal grill bars, 3 knobs, BC, 2SW, AC $35.00

1-513, portable, 1949, plastic, right front rectangular dial, patterned grill area, handle, 3 knobs, BC, AC/DC/battery $35.00

1-514, table, 1949, plastic, right front airplane dial, left horizontal louvers, 2 knobs, AC/DC $35.00

1-516, table-R/P, 1948, leatherette, slanted front slide rule dial, lower grill, 2 knobs, open top phono, BC, AC...............$30.00

1-518, portable, 1948, two-tone case, right front oval recessed dial area, handle, AC/DC/battery..................................$30.00

1-606, table, 1948, plastic, upper slanted slide rule dial, lower horizontal grill bars, 3 knobs, BC, FM, AC/DC $35.00

1-611, portable, 1948, leatherette, upper front slide rule dial, horizontal grill bars, handle, 2 knobs, BC, AC/DC/battery...$30.00

6C51B, table, 1947, plastic, streamline, right front dial, left horizontal wrap-around louvers, 2 knobs, BC, AC/DC $65.00

6D61P, table-R/P, 1947, wood, outer right slide rule dial, 3 knobs, lift top, inner phono, BC, AC $35.00

6E51B, table, 1947, plastic, upper slanted slide rule dial, lower horizontal louvers, 2 knobs, handle, BC, AC/DC...........$40.00

6F26W, table, 1947, wood, upper slanted slide rule dial, lower cloth grill, 4 knobs, BC, SW, AC/DC.........................$40.00

6T61W, table, 1947, wood, right front square dial, left horizontal louvers, 3 knobs, BC, AC/DC $35.00

7E71PR, portable, 1949, "alligator," right front airplane dial, left grill, 2 knobs, handle, AC/DC/battery $30.00

CONTINENTAL
Spiegel, Inc.,
1061 West 35th Street, Chicago, Illinois

1000, table, plastic, streamline, right front dial, left horizontal wrap-around bars, 2 knobs...$95.00

C-45, table-C, 1957, plastic, center round dial knob, right circular louvers, left alarm clock face, BC, 4 tubes, AC $30.00

K6, table, plastic, right front dial, left horizontal wrap-around louvers, 3 knobs, BC, SW $40.00

Piano, table-N, 1940, radio shaped like grand piano, lift-up lid covers dial & G clef grill $295.00

R-20 "Star Raider," console, 1929, walnut finish, highboy, inner dial & knobs, double front doors, stretcher base, AC ..$135.00

R-30 "Star Raider," console, 1929, wood, lowboy, inner front dial & knobs, double doors, stretcher base, AC $135.00

CONTINENTAL ELECTRONICS
Continental Electronics, Ltd.,
81 Pine Street, New York, New York

82 "Sky Weight," table-R/P, 1947, luggage-style, "alligator," lift top, inner phono, 3 knobs, handle, BC, AC $25.00

CORONADO
Coronado,
Minneapolis, Minnesota/
Los Angeles, California

05RA1-43-7755A, console-R/P, 1950, wood, upper front slide rule dial, 4 knobs, center pull-out phono drawer, BC, FM, AC $50.00

05RA1-43-7901A, console-R/P, 1950, wood, inner right slide rule dial, 4 knobs, door, left pull-out phono drawer, BC, FM, AC $60.00

05RA2-43-8230A, table, 1952, plastic, upper front slide rule dial, lower metallic grill, 2 knobs, BC, AC/DC $35.00

05RA2-43-8515A, table, 1950, plastic, lower center raised round dial overlaps large recessed grill area, 2 knobs, AM, FM, AC $35.00

05RA4-43-9876A, portable, 1950, leatherette, upper front slide rule dial, lower metal grill, handle, 2 knobs, BC, AC/DC/battery $30.00

05RA33-43-8120A, table, 1950, plastic, oblong case, right front round dial, left round grill w/horizontal bars, BC, AC/DC...$55.00

05RA37-43-8360A, table, 1950, two-tone plastic, right raised round dial over lattice louvers, 2 knobs, BC, AC/DC $40.00

15RA1-43-7654A, console-R/P, 1951, wood, upper front slide rule dial, 4 knobs, center pull-out phono drawer, BC, FM, AC ..$45.00

15RA1-43-7902A, console-R/P, 1951, wood, inner right slide rule dial, 4 knobs, door, left pull-out phono drawer, BC, FM, AC $70.00

15RA2-43-8230A, table, 1952, plastic, upper front slide rule dial, lower metallic grill, 2 knobs, BC, AC/DC $35.00

15RA33-43-8246A, table, 1952, plastic, center front round dial over checkered grill, 2 knobs, BC $30.00

15RA33-43-8365, table, 1952, plastic, lower front round raised dial overlaps large upper grill area, 2 knobs, BC, AC....$35.00

15RA37-43-9230A, table-R/P, 1952, wood, right front square dial, left grill, 2 knobs, left 2/3 lift top, inner phono, AC $30.00

35RA-43-9856A, portable, 1953, center front round dial over criss-cross grill, 2 knobs, handle, BC, AC/DC/battery ...$30.00

35RA4-43-9856A, portable, 1953, center front round dial over criss-cross grill, 2 knobs, handle, BC, AC/DC/battery ...$30.00

35RA33-43-8125, table, 1953, plastic, right front square dial, left horizontal grill bars, 2 knobs, BC, AC/DC $30.00

35RA33-43-8145 "Ranger," table, 1953, plastic, right front round dial, left lattice grill, 2 knobs, BC, AC/DC $30.00

35RA33-43-8225, table, 1953, plastic, right front dial, left vertical grill bars, center horizontal wrap-around strip, BC, AC/DC $35.00

35RA37-43-8355, table, 1953, plastic, recessed slide rule dial, upper recessed lattice grill, 3 knobs, BC, AC/DC $35.00

35RA40-43-8247A, table-C, 1954, plastic, square case, right side dial knob, large front alarm clock, BC, AC....................$30.00

43-6301, table, 1946, wood, upper slanted slide rule dial, lower cloth grill, 2 knobs, BC, battery..............................$40.00

43-6321, table, 1948, wood, lower front slide rule dial, large upper cloth grill, 2 knobs, BC, battery................................$35.00

43-6451, table, 1946, two-tone wood, upper slanted slide rule dial, large lower cloth grill, 2 knobs, BC, battery **$35.00**

43-6485, table, 1948, wood, upper slanted slide rule dial, large lower cloth grill, 2 knobs, BC, battery **$35.00**

43-6927, console, 1948, wood, upper slanted slide rule dial, large lower cloth grill area, 4 knobs, AC **$75.00**

43-6951, console, 1948, wood, upper slanted slide rule dial, lower cloth grill, 4 knobs, AM/FM, AC **$75.00**

43-7601, console-R/P, 1946, wood, upper slide rule dial, 4 knobs, lower pull-out phono drawer, BC, SW, AC **$80.00**

43-7651, console-R/P, 1946, wood, inner right slide rule dial, 4 knobs, pushbuttons, left pull-out phono drawer, BC, 4 SW, AC **$85.00**

43-7652, console-R/P, 1948, wood, inner right slide rule dial & pushbuttons, left pull-out phono, BC, SW, AC **$85.00**

43-7851, console-R/P, 1948, wood, inner right slide rule dial, 4 knobs, door, left pull-out phono drawer, BC, SW, AC ...**$70.00**

43-8160, table, 1947, plastic, center round dial inside concentric circular louvers, 2 knobs, base, BC, AC/DC................**$90.00**

43-8178, table, 1947, plastic, right half-round dial, wrap-around horizontal bands, 2 knobs, BC, AC/DC **$65.00**

43-8180, table, 1946, plastic, right front dial, left horizontal wrap-around louvers, 2 knobs, BC, AC/DC..........................**$45.00**

43-8190, table, 1947, plastic, contrasting plastic oblong front panel encircles 2 knobs & grill, handle, BC, AC/DC....**$200.00**

43-8213, table, 1946, wood, upper slanted slide rule dial, lower criss-cross grill, 2 knobs, BC, AC/DC **$40.00**

43-8240, table, 1947, plastic, upper slanted slide rule dial, lower horizontal louvers, 2 knobs, BC, AC/DC.................**$45.00**

43-8305, table, 1946, plastic, lower front slide rule dial, upper cloth grill, 2 knobs, curved base, BC, 6 tubes, AC/DC ..**$55.00**

43-8312, table, 1946, plastic, lower front slide rule dial, large upper cloth grill, curved base, BC, 6 tubes, AC/DC **$55.00**

43-8312A, table, 1946, plastic, lower front slide rule dial, large upper cloth grill, curved base, BC, AC/DC **$55.00**

43-8330, table, 1947, wood, lower front slide rule dial, upper recessed horizontal louvers, 2 knobs, BC, AC/DC.......**$45.00**

43-8351, table, 1947, plastic, upper front slide rule dial, lower horizontal louvers, 2 knobs, 6 pushbuttons, BC, AC/DC.....**$50.00**

43-8354, table, 1947, plastic, upper front slide rule dial, lower cloth grill w/2 horizontal bars, 2 knobs, 5 pushbuttons, BC, AC/DC **$45.00**

43-8420, table, 1947, wood, lower front slide rule dial, upper cloth grill w/2 horizontal bars, 2 knobs, BC, AC/DC...............**$35.00**

43-8470, table, 1946, wood, lower front slide rule dial, upper cloth grill w/2 horizontal bars, 2 knobs, BC, AC/DC...............**$35.00**

43-8471, table, 1946, wood, lower front slide rule dial, upper cloth grill w/2 horizontal bars, 2 knobs, BC, AC/DC...............**$35.00**

43-8576, table, 1946, wood, lower front slide rule dial, large upper cloth grill, 4 knobs, BC, SW, AC **$35.00**

43-8685, table, 1947, wood, lower front slide rule dial over large cloth grill area, 3 knobs, BC, AC **$40.00**

43-9196, table-R/P, 1947, wood, front slide rule dial, horizontal louvers, 4 knobs, 3/4 lift top, inner phono, BC, AC.......**$35.00**

43-9201, table-R/P, 1947, wood, front slide rule dial, large grill, 2 knobs, 3/4 lift top, inner phono, BC, AC **$35.00**

43-9865, portable, 1948, inner lower right dial, lattice grill, flip-up front, handle, BC, AC/DC/battery **$40.00**

94RA1-43-6945A, console, 1949, wood, upper front slide rule dial, large lower cloth grill, 4 knobs, BC, FM, AC **$70.00**

94RA1-43-7605A, console-R/P, 1949, wood, upper front slide rule dial, 4 knobs, lower tilt-out phono, BC, SW, AC **$70.00**

94RA1-43-7656A, console-R/P, 1949, wood, inner right slide rule dial, 4 knobs, door, left pull-out phono drawer, BC, FM, AC **$80.00**

94RA1-43-7751A, console-R/P, 1950, wood, upper front dial, 4 knobs, center pull-out phono drawer, lower grill, BC, FM, AC **$65.00**

94RA1-43-8510A, table, 1949, plastic, upper slanted slide rule dial, lower off-center lattice grill, 4 knobs, BC, FM, AC **$45.00**

94RA1-43-8510B, table, 1949, plastic, upper slanted slide rule dial, lower off center lattice grill, 4 knobs, BC, FM, AC...**$45.00**

94RA1-43-8511B, table, 1949, plastic, upper slanted slide rule dial, lower off center lattice grill, 4 knobs, BC, FM, AC...**$45.00**

94RA4-43-8130A, table, 1949, plastic, lower front slide rule dial, upper horizontal louvers, 2 knobs, BC, AC/DC **$30.00**

94RA31-43-8115A "Cub," table, 1950, plastic, right front round dial overlaps lattice wrap-around grill, 2 knobs, BC, AC/DC..**$45.00**

94RA31-43-9841A, portable, 1949, inner slide rule dial, 2 knobs, lattice grill area, fold-down front panel, handle, BC, AC/DC/battery **$35.00**

94RA33-43-8130C, table, 1949, plastic, lower front dial, large upper grill w/horizontal bars, 2 knobs, BC...................**$30.00**

675, tombstone, 1934, wood, front airplane dial w/center hemispheres, 6 tubes, BC, SW **$100.00**

686, table, 1935, wood, right front oval dial, left cloth grill w/horizontal bars, 4 knobs, BC, 2SW **$75.00**

1070A, table, 1940, wood, front slide rule dial, upper cloth grill w/cut-outs, 6 pushbuttons, 4 knobs, BC, SW, AC $65.00

C5D14, table, 1942, plastic, center round dial inside concentric circular louvers, 2 knobs, base, BC, AC/DC.................**$90.00**

RA12-8121-A, table, 1957, plastic, right front round dial, lower knob, left horizontal bars, BC, AC/DC **$20.00**

RA37-43-9240A, table-R/P, 1955, wood, right side dial, large front grill, lift top, inner phono, BC, AC **$25.00**

RA37-43-9855, portable, 1954, plastic, top right dial knob, top left volume knob, front vertical grill bars, handle, BC, AC/DC/battery **$30.00**

RA42-9850A, portable, 1955, plastic, large center front round dial over horizontal grill bars, handle, BC, 4 tubes, battery **$35.00**

RA48-8157A, table, 1958, plastic, right front half-round dial, horizontal grill bars, feet, BC, 4 tubes, AC/DC **$20.00**

RA48-8158A, table, 1958, plastic, lower front slide rule dial, large upper grill, 2 knobs, feet, BC, 5 tubes, AC/DC **$30.00**

RA48-8159A, table, 1958, plastic, lower front slide rule dial, large upper grill, 2 knobs, feet, BC, 6 tubes, AC/DC **$30.00**

RA48-8342A, table, 1957, plastic, recessed front, right dial over lattice grill area, feet, BC, 5 tubes, AC/DC **$30.00**

RA48-8351A, table, 1957, plastic, right side dial knob, large front perforated grill w/crest & "V," BC, 6 tubes, AC/DC........**$45.00**

RA48-8352A, table, 1957, plastic, lower front slide rule dial, upper grill w/center vertical divider, 2 knobs, BC, 6 tubes, AC/DC..$35.00

CORONET

**Crystal Products, Co.,
1519 McGee Trafficway,
Kansas City, Missouri**

C-2, table, 1946, two-tone, slide rule dial & 2 knobs on top of case, front cloth grill w/horizontal bars, BC, AC/DC $50.00

COTO-COIL

**Coto-Coil Co.,
87 Willard Ave., Providence, Rhode Island**

Coto Symphonic, table, 1925, wood, rectangular case, 3 dial black front panel, 4 tubes, battery $150.00

CRESTLINE

ATR 210, portable, plastic, right front dial, horizontal grill bars, lower right side knob, handle, BC....................$45.00

CROSLEY

**The Precision Equipment Company, Inc.,
Peebles Corner, Cincinnati, Ohio
Crosley Manufacturing Company, Cincinnati, Ohio
The Crosley Radio Corporation, Cincinnati, Ohio
Crosley Corporation,
1329 Arlington Street, Cincinnati, Ohio**

The Crosley company was begun in 1921 by Powel Crosley, who believed his radio company should offer the consumer a good quality product at the lowest possible price and he called his sets the "Model T's" of radio. In 1923, Crosley bought out The Precision Equipment Company. The Crosley Radio Corporation enjoyed success until the late 1920s. One of the most sought-after of Crosley sets today is the "Pup", a small 1 tube set made to sell for only $9.75 in 1925 and known as the "Sky Terrier."

02CA, console, 1941, wood, large upper front slanted round dial, lower cloth grill w/vertical bars, pushbuttons, 2 knobs, BC, SW, 10 tubes..$150.00

02CP, console-R/P, 1941, wood, large upper front slanted round dial, center pull-out phono, lower cloth grill w/vertical bars, pushbuttons, 2 knobs, BC, SW, 10 tubes....................$150.00

03CB, console, 1941, wood, large upper front slanted round dial, lower cloth grill w/vertical bars, pushbuttons, 2 knobs, BC, SW, 10 tubes..$150.00

1-N "Litlfella," cathedral, 1932, wood, small case, center front window dial, upper 3-section grill, scalloped base, 3 knobs, AC $190.00

4-29, portable, 1926, leatherette, inner 2 dial front panel, fold-back top, fold-down front, handle, battery $185.00

4-29, table, 1926, two-tone wood, high rectangular case, slanted 2 dial panel, wood lid, 4 tubes, battery $150.00

5-38, table, 1926, wood, 2 styles, high rectangular case, slanted front panel w/3 dials, 5 tubes, battery $100.00

5-50, table, 1926, wood, high rectangular case, right front thumbwheel dial, 5 tubes, battery...$85.00

5-75, console, 1926, mahogany, highboy, upper right front dial, built-in speaker, 5 tubes, battery $160.00

5M3, tombstone, 1934, wood, center front window dial w/metal escutcheon, upper grill w/cut-outs, AC......................$120.00

6-60, table, 1927, wood, high rectangular case, slanted front panel, right thumbwheel dial, battery............................$85.00

6H2, tombstone, 1933, wood, center front round dial, upper cloth grill w/cut-outs, 3 knobs, BC, SW, AC $110.00

7H2, (left) tombstone, 1934, wood, shouldered, center front round dial, upper cloth grill w/cut-outs, 4 knobs, BC, SW $125.00

8H1, console, 1934, wood, upper front round dial, lower cloth grill w/cut-outs, BC, SW, AC $125.00

9-101, table, 1949, plastic, upper front curved slide rule dial, lower "boomerang" louvers, 3 knobs, BC, battery.................**$35.00**

9-102, table, 1948, plastic, upper front curved slide rule dial, lower "boomerang" louvers, 3 knobs, BC, AC.....................**$55.00**

9-103, table, 1949, plastic, lower front slide rule dial, large upper perforated grill area w/center crest, 3 knobs, BC, AC/DC **$40.00**

9-104W, table, 1949, plastic, lower front slide rule dial, large upper grill area w/center crest, 3 knobs, BC, AC/DC **$40.00**

9-105, table, 1949, plastic, lower front slide rule dial, large upper grill area w/center crest, 3 knobs, BC, SW, AC/DC.......**$40.00**

9-106W, table, 1949, plastic, lower front slide rule dial, large upper grill area w/center crest, 3 knobs, BC, SW, AC/DC **$40.00**

9-113, table, 1949, plastic, lower slanted slide rule dial, upper metal perforated grill, 2 knobs, BC, AC/DC.................**$40.00**

9-114W, table, 1949, plastic, lower slanted slide rule dial, upper metal perforated grill, 2 knobs, BC, AC/DC.................**$40.00**

9-117, table, 1948, plastic, large right front square dial, left vertical wrap-over grill bars, 3 knobs, battery **$35.00**

9-118W, table, 1948, plastic, upper front curved slide rule dial, lower "boomerang" louvers, 3 knobs, BC, AC **$55.00**

9-119, table, 1948, plastic, right front round dial, left cloth grill w/horizontal bars, 2 knobs, BC, AC/DC **$45.00**

9-120W, table, 1948, plastic, right front round dial, left cloth grill w/horizontal bars, 2 knobs, BC, AC/DC $45.00

9-121, table, 1949, plastic, raised top w/slide rule dial, lower horizontal wrap-around louvers, 2 knobs, BC, AC/DC **$45.00**

9-122W, table, 1949, plastic, raised top w/slide rule dial, lower horizontal wrap-around louvers, 2 knobs, BC, AC/DC ..**$45.00**

9-201, console-R/P, 1948, wood, 2 upper front slide rule dials, center pull-out phono, lower grill, BC, FM, AC **$90.00**

9-202M, console-R/P, 1948, wood, inner right slide rule dial, 4 knobs, door, left pull-out phono drawer, AM, FM, AC ...**$75.00**

9-203B, console-R/P, 1948, wood, inner right dial, left pull-out phono, lower storage & grill, BC, FM, AC.....................**$70.00**

9-204, console-R/P, 1949, wood, inner right dial, left pull-out phono, lower storage & grill, BC, FM, AC.....................**$70.00**

9-205M, console-R/P, 1949, wood, right tilt-out slide rule dial, 4 knobs, left pull-out phono drawer, BC, FM, AC **$70.00**

9-207M, console-R/P, 1949, wood, right tilt-out slide rule dial, 5 knobs, left pull-out phono drawer, BC, SW, FM, AC **$75.00**

9-209, console-R/P, 1949, walnut, inner slide rule dial, pull-out phono drawer, criss-cross grill, BC, AC.......................**$75.00**

9-209L, console-R/P, 1949, walnut, inner slide rule dial, pull-out phono drawer, criss-cross grill, BC, AC.......................**$75.00**

9-212M, console-R/P, 1949, mahogany, inner right slide rule dial, door, left pull-out phono drawer, criss-cross grill, BC, AC **$75.00**

9-212ML, console-R/P, 1949, mahogany, inner slide rule dial, pull-out phono drawer, criss-cross grill, BC, AC **$75.00**

9-213B, console-R/P, 1949, blonde, inner slide rule dial, pull-out phono drawer, criss-cross grill, BC, AC.......................**$75.00**

9-214M, console-R/P, 1949, wood, right tilt-out slide rule dial, 4 knobs, pull-out phono drawer, BC, FM, AC **$70.00**

9-214ML, console-R/P, 1949, wood, right tilt-out slide rule dial, 4 knobs, left pull-out phono drawer, BC, FM, AC **$70.00**

9-302, portable, 1948, "alligator," metal front panel w/upper slide rule dial, handle, 2 top knobs, BC, AC/DC/battery **$35.00**

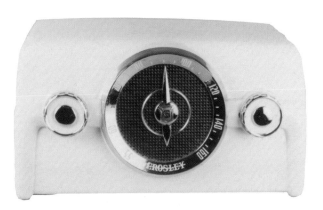

10-135, table, 1950, plastic, center front circular chrome dial with inner metal perforated grill, 2 knobs, BC $100.00

10-136E, table, 1950, plastic, center front circular dial with inner perforated grill, 2 knobs, BC **$100.00**

10-137, table, 1950, plastic, center front circular dial with inner perforated grill, 2 knobs, BC **$100.00**

10-138, table, 1950, plastic, center front circular dial w/inner perforated grill, 2 knobs, BC, AC/DC $100.00

10-145M, table-R/P, 1949, wood, center front round dial, right & left grills, 3 knobs, lift top, inner phono, AC **$40.00**

10-307M, portable, 1949, plastic, upper front slide rule dial, lower horizontal grill bars, handle, 2 knobs, BC, AC/DC/battery **$35.00**

11, table, plastic, right front dial, left horizontal wrap-around louvers, 2 knobs, BC **$45.00**

11-100U, table, 1951, plastic, large center round dial w/inner circular louvers, side "fins," 2 knobs, BC **$115.00**

11-101U, table, 1951, plastic, large round dial w/inner circular louvers, side "fins," 2 knobs, BC, AC/DC **$115.00**

11-102U, table, 1951, plastic, large center round dial w/inner circular louvers, side "fins," 2 knobs, BC.......................**$115.00**

11-104U, table, 1951, plastic, large center round dial w/inner circular louvers, side "fins," 2 knobs, BC, AC/DC.............**$115.00**

11-105U, table, 1951, plastic, large center round dial w/inner circular louvers, side "fins," 2 knobs, BC, AC/DC **$115.00**

11-107U, table, 1952, plastic, center front square dial w/inner checkered grill & crest, 2 knobs, BC, AC/DC............$60.00

11-109U, table, 1952, plastic, center front square dial w/inner checkered grill & crest, 2 knobs, BC. AC/DC............$60.00

11-112U, table, plastic, center front round see-through filigree dial with inner grill area, 2 knobs, rear label states "made exclusively for the leading jewelers of America by Crosley," BC, AC/DC................$125.00

11-114U, table, 1951, plastic, right front round dial knob, left concentric circular louvers w/horizontal center ridge, BC, AC/DC $100.00

11-116U, table, 1951, plastic, right front round dial knob, left concentric circular louvers w/horizontal center ridge, BC, AC/DC $100.00

11-119U, table, 1951, plastic, right front round dial knob, left concentric circular louvers w/horizontal center ridge, BC, AC/DC $100.00

11-123U, table-C, plastic, right front round dial w/inner perforations, left alarm clock, center crest, 5 knobs, BC, AC $110.00

11-126U, table, 1951, plastic, right front dial, left round grill w/center crest, 3 knobs, AM, FM, AC/DC $45.00

11-132U, table, plastic, center front round see-through filigree dial with inner grill area, 2 knobs, rear label states "made exclusively for the leading jewelers of America by Crosley," BC, AC/DC $125.00

11-207MU, console-R/P, 1951, wood, inner right slide rule dial, door, 3 knobs, left pull-out phono drawer, BC, AC $50.00

11-301U, portable, 1951, plastic, flip up semi-circular front w/crest, inner dial, handle, BC, AC/DC/battery $45.00

11-305U, portable, 1951, plastic, flip up semi-circular front w/crest, inner dial, handle, BC, AC/DC/battery $45.00

11-550MU, console-R/P, 1951, wood, inner front round metal dial, lower pull-out phono, double doors, BC, AC $75.00

11AB, table, plastic, right front dial, left horizontal wrap-around louvers, base, 2 knobs $50.00

14AG, table, wood, right front square dial, left grill w/horizontal bars, handle, 3 knobs, AC/DC $55.00

15-16, console, 1937, wood, large upper front round dial, lower cloth grill w/3 vertical bars, 5 knobs, 15 tubes $175.00

16AL, table, 1940, walnut, right front dial, left vertical grill bars, pushbuttons, 3 knobs, 5 tubes, AC/DC $65.00

20AP "Fiver," table, wood, right front square dial, left cloth grill w/diagonal bars, 3 knobs, BC, SW, 5 tubes $45.00

21, table, 1929, metal, rectangular case, center window dial, Deco corner details, 3 knobs, 6 tubes, battery $100.00

22, console, 1929, walnut veneer, highboy, upper front window dial, lower round grill w/cut-outs, 3 knobs, battery $130.00

22-AS, table-R/P, wood, right front dial, left grill w/horizontal bars, lift top, inner phono $35.00

22CA, console, walnut, large upper front slanted round dial, lower cloth grill w/vertical bars, pushbuttons, 2 knobs, BC, SW, 12 tubes..$200.00

22CB, console, 1941, wood, large upper front slanted round dial, lower vertical grill bars, BC, FM, 12 tubes, AC...........$200.00

25AY, console, 1940, walnut, upper front slanted dial, lower vertical grill bars, pushbuttons, BC, SW, 7 tubes, AC $135.00

28AZ "Recordola," console-R/P/Rec/PA, 1940, wood, inner dial, phono, recorder, PA system, front grill w/3 vertical bars, 8 tubes, AC..**$110.00**

31, table, 1929, metal, rectangular case, center window dial, Deco corner details, 3 knobs, 7 tubes, AC **$100.00**

33-BG, table-R/P/Rec, 1940, wood, outer right front square dial, left horizontal louvers, 3 knobs, lift top, inner phono, AC.......**$35.00**

33-S, console, 1929, wood, lowboy, upper front window dial, lower grill w/cut-outs, 3 knobs, AC.......................................**$110.00**

34-S, console, 1929, wood, lowboy, inner dial & controls, double front doors, AC **$125.00**

35AK, table-R/P, 1941, wood, right front square dial, left grill, 3 knobs, lift top, inner phono, AC **$30.00**

36AM, table, 1940, wood, right front dial, left cloth grill w/cut-outs, 2 knobs, BC, battery **$25.00**

41, table, 1929, metal, rectangular case, center window dial, Deco corner details, 3 knobs, 8 tubes, AC **$100.00**

43BT, table, 1940, wood, right front square dial, left horizontal louvers, 3 knobs **$45.00**

46FA, table, 1947, plastic, large center front square dial, right and left horizontal wrap-around louvers, 3 knobs, BC, SW $45.00

46FB, table, 1947, wood, large center front square dial, right & left cloth wrap-around grills, 3 knobs, BC, SW, battery.......**$40.00**

48 "Widgit," cathedral, 1931, repwood case, ornate "carved" front, upper grill w/cut-outs, 2 knobs, 5 tubes.............**$375.00**

50, table, 1924, wood, 1 dial black Bakelite front panel, lift top, 1 tube, battery $150.00

50A, table-amp, 1925, wood, amplifier, black Bakelite front panel, lift top **$175.00**

50/50A, table, 1925, wood, low rectangular case, receiver/amplifier in one unit, lift top, 3 tubes, battery **$300.00**

50 Portable, portable, 1924, wood, inner 1 dial black front panel, fold-back top, fold-down front, storage, battery **$300.00**

51, table, 1924, wood, low rectangular case, 1 dial black front panel, lift top, 2 tubes, battery $125.00

51A, table-amp, 1924, wood, box, 2-stage amplifier **$150.00**

51 Portable, portable, 1924, leatherette, inner 1 dial front panel, fold-back top, fold-down front, handle, battery **$165.00**

51-S "Special," table, 1924, wood, slanted 1 dial black Bakelite front panel, lift top, battery **$115.00**

51SD "Special Deluxe," table, 1924, wood, high rectangular case, left front half-round pointer dial, lift top, 2 tubes, battery **$140.00**

52, table, 1924, wood, low rectangular case, 1 dial black front panel, lift top, 3 tubes, battery **$125.00**

52-FC, table, 1942, wood, right front airplane dial, left cloth grill w/horizontal bars, 3 knobs, 4 tubes.............................**$45.00**

52P, portable, 1924, leatherette, inner 1 dial front panel, fold-down front, handle, battery **$175.00**

52PA, portable, 1941, right front dial over large grill area, 2 knobs, handle, 5 tubes **$25.00**

52-S "Special," table, 1924, wood, high rectangular case, slant front panel with left dial, lift top, battery **$130.00**

52SD "Special Deluxe," table, 1924, wood, high rectangular case, slanted panel, left half-round pointer dial, 3 tubes, battery **$130.00**

52TA, table, 1941, walnut, right front square dial, left cloth grill w/2 horizontal bars, 2 knobs, 5 tubes, AC/DC **$40.00**

52TD, table, 1941, plastic, right front airplane dial, right and left horizontal wrap-around bars, 3 knobs, BC, SW, 5 tubes, AC/DC $40.00

52TL, table, 1942, wood, large center front dial, side grill, 3 knobs, BC, SW, 5 tubes, AC $50.00
52TP, table-R/P, 1942, wood, outer right front airplane dial, left grill area, 3 knobs, lift top, inner phono, BC, SW, AC....$35.00
52TQ, table-R/P, 1941, wood, outer right front airplane dial, left grill area, 3 knobs, lift top, inner phono, AC $35.00
54G "New Buddy," table, 1930, repwood "carved" front panel, lower right dial, upper cloth grill, 2 knobs, AC $250.00
56FA, table, 1948, plastic, large center front dial, right & left horizontal wrap-around louvers, 4 knobs, BC, SW, battery ..$45.00
56PA, portable, 1946, plastic, upper front slide rule dial, lower horizontal louvers, 2 top knobs, handle, BC, AC/DC/battery $45.00

56PB, portable, 1946, upper front slide rule dial, lower horizontal louvers, handle, AC/DC/battery $45.00
56TA-L, table, 1946, plastic, right front dial over horizontal wrap-around grill bars, 3 knobs $40.00
56TC, table, wood, right front square dial, left grill w/horizontal bars, 3 knobs, BC, SW $40.00
56TC-L, table, 1946, wood, right front square dial, left grill w/horizontal wrap-around bars, 3 knobs, BC, SW $40.00
56TD "Duette," table, 1947, plastic, modern, top slide rule dial, lower vertical grill bars, 3 knobs, BC, AC/DC $125.00

56TD-R "Duette," table, 1947, plastic, modern, top slide rule dial, lower vertical grill bars, 3 knobs, BC, AC/DC $125.00
56TD-W "Duette," table, 1947, plastic, modern, top slide rule dial, lower front vertical grill bars, 3 knobs $125.00
56TG, table, 1946, plastic, upper front slide rule dial, lower horizontal wrap-around louvers, 2 knobs, BC, AC/DC $45.00
56TJ, table, 1946, wood, upper slanted slide rule dial, center cloth grill, 2 knobs, BC, AC/DC $35.00
56TN, table, 1948, wood, right front dial, left wrap-around grill w/horizontal bars, 3 knobs, BC, SW, AC/DC................$50.00
56TN-L, table, 1946, wood, right front dial, left wrap-around grill w/horizontal bars, 3 knobs, BC, SW, AC/DC................$50.00
56TP, table-R/P, 1946, wood, right front black dial, left cloth wrap-around grill, 3 knobs, lift top, inner phono, BC, SW, AC ..$35.00
56TP-L, table-R/P, 1948, wood, right front black dial, left cloth wrap-around grill, 3 knobs, lift top, inner phono, BC, SW, AC $35.00
56TR, table-R/P, 1948, wood, center front slide rule dial, right/left wrap-around grills, lift top, inner phono, BC, AC $35.00
56TS, table-R/P, 1947, wood, center front slide rule dial, right/left wrap-around cloth grills, 3 knobs, lift top, inner phono, BC, SW, AC...$35.00
56TU, table, 1946, plastic, upper slide rule dial, lower wrap-around louvers, 2 knobs, handle, BC, AC/DC $55.00
56TU-O, table, 1949, plastic, upper slide rule dial, lower wrap-around louvers, 2 knobs, handle, BC, AC/DC $55.00
56TV-O, table, 1949, wood, upper slide rule dial, large center front grill, BC, AC/DC...$30.00

56TW, plastic, right front square dial, right/left horizontal wrap-around grill bars, base, 3 knobs......................$50.00
56TX, table, 1946, plastic, right front square dial, right/left horizontal wrap-around grill bars, base, 3 knobs $50.00
56TY, table, 1948, wood, upper slide rule dial, lower horizontal grill bars, 2 knobs, BC, AC/DC $50.00
56TZ, table-R/P, 1948, two-tone wood, inner right slide rule dial, 3 knobs, phono, 3/4 lift top, BC, AC $30.00
57TK, table, 1948, plastic, upper front slide rule dial, lower vertical grill bars, 2 knobs, BC, AC/DC $45.00
57TL, table, 1948, plastic, upper front slide rule dial, lower vertical grill bars, 2 knobs, BC, AC/DC $45.00
58 "Buddy Boy," cathedral, 1931, ornate repwood case, thumbwheel tuning, cloth grill w/cut-outs, 2 knobs, AC $350.00
58TK, table, 1948, plastic, right front round dial, left cloth grill w/horizontal bars, 2 knobs, BC, AC/DC $50.00
58TL, table, 1948, plastic, upper slanted slide rule dial, lower vertical grill bars, 2 knobs, BC, AC/DC $45.00
58TW, table, 1948, plastic, upper slanted slide rule dial, lower wrap around louvers, lucite handle, 2 knobs, BC, AC/DC $50.00

59 "Oracle," grandfather clock, 1931, wood, window dial, ornate grill, raised top, Deco clock face, 3 knobs **$450.00**

59 "Show Boy," cathedral, 1931, ornate repwood case, center front window dial, upper grill area, 3 knobs, 5 tubes, AC **$250.00**

61, tombstone, 1934, wood, shouldered, center front round airplane dial, upper grill w/cut-outs, 3 knobs, BC, SW, AC..........**$135.00**

62-148, tombstone, wood w/inlay, lower front round airplane dial, upper grill w/cut-outs, 2 knobs, AC............................**$130.00**

62PB, portable, 1942, leatherette, inner right front dial, left grill, 2 knobs, fold-down front, handle, 6 tubes, AC/DC battery...**$25.00**

63TA "Victory," table, 1946, wood, large red, white & blue center front dial w/stars & stripes, right & left wraparound grills, 4 knobs, BC, SW, 6 tubes, AC **$100.00**

64 MD, console, 1934, wood, upper front round dial, lower cloth grill w/cut-outs, BC, SW, AC...**$110.00**

66CS, console-R/P, 1947, wood, large inner right dial, 4 knobs, phono, lift top, front grill w/2 vertical bars, BC, SW, AC **$75.00**

66-T, table, 1946, wood, large center front square dial, right & left wrap-around grills, 4 knobs, BC, SW **$55.00**

66TA, table, 1946, plastic, large center front dial, right & left horizontal wrap-around grill bars, 4 knobs, BC, SW, AC **$50.00**

66-TC, table, 1946, wood, large center front square dial, right & left wrap-around grills, 4 knobs, BC, SW, AC **$55.00**

66TW, table, 1946, plastic, large center front square black dial, right & left wrap-around louvers, 4 knobs, BC, SW, AC..........**$50.00**

68CP, console-R/P, 1948, wood, inner right slide rule dial, 4 knobs, phono, lift top, front criss-cross grill, BC, SW, AC **$80.00**

68CR, console-R/P, 1948, wood, upper front slide rule dial, center pull-out phono, lower grill, 4 knobs, BC, SW, AC **$90.00**

68TA, table, 1948, plastic, upper front curved slide rule dial, lower "boomerang" louvers, 3 knobs, BC, AC........................**$55.00**

68TW, table, 1948, plastic, upper front curved slide rule dial, lower "boomerang" louvers, 3 knobs, BC, AC........................**$55.00**

72AF, tombstone, 1934, wood, shouldered, lower front round airplane dial, upper cloth grill w/cut-outs, 3 knobs, AC....**$120.00**

72CP, console-R/P, 1942, wood, upper front slanted airplane dial, center pull-out phono, lower grill w/vertical bars, BC, SW, 7 tubes, AC..**$110.00**

75, table, wood, low rectangular case, 3 upper front window dials, lift top, 5 knobs **$115.00**

82-S, console, 1929, wood, highboy, inner dial & controls, double front doors, stretcher base, AC **$130.00**

86CR, console-R/P, 1947, walnut, top slanted dial, center pull-out phono, lower grill, storage, BC, SW, AC **$125.00**

86CS, console-R/P, 1947, mahogany, top slanted dial, center pull-out phono, lower grill, storage, BC, SW, AC **$125.00**

87CQ, console-R/P, 1948, wood, upper slanted slide rule dial, center pull-out phono drawer, lower grill, 4 knobs, BC, SW, FM, AC **$110.00**

88CR, console-R/P, 1948, wood, inner right dial & knobs, left pull-out phono, criss-cross grill, BC, SW, AC......................**$85.00**

88TA, table, 1948, plastic, upper front curved slide rule dial, lower "boomerang" louvers, 3 knobs, BC, FM, AC/DC **$55.00**

88TC, table, 1948, wood, upper curved slide rule dial, lower cloth grill, 3 knobs, BC, FM, AC/DC....................................**$45.00**

117, console, 1936, wood, upper front round dial, lower cloth grill w/center vertical bar, 5 knobs, BC, SW, 9 tubes, AC...**$130.00**

122 "Super Buddy Boy," cathedral, 1931, repwood case, lower window dial, upper 3 section grill, 3 knobs, 7 tubes, AC........**$350.00**

124, cathedral, 1931, wood, low case, center front window dial, upper 3 section grill, 3 knobs, fluted columns, 10 tubes **$200.00**

124 "Playtime," grandfather clock, 1931, wood, front window dial, lower grill w/cut-outs, 3 knobs, BC, SW, AC **$375.00**

125, cathedral, 1932, wood, center front window dial, upper 3 section grill, fluted columns, 3 knobs **$150.00**

125, console, wood, upper front window dial w/escutcheon, lower cloth grill w/cut-outs, 3 knobs **$130.00**

127, tombstone, 1931, wood, center front window dial, upper grill w/cut-outs, scalloped base, curved top, 3 knobs $260.00
129, cathedral, wood, center front window dial w/escutcheon, upper grill w/cut-outs, 3 knobs....................................$250.00
137, console, 1936, wood, upper front large round dial, lower cloth grill w/3 vertical bars, 5 knobs, BC, SW, 10 tubes.......$130.00
140, table-N, 1931, looks like set of books, inner left window dial, right grill, 2 knobs, double doors $300.00

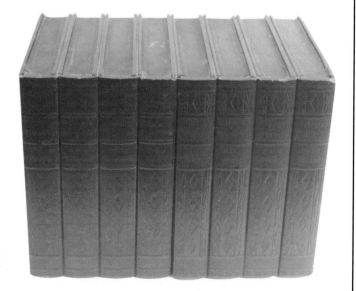

141 "Library Universal," table-N, 1931, looks like set of books, inner right window dial, center round grill, double doors $300.00
146, cathedral, wood, center front window dial, upper 3 section cloth grill, fluted columns, 4 knobs $240.00
146CS, console-R/P, 1947, wood, inner right half-round dial, push-buttons, left pull-out phono drawer, BC, 2SW, FM, AC .$95.00
148, cathedral, wood, center front window dial w/escutcheon, upper cloth grill w/cut-outs, 2 knobs $225.00

148CP, console-R/P, 1948, wood, inner right half-round dial, push-buttons, left pull-out phono drawer, BC, 2SW, FM, AC ..**$95.00**
154, cathedral, 1933, wood, center front window dial w/escutcheon, upper cloth grill with cut-outs, 2 knobs **$200.00**
157, cathedral, 1933, two-tone wood, center front window dial, upper cloth grill w/cut-outs, 3 knobs, AC **$225.00**
160, cathedral, wood, center front window dial, upper cloth grill w/cut-outs, 4 knobs **$265.00**
167, cathedral, 1936, wood, center front window dial, upper grill w/cut-outs, 3 knobs, BC, SW, 5 tubes, AC.................**$190.00**
167, console, 1936, wood, upper front round dial, lower cloth grill w/vertical bars, BC, SW, 13 tubes, AC........................**$130.00**
168, cathedral, 1933, wood, center front window dial, upper cloth grill w/cut-outs, 4 knobs, BC, SW, 7 tubes **$190.00**
169, cathedral, 1934, wood, center front window dial, upper sectioned cloth grill, 2 knobs, AC......................................**$200.00**
176 "Travette," table, metal, Deco case design, right front dial, center 4-section grill, 2 octagonal knobs **$95.00**
179, tombstone, wood, Deco, shouldered, center front window dial, upper sectioned grill, silver flutings, 7 tubes **$250.00**
182 "Travette Moderne," table, wood, Deco, right front dial, center grill w/chrome cut-outs, 2 knobs, 5 tubes, AC/DC.**$160.00**
250, tombstone, 1936, wood, large front round dial, upper cloth grill w/cut-outs, 4 knobs, 2 bands, 5 tubes **$100.00**
251, table, 1936, wood, lower front dial, upper sectioned cloth grill area, 2 bands, 5 tubes, AC/DC **$65.00**
295, table, 1936, wood, right front round dial, left cloth grill w/cut-outs, fluted side, 4 knobs, BC, SW, AC........................**$90.00**
349, tombstone, 1936, wood, lower front round dial, upper sectioned cloth grill, 4 knobs, 2 bands, 5 tubes **$110.00**
395, table, 1936, wood, right front round dial, left cloth grill w/cut-outs, 4 knobs, 2 bands, 5 tubes **$90.00**
401 "Bandbox Jr.," table, 1928, metal, low rectangular case, center window dial w/escutcheon, battery....................**$80.00**
449, tombstone, 1936, wood, center front round dial, upper cloth grill w/2 vertical bars, 4 knobs, 3 bands, 6 tubes.........**$100.00**
495, table, 1936, wood, Deco, off-center round dial, left oblong grill w/Deco cut-outs, BC, SW, 6 tubes, AC **$90.00**
515, tombstone, 1934, two-tone wood, lower round airplane dial, upper grill w/cut-outs, 4 knobs, BC, SW........................**$95.00**
516, tombstone, 1936, wood, small case, lower front red, white & blue dial, upper cloth grill, 4 knobs, BC, SW, AC **$75.00**

517 "Fiver," tombstone, 1934, wood, lower front round airplane dial, upper cloth grill w/cut-outs, 3 knobs, BC, SW, AC **$75.00**

527A, table, C1938, two-tone wood, right front square dial, left cloth grill w/horizontal bars, 2 knobs $45.00

555, tombstone, 1935, wood, lower front round dial, upper sectioned grill, side fluting, BC, SW $110.00

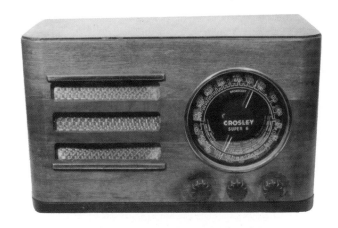

556, tombstone, 1936, wood, lower front round dial, upper sectioned cloth grill, 4 knobs, BC, SW $95.00

587, tombstone, 1939, wood, small case, lower front round dial, upper cloth grill w/2 vertical bars, 2 knobs $80.00

601 "Bandbox," table, 1927, metal, low rectangular case, front dial w/escutcheon, 3 knobs, battery $70.00

608 "Gembox," table, 1928, metal, low rectangular case, center front window dial w/escutcheon, 3 knobs, AC $100.00

609 "Gemchest," console, 1928, metal, upper front window dial, fancy Chinese grill & corner "straps," legs, AC............$350.00

610 "Gembox," table, 1928, metal, low rectangular case, front window dial w/escutcheon, 3 knobs, AC $100.00

612, tombstone, wood, shouldered, center front round dial, upper cloth grill w/cut-outs, 4 knobs $110.00

614EH, tombstone, 1934, wood, shouldered, center front round dial, upper sectioned grill, BC, SW, AC $135.00

614PG, console, 1934, wood, upper front round dial, lower cloth grill w/cut-outs, BC, SW, AC......................................$120.00

617, chairside, 1937, wood, top round dial and knobs, front grill area w/horizontal bars, storage, BC, SW, 6 tubes, AC..$125.00

637 "Super 6," table, 1937, wood, large right round dial, left cloth grill w/horizontal bars, 3 knobs $60.00

637-A, table, 1937, wood, large right round dial, left cloth grill w/horizontal bars, 3 knobs, 2 bands, 6 tubes $60.00

649, console, 1937, wood, upper front round dial, lower cloth grill w/2 vertical bars, 4 knobs, BC, SW, 6 tubes $125.00

649A, table, 1940, plastic, center front vertical dial, right & left wrap-around side louvers, top pushbuttons, AC/DC $85.00

655, tombstone, 1935, wood, center front round dial, upper cloth grill w/cut-outs, fluting, 4 knobs, BC, SW $125.00

699, console, 1936, wood, upper front round dial, lower cloth grill w/vertical bars, 3 bands, 6 tubes $125.00

704 "Jewelbox," table, 1928, metal, low rectangular case, center front dial w/escutcheon, 3 knobs, AC $80.00

704 "Perfecto," side table, 1928, model 704 built into a 6 legged lift top wood table w/drop front panel, AC...................$275.00

705 "Showbox," table, 1928, metal, low rectangular case, front window dial w/escutcheon, 3 knobs, DC $100.00

706 "Showbox," table, 1928, metal, low rectangular case, front window dial w/escutcheon, 3 knobs, AC $100.00

714GA, tombstone, 1934, wood, shouldered, lower round dial, upper grill w/cut-outs, 3 knobs, 3 band, AC................$125.00

714NA, console, 1934, wood, upper front round dial, lower cloth grill w/cut-outs, BC, SW, AC.......................................$120.00

725, tombstone, wood, center front round dial, upper cloth grill w/cut-outs, 4 knobs, BC, SW......................................$125.00

769, console, 1937, wood, upper front large round dial, lower cloth grill w/vertical bar, 7 tubes $135.00

804 "Jewelbox," table, 1929, metal, low rectangular case, center window dial w/escutcheon, 3 knobs, AC $95.00

814FA, tombstone, 1934, wood, center front round dial, upper sectioned grill, 3 knobs, BC, SW, AC $110.00

814QB, console, 1934, wood, upper front round dial, lower cloth grill w/cut-outs, BC, SW, AC......................................$120.00

817, table, 1937, wood, right front round dial, left cloth grill w/horizontal bars, 4 knobs, 3 bands, 8 tubes.........................$60.00

628B, table, 1937, plastic, raised top, lower front slide rule dial, upper horizontal grill bars, 5 pushbuttons, 2 knobs, BC, SW........$60.00

818-A "Super 8," table, wood, right front round dial, left 3-section grill, 5 pushbuttons, 4 knobs, BC, SW, 8 tubes $75.00

819M, console, 1939, wood, upper front slanted dial, lower grill w/3 vertical bars, pushbuttons, 4 knobs, BC, SW, AC **$150.00**

865, console, wood, upper front round dial, lower cloth grill w/center vertical divider, 6 feet, 4 knobs, BC, SW, AC.................**$150.00**

899, console, 1936, wood, upper front round dial, lower cloth grill w/vertical divider, 5 knobs, BC, SW, 8 tubes, AC........**$135.00**

989, console, 1937, wood, upper front large round dial, lower cloth grill with vertical bar, 5 knobs, 9 tubes **$130.00**

1014, tombstone, C1935, wood, shouldered, lower front round dial, upper cloth grill w/cut-outs, 4 knobs **$95.00**

1117, console, wood, upper front round dial, lower cloth grill w/vertical bars, 4 knobs, BC, SW, 11 tubes **$150.00**

1127, console, wood, upper front round dial, lower cloth grill w/vertical bars, 4 knobs, BC, SW, 11 tubes **$145.00**

1199, console, 1937, wood, upper front round dial, lower cloth grill with vertical bar, 5 knobs, 11 tubes **$150.00**

1211, console, 1937, wood, upper front round dial, lower cloth grill with vertical bar, 5 knobs, 12 tubes **$160.00**

1313, console, 1937, wood, upper front round dial, lower cloth grill with vertical bars, 5 knobs, 13 tubes **$170.00**

3716 "WLW," console/PA, 1936, wood, massive console, upper front round dial, 4 chassis, 6 speakers, 37 tubes, 4' 10" high..**$12,000.00**

5519, table, 1939, plastic, center front vertical slide rule dial, right & left vertical grill bars, handle, 2 knobs, 5 tubes **$50.00**

5628-A, table, plastic, lower front slide rule dial, upper horizontal louvers, raised top, 5 pushbuttons, 2 knobs.................**$85.00**

5628-B, table, plastic, slide rule dial, pushbuttons, horizontal louvers, slanted sides, 2 knobs, BC, SW **$85.00**

AC-7, table, 1927, wood, high rectangular case, slanted front panel w/right thumbwheel dial, 6 tubes, AC **$100.00**

AC-7C, console, 1927, wood, upper right front thumbwheel dial, thumbwheel knobs, lower speaker, AC **$140.00**

Ace 3B, table, 1923, wood, low rectangular case, 1 dial front panel, 3 tubes, battery...**$165.00**

Ace 3C, console, 1923, wood, upper Ace 3C table model w/feet removed, lower storage area, battery.........................**$200.00**

Ace 3C, table, 1923, wood, high rectangular case, inner 1 dial panel & speaker, double doors, battery.....................**$175.00**

Arbiter, console-R/P, 1930, walnut veneer w/ornate repwood front panel, center dial, lift top, inner phono, AC **$165.00**

B-429A, portable, 1939, cloth covered, high case, right front square dial, left grill, handle, 2 knobs, 4 tubes, battery **$30.00**

B-439A, portable, 1939, striped case, right front dial, left grill, handle, 2 knobs, 4 tubes, battery **$30.00**

B-549A, portable, 1939, brown striped cloth, right front dial, left grill, handle, 2 knobs, 5 tubes, AC/DC/battery **$30.00**

B-667A, tombstone, 1937, walnut, center front round dial, upper grill w/cut-outs, 4 knobs, 6 tubes, AC/battery **$100.00**

B-5549-A, portable-R/P, 1939, cloth covered, right front dial, left grill, 2 knobs, lift top, inner crank phono, handle, AC/DC/battery **$35.00**

CA-12, console, 1941, wood, upper front slide rule dial, lower cloth grill w/vertical bars, 4 knobs, BC, SW, 11 tubes **$140.00**

Centurion, console, 1935, wood, upper front round airplane dial, lower cloth grill w/cut-outs, BC, SW, 10 tubes **$135.00**

Chum, side table, 1930, walnut veneer w/inlay, 28½" high, front window dial w/escutcheon, 3 knobs **$160.00**

Comrade, side table, 1930, walnut veneer, 29½" high, inner front window dial, double front doors....................................**$140.00**

D10TN, table, 1951, plastic, large center round dial w/inner circular louvers, side "fins," 2 knobs **$115.00**

D-25BE, table-C, 1953, plastic, right round metal dial w/inner perforations, left alarm clock, center crest, 5 knobs, BC, AC ..**$110.00**

D-25CE, table-C, 1953, plastic, right front round dial w/inner perforations, left alarm clock, center crest, 5 knobs, BC, AC **$110.00**

D-25MN, table-C, 1953, plastic, right front round dial w/inner perforations, left alarm clock, center crest, 5 knobs, BC, AC...**$110.00**

D-25WE, table-C, 1953, plastic, right round metal dial w/inner perforations, left alarm clock, center crest, 2 knobs, BC, AC **$110.00**

Director, console, 1930, walnut veneer w/ornate repwood front panel, lowboy, center window dial.............................**$165.00**

E-10BE, table, 1953, plastic, large front dial with center pointer & inner criss-cross grill, 2 knobs, BC, AC/DC..................**$85.00**

E-10WE, table, 1953, plastic, large front dial with center pointer & inner criss-cross grill, 2 knobs, BC, AC/DC..................**$85.00**

E15BE, table, 1953, plastic, upper front dial, perforated grill area w/center horizontal bar, 2 "steering wheel" knobs, crest, BC, AC/DC **$75.00**

E15TN, table, 1953, plastic, upper front dial, perforated grill area w/center horizontal bar, 2 "steering wheel" knobs, crest, BC, AC/DC **$75.00**

E15WE, table, 1953, plastic, upper front dial, perforated grill area w/center horizontal bar, 2 "steering wheel" knobs, crest, BC, AC/DC **$75.00**

E-20-MN, table, 1953, plastic, large center front dial w/inner cloth grill & gold pointer, 2 knobs, AC/DC **$75.00**

E30BE, table, 1953, plastic, right front dial, left round grill with center crest overlaps lower checkered panel, 3 knobs, AM, FM, AC **$35.00**

E30-GN, table, 1953, plastic, right front dial, left round grill with center crest overlaps lower checkered panel, 3 knobs, AM, FM, AC **$35.00**

E30TN, table, 1953, plastic, right front dial, left round grill with center crest overlaps lower checkered panel, 3 knobs, AM, FM, AC **$35.00**

E-90BK, table-C, 1953, plastic, right side dial knob, large front grill w/left square alarm clock, AC **$30.00**

Elf, cathedral, 1931, pressed wood case, ornate "carved" front, upper cloth grill w/cut-outs, 2 knobs **$375.00**

F-5RD, table, 1959, plastic, right side dial & on/off/volume knobs, front lattice grill, BC, AC **$65.00**

F5TWE "Musical Chef," table-timer, 1959, plastic, kitchen radio/timer, right side dial knob, front lattice grill, BC, AC...**$65.00**

F-110BE, portable, 1953, plastic, right front round dial over lattice grill w/crest, handle, BC, battery **$35.00**

F-110BK "Skyrocket," portable, 1953, plastic, right front round dial over lattice grill w/crest, handle, BC, battery **$35.00**

G1465, table, 1938, Catalin, right front dial, left horizontal wrap-around louvers, flared base, 2 knobs ....**$1,000.00+**

Harko Senior, table, 1922, mahogany finish, low rectangular case, 1 dial front panel, 1 tube, battery **$300.00**

JC 6TN, table-C, leatherette, right side dial/volume knobs, right/left side metal perforated grills, center front round alarm clock face, wire stand, BC, AC **$30.00**

JM-8BG "Musical Memories," portable-N, 1956, leather, tubes & transistors, looks like small book, inner thumbwheel dial, metal grill, AM, battery **$165.00**

Mate, console, 1930, walnut veneer w/ornate repwood front panel, upper dial, stretcher base **$165.00**

Minstrel, console, 1931, wood, inner front window dial, lower cloth grill w/cut-outs, double front doors.....................**$135.00**

Pal, consolette, 1931, wood w/ornate repwood front & sides, low-boy, window dial, 5 tubes, 3 knobs, AC **$185.00**

Playmate, console, 1930, walnut veneer, low case, 29 1/2" high, inner front window dial, double doors........................**$140.00**

Prestotune 11, console, 1937, walnut, upper press button tuning dial, lower horizontal louvers, 5 knobs, BC, SW, AC...**$150.00**

Prestotune 12, console-upright, 1937, walnut, upper press button tuning dial, lower horizontal louvers, 5 knobs, BC, SW, AC ...**$150.00**

Prestotune 12, console-low profile, 1937, mahogany w/inlay, top press button tuning dial, front horizontal louvers, BC, SW, 12 tubes, AC..**$160.00**

Pup "Sky Terrier," table, 1924, metal, square case, one top exposed tube, side knobs, battery **$425.00**

RFL-60, table, 1926, mahogany, low rectangular case, 3 dial panel engraved w/woodland scene, 5 tubes, battery ..**$140.00**

RFL-75, table, 1926, mahogany, low rectangular case, slanted ornately engraved 3 dial front panel, battery **$185.00**

RFL-90, console, 1926, mahogany, upper front double dial w/escutcheon, lower built-in speaker, 6 tubes, battery ..**$175.00**

Sheraton, cathedral, 1933, wood, Sheraton-style, center front window dial, pedimented top w/finial, 3 knobs, 5 tubes, AC **$275.00**

T-60GN, table, 1964, plastic, lower front oblong slide rule dial over checkered grill panel, 2 knobs, feet, BC **$20.00**

TA-62, table, 1941, wood, right front dial, left grill w/vertical bars, 5 pushbuttons, 3 knobs, BC, SW, 5 tubes, AC/DC **$55.00**

TH-52, table, 1941, plastic, right front dial, left horizontal wrap-around grill bars, handle, 3 knobs, BC, SW, 8 tubes, AC/DC **$45.00**

TK-52, table, 1941, wood, right front dial, left vertical grill bars, pushbuttons, 3 knobs, BC, SW, 8 tubes, AC/DC **$55.00**

Travo Deluxe, table, 1932, Deco case, right & left front knobs, center cloth grill w/cut-outs, top fluting **$85.00**

Trirdyn, table, 1925, wood, low rectangular case, 2 dial front panel, lift top, battery **$100.00**

Trirdyn 3R3, table, 1924, wood, low rectangular case, 2 dial front panel, lift top, 3 tubes, battery $100.00

Trirdyn 3R3 Special, table, 1924, walnut, low rectangular case, 2 dial front panel, lift top, feet, 3 tubes, battery $110.00

Trirdyn Newport, table, 1925, wood, slanted 2 dial black front panel, 3 tubes, feet, battery $125.00

Trirdyn Regular, table, 1925, wood, low rectangular case, 2 dial front panel, lift top, battery..................................$95.00

Trirdyn Super Regular, table, 1925, wood, low rectangular case, front panel with 2 pointer dials, lift top, battery $130.00

Trirdyn Special, table, 1925, wood, low rectangular case, 2 dial front panel, lift top, battery $125.00

Trirdyn Super Special, table, 1925, wood, low rectangular case, slanted black panel w/2 pointer dials, lift top, battery $150.00

V, table-amp, 1922, wood, low rectangular case, amplifier, black Bakelite front panel, lift top, battery $220.00

V, table, 1922, wood, low rectangular case, 1 dial black Bakelite front panel, lift top, battery $200.00

VI, table, 1923, wood, low rectangular case, 2 dial black Bakelite front panel, lift top, battery $200.00

VI Special, table, 1923, wood, low rectangular case, 2 dial front panel, lift top, rear storage, battery............................$200.00

VIII, table, 1923, wood, low rectangular case, 2 dial black Bakelite front panel, lift top, battery $210.00

VIII Portable, portable, 1923, wood, inner 2 dial panel, storage, fold-down front, handle, 3 tubes, loop antenna, battery.$425.00

X, table, 1922, wood, low rectangular case, 2 dial black Bakelite front panel, lift top, 4 tubes, battery $200.00

XJ, table, 1923, wood, low rectangular case, 2 dial black Bakelite front panel, lift top, battery $210.00

XL, table, 1923, wood, high rectangular case, inner left 2 dial panel, double doors, battery.................................$225.00

XV, table, 1922, wood, high rectangular case, upper 2 dial panel, lower built-in speaker, battery $225.00

CROYDON

30, tombstone, two-tone wood, lower front airplane dial, upper cloth grill w/cut-outs, 3 knobs $145.00

CUTTING & WASHINGTON
Cutting & Washington Radio Corporation, Minneapolis, Minnesota

Cutting & Washington was formed in 1917 by Fulton Cutting and Bowden Washington in the business of making radio transmitters. In 1922 the company marketed its first radio but was out of business by 1924 due to legal difficulties and marketing problems.

11, table, 1922, wood, low rectangular case, 2 dial front panel, lift top, 3 tubes, battery.................................$750.00

11A, table, 1922, wood, low rectangular case, 3 dial black front panel, lift top, battery.................................$650.00

12A, table, 1923, wood, high rectangular case, 2 dial front panel, removable front, battery $650.00

CYARTS

B "Deluxe," table, 1946, Lucite, streamline bullet shape, slide rule dial, rounded left w/round cloth grill, 3 knobs, BC, AC ....$1,000.00+

DAHLBERG
The Dahlberg Company, Minneapolis, Minnesota

4130-D "Pillow Speaker," coin op-N, 1955, plastic, mounts on motel bed headboard, slide rule dial, thumbwheel knobs, moveable pillow speaker, BC, AC $225.00

DALBAR
Dalbar Mfg. Co., 1314 Forest Avenue, Dallas, Texas

100-1000 Series, table, 1946, wood, right front dial, left horizontal grill bars, 4 knobs, BC, SW, AC/DC $35.00

400, table, 1946, wood, right front dial, left diamond-shaped grill, 2 knobs, BC, AC $35.00

Barcombo, Jr., table-R/P, 1946, wood, right front dial, 4 knobs, diamond-shaped grill, lift top, inner phono, BC, AC......$30.00

DAVID GRIMES
David Grimes, Inc., 1571 Broadway, New York City

3XP "Inverse Duplex," table, 1925, wood, rectangular case, slanted 3 dial front panel, 3 tubes, battery $175.00

4DL, table, 1924, wood, 3 inner pointer dials, fold-down front, columns, 4 tubes, battery $225.00

5B "Baby Grand Duplex," table, 1925, wood, low rectangular case, metal front panel w/ 2 pointer dials, 5 tubes, battery $200.00

6D, table, wood, low rectangular case, inner panel w/3 pointer dials, fold-down front, battery $250.00

DAY-FAN
The Dayton Fan & Motor Company, Dayton, Ohio
Day-Fan Electric Company, Dayton, Ohio

Day-Fan began business as the Dayton Fan & Motor Company in 1889 producing fans. The company marketed a line of radio component parts in 1922 and by 1924 was producing complete radio sets. Day-Fan was bought out by General Motors in 1929.

5 (5049), table, 1925, wood, low rectangular case, 1 dial slant front panel, lift top, 5 tubes, battery $90.00

Daycraft, table, 1925, mahogany, low rectangular case, 1 dial slant front panel, right built-in speaker, 5 tubes, battery $125.00

Daygrand, console, 1926, wood, inner 1 dial slanted panel, left built-in speaker, fold-down front, storage, 5 tubes, battery $150.00

Dayola (5112), table, 1925, mahogany, inner 3 dial slanted panel, fold-down front, feet, 4 tubes, battery $110.00

Dayradia (5107), table, 1924, wood, high rectangular case, lower slant front panel, upper built-in speaker, battery $185.00

Dayroyal, console, 1926, mahogany, desk-style, inner 1 dial panel, upper built-in speaker & storage, doors, 5 tubes, battery................$150.00

Daytonia, console, 1926, wood, inner 1 dial slanted panel, fold-down front, right built-in speaker, storage, 5 tubes, battery $150.00

OEM-5, table, wood, low rectangular case, 3 dial black front panel, 5 tubes $125.00

OEM-7 (5106), table, 1925, wood, low rectangular case, 3 dial front panel, lift top, 4 tubes, battery $110.00

OEM-11 (5106) "Duo-Plex," table, 1924, wood, low rectangular case, 3 dial front panel, lift top, 3 tubes, battery $100.00

OEM-12, table, 1925, mahogany finish, low rectangular case, 3 dial front panel, lift top, 4 tubes, battery........................$90.00

DEARBORN

Dearborn Industries, Chicago, Illinois

100, table-R/P, 1947, wood, right front square dial, left cloth grill w/oblong cut-outs, 2 knobs, open top phono, BC, AC...$25.00

DEFOREST

The Radio Telephone Company
49 Exchange Place, New York, New York
Deforest Radio Telephone & Telegraph Company,
1415 Sedgwick Avenue, New York, New York
Deforest Radio Company
Jersey City, New Jersey

Between 1900 and the end of WW I, Lee Deforest and his various companies produced much electrical equipment for the government. By 1922, the company was fully involved in the production of radio sets for the public. After many legal entanglements, the company was sold to RCA in 1933.

D-4 "Radiophone," table, 1923, wood, square case with fold-back top, inner 2 dial panel, 1 exposed tube, battery ..$425.00

D-6, table, 1922, wood, low rectangular case, 2 dial front panel, battery................$1,200.00

D-7 "Radiophone," table, 1922, wood, square case, 2 dial front panel, top loop antenna, 3 tubes, battery $700.00

D-7A, table, 1923, wood, square case, 2 dial black front panel, top loop antenna, 3 tubes, battery $700.00

D-10, table, 1923, leatherette or mahogany, inner 2 dial panel, doors, top loop antenna, 4 tubes, battery...................$650.00

D-12 "Radiophone," table, 1924, leatherette or mahogany cabinet, 2 dial front panel, top loop antenna, 4 tubes, battery.....$600.00

D-14 "Radiophone," table, 1925, wood, tall case, inner slanted 2 dial panel w/5 exposed tubes, loop antenna, battery ..$600.00

D-17A, table, 1925, wood, upper 2 dial front panel, lower built-in speaker, top loop antenna, battery $600.00

D-17L, table, 1925, leatherette, upper 2 dial front panel, lower built-in speaker, top loop antenna, battery $550.00

D-17M, table, 1925, mahogany, upper 2 dial front panel, lower built-in speaker, top loop antenna, battery $600.00

D-556A, table, plastic, upper slanted slide rule dial, large cloth grill w/4 vertical bars, 2 knobs $45.00

DT-600 "Everyman," table, 1922, wood, square case, crystal set, inner panel and storage, lift lid................................$475.00

DT-800, table-amp, 1922, wood, two-step amplifier, inner panel w/2 exposed tubes $450.00

F-5 "Radiophone," table, 1925, wood, low rectangular case, 3 dial front panel, lift top, feet, 5 tubes, battery..............$325.00

F-5-AL, table, 1925, embossed leatherette, low rectangular case, 3 dial front panel, 5 tubes, battery $275.00

F-5-AW, table, 1925, walnut, low rectangular case, 3 dial front panel, 5 tubes, battery $275.00

F-5L, table, 1925, leatherette, upper 3 dial front panel, lower built-in speaker, 5 tubes, battery $225.00

F-5M, table, 1925, mahogany, upper 3 dial front panel, lower built-in speaker, 5 tubes, battery $275.00

MS-1 "Interpanel," table, 1921, 4 units - tuner, audion control, 1-step amp, transmitter, battery..............................$2,500.00+

DELCO

Delco Radio, Division of G. M. Corp.,
Kokomo, Indiana

608, table, 1949, wood, large multi-band slide rule dial over front grill, 4 knobs, BC, SW, AC..$45.00

1102, tombstone, 1935, wood w/inlay, center front dial w/escutcheon, upper grill w/vertical bars, 6 tubes, knobs $110.00

1106, tombstone, 1935, wood, lower front round airplane dial, upper cloth grill w/3 vertical bars, 4 knobs, BC, SW, AC.........$125.00

1107, tombstone, 1935, wood, round airplane dial, upper cloth grill w/3 vertical bars, 4 knobs, BC, SW, AC $125.00

R-1116, table, wood, right front round black dial, left cloth grill w/horizontal bars, 4 knobs $55.00

R-1125, table, 1937, wood, right front airplane dial, left cloth grill w/cut-outs, 2 knobs, AC $50.00

R-1127, table, 1937, wood, right front airplane dial, left cloth grill w/cut-outs, tuning eye, 4 knobs, 3 bands $70.00

R-1134, table, plastic, top right wrap-over slide rule dial, right left wrap-around horizontal bars, 5 pushbuttons, lower right front knob, right side knob, AC $110.00

R-1141, table, wood, lower front slide rule dial, upper cloth grill w/horizontal bars, pushbuttons, 4 knobs, BC, SW **$50.00**

R-1227, table, 1947, plastic, upper slanted slide rule dial, lower horizontal grill bars, decorative case lines, 3 knobs **$55.00**

R-1228, table, 1947, plastic, upper slanted slide rule dial, lower horizontal grill bars, decorative case lines, 3 knobs **$55.00**

R-1229, table, 1947, two-tone wood, upper slanted slide rule dial, lower horizontal louvers, 3 knobs, BC, AC/DC **$40.00**

R-1230, table, 1948, ivory plastic, right front dial, left vertical bars w/center "ribbon candy" cut-out, 2 knobs, BC, AC/DC ..**$75.00**

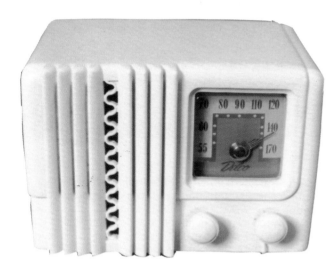

R-1230A, table, 1947, ivory plastic, right front dial, left vertical bars w/center "ribbon candy" cut-out, 2 knobs, BC, AC/DC **$75.00**

R-1231, table, 1948, brown plastic, right front dial, left vertical bars w/center "ribbon candy" cut-out, 2 knobs, BC, AC/DC **$75.00**

R-1231A, table, 1948, brown plastic, right front dial, left vertical bars w/center "ribbon candy" cut-out, 2 knobs, BC, AC/DC..**$75.00**

R-1232, table, 1948, walnut, right front square dial, left vertical grill bars, 2 knobs, BC, AC/DC **$45.00**

R-1233, table, 1948, plastic, right front dial, left vertical bars w/center "ribbon candy" cut-out, 2 knobs, BC, AC/DC ..**$75.00**

R-1235, table, 1946, plastic, upper slanted slide rule dial, lower horizontal louvers, 3 knobs, BC, AC/DC......................**$40.00**

R-1236, table, 1947, plastic, upper slanted slide rule dial, lower horizontal louvers, 3 knobs, BC, AC/DC......................**$40.00**

R-1238, table, 1948, wood & plastic, right front dial, left grill w/circular cut-outs, Lucite handle, 2 knobs, BC, AC/DC......**$60.00**

R-1241, table-R/P, 1949, wood, lower front slide rule dial, large grill, 4 knobs, 3/4 lift top, inner phono, BC, AC.............**$25.00**

R-1242, table-R/P, 1948, wood, right front square dial, 2 knobs, lift top, inner phono, BC, AC/DC **$35.00**

R-1243, table, 1948, wood, upper slanted slide rule dial, large lower grill area, 3 knobs, BC, AC.................................**$35.00**

R-1244, table-R/P, 1948, walnut, lower front slide rule dial, 4 knobs, 3/4 lift top, inner phono, BC, AC **$30.00**

R-1245, console-R/P, 1948, walnut, upper front slide rule dial & grill area, center phono, lower storage, 4 knobs, BC, AC.......**$65.00**

R-1246, console-R/P, 1948, mahogany, upper front slide rule dial & grill area, center phono, storage, 4 knobs, BC, AC....**$65.00**

R-1249, console-R/P, 1949, wood, inner right dial, 4 knobs, door, left pull-out phono drawer, BC, FM, AC.......................**$80.00**

R-1251, console-R/P, 1947, wood, inner right dial, left pull-out phono drawer, lower grill w/cut-outs, BC, SW, AC **$80.00**

R-1254, console-R/P, 1948, wood, inner right slide rule dial, 6 knobs, pushbuttons, left pull-out phono drawer, BC, SW, FM, AC...**$80.00**

R-1407, portable, 1941, inner right front dial, left grill bars, 3 knobs, removable front cover, handle, 6 tubes, AC/DC/battery...**$25.00**

R-1408, portable, 1947, right square dial, left grill w/circular cut-outs, 3 knobs, recessed handle, BC, AC/DC/battery.....**$35.00**

R-1409, portable, 1947, right square dial, left grill w/circular cut-outs, 3 knobs, recessed handle, BC, AC/DC/battery.....**$35.00**

R-1410, portable, 1948, luggage-type, front slide rule dial, 2 knobs, handle, BC, AC/DC/battery **$35.00**

DETROLA
International Detrola Corp.,
1501 Beard Street, Detroit, Michigan

4D, cathedral, 1934, wood, small case, center front round dial, cloth grill w/cut-outs, 3 knobs.........................**$190.00**

7A3, tombstone, 1934, wood, center front round dial, upper cloth grill w/vertical bars, BC, SW, AC **$120.00**

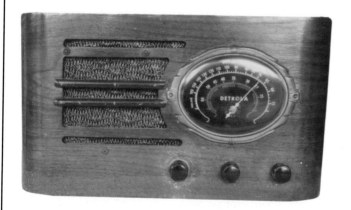

159, table, wood, right front oval dial w/red & yellow bands, left cloth grill w/horizontal bars, 3 knobs, BC, SW, AC **$50.00**

172A "Glen," table, 1937, wood, right front round dial, left grill w/horizontal bars, 3 knobs, 5 tubes, BC, SW, AC/DC ...**$70.00**

173EC "Lark," console, 1937, wood, upper front dial, lower grill w/vertical bars, corner "louvers," 8 tubes, BC, SW, AC ..**$135.00**

174EC "Martin," console, 1937, wood, upper front dial, cloth grill w/vertical bars, corner "louvers," 8 tubes, BC, SW, AC/DC **$135.00**
197 "Pee Wee," table, 1938, plastic, midget, right front dial knob, left wrap-around louvers, 4 tubes, BC, AC ....**$300.00+**

302, cathedral-C, 1938, wood, triangular shaped case, lower right front dial, left cloth grill, upper round clock face, 2 knobs, feet, AC **$325.00**
310, table, wood w/inlay, right front dial, left cloth grill, 6 top push-buttons, handle, 7 tubes, BC, SW, AC **$75.00**
378, portable, 1941, leatherette & plastic, inner dial & knobs, fold-open door, handle, 5 tubes, AC/DC/battery **$50.00**
383, portable, 1941, cloth covered, right front square dial, left grill, handle, 2 knobs, 5 tubes, AC/DC/battery **$30.00**
417, table-R/P, 1941, wood, center front dial, right & left grill areas, lift top, inner phono, 5 tubes **$25.00**
419, table-R/P, 1941, wood, front slide rule dial, grill w/cut-outs, lift top, inner phono, 6 tubes...**$25.00**

218 "Pee Wee," table, 1939, midget, plastic, right front dial knob, left wrap-around louvers, BC, SW, AC........**$300.00+**

558-1-49A, table-R/P, 1946, wood, front dial, horizontal louvers, 3 knobs, lift top, inner phono, BC, AC **$30.00**
568-13-221D, table, 1946, metal, upper right front slide rule dial, left round perforated grill, 3 knobs, BC, SW, AC/DC **$30.00**
571, table, 1946, right front slide rule dial, left horizontal louvers, 2 knobs **$45.00**
571L, table, 1946, wood, upper right front slide rule dial, left cloth grill w/ horizontal bars, 2 knobs, BC, AC/DC **$40.00**
571X-21-94D, table, 1946, right front slide rule dial, left horizontal louvers, 2 knobs, BC, AC/DC **$45.00**
572-220-226A, table, 1946, wood, right front slide rule dial, right & left cloth grill areas w/horizontal bars, 3 knobs, feet, BC, SW, AC...**$40.00**
576-1-6A, table, 1946, wood, upper slanted slide rule dial, lower cloth grill w/vertical bars, 3 knobs, BC, AC/DC.............**$60.00**
579-2-58A, table, 1946, wood, upper slanted slide rule dial, lower cloth grill w/2 horizontal bars, 2 knobs, BC, AC/DC **$45.00**

219 "Super Pee Wee," table, 1938, plastic, Deco, right front dial knob, left wrap-around louvers, 5 tubes, BC, SW...**$350.00+**
258EPC, console-R/P, 1938, wood, upper front dial, lower grill w/horizontal bars & drawer, lift top, inner phono, 8 tubes..........**$150.00**

582, chairside, 1947, wood, top dial, 3 knobs, lift top, inner phono, lower record storage, feet, BC, SW, AC **$85.00**
610-A, table, 1949, wood, right front round dial, horizontal grill bars, rounded corners, 2 knobs, feet, BC, battery **$35.00**
611-A, table, 1948, wood, right front round dial, horizontal grill bars, rounded corners, 4 knobs, feet, BC, SW, battery **$35.00**
3281, table-C, wood, mantle clock style w/arched top, lower right front dial, left cloth grill, upper round clock face, 2 knobs..........**$325.00**
3861, table-R/P, 1941, walnut veneer, right front dial, left grill, knobs, lift top, inner phono, AC **$35.00**
7156, table-R/P, 1948, wood, lower front slide rule dial, horizontal louvers, 4 knobs, 3/4 lift top, inner phono, BC, AC.......**$30.00**
7270, table-R/P, 1947, wood, top slide rule dial, 3 knobs, front grill w/cut-outs, lift top, inner phono, BC, AC.....................**$35.00**

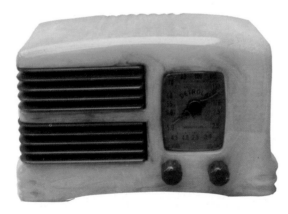

281 "Split Grill," table, 1939, Catalin, right front dial, left 2-section wrap-around horizontal louvers, 2 pinwheel knobs, BC, SW, AC/DC.......................................**$3,000.00+**

DEWALD
Dewald Radio Mfg. Corp.,
440 Lafayette Street
New York, New York
Pierce-Aero, Inc.,
New York

54 "Dynette," portable, leatherette, inner wood panel w/right dial, center grill, removable front, handle $85.00

54A, table, 1933, wood, rounded top, right & left front knobs, center grill w/cut-outs, raised side panels, AC/DC/battery $90.00

60-3, tombstone, 1933, wood, center front window dial w/escutcheon, upper grill w/gothic cut-outs, 3 knobs, 6 tubes, AC/DC $125.00

60-42, console, 1933, wood, upper front window dial w/escutcheon, lower grill w/cut-outs, 6 legs, 3 knobs $145.00

406, table, 1938, plastic, small case, right front round dial, left vertical wrap-over grill bars, "feet," AC $95.00

410, portable, leatherette, left side dial & knob, front rectangular metal grill, handle $30.00

430 "Dynette," table, right front dial, center cloth grill, decorative case designs, 2 knobs $85.00

511, table-R/P, 1949, "alligator," slide rule dial, 4 knobs, lift top, inner phono, handle, BC, SW, AC $30.00

522, table, 1936, wood, Deco, right front dial, left grill w/wrap-over vertical bars, tuning eye, 5 tubes, battery.....................$65.00

530, table, 1939, walnut or ivory plastic, right front dial, left grill w/checker board center, 2 knobs, 5 tubes, BC, AC/DC $65.00

531, table-R/P, 1939, two-tone wood, right front dial, left grill, 2 knobs, lift top, inner phono, AC $35.00

532, table-R/P, 1939, two-tone wood, right front dial, left grill, 2 knobs, lift top, inner phono, AC/DC $35.00

533, table, 1939, wood, right front recessed dial, left wrap-around horizontal louvers, 2 knobs, 5 tubes, AC/DC.................$50.00

534, table, 1939, wood, right front recessed dial, curved left grill w/vertical bars, 2 knobs, 5 tubes, AC/DC $50.00

548 "Organ-Tone," table, 1940, plastic, raised top & flared base, lower front slide rule dial, upper vertical wrap-over grill bars, 4 pushbuttons, 2 knobs, 5 tubes..................$110.00

550 "Dynette," table, 1933, walnut w/inlay, right front dial, center grill w/cut-outs, arched top, 2 knobs, 5 tubes, AC/DC ..$90.00

551 "Deluxe," table, 1933, walnut, right front dial, center grill w/cut-outs, vertical front lines, 2 knobs, AC/DC $85.00

561 "Jewel," table, 1941, Catalin, upper front slide rule dial, lower horizontal grill bars, handle, 2 knobs ....$500.00+

562 "Jewel," table, 1941, Catalin, upper front slide rule dial, lower horizontal grill bars, 2 knobs ....$500.00+

564 "Companionette," portable, 1941, leatherette, inner dial, vertical grill bars, fold-open front, handle, AC/DC/battery....$50.00

565, portable, 1941, leatherette, inner slide rule dial, cloth grill, 2 knobs, front cover, handle, AC/DC/battery $35.00

580, table, 1933, wood, lower front window dial, upper cloth grill w/vertical bars, 3 knobs, 5 tubes, AC $75.00

615, table, 1935, wood, lower front round airplane dial, upper cloth grill, rounded sides, 2 knobs, BC, SW, AC/DC $75.00

643, table, 1939, wood, right front dial, left grill w/horizontal bars, tuning eye, 4 knobs, 6 tubes, BC, SW, AC...................$55.00

645, table, 1939, wood, right front slide rule dial, left horizontal wrap-around grill bars, 3 knobs, 6 tubes, AC/DC $50.00

648, table, 1939, wood, right front dial, curved left w/vertical bars, 6 pushbuttons, 4 knobs, AC/DC $65.00

649, table, 1939, wood, right front dial, left wrap-around horizontal grill bars, 6 pushbuttons, 4 knobs, AC..........................$65.00

669 "Super Six," table-R/P, 1941, wood, right front dial, left horizontal louvers, 2 knobs, lift top, inner phono, AC $35.00

670, table, 1941, wood, upper front slanted slide rule dial, lower grill, 4 knobs, BC, SW, AC/DC $45.00

701, table, 1939, wood, right front dial, left grill w/3 horizontal bars, 6 center pushbuttons, 3 knobs, 7 tubes, AC/DC ..$50.00

708, table, 1941, two-tone wood, upper front slanted slide rule dial, lower grill, 4 knobs, 7 tubes, BC, SW, AC..............$40.00

802, tombstone, 1934, wood, Deco, center front round airplane dial, upper cloth grill w/triangular cut-out, BC, 3SW, AC $125.00

901, tombstone, wood, large case, lower front round airplane dial, upper cloth grill w/vertical bars, 4 knobs.....................$115.00

907, console-R/P, 1940, wood, inner right dial & knobs, left phono, lift top, front grill w/vertical bars $80.00

1200, table, 1937, wood, right front dial, left 3-sectioned cloth grill, 12 tubes, BC, SW $50.00

A-500, table, 1946, plastic, upper front slide rule dial, lower horizontal louvers, 2 knobs, BC, AC/DC.............................$40.00

A-501 "Harp," table, 1946, Catalin, harp-shaped case, upper front slide rule dial, lower cloth grill w/ 5 vertical bars, 2 knobs, 5 tubes, BC, AC/DC ....$600.00+

A-502, table, 1946, Catalin, upper front slide rule dial, lower horizontal louvers, 2 knobs, BC, AC/DC........................$600.00+

A-503, table, 1946, upper front slide rule dial, lower horizontal louvers, 2 knobs, BC, AC/DC $45.00

A-505, table, 1947, upper front slide rule dial, lower horizontal louvers, 4 knobs, BC, SW, AC/DC $40.00

A-507, portable, 1947, leatherette, inner slide rule dial, 2 knobs, fold-down front, handle, BC, AC/DC/battery $35.00

A-509, table, 1948, plastic, upper front slide rule dial, lower horizontal louvers, 2 front knobs, 1 side knob, BC, SW, AC/DC $40.00

A-514, table, 1947, plastic, right front dial, left horizontal wrap-around louvers, 2 knobs, BC, AC/DC $50.00

A-602, table-R/P, 1947, wood, inner slide rule dial, 4 knobs, fold-down front, lift top, handle, BC, AC $30.00

A-605, table-R/P, 1947, wood, front slide rule dial over horizontal louvers, 4 knobs, lift top, inner phono, BC, AC.............$30.00

B-400, portable, 1948, two-tone leatherette, right front square dial, left cloth grill, handle, 2 knobs, BC, battery $30.00

B-401, table, 1948, plastic, right front round dial, left vertical wrap-over grill bars, 2 knobs, BC, AC/DC $60.00

B-402, portable, 1948, plastic, lower front slide rule dial, upper horizontal grill bars, handle, 2 knobs, BC, battery $35.00

B-403, table-C, 1948, Catalin, harp-shaped case, upper front slide rule dial, center clock face, right & left cloth grills, 2 knobs, BC, AC...$600.00+

B-504, portable, 1948, plastic, lower front slide rule dial, upper horizontal louvers, handle, 2 knobs, BC, AC/DC/battery $35.00

B-506, table, 1948, plastic, lower front slide rule dial, upper checkered grill area, 2 knobs, BC, AC/DC.............................$35.00

B-510, table, 1948, plastic, upper front slide rule dial, lower horizontal louvers, 2 front knobs, 1 side knob, BC, 2SW, AC/DC $35.00

B-512, table-C, 1948, Catalin, upper front slide rule dial, center clock face, grill bars on top of case, 5 knobs, BC, AC............$625.00+

B-515, portable, 1949, plastic, lower front slide rule dial, upper horizontal grill bars, handle, 2 knobs, BC, SW, AC/DC/battery $35.00

B-614, table-R/P, 1949, "alligator," slide rule dial, 4 knobs, lift top, inner phono, handle, BC, AC......................................$35.00

C-516, table, 1949, plastic, lower front slide rule dial, upper checkered grill, 2 front knobs, 1 side knob, BC, SW, AC/DC $40.00

C-800, table, 1949, plastic, upper slanted slide rule dial, lower horizontal louvers, 4 knobs, BC, FM, AC/DC $35.00

D-508, portable, 1950, "alligator," upper front slide rule dial, lower grill, handle, telescope antenna, BC, 2SW, AC/DC/battery $35.00

D-517, portable, 1951, plastic, lower front slide rule dial, upper perforated grill, handle, 2 knobs, BC, AC/DC/battery $30.00

D-518, table, 1950, plastic, lower front slide rule dial, upper perforated grill, 2 knobs, BC, AC/DC $35.00

D-519, table, plastic, lower front slide rule dial, upper checkered grill area, 2 knobs, BC $45.00

D-616, table, 1950, plastic, upper front slide rule dial, lower perforated grill, top vents, 2 knobs, BC, AC/DC $35.00

D-E517A, portable, 1952, plastic, lower front slide rule dial, upper checkered grill, handle, 2 knobs, BC, AC/DC/battery $35.00

E-520, table, 1955, plastic, upper front slide rule dial, lower horizontal louvers, 4 knobs, BC, 2SW, AC/DC....................$40.00

E-522, table-R/P, 1951, wood, upper front slide rule dial, horizontal grill bars, 4 knobs, 3/4 lift top, inner phono, BC, AC.......$30.00

F-404, table, 1952, plastic, right front round dial knob, left horizontal wrap-around louvers, BC, AC/DC.........................$45.00

F-405, table, 1953, plastic, upper front slanted slide rule dial, lower horizontal louvers, 4 knobs, BC, 2SW, battery $35.00

G-408, portable, 1953, plastic, lower front round dial, upper vertical grill bars, thumbwheel knob, handle, BC, battery $35.00

H-528, table-C, 1954, plastic, right front round dial, left clock, center checkered panel, 3 knobs, 5 tubes, BC, AC.............$30.00

H-533, table-C, 1954, plastic, right side dial knob, left side on/off/volume knob, front clock, vertical wrap-over grill bars, 5 tubes, BC, AC..$45.00

H-537, table, 1955, plastic, right front dial, left volume, center checkered grill, 3 knobs, BC, SW, AC/DC $40.00

J-802, table, plastic w/contrasting trim, upper front slide rule dial, lower horizontal louvers, 2 knobs, BC, FM $45.00

K-412, table, 1957, plastic, right front dial, recessed left side w/checkered grill, 2 knobs, 4 tubes, BC, AC/DC $25.00

K-545, table-C, 1957, plastic, right front clock, recessed left side w/checkered grill, side knobs, 5 tubes, BC, AC.............$30.00

M-550, table, 1959, plastic, right front dial, recessed left side w/checkered grill, 2 knobs, 5 tubes, BC, AC/DC $25.00

DISTANTONE
Distantone Radio, Inc., Lynbrook, New York

C "Single Control," table, 1926, wood, slant front polished Bakelite panel, one center dial, battery...............................$115.00

DORON
Doron Bros. Electric Co., Hamilton, Ohio

R-5 "Super-Equidyne," table, 1925, wood, low rectangular case, 3 dial front panel, 5 tubes, battery $115.00

DUMONT
Allen B. Dumont Labs, Inc., 2 Main Street Passaic, New Jersey

R-1110, table, plastic, right side dial knob, left side on/off/volume knob, diagonally divided front w/horizontal lines, feet $30.00

RA-346, table, 1956, several variations, including a clock radio version, lower right front dial over lattice grill area w/"tree" design, BC, AC, DC...$125.00

C **RA-354 "Beachcomber,"** portable, 1957, leather case w/front criss-cross grill, right round dial, strap, 4 tubes, BC,
R   AC/DC/battery $35.00

DYNAVOX
**Dynavox Corp., 40-35 21st Street,
Long Island City, New York**

3-P-801, portable, 1948, two-tone leatherette, inner dial, 3 knobs, flip-open door, handle, BC, AC/DC/battery....................$45.00

---

th
pr
m

6-

RF

EAGLE
**Eagle Radio Company,
16 Boyden Place, Newark, New Jersey**

The Eagle Radio Company began business in 1922. After an initial surge of business, the company began to decline and in 1927 was sold to Wurlitzer.

A, table, 1923, wood, low rectangular case, 3 dial front panel, lift top, battery $125.00
B "Neutrodyne," table, 1924, wood, low rectangular case, 3 dial front panel, 5 tubes, battery $145.00
C-1, console, 1925, wood, contains table model F receiver, fold-down front door, lower storage, battery $150.00
C-2, console, 1925, wood, contains table model F receiver, fold-down front door, lower storage, battery $150.00
C-3, console, 1925, wood, contains table model F receiver, fold-down front door, lower storage, battery $150.00
D, table, 1925, wood, low rectangular case, 3 dial black Bakelite front panel, 5 tubes, battery $100.00
F "Neutrodyne," table, 1925, wood, low rectangular case, black Bakelite front panel, 3 window dials, battery $110.00
T51 **H**, table, 1926, wood, low rectangular case, 3 dial front panel, 5 tubes, battery...$100.00
K, console, 1926, wood, inner 3 dial panel w/Eagle emblem, fold-down front door, storage, 5 tubes, battery.........$175.00
K-2, table, 1926, wood, low rectangular case, inner 3 dial panel, fold-down front door, battery $125.00

ECA
**Electrical Corp. of America,
45 West 18th Street, New York, New York**
B20

101, table, 1946, wood, upper front curved slide rule dial, lower horizontal louvers, 2 knobs, BC, AC/DC $35.00
102, table, 1947, plastic, upper front curved slide rule dial, lower vertical grill openings, 2 knobs, BC, AC/DC $45.00
104, table-R/P, 1947, wood, front slide rule dial, lower horizontal louvers, 4 knobs, lift top, inner phono, BC, AC.............$30.00
105, table-R/P, 1947, leatherette, inner slide rule dial, 4 knobs,
555,   phono, lift top, BC, AC..$25.00
106, table-R/P, 1946, wood, front slide rule dial, horizontal louvers, 4 knobs, lift top, inner phono, BC, AC $30.00
108, table, 1946, plastic, shouldered top, upper front curved slide rule dial, lower textured grill, 4 knobs, BC, AC/DC $50.00
121, console-R/P, 1947, wood, top left dial & 4 knobs, right front pull-out phono drawer, BC, AC.................................$95.00
131, table-R/P, 1947, "alligator," inner slide rule dial, 4 knobs, fold-down side door, lift top, handle, BC, AC................$30.00
26, t **132**, table, 1948, wood, upper front slanted slide rule dial, lower criss-cross grill, 4 knobs, BC, AC/DC..........................$35.00

201, table, 1947, two-tone wood, upper front slanted slide rule dial, lower horizontal grill openings, 2 knobs, BC, AC/DC $50.00
204, portable, 1948, "alligator," inner right dial, left grill, 2 knobs, fold-down front, handle, BC, AC/DC/battery.................$30.00

ECHOPHONE
**Echophone Radio, Inc.,
1120 North Ashland Avenue, Chicago, Illinois
The Hallicrafter Co.,
2611 South Indiana Avenue, Chicago, Illinois
Radio Shop, Sunnyvale, California
Echophone Radio Mfg. Co.,
968 Formosa, Los Angeles, California**

The trade name "Echophone" was used on many sets made by different manufacturers.

3, table, 1925, wood, high case, slanted two dial black panel w/3 exposed tubes, lift top, battery $325.00
4, cathedral, 1932, wood, front window dial w/escutcheon, upper cloth grill w/cut-outs, 2 knobs $235.00
4, table, 1925, wood, high case, slanted front panel with 2 pointer dials, 4 exposed tubes, battery $325.00
6, cathedral, wood, right front thumbwheel dial, upper round grill w/lyre cut-out, 2 knobs $195.00

17, upright table, 1932, wood, unusually shaped case with upper front quarter-round window dial, lower cloth grill area with cut-outs, 2 knobs, finials, 2 speakers $350.00
46, console, 1928, wood, rectangular cabinet on 4 legged stand, center front dial w/escutcheon $225.00
60, cathedral, 1931, walnut, lower front quarter-round dial, upper ornate pressed wood grill, 6 tubes, 3 knobs, AC.........$295.00
80, cathedral, 1931, walnut, lower front quarter-round dial w/escutcheon, upper ornate pressed wood grill, 3 knobs, AC...$275.00
81, cathedral, 1931, wood, lower front quarter-round dial w/escutcheon, upper ornate pressed wood grill, 3 knobs, AC...$275.00
90, console, 1931, wood, lowboy, upper front quarter-round dial, lower ornate gothic grill, 3 knobs, AC........................$195.00

AA-207, table, 1938, plastic, right front dial, left horizontal louvers, decorative case lines, 3 knobs, BC, SW, 6 tubes, AC/DC...**$55.00**

AB-182, console, 1937, walnut, upper front dial, lower cloth grill w/vertical bars, BC, SW, 14 tubes, AC **$165.00**

AR-165, chairside-R/P, 1937, wood, Deco, step-down top, rounded front w/horizontal louvers, inner phono, AC **$175.00**

AE-163, table, 1937, wood, raised top, lower front airplane dial, upper cloth grill w/cut-outs, 2 knobs, BC, SW..**$95.00**

AU-190, tombstone, 1938, Catalin, lower front scalloped gold dial, upper cloth grill w/vertical bars, 3 knobs, AC ....**$1,100.00+**

AU-213, table, 1938, walnut, tombstone shape, lower front half-round dial, upper vertical grill bars, 3 knobs, BC, 5 tubes, AC/DC **$145.00**

AX-211 "Little Miracle," table, 1938, plastic, midget, right front dial over horizontal grill bars & front lines, 2 knobs, 5 tubes, AC/DC **$110.00**

AH, table, two-tone wood, right front gold airplane dial, left cloth grill w/horizontal bars, 4 knobs, BC, SW **$45.00**

AL-132, table, 1936, wood with Repwood front panel, right front gold dial, left cloth grill w/cut-outs, 2 knobs, AC **$45.00**

AX-212, table, 1938, walnut or maple, Deco, right front square dial, left round grill w/concentric circle louvers, 2 knobs, 5 tubes, AC/DC **$200.0**

AX-217, table, 1938, walnut or maple, right front square dial, left horizontal louvers, 2 knobs, BC, 5 tubes, AC/DC.........**$40.0**

AX-219, table-R/P, 1938, wood, right front square dial, left horizontal louvers, 2 knobs, open top phono, BC, 5 tubes, AC **$25.0**

AX-221, table-R/P, 1938, wood, right front dial, curved left w/vertical bars, 2 knobs, lift top, inner phono, 5 tubes, AC......**$35.**

AX-221-AC-DC, table-R/P, 1938, wood, right front dial, curved left w/vertical bars, 2 knobs, lift top, inner phono, 5 tubes, AC/DC..**$35.**

AM-169, table, 1937, walnut, right front airplane dial, rounded left side w/vertical bars, 3 knobs, BC, SW, 6 tubes, AC/DC..**$65.00**

AX-222, portable-R/P, 1938, cloth-covered, inner dial & grill, fold-down front, lift top, inner phono, handle, BC, 5 tubes, AC/DC **$30.00**

AX-232, portable-R/P, 1938, "alligator," inner dial/grill/2 knobs, fold-down front, lift top, inner phono, handle, BC, 5 tubes, AC **$30.00**

AX-232 AC-DC, portable-R/P, 1938, "alligator," inner dial/grill/2 knobs, fold-down front, lift top, inner phono, handle, BC, AC/DC **$30.00**

AX-235 "Little Miracle," table, 1938, Catalin, right front square airplane dial, left horizontal louvers, flared base, 2 knobs, BC, 5 tubes, AC/DC ....**$1,000.00+**

AX-238, table, 1939, wood, chest-type, inner right dial, left grill w/horizontal bars, 2 knobs, lift top, BC, AC/DC **$250.00**

B-131, table, 1936, wood, right front gold dial, left cloth grill w/horizontal bars, BC, SW, 6 tubes, AC **$45.00**

BA-199, table, 1938, plastic, center front round dial, cloth grill w/vertical bars, 2 knobs, AC/DC.............................**$85.00**

BB-208, table, 1938, plastic, right front airplane dial, left horizontal louvers, decorative case lines, pushbuttons, 2 knobs, BC, 5 tubes, AC/DC **$55.00**

BB-209, table, 1938, wood, right front airplane dial, left horizontal louvers, pushbuttons, 2 knobs, BC, 5 tubes, AC/DC.....**$50.00**

BD-197 "Mae West," table, 1938, wood, curved case, right front conical dial, left conical grill, 4 knobs, BC, SW, 6 tubes, AC **$450.00**

BF-169, table, 1938, wood, right front dial, curved left w/vertical bars, 3 knobs, BC, SW, 6 tubes, AC/DC **$65.00**

BF-204, table, 1938, wood, right front airplane dial, left wrap-around horizontal louvers, 3 knobs, BC, SW, 6 tubes, AC/DC...**$55.00**

BF-207, table, 1938, walnut or ivory plastic, right front dial, left horizontal louvers, decorative case lines, 3 knobs, BC, SW, 6 tubes, AC/DC **$55.00**

BF-316, table, 1938, wood, right front gold airplane dial, rounded left side w/wrap-around horizontal grill bars, 3 knobs **$75.00**

BJ-200, table, 1938, walnut or ivory plastic, right front dial, left horizontal louvers, decorative case lines, 2 knobs, BC, 6 tubes, AC/DC **$70.00**

BJ-210, table, 1938, wood, right front airplane dial, curved left w/vertical bars, 2 knobs, BC, 6 tubes, AC/DC...............**$65.00**

BJ-214, table, 1938, wood, right front airplane dial, curved left w/horizontal wrap-around louvers, 2 knobs, BC, 6 tubes, AC/DC...**$75.00**

BJ-218, table-R/P, 1938, wood, right front dial, curved left w/horizontal bars, 2 knobs, lift top, inner phono, BC, 6 tubes, AC/DC **$40.00**

BJ-220, table-R/P, 1938, wood, right front dial, left horizontal grill bars, 2 knobs, lift top, inner phono, BC, 6 tubes, AC/DC **$35.00**

BL-200, table, 1938, walnut or ivory plastic, right front gold dial, left horizontal louvers, decorative case lines, 2 knobs, BC, SW, 5 tubes, AC **$70.00**

BL-210, table, 1938, wood, right front airplane dial, curved left w/vertical bars, 2 knobs, BC, 5 tubes, AC **$65.00**

BL-214, table, 1938, wood, right front airplane dial, curved left w/horizontal wrap-around louvers, 2 knobs, BC, 5 tubes, AC **$75.00**

BL-218, table-R/P, 1938, wood, right front dial, curved left w/horizontal bars, 2 knobs, lift top, inner phono, BC, 5 tubes, AC **$40.00**

BL-220, table-R/P, 1938, wood, right front dial, left horizontal bars, 2 knobs, lift top, inner phono, BC, 5 tubes, AC **$35.00**

BM-206, table, 1938, walnut or ivory plastic, right front airplane dial, left horizontal louvers, 2 knobs, BC, 5 tubes, AC/DC **$40.00**

BM-215, table, 1938, two-tone wood, right front gold airplane dial, left horizontal louvers, 2 knobs, 5 tubes, AC/DC..........**$45.00**

BM-216, table-R/P, 1938, wood, right front airplane dial, left horizontal louvers, 2 knobs, open top phono, BC, 5 tubes, AC **$25.00**

BM-242, table-R/P, 1939, wood, right front airplane dial, left horizontal louvers, 2 knobs, lift top, inner phono, 5 tubes, AC **$35.00**

BM-247 "Snow White," table-N, 1938, Snow White and Dwarfs in pressed wood, right front airplane dial, left cloth grill, 2 knobs, BC, 5 tubes, AC/DC................................**$1,200.00+**

BM-258, table, 1937, Catalin, small case, right front airplane dial, left inset horizontal louvers, 2 knobs, 5 tubes, AC/DC ....**$1,000.00+**

BN-216, table-R/P, 1938, wood, right front airplane dial, left horizontal louvers, 2 knobs, open top phono, BC, AC **$25.00**

BQ-223, console-R/P, 1938, wood, upper front conical dial, pushbuttons, lower horizontal grill bars, 4 knobs, left lift top, inner phono, BC, SW, 6 tubes, AC.................................**$175.00**

BQ-225 "Symphony Grand," console, 1938, wood, upper front conical dial, pushbuttons, lower horizontal grill bars, 4 knobs, BC, SW, 6 tubes, AC..**$150.00**

BQ-228, table, 1938, wood, right front conical dial, left horizontal louvers, pushbuttons, 4 knobs, BC, SW, 6 tubes, AC **$100.00**

BR-224, console-R/P, 1938, wood, right front conical dial, pushbuttons, lower horizontal louvers, left lift top, inner phono, BC, SW, 13 tubes, AC..**$200.00**

BR-224-A, console-R/P, 1938, wood, right front conical dial, pushbuttons, lower horizontal louvers, left lift top, inner phono, BC, SW, 13 tubes, AC..**$200.00**

BR-226 "Symphony Grand," console, 1938, wood, upper front conical dial, pushbuttons, lower horizontal louvers, 4 knobs, BC, SW, 13 tubes, AC..**$190.00**

BS-227 "Queen Anne," console, 1938, wood, lowboy, Queen Anne style, upper front conical dial, pushbuttons, tuning eye, lower shell cut-out and horizontal grill bars, BC, SW, 15 tubes, AC..**$300.00**

BT-214, table, 1938, wood, right front airplane dial, rounded left with horizontal grill bars, 2 knobs, 5 tubes, AC/DC..**$70.00**

BT-245, tombstone, 1939, Catalin, lower front scalloped dial, upper 3-section grill with inset horizontal louvers, 3 knobs, 6 tubes, AC/DC......................................**$1,000.00+**

BU-229, table, 1938, wood, right front conical dial, left horizontal grill bars, pushbuttons, tuning eye, 4 knobs, BC, SW, 7 tubes, AC.......**$115.00**

BU-230 "Chippendale," console, 1938, wood, upper front conical dial, lower oval grill w/horizontal louvers, pushbuttons, tuning eye, BC, SW, 7 tubes, AC **$150.00**

BW-231, table, 1938, wood, right front conical dial, left horizontal louvers, 4 knobs, BC, SW, 6 tubes, AC.......................**$85.00**

BX-208, table, 1939, plastic, right front airplane dial, left horizontal louvers, decorative case lines, pushbuttons, 2 knobs, BC, 5 tubes, AC/DC **$55.00**

C-134, tombstone, 1936, walnut, lower front dial, upper cloth grill w/cut-outs and center tuning eye, BC, SW, 8 tubes, AC..**$110.00**

C-138, console, 1936, walnut, upper front dial, tuning eye, lower cloth grill w/vertical bars, 5 knobs, BC, SW, 8 tubes, AC **$150.00**

C-142, console, 1936, walnut, upper front dial, tuning eye, lower cloth grill w/vertical bars, 5 knobs, BC, SW, 8 tubes, AC..**$150.00**

C-145, console-R/P, 1936, walnut, upper front dial, tuning eye, lower cloth grill w/vertical bars, lift top, inner phono, BC, SW, 8 tubes, AC..**$150.00**

CE-259, portable, 1939, luggage-style, center front square dial, side grill, handle, 2 knobs, BC, 5 tubes, battery **$25.00**

CE-260, table, 1939, wood, center front square airplane dial, right & left horizontal louvers, 2 knobs, BC, 5 tubes, battery ..**$35.00**

CF-255 "Emersonette," table, 1939, plastic, midget, right front vertical slide rule dial, horizontal grill bars, 2 knobs, BC, AC/DC ....**$125.00+**

CG-268, table, 1939, walnut or onyx plastic, right front airplane dial, left horizontal wrap-around louvers, 3 knobs, BC, SW, AC/DC **$40.00**

CG-276, table, 1939, wood, right front square dial, left grill w/vertical bars, 3 knobs, BC, SW, AC/DC $55.00

CG-293, console-R/P, 1939, wood, inner right dial & knobs, center phono, lift top, front horizontal bars, BC, SW, AC $80.00

CG-294, console-R/P, 1939, wood, inner right dial & knobs, left phono, lift top, vertical front bars, BC, SW, AC $80.00

CG-318, table, 1939, walnut w/inlay, right front square dial, left vertical grill bars, 3 knobs, BC, SW, 5 tubes, AC/DC $60.00

CH-246, table, 1939, plastic, right front dial, raised left w/horizontal wrap-around louvers, 2 knobs, BC, 5 tubes, AC/DC $60.00

CH-253, table, 1939, ivory, red or brown embossed leatherette, right front half-round dial, left horizontal louvers, 2 knobs, 5 tubes, AC/DC $65.00

CH-256 "Strad," table, 1939, wood, violin shape, front off-center dial, left horizontal louvers, top cut-out, BC, 5 tubes, AC/DC $425.00

CJ-238, table, 1939, wood, chest-type, inner right dial, left horizontal louvers, lift top starts and stops radio, 5 tubes, AC/DC $250.00

CJ-257, kitchen radio, 1939, white finish w/black stripes, right front square airplane dial, left horizontal louvers, top shelf, 2 knobs, BC, 5 tubes, AC/DC $80.00

CL-256 "Strad," table, 1939, wood, violin shape, front off-center dial, left horizontal louvers, top cut-out, BC, AC/DC....$425.00

CQ-269, table, 1939, plastic, right front dial, left horizontal wrap-around louvers, 4 pushbuttons, 3 knobs, AC/DC $50.00

CQ-271, table, 1939, wood, rounded top, right front dial, left vertical bars, 4 pushbuttons, 3 knobs, BC, SW, AC/DC.......$65.00

CQ-273, table, 1939, wood, right front square dial, curved left w/vertical bars, 4 pushbuttons, 3 knobs, AC/DC $75.00

CR-1-303, portable-R/P, 1939, leatherette, inner dial & louvers, fold-down front, handle, lift top, inner phono, AC/DC $35.00

CR-261, table, 1939, walnut or maple, right front square dial, curved left w/vertical grill bars, 2 knobs, BC, 5 tubes, AC/DC $65.00

CR-262, table, 1939, wood, curved front with recessed right dial/left vertical grill bars, 2 knobs, BC, 5 tubes, AC/DC..............$75.00

CR-274, table, 1939, walnut or onyx plastic, right front dial, raised left w/horizontal wrap-around louvers, 2 knobs, BC, 5 tubes, AC/DC $45.00

CR-297, console-R/P, 1939, wood, inner right dial & knobs, left phono, lift top, front vertical grill bars, BC, 5 tubes, AC ..$50.00

CR-303, portable-R/P, 1939, leatherette, inner dial & louvers, fold down front, handle, lift top, inner phono, AC $35.00

CS-268, table, 1939, walnut or onyx plastic, right front dial, left wrap-around horizontal louvers, 3 knobs, BC, SW, AC/DC $45.00

CS-270, table, 1939, wood, rounded top, right front square dial, left vertical grill bars, 3 knobs, BC, SW, AC/DC $65.00

CS-272, table, 1939, wood, right front square dial, curved left w/vertical bars, 3 knobs, BC, SW, AC/DC $65.00

CS-317, table, 1939, walnut, right front square dial, left vertical grill bars, "waterfall" top & base, 6 tubes, AC/DC $60.00

CS-320, table, 1939, two-tone walnut, right front square dial, left vertical grill bars, 3 knobs, BC, SW, AC/DC $55.00

CT-275, portable, 1939, cloth covered w/stripes, right front dial, left grill, handle, 2 knobs, 5 tubes, battery....................$25.00

CU-265, table, 1939, plastic, right square dial over horizontal front bars, 2 knobs, BC, 5 tubes, AC/DC...............................$45.00

CV-1-290, portable-R/P, 1939, cloth covered, inner dial & louvers, fold-down front, lift top, inner phono, AC/DC $30.00

CV-1-291, table-R/P, 1939, wood, right front square dial, curved left w/horizontal bars, lift top, inner phono, 5 tubes, AC/DC $35.00

CV-264, table, 1939, ivory, brown or red embossed design, right front square dial, left horizontal louvers, 2 knobs, BC, AC/DC $45.00

CV-280, portable, 1939, cloth covered, inner right dial, left horizontal louvers, fold-down front, handle, BC, 5 tubes, AC/DC $30.00

CV-289, table-R/P, 1939, wood, right front square dial, left vertical grill bars, lift top, inner phono, BC, 5 tubes, AC $35.00

CV-290, portable-R/P, 1939, cloth covered, inner dial & louvers, fold-down front, lift top, inner phono, BC, 5 tubes, AC ..$30.00

CV-291, table-R/P, 1939, wood, right front square dial, curved left w/horizontal bars, lift top, inner phono, BC, 5 tubes, AC $35.00

CV-295, table, 1939, wood, right front square dial, curved left w/vertical grill bars, 2 knobs, BC, 5 tubes, AC/DC $65.00

CV-296 "Strad," table, 1939, wood, violin shape, right front square dial, left horizontal louvers, top cut-outs, BC, AC/DC $425.00

CV-298 "Strad," table, 1939, wood, violin shape, right front square dial, left horizontal louvers, top cut-outs, BC, 5 tubes, AC/DC $425.00

CV-313, table, 1939, walnut, right front square dial, left vertical grill bars, rounded sides, 2 knobs, BC, 5 tubes, AC/DC $80.00

CV-316, table, 1939, walnut, right front square dial, left horizontal louvers, rounded sides, 2 knobs, BC, 5 tubes, AC/DC...$85.00

CW-279, table, 1939, plastic, right front dial, right & left wrap-around horizontal bars, 4 pushbuttons, 2 knobs, 5 tubes, AC/DC $65.00

CX-263, portable, 1939, cloth covered, right front dial, left horizontal louvers, handle, 2 knobs, BC, 5 tubes, battery........$25.00

CX-283, portable, 1939, cloth covered, right front dial, left horizontal louvers, handle, 2 knobs, BC, 5 tubes, battery........$25.00

CX-284, portable, 1939, cloth covered, inner right dial, left louvers, slide-in door, handle, 2 knobs, BC, 5 tubes, battery $30.00

CX-285, table, 1940, wood, center front dial, right & left horizontal louvers, 2 knobs, BC, 5 tubes, battery $35.00

CX-292, portable-R/P, 1939, cloth covered, right front dial, left louvers, lift top, inner phono, handle, BC, 5 tubes, battery ...$25.00

CX-305, portable, 1939, walnut, right front recessed dial, left horizontal grill bars, handle, 2 knobs, BC, 5 tubes, battery $45.00

CY-269, table, 1939, walnut or onyx plastic, right front dial, left wrap-around horizontal louvers, 4 pushbuttons, 3 knobs, 5 tubes, AC/DC $55.00

CY-286, table, 1939, wood, right front dial, left horizontal grill bars, 4 pushbuttons, 3 knobs, BC, SW, 5 tubes, AC/DC $45.00

CY-288, table, 1939, wood, right front square dial, curved left w/horizontal bars, 4 pushbuttons, 3 knobs, BC, SW, AC/DC $75.00

CZ-282, table, 1939, wood, curved right w/top recessed pushbuttons, left vertical bars, 2 knobs, BC, 5 tubes, AC/DC....$85.00

D-139, console, 1936, walnut, upper front dial, tuning eye, lower cloth grill w/3 vertical bars, 5 knobs, BC, SW, 10 tubes, AC $155.00

D-140, tombstone, 1936, walnut, center front dial, upper cloth grill w/cut-outs and center tuning eye, 5 knobs, BC, SW, 10 tubes, AC $130.00

D-146, console, 1936, walnut, upper front dial, tuning eye, lower cloth grill w/vertical bars, 5 knobs, BC, SW, 10 tubes, AC................$150.00

DA-287, table, 1939, walnut, right front dial, left horizontal bars, 3 knobs, BC, SW, 6 tubes, AC $50.00

DB-247 "Snow White," table-N, 1939, Snow White & Dwarfs in pressed wood, right front dial, left cloth grill, 2 knobs, BC, 5 tubes, AC/DC ....$1,200.00+

DB-296, table, 1939, wood, right front dial, left horizontal louvers, pull-up handle, 2 knobs, BC, 5 tubes, AC/DC $45.00

DB-301, table, 1939, plastic, right front dial, left horizontal louvers, pull-up handle, 2 knobs, BC, 5 tubes, AC/DC $45.00

DB-315, table, 1939, walnut, right front dial, left conical grill, handle, 2 knobs, BC, 5 tubes, AC/DC $75.00

DC-308, portable, 1939, leatherette, right front dial, large left grill, handle, 2 knobs, 5 tubes, battery $25.00

DF-302, portable, 1939, walnut w/inlay, right front dial, left horizontal louvers, handle, BC, 6 tubes, AC/DC/battery $50.00

DF-306, portable, 1939, cloth covered, inner dial & louvers, fold-down front, handle, 2 knobs, BC, 6 tubes, AC/DC/battery $30.00

DH-264, table, 1939, brown embossed design, right front square dial, left horizontal louvers, 2 knobs, BC, 5 tubes, battery...$35.00

DJ-200, table, 1939, plastic, right front airplane dial, left horizontal louvers, decorative case lines, 2 knobs.........................$75.00

DJ-310, portable, 1939, leatherette, right front dial, left horizontal louvers, handle, 2 knobs, BC, 6 tubes, AC/DC/battery...$30.00

DM-331, table, 1939, two-tone wood, right front dial, left two-section grill w/vertical bars, 3 knobs $40.00

DQ-334, table, two-tone wood, right front square dial, left horizontal grill bars, 2 knobs $45.00

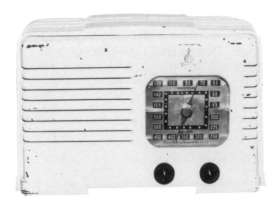

DW-358, table, plastic, right front airplane dial, left horizontal wrap-around grill bars, decorative case lines, 2 knobs $75.00

EC-301, table, 1940, plastic, right front gold dial, left horizontal louvers, handle, 2 knobs, 5 tubes.................................$40.00

EP-375 "5+1," table, 1941, Catalin, right front square dial, 5 left grill bars and 1 right bar, handle, 2 knobs, AC ....$800.00+

F-133, table, 1936, two-tone wood, right front gold dial, left wrap-around grill w/horizontal bars, horizontal decorative metal bands, BC, SW, 6 tubes, AC/DC.................................$85.00

FL-715, table, plastic, right front dial, left horizontal grill bars, 2 knobs, BC, AC/DC $40.00

FU-427, portable, 1941, cloth covered, right front round dial, left horizontal louvers, handle, 2 knobs.............................$30.00

FU-428, portable, 1942, inner right round dial, left horizontal louvers, 2 knobs, fold-down front, handle, AC/DC/battery $30.00

G-127, portable-R/P, 1936, cloth covered, inner front dial and grill, fold-down front, fold-back top, inner phono, BC, SW, 6 tubes, AC/DC..........$30.00

H-130, table, 1936, walnut, right front airplane dial, left cloth grill w/horizontal bars, 2 knobs, 6 tubes, battery.................$30.00

H-137, portable, 1936, walnut w/metal design, upper right front dial, left cloth grill w/cut-outs, handle, 2 knobs, 6 tubes, battery..$45.00

J-106, table, 1935, walnut w/ebony base, lower front oval dial, upper cloth grill w/cut-outs, rounded sides, 2 knobs, 6 tubes, AC/DC $110.00

K-121, table, 1936, walnut, right front airplane dial, left cloth grill w/2 horizontal bars, 4 knobs, 5 tubes, AC.....................$40.00

K-123, table, 1936, walnut, right front airplane dial, left cloth grill w/vertical bars, 4 knobs, 5 tubes, AC $40.00

L-117, tombstone, 1936, wood, lower front dial, upper cloth grill w/vertical bars, 4 knobs, BC, SW, 5 tubes, AC $80.00

L-143, table-R/P, 1936, wood, high case, lower right dial, left grill, lift top, inner phono, BC, SW, AC $45.00

L-150, chairside, 1935, walnut, oval, step-down top w/upper level drawer & lower dial & knobs, 2 band..........................$140.00

L-458, table, 1932, two-tone walnut, right front window dial, center round grill w/cut-outs, 2 knobs...................................$65.00

L-556, cathedral, 1932, two-tone wood, front window dial, upper cloth grill w/cut-outs, AC...$200.00

L-559, table, 1932, wood, chest-type, inner top dial & knobs, lift-up lid, fancy front grill, AC $225.00

LA, table, plastic, decorative case design, right dial, center cloth grill w/cut-outs, 2 knobs...$95.00

M-755, cathedral, 1932, two-tone burl walnut, center front window dial, upper cloth grill w/cut-outs $265.00

Q-236 "Snow White," table-N, 1939, Snow White & Dwarfs in pressed wood, center front dial & cloth grill, 2 knobs, AC ....$1,500.00+

U-5A, tombstone, 1935, plastic, Deco, round dial, cloth grill w/vertical bars, 2 knobs, plastic back, AC............................$200.00

U-6D, table, 1934, wood, lower front round dial, upper cloth grill w/cut-outs, 2 knobs $135.00

U-6F, table, 1936, wood, lower front dial, upper cloth grill w/cutouts, rounded top, rounded sides...............................$135.00

X-175, console-R/P, 1937, wood, Deco, right dial, raised and rounded left side w/horizontal bars, BC, SW, AC.......$285.00

Z-159, upright table, 1937, wood, slanted front panel, center dial, upper grill w/vertical bars, AC.......................................$85.00

EMOR

Emor Radio, Ltd.,
400 East 118th St., New York, New York

100, floor-N, 1947, chrome, Deco, round globe-shaped radio on adjustable floor stand, top grill bars, 5 tubes, BC, SW..$350.00

EMPIRE

Empire Electrical Products, Co.,
102 Wooster Street, New York, New York

30, table, 1933, wood, front dial, center cloth grill w/cut-outs, arched top, 2 knobs, 5 tubes, AC/DC $85.00

EMPRESS

Empire Designing Corp.,
1560 Broadway, New York, New York

55 "Chalet," table-N, 1946, wood, cottage-shaped case, dial in door, 2 knobs in windows, upper lattice grill, BC, 5 tubes, AC/DC (top right) $225.00

ERLA

Electrical Research Laboratories,
2500 Cottage Grove Avenue, Chicago, Illinois

The name Erla is short for Electrical Research Laboratories. The company began in 1921 selling component parts and radio kits and by 1923 they were marketing complete sets. After much financial difficulty, Erla was reorganized as Sentinel Radio Corporation in 1934.

22P, cathedral-C, 1930, wood, scalloped top, lower front horizontal dial, upper cloth grill w/cut-outs and center clock face, 2 knobs, AC..$350.00

30, console, 1929, wood, highboy, lower front window dial w/escutcheon, upper grill w/cut-outs, AC $165.00

271, cathedral, wood, squared top, lower front window dial, upper round grill w/cut-outs, 2 knobs, AC............................$165.00

De Luxe Super-Five, table, 1925, wood, low rectangular case, 3 dial front panel, scalloped molding, feet, battery $145.00

S-11, table, 1925, wood, low rectangular case, slanted front panel w/3 pointer dials, button feet, battery $160.00

ESPEY

Espey Mfg. Co., Inc.,
33 West 46th Street, New York, New York

7-861, end table, 1938, mahogany or walnut, Duncan Phyfe style, drop-leaf, inner dial & controls, BC, SW, 6 tubes, AC ..$145.00

18B, table, 1950, wood, upper front slide rule dial, large center cloth grill, 2 knobs, BC, AC/DC $40.00

31 "Roundabout," table, 1950, two-tone plastic cylindrical fluted case, right front dial, 2 knobs, BC, 5 tubes, AC/DC $150.00

651, table, 1946, plastic, upper front slanted slide rule dial, lower horizontal wrap-around louvers, 2 knobs, BC, AC/DC ..$45.00

861B, portable, 1938, inner right front dial, left grill, removable cover, handle, 3 knobs, BC, SW, 6 tubes, AC..............$25.00

6545, table-R/P, 1946, wood, top slide rule dial, front criss-cross grill, 3 knobs, open top phono, BC, AC $20.00

6547, table-R/P, 1946, wood, front slide rule dial, lower horizontal louvers, 4 knobs, lift top, inner phono, BC, AC $30.00

6613, table, 1947, wood, upper front slanted slide rule dial, lower horizontal louvers, 4 knobs, BC, SW, AC/DC...............$40.00

RR13, table, 1947, wood, upper front slanted slide rule dial, lower cloth grill w/ "X" cut-out, 2 knobs, BC, SW, AC/DC **$50.00**

ESQUIRE
Esquire Radio Corp.,
51 Warren Street, New York, New York

60-10, table, 1947, plastic, right front half-round dial over large grill area, horizontal decorative lines, 2 knobs, BC, AC/DC **$65.00**

65-4, table, 1947, plastic, right half-round dial, left horizontal wrap-around louvers, 2 knobs, BC, AC/DC...........................**$55.00**

511, table-C, 1952, plastic, center front round dial knob, right checkered grill, left alarm clock, BC, AC **$30.00**

520, table-N-C, 1952, plastic clock/radio/lamp, center front round dial, left alarm clock, BC, AC..**$65.00**

550, table-C, 1952, plastic, center front round dial knob, right checkered grill, left alarm clock, BC, AC **$30.00**

550U, table-C, 1952, plastic, center front round dial knob, right checkered grill, left alarm clock, feet **$30.00**

ETHERPHONE
Radio Apparatus Co.,
40 West Montcalm Street, Detroit, Michigan

RX-1, table, 1923, wood, square case, lift top, inner black panel w/1 exposed tube, battery **$400.00**

EVEREADY

1, console, 1928, gumwood w/maple finish, table model #1 on four legs, center front window dial, 3 knobs, AC **$225.00**

1, table, 1927, gumwood w/maple finish, low rectangular case, center front window dial, 3 knobs, AC **$175.00**

2, console, 1928, metal, table model #2 on aluminum legs, center front window dial, 3 knobs, AC **$125.00**

2, table, 1928, metal, low rectangular case w/decorative lines, center front window dial, 3 knobs, AC **$95.00**

3, console, 1928, wood, table model #3 on four legs, center front window dial, 3 knobs **$125.00**

3, table, 1928, wood, low rectangular case, center front window dial w/escutcheon, 3 knobs **$95.00**

20, table, 1928, wood, high rectangular case, upper front window dial, lift top, 3 knobs, 6 tubes, battery.........................**$100.00**

31, table, 1929, wood, low rectangular case, center front dial in carved panel, 3 knobs, AC **$110.00**

32, console, 1929, wood, inner ornate panel w/upper window dial, sliding doors, 7 tubes, 3 knobs, AC............................**$175.00**

33, console, 1929, wood, inner ornate panel w/upper window dial, sliding doors, 7 tubes, 3 knobs, AC...........................**$185.00**

54, console, 1929, wood, inner ornate front panel w/upper window dial, sliding doors, 3 knobs, AC **$210.00**

EXCEL
Excel Corp. of America,
9 Rockefeller Plaza, New York, New York

KR-451, portable, right front dial knob, upper right thumbwheel on/off/volume knob, left grill area w/circular cut-outs, handle, AM, battery **$35.00**

Super T-211, portable, plastic, right front half-round dial, lower right thumbwheel on/off/volume knob, metal perforated grill area, pull-up handle, AM, battery **$40.00**

XL-45, portable, plastic, upper front round dial knob overlaps horizontal grill bars, pull-up handle, 4 tubes, made in Japan, AM, battery **$35.00**

EXCELLO
Excello Products Corporation,
4822 West 16th St., Cicero, Illinois

154, console-R/P, 1931, wood, lower front window dial, upper grill w/cut-outs, lift top, inner phono **$175.00**

172, console, 1931, wood, highboy, ornately carved, inner front window dial, scrolled grill, doors, Queen Anne legs **$250.00**

D, cathedral, 1931, wood, scalloped top, center front window dial, upper cloth grill w/cut-outs, 3 knobs **$310.00**

D-6, console-R/P, 1931, wood, upper front window dial, lower circular grill w/cut-outs, 3 knobs, lift top, inner phono **$125.00**

FADA
Fada Radio & Electric Company,
30-20 Thomson Avenue,
Long Island City, New York
F.A.D. Andrea, Inc.,
1581 Jerome Avenue, New York, New York

Fada was named for its founder — Frank Angelo D'Andrea. The company began business in 1920 with the production of crystal sets. Business expanded until the mid-twenties, but overproduction and internal problems took their toll and by 1932 the company had been sold and the name changed to Fada Radio & Electric Corporation. Fada continued to produce radios through the mid-1940's and is probably best known for the Fada Bullet, their ultra-streamlined Catalin radio made in the 1940's.

5F60, table, 1939, Catalin, small case, right front square airplane dial, left horizontal louvers, 2 fluted knobs, BC, SW, AC ....**$600.00+**

6A39, table, 1948, plastic, right front dial, left horizontal wrap-around louvers, 2 knobs, BC, SW **$60.00**

7, console, 1926, wood, highboy, inner dial & 3 knobs, fold down front, optional side loop antenna, 7 tubes **$250.00**

7 "Seven," table, 1926, wood, low rectangular case, center front dials, loop antenna folds out of left side, 3 knobs, lift top, 7 tubes **$190.00**

10, table, 1928, low rectangular case, center front dial w/escutcheon, 3 knobs, switch, AC............................**$110.00**

11, table, 1928, wood, low rectangular case, center front window dial w/escutcheon, AC...**$135.00**

12, table, 1928, low rectangular case, center front dial w/escutcheon, 3 knobs, switch, DC...........................**$100.00**

16, table, 1928, low rectangular case, center front window dial, 3 knobs, AC $110.00

17, table, 1928, wood, low rectangular case, center front window dial w/escutcheon, AC $135.00

20, table, 1929, two-tone metal, low rectangular case, center front window dial, 3 knobs, AC $110.00

20-T, table, 1938, walnut, right front illuminated dial, left grill w/Deco cut-outs, 6 tubes, AC/DC................................$50.00

20-W, table, 1938, plastic, small right front dial, left cloth grill w/Deco bars, decorative case lines, 2 knobs, BC, 5 tubes, AC $85.00

20-Z, table, 1929, two-tone metal, low rectangular case, center front window dial, 3 knobs, AC $110.00

22, table, 1929, wood, large front bronze escutcheon w/window dial, 3 knobs, 6 tubes, battery $115.00

25, console, 1929, walnut, upper front recessed window dial w/escutcheon, lower grill w/cut-outs, 3 knobs, AC $140.00

25-Z, console, 1929, walnut, upper front recessed window dial w/escutcheon, lower grill w/cut-outs, 3 knobs, AC $130.00

30, console, 1928, wood, highboy, inner window dial, 3 knobs, fold-down front, lower oval grill w/cut-outs, AC $140.00

30J, table, wood, right front airplane dial, left cloth grill w/cut-outs, 4 knobs, AC $50.00

31, console, 1928, wood, inner front window dial, 3 knobs, fold-down front, upper speaker w/doors, AC $190.00

32, console, 1929, walnut, inner front window dial, upper "scallop shell" grill, 3 knobs, double front doors, AC $150.00

33 Series, portable, 1940, cloth covered, inner metal panel w/lower dial and upper vertical grill bars, fold-open front, handle, BC, battery..$50.00

35, console, 1929, walnut, inner front window dial, upper "scallop shell" grill, 3 knobs, double front doors, AC................$150.00

35-B, console, 1929, walnut, inner front window dial, upper "scallop shell" grill, 3 knobs, double front doors, AC...........$150.00

35-C, console, 1929, walnut, inner front window dial, upper "scallop shell" grill, 3 knobs, double front doors, AC...........$150.00

35-Z, console, 1929, walnut, inner front window dial, upper "scallop shell" grill, 3 knobs, double front doors, AC...........$150.00

41, console, 1930, wood, highboy, inner dial & knobs, double front doors, stretcher base......................................$165.00

42, console, 1930, wood, lowboy, ornate center front panel w/upper window dial, lower grill w/cut-outs $180.00

43, cathedral, wood, scalloped top, ornate pressed wood front, center window dial, upper grill, 7 tubes $265.00

44, console, 1930, wood, lowboy, inner dial & knobs, double front sliding doors, stretcher base $180.00

45, console, 1931, wood, lowboy, upper front window dial, lower cloth grill w/cut-outs, 3 knobs $150.00

46, console, 1930, wood, highboy, ornate, inner dial & knobs, double doors, 6 legs, stretcher base $185.00

47, console-R/P, 1930, wood, lowboy, ornate, inner dial & knobs, double front doors $235.00

49, console, 1931, wood, highboy, inner window dial, 3 knobs, grill w/cut-outs, double doors, 6 legs $180.00

51, cathedral, 1931, wood, center front window dial, upper cloth grill w/cut-outs, front pillars..............................$295.00

52, table, 1938, Catalin, right front square airplane dial, left horizontal wrap-around louvers, 2 fluted knobs..............$850.00+

53, table, 1938, Catalin, right front square airplane dial, left horizontal louvers, 2 fluted knobs ....$750.00+

55, table, 1932, wood, upper right front window dial, center cloth grill w/vertical bars, 2 knobs, 5 tubes $85.00

60W, table, plastic, right front airplane dial, left grill w/Deco cut-outs, decorative case lines, 3 knobs $85.00

66, console, wood, 1932, lowboy, two upper window dials, lower cloth grill w/cut-outs, 5 knobs, stretcher base, BC, SW, 10 tubes, AC...$185.00

70, console, 1928, wood, lowboy, inner dial, 3 knobs, fold-down front, lower speaker, doors, side loop antenna, AC $250.00

72, console-R/P, 1928, wood, lowboy, ornate, inner window dial, lower grill w/cut-outs, double front doors, AC $250.00

73, tombstone, 1932, two-tone walnut, center front quarter-round dial, upper cloth grill w/diamond-shaped cut-out, 3 knobs, 7 tubes, AC..$100.00

74, console, 1932, wood, lowboy, upper front quarter-round dial, lower cloth grill w/cut-outs, 3 knobs, stretcher base, 9 tubes, AC $210.00

75, console, 1929, wood, lowboy, inner window dial, fold-down front, lower speaker w/double doors, AC $160.00

76, console, 1932, wood, lowboy, inner quarter-round dial, 3 knobs, cloth grill w/vertical bars, double sliding front doors, stretcher base, 9 tubes, AC..........................$150.00

77, console-R/P, 1929, wood, lowboy, inner front window dial, lower grill w/cut-outs, double front doors, lift top, inner phono, AC $250.00

78, console, 1932, walnut, inner quarter-round dial, 3 knobs, cloth grill w/cut-outs, double sliding front doors, stretcher base, 11 tubes, AC.....................................$150.00

79, console, 1932, wood, highboy, inner dial & knobs, double front doors, 6 legs, stretcher base, 11 tubes, AC $185.00

97, console, 1932, wood, lowboy, upper front quarter-round dial, lower cloth grill w/cut-outs, 6 legs, stretcher base, 3 knobs, 9 tubes, AC...$150.00

98, console, 1933, wood, upper front quarter-round dial, lower cloth grill w/cut-outs, 6 legs, stretcher base, 7 tubes, AC...$150.00

100, portable, "alligator," inner right slide rule dial, 3 knobs, left grill area, fold-down front, handle, AC/DC/battery $30.00

115 "**Bullet,**" table, 1941, Catalin, streamlined, right front round airplane dial, left horizontal grill bars, handle, 2 knobs, BC, 5 tubes, AC/DC ....$600.00+

119, table, plastic, right front airplane dial, left cloth grill w/"T" design, decorative case lines, 3 knobs.........................$55.00

130, table, 1935, wood, right front window dial, center cloth grill w/cut-outs, rounded top, 5 tubes, AC/DC.....................$80.00

136, table, 1941, Catalin, right front airplane dial, left horizontal wrap-around louvers, flared base, handle, 2 knobs, AC ....$1,000.00+

144MT, table, 1940, wood, right front square dial, left cloth grill w/vertical cut-outs, 3 knobs $60.00

150-CA, console, 1935, wood, upper front round dial, lower cloth grill w/cut-outs, BC, SW, AC.....................................$130.00

155, table, 1935, two-tone wood, right front dial, center cloth grill w/cut-outs, 4 tubes, 2 knobs, AC/DC $75.00

160 "**One-Sixty,**" table, 1923, mahogany, low rectangular case, 3 dial black Bakelite front panel, lift top, 4 tubes, battery $120.00

160-A "**One-Sixty,**" table, 1925, wood, low rectangular case, 3 dial black front panel, lift top, 4 tubes, battery $120.00

160-CA, console, 1935, wood, upper front round dial, lower cloth grill w/cut-outs, 6 tubes..................................$130.00

167, table, 1936, wood, lower front dial, upper cloth grill w/cut-outs, BC, SW, 6 tubes, AC/DC....................$85.00

168, table, 1936, wood, lower front dial, upper cloth grill w/cut-outs, BC, SW, 6 tubes, AC/DC....................$85.00

169, table, wood, right front square airplane dial, left grill w/vertical bars, 4 knobs, BC, SW, AC.......................$50.00

170-T, tombstone, 1935, wood, lower front round dial, upper cloth grill w/cut-outs, 4 knobs, BC, SW, AC $100.00

175-A "**Neutroceiver,**" table, 1924, mahogany, low rectangular case, 3 dial slanted front panel, 5 tubes, battery........$150.00

175/90-A "**Neutroceiver Grand,**" console, 1925, wood, model 175-A on a cabinet, 3 dial front panel, double doors, 5 tubes, battery $190.00

177, table, wood, right front slide rule dial, left vertical grill bars, base, 4 knobs, 3 bands $60.00

182G, table-N, 1940, metal, looks like baby grand piano, dial & G-clef speaker grill under keyboard, 2 knobs, BC, 5 tubes, AC/DC $600.00

185-A "**Neutrola,**" table, 1925, wood, inner 3 dial panel, fold-down front, upper speaker, 5 tubes, battery...............$175.00

185/90-A "**Neutrola Grand,**" console, 1925, wood, model 185-A on a cabinet, inner 3 dial panel, speaker, 5 tubes, battery $215.00

192-A "**Neutrolette,**" table, 1925, wood, rectangular case, 3 dial black slanted front panel, battery.....................$150.00

195-A "**Neutro-Junior,**" table, 1924, wood, low rectangular case, 2 dial black front panel, lift top, battery.......................$150.00

209V, table, 1941, ivory plastic, right front dial, left vertical grill bars, 2 knobs, BC, 5 tubes, AC/DC..............................$50.00

209W, table, 1941, walnut plastic, right front dial, left vertical grill bars, 2 knobs, BC, 5 tubes, AC/DC............................$50.00

252 "**Temple,**" table, 1941, Catalin, upper front dial, lower horizontal grill bars, rounded corners, 2 knobs, BC, AC/DC...$325.00+

260B, table, 1936, black plastic, right front dial, left cloth grill w/Deco bars, 2 knobs, BC, 6 tubes, AC/DC $85.00

260D, table, 1936, black plastic w/chrome trim, right front dial, left cloth grill w/Deco bars, 2 knobs, BC, 6 tubes, AC/DC ...$225.00

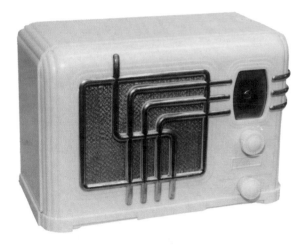

260G, table, 1936, ivory plastic w/gold trim, right front dial, left cloth grill w/Deco bars, 2 knobs, BC, 6 tubes, AC/DC $225.00

260V, table, 1936, ivory plastic, right front dial, left cloth grill w/Deco bars, 2 knobs, BC, 6 tubes, AC/DC $85.00

263W, table, 1936, plastic, small right front dial, left cloth grill w/Deco bars, plastic back, 3 knobs $85.00

265-A "Special," table, 1927, mahogany, low rectangular case, 2 front window dials, 3 knobs, 6 tubes, battery $135.00

290-C, console, 1936, wood, upper front round dial, lower cloth grill w/vertical bars, 6 knobs, tuning eye, BC, SW, 9 tubes, AC..$150.00

290-T, tombstone, 1936, walnut, lower front round dial, upper cloth grill w/cut-outs, 6 knobs, tuning eye, BC, SW, 9 tubes, AC......$165.00

351, table, wood, right front gold dial, left cloth grill w/Deco cut-outs, 4 knobs $55.00

358, table, 1937, wood, right front dial, left cloth grill w/horizontal wrap-around bars, 5 knobs, 6 pushbuttons, feet $75.00

454V, table, 1938, ivory plastic, right front square dial, left cloth grill w/Deco cut-outs, 2 knobs, AC $75.00

480-B, table, 1927, walnut, large front escutcheon w/2 window dials, fold-out loop antenna, 8 tubes $210.00

602, table-R/P, 1947, wood, upper front slide rule dial, lower grill, 4 knobs, lift top, inner phono, BC, AC $30.00

605, table, 1946, plastic, upper front slanted slide rule dial, lower horizontal louvers, 2 knobs...$55.00

605W, table, 1946, plastic, upper front slanted slide rule dial, lower horizontal louvers, 2 knobs, BC, AC/DC $55.00

609W, table, 1946, plastic, right front square dial, left vertical grill bars, 2 knobs, BC, AC/DC...................................$50.00

637, portable-R/P, 1947, leatherette, inner slide rule dial, 4 knobs, phono, 2 fold-back covers, BC, AC $30.00

652 "Temple," table, 1946, Catalin, upper front dial, lower horizontal grill bars, rounded corners, 2 knobs, BC, AC/DC...$475.00+

700, table, 1948, Catalin, right front round dial, left horizontal grill bars, handle, curved sides, 2 knobs, BC, AC/DC......$500.00+

711, table, 1947, Catalin, right front dial, left cloth grill, handle, rounded corners, 2 knobs, AC..................................$500.00+

740, table, 1947, plastic, stepped top, right front dial, left horizontal wrap-around louvers, 2 knobs, BC, AC/DC $55.00

790, table, 1949, plastic, right front square airplane dial, left criss-cross grill w/"T" design, 4 knobs, BC, FM, AC/DC.........$85.00

795, table, 1948, plastic, upper front slide rule dial, lower horizontal louvers, 2 knobs, FM, AC $45.00

830, table, 1950, plastic, upper curved slide rule dial, lower horizontal louvers, 2 knobs, BC, AC/DC $45.00

845, table, 1950, plastic, Deco, right front round dial, left horizontal grill bars, handle, 2 knobs, BC, AC/DC ....$200.00+

855, table, 1950, plastic, lower front slide rule dial, upper recessed horizontal grill bars, 2 knobs, BC, AC/DC......$45.00

1000 "Bullet," table, 1946, Catalin, streamline bullet shape, right front round dial, left horizontal grill bars, handle, 2 knobs, BC, AC/DC ....$600.00+

1001, table, 1947, burl veneer, upper front slanted slide rule dial, lower horizontal louvers, 2 knobs, BC, AC/DC..$50.00

1452A, tombstone, 1934, walnut, front round airplane dial, upper cloth grill w/Deco cut-outs, 4 knobs, 5 tubes, AC $120.00

1452F, console, 1934, walnut, upper front round airplane dial, lower cloth grill w/cut-outs, 4 knobs, AC.....................$135.00

1462D, table, 1935, wood, lower front round airplane dial, upper cloth grill w/cut-outs, 4 knobs, BC, SW, 6 tubes, AC/DC $80.00

1470C, tombstone, 1934, wood, center front round dial, upper cloth grill w/cut-outs, 4 knobs, BC, SW, 7 tubes, AC...$120.00

1470E, console, 1934, wood, upper front round dial, lower cloth grill w/cut-outs, 4 knobs, BC, SW, AC $130.00

A66SC, console, 1939, wood, upper front dial, pushbuttons, lower cloth grill w/vertical bars, BC, SW, AC $150.00

C-34, portable, 1941, leatherette, inner dial, vertical grill bars, flip-open front, handle, BC, 5 tubes, AC/DC/battery $55.00

F55T, table, 1939, walnut, Deco, right front square dial, left horizontal grill bars, 2 knobs, 5 tubes, AC $60.00

KG, console, 1931, wood, lowboy, ornate front, upper window dial, lower cloth grill w/cut-outs, 7 tubes $225.00

L56 "Bell," table, 1939, Catalin, right front dial, left horizontal wrap-around louvers, flared base, handle, 2 knobs, AC ....$1,000.00+

L-96W, table, 1939, plastic, right front square airplane dial, left cloth grill w/Deco cut-outs, handle, 3 knobs, BC, AC/DC $85.00

P-40, portable, 1939, cloth covered, right front recessed dial, left 2-section grill, handle, 2 knobs, 4 tubes, battery $25.00

P41, portable, leatherette, inner slide rule dial, square grill, 2 knobs, slide-out front, handle $25.00

P80, portable, 1947, plastic, inner right dial, Deco grill cut-outs, 3 knobs, flip-up lid, BC, AC/DC/battery $80.00

P82, portable, 1947, leatherette, inner right slide rule dial, 3 knobs, slide-in door, handle, BC, AC/DC/battery $30.00

P-100, portable, 1947, "snakeskin," inner right slide rule dial, 3 knobs, fold-down front, handle, BC, AC/DC/battery $35.00

P111, portable, 1952, plastic, inner right round dial, lattice grill, flip-up front, handle, BC, AC/DC/battery $45.00

P-130, portable, 1951, leatherette, inner slide rule dial, lift front, telescope antenna, handle, BC, 2SW, AC/DC/battery ..$65.00

PL24, portable, 1940, leatherette, inner right dial, left horizontal louvers, slide-up door, handle, BC, SW, 7 tubes, AC/DC/battery $30.00

PL41, portable, 1941, leatherette, inner slide rule dial, lower grill area with Fada logo, 2 knobs, removable front, handle, BC, 5 tubes, AC/DC/battery $30.00

PL50, table-R/P, 1939, wood, right front square dial, left horizontal louvers, lift top, inner phono, AC $30.00

PT-208, table-R/P, 1941, walnut, center front dial, right & left grills, lift top, inner phono, 5 tubes, AC.........................$30.00

RE1843, tombstone, wood, center front quarter-round dial, upper cloth grill w/diamond-shaped cut-out, 3 knobs..$120.00

FAIRBANKS-MORSE
Fairbanks-Morse Home Appliances,
430 South Green Street
Chicago, Illinois

6AC-7, chairside, 1937, two-tone wood, top "Great Circle" dial, tuning eye, front grill w/vertical bars, AC $120.00

9AC-4, console, 1937, wood, upper front round dial w/automatic tuning, lower cloth grill w/vertical bars, AC $165.00

9AC-5, console, 1937, wood, upper front round dial w/automatic tuning, lower cloth grill w/vertical bars, AC $165.00

12-C-6, console, 1936, wood, upper front "semaphore dial," lower grill w/bowed vertical bars, BC, SW, 12 tubes............$185.00

57TO, table, 1936, wood, right front round dial, left cloth grill w/cut-outs, cabinet finished on back $85.00

58-T-1, table, 1936, wood, right front round dial, left grill w/Deco cut-outs, rounded left side, BC, SW, 5 tubes $85.00

72-C-2, console, 1936, wood, upper front round airplane dial, lower cloth grill w/splayed vertical bars, 4 knobs, tuning eye $140.00

91-C-4, console, 1936, wood, upper front "semaphore dial," lower grill w/center vertical bars, BC, SW, 9 tubes $150.00

746, console, 1935, wood, upper front round airplane dial, lower cloth grill w/cut-outs, BC, SW, battery $90.00

814, tombstone, 1934, wood, Deco, lower front half-round dial, upper wrap-over vertical grill bars, BC, 8 tubes $125.00

5106, cathedral, 1934, wood, center front window dial, upper scalloped-top grill w/cut-outs, 3 knobs, 5 tubes $225.00

5312, tombstone, 1934, walnut, Deco, lower front round airplane dial, upper wrap-over vertical grill bars, BC, 5 tubes ...$125.00

5341, console, 1934, wood, upper front round airplane dial, lower cloth grill w/cut-outs, 6 legs, 5 tubes, AC $120.00

7014, tombstone, 1934, wood, Deco, lower front round dial, upper wrap-over vertical grill bars, 4 knobs, 7 tubes $150.00

7040, console, 1934, wood, Deco, upper front round dial, lower cloth grill w/vertical bars, 6 legs, 4 knobs, 7 tubes, AC ..$150.00

7117, tombstone, 1935, wood, lower front round dial, upper cloth grill w/cut-outs, 4 knobs $125.00

7146, console, 1935, wood, upper front round dial, lower cloth grill w/cut-outs, 3 band $120.00

FAIRVIEW
Fairview Electric Shop,
35 Fairview Avenue, Binghamton, New York

J-400 "Lasher Capacidyne," table, 1925, wood, high rectangular case, 3 dial front panel, storage, 5 tubes, battery $140.00

FARNSWORTH
Farnsworth Television & Radio Corp.,
Fort Wayne, Indiana

AC-55, console, 1939, wood, upper front slide rule dial, pushbuttons, lower grill w/2 vertical bars, 7 tubes, AC.............$120.00

AC-70, console, 1940, wood, upper front 3 section dial, pushbuttons, lower grill w/vertical bars, 4 knobs, 8 tubes, AC .$125.00

AC-90, console, 1939, wood, upper front slanted dial, pushbuttons, lower grill w/vertical bars, 4 knobs, 10 tubes, AC $145.00

AC-91, console, 1939, wood, wide cabinet, upper front dial, pushbuttons, lower grill w/2 vertical bars, 10 tubes, AC......$150.00

AK-17, table-R/P, 1939, walnut, right front half-round dial, left wrap-around grill, lift top, inner phono $35.00

AK-59, console-R/P, 1939, wood, inner dial & phono, pushbuttons, lower grill w/center vertical bar, BC, SW, 7 tubes, AC $135.00

AK-76, console-R/P, 1939, wood, inner dial & phono, pushbuttons, lower front grill w/vertical bars, BC, SW, 8 tubes, AC...$145.00

AK-86, console-R/P, 1940, wood, inner dial & phono, pushbuttons, lower front grill w/vertical bars, BC, SW, 8 tubes, AC $145.00

AK-95, console-R/P, 1939, wood, inner dial & phono, pushbuttons, lower front grill w/vertical bars, 10 tubes, AC $155.00

AK-96, console-R/P, 1940, wood, Chippendale design, inner dial & phono, pushbuttons, front grill cut-outs, BC, SW, 10 tubes, AC $135.00

AT-11, table, 1939, plastic, right front half-round dial, left horizontal wrap-around louvers, handle, 2 knobs, 5 tubes, AC/DC $110.00

AT-12, table, 1939, plastic, right front half-round dial, left horizontal wrap-around louvers, handle, 2 knobs, 5 tubes, AC/DC $110.00

AT-15, table, 1939, plastic, right front half-round dial, top pushbuttons, left horizontal wrap-around louvers, handle, 2 knobs, 5 tubes, AC/DC $110.00

AT-16, table, 1939, wood, Deco, step-down top, right front half-round dial, top pushbuttons, left grill w/horizontal bars, 5 tubes, AC/DC $85.00

AT-31, portable, 1939, cloth covered, inner right slide rule dial, left grill, 3 knobs, fold-down front, handle, 5 tubes, AC/DC/battery $25.00

AT-50, table, 1939, wood, lower front slide rule dial, pushbuttons, upper grill w/horizontal bars, 4 knobs, BC, SW, 7 tubes..$70.00

BC-80, console, 1940, wood, upper front dial, lower cloth grill w/vertical bars and cut-outs, pushbuttons $125.00

BC-81, console, 1940, wood, upper front slide rule dial, pushbuttons, lower grill w/vertical bars, BC, SW, 8 tubes, AC ..$125.00

BC-82, console, 1940, wood, upper front slide rule dial, lower cloth grill w/center vertical divider, pushbuttons, BC, SW, AC $140.00

BC-102, console, 1940, wood, upper front slide rule dial, pushbuttons, lower grill w/vertical bars, BC, SW, 10 tubes, AC...$135.00

BC-103, console, 1940, wood, upper front dial, lower cloth grill w/center vertical bars, pushbuttons, BC, SW, 10 tubes, AC $125.00

BK-69, table-R/P, 1941, wood, right front slide rule dial, pushbuttons, left grill, lift top, inner phono, AC.........................$35.00

BK-73, chairside-R/P, 1940, walnut, top dial & knobs, front horizontal louvers, lift top, inner phono, side storage, 7 tubes, AC..$125.00

BK-88, console-R/P, 1940, wood, front tilt-out dial panel, lower horizontal grill bars, lift top, inner phono, 8 tubes, AC $150.00

BKR-84, table-R/P/Rec, 1940, wood, right front slide rule dial, pushbuttons, left grill, lift top, inner phono & recorder, AC $35.00

BT-20, table, 1940, plastic, right front airplane dial, raised left horizontal wrap-around louvers, 3 knobs, rounded top, BC, SW, 6 tubes, AC/DC $50.00

BT-22, table, 1940, wood, right front slide rule dial, pushbuttons, left grill w/vertical bars, 3 knobs, BC, SW, 6 tubes, AC/DC $70.00

BT-40, table, 1940, two-tone wood, right front dial, left horizontal louvers, battery $40.00

BT-54, table, 1942, wood, right front dial, left cloth grill w/cut-outs, 2 knobs $35.00

BT-55, table, 1940, wood, right front slide rule dial, left grill w/cut-outs, pushbuttons, 2 knobs, AC $65.00

BT-57, table, 1940, wood, right front slide rule dial, left horizontal grill bars, 3 knobs $45.00

BT-61, table, 1940, wood, right front slide rule dial, left grill w/cut-outs, pushbuttons, 3 knobs, AC $55.00

BT-68, portable, 1946, leatherette, inner dial & grill w/cut-outs, fold-down front, 2 knobs, handle, 6 tubes, AC/DC/battery...$45.00

BT-70, table, 1940, wood, lower front slide rule dial, upper cloth grill, pushbuttons, 4 knobs, AC.....................................**$50.00**

BT-71, table, 1940, wood, lower front slide rule dial, upper cloth grill w/cut-outs, pushbuttons, 4 knobs, AC **$50.00**

BT-1010, table, wood, right front slide rule dial w/plastic escutcheon, left horizontal louvers, 4 knobs, BC, SW, 10 tubes, AC..**$50.00**

CC-70, console, 1941, wood, upper front dial, lower grill w/vertical bars, pushbuttons, 4 knobs, 7 tubes **$120.00**

CC-90, console, 1941, wood, upper front dial, lower grill w/cut-outs, pushbuttons, 9 tubes, AC **$120.00**

CK-58, table-R/P, 1941, wood, upper front slide rule dial, lower grill, 2 knobs, lift top, inner phono, 5 tubes, AC.............**$35.00**

CK-66, table-R/P, 1941, wood, front slide rule dial, lower grill area, 4 knobs, lift top, inner phono, 6 tubes, AC **$35.00**

CK-73, chairside-R/P, 1941, wood, top dial & knobs, front horizontal wrap-around grill bars, lift top, inner phono, side storage, BC, SW, 7 tubes, AC **$135.00**

CT-41, table, 1941, mahogany plastic, right front dial, left horizontal wrap-around louvers, 2 knobs, BC, 4 tubes, battery..**$40.00**

CT-42, table, 1941, walnut, right front slide rule dial, left grill w/Deco cut-outs, 2 knobs, BC, 4 tubes, battery **$35.00**

CT-43, table, 1941, two-tone mahogany plastic, right front dial, left horizontal wrap-around louvers, 2 knobs, BC, 4 tubes, battery ..**$40.00**

CT-50, table, 1941, mahogany plastic, upper front slide rule dial, lower horizontal louvers, handle, 2 knobs, 5 tubes, AC ...**$50.00**

CT-51, table, 1941, ivory plastic, upper front slide rule dial, lower horizontal louvers, handle, 2 knobs, 5 tubes, AC **$50.00**

CT-52, table, 1941, mahogany plastic w/gold trim, upper front slide rule dial, lower horizontal louvers, handle, 2 knobs, BC, SW, 5 tubes, AC **$50.00**

CT-53, table, 1941, ivory plastic w/brown trim, upper front slide rule dial, lower horizontal louvers, handle, 2 knobs, BC, SW, 5 tubes, AC **$50.00**

CT-54, table, 1941, walnut, upper front slide rule dial, lower 3-section wrap-around grill, 2 knobs, BC, SW, 5 tubes, AC...**$55.00**

CT-59, portable, 1941, leatherette & plastic, inner dial & horizontal grill bars, flip-open front, handle, BC, 5 tubes, AC/DC/battery ...**$65.00**

CT-60, portable, 1941, leatherette, luggage-type, inner right front dial, left grill, 2 knobs, fold-down front, handle, BC, 6 tubes, AC/DC/battery **$30.00**

CT-61, table, 1941, mahogany plastic, upper front slide rule dial, lower grill, handle, 2 knobs, 6 tubes, AC **$50.00**

CT-62, table, 1941, ivory plastic, upper front slide rule dial, lower grill, handle, 2 knobs, 6 tubes, AC................................**$50.00**

CT-63, table, 1941, mahogany plastic, upper front slide rule dial, lower grill, 2 knobs, BC, SW, 6 tubes, AC **$45.00**

CT-64, table, 1941, wood, upper front slide rule dial, lower cloth grill w/horizontal bars, 2 knobs, BC, SW, 6 tubes **$50.00**

EC-260, console, 1946, wood, dial & 3 knobs on top of case, front cloth grill, BC, AC **$100.00**

EK-264, console-R/P, 1946, wood, dial & 3 knobs on top of case, front criss-cross grill, lift top, inner phono, BC, 6 tubes, AC **$125.00**

EK-264WL, console-R/P, 1946, wood, dial & knobs on top of case, front criss-cross grill, lift top, inner phono, BC, 6 tubes, AC...........**$125.00**

ET-060, table, 1946, plastic, upper front slide rule dial, lower wrap-around checkered grill, 2 knobs, BC, SW, AC/DC..........**$40.00**

ET-061, table, 1946, plastic, upper front slide rule dial, lower wrap-around checkered grill, 2 knobs, BC, SW, AC/DC..........**$50.00**

ET-063, table, 1946, wood, upper front slide rule dial, lower cloth grill w/ cutouts, curved sides, BC, SW, AC/DC **$60.00**

ET-064, table, 1946, plastic, upper slanted pointer dial, lower cloth grill w/metal insert, 2 knobs, BC, AC/DC **$90.00**

ET-065, table, 1946, plastic, upper slanted pointer dial, lower grill w/metal insert, handle, 2 knobs, BC, AC/DC $80.00

ET-066, table, 1946, wood, upper front pointer dial, lower cloth grill w/"X" cut-outs, scalloped base, 2 knobs, BC, AC/DC **$60.00**

ET-067, table, 1946, wood, upper front slide rule dial, lower grill, vertical fluting on case top, 2 knobs, AC **$35.00**

GK-102, console-R/P, 1947, wood, inner right slide rule dial, 4 knobs, pushbuttons, left phono, lift top, BC, FM, AC...**$100.00**

GK-111, console-R/P, 1949, wood, inner right dial, pushbuttons, 4 knobs, left pull-out phono drawer, BC, FM, AC **$80.00**

GK-141, console-R/P, 1947, wood, inner right slide rule dial, 5 knobs, 8 pushbuttons, left phono, lift top, BC, SW, FM, AC..........**$80.00**

GP-350, portable, metal & leatherette, inner right round dial, left metal grill, 2 knobs, flip-open front, BC, AC/DC **$45.00**

DT-55, table, 1942, wood, upper front slide rule dial, lower 3-section wrap-around grill, 2 knobs $50.00

GT-050, table, 1948, plastic, Deco design, right front round dial, horizontal wrap-around louvers, 2 knobs, BC, AC/DC...$125.00

GT-051, table, 1948, plastic, Deco design, right front round dial, horizontal wrap-around louvers, 2 knobs, BC, 5 tubes, AC/DC..$125.00

GT-064, table, 1948, plastic, upper front slanted dial, lower cloth grill, vertical fluting, 2 knobs, BC, AC/DC $45.00

GT-065, table, 1948, plastic, upper front slanted dial, lower cloth grill, vertical fluting, handle, 2 knobs, BC, AC/DC $45.00

FEDERAL

**Federal Telephone & Radio Corporation,
591 Broad Street, Newark, New Jersey
Federal Telephone & Telegraph Company,
Buffalo, New York
Federal Radio Corporation (Division of the Federal
Telephone Manufacturing Corp.), Buffalo, New York**

Federal Telephone & Telegraph began in 1908 with the manufacture of telephones and soon began to produce radio parts as well. The company produced its first complete radio in 1921 and began to manufacture a high quality, relatively expensive line of sets. As time went on and less complicated radios began to appear on the market, Federal's business declined and by 1929 the company had been sold.

57, table, 1922, metal, 1 dial polished black Bakelite front panel, top right door, 4 tubes, battery $575.00

58 DX, table, 1922, metal or wood, polished black Bakelite front panel, top right door, 4 tubes, battery..........................$750.00

59, table, 1923, metal or wood, polished black Bakelite front panel, lift top, 4 tubes, battery $900.00

61, table, 1924, metal or wood, polished black Bakelite front panel, lift top, 6 tubes, battery $1,200.00

102, portable, 1924, wood, rectangular case, inner Bakelite panel, removable front, handle, 4 tubes, battery....$550.00

110, table, 1924, metal or wood, polished black Bakelite front panel, lift top, 3 tubes, battery $750.00

141, table, 1925, mahogany, inner 2 dial Bakelite front panel, double front doors, 5 tubes, battery $475.00

142, table, 1925, wood, rectangular case, right two dial panel, left built-in speaker, 5 tubes, battery $425.00

143, console, 1925, wood, lowboy, inner right two dial panel, left built-in speaker, 5 tubes, battery $450.00

144, console, 1925, wood, lowboy, inner right two dial panel, left built-in speaker, 5 tubes, battery $450.00

301, console-R/P/Rec, 1940, wood, inner right dial, left phono & recorder, lift top, front grill, AC..................................$100.00

306, console-R/P/Rec, 1940, wood, inner right dial, left phono & recorder, lift top, AC $100.00

1024TB, table, 1948, black Catalin, upper front slanted slide rule dial, large lower wire mesh grill, 3 knobs, AC/DC $425.00

1028T, table, wood, right front dial with red pointer, left criss-cross grill, 3 knobs $45.00

1030T, table, 1946, wood, upper slanted slide rule dial, lower grill, 3 knobs, BC, SW, AC/DC....................................$40.00

1040T, table, 1947, plastic, right front dial, horizontal wrap-around grill bars, 2 knobs, BC, AC/DC $45.00

1040-TB, table, 1947, plastic, right front dial, horizontal wrap-around grill bars, 2 knobs, BC, AC/DC..........................$45.00

6001-PO, portable, "alligator," inner right slide rule dial, left grill, fold-down front, handle, BC, AC/DC/battery.................$40.00

A-10 "Orthosonic," table, 1925, mahogany, low rectangular case, slanted 3 dial front panel, 5 tubes, battery $125.00

B-20 "Orthosonic," table, 1925, mahogany, low rectangular case, slanted panel w/3 window dials, 5 tubes, battery $100.00

B-30 "Orthosonic," table, 1925, mahogany, slanted front panel w/3 window dials, rounded top speaker, 5 tubes, battery $240.00

B-35 "Orthosonic," console, 1925, mahogany, inner right 3 dial panel, left built-in speaker, fold-down front, storage, battery..$175.00

B-36 "Orthosonic," console, 1925, mahogany, inner right 3 dial panel, left built-in speaker, fold-down front, storage, battery..$185.00

C-20 "Orthosonic," table, 1925, mahogany, low rectangular case, slanted front panel w/2 dials, 3 knobs, battery $100.00

C-30 "Orthosonic," table, 1925, mahogany, slanted front panel w/2 dials, rounded top speaker, 7 tubes, battery.........$250.00

E-10 "Orthosonic," table, 1926, mahogany, low rectangular case, center window dial w/escutcheon, 6 tubes, battery $110.00

H-10-60 "Orthosonic," table, 1928, wood, low rectangular case, center front window dial w/escutcheon, 3 knobs, AC $130.00

FENTONE

L. T. Labs, Beach & Sheridan Rd., Waukegan, IL

M-1851, portable, plastic, right front thumbwheel dial, left thumbwheel volume, center horizontal grill bars, handle, telescoping antenna, AC/battery $35.00

FERGUSON

J. B. Ferguson, 80 Beaver St., New York, New York
Ferguson Radio & Television Co., Inc., 745 Broadway, New York, New York

3, table, 1925, wood, low rectangular case, 3 dial front panel, 4 tubes, battery...$125.00
4, table, 1925, wood, low rectangular case, slanted 2 dial front panel, 4 tubes, battery $125.00
6, table, 1925, wood, low rectangular case, 2 dial front panel, battery storage, battery $115.00
8, table, 1925, wood, rectangular case, slanted front panel w/window dial, 2 knobs, 6 tubes, battery...............................$135.00
12, table, 1926, wood, low rectangular case, right & left front window dials, 3 knobs, battery $115.00
214, table, 1937, walnut, slanted front, right airplane dial, left grill w/cut-outs, 3 knobs, tuning eye, BC, SW, 14 tubes, AC/DC $90.00

FERRAR

Ferrar Radio & Television Corp., 55 West 26th Street, New York, New York

C-81-B, console, 1947, two-tone wood, upper front slide rule dial, lower grill, 4 knobs, BC, SW, AC/DC...........................$100.00
T-61-B, table, 1948, wood, right front slide rule dial, left horizontal grill bars, 3 knobs, BC, SW, AC/DC $25.00
TA61B, table, 1948, wood, upper front slanted slide rule dial, lower diamond shaped grill, BC, SW, AC $45.00

FIDELITY

N31, table, plastic, right front round dial over large lattice grill area, feet, BC, AC $25.00

FIRESTONE

The Firestone Tire & Rubber Company, 1200 Firestone Parkway, Akron, Ohio

4-A-1 "Mercury," table, 1948, plastic, lower front slanted slide rule dial, upper horizontal louvers, 2 knobs, BC, AC.....$45.00
4-A-2, table, 1947, plastic, upper front slide rule dial, lower horizontal louvers, 2 knobs, BC, AC/DC $45.00
4-A-3 "Diplomat," table, 1948, plastic, right front dial, left vertical wrap-over grill bars w/lower loops, 2 knobs, 6 tubes, BC, AC/DC $50.00
4-A-10 "Reporter," table, 1947, plastic, upper front slide rule dial, lower horizontal wrap-around louvers, 2 knobs, BC, AC/DC..$50.00
4-A-11, table, 1948, plastic, lower front slide rule dial, upper horizontal wrap-around louvers, 2 knobs, BC, AC/DC $50.00
4-A-12 "Narrator," table, 1948, plastic, elongated base, lower slide rule dial, upper horizontal wrap-around louvers, 2 thumbwheel knobs, AM, FM, AC/DC..........................$55.00
4-A-15, console-R/P, 1948, wood, inner right slide rule dial, pushbuttons, lift top, left pull-out phono drawer, BC, SW, FM, AC..$80.00
4-A-17, table-R/P, 1948, wood, outer top right dial, 3 knobs, front grill w/cut-outs, lift top, inner phono, BC, AC $30.00
4-A-20, table, 1947, wood, upper front slanted slide rule dial, lower cloth grill w/ "X" cut-out, 3 knobs, BC, SW, AC/DC........$45.00
4-A-21, table, 1947, wood, right front slide rule dial, left cloth grill w/cut-outs, 4 knobs, 6 pushbuttons, BC, SW, AC $50.00
4-A-23, table, 1946, wood, upper front slanted slide rule dial, lower cloth grill, 4 knobs, 6 pushbuttons, BC, 2SW, AC..........$65.00
4-A-24, table, 1947, wood, upper front slanted slide rule dial, lower cloth grill w/"X" cut-out, 2 knobs, BC, battery.......$45.00
4-A-25, table, 1947, plastic, upper front slide rule dial, lower horizontal louvers, 2 knobs, BC, AC/DC $40.00
4-A-26 "Newscaster," table, 1948, plastic, upper front slanted slide rule dial, lower horizontal louvers, 2 knobs, BC, AC/DC..$45.00
4-A-27, table, 1947, plastic, lower front slanted slide rule dial, upper horizontal louvers, 2 knobs, BC, AC/DC $50.00
4-A-30, console, 1949, wood, upper front slide rule dial, lower cloth grill w/vertical bars, pushbuttons, 4 knobs $120.00
4-A-31, console-R/P, 1947, wood, upper front slanted slide rule dial, 3 knobs, lower tilt-out phono drawer, BC, AC.......$95.00
4-A-37, console-R/P, 1947, wood, upper front slide rule dial, 4 knobs, 6 pushbuttons, lower tilt-out phono, BC, SW, AC.............$100.00

4-A-41, table, 1948, plastic, upper front slanted slide rule dial, lower horizontal louvers, 2 knobs, BC, AC/DC..............**$40.00**

4-A-42 "Georgian," console-R/P, 1947, wood, upper front slide rule dial, 4 knobs, 6 pushbuttons, lower tilt-out phono, BC, FM, AC **$100.00**

4-A-60, console-R/P, 1948, wood, inner right slide rule dial, 4 knobs, left pull-out phono drawer, BC, FM, AC **$85.00**

4-A-61 "Cameo," table, 1948, plastic, lower front slanted slide rule dial, upper horizontal louvers, 2 knobs, BC, AC/DC.......**$50.00**

4-A-62, console-R/P, 1949, wood, inner right black dial, 3 knobs, left lift top, inner phono, BC, FM, AC **$60.00**

4-A-64 "Contemporary," console-R/P, 1949, wood, upper right front dial, 3 knobs, left lift top, inner phono, BC, FM, AC..**$65.00**

4-A-66, console-R/P, 1949, wood, inner top right slide rule dial, 4 knobs, front pull-out phono, BC, FM, AC......................**$65.00**

4-A-67, table, 1949, plastic, upper front slanted slide rule dial, lower horizontal louvers, 2 knobs, BC, battery **$30.00**

4-A-68, table, 1949, plastic, right front round dial knob, left checkerboard grill, ridged base, BC, AC/DC **$35.00**

4-A-69 "Sunrise," table-C, 1949, plastic, upper front slide rule dial, center electric clock, grill on case top, 4 knobs, BC, AC **$45.00**

4-A-70, table, 1951, plastic, right front half-round dial w/large tuning knob, left horizontal grill bars, BC, AC/DC...............**$40.00**

4-A-71, table-R/P, 1949, wood, center front dial, right & left horizontal louvers, 4 knobs, lift top, inner phono, BC, AC ...**$30.00**

4-A-78, table, 1950, plastic, oblong front panel, right half-round dial, left grill, 2 knobs, BC, AC/DC................................**$45.00**

4-A-86, console-R/P, 1951, wood, inner right front slide rule dial, 4 knobs, lower pull-out phono drawer, left storage, BC, FM, AC..**$80.00**

4-A-87, console-R/P, 1951, wood, upper front slide rule dial, 4 knobs, center pull-out phono drawer, lower grill, BC, AC..**$50.00**

4-A-89, table, 1950, plastic, large front half-round dial, lower panel w/vertical lines & 2 knobs, BC, AC/DC.........................**$35.00**

4-A-92, table-C, 1951, plastic, right front dial, left clock, center vertical wrap-over grill bars, right side knob, BC, AC **$35.00**

4-A-108, table, 1953, plastic, center front half-round dial surrounded by perforated grill area, 2 knobs, feet, BC, AC/DC...**$35.00**

4-A-110, table-C, 1953, wood, right front square dial, left alarm clock, center lattice grill, 5 knobs, BC, AC.....................**$35.00**

4-A-115, table, 1953, wood, center front round dial over large woven grill, 2 knobs, BC, AC/DC..................................**$40.00**

4-A-124, table, metal, right front round dial knob overlaps vertical grill bars w/center wedge-shaped divider, lower left on/off/volume knob, BC $65.00

4-A-134, table-C, 1956, plastic, right side round dial knob, left front clock, right lattice grill, BC, AC **$25.00**

4-A-143, table, 1956, plastic, lower front dial, large upper grill w/center strip, twin speakers, 2 knobs, BC, 5 tubes, AC/DC **$45.00**

4-A-149, table, 1957, plastic, right front round dial, left horizontal bars, BC, 4 tubes, AC/DC **$25.00**

4-A-152, table-R/P, 1957, right side dial knob, large front grill, 3/4 lift top, inner phono, handle, BC, 5 tubes, AC **$20.00**

4-A-153, table, 1957, plastic, center front vertical slide rule dial & tone control, right & left lattice grills, 2 knobs, BC, 6 tubes, AC/DC **$20.00**

4-A-154, table-C, 1957, plastic, front off-center vertical dial, right square clock, 3 knobs, BC, 5 tubes, AC.......................**$25.00**

4-A-159, table, 1957, plastic, right front vertical slide rule dial, large left lattice grill, 2 knobs, BC, 5 tubes, AC/DC.......**$20.00**

4-A-160, table-C, 1957, plastic, right side round dial knob, front alarm clock, left step-down top, BC, 4 tubes, AC.........**$20.00**

4-A-162, table-C, 1957, plastic, lower front dial, center square clock face w/day-date, 5 knobs, BC, 5 tubes, AC **$25.00**

4-A-163, table, 1957, plastic, right front dial knob over random patterned panel, left checkered grill, feet, AC/DC **$20.00**

4-A-164, table-C, 1957, plastic, right side dial knob, off-center clock over checkered panel, BC, 5 tubes, AC **$25.00**

4-A-167, table-C, 1958, plastic, right front round dial, left square clock, side half-round cut-outs, feet, BC, 5 tubes, AC...**$20.00**

4-A-175, table-R/P, 1958, right side dial knob, large front grill, 3/4 lift top, inner phono, handle, BC, 5 tubes, AC **$25.00**

4-A-176, table, 1958, plastic, right front dial knob w/wedge-shaped pointer, left lattice grill, right side knob, BC, 4 tubes, AC **$20.00**

4-A-179, table-C, 1958, plastic, right side dial knob, left front clock, right horizontal louvers, BC, 5 tubes, AC **$20.00**

4-C-3, portable, 1947, leatherette, inner front slide rule dial, 2 knobs, fold-back top, lower grill, BC, AC/DC/battery **$25.00**

4-C-5, portable, 1948, top right dial knob, top left on/off/volume knob, rounded center top, rounded sides, strap, BC, AC/DC/battery $35.00

4-C-13, portable, 1949, lower right front dial knob, upper horizontal wrap-around grill bars, handle, BC, AC/DC/battery..**$35.00**

4-C-16, portable, 1951, plastic, lower front slide rule dial, upper vertical grill bars, flex handle, 2 knobs, BC, AC/DC/battery **$35.00**

4-C-18, portable, 1950, leatherette, center front slide rule dial over large grill area, handle, 2 knobs, BC, AC/DC/battery **$25.00**

4-C-19, portable, 1952, plastic, "alligator" front panel w/center circular louvers, side knobs, flex handle, BC, AC/DC/battery **$40.00**

4-C-21, portable, 1952, two-tone leatherette, center front round dial with inner perforated grill, handle, 2 knobs, BC, AC/DC/battery **$35.00**

4-C-22, portable, 1954, plastic, lower front round dial, upper vertical grill bars, thumbwheel on/off/volume knob, handle, BC, 4 tubes, battery $30.00

4-C-29, portable, 1956, plastic, hybrid/tubes and transistors, right front dial, left checkered grill, handle, BC, battery $250.00

4-C-30, portable, 1957, leather, right front slide rule dial, left grill, lower map, telescope antenna, handle, BC, SW, 5 tubes, AC/DC/battery $40.00

4-C-31, portable, 1957, leather case w/front grill cut-outs, upper right round dial, right side thumbwheel knob, handle, helmet logo, BC, 4 tubes, battery...$30.00

4-C-32, portable, 1957, leather case w/front grill cut-outs, upper right round dial, right side thumbwheel knob, handle, helmet logo, BC, 4 tubes, AC/DC/battery...............................$30.00

4-C-35, portable, 1958, leatherette, upper front slide rule dial, lower map/grill area, telescope antenna, handle, BC, SW, 5 tubes, AC/DC/battery $40.00

S-7403-2, table, plastic, right front dial, left vertical wrap-over grill bars w/lower loops, 2 knobs, 6 tubes $50.00

S-7403-3, table, wood, right front slide rule dial, left horizontal grill bars, handle, 2 knobs $40.00

S-7426-6, table, plastic, right front dial w/statue & globe, horizontal grill bars, 2 knobs, BC, AC $45.00

FIVE STARS

M-1832, portable, plastic, right front dial, upper right thumbwheel on/off/volume knob, left lattice grill area, handle, BC, 4 tubes, battery $40.00

FLUSH WALL

Flush Wall Radio Co.,
58 East Park Street
Newark, New Jersey

5P, wall radio, 1947, Catalin front panel, right dial, left horizontal grill openings, 2 knobs, BC, AC/DC $200.00

FRANKLIN

Franklin Radio Corporation, Dayton, Ohio

105, cathedral, wood, center front dial, upper cloth grill w/cut-outs, 4 tubes...$200.00

FREED-EISEMANN

Freed Radio Corporation,
200 Hudson Street, New York, New York
Freed-Eisemann Radio Corporation,
255 Fourth Avenue, New York, New York

The Freed-Eisemann Radio Corporation began in 1922. Business was good for the company until 1924 when, with the onslaught of less expensive radios from the competition, the company began to decline. Most of the Freed-Eisemann stock was sold to the Freshman Company in 1928 and the final blow was the stock market crash in 1929. Two later companies also formed by the Freed Brothers were The Freed Television and Radio Corporation begun in 1931 and The Freed Radio Corporation begun in 1940.

10, table, 1926, wood, low rectangular case, 3 dial black front panel, 5 tubes, battery..$100.00

11 "Electric 11," console, 1927, wood, fold-down front, inner window dial, lower double doors, inner grill, 6 tubes, AC...$200.00

11 "Electric 11," table, 1927, wood, low rectangular case, inner window dial, fold-down front, 6 tubes, AC $135.00

26, portable, 1937, leatherette or cloth, inner right dial, left grill, fold-down front, handle, AC/DC....................................$30.00

27D, table, 1937, wood, right front airplane dial, left grill w/cut-outs, tuning eye, BC, SW, AC/DC $75.00

28, table, 1937, two-tone wood, right front square airplane dial, left grill w/horizontal bar, BC, SW, AC..........................$45.00

29-D, table, 1937, walnut, right front airplane dial, left grill w/horizontal bars, tuning eye, 4 knobs, BC, SW, 11 tubes, AC/DC $65.00

30, table, 1926, mahogany, slanted front panel, 2 window dials w/escutcheons, 6 tubes, battery...............................$125.00

30-D, table, 1937, wood, right front airplane dial, left grill w/horizontal bars, tuning eye, 3 knobs, BC, SW, 10 tubes, AC/DC $65.00

40, table, 1926, wood, high rectangular case, slanted front, center window dial w/escutcheon, 6 tubes, battery $115.00

46, console-R/P, 1947, wood, inner right slide rule dial, 6 knobs, left phono, lift top, doors, BC, 2SW, FM, 20 tubes, AC...$65.00

48, table, 1926, wood, inner center dial w/escutcheon, fold-down front, side columns, 6 tubes, battery $125.00

50, table, 1926, mahogany, inner center dial w/escutcheon, fold-down front, side columns, 7 tubes, battery..................$120.00

51, table, 1941, walnut, right & left front vertical slide rule dials, large center grill area, tuning eye, 5 knobs, BC, SW, FM, 14 tubes, AC..$70.00

350, table, 1933, walnut w/black & silver trim, right front window dial, center grill w/cut-outs, 3 knobs, 5 tubes, AC $85.00

800, table, 1926, wood, low rectangular case, slanted front w/center dial, loop antenna, 8 tubes $185.00

800-C-8, "roller" console, 1927, wood, console on roller wheels, center front dial, lower speaker grill w/cut-outs, top loop antenna, 8 tubes...$300.00

850, console, 1926, wood, tall Italian Renaissance cabinet, inner dial, fold-down front, upper speaker w/doors, 8 tubes ...$275.00

BG-357-P, table, 1936, silver, pink, green or blue mirror glass, center front round dial surrounded by vertical grill bars, 2 knobs, 5 tubes, AC/DC....................................$1,000.00+

FE-15, table, 1924, wood, low rectangular case, 3 dial black front panel, lift top, 5 tubes, battery $125.00

FE-18, table, 1925, wood, high rectangular case, 3 dial slanted front panel, storage, 5 tubes, battery.........................$125.00

FE-24, table, 1937, wood, right front dial, left grill w/cut-outs, 5 tubes, AC/DC $50.00

FE-28, table, 1937, wood, right front square airplane dial, left cloth grill w/horizontal bars, 3 knobs, BC, SW $50.00

FE-30, table, 1925, wood, low rectangular case, inner three dial panel, fold-down front, battery $135.00
FE-60, table, 1936, two-tone wood, right front dial, left grill w/bars, 6 tubes, AC/DC $50.00
FM-40, table, 1940, walnut, right & left front vertical slide rule dials, large center grill area, 5 knobs, AM, FM, 13 tubes, AC/DC $70.00
NR-5, table, 1923, mahogany, low rectangular case, 3 dial black front panel, lift top, 5 tubes, battery $110.00
NR-6, table, 1924, wood, low rectangular case, 3 dial front panel, lift top, 5 tubes, battery $120.00
NR-7, table, 1925, wood, low rectangular case, 3 dial black front panel, lift top, 6 tubes, battery $100.00
NR-8, console, 1927, wood, inner panel w/2 window dials, upper speaker, double doors, 6 tubes, battery $175.00
NR-8, table, 1927, mahogany, slanted front panel with 2 window dials, 6 tubes, battery $115.00
NR-9, console, 1927, wood, inner panel w/window dial, fold-down front, upper speaker, 6 tubes, battery $165.00
NR-9, table, 1927, wood, slant front panel w/window dial & brass escutcheon, 3 knobs, 6 tubes, battery.........................$90.00

NR-12, table, 1924, wood, low rectangular case, 2 dial black front panel, lift top, 4 tubes, battery $200.00
NR-20, table, 1924, wood, low rectangular case, inner 3 dial panel, fold-down front, columns, battery $200.00
NR-45, table, 1925, wood, low rectangular case (2 versions), 3 dial black front panel, 6 tubes, battery......................$195.00
NR-55, console, 1929, walnut veneer, upper front window dial, lower grill w/cut-outs, 3 knobs, 8 tubes, AC $160.00
NR-60, console, 1927, wood, inner dial w/large escutcheon, 3 knobs, drop front, lower cloth grill w/cut-outs, double doors, AC $150.00
NR-60, table, 1927, wood, low rectangular case, front window dial, 3 knobs, 7 tubes, AC $100.00
NR-66, table, 1927, wood, low rectangular case, front window dial, 6 tubes, 3 knobs, battery $100.00
NR-67, table, wood, low rectangular case, inner front window dial w/large escutcheon, fold-down front, lift top $120.00
NR-77, table, 1927, wood, low rectangular case, front window dial, right side fold-out loop antenna, 7 tubes, battery...$110.00
NR-78, console, 1929, walnut, highboy, upper front window dial, lower grill w/cut-outs, 3 knobs, 8 tubes, AC $130.00
NR-79, console, 1929, walnut, highboy, center front window dial, upper grill w/cut-outs, 3 knobs, 8 tubes, AC...............$135.00
NR-85, table, 1928, metal, rectangular case w/decorative decals, center front thumbwheel dial, AC $165.00
NR-90, console, 1929, walnut, upper front dial, lower cloth grill w/cut-outs, stretcher base, 8 tubes, AC $150.00
NR-95, console-AC, 1929, walnut, highboy, inner window dial, upper grill w/cut-outs, doors, 9 tubes, AC $150.00

NR-95, console-DC, 1929, walnut veneer, highboy, inner window dial, upper grill w/cut-outs, doors, DC $135.00

———————————————————————

FRESHMAN
Chas. Freshman Co., Inc.,
Freshman Building
240-248 West 40th Street,
New York, New York

In 1922 the Charles Freshman Company was formed for the manufacture of radio parts. The popular, low-cost Freshman Masterpiece was introduced in 1924 in both kit as well as a completed radio form. The company was plagued by quality control problems and by 1928, in spite of a merger with Freed-Eisemann, the stock market crash dealt the final blow.

5-F-2, table, 1925, wood, low rectangular case, slanted 3 dial front panel, battery..$100.00
5-F-4, table, 1925, mahogany, low rectangular case, slanted 3 dial front panel, battery $100.00
5-F-5, table, 1925, mahogany, low rectangular case, 3 dial front panel, left built-in speaker, battery $145.00
6-F-1 "Masterpiece," console, 1926, mahogany, inner 3 dial panel, fold-down front, upper speaker grill w/cut-outs, lower storage, battery $185.00
6-F-2 "Masterpiece," console, 1926, burled walnut, inner 3 dial panel, fold-down front, upper speaker grill w/cut-outs, lower storage, battery $185.00
6-F-3 "Masterpiece," console, 1926, mahogany, right 3 dial front panel, left built-in speaker, lower storage, battery.......$160.00
6-F-4 "Masterpiece," console, 1926, mahogany, right 3 dial front panel, left built-in speaker, lower storage, battery.......$160.00
6-F-5 "Masterpiece," table, 1926, mahogany, low rectangular case, right 3 dial front panel, left built-in speaker, battery...$140.00
6-F-6 "Masterpiece," table, 1926, wood, low rectangular case, 3 dial slanted front panel, 5 tubes, battery $100.00
6-F-9 "Masterpiece," console, 1926, mahogany, inner right 3 dial panel, left built-in speaker, fold-down front, lower storage, battery $190.00
6-F-10 "Masterpiece," console, 1926, walnut, inner right 3 dial panel, left built-in speaker, fold-down front, lower storage, battery $190.00
6-F-11 "Masterpiece," console, 1926, mahogany, inner 3 dial panel, fold-down front, lower double doors, inner speaker, battery $200.00
6-F-12 "Masterpiece," console, 1926, walnut, inner 3 dial panel, fold-down front, lower double doors, inner speaker, battery $200.00
7-F-2, table, 1927, wood, low rectangular case, center front window dial w/escutcheon, 6 tubes, battery $85.00
7-F-3, console, 1927, mahogany, upper front window dial, lower built-in speaker w/round grill, battery.........................$150.00
7-F-5, console, 1927, mahogany, inner window dial, fold-down front, lower double doors, inner speaker, battery $185.00
21 "Earl," table, 1929, metal, low rectangular case, front window dial w/escutcheon, 8 tubes, AC $85.00
22 "Earl," console, 1929, walnut finish, highboy, upper front window dial, lower grill w/circular cut-outs, 8 tubes, AC ...$185.00
31 "Earl," console, 1929, walnut finish, upper front window dial, lower grill w/cut-outs, stretcher base, 8 tubes, AC $185.00
32 "Earl," console, 1929, highboy, walnut finish, inner front window dial, double doors, stretcher base, 8 tubes, AC....$200.00
41 "Earl," console, 1929, wood, highboy, inner window dial and speaker grill w/cut-outs, double doors, AC $185.00
Concert, table, 1925, mahogany, tall case, inner 3 dial panel, fold-down front, upper built-in speaker $165.00

F-1 "Equaphase," table, 1927, wood, low rectangular case, center front dial, 6 tubes, battery..................................**$95.00**

Franklin "Masterpiece," console, 1927, mahogany, inner right 3 dial panel, left built-in speaker, fold-down front, lower storage, battery **$190.00**

Franklin "Masterpiece," table, 1927, mahogany, right 3 dial panel, left built-in speaker, fold-down front, battery.....**$140.00**

G-4 "Equaphase," console, 1927, wood, inner front dial & round speaker grill, double doors, lower storage, AC...........**$185.00**

G-7 "Equaphase," console, 1927, wood, inner dial, fold-down front, lower double doors, inner speaker, AC **$165.00**

M, table, metal, center front window dial w/escutcheon, lift-off top, 2 knobs, switch, AC..................................**$85.00**

Masterpiece, table, 1925, wood, 2 styles, low rectangular case, 3 dial front panel, lift top, 5 tubes, battery **$100.00**

Masterpiece w/speaker, table, 1925, wood, low rectangular case w/built-in speaker, 3 dial panel, lift top, battery **$125.00**

N-12, console, 1928, walnut, lowboy, upper front window dial, lower grill w/cut-outs, stretcher base, AC **$165.00**

Q-15 "Little Giant of the Air," table, 1928, metal, center front dial knob, lift-off top, AC **$80.00**

—————————

GAROD

Garod Radio Corporation,
70 Washington Street, Brooklyn, New York
Garod Corporation,
8 West Park Street, Newark, New Jersey

The name Garod is short for the original Gardner-Rodman Corporation which manufactured crystal sets in 1921. The name was changed to the Garod Corporation in 1923 when the company began to produce radios. Due to legal and quality control problems, the original company was out of business by 1927 but the Garod name had appeared once again in radio manufacturing by 1933.

1B55L, table, 1940, Catalin, right square airplane dial over horizontal wrap-around grill bars, recessed handle, 2 knobs ..**$900.00+**

3P85, table-R/P, 1941, wood, right front dial, left vertical grill bars, 3 knobs, lift top, inner phono, BC, SW, 8 tubes, AC......**$35.00**

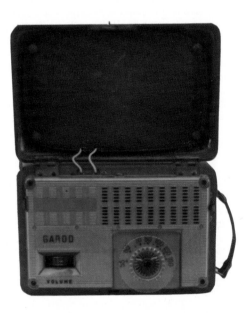

4A-1B, portable, 1947, inner right dial, upper grill w/horizontal slots, lower left volume control, flip-up front, handle, BC, AM/battery..**$45.00**

4A-2B, portable, 1947, inner right dial, upper grill w/horizontal slots, lower left volume control, flip-up front, handle, BC, AM/battery **$45.00**

4B-1, portable, 1948, plastic, inner left dial, geometric grill design, flip-up front, handle, BC, battery..............................**$35.00**

5A1 "Ensign," table, 1947, plastic, upper front slide rule dial, lower grill area w/vertical bars, rounded corners, 2 knobs, BC, AC/DC..**$55.00**

5A2, table, 1946, plastic, upper front slide rule dial, lower inset vertical grill design, 2 knobs, BC, 5 tubes, AC/DC **$50.00**

5A2-Y, table, 1946, plastic, upper front slide rule dial, lower inset vertical grill design, 2 knobs, BC, 5 tubes, AC/DC **$50.00**

5A3, table, 1948, plastic, right front dial, horizontal louvers, rounded corners, 2 knobs, BC, AC/DC **$35.00**

5A4 "Thriftee," table, 1948, plastic, upper front slanted slide rule dial, lower horizontal wrap-around grill bars, 2 knobs, BC, AC/DC..**$40.00**

5AP1-Y "Companion," table-R/P, 1947, plastic, upper front slide rule dial, lower vertical grill bars, 2 knobs, open top phono, BC, AC..**$55.00**

5D-2, portable, 1947, "alligator," inner right vertical dial, 2 knobs, left horizontal louvers, flip-up front, BC, AC/DC/battery..**$35.00**

5D-3A, portable, 1947, metal, inner right triangular slide rule dial, 2 knobs, left grill, flip-up lid, BC, AC/DC/battery **$35.00**

5D-5, portable, 1948, metal, inner right triangular slide rule dial, 2 knobs, left grill, flip-up lid, BC, AC/DC/battery **$35.00**

5RC-1 "Radalarm," table-C, 1948, plastic, right front dial, left alarm clock, center horizontal louvers, 5 knobs, BC, AC **$35.00**

6A-2, table, 1947, wood, upper front slide rule dial, lower horizontal louvers, 2 knobs, BC, AC/DC **$40.00**

6AU-1 "Commander," table, 1946, Catalin, upper front slide rule dial, lower horizontal wrap-around louvers, handle, 2 knobs, BC, AC/DC..**$650.00+**

6BU-1A, table, 1947, plastic, lower front slide rule dial, upper horizontal louvers, 2 knobs, flared base, BC, AC/DC **$50.00**

6DPS-A, console-R/P, 1947, wood, inner right front slide rule dial 4 knobs, left pull-out phono drawer, legs, BC, SW, AC ..**$80.00**

8A4, table, 1938, wood, step-down top, right front airplane dial, left cloth grill w/horizontal wrap-around bars, 4 knobs, BC SW, AC/DC **$65.00**

11FMP, console-R/P, 1948, wood, inner right slide rule dial, 4 knobs, door, left pull-out phono drawer, legs, BC, SW, FM AC **$80.00**

62B, table, 1947, plastic, lower front slide rule dial, upper horizontal louvers, flared base, 4 knobs, BC, SW, AC/DC........**$50.00**

126, table, 1940, Catalin, upper front dial, lower cloth grill w/overlapping circle cut-outs, handle, 2 knobs ....**$1,800.00+**

306, table-R/P, 1948, wood, center front dial, 4 knobs, 3/4 lift top inner phono, BC, AC **$30.00**

309-P8, console-R/P, 1938, wood, large front dial area, lower grill w/center vertical bar, lift top, inner phono, AC............**$125.00**

711-P, table-R/P, 1941, walnut veneer, right front dial, left vertical grill bars, lift top, inner phono, 7 tubes, AC **$45.00**

769, table, 1935, wood, Deco, right front dial, pushbuttons, step down left grill w/vertical bars, BC, SW **$115.00**

1450, table, 1940, Catalin, arched top, right front square airplane dial, left cloth grill w/horizontal bars, handle, 2 knobs ...**$850.00+**

4159, table, 1938, wood, right front slide rule dial, pushbuttons left rounded grill w/horizontal bars, 15 tubes, AC **$65.00**

BP20, portable, 1941, leatherette, inner dial and horizontal grill bars, flip-open front, handle, AC/DC/battery **$35.00**

EB, console-R/P, 1926, wood, inner 3 dial panel, fold-down front lower storage & phono, doors, battery **$185.00**

M, table, 1925, wood, low rectangular case, 3 dial slanted front panel..**$95.00**

RAF, table, 1923, mahogany, low rectangular case, 3 dial front panel, lift top, 5 tubes, battery **$195.00**

V, table, 1923, mahogany, low rectangular case, 3 dial slanted front panel, feet, 5 tubes, battery...............................**$100.00**

—————————

GENERAL ELECTRIC
General Electric Co., Electronics Department, Bridgeport, Connecticut

GE began manufacturing radios in 1919 and marketed them through RCA until 1930, when they began to use their own General Electric trademark on their products.

41 "**Musaphonic,**" console-R/P, 1948, wood, inner right slide rule dial, 5 knobs, 9 pushbuttons, left pull-out phono drawer, double doors, BC, 3SW, 2FM, AC......................................$95.00

42 "**Musaphonic,**" console-R/P, 1948, wood, inner slide rule dial, 5 knobs, 9 pushbuttons, pull-out phono, BC, 3SW, 2FM, AC..$95.00

43 "**Musaphonic,**" console-R/P, 1948, wood, inner slide rule dial, 5 knobs, 9 pushbuttons, pull-out phono, BC, 3SW, 2FM, AC..$95.00

44 "**Musaphonic,**" console-R/P, 1948, wood, inner slide rule dial, 5 knobs, 9 pushbuttons, pull-out phono, BC, 3SW, 2FM, AC..$95.00

45 "**Musaphonic,**" console-R/P, 1948, wood, inner slide rule dial, 5 knobs, 9 pushbuttons, pull-out phono, BC, 3SW, 2FM, AC..$95.00

50, table-C, 1946, plastic, lower right front dial, upper lattice grill, left square clock, 4 knobs..............................$40.00

50W, table-C, 1948, ivory plastic, lower right front dial, upper lattice grill, left square clock, 4 knobs...............................$40.00

54, table, 1940, plastic, Deco, right front vertical slide rule dial, left round grill w/horizontal bars, 4 knobs...........................$85.00

60, table-C, 1948, mahogany plastic, upper front thumbwheel dial, left clock, right horizontal grill bars, BC, AC $45.00

62, table-C, 1948, ivory plastic, upper front thumbwheel dial, left clock, right horizontal grill bars, BC, AC $45.00

65, table-C, 1949, plastic, upper front thumbwheel dial knob, left round alarm clock, right vertical grill bars, AC $40.00

66, table-C, 1949, plastic, upper front thumbwheel dial, left round alarm clock, right horizontal louvers, BC, AC $40.00

67, table-C, 1949, plastic, upper front thumbwheel dial, left round alarm clock, right horizontal louvers, BC, AC...$40.00

100, table, 1946, plastic, lower front half-round dial, upper horizontal wrap-around grill bars, 2 knobs, BC, AC/DC $45.00

102, table, 1948, brown plastic, lower front slide rule dial, upper horizontal grill bars, 2 knobs, BC, AC/DC $35.00

102W, table, 1948, ivory plastic, lower front slide rule dial, upper horizontal grill bars, 2 knobs, BC, AC/DC $35.00

103, table, 1946, wood, lower front black dial, upper "woven" grill, 2 knobs, BC, AC/DC $50.00

106, table-R/P, 1946, wood, right front round black dial, 3 knobs, lift top, inner phono, BC, AC...$30.00

107, table, 1948, brown plastic, lower front slide rule dial, upper horizontal wrap-around louvers, 2 knobs, BC, AC/DC ..$45.00

107W, table, 1948, ivory plastic, lower front slide rule dial, upper horizontal wrap-around louvers, 2 knobs, BC, AC/DC ..$45.00

113, table, 1948, plastic, right front half-round dial, left horizontal grill bars, 2 knobs, BC, AC/DC $35.00

114, table, 1946, brown plastic, lower front slide rule dial, upper horizontal louvers, 2 knobs, BC, AC/DC $45.00

114W, table, 1946, ivory plastic, lower front slide rule dial, upper horizontal louvers, 2 knobs, BC, AC/DC $45.00

115, table, 1948, brown plastic, lower front slide rule dial, upper plastic perforated grill, 2 knobs, BC, AC/DC..$40.00

115W, table, 1948, ivory plastic, lower front slide rule dial, upper plastic perforated grill, 2 knobs, BC, AC/DC $40.00

119W, console-R/P, 1948, wood, inner right dial, 3 knobs, phono, lift top, front criss-cross grill, BC, AC $55.00

135, table, 1950, plastic, lower front slide rule dial, upper recessed vertical grill bars, 2 knobs, BC, AC/DC $40.00

136, table, 1950, plastic, lower front slide rule dial, upper recessed vertical grill bars, 2 knobs, BC $40.00

140, portable, 1947, metal & plastic, inner metal panel w/dial & grill, flip-open door, pull-up handle, BC, AC/DC/battery $40.00

143, portable, 1949, plastic, lower front slide rule dial, upper horizontal louvers, 2 thumbwheel knobs, BC, AC/DC/battery.......$45.00

145, portable, 1949, inner slide rule dial, lattice grill, 2 knobs, lift-up top, handle, BC, AC/DC/battery $35.00

150, portable, 1949, leatherette, upper front slide rule dial, lower horizontal grill bars, handle, 2 knobs, BC, AC/DC/battery......$35.00

160, portable, 1949, plastic, upper front slide rule dial, lower lattice grill, handle, 2 thumbwheel knobs, BC, AC/battery $30.00

165, portable, 1950, maroon plastic, upper front slide rule dial, lower horizontal grill bars, 2 knobs, handle, BC, AC/DC/battery ..$35.00

180, table, 1947, wood, right front dial over cloth grill w/horizontal bars, 2 knobs, rounded corners, feet, BC, battery.........$30.00

200, table, 1946, plastic, lower front black dial, upper horizontal wrap-around grill bars, 2 knobs, BC, AC/DC $35.00

201, table, 1946, plastic, lower front black rectangular dial, upper metal criss-cross grill, 2 knobs, BC $45.00

202, table, 1947, plastic, lower front rectangular dial, upper metal criss-cross grill, 2 knobs, BC $45.00

203, table, 1946, wood, lower front black rectangular dial, upper metal woven grill, 2 knobs, BC, AC/DC $45.00

210, table, 1948, mahogany plastic, right front round dial, recessed cloth grill, 2 knobs, BC, FM, AC/DC $30.00

211, table, 1948, ivory plastic, right front round dial, recessed cloth grill, 2 knobs, BC, FM, AC/DC $30.00

212, table, 1948, wood, right front dial over plastic wrap-around panel, cloth grill, 2 knobs, AM, FM, AC/DC $30.00

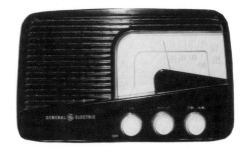

218, table, 1951, plastic, right front dial, lattice grill, lower diagonal panel w/3 knobs, BC, FM, AC/DC $35.00

220, table, 1946, plastic, lower front slide rule dial, checkered grill area, top vertical fluting, 2 knobs, BC, SW, AC/DC.......$40.00

221, table, 1946, wood, large lower slide rule dial, upper criss-cross grill, 2 knobs, BC, SW, AC/DC............................$50.00

226, table, 1950, plastic, lower front slide rule dial, upper recessed checkered grill, 2 knobs, BC, AC/DC $45.00

250, portable, 1946, metal, inner top slide rule dial, 4 knobs, flip back lid, lower horizontal louvers, BC, AC/battery $35.00

254, portable, 1948, cloth covered, inner right dial, 2 knobs, left grill, fold-down front, handle, BC, AC/DC/battery $30.00

260, portable, 1947, metal, inner top slide rule dial, 1 knob, 12 pushbuttons, flip-up lid, lower horizontal louvers, BC, 5SW, AC/battery $50.00

280, table, 1947, wood, right front dial over large grill w/2 horizontal bars, 4 knobs, rounded corners, BC, SW, battery $30.00

303, table-R/P, 1947, wood, upper front slide rule dial, lower horizontal louvers, 4 knobs, lift top, inner phono, BC, AC ...$30.00

304, table-R/P, 1948, wood, upper front slide rule dial, lower horizontal grill bars, 4 knobs, lift top. inner phono, BC, AC ..$30.00

321, table, 1946, wood, center front slide rule dial, upper metal "woven" grill, 2 knobs, 5 pushbuttons, BC, AC/DC $40.00

324, console-R/P, 1949, mahogany, right front tilt-out slide rule dial, 4 knobs, left pull-out phono drawer, lower grill & storage BC, FM, AC $70.00

328, console-R/P, 1949, blonde wood, right front tilt-out slide rule dial, 4 knobs, left pull-out phono drawer, lower grill & storage, BC, FM, AC **$70.00**

356, table, 1948, plastic, step-down top, upper front slide rule dial, lower horizontal louvers, 2 knobs, BC, FM, AC/DC.......**$45.00**

376, console-R/P, 1948, wood, left tilt-out slide rule dial & 4 knobs, right pull-out phono drawer, lower grill, BC, FM, AC **$70.00**

400, table, 1950, plastic, slanted right front dial, left vertical grill bars, 2 knobs, BC, AC/DC...**$35.00**

405, table, 1951, plastic, flared base, lower front slide rule dial, upper vertical grill bars, 2 knobs, BC................$40.00

408, table, 1950, plastic, center front raised half-round dial over horizontal bars, 2 thumbwheel knobs, BC, FM, AC/DC...**$40.00**

409, table, 1952, plastic, center front raised half-round dial over horizontal bars, 2 thumbwheel knobs, BC, FM, AC/DC..$40.00

410, table, 1951, wood, lower front slide rule dial, large upper grill, 2 knobs, feet, AM, AC/DC **$30.00**

411, table, 1950, plastic, large right front dial, left vertical grill bars, 2 knobs, BC **$35.00**

412, table, 1952, plastic, large right front dial, left vertical grill bars, 2 knobs, BC, AC/DC **$35.00**

414, table, 1950, plastic, large right front dial, left horizontal grill bars, 2 knobs, BC, AC/DC...**$35.00**

415F, table, 1953, plastic, large right front dial, left horizontal grill bars, 2 knobs, BC, AC/DC..**$35.00**

417, console-R/P, 1947, wood, inner right slide rule dial, 5 knobs, 12 pushbuttons, left phono, fold-down front, lower grill area, BC, 2SW, 2FM, AC **$95.00**

417A, console-R/P, 1947, wood, inner right slide rule dial, 5 knobs, 12 pushbuttons, left phono, fold-down front, lower grill area, BC, 2SW, 2FM, AC **$95.00**

419, table, 1954, plastic, right front round dial over large checkered grill area w/horizontal & vertical bars, 2 knobs, feet, BC, AC/DC **$20.00**

422, table, 1951, plastic, lower front slide rule dial, upper recessed vertical grill bars, 2 knobs, BC, AC/DC..........**$35.00**

423, table, 1951, plastic, lower front slide rule dial, upper recessed vertical grill bars, 2 knobs, BC, AC/DC..........**$35.00**

428, table, 1955, plastic, raised center w/half-round dial, vertical front bars, feet, 2 knobs, BC, AC/DC **$30.00**

430, table, 1952, wood, right front rectangular dial, left horizontal grill bars, 2 knobs, BC **$35.00**

440, table, 1954, plastic, center front raised half-round dial over horizontal bars, 2 thumbwheel knobs, BC, FM, AC/DC..**$45.00**

442, table, 1951, plastic, lower front slide rule dial, upper recessed grill w/vertical bars, 2 knobs, BC, AC............**$40.00**

453, table, 1956, plastic, right front round dial over large checkered grill area w/horizontal & vertical bars, 2 knobs, feet, BC, AC/DC **$20.00**

500, table-C, 1950, plastic, upper front thumbwheel dial, left round clock, right horizontal grill bars, BC, AC **$45.00**

502, console-R/P, 1948, wood, inner right slide rule dial, 5 knobs, 9 pushbuttons, door, left pull-out phono drawer, lower grill area, BC, 3SW, 2FM, AC **$100.00**

507, table-C, 1950, plastic, upper front thumbwheel dial, left alarm clock, right vertical grill bars, BC, AC **$45.00**

510, table-C, 1951, plastic, upper front thumbwheel dial, left alarm clock, right circular louvers, BC, AC **$45.00**

511, table-C, 1951, plastic, upper front thumbwheel dial, left alarm clock, right circular louvers, BC, AC **$45.00**

514, table-C, 1953, plastic, upper front thumbwheel dial, left round alarm clock, right horizontal grill bars, BC, AC..$45.00

515, table-C, 1951, plastic, upper front thumbwheel dial, left round alarm clock, right vertical grill bars, BC, AC **$45.00**

515F, table-C, 1951, plastic, upper front thumbwheel dial, left round alarm clock, right vertical grill bars, BC, AC **$45.00**

516, table-C, 1951, plastic, upper front thumbwheel dial, left round alarm clock, right vertical grill bars, BC, AC **$45.00**

516F, table-C, 1951, plastic, upper front thumbwheel dial, left round alarm clock, right vertical grill bars, BC, AC **$45.00**

517F, table-C, 1951, plastic, upper front thumbwheel dial, left round alarm clock, right vertical grill bars, BC, AC **$45.00**

518F, table-C, 1951, plastic, upper front thumbwheel dial, left round alarm clock, right vertical grill bars, BC, AC ..$45.00

521, table-C, 1950, upper front thumbwheel dial, wrap-around panel w/right horizontal grill bars & left round alarm clock, BC, AC..$50.00

535, table-C, 1951, plastic, right front square dial, left square alarm clock, center vertical bars, 5 knobs, AC.........$30.00
542, table-C, 1953, plastic, upper front thumbwheel dial, right vertical grill bars, left round alarm clock, BC, AC $45.00
543, table-C, 1953, plastic, upper front thumbwheel dial, right vertical grill bars, left round alarm clock, BC, AC $45.00

546, table-C, 1953, plastic, lower front slide rule dial, right & left vertical grill bars, center clock, 5 knobs, AC $30.00
548, table-C, 1953, plastic, lower front slide rule dial, right & left vertical grill bars, center clock, 5 knobs, AC.................$30.00
549, table-C, 1953, plastic, lower front slide rule dial, right & left vertical grill bars, center clock, BC, AC $30.00
551, table-C, 1953, plastic, lower front slide rule dial, right & left vertical grill bars, center clock, 4 knobs, BC, AC..........$30.00
573, table-C, plastic, lower front slide rule dial, right & left vertical grill bars, center clock, BC, AC.....................................$30.00
590, table-C, 1955, plastic, right front dial, left clock, raised center lattice grill, 5 knobs, BC, 6 tubes, AC $25.00
600, portable, 1950, plastic, lower front slide rule dial, upper recessed horizontal grill bars, handle, 2 thumbwheel knobs, BC, battery $35.00
601, portable, 1950, maroon plastic, lower front slide rule dial, upper recessed horizontal grill bars, 2 thumbwheel knobs, handle, BC, AC/DC/battery $35.00
603, portable, 1950, tan plastic, lower front slide rule dial, upper recessed horizontal grill bars, 2 thumbwheel knobs, handle, BC, AC/DC/battery $35.00
604, portable, 1950, green plastic, lower front slide rule dial, upper recessed horizontal grill bars, 2 thumbwheel knobs, handle, BC, AC/DC/battery $35.00
610, portable, 1951, plastic, upper front half-round dial, lower vertical grill bars, handle, 2 knobs, BC, AC/DC/battery $35.00

636, portable, 1955, plastic, large right front dial knob, left metal perforated grill, fold-down handle, BC, battery $30.00
637, portable, 1955, plastic, large right front dial knob, left metal perforated grill, fold-down handle, BC, battery $30.00

648, portable, plastic, large right front dial with center crest overlaps perforated grill area, fold-down handle, BC...**$40.00**

650, portable, 1950, maroon plastic, upper front slide rule dial, lower horizontal grill bars, handle, 2 thumbwheel knobs, BC, AC/DC/battery **$35.00**

660 & 660A "Convertible," portable-C, plastic, combination clock (660A) and removable portable radio (660), radio has right side knobs, front metal perforated grill area and fold-down handle...**$50.00**

741, console-R/P, 1952, wood, inner right dial, 3 knobs, lower pull-out phono drawer, double doors, BC, AC.............**$55.00**

752, console-R/P, 1951, wood, inner right dial, 4 knobs, lower pull-out phono drawer, double doors, BC, FM, AC.......**$60.00**

755, console-R/P, 1951, wood, inner right dial, 2 knobs, lower pull-out phono drawer, BC, FM, AC **$70.00**

870, table, 1956, plastic, right front round dial, raised left lattice grill area, 3 knobs, BC, 6 tubes **$35.00**

895, table-C, 1956, plastic, right front dial knob and left square clock over large checkered panel, feet, BC, AC............**$25.00**

A-52, tombstone, wood, center front dial w/oval escutcheon, upper cloth grill w/cut-outs, 4 knobs **$115.00**

A-53, tombstone, 1935, walnut finish, center front window dial, upper cloth grill w/cut-outs, 3 knobs, BC, SW, AC **$115.00**

A-54, table, 1936, two-tone walnut, step-down top, upper right front window dial, left grill w/cut-outs, 4 knobs, BC, SW, 5 tubes, AC/DC **$65.00**

A-55, console, 1936, wood, upper front dial w/oval escutcheon, lower cloth grill w/center vertical bars, 4 knobs, BC, SW, 5 tubes..**$115.00**

A-63, tombstone, 1935, walnut veneer, Deco, center front window dial, upper cloth grill w/vertical bars, BC, SW, AC.......**$125.00**

A-64, tombstone, 1935, wood, center front horizontal pointer dial, upper cloth grill w/cut-outs, arched top, 4 knobs **$115.00**

A-65, console, 1935, walnut-veneer, upper front window dial, lower cloth grill w/vertical bars, 4 knobs, BC, SW, AC **$120.00**

A-67, console, 1935, wood, upper front horizontal pointer dial, lower cloth grill w/scrolled cut-outs, 4 knobs, BC, SW **$150.00**

A-70, tombstone, 1935, wood, center front horizontal pointer dial, upper & lower cloth grill areas w/vertical bars, fluting, BC, SW, AC **$125.00**

A-75, console, 1935, walnut-veneer, upper front horizontal pointer dial, lower cloth grill w/3 vertical bars, BC, SW, AC **$145.00**

A-82, tombstone, 1935, walnut, lower front horizontal pointer dial, upper cloth grill w/cut-outs, BC, SW, AC...................**$125.00**

A-83, tombstone, 1936, wood, center front horizontal pointer dial, upper & lower cloth grills w/vertical bars, BC, SW, 8 tubes **$130.00**

A-85, console, 1936, wood, upper front horizontal pointer dial, lower cloth grill w/vertical bars, BC, SW, 8 tubes **$140.00**

A-87, console, 1935, wood, upper front horizontal pointer dial, lower vertical grill bars, 3 knobs, feet, 4 band, AC **$150.00**

A-125, console, 1935, wood, upper front horizontal pointer dial, lower grill w/rectangular cut-outs, fluted sides, base, 5 band, AC **$185.00**

BX, table, 1932, metal case w/lacquer finish, right front dial, center round grill, 2 knobs, 4 tubes, AC/DC.......................**$75.00**

C403, table-C, antique white plastic, large right front dial knob over horizontal bars, left alarm clock, feet, BC, AC.......**$10.00**

C404, table-C, Wedgwood blue plastic, large right front dial knob over horizontal bars, left alarm clock, feet, BC, AC.......**$10.00**

C405, table-C, gray/white plastic, right front round dial knob over horizontal bars, off-center raised clock area, feet, BC, AC **$10.00**

C405D, table-C, gray/white plastic, right front round dial knob over horizontal bars, off-center raised clock area, feet, BC, AC **$10.00**

C407, table-C, rose beige/white plastic, right front round dial knob over horizontal bars, off-center raised clock area, feet, BC, AC **$10.00**

C415, table-C, 1958, plastic, raised clock/dial panel, lower front slide rule dial, upper clock, right & left vertical bars, BC, 5 tubes, AC...**$30.00**

C-415C, table-C, 1958, plastic, raised clock/dial panel, lower front slide rule dial, upper clock, right & left vertical grill bars, BC, AC **$30.00**

C433, table-C, antique white plastic, raised clock/dial panel, lower front slide rule dial, upper clock, right & left vertical bars, feet, BC **$15.00**

C434, table-C, rose beige plastic, raised clock/dial panel, lower front slide rule dial, upper clock, right & left vertical bars, feet, BC **$15.00**

C434C, table-C, plastic, raised clock/dial panel, lower front slide rule dial, upper clock, right & left vertical bars, feet, BC $15.00
C436, table-C, antique white plastic, right front dial over checkered grill panel, left alarm clock, feet, BC, AC $10.00
C437, table-C, pink plastic, right front dial over checkered grill panel, left alarm clock, feet, BC, AC..............................$10.00

C437A, table-C, pink plastic, right front dial over checkered grill panel, left alarm clock, feet, BC, AC $10.00
C438, table-C, mint green plastic, right front dial over checkered grill panel, left alarm clock, feet, BC, AC $10.00
C495A, table-C, 1962, pink/white plastic, right front vertical slide rule dial, left alarm clock, center textured panel, BC, AC $20.00

C496A, table-C, 1962, cocoa/white plastic, right front vertical slide rule dial, left alarm clock, center textured panel, BC, AC...$20.00
C510, table-C, antique white plastic, right front vertical dial, left alarm clock, center textured grill area, AM, FM, AC $15.00

C510A, table-C, plastic, right front vertical dial, left alarm clock, center textured grill area, AM, FM, AC $15.00
E-50, table, 1937, wood, center front horizontal dial w/surrounding 4-section cloth grill, 4 knobs, 2 bands, 5 tubes, AC $55.00

E-52, table, 1937, wood, center front horizontal dial w/surrounding 4-section cloth grill, 4 knobs, BC, SW, AC $55.00

E-61, tombstone, 1936, wood, rounded top, center front horizontal slide rule dial, upper cloth grill w/cut-outs, 4 knobs, BC, SW, AC...$150.00
E-71, tombstone, 1936, two-tone wood, center front horizontal dial, large cloth grill w/cut-outs, 4 knobs, BC, SW, AC $130.00
E-72, table, 1936, wood, left front horizontal dial, right cloth grill w/3 vertical bars, 4 knobs, AC $40.00
E-81, tombstone, 1936, wood, center front horizontal dial, upper grill w/cut-outs, 4 knobs, BC, SW, 8 tubes, AC $125.00
F-51, table, 1937, plastic, Deco, right front vertical dial, rounded left side, horizontal wrap-around bars, 4 knobs, 5 tubes, AC $125.00
F-53, table, 1937, wood, center front rectangular slide rule dial, upper & lower grills w/horizontal bars, 4 knobs, BC, SW, AC $60.00

F-63, table, 1937, walnut, left front gold dial, streamlined right side w/Deco grill cut-outs, 4 knobs, BC, SW, 6 tubes, AC **$85.00**
F-65, console, 1937, wood, upper front rectangular dial, lower cloth grill w/3 vertical bars, BC, SW, 6 tubes, AC........**$125.00**
F-66, console, 1937, wood, upper front rectangular dial, lower cloth grill w/3 vertical bars, BC, SW, 6 tubes, AC........**$125.00**
F-70, table, 1937, wood, left front rectangular dial, right cloth grill w/4 horizontal bars, 4 knobs, BC, SW, 7 tubes, AC **$65.00**
F-74, table, 1938, wood, left front rectangular dial, tuning eye, right grill w/2 horizontal bars, 4 knobs, BC, SW, AC **$85.00**
F-75, console, 1937, wood, upper front rectangular dial, lower cloth grill w/vertical bars, BC, SW, 7 tubes, AC...........**$125.00**

F-81, tombstone, 1937, wood, lower front rectangular dial, upper cloth grill w/horizontal bars, 4 knobs, BC, SW, 8 tubes, AC **$145.00**
F-86, console, 1937, wood, upper front rectangular dial, lower cloth grill w/3 vertical bars, BC, SW, 8 tubes, AC........**$135.00**
F-96, console, 1937, wood, upper front rectangular dial, pushbuttons, lower cloth grill w/2 vertical bars, 5 knobs, 9 tubes, AC **$145.00**
F-107, console, 1937, wood, upper front rectangular dial, lower cloth grill w/vertical bars, pushbuttons, BC, SW, 10 tubes, AC ..**$165.00**
F-109, console-R/P, 1937, wood, upper front dial, lower cloth grill w/vertical bars, inner phono, BC, SW, 10 tubes, AC **$165.00**

F-135, console, 1937, wood, upper front rectangular dial, lower cloth grill w/vertical bars, pushbuttons, BC, SW, 13 tubes, AC **$200.00**
F-665, chairside, 1937, walnut, top rectangular dial & knobs, front grill w/vertical bars, step-down top, BC, SW, 6 tubes, AC **$130.00**
FB-52, cathedral, wood, center front rectangular dial, cloth grill w/vertical bars, battery **$100.00**
FB-77, console, 1938, wood, upper front rectangular dial, lower cloth grill w/3 vertical bars, 4 knobs, battery...............**$115.00**

FD-100, cathedral, wood, center front slide rule dial, upper cloth grill w/vertical bars, 4 knobs, BC, 10 tubes, AC/DC **$175.00**
FE-112, table, 1940, wood, right front rectangular dial, left cloth grill w/horizontal wrap-around bars, tuning eye, 4 knobs, BC, 2SW, LW, 11 tubes, AC **$100.00**
G-50, table, 1937, wood, right front round telephone dial, left cloth grill w/vertical bars, 2 knobs, BC, 5 tubes, AC **$65.00**
G-53, table, 1938, wood, 2 right front slide rule dials, pushbuttons, left grill w/vertical wrap-over bars, BC, SW, 5 tubes, AC **$60.00**
G-55, console, 1938, wood, upper front round telephone dial, lower cloth grill w/2 vertical bars, BC, 5 tubes, AC......**$120.00**
G-56, console, 1938, wood, 2 upper front dials, lower grill w/vertical bars, pushbuttons, BC, SW, 5 tubes, AC...............**$120.00**
G-61, table, 1938, wood, rounded right w/3 dials, left wrap-around grill w/horizontal bars, pushbuttons, BC, SW, 6 tubes, AC **$85.00**
G-64, table, 1939, wood, 2 right front slide rule dials, left wrap-around cloth grill w/horizontal bars, pushbuttons, 4 knobs, BC, SW, AC..**$80.00**
G-68, console-R/P, 1938, wood, inner dial & phono, front grill w/vertical bars, lift top, BC, SW, 6 tubes, AC **$130.00**
G-76 "Radiogrande," console, 1938, wood, upper front dial, pushbuttons, tuning eye, large lower grill w/cut-outs, BC, SW, AC **$215.00**
G-78, console, 1939, wood, upper front rectangular dial, lower cloth grill w/horizontal bars, pushbuttons, 4 knobs, BC, SW..**$150.00**
G-85, console, 1938, wood, upper front dial, lower cloth grill w/horizontal & vertical bars, tuning eye, 10 pushbuttons, BC, SW, 8 tubes, AC...**$165.00**
G-87A, console, 1933, wood, lowboy, upper front window dial, lower cloth grill w/cut-outs, BC, 8 tubes, AC **$140.00**
G-97, console, 1938, wood, upper front dial, lower cloth grill w/vertical bars, 7 pushbuttons, right top pop-up station timer, BC, SW, 9 tubes, AC **$185.00**

G-105, console, 1938, wood, upper front dial, lower cloth grill w/vertical bars, tuning eye, 14 pushbuttons, BC, SW, 10 tubes, AC..**$185.00**

GB-400, portable, 1948, luggage-style, front thumbwheel dial & volume knobs, center grill, handle, BC, battery.............**$35.00**

GB-401, table, 1939, two-tone wood, slanted front w/vertical wrap-over bars, 2 thumbwheel knobs, battery **$40.00**

GD-41, table, 1938, two-tone wood, right front airplane dial, left cloth grill w/3 section cut-outs, 2 knobs, AC/DC...........**$50.00**

GD-52, table, 1938, wood, slanted front w/thumbwheel dial & volume knobs, center grill, 6 pushbuttons, BC, 5 tubes, AC.........**$70.00**

GD-60, table, 1938, wood, slanted front w/thumbwheel dial & volume knobs, center grill, 6 pushbuttons, BC, AC...........**$70.00**

GD-63, table, 1939, wood, slanted front w/vertical wrap-over bars, thumbwheel dial & volume knobs, pushbuttons, BC **$70.00**

GD-500, table, 1939, plastic, right front round "compass" dial, left grill w/vertical wrap-over bars **$60.00**

GD-520, table, 1939, plastic, Deco, small case, right front metal dial panel, left wrap-around horizontal bars, 2 knobs..**$150.00**

GD-600, table, 1938, wood, right front rectangular dial, left cloth grill w/vertical wrap-over bars, 2 knobs $60.00

H-32, console, 1931, walnut, lowboy, upper front window dial, lower grill w/scrolled cut-outs, AC **$145.00**

H-71, console-R/P, 1931, wood, lowboy, inner front dial & grill, double doors, lift top, inner phono, 9 tubes, AC **$285.00**

H-87, console, 1939, wood, upper front slanted dial, pushbuttons, lower cloth grill w/bars, rounded sides, BC, SW, 8 tubes, AC **$165.00**

H-91 "Longfellow, grandfather clock, 1931, mahogany, Colonial design, inner dial & knobs, front door, upper clock face, 10 tubes, AC **$500.00**

H-500, table, 1939, plastic, Deco, step-down top, center front thumbwheel dial, left front lattice grill, AC **$115.00**

H-502, table, 1939, plastic, Deco, step-down top, center front thumbwheel dial, left lattice grill area, AC **$115.00**

H-520, table, 1939, plastic, Deco, step-down top, center front thumbwheel dial, left front lattice grill, BC, 5 tubes, AC **$115.00**

H-530, tombstone, 1939, wood, small case, lower right front dial, upper 2-section cloth grill, chassis mounted sideways, BC **$95.00**

H-531, tombstone, 1939, wood, small case, lower right front dial, upper 2-section cloth grill, chassis mounted sideways, BC **$95.00**

H-600, table, 1939, swirled plastic, right front square dial, left lattice grill, horizontal case lines, 2 knobs, AC **$100.00**

H-610, table, 1939, swirled plastic, right front square dial, 4 pushbuttons, left lattice grill, horizontal case lines, 2 knobs, AC **$65.00**

H-620, table, 1939, plastic, right front square dial, left horizontal louvers, 3 knobs, BC, SW, AC **$60.00**

H-620U, table, 1939, plastic, right front square dial, left horizontal louvers, 3 knobs, BC, SW, 6 tubes, AC **$60.00**

H-630, table, 1939, wood, right front dial, 4 pushbuttons, left cloth wrap-over grill, 3 knobs, BC, SW, AC **$50.00**

H-632, table, 1939, wood, center front dial, pushbuttons, right & left side wrap-around grills, 3 knobs, BC, SW, AC **$60.00**

H-634, table, 1939, wood, right front rectangular dial, pushbuttons, left wrap-around grill, BC, 2SW **$60.00**

H-639, table-R/P, Deco, right front dial, pushbuttons, rounded left side w/wrap-around horizontal grill louvers, lift top, inner phono, AC **$50.00**

HB-402, portable, 1939, right front dial, left grill area, 2 knobs, handle...**$25.00**

HB-412, portable, 1939, leatherette, inner right front dial, left grill, fold-up front, handle, AC/DC/battery **$30.00**

HJ-624, table, 1939, wood, right front dial, pushbuttons, left wrap-around grill w/horizontal bars, thumbwheel knobs **$85.00**

J-51, table, 1940, wood, upper front slide rule dial, lower horizontal louvers, 2 knobs, BC, AC **$40.00**

J-53, table, 1940, two-tone wood, upper front slide rule dial, lower horizontal louvers, 2 knobs, BC, AC/DC **$45.00**

J-54, table, mottled brown plastic, upper front slide rule dial, lower horizontal louvers, 2 knobs, BC..............................**$45.00**

J-54W, table, ivory plastic, upper front slide rule dial, lower horizontal louvers, 2 knobs, BC..............................**$45.00**

J-62, table, 1941, mahogany, upper front slide rule dial, lower cloth grill w/criss-cross cut-outs, side handles, decorative molding, 3 knobs, AC **$60.00**

J-64, table, two-tone wood, large front slide rule dial, rounded left grill w/horizontal bars, 5 pushbuttons, 4 knobs, BC, SW..$60.00

J-71, table, wood, large center front slide rule dial, right & left wrap-around horizontal grill bars, 6 pushbuttons, 4 knobs, BC, SW **$85.00**

J-72, cathedral, 1932, wood, lower front window dial, upper cloth grill w/cut-outs, 3 knobs, AC **$200.00**

J-80, cathedral, 1932, wood, center front window dial, cloth grill w/cut-outs, fluted columns, 3 knobs, AC **$295.00**

J-82, cathedral, 1932, wood, center front window dial, cloth grill w/cut-outs, fluted columns, 3 knobs, AC **$295.00**

J-86, console, 1932, wood, lowboy, upper front window dial, lower grill w/cut-outs, stretcher base, AC.............................**$140.00**

J-88, console-R/P, 1932, wood, lower front window dial, upper grill w/cut-outs, 3 knobs, inner phono, 8 tubes, AC **$140.00**

J-100, cathedral, 1932, wood, front window dial, upper cloth grill w/cut-outs, 3 knobs, 10 tubes, AC...............................**$295.00**

J-501W, table, 1941, ivory plastic, upper front slide rule dial, lower horizontal louvers, 2 knobs, AC/DC **$45.00**

J-620, table, 1941, blond mahogany, upper front slide rule dial, lower cloth grill w/criss-cross cut-outs, side handles, decorative molding, 3 knobs, AC......................$60.00

J-644, table, 1941, plastic, right front dial, left horizontal louvers, rounded top, 2 knobs, AC......................$40.00

J-805, console, 1940, wood, upper front slide rule dial, lower cloth grill w/bars, 6 pushbuttons, 4 knobs, BC, SW, AC $145.00

J-809, console-R/P, 1940, mahogany, inner right front slide rule dial, door, left pull-out phono drawer, lower grill area, BC, SW, 8 tubes, AC......................$100.00

JB-410, portable, 1940, leatherette/plastic, inner dial and horizontal grill bars, fold-open front, handle, battery $40.00

JB-420, table, 1940, mahogany plastic, right front dial over horizontal wrap-around grill bars, 2 knobs, BC, AC $45.00

JCP-562, table, 1942, wood, right front dial, left cloth grill, 2 knobs $35.00

JFM-90, table, wood, FM only, center front black dial, 6 pushbuttons, rounded front corners, 2 knobs......................$30.00

K-40-A, table, 1933, walnut, right front dial, center cloth grill w/cut-outs, lower scalloped molding, 2 knobs, 4 tubes, AC/DC......................$85.00

K-41, table, 1933, metal, right front dial, center round cloth grill, decorative case lines, 2 knobs, AC $75.00

K-43, cathedral, 1933, wood, low case, center front dial surrounded by cloth grill w/cut-outs, 4 knobs, BC, SW, AC.......$165.00

K-50, cathedral, 1933, wood, lower right front window dial, upper cloth grill w/cut-outs, 3 knobs, 5 tubes, AC $150.00

K-50-P, cathedral, 1933, wood, lower right front window dial, upper cloth grill w/cut-outs, 4 knobs, AC...............$150.00

K-51, table, 1932, wood, inner front window dial, cloth grill w/cut-outs, double sliding carved doors, 5 tubes, AC $200.00

K-51-P, table, 1932, wood, inner front window dial, cloth grill w/cut-outs, double sliding carved doors, AC $200.00

K-52, cathedral, 1933, wood, lower right front window dial, upper cloth grill w/cut-outs, 4 knobs, BC, SW, 5 tubes, AC...$225.00

K-53-M, table, 1933, wood, right front window dial, left & right quarter-round grill cut-outs, 4 knobs, AC......................$90.00

K-54 "Music Box," table-R/P, 1932, ornate case, right side controls, front grill w/cut-outs, lift top, inner phono, 5 tubes, AC......................$95.00

K-60, cathedral, 1933, wood, mantle-clock design, lower front window dial, upper round cloth grill w/cut-outs, handle, 6 tubes, AC $250.00

K-60-P, cathedral, 1933, wood, mantle-clock design, lower front window dial, upper round cloth grill w/cut-outs, handle, 4 knobs......................$250.00

K-62, console, 1931, wood, lowboy, center front window dial, lower cloth grill w/cut-outs, 3 knobs, 6 legs, 9 tubes, AC $150.00

K-63, cathedral, 1933, wood, mantle-clock design, lower front window dial, upper cloth grill w/cut-outs, 4 knobs, BC, SW, 6 tubes, AC $250.00

K-64, cathedral, 1933, wood, mantle-clock design, round dial, upper cloth grill w/cut-outs, handle, 4 knobs, BC, SW, 6 tubes, AC......................$250.00

K-65, console, 1933, walnut, upper front window dial, lower cloth grill w/cut-outs, 6 legs, stretcher base, 6 tubes, AC $145.00

K-70, cathedral, wood, lower front window dial w/escutcheon, upper 3-section cloth grill, 3 knobs......................$160.00

K-80, tombstone, 1933, wood, center front round dial, upper cloth grill w/cut-outs, angled top, 4 knobs, BC, SW, 8 tubes, AC $250.00

K-82 "Georgian," grandfather clock, 1931, mahogany, Colonial design, inner dial & controls, front door, upper clock face, 9 tubes, AC..**$400.00**

K-85, console, 1933, wood, upper front round dial, lower cloth grill w/cut-outs, 6 legs, 4 knobs, BC, SW, 8 tubes, AC **$165.00**

K-106, console, 1933, wood, upper front window dial, lower grill w/cut-outs, 6 legs, 5 knobs, 10 tubes, AC **$150.00**

K-126, console, 1933, wood, upper front window dial, lower cloth grill w/cut-outs, 6 legs, BC, SW, 12 tubes, AC **$175.00**

L-50, table, 1932, ornate "carved" front & sides, right dial, center grill, 2 knobs, handle, 5 tubes, AC/DC **$150.00**

L-500, table, 1941, mahogany plastic, upper front slide rule dial, lower horizontal louvers, 2 knobs, BC, AC/DC.............**$40.00**

L-550, table, 1941, ivory plastic, upper front slide rule dial, lower horizontal louvers, 2 knobs, BC, AC/DC **$40.00**

L-570, table, 1941, Catalin, upper front slide rule dial, lower horizontal louvers, handle, 2 ribbed knobs, BC ....**$550.00+**

L-600, table, 1941, mahogany plastic, upper front slide rule dial, lower horizontal louvers, 2 knobs, BC **$40.00**

L-604, table, 1941, two-tone walnut, upper front slanted slide rule dial, lower horizontal louvers, BC, AC **$40.00**

L-610, table, 1941, ivory plastic, upper front slanted slide rule dial, lower horizontal louvers, 2 knobs, BC, AC **$40.00**

L-613, table, two-tone wood, upper front slanted slide rule dial, lower horizontal louvers, 2 knobs, BC, SW **$45.00**

L-621, table, 1941, mahogany plastic, upper front slide rule dial, lower double grill w/horizontal louvers, 2 knobs, BC, SW, 6 tubes, AC/DC **$50.00**

L-624, table, 1941, ivory plastic, upper front slanted slide rule dial, lower double grill w/horizontal louvers, 2 knobs, BC, SW, AC **$50.00**

L-630, table, 1940, two-tone wood, upper front slide rule dial, lower cloth grill w/center horizontal bar, 4 knobs, BC, SW **$45.00**

L-632, table, 1941, wood, upper front slanted slide rule dial, lower horizontal louvers, 2 knobs, BC, SW...........................**$45.00**

L-633, table, 1941, walnut, upper front slanted slide rule dial, lower horizontal grill bars, rounded front sides, AC......**$55.00**

L-640, table, 1941, wood, upper front slide rule dial, lower grill area, 5 pushbuttons, 4 knobs, BC, 2SW, AC **$60.00**

L-641, table, 1942, wood, upper front slide rule dial, lower grill w/horizontal bars & center oval, 4 knobs, BC, SW........**$45.00**

L-652, table, wood, large center front slide rule dial, 5 pushbuttons, top louvers, 2 knobs, BC **$50.00**

L-740, table, 1941, walnut, center front slide rule dial, 5 pushbuttons, top grill bars, 4 knobs, BC, SW, 7 tubes, AC........**$75.00**

L-915, console, 1940, walnut, upper front slanted slide rule dial, pushbuttons, lower grill w/vertical bars, BC, SW, 9 tubes, AC ..**$125.00**

L-916, console, 1941, wood, upper front slanted slide rule dial, pushbuttons, lower grill w/vertical bars, BC, 2SW, AC ..**$120.00**

LB-412, portable, 1941, two-tone case, inner dial and grill bars, fold-open front, handle, BC **$45.00**

LB-502, portable, 1941, plastic, inner dial and horizontal grill bars, fold-open front, handle, AC/DC/battery **$45.00**

LB-530, portable, 1940, leatherette, inner slide rule dial & knobs, fold-open top, front horizontal louvers, handle, AC/battery.......**$30.00**

LB-530X, portable, 1940, leatherette, inner slide rule dial & knobs, fold-open top, front horizontal louvers, handle, AC/battery **$30.00**

LB-603, portable, 1941, two-tone leatherette, inner right dial over horizontal grill bars, fold-up front, handle, AC/DC/battery........**$35.00**

LB-700, portable, 1940, cloth covered, upper front dial, lower horizontal grill bars, handle, BC, AC/DC/battery **$30.00**

LB-702, portable, 1941, cloth covered, inner top dial & knobs, lift-up lid, front horizontal grill bars, battery **$25.00**

LC-619, console-R/P, 1941, two-tone walnut, inner right front slide rule dial, left lift top, inner phono, BC, SW, 6 tubes.....**$130.00**

LC-638, table-R/P, 1941, walnut, front slide rule dial, horizontal louvers, 4 knobs, lift top, inner phono, 6 tubes, AC.......**$35.00**

LC-648, console-R/P, 1941, two-tone walnut, inner right front slide rule dial, door, left lift top, inner phono, BC, 6 tubes ...**$120.00**

LC-658, table-R/P, 1941, mahogany veneer, outer front dial & grill, 4 knobs, lift top, inner phono, BC, 6 tubes, AC......**$30.00**

LC-679, table-R/P, 1942, wood, center front dial, 6 pushbuttons, 2 knobs, right & left side wrap-around cloth grills w/horizontal bars, lift top, inner phono, AC......................................**$40.00**

LF-115, console, 1940, walnut, upper front slanted slide rule dial, pushbuttons, lower grill w/vertical bars, BC, FM, SW, 11 tubes **$135.00**

LF-116, console, 1940, walnut, upper front slanted slide rule dial, pushbuttons, lower grill w/vertical bars, BC, FM, SW, 11 tubes...**$125.00**

LFC-1118, console-R/P, 1940, walnut, inner right front slide rule dial, pushbuttons, door, left lift top, inner phono, BC, FM, SW, 11 tubes...**$150.00**

LFC-1128, console-R/P, 1940, walnut, inner right front slide rule dial, pushbuttons, door, left pull-out phono drawer, BC, FM, SW, 11 tubes **$140.00**

M-51A, tombstone, 1935, two-tone wood, rounded top, lower front square airplane dial, cloth grill w/vertical bars, 4 knobs ..**$125.00**

M-61, tombstone, 1934, wood, shouldered, center square airplane dial, upper grill w/vertical bars, BC, SW, AC **$135.00**

M-81, tombstone, 1934, wood, center front square airplane dial, upper grill w/vertical bars, 5 knobs, BC, SW, 8 tubes, AC...........**$125.00**

L-660, table, 1941, wood, front slide rule dial w/chrome escutcheon, 5 pushbuttons, 2 knobs, BC, AC.........$60.00

L-678, table-R/P, 1941, wood, center front dial, right & left wrap-around grills, lift top, inner phono, AC **$35.00**

M-103, table, plastic, lower front curved slide rule dial, upper horizontal louvers, 2 knobs, BC.............................$45.00

P-671, portable, 1958, black/white plastic, right side dial knob, horizontal front grill bars with GE logo, handle, AC/DC/battery **$20.00**

P-672, portable, 1958, terra cotta/white plastic, right side dial knob, horizontal front grill bars with GE logo, handle, AC/DC/battery **$20.00**

P-673, portable, 1958, turquoise/white plastic, right side dial knob, horizontal front grill bars with GE logo, handle, AC/DC/battery **$20.00**

P-700, portable, plastic, large right front dial, left grill w/horizontal bars, fold-down handle, BC............................**$25.00**

P-735A, portable, 1958, plastic, right side dial knob, left side on/off/volume knob, large front grill area, handle, BC, 4 tubes, AC/DC/battery **$25.00**

S-22 "Junior," console, 1931, wood, lowboy, upper front window dial, lower cloth grill w/cut-outs, 8 tubes, 3 knobs **$125.00**

S-22 "Junior," tombstone, 1931, walnut, lower window dial, upper floral cloth grill, top, brass handle, columns, 3 knobs, 8 tubes, AC **$175.00**

S-22 "Junior," tombstone/stand, 1931, walnut, model S-22 with removable 4 legged stand **$210.00**

S-22A, tombstone, 1932, wood, lower front window dial, upper floral cloth grill, columns, 3 knobs, 8 tubes **$165.00**

S-22C, tombstone, 1934, wood, lower front window dial, upper floral cloth grill, columns, 3 knobs, 8 tubes, AC **$165.00**

S-22X "Junior," tombstone-C, 1931, wood, lower front window dial, upper cloth grill w/cut-outs & center clock, columns, top metal handle, 3 knobs, 8 tubes, AC **$225.00**

S-42 "Junior," console, 1931, walnut, upper front window dial, lower cloth grill w/cut-outs, 3 knobs, 8 tubes...............**$130.00**

S-42B, console, 1931, walnut, upper front window dial, lower cloth grill w/vertical bars, 3 knobs, 8 tubes, battery **$95.00**

T-12 "Midget," cathedral, 1931, wood, lower front window dial w/escutcheon, upper cloth grill w/cut-outs, 3 knobs, 4 tubes, AC **$165.00**

T-101, table, slate gray plastic, large left front dial over horizontal grill bars, feet, BC...**$10.00**

T-102, table, honey beige plastic, large left front dial over horizontal grill bars, feet, BC **$10.00**

T-103, table, mint green plastic, large left front dial over horizontal grill bars, feet, BC **$10.00**

T-115A, table, 1958, plastic, raised upper front slide rule dial, large lower lattice grill, 2 knobs, BC, 6 tubes, AC/DC ...**$10.00**

T-125A, table, 1959, pink plastic, right front dial knob, center lattice grill, left on/off/volume knob, BC, AC/DC **$10.00**

T-125C, table, 1959, pink plastic, right front round dial, center lattice grill, left on/off/volume knob, feet, AC/DC **$10.00**

T-126, table, 1959, beige plastic, right front dial knob, center lattice grill, left on/off/volume knob, BC, AC/DC................**$10.00**

T-126A, table, 1959, beige plastic, right front dial knob, center lattice grill, left on/off/volume knob, BC, AC/DC **$10.00**

T-126C, table, 1959, beige plastic, right front round dial, center lattice grill, left on/off/volume knob, feet, AC/DC **$10.00**

T-127, table, 1959, antique white plastic, right front dial knob, center lattice grill, left on/off/volume knob, BC, AC/DC.......**$10.00**

T-127A, table, 1959, white plastic, right front dial knob, center lattice grill, left on/off/volume knob, BC, AC/DC...............**$10.00**

T-127C, table, 1959, off-white plastic, right front round dial, center lattice grill, left on/off/volume knob, feet, AC/DC...............**$10.00**

T-128, table, 1959, yellow plastic, right round dial, center lattice grill, left on/off/volume knob, feet, AC/DC **$10.00**

T-128C, table, 1959, yellow plastic, right front round dial, center lattice grill, left on/off/volume knob, feet, AC/DC **$10.00**

T-129C, table, 1959, turquoise plastic, right round dial, center lattice grill, left on/off/volume knob, feet, AC/DC..............**$10.00**

T-140D, table, 1966, sage green plastic, large right front dial overlaps dual speaker lattice grill area, feet, BC **$10.00**

T-141, table, 1966, rose beige plastic, large right front dial overlaps dual speaker lattice grill area, feet, BC **$10.00**

T-141D, table, 1966, rose beige plastic, large right front dial overlaps dual speaker lattice grill area, feet, BC **$10.00**

T-142, table, 1966, antique white plastic, large right front dial overlaps dual speaker lattice grill area, feet, BC **$10.00**

T-142D, table, 1966, antique white plastic, large right front dial overlaps dual speaker lattice grill area, feet, BC **$10.00**

T-143, table, 1966, walnut grain plastic, large right front dial overlaps dual speaker lattice grill area, feet, BC **$10.00**

T-150 "Musaphonic," table, 1962, mahogany, lower front slide rule dial, large upper grill area, 4 knobs, AM, FM.........**$15.00**

T-151 "Musaphonic," table, 1962, walnut, lower front slide rule dial, large upper grill area, 4 knobs, AM, FM.................**$15.00**

T-151B "Musaphonic," table, 1962, wood, lower front slide rule dial, large upper grill area, 4 knobs, AM, FM.................**$15.00**

T-165, table, 1961, Wedgwood blue/white plastic, lower right front dial panel over large textured grill area, BC **$15.00**

T-166, table, 1961, mocha/beige plastic, lower right front dial panel over large textured grill area, BC.................**$15.00**

T-170, table, 1961, cocoa/beige plastic, right front vertical dial, large left lattice grill area, 4 knobs, AM, FM **$15.00**

T-171, table, 1961, antique white plastic, right front vertical dial, large left lattice grill area, 4 knobs, AM, FM **$15.00**

T-180, table, antique white plastic, right front dial panel over large grill area w/horizontal bars, feet, FM **$10.00**

T-185, table, Wedgwood blue/white plastic, lower right front dial panel over large textured grill area, FM.................**$10.00**

T-186, table, cocoa/beige plastic, lower right front dial panel over large textured grill area, FM **$10.00**

T-186A, table, cocoa/beige plastic, lower right front dial panel over large textured grill area, 2 knobs, FM **$10.00**

T-210 "Musaphonic," table, 1961, mocha/beige plastic, lower front slanted slide rule dial, large upper cloth grill area, dual speakers, 4 knobs, AM, FM, AC/DC **$20.00**

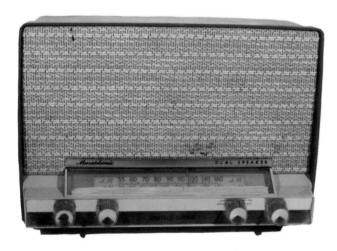

T-210B "Musaphonic," table, 1961, mocha/beige plastic, lower front slanted slide rule dial, large upper cloth grill area, dual speakers, 4 knobs, AM, FM, AC/DC **$20.00**

YRB-60-2, table, 1948, plastic, right front dial printed on flocked grill, horizontal wrap-around bands, BC, AC/DC **$55.00**

YRB 79-2, table, 1948, plastic, lower front slide rule dial, upper recessed horizontal louvers, 2 knobs, BC, AC/DC **$40.00**

YRB 83-1, table, 1948, wood, lower front slide rule dial, upper horizontal louvers, 2 knobs, BC, AC/DC **$45.00**

X-415, table, 1948, wood, center front multi-band dial, upper step-back top w/horizontal louvers, 5 knobs, AC **$75.00**

GENERAL IMPLEMENT
General Implement Corp., Terminal Tower, Cleveland, Ohio

9A5, table, 1948, plastic, right front square dial, left horizontal grill bars, handle, 2 knobs, BC, AC/DC **$85.00**

GENERAL MOTORS

201 "Pioneer," console, 1931, wood, lowboy, inner dial & knobs, double doors, lower grill area, 7 tubes, battery **$110.00**

219A, side table, wood, inner window dial, 3 knobs, fold-down front door, stretcher base.................**$120.00**

250 "Little General," cathedral, 1931, walnut, lower front window dial, upper scalloped grill w/cut-outs, 7 tubes, 3 knobs, AC.................**$250.00**

250A "Little General," cathedral, 1931, wood, lower front window dial, upper cloth grill w/cut-outs, 7 tubes, 3 knobs, AC ..**$250.00**

251 "Valere," console, 1931, wood, lowboy, upper front window dial, lower cloth grill w/cut-outs, 3 knobs, AC.................**$130.00**

252 "Cosmopolitan," console, 1931, wood, inner front dial, 3 knobs, small sliding door, lower vertical grill bars, 10 tubes, AC **$135.00**

281, ashtray/remote control unit, metal, looks like an ashtray on floor stand, upper window dial, 2 knobs **$185.00**

GENERAL TELEVISION
General Radio & Television Corp., Chicago, Illinois

4B5, table, 1947, plastic, right front square dial, left horizontal louvers, 2 knobs, BC, AC/DC.................**$35.00**

6C5, table, 1948, plastic, right front square dial, left cloth grill w/3 vertical bars, 2 knobs, BC **$45.00**

9B6P, table, 1948, plastic, right front square dial over large metal wrap-around perforated grill, handle, 2 knobs, BC, AC/DC.................**$40.00**

14A4F, table, 1946, plastic, right front square dial, left horizontal louvers, 2 knobs, BC, battery $35.00

17A5, table, 1946, wood, right front square dial, left plastic horizontal grill louvers, zig-zag strip on base, 2 knobs, BC, AC/DC ..$45.00

19A5, table, 1946, wood, right front square dial outlined in plastic, left plastic horizontal louvers, 2 knobs, BC, AC/DC $40.00

21A4, portable, 1947, luggage-style, cloth w/lower stripes, right front square dial, left grill, handle, 2 knobs, BC, battery...$25.00

22A5C, table-R/P, 1947, wood, right front square dial, 2 knobs, left grill, lift top, inner phono, BC, AC $30.00

23A6, portable, 1947, luggage-style, cloth covered, right front square dial, left grill, 2 knobs, handle, BC, AC/DC/battery $25.00

24B6, table, 1948, wood, right front square dial, left horizontal grill bars, handle, 2 knobs, BC, AC/DC $50.00

25B5, portable, 1947, two-tone, right front square dial over large perforated grill, 2 knobs, handle, BC, AC/DC/battery $30.00

26B5, portable, 1947, two-tone leatherette, right front dial panel over large grill area, handle, 2 knobs, BC, AC/DC/battery $30.00

27C5, table, 1948, plastic, right front square dial, left cloth grill w/3 vertical bars, 2 knobs, BC, AC/DC $45.00

27C5L, table, 1948, plastic, right front square dial, left cloth grill w/3 vertical bars, 2 knobs, BC, AC/DC..........................$45.00

49, table, wood, right front square dial, left cloth grill, plastic grill bars/dial bezel/handle/knobs, AC/DC $60.00

526, table, 1940, wood, right front dial, left grill w/horizontal bars, plastic dial bezel/handle/knobs, BC, AC/DC ...$50.00

534 "Grand Piano," table-N, wood, looks like grand piano, inner right dial, left G-clef grill, lift top, 5 tubes, 2 knobs, BC, AC/DC...$295.00

591, table, 1940, Catalin w/plastic trim, right front dial, left horizontal grill bars, handle, 2 knobs...................................$650.00+

GILFILLAN
Gilfillan Bros. Inc.,
1815 Venice Boulevard,
Los Angeles, California

The Gilfillan company, originally formed as a smelting and refining outfit, began to manufacture and sell radio parts in 1922 and by 1924 they were advertising complete radios and soon grew to be one of the largest radio manufacturers on the West coast. The last radios made by Gilfillan were produced in 1948.

5, cathedral, 1932, wood, lower front window dial, upper cloth grill w/cut-outs, scrolled top, 3 knobs, 5 tubes, AC $275.00

5-F, table, 1941, plastic, right front dial, left horizontal louvers, 5 tubes, 2 knobs $45.00

5-L, portable, 1941, striped, right front square dial over horizontal grill bars, handle, 2 knobs, 5 tubes, AC/DC $35.00

10, table, 1926, carved walnut, rectangular case, slanted front panel w/center dial, 5 tubes, battery............................$150.00

16H, table, wood, right front dial, left cloth grill w/"X" cut-out, handle, 2 knobs, BC, AC/DC......................................$45.00

20, console, 1926, mahogany, lowboy, upper slanted panel w/center dial, lower built-in speaker, 6 tubes, battery...........$195.00

56B, table, 1946, wood, metal front panel w/right square dial & left perforated grill, 2 knobs, BC, AC/DC............................$50.00

56B-CB, table, 1946, wood, metal front panel w/right square dial & left perforated grill, 2 knobs, BC, AC/DC........$50.00

58M, table, 1948, plastic, Deco, rounded right w/half-round dial, left horizontal wrap-around louvers, 2 knobs, BC, AC/DC **$125.00**

58W, table, plastic, Deco, rounded right w/half-round dial, left horizontal wrap-around louvers, 2 knobs, BC, AC/DC **$125.00**

63X, tombstone, 1935, wood, center front round dial, upper grill w/cut-outs, 4 knobs, 3 band, AC **$125.00**

66AM, table, 1946, wood, upper front slanted slide rule dial, lower cloth grill, 2 knobs, BC, AC....................................**$35.00**

66B "Overland," portable, 1946, leatherette, metal front panel w/right dial & left perforated grill, double doors, handle, 2 knobs, BC, AC/DC/battery...............................**$50.00**

66PM "El Dorado," table-R/P, 1946, wood, inner right vertical dial, 4 knobs, left phono, front grill, lift top, BC, AC.......**$25.00**

66S, table, 1939, wood, upper front dial, right & left side wrap-around grills w/horizontal bars, AC **$65.00**

68-48, console-R/P/Rec, 1949, wood, inner right slide rule dial, 4 knobs, left pull-out phono/recorder drawer, doors, lower grill, BC, AC **$70.00**

68B-D, portable, 1948, "alligator," metal front panel w/right square dial & left perforated grill, handle, 2 knobs, BC, AC/DC/battery **$35.00**

68F, table, 1948, wood, metal front panel w/right square dial & left perforated grill, 3 knobs, AM, FM, AC/DC.....................**$45.00**

80, table, 1927, wood, low rectangular case, center front window dial, 3 knobs, 6 tubes, AC **$150.00**

86U, tombstone, 1947, wood, center front slide rule dial, upper grill, 4 knobs, 6 pushbuttons, BC, 2SW, AC **$70.00**

100, console, 1929, wood, lowboy, inner front dial, lower cloth grill w/cut-outs, doors, 8 tubes, AC **$165.00**

105, console, 1929, wood, lowboy, upper front window dial, lower cloth grill, fluted columns, 3 knobs, AC **$130.00**

108-48, console-R/P/Rec, 1949, wood, inner right front slide rule dial, 5 knobs, left pull-out phono/recorder drawer, doors, BC, FM, AC **$70.00**

119, console, 1940, wood, lowboy, half-round Hepplewhite-style, upper front slide rule dial, AC **$300.00**

GN-1 "Neutrodyne," table, 1924, wood, low rectangular case, inner panel, fold-down front, doors, 5 tubes, battery ...**$165.00**

GN-2 "Neutrodyne," table, 1924, wood, low rectangular case, 3 dial front panel, 5 tubes, battery **$130.00**

GN-3 "Neutrodyne," table, 1925, wood, high rectangular case, 2 dial slant front panel with 4 exposed tubes, battery **$195.00**

GN-5 "Neutrodyne," table, 1925, mahogany, low rectangular case, 3 dial front panel, 5 tubes, battery **$140.00**

GN-6, table, 1925, mahogany, tall case, slanted front panel w/2 dials and 4 exposed tubes, battery..............................**$200.00**

GLOBAL

GR-7000, portable, plastic, right front dial, upper right thumbwheel on/off/volume knob, left grill w/horizontal bars, made in Japan, BC, 4 tubes, battery..........................**$50.00**

GLOBE

Globe Electronics, Inc.,
225 West 17th Street,
New York, New York

5BP1, portable, 1947, luggage-style, inner left dial, right 2-section grill, 3 knobs, fold-down front, handle, BC, AC/DC/battery..........**$35.00**

6P1, table-R/P, 1947, wood, front slanted slide rule dial, lower grill, 2 knobs, 3/4 lift top, inner phono, BC, AC..............**$35.00**

6U1, table, 1947, wood, upper front slanted slide rule dial, lower cloth grill, 2 knobs, BC, AC/DC **$35.00**

7CP-1, console-R/P, 1947, wood, center front square dial, 2 knobs, 4-section grill area, lower record storage, lift top, inner phono, BC, AC **$50.00**

51, table, 1947, swirled plastic, right front round dial, left horizontal wrap-around louvers, 2 knobs, BC, AC/DC **$85.00**

62C, table-R/P, 1947, wood, upper front slanted slide rule dial, 4 knobs, lower grill, 3/4 lift top, inner phono, BC, SW, AC..**$35.00**

85, table-C, 1948, wood, large raised electric clock, right thumbwheel dial, left thumbwheel on/off/volume knob, BC, AC..**$65.00**

454, portable, 1948, inner dial, geometric grill, 2 knobs, flip-open front, handle, BC, 4 tubes, AC/DC/battery **$45.00**

456, portable, 1948, leatherette, lower front slide rule dial, upper grill, handle, 2 knobs, BC, battery **$20.00**

457, table, 1948, plastic, right front half-round dial, left horizontal wrap-around louvers, 2 knobs, BC, AC/DC **$75.00**

500, portable, 1947, leatherette, inner top slide rule dial, 2 knobs, fold-up lid, lower front horizontal louvers, BC, AC/DC...**$30.00**

517, table-R/P, 1947, leatherette, left front dial, right perforated grill, 2 knobs, open top phono, BC, AC/DC **$15.00**

552, table, 1947, plastic, streamline, right front dial over horizontal wrap-around louvers, 2 knobs, BC, AC/DC................**$115.00**

553, table, 1947, plastic, right front half-round dial, left horizontal wrap-around louvers, 2 knobs, BC, AC/DC **$75.00**

558, table-C, 1948, wood, large raised electric clock, right thumbwheel dial, left thumbwheel on/off/volume knob, BC, AC..**$65.00**

559, table-N, 1948, horse stands on wood base, 2 thumbwheel knobs, horizontal grill slats, BC, AC/DC **$200.00**

GLOBE TROTTER
Globe Trotter Radio Co.

Globe Trotter, table-N, 1936, looks like a world globe on a stand, tunes by turning globe, 6-color maps, 4 tubes, AC/DC..**$450.00**

GLORITONE

5T10, table, plastic, lower front slide rule dial, upper 2-section grill area w/horizontal bars, twin speakers, 2 knobs, BC..**$25.00**

9B, console, 1932, wood, lowboy, upper front quarter-round dial, lower grill w/cut-outs, 9 tubes, 6 legs **$140.00**

24, cathedral, 1933, wood, center front window dial, upper cloth grill w/cut-outs, fluted columns, 4 tubes, 2 knobs **$225.00**

25A, table, 1932, wood, rectangular case, right front window dial, center cloth grill w/cut-outs, 5 tubes **$65.00**

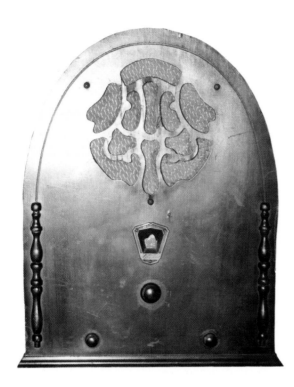

26, cathedral, 1931, wood, center front window dial, upper grill w/cut-outs, side columns, 3 knobs, 5 tubes ...**$150.00**

26-P, cathedral, 1929, wood, center front window dial w/escutcheon, upper cloth grill w/cut-outs, 3 knobs **$160.00**

27, cathedral, 1930, wood, modern, 2 or more versions, lower right front thumbwheel dial, upper grill w/cut-outs, AC **$175.00**

27S, console, 1930, wood, lowboy, upper left front dial, lower "clover-leaf" grill cut-outs, rounded top **$200.00**

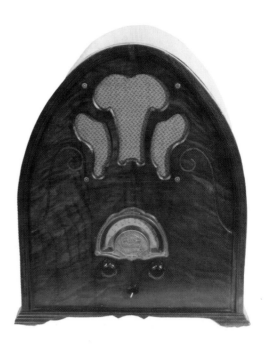

99, cathedral, 1931, wood, lower front half-round dial w/escutcheon, upper 3-section cloth grill, 3 knobs **$225.00**

99A, cathedral, 1931, wood, lower front half-round dial w/escutcheon, upper 3-section cloth grill, 3 knobs **$225.00**

305, cathedral, two-tone wood, center front window dial, upper cloth grill w/cut-outs, 2 knobs **$225.00**

—————————————————————————

GOODYEAR

015060, table, tall case, two-tone wood, center front dial w/plastic escutcheon, tuning eye, 5 pushbuttons, 4 knobs, BC, SW, AC...**$65.00**

—————————————————————————

GRANCO

**Granco Products, Inc.,
36-17 20th Avenue, Long Island City, New York**

601, table, 1959, plastic, upper right front window dial, lower lattice grill, 2 knobs, Hi-Fi, FM, 5 tubes, AC $20.00

610, table, 1955, plastic, center front horizontal dial over horizontal grill bars, 2 knobs, FM, 6 tubes, AC/DC $10.00

611, table, 1959, plastic, center front horizontal dial over large lattice grill, 2 knobs, Hi-Fi, FM, 6 tubes, AC/DC $15.00

704, table, 1962, plastic, lower left front 2-band dial panel over large lattice grill, feet, AM, FM......................................$20.00

720, table, 1955, plastic, center front horizontal dial over horizontal grill bars, 2 knobs, AM, FM, 7 tubes, AC/DC............$15.00

750, table-R/P, 1956, wood, lower front slide rule dial, large upper grill area, 4 knobs, 3/4 lift top, inner 3 speed phono, BC, FM, 7 tubes, AC...$25.00

770, table-C, 1957, plastic, left front dial over horizontal bars, right round alarm clock, 2 knobs, BC, FM, 7 tubes, AC $25.00

RP-1220, console-R/P, 1958, wood, inner right front dial, 5 knobs, fold-down door, large lower grill area, left lift top, inner phono, hi-fi, BC, FM, 12 tubes, AC...$75.00

GRANTLINE

**W. T. Grant Co.,
1441 Broadway, New York, New York**

500, table, 1946, plastic, small right front dial, left horizontal grill bars, 2 knobs, BC, AC/DC...$45.00

501, table, 1946, plastic, small right front dial, left horizontal grill bars, 2 knobs, BC, 5 tubes, AC/DC...............................$45.00

501A, table, 1946, plastic, small right front dial, left horizontal grill bars, 2 knobs, BC, AC/DC.......................................$45.00

501-7, table, 1948, plastic, arched dial at top of semi-circular front grill design, 2 knobs, BC, AC/DC $50.00

502, Series A, table, plastic, Deco, right front slide rule dial, left round grill w/horizontal bars, 4 pushbuttons, right side knob, 5 tubes $120.00

504-7, table, 1947, plastic, right front round dial over horizontal louvers, 2 knobs, BC, AC/DC $30.00

508-7, portable, 1948, plastic, arched dial at top of semi-circular front grill design, handle, 2 knobs, BC, AC/DC/battery...$40.00

510A, portable, 1947, upper front slide rule dial, lower metal grill, 2 knobs on top of case, handle, BC, AC/DC/battery $30.00

605, table, 1946, plastic, streamline, right front half-round dial, left horizontal wrap-around grill bars, right side knob, 6 pushbuttons, BC, AC/DC $165.00

606, table, 1946, plastic, streamline, right front half-round dial, left horizontal wrap-around grill bars, right side knob, 6 pushbuttons, BC, AC/DC $165.00

651, table, 1947, plastic, upper front slanted slide rule dial, lower horizontal wrap-around louvers, 2 knobs, BC, AC/DC ..$45.00

5610, end table, 1948, wood, front slide rule dial, 2 knobs, grill cut-outs, raised top edge, BC, AC/DC..........................$95.00

6541, table-R/P, wood, upper front slanted slide rule dial, lower horizontal grill bars, 3 knobs, lift top, inner phono, AC ..$30.00

6547, table-R/P, 1947, upper front slanted slide rule dial, lower horizontal grill bars, 4 knobs, lift top, inner phono, BC, AC..$30.00

GRAYBAR

Graybar Electric Co.

310, table, 1928, wood, low rectangular case, center front dial, lift top, 7 tubes, 2 knobs, 1 switch, AC $85.00

330, table, 1929, wood, low rectangular case, center front window dial, lift top, 2 knobs, 1 switch, AC.....................................$85.00

GB-4, cathedral, 1931, wood, lower front window dial w/escutcheon, upper 3-section cloth grill, 3 knobs, AC $135.00

GREBE

**A. H. Grebe,
10 Van Wyck Avenue,
Richmond Hill, New York**

A. H. Grebe began as a young man to produce crystal sets and by 1920 had formed A. H. Grebe & Company. The popular Grebe Synchrophase, introduced in the mid-twenties, was the highlight of the company's career. The ever-present Doctor Mu, the oriental "sage of radio," and his advice on life was a regular feature of Grebe advertising. By 1932, the original Grebe company was out of business.

60, cathedral, 1933, walnut, center front window dial w/escutcheon, upper grill w/cut-outs, 3 knobs, 6 tubes $250.00

80, tombstone, 1933, walnut, center front window dial w/escutcheon, upper grill w/cut-outs, 3 knobs, 8 tubes $160.00

84, console, 1933, walnut, lowboy, inner front window dial, lower grill cut-outs, sliding doors, 6 legs, 8 tubes $175.00

160, console, 1930, wood, lowboy, upper front window dial & carvings, lower cloth grill w/cut-outs, AC.....................$175.00

206-L, table, 1937, wood, step-down top, right front airplane dial, left cloth grill w/3 vertical bars, 4 knobs, 6 tubes, AC $85.00

270, console, 1929, wood, lowboy, upper front window dial, lower cloth grill w/cut-outs, stretcher base $150.00

285, console, 1929, wood, upper front window dial, lower cloth grill w/cut-outs, sliding doors, AC $175.00

309-L, table, 1937, wood, step-down top, large right front telephone dial, left cloth grill w/cut-outs, 5 knobs, BC, SW, 9 tubes, AC..$125.00

370-C, table, 1936, wood, large center front dial, right & left cloth wrap-around grills w/horizontal bars, 4 knobs, BC, SW, 7 tubes, AC...$90.00

450, console-R/P, 1929, wood, front window dial, lower cloth grill w/cut-outs, stretcher base, inner phono, AC $160.00

3016-4, console, 1937, walnut, upper front telephone dial, lower cloth grill w/vertical bars, 5 knobs, BC, SW, 16 tubes, AC.......$250.00

AC-Six, table, 1928, wood, low rectangular case, front window dial w/escutcheon, 7 tubes, AC $175.00

AHG-9, tombstone, 1935, wood, lower front round airplane dial, upper cloth grill w/3 vertical bars, 5 knobs, BC, SW, 9 tubes.......$145.00

AHG-90, console, 1935, wood, upper front round airplane dial, lower cloth grill w/vertical bars, BC, SW, 9 tubes $125.00

AHG-120, console, 1935, wood, upper front round airplane dial, lower cloth grill w/cut-outs, BC, SW, 12 tubes............$140.00

Challenger 5, table, 1938, plastic, center front square dial, right & left wrap-around grills w/horizontal bars, 5 tubes, AC/DC..$50.00

CR-3, table, 1920, wood, 2 styles, low rectangular case, 2 dial black front panel, lift top, battery $450.00

CR-3A, table, 1920, wood, low rectangular case, 2 dial front panel, 1 exposed tube, battery, very rare...............**$3,000.00+**
CR-5, table, 1921, wood, low rectangular case, 2 dial black Bakelite front panel, battery.................................**$500.00**
CR-8, table, 1921, wood, low rectangular case, 3 dial black Bakelite front panel, battery...............................**$500.00**

CR-9, table, 1921, wood, low rectangular case, 2 dial black Bakelite panel, lift top, 3 tubes, battery..................$500.00
CR-12, table, 1923, wood, low rectangular case, 2 dial black Bakelite front panel, 4 tubes, battery **$600.00**
CR-13, table, 1923, wood, low rectangular case, 3 dial black Bakelite front panel, lift top, battery **$650.00**

CR-14, table, 1923, wood, low rectangular case, 2 dial black Bakelite panel, lift top, 3 tubes, battery..................$550.00
CR-18, table, 1926, wood, rectangular case, 2 front thumbwheel dials, top exposed meter coils, battery **$750.00**
MU-1 w/chain "Synchrophase," table, 1925, wood, rectangular case, 3 diamond-shaped thumbwheel dials, with dial chain, battery **$225.00**
MU-1 w/o chain "Synchrophase," table, 1925, wood, rectangular case, 3 diamond-shaped thumbwheel dials, w/o dial chain, battery **$225.00**
SK-4, console, 1930, wood, lowboy, large front dial escutcheon w/thumbwheel tuning, lower round grill w/cut-outs, AC..**$170.00**
Synchronette, table, 1933, wood w/inlay, Deco, right front dial, center grill w/cut-outs, stepped top, 5 tubes, 2 knobs, AC **$85.00**
Synchrophase Seven, table, 1927, two-tone wood, low rectangular case, center thumbwheel dial, front pillars, battery **$175.00**

———————————

GRUNOW
General Household Utilities Co.,
Chicago, Illinois

7C, console, wood, upper front round airplane dial, lower shield-shaped grill w/2 vertical bars, 5 knobs **$125.00**
450, tombstone, 1934, wood, small case, lower front dial, large grill w/chrome cut-outs, BC, SW, AC.........................**$185.00**

470, tombstone, 1935, walnut, rounded shoulders, lower front dial, upper grill w/cut-outs, 4 tubes, AC **$95.00**

500, tombstone, 1933, wood, step-down top, center front window dial, upper cloth grill w/chrome cut-outs, 2 knobs, AC $250.00

501, table, 1933, two-tone wood, right front window dial, center grill w/chrome cut-outs, 2 knobs, AC.................$150.00
520, table, 1935, right & left front windows w/escutcheons, center grill w/vertical chrome bars, 5 tubes, AC/DC..............**$125.00**
566, table, 1935, wood, right front round dial, left cloth grill w/horizontal bars, 2 knobs **$75.00**
570, tombstone, two-tone wood, lower front round dial, upper cloth grill w/cut-outs, 5 tubes, 3 knobs **$120.00**
580, tombstone, 1935, walnut, center front round dial, upper grill w/cut-outs, 4 knobs, BC, SW, 5 tubes, AC **$125.00**
581, console, 1935, wood, upper front round dial, lower cloth grill w/cut-outs, 4 knobs, AC **$140.00**
588, table, 1937, wood, right front Tele-dial, left wrap-around grill w/center horizontal bar, 3 knobs, 5 tubes **$85.00**
589, console, 1937, wood, upper front Tele-dial, lower round cloth grill w/2 vertical bars, 4 knobs, BC, SW, 5 tubes, AC..**$200.00**
594, table, 1937, ivory finish, "violin-shape," center front round chrome grill w/center airplane dial, 5 tubes, 2 knobs ..**$120.00**
640, tombstone, 1935, wood, center front round dial, upper cloth grill w/cut-outs, 4 knobs, BC, SW, 6 tubes, AC **$110.00**

641, console, 1935, two-tone wood, upper front round dial, lower cloth grill with cut-outs, 6 tubes, AC **$125.00**

653, console, 1937, walnut, upper front slanted Tele-dial, lower cloth grill w/vertical bars, 4 knobs, 6 tubes, AC...........**$200.00**

654, upright table, 1937, wood, upper front round airplane dial, lower horizontal grill bars, 4 knobs, BC, SW, 6 tubes, AC **$100.00**

660, tombstone, 1934, wood, lower front round dial, upper cloth grill w/cut-outs, fluting, 4 knobs, BC, SW, 6 tubes.......**$140.00**

671, console, 1934, wood, upper front round dial, lower grill with cut-outs, 4 knobs, BC, SW, 6 tubes, AC **$130.00**

681, console, 1935, wood, upper front round dial, lower cloth grill with vertical bars, 4 knobs, 6 tubes, AC **$130.00**

700, tombstone, 1933, wood, step-down top, center front window dial, upper cloth grill w/chrome cut-outs, 5 knobs, 7 tubes, AC..**$235.00**

750, tombstone, 1934, wood, step-down top, center front round dial, upper cloth grill w/cut-outs, BC, 3SW, AC **$125.00**

761, console, 1935, wood, upper front round dial, lower cloth grill w/2 vertical bars, 5 knobs, BC, SW, 7 tubes, AC **$125.00**

871, console, 1935, wood, upper front round dial, lower cloth grill with 2 vertical bars, 5 knobs, BC, SW, 8 tubes, AC **$130.00**

1081, console, 1937, two-tone walnut, upper front Tele-dial, lower grill w/vertical bars, BC, SW, 10 tubes, AC **$250.00**

1171, console, 1935, wood, upper front round dial, lower cloth grill w/2 vertical bars, 5 knobs, BC, SW, 11 tubes, AC **$165.00**

1183, console, 1937, wood, upper front Tele-dial, lower cloth grill w/6 vertical bars, 4 knobs, BC, SW, 11 tubes, AC **$275.00**

1191, console, 1936, wood, upper front round dial, tuning eye, lower cloth grill w/horizontal bars, BC, SW, 11 tubes, AC **$180.00**

1241, console, 1935, wood, upper front round dial, lower cloth grill with 2 vertical bars, BC, SW, 12 tubes, AC **$170.00**

1291, console, 1936, wood, upper front Tele-dial, lower cloth grill w/5 vertical bars, 4 knobs, BC, 3SW, 12 tubes, AC **$300.00**

1541, console, 1936, wood, upper front Tele-dial, lower cloth grill w/7 vertical bars, 5 knobs, BC, SW, 15 tubes, AC **$350.00**

GUILD
**Guild Radio & Television Co.,
460 North Eucalyptus Avenue,
Inglewood, California**

380T "Town Crier," table-N, wood, looks like an old lantern, inner vertical slide rule dial, 4 knobs, front door, AM/FM......$100.00

484 "Spice Chest," table-N, 1956, wood, spice chest design, inner slide rule dial, 3 knobs, double front shutter or panel doors, 2 drawers, BC, AC/DC **$95.00**

556 "Country Belle," wall-N, 1956, wood, looks like an old wall telephone, side crank tunes stations, 2 side knobs, AC ..**$65.00**

638B-A "Buccaneer Chest," table-N, 1965, wood, looks like an old treasure chest, inner panel with Old World map, slide rule dial, 4 knobs, leather straps, AM, FM, 7 tubes, AC $125.00

785 **"Grafonola,"** table-R/P-N, 1959, wood, looks like an old crank phonograph complete w/horn, top phono, side louvers, BC, AC **$125.00**
818 **"Bonnet Box,"** console-R/P-N, wood, looks like an old dry sink, inner radio & phono, lift lid, AM, FM **$175.00**
921ML **"New Englander,"** console-R/P-N, wood, looks like a roll-top desk, top compartment w/fold-back lid contains radio controls, phono is under roll-top, front grill, AM, FM **$300.00**
T/K 1577 **"Teakettle,"** table-N, wood, china & brass, looks like an old tea kettle, top lifts for controls, bottom speaker **$125.00**

GULBRANSEN
**Gulbransen Co.,
816 North Kedzie Avenue,
Chicago, Illinois**

130, cathedral, 1931, wood, center front window dial, upper cloth grill w/lyre cut-out, fluted columns, 3 knobs, AC..........**$400.00**
135, console, 1931, wood, lowboy, upper front window dial, lower grill w/cut-outs, stretcher base, AC.............................**$130.00**
235, console, 1931, wood, upper front window dial, lower cloth grill w/cut-outs, stretcher base, AC..............................**$130.00**
9950, console, 1930, wood, highboy, upper front window dial, speaker grill underneath cabinet, AC **$150.00**

HALLDORSON
**Halldorson Co.,
1772 Wilson Ave., Chicago, Illinois**

RD-400, table, 1925, wood, low rectangular case, 2 dial front panel, 4 tubes, battery..**$95.00**
RF-500, table, 1925, wood, low rectangular case, 3 dial front panel, 5 tubes, battery..**$100.00**

HALLICRAFTERS
**The Hallicrafters Co.,
5th & Kostner Avenues, Chicago, Illinois**

The Hallicrafters Company was formed by Bill Halligan in 1933 for the manufacture of receivers and phonos for other companies. By 1935, Hallicrafters was producing its own ham radio equipment. During WW II, the company had many military contracts. Hallicrafters enjoyed a reputation for reasonable prices which they were able to offer due to their large volume of business.

5R10, table, 1951, metal, large center front slide rule dial, top left perforated grill, 4 knobs, BC, 3SW, AC/DC........**$50.00**
5R10A, table, 1952, metal, large center front slide rule dial, top left perforated grill, 4 knobs, multi-band, AC/DC **$50.00**
5R14, table, 1951, plastic, center front round metal dial ring over perforated grill panel, 2 knobs, BC, AC/DC **$40.00**
5R24, portable, 1952, center front round dial over woven grill, handle, 2 knobs, BC, AC/DC/battery **$35.00**
5R30A "Continental," table, 1952, right front slide rule dial, left checkered perforated grill, 3 knobs, BC, SW, AC/DC ...**$40.00**
5R50, table-C, 1952, right front slide rule dial, left square alarm clock, top checkered grill, 6 knobs, BC, SW, AC **$45.00**
5R60, table, 1955, mahogany plastic, left front round dial, right checkered grill, 2 center knobs, feet, BC **$35.00**
5R61, table, 1955, ivory plastic, right front round dial, left checkered grill, 2 center knobs, feet, BC **$35.00**
EC-306, table-R/P, 1948, wood, center front dial, right & left grills, lift top, inner phono, BC, SW, AC **$40.00**
EX-306, table-R/P, 1948, wood, center front dial, right & left grills, lift top, inner phono, BC, SW, AC **$40.00**
S-55, table, 1949, metal, center front slide rule dial, top wrap-over perforated grill, 4 knobs, BC, FM, AC/DC **$40.00**
S-58, table, 1949, metal, left rectangular front slide rule dial, right perforated grill w/"h" logo, 4 knobs, BC, FM, AC...........**$55.00**
S-80, table, 1952, upper front slanted slide rule dial, lower perforated grill w/"h" logo, 3 knobs, BC, SW **$45.00**
TW-25, portable, 1953, leatherette, large center front round metal dial ring over perforated grill panel, handle, 2 knobs, BC **$35.00**

TW100, portable, British tan leather, large center front metal dial ring overlaps lower grill cut-outs, upper right thumbwheel on/off/volume knob, handle, BC.....................**$35.00**

TW101, portable, Cordovan leather, large center front metal dial ring overlaps lower grill cut-outs, upper right thumbwheel on/off/volume knob, handle, BC **$35.00**

TW102, portable, champagne leather, large center front metal dial ring overlaps lower grill cut-outs, upper right thumbwheel on/off/volume knob, handle, BC **$35.00**

TW103, portable, cherry red leather, large center front metal dial ring overlaps lower grill cut-outs, upper right thumbwheel on/off/volume knob, handle, BC **$45.00**

TW104, portable, cloud blue leather, large center front metal dial ring overlaps lower grill cut-outs, upper right thumbwheel on/off/volume knob, handle, BC **$45.00**

TW105, portable, bonanza yellow leather, large center front metal dial ring overlaps lower grill cut-outs, upper right thumbwheel on/off/volume knob, handle, BC **$45.00**

TW-500, portable, 1954, leatherette, inner multi-band slide rule dial, lattice grill, flip-up front w/map, telescope antenna, handle, AC/DC/battery **$75.00**

TW-1000 "World Wide," portable, 1953, leatherette, inner multi-band slide rule dial, flip-up front w/map, telescope antenna, handle, 8 bands, AC/DC/battery......................**$125.00**

TW-2000 "World Wide," portable, 1955, leatherette, inner multi-band slide rule dial, flip-up front w/map, telescope antenna, handle, 8 bands, AC/DC/battery **$125.00**

———————————————

HALSON

Halson Radio Mfg. Co.,
New York, New York

10, table, 1938, two-tone wood, rectangular dial, left cloth wrap-around grill w/vertical bars, 3 knobs, BC, SW, 6 tubes, AC/DC **$55.00**

43B-A, table, 1933, walnut, step-down top, right front dial, center round grill w/cut-outs, 2 knobs, 4 tubes, AC/DC......................**$85.00**

610, tombstone, 1934, wood, center front round dial, upper cloth grill w/cut-outs, 3 knobs, BC, SW, AC **$125.00**

A5, table, 1938, Catalin, small case, right front round dial, left cloth grill w/horizontal wrap-around bars, 2 knobs ..**$700.00+**

CR53, table, wood w/inlay, right front dial, center cloth grill w/cut-outs, 2 knobs, BC **$85.00**

T10, table, 1937, wood, right front dial, left cloth grill w/cut-outs, 2 knobs, BC, AC......................**$45.00**

———————————————

HANSEN

Hansen Storage Co.,
120 Jefferson St., Milwaukee, Wisconsin

American Crest, table, 1925, wood, low rectangular case, 2 dial front panel, 6 tubes, battery **$125.00**

Bluebird, table, 1925, wood, step-down case, slanted two dial panel, 4 tubes, battery......................**$125.00**

Gold Finch, table, 1925, wood, low rectangular case, 2 dial front panel, 5 tubes, battery......................**$110.00**

———————————————

HARMONY

Harmony Mfg. Co.,
2812 Griffith Ave., Cincinnati, Ohio

5, table, 1925, wood, low rectangular case, front panel w/left dial, 5 tubes, battery......................**$110.00**

———————————————

HARPERS

GK-301, portable, 1962, plastic, right front thumbwheel dial knob overlaps wedge-shaped metal perforated grill area, right side knob, fold-down handle, BC, battery........**$45.00**

———————————————

HARTMAN

Hartman Electrical Mfg. Co.,
31 E. Fifth St.,
Mansfield, Ohio

12-A, console, 1925, wood, lowboy, inner left dial panel, right speaker grill w/cut-outs, fold-down front, lower storage, 5 tubes, battery **$180.00**

12-B, table, 1925, wood, low rectangular case, left dial panel, right speaker grill w/cut-outs, 5 tubes, battery......................**$150.00**

12-C, table, 1925, wood, low rectangular case, center 3 dial panel, 5 tubes, battery......................**$125.00**

———————————————

HERALD

P-156S, portable, plastic, right front thumbwheel dial knob, upper right thumbwheel on/off/volume knob, left lattice grill, fold-down handle, BC......................**$45.00**

———————————————

HETEROPLEX
Heteroplex Mfg. Co.,
423 Market St.,
Philadelphia, Pennsylvania

De Luxe, table, 1925, wood, low rectangular case, 2 dial front panel, top door, 3 tubes, battery..................................$115.00

HITACHI
Electronic Utilities Co., Div. of the Sampson Company,
2244 South Western Avenue, Chicago, Illinois

H-501, table, plastic, right front dial panel, left lattice grill area, feet, 2 knobs, switch, BC, SW, 5 tubes $30.00

HOFFMAN
Hoffman Radio Corp.,
3430 South Hill Street,
Los Angeles, California

A-200, table, 1946, plastic, upper front slide rule dial, lower horizontal louvers, 2 knobs, BC, AC/DC $45.00
A-300, table, 1946, wood, upper front slanted slide rule dial, lower horizontal louvers, 3 knobs, BC, AC..............................$35.00
A-301, table, wood, upper front slanted slide rule dial, pushbuttons, lower horizontal louvers, 3 knobs, BC $40.00
A-309, table, 1947, wood, upper front slide rule dial, lower cloth grill w/metal cut-outs, 2 knobs, BC, AC/DC..................$45.00
A-401, table-R/P, 1947, wood, upper front slide rule dial, lower grill, 3 knobs, lift top, inner phono, BC, AC....................$30.00
A-500, console-R/P, 1946, wood, lowboy style, inner slide rule dial, 3 knobs, 6 pushbuttons, lift top, BC, AC $65.00
A-501, console-R/P, 1946, wood, inner right slide rule dial, 5 knobs, pushbuttons, door, lower front grill w/horizontal bars, BC, 2SW, AC..$100.00
A-700, portable, 1947, upper front slide rule dial, lower lattice grill, handle, 2 knobs, BC, AC/DC/battery............................$40.00
B-400, table-R/P, 1947, wood, upper front dial, lower grill, 2 knobs, 3/4 lift top, inner phono, BC, AC $30.00
B-1000, console-R/P, 1947, wood, modern, tilt-out front, inner left dial, knobs, pushbuttons & right phono, BC, 2SW, AC $90.00
B-8002, console-R/P, 1958, wood, inner left dial, right phono, lift top, large front grill area, feet, BC, FM, 14 tubes, AC $50.00

C-501, console-R/P, 1948, wood, modern, inner right slide rule dial, 5 knobs, pushbuttons, door, left lift top, inner phono, BC, 2SW, AC...$85.00
C-502, console-R/P, 1948, wood, modern, inner right slide rule dial, 5 knobs, 6 pushbuttons, door, left lift top, inner phono, BC, FM, 15 tubes, AC $95.00
C-503, console-R/P, 1948, wood, modern, inner right slide rule dial, 5 knobs, 6 pushbuttons, door, left lift top, inner phono, BC, 2SW, 14 tubes, AC $95.00
C-507, console-R/P, 1948, wood, inner right slide rule dial, 4 knobs, left pull-out phono drawer, front doors fold open, BC, FM, 10 tubes, AC $75.00
C-514, console-R/P, 1948, wood, inner right slide rule dial, 5 knobs, pushbuttons, left lift top, inner phono, BC, FM, 18 tubes, AC...$125.00
C-518, console-R/P/Rec, 1949, wood, inner right slide rule dial, 5 knobs, pushbuttons, doors, left pull-out phono & recorder drawers, BC, FM, 21 tubes, AC...............................$150.00
C-1007, console-R/P/Rec, 1949, wood, inner right slide rule dial, 5 knobs, pushbuttons, doors, left pull-out phono & recorder drawers, BC, FM, 23 tubes, AC...............................$180.00

HORN
Herbert H. Horn Radio Manufacturing Co.,
1625-29 South Hill Street, Los Angeles, California

Riviera PR, console-R/P, 1935, wood, Deco, tubular cabinet, inner front dial, double doors, lift top, inner phono, 6 tubes $500.00
Riviera R, console, 1935, wood, Deco, tubular cabinet, inner front dial & knobs, lower grill, double doors, 6 tubes $500.00

HOWARD
Howard Radio company,
451-469 East Ohio Street, Chicago, Illinois

Howard began selling radio parts in 1922 and complete sets in 1924. By 1949, the company was out of business.

4BT, table, 1939, wood, upper front dial, lower cloth grill w/cut-outs, 3 knobs, battery.....................................$35.00
20, cathedral, 1931, wood, center front window dial, upper grill w/cut-outs, 3 knobs, 7 tubes, AC...............................$250.00
40, console, 1931, wood, lowboy, upper front window dial, lower grill w/cut-outs, stretcher base...................................$135.00
60, console-R/P, 1931, wood, front window dial, lower grill cut-outs, lift top, inner phono, 3 knobs, 9 tubes, AC..........$145.00
150, table, 1925, wood, low rectangular case, slanted 3 dial front panel, 5 tubes, battery.......................................$95.00
200, table, 1925, wood, low rectangular case, 3 dial front panel, 6 tubes, battery..$110.00
214, console, 1937, walnut, upper front oval dial, lower cloth grill w/vertical bars, tuning eye, 5 knobs, BC, SW, 14 tubes, AC...$150.00
218, console, 1937, walnut, upper front round dial, lower cloth grill w/vertical bars, tuning eye, BC, SW, 11 tubes, AC $125.00
225, table, 1937, wood, right front dial, left wrap-over cloth grill w/vertical cut-outs, 4 knobs, BC, SW, AC $65.00
250, console, 1925, wood, lowboy, inner 3 dial panel, fold-down front, built-in speaker, 5 tubes, battery.......................$160.00
250, table, 1937, two-tone wood, right front dial, left vertical grill cut-outs, 4 knobs, BC, SW, AC $60.00
256, table, 1937, walnut, right front round dial, left cloth grill w/cut-outs, 5 knobs, AC...$40.00
259-T, table, 1937, walnut w/inlay, right front round dial, left cloth grill w/vertical bars, 7 tubes, AC/DC............................$45.00
266-T, table, 1937, walnut, right front round dial, left cloth grill w/cut-outs, 4 knobs, 6 tubes, AC..................................$45.00

268, table, 1936, wood, step-down top, large right front round dial, left cloth grill w/vertical bars, tuning eye, 4 knobs, BC, SW, 7 tubes, AC...$70.00

303, console, 1939, walnut, upper front rectangular dial, 4 pushbuttons, lower grill w/center vertical bar, 6 tubes, AC........$125.00

305, table, 1939, two-tone wood, lower front slide rule dial, pushbuttons, large upper grill, 4 knobs, BC, SW, AC $55.00

307, table, 1940, two-tone wood, lower front slide rule dial, large upper grill, BC, SW, 5 tubes, AC $55.00

307-TP, table-R/P, 1941, wood, lower right front slide rule dial, left grill, lift top, inner phono, AC $30.00

308-C, console, 1939, wood, upper front slide rule dial, pushbuttons, lower cloth grill w/center vertical bar, BC, SW, 8 tubes, AC $135.00

308-TT, console, 1939, walnut, slanted top, pushbuttons, tuning eye, front horizontal grill bars, 4 knobs, BC, SW, 8 tubes, AC $165.00

318-D, console, 1938, walnut, upper front slide rule dial, lower cloth grill w/vertical bars, tuning eye, pushbuttons, 4 knobs, BC, SW, 7 tubes, AC...$125.00

368, table, 1937, wood, right front dial, left wrap-over cloth grill w/vertical bars, 4 knobs, BC, SW, 8 tubes, AC $60.00

375, table, 1938, wood, large right front slide rule dial, left wraparound cloth grill w/cut-outs, pushbuttons, 4 knobs, BC, SW, AC $75.00

400, console, 1937, wood, upper front dial, lower cloth grill w/horizontal bars, 4 knobs, BC, SW, 12 tubes, AC...............$140.00

418, console, 1938, wood, upper front slide rule dial, lower cloth grill w/cut-outs, pushbuttons, 4 knobs, BC, SW, 11 tubes, AC $135.00

425, console, 1937, wood, upper front dial, lower cloth grill w/horizontal bars, 4 knobs, BC, SW, 14 tubes, AC...............$150.00

468, table, 1938, wood, right front slide rule dial, left wraparound cloth grill w/cut-outs, pushbuttons, BC, SW, 8 tubes, AC $65.00

472AC, chairside-R/P, 1948, wood, top dial & knobs, upper front grill, lower pull-out phono drawer, storage, BC, FM, AC ...$75.00

472AF, console-R/P, 1948, wood, right front pull-out radio drawer, left pull-out phono drawer, lower criss-cross grill, BC, FM, AC...$85.00

472C, chairside-R/P, 1948, wood, top dial & knobs, upper front grill, lower pull-out phono drawer, storage, BC, FM, AC $75.00

472F, console-R/P, 1948, wood, right front pull-out radio drawer, left pull-out phono drawer, lower criss-cross grill, BC, FM, AC...$85.00

474, table, 1948, plastic, right front square dial over horizontal wrap-around bars, 3 knobs, BC, FM, AC/DC $40.00

518-S, console, 1940, walnut, upper front rectangular dial, lower horizontal grill bars, tuning eye, 6 pushbuttons, 4 knobs, BC, SW, 12 tubes, AC..$150.00

575, table, 1939, two-tone walnut, center front slide rule dial, upper grill, 6 pushbuttons, 4 knobs, BC, SW, 6 tubes, AC...$55.00

580, table, 1940, wood, center front slide rule dial, upper grill, 6 pushbuttons, tuning eye, 4 knobs, BC, SW, 8 tubes, AC $65.00

700, table, 1940, plastic, right front dial over horizontal wraparound louvers, 2 knobs, BC, 5 tubes, AC $40.00

718-APC, console-R/P, 1940, walnut, inner right front slide rule dial, pushbuttons, 4 knobs, tuning eye, inner left phono, doors, front grill w/vertical bars, BC, SW, 12 tubes, AC...$95.00

718C, console, 1941, walnut, upper front rectangular dial, lower vertical grill bars, 6 pushbuttons, 4 knobs, BC, SW, 12 tubes, AC..$130.00

718-FM, console, 1941, wood, upper front slide rule dial, lower cloth grill w/vertical bars, pushbuttons, 4 knobs, BC, SW, 14 tubes, AC...$130.00

780, table, 1941, two-tone wood, upper front slanted slide rule dial, lower criss-cross grill, 6 knobs, BC, SW, AC $50.00

808CH, chairside-R/P, 1941, wood, top dial & knobs, front grill w/cut-outs, lift top, inner phono, storage, BC, SW, 8 tubes, AC $120.00

901A, table, 1946, two-tone wood, right front dial, left horizontal louvers, 2 knobs $30.00

901A-I, table, 1946, plastic, right front square dial, left horizontal louvers, horizontal wrap-around bars, 2 knobs, BC, 5 tubes, AC/DC $50.00

901AP, table-R/P, 1946, wood, right front square dial, left grill w/horizontal bars, 3 knobs, lift top, inner phono, BC, AC..$30.00

906, table, 1947, wood, lower front slide rule dial, upper 2-section criss-cross grill, BC, AC...$45.00

906C, chairside-R/P, 1947, wood, dial & 4 knobs on top of case, upper front grill, lower pull-out phono drawer, record storage, BC, AC...$75.00

906-S, table, 1948, wood, lower front slide rule dial, upper 2-section criss-cross grill, BC, SW, AC $50.00

906-SB, table, 1948, wood, lower front slide rule dial, upper 2-section criss-cross grill, BC, SW, AC............................$50.00

909M, console-R/P, 1947, wood, right pull-out radio drawer, left pull-out phono drawer, lower criss-cross grill, BC, SW, AC...$75.00

920, table, 1946, plastic, right front square dial, left horizontal louvers, horizontal wrap-around bars, 3 knobs, BC, 4 tubes, battery $35.00

A, table, 1925, wood, low rectangular case, 3 dial front panel, 5 tubes, battery...$135.00

F-17, console, 1934, wood, lowboy, upper front round dial, lower cloth grill w/cut-outs, 6 legs, BC, SW, AC $125.00

HUDSON

Series OEL, console, wood, large upper front red dial, lower cloth grill w/center vertical bars, tuning eye, 4 knobs, BC, SW, AC $140.00

HUDSON-ROSS

Three Little Pigs, cathedral, 1933, ivory or green wood, center front dial, upper grill w/hand-painted 3 Little Pigs cut-out, side pig figures, 2 knobs $425.00

HYMAN
Henry Hyman & Co., Inc.,
476 Broadway, New York, New York

V-60 "Bestone," table, 1925, wood, high rectangular case, 2 dial front panel, 4 tubes, battery $130.00

JACKSON
Jackson Ind., Inc.,
58E Cullerton Street, Chicago, Illinois

150, console-R/P, 1951, wood, inner front slide rule dial, 4 knobs, lower pull-out phono drawer, double doors, BC, AC $50.00
254, console-R/P, 1952, wood, inner right front vertical slide rule dial, left pull-out phono drawer, double front doors, BC, AC $50.00
255, console-R/P, 1952, wood, inner right front vertical slide rule dial, 4 knobs, left pull-out phono drawer, double doors, AM, FM, AC $50.00
350, console-R/P, 1951, wood, inner front slide rule dial, 4 knobs, lower pull-out phono drawer, double doors, BC, FM, AC $55.00
DP-51, portable-R/P, 1952, luggage-style, inner right dial, lattice grill, left phono, lift top, handle, BC, AC.....................$20.00
JP-50, portable-R/P, 1952, luggage-style, inner right dial, lattice grill, 3 knobs, left phono, lift top, handle, BC, AC $20.00
JP-200, portable-R/P, 1952, leatherette, luggage-style, inner right half-round dial, left phono, lift top, handle, BC, AC $20.00

JACKSON-BELL
Jackson-Bell Company,
Los Angeles, California

The Jackson-Bell Company began business in 1926 selling radios. The company is best known for its midget radios manufactured from 1930 to 1932 with which they grew to be one of the largest radio producers on the West Coast. Jackson-Bell was out of business by 1935.

4, cathedral, wood, front window dial w/escutcheon, upper cloth grill w/cut-outs, 3 knobs...$200.00
4 "Peter Pan," cathedral, 1935, wood, front window dial, upper grill w/Peter Pan cut-out, pointed top, 3 knobs, AC $295.00
6, table, 1930, wood, center front window dial, right & left scenic tapestry grills, 3 knobs, AC..$195.00
25 "Peter Pan," tombstone, 1932, wood, shouldered, front window dial, upper cloth grill w/Peter Pan cut-out, 3 knobs, AC $295.00
25AV "Pandora," table, 1932, wood, chest-style, carved case, lift top, inner window dial, 3 knobs, storage, 5 tubes, AC $275.00
26-SW, tombstone, 1932, wood, shouldered, lower front window dial, upper grill w/cut-outs, 3 knobs, 6 tubes $150.00
34, table, C1933, blue mirror glass case, center front round dial surrounded by grill cut-outs, 2 knobs, AC $1,200.00
38, console, 1932, wood, lowboy, upper front window dial, lower cloth grill w/cut-outs, 6 legs, 8 tubes $140.00
54 "Peter Pan," tombstone, 1935, wood, shouldered, lower front window dial, upper cloth grill w/Peter Pan cut-out, 3 knobs..$295.00
59, cathedral, 1929, wood, right front thumbwheel dial, center Deco "sun-burst" grill cut-outs, pointed top, 7 tubes, AC $175.00
60, cathedral, 1929, wood, right front thumbwheel dial, center Deco "sun-burst" grill cut-outs, pointed top, AC $175.00
62, cathedral, 1930, wood, lower front window dial, upper round "sun-burst" grill, pointed top, 3 knobs, 6 tubes, AC $175.00
62, cathedral, 1930, wood, lower front window dial, upper cloth grill w/swan cut-outs, 3 knobs, AC $300.00

68, cathedral, 1931, wood, center front window dial, upper cloth grill w/tulip cut-outs, 3 knobs, 8 tubes, AC ...$250.00
84, cathedral, 1931, wood, front window dial, upper cloth grill w/Peter Pan cut-out, 3 knobs, 4 tubes $295.00
87, cathedral, 1931, wood, lower front half-round dial, upper cloth grill w/tulip cut-outs, decorative spindles, 3 knobs, AC ..$250.00

JEFFERSON-TRAVIS
Jefferson-Travis, Inc.,
380 Second Avenue, New York, New York

MR-3, portable, 1947, leatherette, right front slide rule dial, left round grill w/"JT" cut-out, handle, 3 knobs, BC, SW, AC/DC/battery $30.00

JEWEL
Jewel Radio Corp.,
583 Sixth Avenue, New York, New York

300, table, 1947, plastic, right front round dial, left horizontal wrap-around louvers, 2 knobs, BC, AC/DC $45.00
304 "Pixie," portable, 1948, "alligator," inner right dial, flip-open lid, outer perforated grill, strap, BC, battery...................$50.00
501, table, 1947, wood, upper front slanted slide rule dial, lower horizontal grill openings, 2 knobs, BC, AC/DC.............$35.00
502, table, 1947, wood w/inlay, upper front slanted slide rule dial, lower horizontal louvers, 2 knobs, BC, AC/DC.............$40.00
504, table, 1947, wood, upper front slanted slide rule dial, lower grill w/large block openings, 2 knobs, BC, AC/DC $40.00
505 "Pin Up," wall-C, 1947, plastic, lower right front window dial, 2 right side knobs, center clock over vertical wrap-over bars, BC, AC $85.00
801 "Trixie," portable, 1948, "alligator," inner right dial, 3 knobs, fold-open door, strap, BC, AC/DC/battery $50.00
814, portable, 1948, plastic, lower front recessed dial panel, 2 knobs, top grill bars, strap, BC, battery $40.00
915, table-C, 1950, plastic, right front round dial, left clock, center perforated grill, 4 knobs, BC, AC $35.00
920, table-C, 1949, plastic, right front round dial, left clock, center horizontal grill bars, 4 knobs, BC, AC........................$35.00

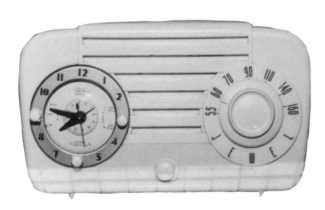

935, table-C, 1949, plastic, right front round dial, left clock, center horizontal bars, 5 knobs, BC, AC $35.00

940, table-C, plastic, right front square dial, left clock, center lattice grill, 6 knobs, BC, AC.................................$30.00

949, portable, 1950, leatherette, center front round dial over cloth grill, handle, 2 knobs, BC, AC/DC/battery $25.00

955, table, 1950, plastic, step-down right side, right front dial, left lattice grill, 2 knobs, BC, AC/DC...................................$50.00

956, table, 1951, plastic, right front see-through dial, left checkered grill, center tuning knob, BC, AC/DC....................$30.00

960, table, 1950, plastic, dial markings over large front checkered grill area, large dial pointer, 2 knobs, BC, AC/DC $30.00

5007, table, 1952, plastic, right front dial, left checkered grill, large center dial knob, BC, AC $30.00

5010, portable, 1950, leatherette, center front dial, right & left cloth grill areas, handle, 2 knobs, BC, AC/DC/battery...$25.00

5020, table-R/P, 1951, wood, outer front half-round dial over large grill area, 3 knobs, lift top, inner phono, BC, AC $35.00

5040, table-C, 1952, plastic, upper right & left thumbwheel knobs, center front round alarm clock, BC, AC $50.00

5050, portable, 1951, plastic, top left dial, top right checkered grill area, handle, 3 knobs, BC, AC/DC/battery....................$45.00

5057U "Wakemaster," table-C, 1950, plastic, right front slide rule dial, center clock, right & left checkered grill areas, 5 knobs, BC, AC $45.00

5125U, table-C, 1953, plastic, large right side dial knob, center front alarm clock, left checkered grill, BC, AC $30.00

5200, table, 1953, plastic, right half-round dial, left diagonal grill bars, 2 knobs, feet, BC, AC/DC...................................$35.00

5205, table/lamp, 1953, plastic, right front dial knob, center vertical bars, slanted top w/built-in lamp, BC, AC $60.00

5250, table-C, 1953, plastic, upper right & left thumbwheel knobs, center front alarm clock, side bars, BC, AC $50.00

5310, portable, 1953, plastic, large center front round dial over horizontal grill bars, handle, BC, battery $30.00

KADETTE
International Radio Corporation,
Ann Arbor, Michigan

24 "Clockette," "Futura," table, 1937, wood, clock-style case, center front round metal dial ring with inner metal screen grill, feet, 2 knobs, AC...$125.00

35, table, 1936, wood, lower front round telephone dial, upper grill w/horizontal bars, 2 knobs, BC, 5 tubes, AC..............$120.00

36, table, 1935, wood, right front square dial, left grill w/horizontal bars, 4 knobs, BC, SW, AC $45.00

41 "Jewel," table, 1935, walnut Bakelite, right front dial, center grill w/plastic cut-outs, 2 knobs, AC/DC $175.00

43 "Jewel," table, 1935, ivory plastic, right front dial, center grill w/plastic cut-outs, 2 knobs, AC/DC $200.00

44 "Jewel," table, 1935, red plastic, right front dial, center grill w/plastic cut-outs, 2 knobs, AC/DC $300.00

47 "Jewel," table, 1935, black plastic, right front dial, center grill w/plastic cut-outs, 2 knobs, AC/DC.................$250.00

48 "Jewel," table, 1935, marble plastic, right front dial, center grill w/plastic cut-outs, 2 knobs, AC/DC $250.00

66X, table, 1936, wood, lower front dial, upper cloth grill w/horizontal bars, 3 knobs, 6 tubes...........................$50.00

76, table, 1936, wood, lower front dial, upper cloth grill w/wrap-over vertical bars, 6 tubes, AC/DC $70.00

77, tombstone, 1936, wood, lower front airplane dial, upper grill w/horizontal & vertical bars, BC, SW, 7 tubes, AC/DC...$90.00

86, table, 1936, wood, lower front dial, upper cloth grill w/horizontal bars, 3 knobs, 6 tubes, AC/DC $85.00

87, table, 1936, wood, right front round dial over horizontal grill bars, 3 knobs, BC, SW, AC $50.00

96, table, two-tone wood, right front round dial, left round grill w/3 vertical bars, 3 knobs, BC/SW.................................$55.00

400, table, 1936, wood, lower front dial, upper cloth grill w/horizontal bars, 3 knobs, battery $40.00

630, table, 1938, two-tone mahogany, right front vertical dial, left cloth grill w/horizontal bars, 4 knobs, BC, SW, 6 tubes, AC $55.00

635, tombstone, 1938, wood, lower front dial, upper grill w/horizontal louvers, 4 knobs, BC, SW, 6 tubes, AC $75.00

735, table, 1938, wood, right front vertical dial, left cloth grill w/horizontal bars, 4 knobs, BC, SW.............................$55.00

845, table, 1938, walnut, right front dial, left checkerboard grill, 4 knobs, BC, SW, 8 tubes, AC $65.00

950, table, 1938, wood, large right front slide rule dial, curved left w/wrap-around horizontal grill bars, 4 knobs, BC, SW, 9 tubes, AC...$65.00

1019, table, wood, right front gold airplane dial, left cloth grill w/3 horizontal bars, 3 knobs, BC, SW, 10 tubes, AC...........$50.00

K-25 "Clockette," table, 1937, Catalin, clock-style case, center front round metal dial w/inner metal screen grill, 2 knobs ..$1,000.00+

K-150, table, 1937, walnut plastic, lower front dial, upper grill w/vertical bars, oval medallions, 5 tubes, AC/DC.......$100.00

K-151, table, 1937, ivory plastic, lower front dial, upper grill w/vertical bars, oval medallions, 5 tubes, AC/DC $120.00

K-1024, table, 1937, two-tone walnut & maple, right front airplane dial, left rectangular grill area, 3 knobs, 10 tubes, AC/DC $75.00

K-1030, table, 1937, wood, right front airplane dial, left oblong grill w/center horizontal bars, 6 pushbuttons, 2 knobs, BC, SW...$60.00

K-1035, 1937, wood, right front airplane dial, left grill w/horizontal louvers, 6 pushbuttons, 2 knobs, BC, SW, 10 tubes $60.00

K-1140, 1937, wood, right front airplane dial, left grill w/horizontal louvers, 6 pushbuttons, 3 knobs, BC, SW, 11 tubes $60.00

L "Classic," table, 1936, 3 plastics, lower front dial, back/front grills w/horizontal bars, 2 knobs, 6 tubes, AC/DC .....$800.00+

L-29, table, 1939, walnut, upper front dial, top raised circular grill area, 2 top knobs, BC, 5 tubes, AC.............................$150.00

S947 "Kadette Jr," table, 1933, plastic, pocket-size, Deco, thumbwheel dial knob, center front grill cut-outs, BC, 2 tubes, AC/DC $300.00

The Colonial "Clockette," table, 1937, wood, clock-style case, large center front round metal dial, side fluting, 2 knobs, 5 tubes, AC...$125.00

The Modern "Clockette," table, 1937, wood, Deco, clock-style case, large center front round metal dial, 2 knobs, AC ..$125.00

Topper, table, 1940, plastic, upper front slide rule dial, top speaker "dome" grill & 2 knobs, AC/DC $195.00

KELLOGG
Kellogg Switchboard & Supply Company,
1066 West Adams Street,
Chicago, Illinois

The Kellogg Switchboard & Supply Company began in 1897 producing telephone equipment and by 1922 was manufacturing radio parts. Experiencing some financial difficulty in the late 1920's, Kellogg discontinued radio production in 1930.

504 "Wavemaster," table, 1925, wood, low rectangular case, 1 dial front panel, lift top, feet, battery $245.00

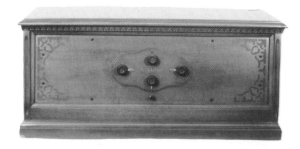

507 "Wavemaster," table, 1926, wood, low rectangular case, center front escutcheon with 4 knobs, 6 tubes, battery.....$135.00

521, console, 1928, wood, lowboy, upper front dial & escutcheon, lower grill w/cut-outs, stretcher base $175.00

523, console, 1929, wood, lowboy, inner front window dial & knobs, double doors, stretcher base, 9 tubes, AC $225.00

KENNEDY
The Colin B. Kennedy Company, Inc.,
Rialto Building,
San Francisco, California

The Colin B. Kennedy Company was formed in 1919 for the production of radios. Business boomed until the mid-twenties when sales began to decline due to lower priced competitive models and, by 1926, the company had declared bankruptcy.

20, table, 1925, mahogany, slanted front panel, center large round dial, 4 knobs, 5 tubes, battery $200.00

42 "Coronet," upright table, 1931, walnut, right front window dial, upper grill w/"tulip" cut-outs, flared base, 3 knobs......$250.00

52A, cathedral, wood, center front window dial, upper cloth grill w/cut-outs, 3 knobs $325.00

62, (right) console, wood, lowboy, upper front quarter-round dial, lower cloth grill w/cut-outs, 4 knobs, 6 legs, 2 speakers, 10 tubes, AC $175.00

110 "Universal," table, 1922, wood, low rectangular case, black Bakelite front panel, 3 tubes, battery $1,100.00

110/525, table, 1922, wood, 2 units, receiver & two-stage amp, black front panels, battery $1,500.00

164, console, 1932, wood, lowboy, upper front quarter-round dial, lower grill w/cut-outs, 6 legs, 10 tubes..........$175.00

220, table, 1921, wood, square case, black Bakelite front panel, lift top, 1 tube, battery $900.00

220/525, table, 1922, wood, 2 units – receiver & 2 stage amp, black front panels, lift tops, battery $1,300.00

266, console, 1932, wood, lowboy, upper front quarter-round dial, lower grill w/cut-outs, 6 legs, 12 tubes $200.00

281/521, table, 1921, mahogany, 2 units - receiver & 2 stage amp, 3 dial receiver panel, lift tops, battery $975.00

311, portable, 1923, oak, inner left control panel w/1 exposed tube, right storage, lift top, handle, battery $600.00

366A, console, 1932, wood, lowboy, inner front quarter-round dial, lower grill w/cut-outs, double front doors, 6 legs, 12 tubes $200.00

525, table/amp, 1921, wood, tall rectangular case, 2 stage amp..$400.00

III, portable, 1923, leatherette, inner black panel w/3 exposed tubes, lift-off cover w/storage, handle, battery............$475.00

V, table, 1923, wood, high rectangular case, 2 dial slant front panel, 3 exposed tubes, battery $375.00

VI, table, 1924, wood, tall rectangular case, 2 dial slant front panel, 4 exposed tubes, battery $425.00

X, table, 1923, mahogany, inner 2 dial slanted panel, 3 exposed tubes, fold-up top, lower speaker grill w/cut-outs, battery $600.00

XI, table, 1924, mahogany, inner 2 dial slanted panel, 4 exposed tubes, fold-up top, lower speaker grill w/cut-outs, battery ..$600.00

XV, table, 1924, wood, tall rectangular case, 2 dial slant front panel, 5 exposed tubes, battery $425.00

XXX, table, 1925, wood, rectangular case, slant front panel w/2 window dials, battery $375.00

KENT

402A, table, metal, midget, right front dial over horizontal wrap-around bars, 3 tubes, BC $85.00

422, table, metal, midget, right front dial over horizontal wrap-around bars, handle, BC, AC/DC $85.00

422A, table, metal, midget, right front dial over horizontal wrap-around bars, handle, BC, 4 tubes, AC/DC $85.00

KING

King Quality Products, Inc., Buffalo, New York
King-Buffalo, Inc., Buffalo, New York
King-Hinners Radio Co., Inc., Buffalo, New York
King Manufacturing Corporation, Buffalo, New York

King Quality Products, Inc., began business in 1924. The company was owned by Sears, Roebuck and in the mid-twenties produced radios with both the Sears Silvertone as well as the King label. By the early 1930's, King was out of business.

4, upright table, wood, small case, lower half-round dial, upper round grill w/cut-outs, 2 knobs...................................$195.00

10, table, wood, low rectangular case, 3 dial black front panel, 5 tubes, battery $125.00

25, table, 1925, wood, low rectangular case, 3 dial front panel, 5 tubes, battery..$115.00

25-C, console, 1925, wood, inner right 3 dial panel & left speaker grill w/cut-outs, fold-down front, lower storage, battery..$195.00

30, table, 1925, wood, low rectangular case, slanted 3 dial front panel, 5 tubes, battery..$100.00

30-S, table, 1925, wood, low rectangular case, left front slanted 3 dial panel, right speaker grill w/cut-outs, battery $140.00

61, table, 1926, two-tone wood, low rectangular case, 3 dial front panel, 6 tubes, battery..$110.00

61-H, console, 1926, wood, inner left 3 dial panel & right speaker grill w/cut-outs, fold-down front, lower storage, battery...$180.00

62, table, 1926, two-tone wood, rectangular case, oval front panel w/window dial, 3 knobs, battery..................................$100.00

71 "Commander," table, 1926, wood, low rectangular case, center front window dial, loop antenna, feet, 6 tubes, battery $175.00

80 "Baronet," table, 1927, wood, low rectangular case, center front dial, 3 knobs, fluted columns, 6 tubes, battery $120.00

80-H "Viking," console, 1927, wood, inner right 1 dial panel & left speaker grill w/cut-outs, fold-down front, lower storage, 6 tubes, battery...$200.00

81 "Crusader," table, 1927, two-tone wood, low rectangular case, oval front panel w/1 dial, 3 knobs, 6 tubes, battery $100.00

81-H "Chevalier," console, 1927, walnut, highboy, inner 1 dial oval panel & upper round grill, double doors, 6 tubes, battery $185.00

FF, table, 1929, two-tone metal, low rectangular case, center front window dial, 3 knobs, 6 tubes, AC $85.00

KINGSTON
Kingston Radio, Kokomo, Indiana

Founded in 1933, Kingston manufactured many farm battery radios which were sold under other labels, such as Airline and Truetone. The company was out of business by 1951.

55, table, 1934, wood, step-down sides, right front dial, center cloth grill w/cut-outs, 2 knobs, 5 tubes, AC/DC $80.00

600A, tombstone, 1934, wood, Deco, center front window dial, upper cloth grill w/cut-outs, 3 knobs, 6 tubes $125.00

600B, console, 1934, wood, Deco, upper front dial, lower grill area, 3 knobs, 6 tubes $150.00

KITCHENAIRE
The Radio Craftsmen, Inc.,
1341 South Michigan Avenue,
Chicago, Illinois

No #, wall, 1946, metal, kitchen wall set w/right & left side shelves, 2 knobs, herringbone grill, top louvers, BC, AC/DC $200.00

KNIGHT
Allied Radio Corp.,
833 West Jackson Boulevard,
Chicago, Illinois

4D-450, portable, 1948, leatherette & plastic, upper front slide rule dial, lower lattice grill, handle, 2 knobs, BC, battery $30.00

4G-420, table-R/P, 1950, front slide rule dial, 3 knobs, lift top, inner phono, BC, AC $25.00

5A-152, table, 1947, plastic, upper front slanted slide rule dial, lower horizontal louvers, 2 knobs, BC, AC/DC $35.00

5A-154, table, 1947, two-tone wood, upper front slanted slide rule dial, lower horizontal louvers, 2 knobs, BC, AC/DC $45.00

5A-190, table, 1947, plastic, step-down top, right front dial, left horizontal grill bars, 2 knobs, BC, AC/DC $60.00

5B-160, table-R/P, 1947, leatherette, slanted slide rule dial, front horizontal louvers, 3 knobs, open top phono, BC, AC...$20.00

5B-175, table, 1947, plastic, right front square dial, left vertical wrap-over louvers, 2 knobs, BC, AC/DC $45.00

5B-185, table-R/P, 1947, wood, upper front dial, lower criss-cross grill, 2 knobs, lift top, inner phono, BC, AC............$35.00

5C-290, portable, 1947, leatherette, top dial, lower horizontal louvers, 3 knobs, handle, BC, AC/DC/battery $20.00

5D-250, table, 1949, plastic, raised top, upper front slanted slide rule dial, lower horizontal louvers, 2 knobs, BC, AC/DC..$50.00

5D-455, portable, 1948, leatherette/plastic, upper front slide rule dial, lower lattice grill, handle, 2 knobs, BC, AC/DC/battery..$30.00

5F-525, table, 1949, plastic, right front round dial, left checkerboard grill, ridged base, 2 knobs, BC, AC/DC $40.00

5F-565, portable, 1949, leatherette, right front square dial, horizontal louvers, handle, 3 knobs, BC, AC/DC/battery.....$40.00

5H-570, table, 1951, plastic, diagonally divided front panel with right round dial, 2 knobs, BC, AC/DC $25.00

5H-605, table-C, 1951, plastic, lower right front dial knob over horizontal bars, upper square clock, BC, AC............$45.00

5H-700, table-R/P, 1951, right front square dial, left grill, 3 knobs, switch, 3/4 lift top, inner phono, BC, AC $20.00

5J-705, table, 1952, plastic, right front square dial, left vertical wrap-over grill bars, 2 knobs, BC, AC $45.00

5K-715, table-C, 1953, wood, right front square dial, left square alarm clock, raised center w/vertical wrap-over grill bars, BC, AC..$45.00

6A-122, table, 1946, wood, upper front slanted slide rule dial, lower cloth grill, 4 knobs, BC, SW, AC/DC $40.00

6A-127, portable, 1946, leatherette, upper front slanted slide rule dial, lower criss-cross grill, 3 knobs, handle, BC, AC/DC/battery $35.00

6A-195, table, 1947, plastic, right front square dial, left vertical wrap-over grill bars, 2 knobs, BC, SW, AC/DC $45.00

6C-225, table, 1947, plastic, upper front slide rule dial, lower horizontal louvers w/center bar, 3 knobs, BC, AC/DC........$50.00

6D-235, table, 1949, wood, curved sides, right front dial, left vertical grill bars, 3 knobs, BC, AC/DC $60.00

6D-360, console-R/P, 1948, two-tone wood, upper front slide rule dial, 5 knobs, center pull-out phono drawer, lower grill, BC, SW, AC...$110.00

6H-580, table, 1951, plastic, large front dial w/horizontal decorative lines, 2 knobs, BC, AC/DC............$25.00

6K-718, portable, 1953, two-tone leatherette, center front round dial w/inner perforated grill, handle, 2 knobs, BC, AC/DC/battery $35.00

7B-220, table, 1947, wood, upper front slanted slide rule dial, lower criss-cross grill, 4 knobs, BC, FM, AC/DC $45.00

7D-405, table-R/P, 1948, wood, upper front slide rule dial, lower grill, 4 knobs, lift top, inner phono, BC, AC $30.00

8B-210, table-R/P, 1947, wood, front dial, 4 knobs, 3/4 lift top, inner phono, BC, AC $30.00

11C-300, console-R/P, 1947, wood, inner right slide rule dial, 4 knobs, fold-down door, left pull-out phono drawer, lower grill, BC, FM, AC $75.00

11D-302, console-R/P, 1949, wood, inner right slide rule dial, 4 knobs, door, left fold-down phono, lower grill, BC, FM, AC $75.00

49-J6, table, 1940, plastic, right front dial, left horizontal wrap-around bars, pushbuttons, 3 knobs $50.00

68B-151K, table, wood, right front black oval dial, left cloth grill w/cut-outs, tuning eye, 4 knobs, battery $60.00

94S-445, table-C, 1955, wood, right front square dial, left square alarm clock, center horizontal grill bars, BC, 5 tubes, AC $35.00

96-326, table-R/P/Rec, 1951, leatherette, inner left dial, phono, recorder, lift top, handle, BC, AC............$30.00

449, portable, 1950, leatherette, left front slide rule dial, lower horizontal grill bars, handle, 2 knobs, BC, AC/DC/battery ..$25.00

2117, tombstone, wood, lower front large round dial w/center sailing ship, upper cloth grill w/cut-outs, 4 knobs, BC, SW $115.00

B17115, portable, 1941, leatherette, inner right front dial, left grill w/horizontal bars, 2 knobs, fold-in front, handle, 6 tubes, AC/DC/battery $25.00

KODEL
The Kodel Manufacturing Company,
118 Third Street, West, Cincinnati, Ohio
The Kodel Radio Corporation,
503 East Pearl Street, Cincinnati, Ohio

The Kodel Manufacturing Company was formed in 1924 by Clarence Ogden, an inventor of battery chargers. The company's radio business boomed along with their production of battery eliminators. The advent of AC radio, however, was the beginning of the end for Kodel and they were out of business by the 1930's.

Big Five "Logodyne," console, 1925, mahogany, desk-style, inner 3 dial panel, fold-down front, right built-in speaker, battery $175.00

Big Five "Logodyne," table, 1925, mahogany, low rectangular case, slanted 3 dial front panel, 5 tubes, battery........$120.00

C-11 "Gold Star," table, 1924, leatherette, tall rectangular case, 1 dial front panel, 1 tube, battery................$165.00

C-12 "Gold Star," table, 1924, wood, rectangular case, center front dial, 2 tubes, battery.............................$140.00

C-13 "Gold Star," table, 1924, wood, low rectangular case, 2 dial front panel, 3 tubes, battery $155.00

C-14, table, 1924, wood, low rectangular case, 2 dial front panel, 4 tubes, battery.............................$130.00

Standard Five "Logodyne," console, 1925, mahogany, slanted 3 dial center panel, right built-in speaker, door, 5 tubes, battery..$175.00

Standard Five "Logodyne," table, 1925, mahogany, low rectangular case, 3 dial front panel, 5 tubes, battery $120.00

KOLSTER

Federal Telegraph Company,
Woolworth Building, New York, New York
Federal-Brandes, Inc., Newark, New Jersey

To avoid any confusion with the rival Federal Telephone & Telegraph Company, the Federal Telegraph Company used the Kolster name for its radio line which began in 1925. Plagued with internal problems from the beginning and after many reorganization attempts, Kolster was out of business by 1930.

6D, table, 1926, wood, rectangular case, center front dial w/escutcheon, lift top, 3 knobs, 6 tubes, battery $75.00
6E, console, 1926, wood, lowboy, upper front dial, center grill w/fleur-de-lis cut-outs, lower storage, battery.............$165.00
6G, console, 1926, wood, inner front dial, 3 knobs, lower grill, double doors, storage, battery $185.00
6H, console, 1926, wood, lowboy, inner front dial, 3 knobs, lower grill, double doors, storage, 6 tubes, battery $185.00

6J, table, 1927, wood, low rectangular case, center front window dial w/large escutcheon, 3 knobs, AC $135.00
7A, table, 1926, two-tone wood, low rectangular case, center front dial, 3 knobs, battery $100.00
7B, table, 1926, two-tone wood, center front dial, upper built-in speaker, 3 knobs, battery $130.00
8A, table, 1926, wood, center front window dial w/escutcheon, 3 knobs, 8 tubes, battery $110.00
8B, console, 1926, wood, center front window dial, upper built-in speaker, left side loop antenna, battery $200.00
8C, console, 1926, wood, inner dial, fold-down front, upper speaker, built-in loop antenna, battery.................$250.00

K-20, table, 1928, wood & metal, rectangular case, center front window dial, 3 knobs, carvings, paw feet, AC $100.00

K-21, table, 1928, wood, rectangular case, center front window dial, front carvings, paw feet, 3 knobs $100.00
K-43, console, 1929, wood, inner dial w/escutcheon, lower grill w/cut-outs, double front doors $150.00
K-44, console, 1929, walnut, inner dial w/escutcheon, lower grill w/cut-outs, double front doors, stretcher base $150.00
K-45, console, 1928, wood, lowboy, right side window dial & knobs, large front floral grill cloth, 11 tubes, AC.........$400.00
K-48, console, wood, lowboy, upper front window dial w/escutcheon, lower grill w/cut-outs, 3 knobs $135.00
K-60, tombstone, 1931, wood, center front window dial, upper cloth grill w/repwood cut-outs, 3 knobs, AC $145.00
K-70, console, 1931, wood, upper front window dial, lower cloth grill w/cut-outs, 3 knobs, 8 tubes $145.00
K-80, console, wood, carved front panel w/upper window dial, lower cloth grill w/2 vertical bars, 3 knobs $150.00
K-90, console, wood, inner front window dial, lower cloth grill w/2 vertical bars, 3 knobs, double sliding doors $150.00
K-100, console, 1932, wood, upper front window dial, lower cloth grill w/cut-outs, 3 knobs, 7 tubes $140.00
K-110, tombstone, 1932, wood, shouldered, center front window dial, upper cloth grill w/cut-outs, 3 knobs, 8 tubes, AC ..$120.00
K-114, tombstone, 1932, wood, shouldered, center front window dial, upper cloth grill w/cut-outs, 3 knobs, 9 tubes, battery $100.00
K-120, console, 1932, wood, lowboy, upper front window dial, lower cloth grill w/cut-outs, 3 knobs, 8 tubes $100.00
K-124, console, 1932, wood, upper front window dial, lower cloth grill w/cut-outs, 3 knobs, 9 tubes, battery $90.00
K-130, console, 1932, wood, lowboy, upper front window dial, lower cloth grill w/cut-outs, 6 legs, 9 tubes, AC $150.00
K-140, console, 1932, wood, lowboy, upper front window dial, lower grill w/cut-outs, doors, 3 knobs, 6 legs, 10 tubes, AC $185.00

KRAFT
Kraft Mfg. & Dist. Co.

Puppytune, table-lamp, 1949, radio/lamp shaped like puppy, right square dial, left grill, 2 knobs, BC, AC/DC $175.00

LAFAYETTE
Radio Wire Television, Inc.,
100 Sixth Avenue,
New York, New York

60, tombstone, 1935, wood, center front round dial, upper cloth grill w/horizontal bars, 4 knobs, BC, SW $135.00
B14, table, 1937, two-tone wood, right front oval dial, left wrap-around grill w/horizontal bars, tuning eye, BC, SW, 8 tubes, AC....$75.00
B18, console, 1938, wood, upper front oval dial, lower cloth grill w/2 vertical bars, tuning eye, BC, SW, 8 tubes, AC $135.00
B20, console-R/P, 1938, wood, front oval dial, lower cloth grill w/vertical bars, tuning eye, lift top, inner phono, BC, SW, 8 tubes, AC...$135.00
B25, table, 1938, two-tone wood, right front round dial, left wrap-around cloth grill w/horizontal bars, tuning eye, pushbuttons, BC, SW, 8 tubes, AC..$75.00
B26, console, 1938, wood, upper front round dial, lower cloth grill w/2 vertical bars, tuning eye, pushbuttons, BC, SW, 8 tubes, AC $150.00
B34, console, 1938, wood, step-down top, upper front round dial, lower cloth grill w/center vertical bar, tuning eye, pushbuttons, BC, SW, 11 tubes, AC................................$150.00
B38, console-R/P, 1938, walnut, front round dial, lower cloth grill w/vertical bars, tuning eye, pushbuttons, lift top, inner phono, BC, SW, 11 tubes, AC...$150.00

B44, console, 1938, wood, upper front round dial, lower cloth grill w/center vertical bars, tuning eye, pushbuttons, BC, SW, 13 tubes, AC...$175.00

B101, console, 1940, walnut, upper front slide rule dial, lower cloth grill w/vertical bars, pushbuttons, 4 knobs, BC, SW, 9 tubes, AC...$125.00

B102, console-R/P, 1940, walnut, inner right dial, pushbuttons & knobs, inner left phono, lift top, front grill w/horizontal bars, BC, SW, 9 tubes, AC.....................$135.00

B103, table, 1940, wood, right front slide rule dial, left horizontal grill bars, pushbuttons, 4 knobs, BC, SW, 9 tubes, AC ..$65.00

BA1, chairside, 1938, wood, top round dial and 3 knobs, rounded front w/lower horizontal grill bars, storage, BC, SW, 7 tubes, AC/DC $135.00

BA2, table, 1938, two-tone walnut, right front airplane dial, left wrap-around horizontal grill bars, tuning eye, 4 knobs, BC, SW, 8 tubes, AC/DC.................................$75.00

BA19, table, 1938, wood, right front round airplane dial, left cloth grill w/horizontal bars, tuning eye, 3 knobs, BC, SW, 7 tubes, AC/DC $70.00

BB-27, table, 1939, wood, right front dial, curved left wrap-around grill, pushbuttons, tuning eye, 6 tubes, AC/DC.............$65.00

C-3, table, 1938, ivory plastic, large center front airplane dial, right & left side wrap-around grills w/horizontal bars, BC, 6 tubes, AC/DC $75.00

C-4, table, 1938, red plastic, large center front airplane dial, right & left side wrap-around grills w/horizontal bars, BC, 6 tubes, AC/DC $90.00

C-5, table, 1938, black plastic, large center front airplane dial, right & left side wrap-around grills w/horizontal bars, BC, 6 tubes, AC/DC $75.00

C57, table, 1938, wood, right front dial, left cloth grill w/horizontal bars, tuning eye, 5 knobs, BC, SW, 9 tubes, AC/DC $60.00

C69 "Little Symphony," table-R/P, 1938, wood, left front dial, right cloth grill w/3 vertical bars, tuning eye, 5 knobs, lift top, inner phono, BC, SW, 9 tubes, AC/DC..........................$50.00

C77, table, 1938, wood, right front dial, left cloth grill w/horizontal bars, tuning eye, 5 knobs, BC, SW, 12 tubes, AC/DC ..$70.00

C81, table, 1938, wood, right front dial, left cloth grill w/horizontal bars, tuning eye, 5 knobs, BC, SW, 12 tubes, AC.........$70.00

C82, console, 1938, wood, upper front dial, lower cloth grill w/center vertical bars, tuning eye, 5 knobs, BC, SW, 16 tubes, AC/DC ..$175.00

C85, table, 1938, wood, right front dial, left cloth grill w/horizontal bars, tuning eye, 5 knobs, BC, SW, 9 tubes, AC...........$55.00

C86 "Little Symphony," table-R/P, 1938, wood, left front dial, right cloth grill w/3 vertical bars, tuning eye, 5 knobs, lift top, inner phono, BC, SW, 9 tubes, AC................................$50.00

C89, console, 1938, wood, upper front dial, lower cloth grill w/center vertical bars, tuning eye, 5 knobs, BC, SW, 16 tubes, AC..$175.00

C-117, table, 1940, wood, right front slide rule dial, left grill w/vertical bars, tuning eye, 4 knobs, BC, SW, 7 tubes, AC ...$55.00

C-119, table, wood, right front slide rule dial, left grill w/horizontal louvers, 4 knobs, BC, SW, 10 tubes, AC/DC $45.00

C-121, portable, 1940, brown & white leatherette, inner right front dial, left cloth grill, fold-in front, handle, BC, 5 tubes, AC/DC/battery $25.00

C-121BL, portable, 1940, blue & white leatherette, inner right front dial, left cloth grill, fold-in front, handle, BC, 5 tubes, AC/DC/battery $25.00

C-121BR, portable, 1940, brown leatherette, inner right front dial, left cloth grill, fold-in front, handle, BC, 5 tubes, AC/DC/battery $25.00

C-125, portable, 1940, leatherette, inner right front dial, left cloth grill, 3 knobs, fold-in front, handle, BC, SW, 7 tubes, AC/DC/battery $25.00

C-127, table, 1940, walnut, right front dial, left grill w/horizontal bars, 5 knobs, BC, SW, 13 tubes, AC/DC $50.00

CC-35, console-R/P, 1940, walnut, inner right dial panel, left phono, lift top, double front doors cover grill, BC, SW, 15 tubes, AC..$120.00

CC-39, console-R/P, 1940, wheat finish, inner right dial panel, left phono, lift top, double front doors cover grill, BC, SW, 15 tubes, AC..$120.00

CC-55, portable, 1939, striped cloth covered, right front dial, left grill, handle, 2 knobs, AC/DC/battery $30.00

D21, table, 1938, wood, right front airplane dial, left wrap-over cloth grill w/center vertical divider, 3 knobs, BC, SW, 5 tubes, AC $40.00

D-22, table, 1938, wood, right front airplane dial, left wrap-over cloth grill w/center vertical divider, tuning eye, 3 knobs, BC, 5 tubes, battery....................................$40.00

D-23, table, 1938, wood, right front airplane dial, left cloth grill w/horizontal bars, 3 knobs, BC, SW, 6 tubes, AC/DC...$40.00

D32, table, 1938, wood, right front dial, left wrap-around cloth grill w/2 horizontal bars, 5 knobs, BC, SW, 6 tubes, AC/battery......$45.00

D35, table, 1938, wood, right front airplane dial, left cloth grill w/horizontal & vertical bars, tuning eye, 4 knobs, BC, SW, 6 tubes, AC..$60.00

D36, table, 1938, wood, right front airplane dial, left wrap-around cloth grill w/horizontal bars, tuning eye, 4 knobs, BC, SW, 6 tubes, AC..$60.00

D40, console, 1938, wood, upper front airplane dial, lower cloth grill w/cut-outs, tuning eye, BC, SW, 6 tubes, AC $125.00

D41, table, 1938, wood, right front airplane dial, left wrap-over cloth grill w/center vertical divider, 4 knobs, BC, SW, 6 tubes, battery $35.00

D48, table, 1938, wood, right front airplane dial, left wrap-over cloth grill w/center vertical divider, tuning eye, 3 knobs, BC, SW, 7 tubes, AC/DC..................................$55.00

D49, table, 1938, wood, right front airplane dial, left cloth grill w/cut-outs, tuning eye, 4 knobs, BC, SW, 7 tubes, AC...$60.00

D50, table, 1938, wood, right front airplane dial, left wrap-over cloth grill w/vertical bars, tuning eye, 4 knobs, BC, SW, 8 tubes, AC..$60.00

D51, table, 1938, wood, right front telephone dial, left cloth grill w/vertical bars, tuning eye, 4 knobs, BC, SW, 8 tubes, AC $100.00

D53, console, 1938, wood, upper front airplane dial, lower cloth grill w/center vertical divider, tuning eye, 4 knobs, BC, SW, 8 tubes, AC...$120.00

D54, console, 1938, wood, upper front telephone dial, lower cloth grill w/3 center vertical bars, tuning eye, 4 knobs, BC, SW, 8 tubes, AC...$175.00

D-55, console-R/P, 1938, wood, front airplane dial, lower cloth grill w/center vertical bars, tuning eye, 4 knobs, lift top, inner phono, BC, SW, 8 tubes, AC..........................$120.00

D-68, table, 1938, wood, right front dial, left grill w/horizontal bars, tuning eye, pushbuttons, 3 knobs, 7 tubes, AC/DC.......$65.00

D-73, table, 1939, plastic, streamline, right front dial, curved left with horizontal wrap-around louvers, 3 knobs, 6 tubes, AC/DC $100.00

D-131, table, 1940, walnut plastic, right front dial, left vertical grill bars, 2 knobs, 4 tubes, AC/DC $40.00

D-132, table, 1940, ivory plastic, right front dial, left vertical grill bars, 2 knobs, 4 tubes, AC/DC $40.00

D-133 "Little Giant," table-R/P, 1940, brown leatherette, right front airplane dial, left grill area, two knobs, lift top, inner phono, AC $25.00

D-139, table, 1940, walnut plastic, streamline, right front airplane dial, curved left w/horizontal wrap-around louvers, 2 knobs, 5 tubes, AC/DC $100.00

D-140, table, 1940, ivory plastic, streamline, right front airplane dial, curved left w/horizontal wrap-around louvers, 2 knobs, 5 tubes, AC/DC $100.00

DA-28, table, 1938, wood, right front dial, left cloth grill w/horizontal & vertical bars, 4 knobs, BC, SW, 7 tubes, battery....................$35.00

E-186, table, 1940, walnut plastic, right front airplane dial, left horizontal wrap-around louvers, 3 knobs, BC, SW, 6 tubes, AC/DC....................$45.00

E-187, table, 1940, ivory plastic, right front airplane dial, left horizontal wrap-around louvers, 3 knobs, BC, SW, 6 tubes, AC/DC....................$45.00

E-188, table, 1940, two-tone walnut, right front airplane dial, left grill w/3 vertical bars, 3 knobs, BC, SW, 6 tubes, AC/DC....................$50.00

E-189, table, 1940, two-tone walnut, right front slide rule dial, left horizontal grill bars, tuning eye, pushbuttons, 4 knobs, BC, SW, 9 tubes, AC....................$80.00

E-191 "Veri-Own," portable, 1940, leatherette, inner dial and vertical grill bars, fold-open door, handle, BC, battery.......$40.00

EB-52, table, 1938, wood, right front dial, left cloth grill w/2 vertical bars, 3 knobs, 5 tubes, battery....................$35.00

EB-56, table, 1938, wood, right front telephone dial, left wrap-around cloth grill w/2 horizontal bars, 3 knobs, 5 tubes, AC....................$75.00

EB58, table, 1938, two-tone wood, right front telephone dial, left wrap-around cloth grill w/2 horizontal bars, 3 knobs, 6 tubes, AC/DC....................$75.00

EB65, chairside-R/P, 1938, wood, Deco, fold-back top, top telephone dial, front round cloth grill w/vertical bars, inner phono, BC, SW, 6 tubes, AC....................$185.00

EB66, table, 1938, three-tone wood, right front telephone dial, left cloth grill, 4 knobs, BC, SW, 7 tubes, AC/DC................$75.00

EB67, table, 1938, wood, right front telephone dial, left cloth grill w/Deco cut-outs, 4 knobs, BC, SW, 7 tubes, battery $50.00

EB70, table, 1938, two-tone wood, right front telephone dial, left cloth grill area, 4 knobs, BC, SW, 6 tubes, AC.............$75.00

FA-10, table, 1938, ivory plastic, Deco case w/step-down sides, front airplane dial, upper vertical grill bars, tuning eye, 4 knobs, BC, SW, 7 tubes, AC/DC....................$1,000.00+

FA-11, table, 1938, red plastic, Deco case w/step-down sides, front airplane dial, upper vertical grill bars, tuning eye, 4 knobs, BC, SW, 7 tubes, AC/DC....................$1,000.00+

FA-12, table, 1938, ebony plastic, Deco case w/step-down sides, front airplane dial, upper vertical grill bars, tuning eye, 4 knobs, BC, SW, 7 tubes, AC/DC....................$1,000.00+

FA-15W, table, 1947, wood, small right front vertical slide rule dial, left horizontal louvers, 2 knobs, BC, AC/DC.........$35.00

FE-141, table, 1940, walnut plastic, Deco, step-down top, right front half-round dial, left horizontal bars, base, 6 pushbuttons, right side knob, 6 tubes, AC/DC $150.00

FE-142, table, 1940, ivory plastic, Deco, step-down top, right front half-round dial, left horizontal bars, base, 6 pushbuttons, right side knob, 6 tubes, AC/DC $150.00

FE-143, table, 1940, walnut plastic, Deco, step-down top, right front dial, left horizontal bars, pushbuttons, right side knob, 5 tubes, AC/DC $150.00

FE-144, table, 1940, ivory plastic, Deco, step-down top, right front dial, left horizontal bars, pushbuttons, right side knob, 5 tubes, AC/DC $150.00

FE-145, console-R/P, 1940, walnut veneer, inner right dial/left phono, lift top, double front grill doors, BC, SW, 11 tubes, AC....................$125.00

FE-146, console-R/P, 1940, wood, inner right dial/left phono, lift top, front grill area, BC, SW, 11 tubes, AC.................$125.00

FE-147, console-R/P, 1940, mahogany, inner right dial/left phono, lift top, double front doors, inner grill & storage, BC, SW, 11 tubes, AC....................$125.00

FE-147R, console-R/P, 1940, mahogany, inner right dial/left phono, lift top, double front doors, inner grill & storage, BC, SW, 11 tubes, AC....................$125.00

FE-149, console, 1940, walnut, upper front slanted slide rule dial, lower cloth grill w/center vertical divider, tuning eye, 8 pushbuttons, 3 knobs, BC, SW, 11 tubes, AC $150.00

FE-151, console-R/P, 1940, mahogany, inner front dial & grill, double doors, lift top, inner phono, BC, SW, 11 tubes, AC $125.00

FE-152, console-R/P, 1940, walnut, inner front dial & grill, double doors, lift top, inner phono, BC, SW, 11 tubes, AC $125.00

FE-154, console-R/P, 1940, bleached mahogany, inner front dial & grill, double doors, lift top, inner phono, BC, SW, 11 tubes, AC....................$125.00

FE-155, console-R/P, 1940, wood, inner right dial/left phono, lift top, double front doors, inner grill & storage, BC, SW, 11 tubes, AC....................$125.00

FE-156, console-R/P, 1940, wood, inner right dial/left phono, lift top, double front grill doors, BC, SW, 11 tubes, AC $125.00

FS16, table, 1938, wood, right front dial, left grill w/2 horizontal bars, 2 knobs, BC, 5 tubes, AC/DC....................$35.00

FS29, table, 1938, walnut, right front airplane dial, left grill w/cut-outs, 3 knobs, BC, SW, 10 tubes, AC/DC....................$45.00

FS30, table, 1938, two-tone wood, right front airplane dial, left grill w/cut-outs, tuning eye, 3 knobs, BC, SW, 11 tubes, AC/DC....................$65.00

FS47, console, 1938, wood, upper front dial, lower cloth grill w/center vertical divider, tuning eye, 4 knobs, BC, SW, 11 tubes, AC/DC....................$130.00

FS-60, table-R/P, 1938, walnut, right front dial, left cloth grill w/curved cut-outs, 4 knobs, lift top, inner phono, BC, 5 tubes, AC/DC....................$30.00

J62C, table-R/P, 1947, wood, front slanted slide rule dial, lower grill, 4 knobs, 3/4 lift top, inner phono, BC, SW, AC.....$35.00

JS-129, console, 1940, walnut, upper front dial, lower grill w/2 vertical bars, tuning eye, 5 knobs, BC, SW, 8 tubes, AC ..$150.00

JS-130, portable, 1940, brown/white leatherette, inner right dial, left grill, 2 knobs, slide-in front, handle, BC, 6 tubes, AC/DC/battery....................$25.00

JS-130BL, portable, 1940, blue/white leatherette, inner right dial, left grill, 2 knobs, slide-in front, handle, BC, 6 tubes, AC/DC/battery....................$25.00

JS-135, table, 1940, walnut, right front airplane dial, left grill area, 4 knobs, BC, SW, 6 tubes, AC $45.00

JS-168 "Symphonette," table-R/P, 1940, two-tone walnut, right front dial, left grill w/center vertical bar, tuning eye, 5 knobs, BC, SW, 9 tubes, AC/DC....................$45.00

JS-173, table, 1940, two-tone walnut, right front dial, left grill w/center vertical bar, tuning eye, 5 knobs, BC, SW, 8 tubes, AC $65.00

JS-175 "Symphonette," table-R/P, 1940, two-tone walnut, right front dial, left grill w/center vertical bar, tuning eye, 5 knobs, BC, SW, 8 tubes, AC $45.00

JS-176, table-R/P/Rec, 1940, wood, right front dial, left grill w/center vertical bar, tuning eye, 5 knobs, lift top, inner phono/recorder, BC, SW, 9 tubes, AC $55.00

JS-177, table, 1940, walnut plastic, right front airplane dial, left grill w/concentric squares, handle, 2 knobs, BC, 5 tubes, AC/DC $45.00

JS-178, table, 1940, ivory plastic, right front airplane dial, left grill w/concentric squares, handle, 2 knobs, BC, 5 tubes, AC/DC $45.00

JS-179, table, 1940, walnut plastic, right front airplane dial, left cloth grill w/cut-outs, handle, 3 knobs, 5 tubes, AC/DC **$50.00**

JS-180, table, 1940, ivory plastic, right front airplane dial, left cloth grill w/cut-outs, handle, 3 knobs, 5 tubes, AC/DC **$50.00**

JS-181, table, 1940, walnut plastic, right front airplane dial, left cloth grill w/cut-outs, handle, 4 knobs, BC, SW, 6 tubes, AC/DC **$50.00**

JS-182, table, 1940, ivory plastic, right front airplane dial, left cloth grill w/cut-outs, handle, 4 knobs, BC, SW, 6 tubes, AC/DC **$50.00**

JS-183, table, 1940, two-tone walnut, right front dial, left horizontal grill bars, tuning eye, 4 knobs, BC, 8 tubes, AC **$60.00**

M-31, tombstone, 1938, wood, lower front round airplane dial, upper cloth grill w/cut-outs, 4 knobs, BC, SW, 6 tubes, 32 volt power..**$50.00**

M31-71, cathedral, wood, shouldered, center front half-round dial, upper 3-section cloth grill, 3 knobs.................$140.00

M42, console, 1938, wood, large upper front round dial, lower cloth grill w/3 vertical bars, tuning eye, 4 knobs, BC, SW, 12 tubes, AC...**$175.00**

MC10B, table, 1947, plastic, right front dial, left horizontal louvers, 2 knobs, BC, AC/DC...................................**$45.00**

MC11, table, 1947, two-tone, rounded top, upper front slanted slide rule dial, lower grill, 3 knobs, BC, AC/DC **$40.00**

MC12, table, 1947, plastic, upper front slanted slide rule dial, lower horizontal wrap-around louvers, 3 knobs, BC, 2SW, AC/DC **$40.00**

MC13, table-R/P, 1947, wood, center front square dial, right/left cloth grills, 2 knobs, lift top, inner phono, BC, AC **$25.00**

MC16, table, 1947, plastic, Deco, right front dial, left horizontal wrap-around louvers, 2 knobs, BC, AC/DC **$70.00**

S-49, table-R/P, 1940, wood, small right front dial, left cloth grill, 2 knobs, lift top, inner phono, BC, 5 tubes, AC **$25.00**

S-161 "Mini-Portable," portable, 1940, leatherette, top right dial knob, top left on/off/volume knob, front grill, handle, BC, 4 tubes, battery..**$30.00**

S-165, table, 1940, walnut, upper front slide rule dial, lower grill area, 2 knobs, BC, 5 tubes, AC/DC.............................**$35.00**

SB7, table, 1938, walnut, right front dial, left cloth grill w/horizontal bars, 2 knobs, BC, 5 tubes, AC **$40.00**

SB8, table, 1938, walnut, right front dial, left cloth grill w/horizontal bars, tuning eye, 2 knobs, BC, 6 tubes, AC **$40.00**

LAMCO
La Magna Mfg. Co., Inc.,
51 Clinton Place,
East Rutherford, New Jersey

1000, table, 1947, plastic, right front round dial, left horizontal wrap-around louvers, 2 knobs, BC, AC/DC..................**$45.00**

3000, portable, 1948, two-tone leatherette, right front dial, left cloth grill, handle, 2 knobs **$35.00**

———————————————————————————————

LASALLE
LaSalle Radio Products Co.,
140 Washington Street,
New York, New York

LTUC "Trans-Universe," tombstone, 1935, wood, center front octagonal dial, upper cloth grill w/cut-outs, 3 knobs, BC, SW, 7 tubes, AC **$115.00**

———————————————————————————————

LEARADIO
Lear Incorporated,
110 Ionia Avenue, N. W., Grand Rapids, Michigan

561, table, 1946, wood, upper front slide rule dial, lower cloth grill, 2 knobs, BC, AC/DC $35.00

566, table, 1946, plastic, upper front slide rule dial, lower horizontal louvers w/ stylized "X," 2 knobs, BC $65.00

567, table, 1946, plastic, upper front slide rule dial, lower horizontal louvers w/ stylized "X," 2 knobs, BC, AC/DC............$65.00

1281-PC, console-R/P, 1948, wood, right front tilt-out slide rule dial, 4 knobs, left pull-out phono drawer, BC, FM, 12 tubes, AC $100.00

6611PC, console-R/P, 1946, wood, right front pull-out drawer w/dial & 4 knobs, left pull-out phono drawer, BC, 2SW, 6 tubes, AC...$80.00

6615, table, 1946, wood, upper front slanted slide rule dial, lower cloth grill w/horizontal bars, 3 knobs $40.00

6616, table, 1946, plastic, upper front slide rule dial, lower horizontal louvers, 3 knobs, BC, AC/DC $35.00

6617PC, table-R/P, 1947, wood, chest-type, inner right slide rule dial, 3 knobs, left phono, lift top, BC, AC......................$35.00

RM-402C "Learavian," portable, 1948, striped cloth, top slide rule dial, 3 knobs, handle, BC, SW, LW, AC/DC/battery $40.00

LEE
John Meck Industries,
Plymouth, Indiana

400, table, 1948, flocked case, right front half-round dial/left on/off/volume markings printed on flocked grill, 2 plastic knobs, BC $150.00

LEWOL

4L "Best," table, 1934, embossed leather, right front dial, center "leaf" cut-out, angled top, 2 knobs, BC, 4 tubes, AC/DC $175.00

LEWYT
Lewyt Corp.,
60 Broadway, Brooklyn, New York

615A, table-R/P, 1947, wood, inner right slide rule dial, 4 knobs, left phono, lift top, front grill, BC, AC $25.00

711, portable, 1948, lower front dial, upper grill w/circular cut-outs, molded handle, 3 recessed knobs, BC, AC/DC/battery..$40.00

LEXINGTON
Bloomingdale Bros.,
60th Street & Lexington Avenue.,
New York, New York

6545, table-R/P, 1947, wood, top slide rule dial, front criss-cross grill, 3 knobs, open top phono, BC, AC $20.00

LIBERTY
American Communications Co.,
306 Broadway, New York, New York

507A, table, 1947, plastic, right front square dial, left horizontal wrap-around louvers, 2 knobs, BC, AC/DC..................$45.00

A6P, table, 1947, plastic, right front square dial, left horizontal wrap-around louvers, 2 knobs, BC, AC/DC.................$45.00

LIBERTY TRANSFORMER
Liberty Transformer Co.,
555 N. Parkside Ave.,
Chicago, Illinois

Sealed Five, table, 1925, wood, low rectangular case, 3 dial front panel, 5 tubes, battery...$120.00

LINCOLN
Allied Radio Corp.,
833 West Jackson Boulevard,
Chicago, Illinois

5A-110, table, 1946, wood, lower front slanted slide rule dial, large upper cloth grill, 2 knobs, BC, AC/DC $30.00

S13L-B, table, 1946, wood, upper front slanted slide rule dial, lower cloth grill w/"X" cut-out, 2 knobs, BC, SW, AC/DC..........$45.00

LOFTIN-WHITE

G, cathedral, wood, shouldered, lower front window dial upper round grill w/lyre cut-out, finials, 2 knobs, 5 tubes, AC $275.00

LOG CABIN

Log Cabin, table-N, c1935, wood, looks like log cabin, knobs in windows, speaker grill in door, 4 tubes, AC/DC $200.00

LYRIC
The Rauland Corp.,
4245 Knox Avenue, Chicago, Illinois

546T, table, 1946, plastic, right front square dial, left cloth grill w/criss-cross center, 2 knobs, BC, AC/DC $45.00

J, cathedral, two-tone wood, scalloped top, lower front half-round dial, upper cloth grill w/cut-outs, 3 knobs ...$285.00

MAGIC-TONE
Radio Development & Research Corp.,
233 West 54th Street,
New York, New York

501, table, 1946, wood, upper front slide rule dial, lower grill w/4 horizontal bars, 2 knobs, BC, AC/DC $40.00

504, table-N, 1947, liquor bottle shape, dial on neck, controls in cap, base, BC, AC/DC..$350.00

510, portable, 1948, "snakeskin," purse-type, dial on top of case, strap, right side knob, BC, 4 tubes, battery $60.00

900, table-N, 1948, keg lamp, keg front "spigot" is dial, keg top knob is volume control, base, BC, AC/DC...................$250.00

MAGNAVOX
The Magnavox Company,
Oakland, California

The Magnavox Company was formed in 1917 for the manufacture of microphones and loudspeakers and, during WW I, the company did much business with the US government. Magnavox soon began to produce radios but lost money throughout the 1920's due to many internal problems.

10, table, 1925, wood, low rectangular case, center front dial, 5 tubes, battery..$165.00

25, table, 1925, wood, high rectangular case, lower 1 dial panel, upper built-in speaker grill, battery $210.00

28M, end table-R/P, 1941, wood, top dial & knobs, front grill w/cut-outs, lift top, inner phono, 7 tubes, AC..............$115.00

75, console, 1925, mahogany, inner 1 dial panel, fold-down front, upper built-in speaker grill, 5 tubes, battery $275.00

154B, console-R/P, 1947, wood, inner right dial, 5 knobs, 6 pushbuttons, door, left pull-out phono drawer, BC, SW, 10 tubes, AC...$85.00

155B "Regency Symphony," console-R/P, 1947, wood, inner right dial, 5 knobs, 8 pushbuttons, door, left lift top, inner phono, BC, SW, 13 tubes, AC.......................................$95.00

AM-20, table-C, plastic, large right side dial knob, left front square clock face over horizontal grill bars, left side knob, BC, AC..$25.00

D, table, 1925, wood, high rectangular case, lower front pull-out chassis drawer, upper built-in speaker grill, battery $175.00

FM40, table, 1961, wood, lower front slide rule dial, large upper grill area w/2 speakers, 4 knobs, 7 tubes $20.00

J "Junior," table, 1925, wood, square case, center front dial, 3 knobs, lift top, 5 tubes, battery $150.00

T, table, 1925, wood, inner right pull-out chassis drawer, left speaker, fold-down front, 5 tubes $145.00

TRF-5, table, 1924, wood, low rectangular case, center front round dial, side cut-outs, feet, 5 tubes, battery $160.00

TRF-50, table, 1924, wood, inner dial & knobs, built-in speaker, double doors w/carvings, 5 tubes, battery..................$250.00

MAGUIRE
Maguire Industries, Inc.,
West Putnam,
Greenwich, Connecticut

6L, table, plastic, step-back right w/slide rule dial, left horizontal wrap-around louvers, 3 knobs, BC, SW $45.00

500BW, table, 1946, plastic, left front round dial, horizontal louvers, 2 knobs, BC, AC/DC $35.00

561DW, table, 1946, plastic, left front round dial, horizontal grill bars, 2 knobs, BC, AC/DC $40.00

571, table, 1948, plastic, left front round dial, horizontal louvers, 2 knobs, BC, AC/DC $40.00

661, table, 1947, plastic, left front round dial, horizontal wrap-around bars, 2 knobs, handle, BC, AC/DC..................$55.00

700A, table-R/P, 1946, wood, lower front slide rule dial, upper horizontal louvers, 3 knobs, 3/4 lift top, inner phono, BC, AC $35.00

700E, table-R/P, 1947, wood, lower front slide rule dial, upper criss-cross grill, 3 knobs, 3/4 lift top, inner phono, BC, AC $30.00

MAJESTIC
Grigsby-Grunow Company,
5801 Dickens Avenue, Chicago, Illinois
Majestic Radio & Television Corporation,
St. Charles, Illinois

The Grigsby-Grunow Company was formed in 1928. The company's radio sales were extraordinary due to the superiority of their speakers over that of others on the market. However, the Depression soon caught up with Grigsby-Grunow, and by 1933 the company was bankrupt. The business was re-formed into the Majestic Radio & Television Corporation which made the Majestic line and General Household Utilities which made the Grunow line until 1937.

1 "Charlie McCarthy," table-N, 1938, plastic, small right front slide rule dial, rounded left w/Charlie McCarthy figure, 2 knobs, BC, 6 tubes, AC **$1,200.00**

1A-59, table, 1939, two-tone wood, right front slide rule dial, left horizontal wrap-around louvers, 2 knobs, 5 tubes, AC..**$50.00**

1BR50-B, portable, 1939, luggage-type, striped cloth, front dial, grill & knobs, handle, AC/DC/battery **$30.00**

2C60-P, console-R/P, 1939, wood, Deco, upper slide rule dial, pushbuttons, fold-down front, inner phono, BC, SW, AC........**$165.00**

3BC90-B, console, 1939, walnut, Deco, upper front slanted slide rule dial, lower vertical grill bars, pushbuttons, tuning eye, BC, SW, 9 tubes..**$200.00**

3-C-80, console, 1939, wood, upper front slide rule dial, lower grill & decorative horizontal bars, pushbuttons, BC, SW, AC ..**$165.00**

4L1, portable, 1955, plastic, center front round dial w/eagle, top right thumbwheel on/off/volume knob, handle, BC, 4 tubes, battery **$35.00**

5A410, table, 1946, plastic, upper front raised slide rule dial, lower horizontal wrap-around louvers, 2 knobs, BC..$80.00

5A430, table, 1946, wood, small upper front slide rule dial, lower cloth grill, 2 knobs, BC, AC/DC **$35.00**

5A445, table-R/P, 1947, wood, right front dial, left criss-cross grill, 3 knobs, lift top, inner phono, BC, AC **$30.00**

5A445R, table-R/P, 1947, wood, right front dial, 3 knobs, left grill, lift top, inner phono, BC, AC..**$30.00**

5AK711, table, 1947, plastic, low case, slide rule dial, top vertical grill bars, 2 knobs, BC, AC/DC **$110.00**

5AK780, end table-R/P, 1947, step down end table, top dial & 3 knobs, phono in base w/lift top, BC, AC **$75.00**

5C-2, table-C, 1952, plastic, upper front dial, center clock, right & left vertical bars, 5 knobs, BC, AC................................**$45.00**

5LA5, table, 1951, plastic, upper front raised slide rule dial, lower horizontal wrap-around louvers, 2 knobs, BC, AC/DC ...**$80.00**

5LA7, table, 1951, plastic, raised top, upper front slanted slide rule dial, lower horizontal wrap-around louvers, 2 knobs, BC, AC/DC **$60.00**

5M1, portable, 1955, plastic, center front round dial w/eagle, top right thumbwheel on/off/volume knob, fold-down handle, BC, 4 tubes, AC/DC/battery **$35.00**

5T, table-C, 1939, plastic, Deco, center round dial surrounds clock face, rear grill, 2 knobs, BC, 5 tubes, AC/DC ..$150.00

6FM714, table, 1948, plastic, raised top, upper front slanted slide rule dial, lower right & left horizontal wrap-around louvers, 2 knobs, BC, FM, AC/DC **$60.00**

6FM773, console-R/P, 1949, wood, inner right dial, 2 knobs, left phono, lift top, front criss-cross grill, BC, FM, AC.........**$55.00**

7C40, table-R/P, 1942, walnut, right front dial, left vertical grill bars, 3 knobs, lift top, inner phono, 7 tubes, AC **$35.00**

7C432, table, 1947, wood, upper front slide rule dial, lower horizontal louvers, 4 knobs, tubular feet, BC, AC...............**$40.00**

7C447, table-R/P, 1947, wood, inner right vertical dial, 4 knobs, left phono, lift top, front criss-cross grill, BC, AC **$30.00**

7FM888, console-R/P, 1949, wood, inner right slide rule dial, 2 knobs, left pull-out phono drawer, doors, BC, FM, 7 tubes, AC/DC **$70.00**

7JK777R, console-R/P, 1947, wood, inner right dial, 4 knobs, left phono, lift top, front criss-cross grill, BC, AC.................**$65.00**

7JL866, end table-R/P, 1949, wood, step-down top, slide rule dial, 4 knobs, front pull-out phono drawer, BC, AC..............**$90.00**

7K60, console, 1941, wood, upper front dial, lower grill w/vertical bars, 3 knobs, 7 tubes **$125.00**

7P420, portable, 1947, leatherette, inner right dial, left grill w/eagle, fold-down front, handle, telescope antenna, BC, AC/DC/battery $45.00

7T11, table, 1942, plastic, right front airplane dial, curved left w/horizontal wrap-around bars, 3 knobs, 7 tubes, AC/DC...$125.00

7YR752, table-R/P/Rec, 1947, wood, outer right front dial, left cloth grill, 3 knobs, lift top, inner phono/recorder, BC, AC..$25.00

8FM744, table, 1947, wood, curved top, front slide rule dial over large cloth grill area, 2 knobs, BC, FM, AC/DC $40.00

8FM775, console-R/P, 1947, wood, upper front slide rule dial, lower pull-out phono drawer, 3 knobs, BC, FM, AC $55.00

8FM776, console-R/P, 1947, wood, inner right slide rule dial, 3 knobs, left pull-out phono drawer, double doors, BC, FM, AC..$65.00

8FM889, console-R/P, 1949, wood, inner right slide rule dial, 3 knobs, left pull-out phono drawer, double doors, BC, FM, AC..$75.00

8JL885, console-R/P, 1948, wood, upper front slide rule dial, center pull-out phono drawer, lower grill, 5 knobs, BC, SW, AC..$85.00

8S452, table-R/P, 1946, wood, inner right dial & knobs, horizontal wrap-around louvers, BC, SW, AC $40.00

8S473, console-R/P, 1946, wood, inner right dial & knobs, left phono, lift-top, front criss-cross grill, BC, SW, AC.........$85.00

10FM891, console-R/P, 1949, wood, inner right slide rule dial, 4 knobs, left pull-out phono, double doors, BC, SW, FM, AC..$75.00

12FM475, console-R/P, 1947, wood, inner right dial & knobs, left phono, lift top, front criss-cross grill, BC, SW, FM, AC ..$80.00

12FM895, console-R/P, 1949, wood, inner right slide rule dial, 4 knobs, left pull-out phono drawer, double doors, BC, SW, FM, AC $80.00

15, tombstone, 1932, wood, shouldered, center front window dial, upper cloth grill w/cut-outs, 3 knobs, 5 tubes, AC $120.00

15A, tombstone, 1932, wood, shouldered, center front window dial, upper cloth grill w/cut-outs, 3 knobs, 5 tubes ...$120.00

30, cathedral, wood, shouldered, right front window dial w/escutcheon, upper cloth grill w/cut-outs, small finials, 2 knobs, AC $175.00

31, cathedral, 1931, walnut, shouldered, right front window dial, upper cloth grill with cut-outs, small finials, 2 knobs, 6 tubes..$175.00

44 "Duo-Chief," table, 1933, wood, lower left front dial, upper grill w/aluminum cut-outs, 2 knobs, BC, SW, 4 tubes, AC $175.00

49 "Duo-Modern," table, 1933, two-tone wood, lower left front dial, upper cloth grill w/aluminum cut-outs, 2 knobs, BC, SW, 4 tubes, AC $175.00

50, cathedral, 1931, wood, shouldered, right front window dial, upper cloth grill w/cut-outs, small finials, 2 knobs, 8 tubes $175.00

50, cathedral/stand, 1931, wood w/stand, shouldered, right front window dial, upper cloth grill w/cut-outs, small finials, 2 knobs, 8 tubes..$225.00

52, cathedral/stand, 1930, wood w/stand, shouldered, right front window dial, upper cloth grill w/cut-outs, top spires, 8 tubes, 2 knobs..$225.00

52, table, 1938, plastic, upper right front dial, left grill w/2 horizontal bars, 2 knobs, BC, 5 tubes, AC/DC $60.00

55 "Duette," table, 1933, two-tone wood, left front dial & knobs, grill w/aluminum lyre-shaped cut-out, BC, SW, 5 tubes, AC $200.00

56 "Ardmore," cathedral, 1933, wood, peaked top, center front window dial, upper cloth grill w/cut-outs, 3 knobs, finials...$200.00

57 "Berkshire," console, 1933, wood, lowboy, upper front window dial, lower cloth grill w/cut-outs, 3 knobs $135.00

59 "Studio," tombstone, 1933, two-tone wood, Deco, step-down top, lower front dial & knobs, upper grill w/vertical aluminum bars, BC, SW, 5 tubes, AC..$325.00

60, table, two-tone wood, Deco, right front oval dial, left cloth grill w/cut-outs, 4 knobs $85.00

67 "Barclay," console, 1933, wood, lowboy, upper front window dial, lower cloth grill w/cut-outs, decorative fluting, 6 legs, 6 tubes...$135.00

68 "Plaza," console, 1933, wood, upper front window dial, lower cloth grill w/cut-outs, decorative fluting and carvings, 6 tubes ..$135.00

69 "Savoy," console, 1933, wood, upper front window dial, lower cloth grill w/scrolled cut-outs, 6 tubes.........................$145.00

71, console, 1928, walnut, upper front window dial, lower oval cloth grill w/cut-outs, 3 knobs, BC, 7 tubes, AC $175.00

71B, console, 1929, wood, lowboy, upper front window dial w/oval escutcheon, lower round cloth grill w/cut-outs, 3 knobs, AC $175.00

75 "Queen Anne," console, 1933, walnut w/oriental wood front panel, upper front window dial, lower grill w/cut-outs, Queen Anne legs **$165.00**

76, table, 1936, wood, step-down top, front oval dial w/escutcheon, left grill, tuning eye, BC, SW, 7 tubes, AC **$80.00**

77, console, 1933, wood, upper front window dial, lower grill w/cut-outs, Queen Anne legs, 3 knobs, 7 tubes.........**$150.00**

80FMP2, console-R/P, 1951, wood, inner right slide rule dial, 2 knobs, door, left pull-out phono drawer, lower grill, BC, FM, AC **$75.00**

86 "Hyde Park," console, 1931, walnut, upper front window dial, lower cloth grill w/scrolled cut-outs, 3 knobs, 8 tubes, AC...**$140.00**

90, console, 1929, wood, lowboy, upper front window dial, lower cloth grill, 3 knobs, stretcher base **$135.00**

90-B, console, 1929, wood, lowboy, upper front window dial, lower cloth grill, 3 knobs, stretcher base................$135.00

91, console, 1929, walnut, lowboy, upper front window dial, lower cloth grill w/cut-outs, 3 knobs, stretcher base, AC **$130.00**

92, console, 1929, walnut, highboy, inner front window dial, oval cloth grill w/cut-outs, double doors, 3 knobs, AC **$140.00**

93, console, 1930, wood, lowboy, front window dial, lower cloth grill w/cut-outs, 3 knobs, stretcher base, AC **$140.00**

102, console-R/P, 1930, wood, lowboy, front window dial, lower cloth grill w/cut-outs, lift top, inner phono, storage **$150.00**

103, console-R/P, 1930, wood, lowboy, inner front window dial, lower cloth grill w/cut-outs, double doors, lift top, inner phono ...**$150.00**

130, console, 1930, walnut, lowboy, upper front window dial, lower cloth grill w/cut-outs, AC **$130.00**

130, portable, 1939, leatherette, small case, upper front round dial, angled top, handle, 2 knobs, BC, battery...............**$75.00**

131, console, 1930, wood, lowboy, upper front window dial, lower cloth grill w/cut-outs, AC.....................................**$130.00**

132, console, 1930, wood, highboy, inner front window dial, upper grill w/cut-outs, double doors, stretcher base..............**$150.00**

151 "Havenwood," tombstone, 1931, wood, shouldered, center front window dial, upper cloth grill w/cut-outs, 3 knobs..**$130.00**

153 "Ellswood," console, wood, lowboy, upper front window dial, lower cloth grill w/cut-outs, 3 knobs............................**$140.00**

155 "Castlewood," console-R/P, wood, lowboy, upper front window dial, lower cloth grill w/cut-outs, 3 knobs, lift top, inner phono **$130.00**

156 "Sherwood," grandfather clock, wood, front window dial, upper clock face, rounded top, finials, lower door w/inner storage, AC **$450.00**

161, tombstone, wood, step-down top, right front window dial, center cloth grill w/chrome cut-outs, 2 knobs **$235.00**

167, tombstone, 1939, wood, lower front large round dial, upper cloth grill w/5 vertical bars, BC, SW, AC **$95.00**

181, console-R/P, 1929, walnut, lowboy, inner front window dial, lower round grill w/cut-outs, 3 knobs, double doors, phono, AC **$150.00**

194 "Gothic," cathedral, 1933, walnut finish, lower right front dial, upper cloth grill w/cut-outs, BC, SW, 4 tubes, AC **$195.00**

195 "Gothic," cathedral, 1933, walnut finish, front window dial, upper cloth grill w/cut-outs, 2 knobs, BC, SW, 5 tubes, AC **$250.00**

196 "Gothic," cathedral, 1933, wood, front window dial, upper cloth grill w/cut-outs, fluted columns, BC, 6 tubes, AC **$250.00**

200, console, 1932, wood, lowboy, upper front quarter-round dial, lower cloth grill w/cut-outs, 3 knobs, stretcher base...$125.00

201 "Sheffield," tombstone, 1932, wood, Deco, lower front quarter-round dial, upper cloth grill w/cut-outs, 3 knobs, 8 tubes **$130.00**

203 "Fairfax," console, 1932, wood, lowboy, Early English design, upper front quarter round dial, lower cloth grill w/cut-outs, stretcher base, 8 tubes **$150.00**

211 "Whitehall," console, 1932, wood, highboy, Jacobean design, lower front quarter-round dial, upper cloth grill w/cut-outs, 10 tubes **$150.00**

214 "Stratford," console, 1932, wood, lowboy, Art-Modern design, upper front quarter-round dial, lower cloth grill w/cut-outs, 10 tubes **$150.00**

215 "Croydon," console, 1932, wood, highboy, Early English design, front quarter-round dial, upper 2-section cloth grill w/cut-outs, 10 tubes **$200.00**

233, console-R/P, 1930, wood, lowboy, inner front window dial/grill, double doors, lift top, inner phono, AC.........**$175.00**

250-MI "Zephyr," table, 1939, plastic, raised top, upper front slide rule dial, lower horizontal wrap-around louvers, top pushbuttons, 2 knobs **$100.00**

251 "Cheltenwood," tombstone/stand, 1933, wood, front quarter-round dial, upper cloth grill w/cut-outs, 3 knobs, stretcher base **$150.00**

253 "Brentwood," console, wood, lowboy, Jacobean design, upper front quarter-round dial, lower cloth grill w/cut-outs, 3 knobs, stretcher base **$150.00**

259-EB, table, 1939, walnut, front slide rule dial, curved left grill w/cut-outs, pushbuttons, 2 knobs, BC, SW, AC **$85.00**

291, tombstone, 1932, two-tone walnut, peaked top, Art Moderne design, lower front quarter-round dial, upper cloth grill w/cut-outs, 3 knobs, 9 tubes **$175.00**

293, console, 1933, wood, lowboy, upper front quarter-round dial, lower cloth grill w/cut-outs, 3 knobs, 6 legs, 9 tubes......................................**$150.00**

304, console, 1932, wood, inner front quarter-round dial, large lower cloth grill w/cut-outs, 3 knobs, double doors, 6 legs, stretcher base......................................**$160.00**

310A, tombstone, wood, center front window dial w/escutcheon, large cloth grill area w/cut-outs, 3 knobs **$110.00**

311, tombstone, 1932, wood, center front window dial, large cloth grill area w/cut-outs, 3 knobs, 7 tubes......................................**$110.00**

314, console, 1932, wood, lowboy, upper front window dial, large cloth grill area w/cut-outs, 3 knobs, 6 legs, stretcher base, 7 tubes......................................**$175.00**

324, console, 1932, wood, lowboy, inner front quarter-round dial, lower 2-section cloth grill w/cut-outs, 3 knobs, double doors, 6 legs, stretcher base, 12 tubes **$195.00**

331, cathedral, 1933, wood, shouldered, center front window dial, upper grill w/gothic cut-outs, 3 knobs, 7 tubes, AC **$265.00**

336, console, 1933, wood, lowboy, upper front window dial, lower cloth grill w/cut-outs, 3 knobs, 7 tubes, AC **$135.00**

344, console, 1933, wood, lowboy, inner window dial, doors, lower cloth grill w/criss-cross cut-outs, twin speakers, 6 legs, 11 tubes, AC $140.00

351 "Collingwood," console, 1932, wood, lowboy, Tudor design, inner front quarter-round dial, lower cloth grill w/cut-outs, double doors, 10 tubes......................................**$160.00**

353 "Abbeywood," console-R/P, 1932, wood, ornate Charles II design, inner front dial & knobs, doors, right & left cloth grills w/cut-outs, lift top, inner phono, 10 tubes..................**$235.00**

363, console, 1933, wood, lowboy, upper front quarter-round dial, pipe organ front panel w/illuminated stained glass insert, lower grill w/gothic cut-outs, 6 legs, 11 tubes, AC **$250.00**

370, table, 1933, wood, rounded top, right front window dial, center cloth grill w/cut-outs, 2 knobs, AC **$90.00**

371, table, 1933, wood, rounded top, right front window dial, center grill w/gothic cut-outs, 2 knobs, 5 tubes **$90.00**

373, table, 1933, wood, rounded top, right front window dial, upper grill w/illuminated glass insert, 2 knobs, 5 tubes, AC **$175.00**

381 "Treasure Chest," table-N, 1933, wood w/repwood trim, looks like treasure chest, inner dial, speaker in lid, AC.........**$225.00**

393, console, 1933, wood, lowboy, upper front window dial, lower cloth grill w/"peacock" cut-out, 6 legs, 3 knobs, 8 tubes, AC **$185.00**

400, table, 1941, plastic, raised top, upper front slide rule dial, lower horizontal wrap-around louvers, 2 knobs, 5 tubes, AC/DC **$80.00**

411 "DeLuxe," table, 1933, wood w/inlay, Deco, front dial & knobs, center grill w/aluminum cut-outs, 6 tubes, AC/DC **$150.00**

448-2, table, 1940, wood, right front slide rule dial, left vertical wrap-over bars, battery **$45.00**

461 "Master Six," tombstone, 1933, wood, front window dial, upper chrome grill, vertical fluted front bar, top & side fluting, 6 tubes, AC......................................**$150.00**

463 "Century Six," table, 1933, walnut, right front window dial, left grill w/Deco chrome cut-outs, left side knob, 6 tubes, AC **$200.00**

511, table, 1938, plastic, center front slide rule dial surrounded by circular grill area w/horizontal louvers, 2 knobs, BC, 5 tubes, AC **$800.00**

560 "Chatham," console, 1933, birch & walnut, lowboy, upper front window dial, lower cloth grill with vertical bars, stretcher base......................................**$130.00**

566 "Tudor," console, 1933, oak, antique finish, upper front window dial, geometric grill cut-outs, stretcher base **$135.00**

599 "Radiograph," table-R/P, 1931, walnut, left front dial & knobs, center cloth grill w/cut-outs, lift top, inner phono, 5 tubes......................................**$75.00**

651, table, 1937, plastic, front round airplane dial, curved left w/wrap-around horizontal bars, 3 knobs, BC, 5 tubes, AC/DC $125.00

666 "Ritz," console, 1933, two-tone wood, Deco, upper front window dial, "V" shaped grill with vertical cut-outs **$185.00**

5H11U, table, 1950, plastic, large center front round dial w/stylized "M" logo over dotted grill, 2 knobs, BC, AC/DC **$30.00**

5H12, table, 1952, plastic, large center front round dial w/stylized "M" logo over dotted grill, 2 knobs, BC, AC/DC **$30.00**

5J1 "Jewel Box," portable, 1950, plastic, inner right dial, center Oriental pattern grill, flip-up front, handle, BC, AC/DC/battery **$85.00**

5L1 "Music Box," portable, 1950, two-tone plastic, right front dial, center checkered grill, handle, 2 knobs, BC, AC/DC/battery **$30.00**

5L1U, portable, 1950, two-tone plastic, right front dial, center checkered grill, handle, 2 knobs, BC **$30.00**

5M1 "Playmate Jr.," portable, 1950, metal, small case, inner right dial, 2 knobs, flip-up front, handle, BC, AC/DC/battery **$45.00**

5M1U, portable, 1950, metal, small case, inner right dial, 2 knobs, flip-up front, handle, BC, AC/DC/battery **$45.00**

5P21N, portable, plastic, upper right front dial knob overlaps lower horizontal grill bars, stylized "M" logo, handle, BC...**$25.00**

5P23WB-1, portable, leatherette & plastic, upper right front dial knob overlaps V-shaped grill area w/vertical bars, handle, BC **$40.00**

5P31A, portable, 1957, leatherette & plastic, upper right front dial knob, lower lattice grill area, rotatable handle, BC **$30.00**

5P22RW-1, portable, leatherette, right front round dial knob, lower horizontal bars, handle, AC/DC/battery **$35.00**

5P32Y, portable, leatherette, upper right front dial knob, lower perforated grill area w/lower left "M" logo, handle, BC.........**$30.00**

5R1, table, 1951, plastic, right front round dial w/center "M" logo, lower "high-low" checkered panel, 2 knobs, BC...$40.00

5R11U, table, 1950, plastic, right front round dial, lower "hi-low" checkered panel, 2 knobs, BC, AC/DC $40.00

5R23G, table-R/P, 1958, front dial and knobs over large perforated grill, slanted lift top, inner phono, BC, 5 tubes, AC...$35.00

5T, tombstone, 1937, wood, lower front dial w/escutcheon, upper grill w/bars, 4 knobs, BC, SW, 5 tubes $100.00

5T11M, table, 1959, plastic, right front round dial, left lattice grill, 2 knobs, BC, 5 tubes, AC/DC $20.00

5T13P, table, 1959, plastic, lower right front dial knob, upper & lower vertical bars, feet, BC, 5 tubes, AC/DC $30.00

5T22Y, table, 1957, plastic, lower right front round raised dial area, horizontal grill bars, left knob, BC, AC/DC $30.00

5X11U, table, 1950, plastic, center front round dial w/inner perforated grill, metal stand, 2 knobs, BC, AC/DC $40.00

5X12U, table, 1950, plastic, center front round dial w/inner perforated grill, metal stand, 2 knobs, BC, AC/DC $40.00

5X21U, table, 1951, plastic, center front round dial w/inner perforated grill, metal stand, 2 knobs, BC, AC/DC $40.00

6F11, console-R/P, 1950, wood, upper front half-round dial, 4 knobs, lower pull-out phono drawer, BC, AC $50.00

6L1 "Town & Country," portable, 1950, plastic, "U"-shaped dial w/inner perforated grill, handle, 2 knobs, BC, AC/DC/battery...$35.00

6P34E "700 Ranger," portable, 1957, leatherette, upper right front dial, lower metal perforated grill w/stylized "M" logo, handle, AC/DC/battery $35.00

6X11U, table, 1950, plastic, center front round dial w/inner perforated grill, 2 knobs, BC, AC/DC.........................$40.00

7F11, console-R/P, 1950, wood, inner right half-round dial, 4 knobs, left pull-out phono, double doors, BC, AC $55.00

7XM21, table, plastic, large half-round dial, lower "hi-low" grill area with large pointer, 2 knobs, BC, FM, AC/DC $30.00

8FM21, console-R/P, 1951, wood, upper half-round dial, 4 knobs, lower pull-out phono drawer, BC, FM, AC $50.00

8S-515, portable, leatherette, upper right front dial, lower metal perforated grill w/stylized "M" logo, rotatable handle, BC $40.00

6-T, table, 1937, wood, right front dial w/large escutcheon, left cloth grill w/3 vertical bars, 4 knobs, BC, SW, 6 tubes, AC..$85.00

6T15S "Custom 6," table, 1959, plastic, lower right front dial knob, upper vertical grill bars, BC, 6 tubes, AC/DC $30.00

8S-534, portable, leatherette, right front half-round dial, vertical grill bars, rotatable handle, BC $35.00

9A, chairside, 1937, two-tone wood, oval Deco case, top dial & knobs, tuning eye, front vertical grill bars **$150.00**

9FM21, console-R/P, 1950, wood, inner right half-round dial, 4 knobs, left pull-out phono, doors, open storage, BC, FM, AC **$50.00**

10-Y-1, console, 1937, wood, upper front dial, lower cloth grill w/vertical bars, tuning eye, BC, SW, 10 tubes, AC **$160.00**

12-Y-1, console, 1937, walnut, upper front dial, lower cloth grill w/vertical bars, tuning eye, BC, SW, 12 tubes, AC **$175.00**

17-FM-41, console, 1941, wood, upper front slide rule dial, lower vertical grill bars, tuning eye, pushbuttons, BC, SW, AC...**$145.00**

40-60W, table, 1940, wood, right front square dial, left cloth grill, wooden handle, 3 knobs, AC/DC **$50.00**

40-65BP "Headliner," portable, 1940, cloth covered, right front dial, left cloth grill, handle, 2 knobs, BC, 6 tubes, AC/DC/battery **$25.00**

40BK, console, 1940, wood, upper front dial, lower cloth grill w/vertical bars, 3 knobs..**$110.00**

40BW, table, 1940, two-tone wood, right front square dial, raised left grill w/cut-outs, 3 knobs **$65.00**

41A, table, 1939, plastic, Deco, right front dial, raised left grill w/graduated horizontal louvers, 3 knobs, 4 tubes, battery..**$60.00**

41B, table, 1939, plastic, right front dial, curved left grill w/horizontal louvers, 3 knobs, BC, 4 tubes, battery **$35.00**

41D-1, portable, 1939, London tan leatherette, right front dial, left grill, handle, 2 knobs, BC, 4 tubes, battery...............**$25.00**

41D-2, portable, 1939, tan striped cloth, right front dial, left grill, handle, 2 knobs, BC, 4 tubes, battery **$25.00**

41E, table, 1939, two-tone wood, right front dial, left grill w/cut-outs, 3 knobs, BC, 4 tubes, battery **$40.00**

41F, table, 1939, two-tone wood, right front dial, left grill w/cut-outs, 3 knobs, BC, 4 tubes, battery **$40.00**

41S "Sporter," portable, 1939, leatherette, "camera-case" style, top dial & knobs, front grill, carrying strap, 4 tubes, battery **$40.00**

42B1, portable, 1953, two-tone, top right dial knob, top left on/off/volume knob, front vertical grill bars, handle, BC, battery **$25.00**

45B12, table, 1946, two-tone wood, right front dial, left cloth grill, 3 knobs, BC, battery..**$30.00**

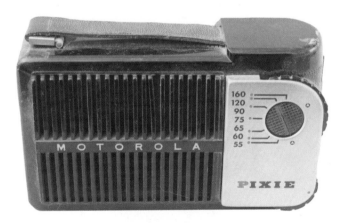

45P1 "Pixie," portable, 1956, plastic, right front metal dial plate, vertical grill bars, 2 thumbwheel knobs, handle, BC, 4 tubes, battery **$250.00**

45P2 "Pixie," portable, 1956, plastic, right front metal dial plate, vertical grill bars, 2 thumbwheel knobs, handle, BC, 4 tubes, battery **$250.00**

47B11, table, 1947, wood, right front half-round dial, left cloth grill w/center "Motorola" logo, 3 knobs, BC, battery **$30.00**

48L11, portable, 1948, plastic, right front dial knob/left volume knob over center graduated horizontal louvers, handle, 2 knobs, BC, battery...**$35.00**

49L11Q, portable, 1949, plastic, right front dial knob/left volume knob over center metal grill, flex handle, BC, battery **$35.00**

50X1, table, 1940, plastic, right front dial, left horizontal louvers, 2 knobs, BC, 5 tubes, AC/DC...**$35.00**

50XC "Circle Grill," table, 1940, Catalin, Deco, right front square dial, left round grill, handle, 2 hexagonal knobs, BC ..**$2,000.00+**

50XC1 "Circle Grill," table, 1940, Catalin, Deco, right front square dial, left round grill, handle, 2 hexagonal knobs, BC ..**$2,000.00+**

50XC4 "Circle Grill," table, 1940, Catalin, Deco, right front square dial, left round grill, handle, 2 hexagonal knobs, BC ....**$2,000.00+**

50XH1, table, plastic, right front dial, left horizontal louvers, 2 knobs, BC..**$40.00**

51A, table, 1939, plastic, Deco, right front dial, raised left grill w/graduated horizontal louvers, 2 knobs, BC, 5 tubes, AC/DC...**$75.00**

51C, table, 1939, plastic, Deco, right front dial, raised left grill w/graduated horizontal louvers, 2 knobs, BC, 5 tubes, AC/DC...**$75.00**

51D, portable, 1941, cloth covered, inner right dial, left grill, fold-down front, handle, BC, 5 tubes, AC/DC/battery..........**$30.00**

51X15 "S Grill," table, 1939, Catalin, right front square dial, left cloth grill w/curved bars, tubular handle, 2 knobs, BC, AC ..**$3,000.00+**

51X16 "S Grill," table, 1939, Catalin, right front square dial, left cloth grill w/curved bars, tubular handle, 2 knobs, BC, AC ....**$3,000.00+**

51X17, table, 1941, two-tone leatherette, right front square dial, left horizontal louvers, 2 knobs, BC, 5 tubes, AC/DC **$40.00**

51X18, table, 1941, ivory, upper front slanted slide rule dial, lower grill, 2 knobs, 5 tubes, AC **$40.00**

51X19, table, 1942, wood, right front square dial, left horizontal plastic louvers, 2 knobs, BC, 5 tubes, AC/DC $40.00

51X20, table, two-tone wood, upper front slanted slide rule dial, lower woven grill, 2 knobs, BC $45.00

52, table, 1939, Catalin, right front dial, left grill w/7 vertical louvers, 2 hexagonal knobs, BC ....**$1,000.00+**

52B1U, portable, 1953, plastic, top left dial knob, top right on/off/volume knob, front vertical grill bars, handle, BC, 4 tubes, AC/DC/battery **$30.00**

52BW, table, 1940, walnut, right front slide rule dial, left horizontal louvers, 4 knobs, BC, SW, 5 tubes, battery..................**$30.00**

52C1, table-C, 1953, plastic, right front dial, left alarm clock, center vertical bars, 4 knobs, BC, AC **$20.00**

52C4, table, 1939, Catalin, right front dial, left grill w/7 vertical louvers, 2 hexagonal knobs, BC ....**$1,000.00+**

52C6, table-C, 1952, plastic, right front dial, left alarm clock, center vertical grill bars, 5 knobs, BC, AC..........................**$20.00**

52CW1, table/wall-C, 1953, plastic, side dial knob, large upper front alarm clock, lower checkered panel w/"M" logo, BC, AC **$25.00**

52H, table, 1952, plastic, upper front dial w/stick pointer & center knob, lower vertical bars, BC, AC/DC **$30.00**

52H11U, table, 1952, plastic, upper front dial w/stick pointer & center knob, lower vertical bars, BC, AC/DC **$30.00**

52L1, portable, 1953, plastic, top right dial knob, top left on/off/volume knob, front lattice grill & stylized "M," handle, BC, 4 tubes, AC/DC/battery **$30.00**

52M1U, portable, 1952, small case, inner right round dial knob, lower lattice grill, stylized "M" cut-out, flip-up front, BC, AC/DC/battery **$40.00**

52M2U, portable, 1952, small case, inner right round dial knob, lower lattice grill, stylized "M" cut-out, flip-up front, BC, AC/DC/battery $40.00

52R12A, table, 1952, plastic, right front round dial knob, left round grill disc w/stylized "M," BC, AC/DC **$25.00**

52R12U, table, 1952, plastic, right front round dial knob, left round grill disc w/stylized "M," BC, AC/DC **$25.00**

52R14, table, 1952, plastic, right front round dial knob, left round grill disc w/stylized "M," BC, AC/DC **$25.00**

52X110, table, plastic, upper front raised slide rule dial, large lower perforated grill area, 2 knobs, BC $30.00

53A, table, 1939, two-tone wood, right front dial, left horizontal wrap-around grill bars, 2 knobs, BC, 5 tubes, AC/DC ...**$60.00**

53C, table, 1939, plastic, Deco, right front dial, raised left grill w/graduated horizontal louvers, 2 knobs, BC, 5 tubes, AC/DC...**$75.00**

53C1, table-C, 1954, plastic, right front dial, left alarm clock, side horizontal bars, 3 knobs, BC, 5 tubes, AC **$30.00**

53C1B, table-C, 1954, plastic, right front dial, left alarm clock, side horizontal bars, feet, 3 knobs, BC **$30.00**

53D1, table-C-N, 1954, clock/radio/desk set, center radio unit w/round alarm clock, right & left pen holders, 5 knobs, BC, 5 tubes, AC..**$50.00**
53F2, table-R/P, 1954, plastic, top round dial, vertical front grill bars, lift top, inner phono, BC, 5 tubes, AC **$40.00**
53H1, table, 1954, ebony plastic, modern, lower front slide rule dial, large upper perforated grill area w/center logo, 2 knobs, BC, AC **$65.00**
53H3, table, 1954, green plastic, modern, lower front slide rule dial, large upper perforated grill area w/center logo, 2 knobs, BC, AC **$65.00**
53LC, portable-C, 1953, plastic, upper right dial/left clock, large lower grill area w/center logo, handle, side knobs, AC/DC/battery ..**$40.00**
53LC1, portable-C, 1953, plastic, upper right dial/left clock, large lower grill area w/center logo, handle, side knobs, AC/DC/battery ..**$40.00**

53X, table, 1954, plastic, large half-round dial on case top, front horizontal grill bars w/logo, BC, 5 tubes, AC/DC........$40.00
53X1, table, 1954, plastic, large half-round dial on case top, front horizontal grill bars w/logo, BC, 5 tubes, AC/DC..........**$40.00**
55B1, portable, 1955, leatherette, upper front dial & on/off/volume knobs, center lattice grill area, rotatable handle, BC, 5 tubes **$30.00**
55B1U, portable, 1955, leatherette, upper front dial & on/off/volume knobs, center lattice grill area, rotatable handle, BC, 5 tubes...**$30.00**
55F11, table-R/P, 1946, wood, upper front slide rule dial, lower grill area, 2 knobs, lift top, inner phono, BC, AC **$30.00**

55L2, portable, 1956, leatherette, right front round dial knob, "V" shaped checkered grill area, rotatable handle, BC, AC/DC/battery $40.00

55L2U, portable, 1956, leatherette, right front round dial knob, "V" shaped checkered grill area, rotatable handle, BC, AC/DC/battery $40.00
55L3, portable, 1956, leatherette, right front round dial knob, "V" shaped checkered grill area, rotatable handle, BC, AC/DC/battery **$40.00**

55L3U, portable, 1956, leatherette, right front round dial knob, "V" shaped checkered grill area, rotatable handle, BC, AC/DC/battery $40.00
55L4, portable, 1956, leatherette, right front round dial knob, "V" shaped checkered grill area, rotatable handle, BC, AC/DC/battery **$40.00**
55M2, portable, 1956, leatherette, right front dial knob, plastic lattice grill area, rotatable handle, BC, AC/DC/battery **$35.00**
55X13A, table, 1946, two-tone wood, upper front dial, lower cloth grill, 2 knobs, BC, AC/DC **$40.00**
56B1, portable, 1959, leatherette, right front dial knob, center plastic grill w/"V" louvers, rotatable handle, BC, AC/DC/battery **$35.00**
56CJ, table-C, 1956, plastic, left front dial, right alarm clock, center panel with "M" logo, 5 knobs, BC, AC **$25.00**
56CS2A, table-C, plastic, lower right front dial knob over vertical grill bars, left alarm clock, feet, BC, AC/DC.................**$20.00**
56H1, table, 1956, plastic, lower front conical dial over large textured grill area, 2 knobs, feet, BC, 5 tubes **$65.00**

56H4, table, 1956, plastic, lower front conical dial over large textured grill area, 2 knobs, feet, BC, 5 tubes **$65.00**

56L1, **portable, 1959, leatherette, right front half-round dial, vertical grill bars, rotatable handle, BC, AC/DC/battery ...$35.00**
56L2, portable, 1959, leatherette, right front half-round dial, vertical grill bars, rotatable handle, BC, AC/DC/battery **$35.00**

56L2A, portable, 1959, leatherette, right front half-round dial, vertical grill bars, rotatable handle, BC, AC/DC/battery $35.00

56L4, portable, 1959, leatherette, right front half-round dial, vertical grill bars, rotatable handle, BC, AC/DC/battery **$35.00**

56M1, portable, 1959, leatherette, right front chrome dial plate, lattice grill area, rotatable handle, BC, AC/DC/battery **$40.00**

56M3, portable, 1959, leatherette, right front chrome dial plate, lattice grill area, roratable handle, BC, AC/DC/battery **$40.00**
56X1, table, 1940, plastic, right front dial, left horizontal wraparound louvers, 2 knobs, BC, 5 tubes, AC/DC **$45.00**
56X11, table, 1947, walnut plastic, right front square dial, left horizontal louvers, 2 knobs, BC, AC/DC **$35.00**
56X12, table, 1947, plastic, slanted sides, upper front slide rule dial, lower horizontal louvers, 2 knobs, BC, AC/DC...**$45.00**
56XA1, table, 1940, plastic, right front dial, left horizontal wraparound louvers, 2 knobs, BC, 5 tubes, AC/DC **$45.00**
56XAW, table, 1940, walnut, right front dial, left cloth grill w/cut-out, 4 top right pushbuttons, 2 knobs, BC, 5 tubes, AC/DC **$50.00**
57A, table, plastic, lower right round dial knob over horizontal front bars, center "M" logo, BC **$25.00**
57CE, table-C, 1957, plastic, lower right front dial knob over vertical grill bars, left alarm clock, feet, BC, 5 tubes, AC **$20.00**

57R4, table, plastic, lower right front dial over horizontal grill bars, 2 "steering wheel" knobs, feet, BC $35.00

57X11, table, 1947, plastic, slanted sides, upper front slide rule dial, lower horizontal louvers, 2 knobs, BC, AC/DC ...$45.00

57X12, table, 1947, ivory plastic, slanted sides, upper front slide rule dial, lower horizontal louvers, 2 knobs, BC **$45.00**

58A11, table, 1948, plastic, right front square dial, left horizontal louvers, 2 knobs, BC, AC/DC **$35.00**

58FRC, table-R/P, 1940, wood, right front slide rule dial, left cloth grill w/cut-outs, 3 knobs, lift top, inner phono, BC, 5 tubes........**$35.00**

58G11, table, 1949, plastic, right front square dial, left horizontal louvers, 2 bullet knobs, BC, AC/DC **$30.00**

58L11, portable, 1948, plastic, right front dial knob /left volume knob over center graduated horizontal louvers, handle, BC, AC/DC/battery..$35.00

58R11, table, 1948, plastic, raised center panel w/right round dial & left lattice grill, 2 knobs, BC, AC/DC **$35.00**

58R11A, table, 1949, plastic, raised center panel w/right round dial & left lattice grill, 2 knobs, BC, AC/DC...................**$35.00**

58X, table, 1949, plastic, upper front slide rule dial, lower trapezoid cloth grill w/3 vertical bars, 2 knobs, BC **$40.00**

58X11, table, 1949, plastic, upper front slide rule dial, lower trapezoid cloth grill w/3 vertical bars, 2 knobs, BC, AC/DC ...**$40.00**

59F11, portable-R/P, 1949, leatherette, inner dial, 3 knobs, phono, record storage, lift top, handle, BC, AC............**$20.00**

59H11U, table, 1950, plastic, dial numerals on horizontal grill bars, stick pointer, 2 knobs, BC, AC/DC **$30.00**

59L12Q, portable, 1949, plastic, right dial/left volume knobs over center wedged-shaped grill, flex handle, BC, AC/DC/battery **$35.00**

59R11, table, 1949, plastic, right front round dial over checkered grill area, recessed base, 2 knobs, BC, AC/DC **$25.00**

59T-4, table, 1938, wood, 2 top thumbwheel knobs & 4 pushbuttons, front cloth grill w/cut-outs, 5 tubes, AC **$65.00**

59T-5, table, 1938, wood, right front slide rule dial, left grill w/Deco cut-outs, pushbuttons, 4 knobs, 5 tubes, AC.................**$75.00**

59X11, table, 1950, plastic, large front half-round dial over horizontal grill bars, 2 knobs, BC, AC/DC **$30.00**

59X21U, table, 1950, plastic, large front half-round dial over horizontal grill bars, 2 knobs, BC, SW, 5 tubes, AC/DC......**$30.00**

61A, table, 1939, plastic, right front dial, left horizontal wraparound louvers, 5 pushbuttons, 2 knobs, BC, AC/DC ...**$65.00**

61B, table, 1939, plastic, right front dial, left horizontal wraparound louvers, 5 pushbuttons, 3 knobs, BC, SW, AC/DC...**$65.00**

61C, table, 1939, wood, right front slide rule dial, left grill w/horizontal bars, pushbuttons, 4 knobs, BC, SW, 6 tubes, AC...**$60.00**

61-CA, table, 1940, wood, right front slide rule dial, left grill w/horizontal bars, pushbuttons, 4 knobs, 6 tubes **$60.00**

61D, console, 1939, wood, upper front slide rule dial, lower grill w/3 vertical bars, 6 pushbuttons, BC, SW, 6 tubes, AC **$125.00**

61E, table, 1939, plastic, right front dial, left horizontal wraparound louvers, 5 pushbuttons, 2 knobs, BC, AC/DC ...**$65.00**

61F, table-R/P, 1939, wood, right front slide rule dial, left grill w/cut-outs, lift top, inner phono, 6 tubes, AC.................**$45.00**

61F23, console-R/P, wood, inner right dial, left phono, 4 knobs, double lift top, front cloth grill w/vertical bars, AC..........**$85.00**

61K23, console, 1942, wood, upper front slide rule dial, lower cloth grill w/vertical bars, pushbuttons, 4 knobs, BC, SW, 6 tubes, AC...**$115.00**

62B, table, 1939, plastic, right front dial, left horizontal wraparound louvers, 5 pushbuttons, 3 knobs, BC, SW, AC/DC...**$65.00**

62C1, table-C, 1952, plastic, right front dial, center divider panel, left alarm clock, 5 knobs, BC, AC **$20.00**

62CW1, table-C, 1953, wood, lower front slide rule dial, large upper clock face, side knobs & grill, BC, AC **$45.00**

62E, table, 1939, plastic, right front dial, left horizontal wraparound louvers, 5 pushbuttons, 2 knobs, BC, AC/DC ...**$65.00**

62FI, console-R/P, 1940, wood, inner right slide rule dial, left phono, lift top, front cloth grill w/2 vertical bars, 6 tubes, AC...**$85.00**

62T1, table, 1940, walnut, right front slide rule dial, left cloth grill w/horizontal bars, pushbuttons, 4 knobs, 6 tubes **$60.00**

62X21, table, 1954, plastic, upper front dial w/stick pointer, lower vertical grill bars, stylized "M" logo, 2 knobs, BC, SW, AC/DC...**$30.00**

63E, table, 1939, wood, right front dial, left grill w/vertical bars, 5 pushbuttons, 2 knobs, BC, AC **$60.00**

63X21, table, 1954, plastic, lower front slide rule dial, large upper grill area, 2 knobs, 6 tubes, AC/DC **$25.00**

64X, table, plastic, lower front slide rule dial, large upper grill area w/2 round speaker cut-outs under horizontal bars, 2 knobs, BC **$25.00**

64X2, table, plastic, lower front slide rule dial, large upper grill area w/2 round speaker cut-outs under horizontal bars, 2 knobs, BC **$25.00**

65F11, table-R/P, 1946, wood, outer front dial & grill, 2 knobs, lift top, inner phono, BC, AC **$30.00**

65L11, portable, 1946, cloth covered, inner right dial, left cloth grill, 2 knobs, flip-up lid, BC, AC/DC/battery.................**$35.00**

65T21, table, 1946, wood, right front slide rule dial over large cloth grill, 4 knobs, BC, SW, 6 tubes, AC **$45.00**

65X11, table, 1946, brown plastic, upper front slide rule dial, lower horizontal louvers, 2 knobs, BC, 6 tubes.......................**$40.00**

67F11, table-R/P, 1948, plastic, outer front vertical dial, right & left grill areas, 2 knobs, pushbuttons, lift top, inner phono, BC, AC **$45.00**

67F12, table-R/P, 1948, walnut, outer front vertical dial, right & left grill areas, 2 knobs, pushbuttons, lift top, inner phono, BC, AC...**$30.00**

67F12B, table-R/P, 1948, blonde, outer front vertical dial, right & left grill areas, 2 knobs, pushbuttons, lift top, inner phono, BC, AC **$35.00**

67F14, console-R/P, 1949, wood, step-down top, slide rule dial, 4 knobs, center pull-out phono drawer, lower storage, BC, AC **$90.00**

67F61BN, table-R/P, 1948, wood, right front slide rule dial, left cloth grill, 4 knobs, lift top, inner phono, BC, 5SW, AC...**$45.00**

67L11, portable, 1948, "alligator," inner slide rule dial, center grill, 2 square knobs, lift-up front, BC, AC/DC/battery...........**$40.00**

67T11, table, wood, upper front slide rule dial overlaps large criss-cross grill area, 2 knobs, BC **$35.00**

67X11, table, 1947, walnut plastic, upper front slide rule dial, lower horizontal wrap-around louvers, 2 knobs, BC, AC/DC **$35.00**

67X12, table, 1947, ivory plastic, upper front slide rule dial, lower horizontal wrap-around louvers, 2 knobs, BC, AC/DC ..**$35.00**

67X13, table, 1947, wood, upper front slide rule dial, lower cloth grill, 2 knobs, BC, AC/DC **$35.00**

67XM21, table, 1948, plastic, upper front wrap-over slide rule dial, lower horizontal wrap-around louvers, 2 knobs, BC, FM, AC/DC **$35.00**

68F11, table-R/P, 1949, plastic, outer vertical slide rule dial, right & left grill areas, lift top, inner phono, BC, AC **$45.00**

68F12, table-R/P, 1949, wood, outer front vertical slide rule dial, right & left grill areas, lift top, inner phono, BC, AC **$35.00**

68F14, console-R/P, 1949, wood, upper front vertical slide rule dial, criss-cross grill, lift top, inner phono, lower storage, BC, AC **$65.00**

68L11, portable, 1948, plastic coated cloth w/aluminum trim, suitcase-style, dial moves inside handle, top thumbwheel knobs, BC, AC/DC/battery **$60.00**

68T11, table, 1949, plastic, upper front slanted slide rule dial, large lower cloth grill, 2 knobs, AM, AC........................**$40.00**

68X11, table, 1949, two-tone plastic, upper front slanted slide rule dial, lower grill w/geometric cut-outs, 2 knobs, BC, AC/DC..**$65.00**

68X11Q, table, 1949, two-tone plastic, upper front slanted slide rule dial, lower grill w/geometric cut-outs, 2 knobs, BC, AC/DC..**$65.00**

69L11, portable, 1949, plastic coated cloth w/aluminum trim, suitcase-style, dial moves inside clear handle, top thumbwheel knobs, BC, AC/DC/battery..**$60.00**

69X11, table, 1950, plastic, large front half-round dial w/stick pointer and inner woven grill area, 2 knobs, BC, AC/DC **$40.00**

71-A, table, 1940, walnut, right front slide rule dial, left wrap-around grill bars, pushbuttons, 4 knobs, BC, SW **$60.00**

72XM21, table, 1952, plastic, large front half-round dial w/inner checkered grill area, stylized "M" logo, 2 knobs, BC, AC/DC..**$25.00**

75F21, console-R/P, 1947, wood, upper front slanted slide rule dial, center pull-out phono drawer, lower cloth grill, 4 knobs, BC, SW, AC **$100.00**

75F31, console-R/P, 1947, wood, inner right slide rule dial, 4 knobs, 6 pushbuttons, left phono, 2 lift tops, BC, SW, FM, AC **$80.00**

76F31, console-R/P, 1948, wood, inner right slide rule dial & knobs, left pull-out phono, fold-down front, BC, FM, AC...........**$75.00**

77FM21, console-R/P, 1948, wood, step-down top, wrap-over slide rule dial, 4 knobs, center front pull-out phono drawer, lower storage, BC, FM, AC..**$90.00**

77FM22, console-R/P, 1949, wood, right front vertical slide rule dial, 4 knobs, left lift top, inner phono, lower storage, BC, FM, AC **$65.00**

77FM22M, console-R/P, 1948, wood, step-down top, wrap-over slide rule dial, 4 knobs, center front pull-out phono, lower storage, BC, FM, AC **$90.00**

77FM22WM, console-R/P, 1948, wood, step-down top, wrap-over slide rule dial, 4 knobs, center front pull-out phono, lower storage, BC, FM, AC **$90.00**

77FM23, console-R/P, 1948, wood, step-down top, wrap-over slide rule dial, 4 knobs, center front pull-out phono, lower storage, BC, FM, AC **$90.00**

77XM21, table, 1948, walnut plastic, upper front slide rule dial, lower horizontal wrap-around louvers, 2 knobs, BC, FM, AC/DC **$50.00**

77XM22, table, 1948, walnut, top wrap-over slide rule dial, lower cloth wrap-around grill, 2 knobs, BC, FM, AC/DC......**$40.00**

77XM22B, table, 1948, blonde, top wrap-over slide rule dial, lower cloth wrap-around grill, 2 knobs, BC, FM, AC/DC **$40.00**

78F11, console-R/P, 1949, wood, step-down top, upper front slide rule dial, 4 knobs, center pull-out phono drawer, lower criss-cross grill, BC, AC **$90.00**

78F12M, console-R/P, 1949, wood, right front vertical slide rule dial, 4 knobs, lift top, inner phono, lower storage, BC, AC **$65.00**

78FM21, console-R/P, 1949, wood, step-down top, upper front slide rule dial, 4 knobs, center pull-out phono drawer, lower storage, BC, AC **$90.00**

78FM22, console-R/P, 1948, wood, right front vertical slide rule dial, left phono, lower grill & storage, BC, FM, AC **$75.00**

79FM21R, console-R/P, 1950, wood, upper front half-round dial, 4 knobs, lower pull-out phono drawer, BC, FM, AC **$80.00**

79XM21, table, 1950, plastic, large front half-round dial w/inner stick pointer & grill, 2 knobs, AM, FM, AC/DC..............**$50.00**

81C, console, 1939, wood, slide rule dial, lower grill w/vert bars, 6 pushbuttons, 8 tubes, BC, SW, AC **$135.00**

81F21, console-R/P, 1941, wood, upper slide rule dial, 5 pushbuttons, pull-out phono drawer, BC, SW, AC **$120.00**

81K31, console, wood, upper front slide rule dial, lower cloth grill w/center vertical divider, pushbuttons, 4 knobs, BC, SW, AC...**$130.00**

82A, console, 1939, wood, slide rule dial, automatic tuning clock, vertical grill bars, 4 knobs, 8 tubes, BC, SW, AC **$185.00**

85F21, console-R/P, 1946, wood, slanted slide rule dial, 4 knobs, 6 pushbuttons, pull-out phono, BC, SW, AC **$100.00**

85K21, console, 1946, wood, slanted slide rule dial, cloth grill, 4 knobs, contrasting veneer, BC, SW, AC **$100.00**

88FM21, console-R/P, 1949, wood, inner right slide rule dial, 4 knobs, left pull-out phono drawer, BC, FM, AC **$65.00**

95F31, console-R/P, 1947, wood, right tilt-out slide rule dial, 4 knobs, inner left phono, BC, SW, FM, AC **$75.00**

99FM21R, console-R/P, 1949, wood, inner right slide rule dial, 4 knobs, left pull-out phono, storage, BC, FM, AC **$60.00**

107F31, console-R/P, 1948, wood, tilt-out dial, 4 knobs, pushbuttons, pull-out phono drawer, BC, SW, FM, AC **$80.00**

107F31B, console-R/P, 1948, wood, tilt-out dial, 4 knobs, pushbuttons, pull-out phono drawer, BC, SW, FM, AC.........**$80.00**

496BT-1, table, 1939, wood, right front dial, left grill w/horizontal cut-outs, 4 tubes, 3 knobs, battery **$40.00**

A-1, portable, 1941, maroon metal & chrome, set turns on when lid is opened, handle, BC, battery **$50.00**

B-150, bike radio, 1940, mounts on bike handlebars, horizontal grill bars, separate battery pack **$85.00**

C5G, table-C, 1959, plastic, center round dial, pushbuttons, left alarm clock, right vertical bars, AM **$15.00**

MURDOCK
Wm. J. Murdock Company,
430 Washington Avenue,
Chelsea, Massachusetts

The Wm. J. Murdock Company began business making radio parts and related items and the company produced its first complete radio in 1924. The Murdock model 200, circa 1925, featured a very unusual loud speaker which screwed into the top of the set. By 1928, the company was out of the radio production business.

100, table, 1924, wood, low rectangular case, 3 dial front panel, top screw-in horn speaker, 5 tubes, battery **$175.00**

101, table, 1925, wood, low rectangular case, 3 dial front panel, 5 tubes, battery..**$125.00**

200 "Neutrodyne," table, 1925, wood, low rectangular case, 3 dial panel, top screw-in horn speaker, 5 tubes, battery.......**$175.00**

201, table, 1925, wood, low rectangular case, 3 dial front panel, 5 tubes, battery..**$125.00**

203, table, 1925, wood, low rectangular case, 3 dial front panel, 6 tubes, battery..**$135.00**

204, console, 1925, wood, inner 2 dial panel, fold-down front, upper speaker grill, lower storage, battery **$250.00**

CS-32, table, 1923, wood, low rectangular case, 3 dial black bakelite front panel, 5 tubes, battery **$175.00**

MURPHY
G. C. Murphy Co.,
531 5th Ave., McKeesport, Pennsylvania

113, table, 1946, wood, slant front, lower dial, upper horizontal louvers, 2 knobs, BC, AC/DC **$35.00**

MUSIC MASTER
Music Master Corporation,
Tenth and Cherry Streets,
Philadelphia, Pennsylvania

The Music Master Corporation was formed in 1924 in the business of manufacturing horns for radios. The company began to produce radios in 1925 but, due to mismanagement and financial difficulties, was out of business by 1926.

60, table, 1925, mahogany, low rectangular case, 3 dial front panel, 5 tubes, battery...**$125.00**

100, table, 1925, mahogany, low rectangular case, slanted 3 dial front panel, feet, 5 tubes, battery **$135.00**

140, table, 1925, wood, high rectangular case, center front dial over stylized "M" logo, lift top, battery........................**$400.00**

175, table, 1925, mahogany, rectangular case, upper slanted 2 dial panel, lower speaker grill w/cut-outs, 6 tubes, battery **$295.00**

215, console, 1925, mahogany, upper slanted 2 dial panel, lower speaker grill w/cut-outs, spinet legs, 6 tubes, battery..**$350.00**

250, table, 1925, mahogany, low rectangular case, front window dial, 7 tubes, battery **$195.00**

460, console, 1925, mahogany, inner slanted 1 dial panel, fold-down front, bowed legs, 7 tubes, battery....................**$265.00**

MUSICAIRE

576, table, 1946, wood, front plastic panel w/upper slide rule dial, lower cloth grill w/wooden vertical bars, 3 knobs, BC, 6 tubes, AC $75.00

576-1-6A, table, 1946, wood, front plastic panel w/upper slide rule dial, lower cloth grill w/wooden vertical bars, 3 knobs, BC, 6 tubes, AC...$75.00

NARRAGANSETT

Beer Barrel, table-N, wood, looks like beer barrel, lower front knobs and perforated grill area, center lighted oval Narragansett name & logo, top "ice" & two beer bottles, BC...........$175.00

NATIONAL UNION
National Union Radio Corp.,
Newark, New Jersey

571, table, 1947, wood, upper right front slide rule dial overlaps large lattice grill, 2 knobs, BC, AC/DC............................$30.00
G-613, portable, 1947, leatherette, upper front slide rule dial, lower cloth grill, handle, 2 knobs, 1 switch, BC, AC/DC/battery $30.00
G-619 "Presentation," table, 1947, wood, upper front slanted slide rule dial, lower cloth grill, 2 knobs, BC, AC/DC.....$35.00

NAYLOR

Sterling Five, table, wood, low rectangular case, 2 dial black bakelite front panel, 5 tubes, battery $125.00

NEUTROWOUND
Neutrowound Radio Mfg. Co.,
Homewood, Illinois

1926, table, 1926, metal, very low rectangular case w/3 top raised dial areas, 6 tubes w/top caps, battery.......................$450.00
1927, table, 1927, metal, very low rectangular case w/3 top raised dial areas, 6 tubes w/top caps, battery.......................$450.00

Super Allectric, table, 1927, wood, low rectangular case, upper slanted panel w/off-center thumbwheel dial, lower knobs & meter, 6 tubes, AC......................................$200.00

NEW YORKER

5C1, table-C, plastic, step-down top, right front dial knob overlaps lattice grill area, left alarm clock, feet, BC $25.00

OLYMPIC
Olympic Radio & TV/Hamilton Radio,
510 Avenue of the Americas, New York, New York

6-501, table, 1946, plastic, right front round slanted dial, left horizontal wrap-around louvers, 2 knobs, BC, AC/DC $65.00
6-501W, table, 1946, plastic, right front round slanted dial, left horizontal wrap-around louvers, 2 knobs, BC, AC/DC $65.00
6-502, table, 1946, wood, right front slanted panel w/round dial, horizontal wrap-around grill bars, 2 knobs, BC, AC/DC $45.00
6-502P, table, 1946, wood, right front slanted panel w/round dial, left vertical grill bars, 2 knobs, BC, AC/DC...................$45.00
6-504L, table-R/P, 1946, top right round dial, 3 knobs, left flip-up top covers phono only, BC, AC $20.00

6-601W, table, 1946, plastic, upper front slanted slide rule dial, lower horizontal grill bars, 4 knobs, BC, SW, AC **$40.00**

6-604W, table, 1947, plastic, upper front slanted slide rule dial, lower horizontal wrap-around louvers, 4 knobs, BC, SW, AC/DC **$40.00**

6-606, portable, 1946, leatherette, luggage style, front plastic panel w/slide rule dial & horizontal grill bars, handle, 2 knobs, BC, 6 tubes, AC/DC/battery **$35.00**

6-606-A, portable, 1947, leatherette, luggage style, front plastic panel w/slide rule dial & horizontal grill bars, handle, 2 knobs, BC, 6 tubes, AC/DC/battery **$35.00**

6-606-U, portable, 1947, luggage style, front plastic panel w/slide rule dial & horizontal grill bars, handle, 2 knobs, BC, AC/DC/battery **$35.00**

6-617, table-R/P, 1946, wood, front slanted slide rule dial, 4 knobs, horizontal louvers, lift top, inner phono, BC, AC **$35.00**

7-421W, table, 1949, plastic, right front round slanted dial, left horizontal wrap-around louvers, 2 knobs, BC, AC/DC **$65.00**

7-435V, table, 1948, plastic, right front round slanted dial, left horizontal wrap-around louvers, 3 knobs, BC, SW, AC/DC..**$65.00**

7-526, portable, 1947, leatherette, front plastic panel w/slide rule dial & horizontal grill bars, handle, 2 knobs, BC, AC/DC/battery **$35.00**

7-532W, table, 1948, plastic, upper front slide rule dial, lower horizontal wrap-around louvers, 4 knobs, BC, FM, AC/DC ..**$45.00**

7-537, table, 1948, plastic, right front round slanted dial, left horizontal wrap-around louvers, 3 knobs, BC, FM, AC/DC ..**$65.00**

7-622, table-R/P, 1948, wood, upper front slide rule dial, lower horizontal grill bars, 4 knobs, lift top, inner phono, BC, AC **$30.00**

7-638, console-R/P, 1948, wood, upper front slide rule dial, cloth grill w/cut-outs, 4 knobs, lift top, inner phono, lower storage, AC **$60.00**

7-724, console-R/P, 1947, wood, inner right slide rule dial, 4 knobs, storage, door, left lift top, inner phono, BC, SW, AC **$70.00**

7-925, console-R/P, 1948, wood, inner right slide rule dial, 4 knobs, door, left pull-out left phono drawer, BC, FM, AC **$70.00**

8-451, portable, 1948, inner right slide rule dial, left lattice grill, 2 knobs, flip-up top, handle, BC, battery **$45.00**

8-533W, table, 1949, plastic, upper front slanted slide rule dial, lower horizontal wrap-around louvers, 4 knobs, BC, FM, AC/DC **$45.00**

8-618, table-R/P, 1948, wood, upper front slanted slide rule dial, lower horizontal grill bars, 4 knobs, lift top, inner phono, BC, SW, AC **$30.00**

8-934, console-R/P, 1948, wood, inner right slide rule dial, 4 knobs, lower storage, door, left lift top, inner phono, BC, FM, AC **$70.00**

402, table-C, 1955, plastic, right side dial knob over horizontal bars, center front alarm clock, feet, BC, 5 tubes, AC **$40.00**

412, table-R/P, 1959, two-tone, center front dial, 3 knobs, 3/4 lift top, inner phono, high-fidelity, BC, 5 tubes, AC/DC **$20.00**

445, portable, 1954, plastic, top dial and on/off/volume knobs, large front checkered grill area, BC...............................**$35.00**

450, portable, 1957, plastic, right front round dial overlaps horizontal grill bars, top right thumbwheel on/off/ volume knob, fold-down handle, made in Japan, BC, battery **$30.00**

450-V, portable, 1957, plastic, right front round dial overlaps horizontal grill bars, top right thumbwheel on/off/volume knob, fold-down handle, BC, battery **$30.00**

461, portable, 1959, plastic, large round front dial overlaps lower perforated grill area, fold-down handle, telescope antenna, BC, 4 tubes, AC/DC/battery **$35.00**

465, table-C, 1959, plastic, right front dial panel, left alarm clock, center lattice grill, feet, BC, 4 tubes, AC........................**$20.00**

489, portable, 1951, inner slide rule dial, left lattice grill, 2 knobs, set plays when flip-up front opens, BC, battery **$45.00**

501, table-R/P, two-tone wood, right front square dial, left cloth grill, 3 knobs, lift top, inner phono, AC..........................**$35.00**

552, table, 1960, plastic, raised top w/slide rule dial, lower checkered grill area, 2 knobs, AM **$25.00**

555, table-C, 1959, plastic, lower front slide rule dial, upper checkered grill w/center alarm clock, 4 knobs, feet, BC, 5 tubes, AC **$25.00**

689M, console-R/P, 1959, wood, inner right dial, left 4 speed phono, lift top, large front grill area, high fidelity, BC, FM, 7 tubes, AC **$30.00**

FM-15, table, 1960, plastic, trapezoid case, upper front slide rule dial over large checkered grill, 3 knobs, AM/FM **$25.00**

LP-163, table, plastic, right front round slanted dial, left horizontal wrap-around louvers, 2 knobs **$65.00**

LP-3244, table, plastic, large center front dial overlaps textured grill area, lower "Olympic" logo, feet, 2 knobs, BC **$40.00**

PT-51, portable, 1941, leatherette, inner right dial, left cloth grill, 2 knobs, slide-in door, handle, BC, 5 tubes, AC/DC/battery...**$25.00**

PQ-61, portable, 1941, leatherette, inner right dial, left grill, 2 knobs, fold-down front, handle, BC, 6 tubes, AC/DC/battery **$25.00**

OPERADIO
The Operadio Corporation,
Chicago, Illinois

1925, portable, 1925, leatherette, inner 2 dial panel, lower grill w/"sun-burst" cut-out, removable cover contains antenna, 6 tubes, battery **$250.00**

OZARKA
Ozarka, Inc.,
804 Washington Boulevard,
Chicago, Illinois

Ozarka, Incorporated began manufacturing radios in 1922. Despite the stock market crash, Ozarka's business remained strong. However, the company was out of business by 1932.

78 "Armada," table, wood, looks like treasure chest, center front window dial, 3 knobs, 6 tubes, side handles **$325.00**

89, table, 1928, metal, low rectangular case, center front window dial w/thumbwheel tuning, 9 tubes **$175.00**

95, cathedral, 1932, wood, fancy scrolled cabinet, center front window dial, upper cloth grill w/cut-outs, 3 knobs, feet, 8 tubes...**$500.00**

Corona, table, wood, low case w/curved sides & carvings, center front dial, 6 tubes, 3 knobs, battery **$275.00**

J-1 "Junior," table, 1925, wood, slanted top with 5 exposed tubes, lower built-in speaker grill w/cut-outs **$325.00**

Minuet, console, wood, upper front dial, large lower speaker grill w/cut-outs, 6 tubes, 3 knobs, battery..........................**$250.00**

S-1 "Senior," table, 1925, wood, high rectangular case, 3 dial slanted front panel, battery **$225.00**

S-5 "Senior," table, wood, high rectangular case, slanted 3 dial panel, lift top, 5 tubes, battery **$250.00**

S-7 "Senior," table, wood, high rectangular case, slanted 3 dial panel, lift top, 7 tubes, battery **$250.00**

V-16, console, 1932, wood, large gothic cabinet w/carvings, upper front window dial, lower cloth grill w/cut-outs, 16 tubes, 2 speakers, 4 knobs, AC **$500.00**

PACKARD-BELL
Packard-Bell Company,
1115 South Hope Street, Los Angeles, California

Packard-Bell began business in 1933, during the Depression and always enjoyed a reputation for good quality radios. Packard-Bell had many government contracts during WW II for electrical equipment. The company was sold in 1971.

5D8, table, 1948, plastic, right front dial, left horizontal louvers, handle, 2 knobs, BC, AC/DC.......................................**$45.00**

5DA, table, 1947, plastic, right front dial, left horizontal louvers, handle, 2 knobs, BC, AC/DC.......................................**$45.00**

5FP, table, 1946, plastic, right front dial, left horizontal louvers, 2 knobs, BC, AC...**$40.00**

5R, table, 1957, plastic, dial numerals over large front checkered grill area, 2 knobs, BC, AC/DC **$35.00**

5R1, table, 1957, plastic, dial numerals over large front checkered grill area, 2 knobs, BC, 5 tubes, AC/DC **$35.00**

5R5, table, 1959, plastic, dial numerals over front horizontal bars, large dial pointer, feet, BC **$25.00**

6RC1, table-C, 1958, plastic, lower front slide rule dial, upper horizontal louvers w/center alarm clock, BC, 6 tubes, AC...**$20.00**

47, table, 1935, wood, center front round airplane dial, right & left horizontal wrap-around louvers, 5 knobs, BC, SW........**$80.00**

65A, table, 1940, wood, right front square dial, left cloth grill w/horizontal bars, handle, 3 knobs **$50.00**

100, table, 1949, plastic, right front dial, left grill w/horizontal bars, decorative case lines, handle, 2 knobs, BC, AC/DC **$45.00**

100A, table, 1949, plastic, right front dial, left grill w/horizontal bars, decorative case lines, handle, 2 knobs, BC, 5 tubes, AC/DC **$45.00**

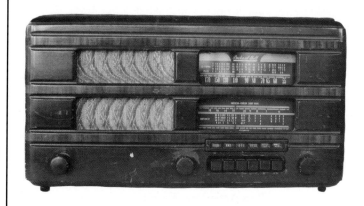

464, table, wood, two right front dial scales, left 2-section cloth grill, 6 pushbuttons, 3 knobs, BC, SW, AC......**$75.00**

471, portable, 1947, luggage-style, leatherette, right front dial, left grill, 3 knobs, handle, BC, AC/DC/battery **$25.00**

501, table, plastic, large right front dial, left horizontal louvers, handle, BC, AC/DC **$45.00**

531, table, 1954, plastic, large center front dial over perforated grill, 2 knobs, BC, AC/DC **$25.00**

551, table, 1946, plastic, upper front curved slide rule dial, lower vertical grill bars, 2 top knobs under handle, BC, AC ...**$65.00**

561, table-R/P, 1946, leatherette, inner left front dial, right grill, 3 knobs, fold-up lid, inner phono, BC, AC **$25.00**

568, portable-R/P, 1947, leatherette, inner right front dial, left grill, 3 knobs, fold-up lid, inner phono, BC, AC $25.00

572, table, 1947, two-tone wood, upper front curved dial, lower horizontal louvers, 2 top knobs under handle, BC, AC/DC $65.00

621, table-C, 1952, plastic, right front square dial, left alarm clock, top grill bars, 5 knobs, BC, AC $25.00

631, table, 1954, plastic, large front perforated metal grill w/raised dial numerals, 2 knobs, BC $25.00

651, table, 1946, wood, upper front curved slide rule dial, lower horizontal louvers, 2 top knobs under handle, BC, SW, AC $65.00

661, table-R/P, 1946, wood, upper front dial, lower grill, 4 knobs, 3/4 lift top, inner phono, BC, AC $25.00

662, console-R/P, 1947, wood, desk-style, inner slide rule dial, 4 knobs, phono, fold-up top, BC, AC...........................$100.00

682, table, 1949, right front square dial, left criss-cross grill, handle, 3 knobs, BC, AC/DC $45.00

771, table, 1948, wood, upper front slanted slide rule dial, lower criss-cross grill, 4 knobs, BC, SW, AC $40.00

861 "Phonocord," console-R/P/Rec/PA, 1947, wood, inner slide rule dial, 4 knobs, phono/recorder/PA, lift top, front criss-cross grill, BC, AC $90.00

880, console-R/P, 1948, wood, inner right slanted slide rule dial, 4 knobs, left phono, fold-up front, BC, AC $90.00

880-A, chairside-R/P, 1948, wood, top slide rule dial, 4 knobs, slide-in lid, inner phono, lower storage area, BC, AC....$85.00

881-A, console-R/P/Rec, 1948, wood, inner right slanted slide rule dial, 4 knobs, left phono/recorder, fold-up front, BC, AC $90.00

881-B, chairside-R/P/Rec, 1948, wood, top slide rule dial, 4 knobs, slide-in lid, inner phono/recorder, lower storage area, BC, AC $85.00

884, table-R/P, 1949, upper front slide rule dial, lower criss-cross grill, 4 knobs, lift top, inner phono, BC, FM, AC $30.00

892, console-R/P, 1949, wood, upper front slide rule dial, 4 knobs, center pull-out phono, lower criss-cross grill, BC, FM, AC...$55.00

1052A, table-R/P/Rec/PA, 1946, inner left front dial, right grill, phono/recorder/PA, fold-up top, BC, 10 tubes, AC $30.00

1054-B, console-R/P/Rec/PA, 1947, wood, top slanted slide rule dial, center front pull-out phono/recorder/PA drawer, BC, SW, AC $65.00

1063, console-R/P/Rec/PA, 1947, wood, inner right dial, 4 knobs, 6 pushbuttons, left phono/recorder/PA, lift top, drop front, BC, SW, 10 tubes, AC...$90.00

1181, console-R/P/Rec, 1949, wood, inner right slanted slide rule dial, 5 knobs, left phono/recorder, fold-back top, BC, FM, AC $90.00

1273, console-R/P, 1948, wood, center front pull-out drawer w/slide rule dial, 5 knobs, phono, BC, FM, AC $80.00

PAN AMERICAN
Pan American Electric Co.,
132 Front Street, New York, New York

"Clock," table-N, 1946, wood, arched case looks like mantle clock, round plastic dial, 2 knobs, 5 tubes, AC/DC........$85.00

PARAGON

Adams-Morgan Co., 16 Alvin Place,
Upper Montclair, New Jersey
The Paragon Electric Corporation,
Upper Montclair, New Jersey

The Adams-Morgan Company began business in 1910 selling wireless parts. By 1916 their first Paragon radio was marketed. After much internal trouble between the company executives leading to the demise of the Adams-Morgan Company and the creation of the Paragon Electric Corporation in 1926, the company finally went out of business completely in 1928.

DA-2, table, 1921, oak, detector/2-stage amplifier, black front panel..$450.00

RA-10, table, 1921, oak, low rectangular case, 2 dial black front panel, battery...$550.00

RA10/DA2, table, 1921, two rectangular case units, RA 10-receiver & DA 2-two stage amplifier, battery.....................$1,000.00

RB-2, table, 1923, mahogany, low rectangular case, 3 dial black front panel, lift top, battery $475.00

RD-5, table, 1922, wood, low rectangular case, battery ..$600.00

RD5/A2, table, 1922, two rectangular case units, RD5-receiver & A2-two stage amplifier, battery $1,000.00

Two, table, 1924, mahogany finish, low rectangular case, 1 center front dial, 2 tubes, battery..$300.00

IIIA, table, 1924, wood, inner black Bakelite panel, double front doors, lift top, 3 tubes, battery $500.00

PARSON'S
Parson's Laboratories, Inc.,
1471 Selby Ave., St Paul, Minnesota

66A, table, 1932, wood, right front half-round dial w/escutcheon, left scalloped cloth grill, 6 tubes, battery $65.00

PATHE
Pathe Phonograph & Radio Corp.,
20 Grand Ave., Brooklyn, New York

B-5, table, 1925, wood, low rectangular case, slanted 3 dial front panel, 5 tubes, battery...$125.00

Minute Man, table, 1925, wood, low rectangular case, 3 dial front panel, 5 tubes, battery...$125.00

PEERLESS

LP400, portable, plastic, right front dial knob, left lattice grill area, fold-down handle, BC, battery $35.00

PENNCREST

621-5121, table, 1963, plastic, large right front round dial overlaps horizontal grill bars, BC, 5 tubes, AC/DC $10.00
626-5844, table, 1962, wood, right front round dial, left grill w/logo, 3 knobs, AM, FM, 6 tubes, AC/DC $10.00
626-5845, table, 1962, wood, right front round dial, left grill w/logo, 3 knobs, AM, FM, 6 tubes, AC/DC $10.00
3123, table-C, 1964, plastic, lower right front dial knob overlaps upper lattice grill area, left clock, BC, 5 tubes $10.00
3129, table-C, 1964, plastic, top right dial knob, front off-center clock over horizontal grill bars, feet, AM, 5 tubes, AC $15.00
3622, table-C, 1962, plastic, right front dial overlaps horizontal wrap-around grill bars, left clock, feet, AM, 5 tubes, AC $15.00
3625, table-C, 1964, plastic, top right dial knob, front off-center clock, feet, AM, 5 tubes, AC $15.00
3845, table-C, 1962, plastic, right front dial, center clock, left grill area w/logo, AM, FM, 6 tubes $15.00
3934, table-C, 1965, walnut finish, right front dial panel, left clock, center lattice grill area, feet, AM, FM, 5 tubes, AC........$15.00
5335, table, 1965, right front dial panel, large left criss-cross grill area, feet, AM, FM, 6 tubes, AC $10.00
5340, table, 1962, plastic, lower right front dial panel overlaps large textured grill area, feet, AM, FM, 6 tubes, AC/DC..$10.00
5343, table, 1962, plastic, lower right front dial panel overlaps large textured grill area, feet, AM, FM, 7 tubes, AC/DC..$10.00
5836, table, 1963, wood, lower left front slide rule dial panel overlaps large grill area, upper left logo, 2 speakers, 4 knobs, AM, FM, 5 tubes, AC/DC $15.00
5837, table, 1963, wood, lower left front slide rule dial panel overlaps large grill area, upper left logo, 2 speakers, 4 knobs, AM, FM, 5 tubes, AC/DC $15.00

PEPSI

Pepsi Bottle, table-N, plastic, looks like large Pepsi bottle, base, AC $600.00

PCR-5 "Cooler," table-N, plastic, looks like Pepsi-Cola cooler, right side dial knob looks like bottle cap, lower front horizontal grill bars, upper Pepsi logo, BC $575.00

PERRY

3856, cathedral, 1932, wood, center front quarter-round dial w/escutcheon, upper cloth grill w/cut-outs, 3 knobs, AC $250.00

PERWAL

Perwal Radio & Television Co.,
140 North Dearborn Street,
Chicago, Illinois

51, table, 1937, wood, right front 3 color dial, left cloth grill with Deco cut-outs, 4 tubes, AC/DC $55.00
52, table, 1937, two-tone wood, center front airplane dial, top grill w/cut-outs, 3 knobs, 5 tubes, AC/DC $70.00
581, table, 1937, center front round airplane dial, top grill with cut-outs, 2 knobs, 5 tubes, AC/DC $70.00
741, table, 1937, wood, right front round dial, tuning eye, left grill w/vertical bars, 3 knobs, BC, SW, 7 tubes, AC/DC $75.00

PFANSTIEHL

Pfanstiehl Radio Co.,
11 South La Salle Street, Chicago, Illinois
Fansteel Products Company, Inc.,
North Chicago, Illinois

The Pfanstiehl Radio Company was formed in 1924 and in that same year marketed its first radio. During the late 1920's business gradually declined and by 1930, the company was out of the radio business.

7 "Overtone," table, 1924, wood, low rectangular case, 3 dial front panel, 5 tubes, battery $110.00
8, table, 1924, wood, low rectangular case, slanted 2 dial front panel, 5 tubes, battery...$100.00
10 "Overtone," table, 1924, wood, low rectangular case, 1 dial front panel, 6 tubes, battery $95.00
10-C, console, 1924, wood, highboy, inner 1 dial panel, fold-down front, upper speaker, 6 tubes, battery $185.00
10-S "Overtone," console, 1924, wood, 1 dial front panel & left built-in speaker on detachable stand, 6 tubes, battery...$135.00
18, table, 1926, wood, low rectangular case, front panel w/half-round double-pointer dial, 3 knobs, 5 tubes, battery ...$100.00
20, table, 1926, wood, rectangular case, 1 dial front panel, 6 tubes, battery..$95.00

50, table, 1927, wood, low rectangular case, center window dial w/escutcheon, 7 tubes, AC...$100.00

PHILCO
Philadelphia Storage Battery Company,
Ontario & C Streets,
Philadelphia, Pennsylvania
Philco Corp.,
Tioga & C Streets,
Philadelphia, Pennsylvania

Philco began business in 1906 as the Philadelphia Storage Battery Company, a maker of batteries and power supplies. In 1927 the company produced its first radio and grew to be one of the most prolific of all radio manufacturers.

14LZX "Lazy X," chairside/remote speaker, 1933, wood, Queen Anne-style chairside unit w/inner top dial & knobs connects to remote speaker unit w/25 ft. cable $300.00

14-X, console, 1933, walnut, upper front dial, lower inclined grill w/3 vertical bars, fluted columns, BC, SW, AC $135.00

15DX, console, 1932, wood, inner front dial & controls, bowed tambour doors, lower inclined grill, 11 tubes $225.00

15X, console, 1932, walnut, upper front window dial, lower inclined grill w/vertical columns, 11 tubes, AC $200.00

16B, cathedral, 1933, two-tone wood, center front window dial, upper cloth grill w/cut-outs, BC, SW, AC.....................$200.00

16B, tombstone, 1933, two-tone wood, center front window dial, upper cloth grill w/cut-outs, BC, SW, 11 tubes, AC $200.00

16-L, console, 1933, wood, lowboy, upper front window dial, lower cloth grill w/cut-outs, BC, SW, 11 tubes, AC $145.00

16RX, chairside/remote speaker, 1933, wood, chairside unit w/top dial & knobs, remote speaker w/inclined grill, BC, SW, 11 tubes, AC $300.00

16-X, console, 1933, wood, upper front window dial, lower cloth grill w/vertical bars, 4 knobs, BC, SW, 11 tubes, AC ..$145.00

17, cathedral, wood, center front window dial, upper cloth grill w/cut-outs, 4 knobs, 11 tubes $225.00

17-D, console, 1933, wood, highboy, inner front dial & controls, double doors, 6 legs, BC, SW, AC $165.00

18-B, cathedral, 1933, two-tone wood, center front window dial, 3-section cloth grill, 4 knobs, BC, 8 tubes, AC $250.00

18-H, console, 1933, wood, lowboy, upper front window dial, lower cloth grill w/cut-outs, 6 legs, 8 tubes, AC ...$150.00

18-L, console, 1933, wood, lowboy, upper front window dial, lower cloth grill w/cut-outs, BC, SW, AC $130.00

18MX, console, 1934, mahogany w/black trim, upper front window dial, lower cloth grill w/2 vertical bars, BC, 8 tubes, AC $135.00

19, cathedral, wood, recessed front panel w/center window dial, upper cloth grill w/cut-outs, 4 knobs, 6 tubes $225.00

19-H, console, 1933, wood, lowboy, upper front window dial, lower cloth grill w/cut-outs, 6 legs, AC.......................$145.00

19T, table, 1938, wood, upper front slide rule dial, lower cloth grill w/zig-zag cut-outs, right side knobs, top pushbuttons...$65.00

20, cathedral, 1930, wood, center front window dial, upper cloth grill w/scrolled cut-outs, 3 knobs, 7 tubes, AC............$200.00

20, console, 1930, wood, small case, lowboy, upper front window dial, lower cloth grill, 3 knobs, 7 tubes $125.00

20 Deluxe, cathedral, 1931, two-tone wood, center front window dial, upper cloth grill w/scrolled cut-outs, 3 knobs $200.00

20B, cathedral, 1930, wood, center front window dial, upper cloth grill w/scrolled cut-outs, 3 knobs, 7 tubes, AC ..$225.00

21B, cathedral, 1930, wood, center front window dial, upper cloth grill w/cut-outs, fluted columns, 3 knobs, 7 tubes $275.00

22L, console-R/P, 1932, wood, lowboy, front window dial, lower cloth grill w/cut-outs, lift top, inner phono, 6 legs, 7 tubes, AC $145.00

28C, table, 1934, wood, front window dial, right & left "butterfly wing" grills, 4 knobs, BC, SW, 6 tubes, AC/DC $135.00

28L, console, 1934, wood, lowboy, upper front window dial, lower cloth grill w/cut-outs, 4 knobs, BC, SW, 6 tubes, AC/DC $140.00

29TX, table/remote speaker, 1934, wood, table set w/front window dial, remote speaker cabinet w/grill cut-outs, BC, SW, AC $200.00

29X, console, 1934, wood, upper front window dial, lower inclined grill w/3 vertical columns, 4 knobs, BC, SW, 6 tubes, AC $150.00

32L, console, 1934, wood, lowboy, upper front window dial, lower cloth grill w/cut-outs, 4 knobs, BC, 6 tubes, DC $100.00

34L, console, 1934, wood, lowboy, upper front window dial, lower cloth grill w/cut-outs, 4 knobs, BC, SW, 7 tubes, battery ..$100.00

37-9, console, 1937, two-tone wood, upper front round automatic tuning dial, lower cloth grill w/3 vertical bars, 9 tubes ...$175.00

37-10, console, 1937, two-tone wood, upper front round automatic tuning dial, lower cloth grill w/3 vertical bars, 9 tubes...$175.00

37-11, console, 1937, two-tone wood, upper front round automatic tuning dial, lower cloth grill w/4 vertical bars, 10 tubes ..**$175.00**

37-33, cathedral, 1937, two-tone wood, lower round dial, upper grill w/vertical cut-outs, 5 tubes, battery **$100.00**

37-33, console, 1937, wood, upper front round dial, lower cloth grill w/cut-outs, BC, 5 tubes, battery............................**$100.00**

37-34, cathedral, 1937, wood, center front round dial, upper cloth grill w/cut-outs, 4 knobs, BC, 5 tubes, battery **$100.00**

37-34, console, 1937, wood, upper front round dial, lower cloth grill w/cut-outs, BC, 5 tubes, battery............................**$100.00**

37-38, tombstone, 1937, wood, shouldered, center front round dial, upper cloth grill w/cut-outs, 4 knobs, battery **$70.00**

37-38, console, 1937, wood, upper front round dial, lower cloth grill w/3 vertical bars, BC, SW, 6 tubes, battery **$100.00**

37-60, cathedral, 1937, wood, center front round dial, upper cloth grill w/cut-outs, 4 knobs, BC, SW, 5 tubes, AC............$130.00

37-60, console, 1937, wood, upper front round dial, lower cloth grill w/cut-outs, BC, SW, 5 tubes, AC.........................**$130.00**

37-61, cathedral, 1937, wood, center front round dial, upper cloth grill w/cut-outs, 4 knobs, BC, SW, 5 tubes, AC $140.00

37-61, console, 1937, wood, upper front round dial, lower cloth grill w/cut-outs, BC, SW, 5 tubes, AC **$130.00**

37-61, tombstone, 1937, wood, center front round dial, upper cloth grill w/cut-outs, BC, SW, AC............................**$130.00**

37-62, table, 1937, two-tone wood, right front round dial, left cloth grill w/Deco cut-outs, 3 knobs, 5 tubes, AC $75.00

37-63, table, 1937, wood, right front round dial, left cloth grill w/Deco cut-outs, 3 knobs **$80.00**

37-84, cathedral, 1937, wood, lower front round dial, upper cloth grill w/vertical bars, 2 knobs, 4 tubes, AC $110.00

37-89, cathedral, 1937, wood, center front round dial, upper cloth grill w/cut-outs, 4 knobs, BC, 6 tubes, AC **$150.00**

37-89, console, 1937, wood, upper front round dial, lower cloth grill w/cut-outs, BC, 6 tubes, AC.................................**$130.00**

37-93, cathedral, 1937, wood, lower front round dial, upper cloth grill w/vertical bars, 2 knobs, 5 tubes **$110.00**

37-116, console, 1937, wood, upper front automatic tuning dial, lower cloth grill w/5 vertical bars, lower right & left front cut-outs, BC, SW, 15 tubes, AC **$250.00**

37-600, table, 1937, wood, finished front & back, right front round dial, left cloth grill w/Deco cut-outs, 2 knobs, top cut-outs, AC **$75.00**

37-602, table, 1937, wood, finished front & back, right front round dial, left cloth grill w/Deco cut-outs, 2 knobs, top cut-outs, 5 tubes, AC/DC $75.00

37-604, table, 1937, wood, dial & knobs on top of case, front round cloth grill w/horizontal bars, 5 tubes, AC/DC ..$110.00

37-610, console, 1937, wood, upper front round dial, lower cloth grill w/3 vertical bars, 4 knobs, BC, SW, 5 tubes, AC...$125.00
37-610, table, 1937, wood, Deco, off-center round dial, rounded left, cloth grill w/horizontal bars, BC, SW, 5 tubes, AC $125.00

37-610, tombstone, 1937, wood, 2 styles, center front round dial, upper cloth grill w/cut-outs, 4 knobs, BC, SW, 5 tubes, AC $110.00
37-611, console, 1937, wood, upper front round dial, lower cloth grill w/cut-outs, BC, SW, 5 tubes, AC/DC...................$130.00
37-611, table, 1937, wood, Deco, off-center round dial, rounded left, cloth grill w/horizontal bars, BC, SW, 5 tubes, AC/DC $125.00
37-611, tombstone, 1937, wood, shouldered, center front round dial, upper cloth grill w/cut-outs, 4 knobs, BC, SW, 5 tubes, AC/DC $110.00
37-620, console, 1937, wood, various styles, upper front round dial, lower cloth grill, BC, SW, 6 tubes, AC $130.00
37-620, tombstone, 1937, two-tone wood, various styles, center front dial, cloth grill w/cut-outs, 4 knobs, BC, SW, AC ..$110.00
37-623, console, 1937, wood, upper front round dial, lower cloth grill w/3 vertical bars, BC, SW, 6 tubes, battery $100.00
37-624, console, 1937, wood, upper front round dial, lower cloth grill w/3 vertical bars, BC, SW, 6 tubes, battery $100.00
37-624, tombstone, 1937, two-tone wood, rounded shoulders, round dial, grill cut-outs, 4 knobs, BC, SW, battery $85.00
37-630, (right) console, 1937, wood, recessed front, upper round dial, lower cloth grill w/3 vertical bars, 4 knobs, BC, SW, 6 tubes, AC $135.00
37-630, table, 1937, wood, Deco, right front round dial, left cloth grill w/Deco cut-outs, 4 knobs, BC, SW, 6 tubes, AC $90.00

37-640, console, 1937, wood, upper front round dial, lower cloth grill w/vertical bars, BC, SW, 7 tubes, AC **$135.00**

37-640, tombstone, 1937, wood, rounded shoulders, center front round dial, upper cloth grill w/vertical cut-outs, 4 knobs, BC, SW, 7 tubes, AC..**$125.00**

37-641, console, 1937, wood, upper front round dial, lower cloth grill w/vertical bars, 4 knobs, BC, SW, 7 tubes, AC/DC...**$125.00**

37-641, tombstone, 1937, wood, rounded shoulders, center front round dial, upper cloth grill w/vertical cut-outs, 4 knobs, BC, SW, 7 tubes, AC/DC....................................**$125.00**

37-643, tombstone, 1937, wood, rounded shoulders, center front round dial, upper cloth grill w/cut-outs, 4 knobs, 9 tubes, battery **$85.00**

37-650, console, 1937, wood, upper front round dial, lower cloth grill w/3 vertical bars, BC, SW, 8 tubes, AC **$130.00**

37-650, tombstone, 1937, wood, various styles, center front dial, upper cloth grill w/cut-outs, 4 knobs, BC, SW, 9 tubes, AC **$135.00**

37-660, console, 1937, wood, upper front round dial, lower cloth grill w/cut-outs, 6 feet, BC, SW, 9 tubes, AC..............**$150.00**

37-660, tombstone, 1937, wood, rounded shoulders, center front round dial, upper cloth grill w/cut-outs, 4 knobs, BC, SW, 9 tubes, AC **$135.00**

37-665, tombstone, 1937, wood, rounded shoulders, center front round dial, upper cloth grill w/cut-outs, 4 knobs, BC, 2SW, 9 tubes, AC **$135.00**

37-670, console, 1937, wood, upper front round dial, lower cloth grill w/4 vertical bars, BC, SW, 11 tubes, AC **$175.00**

37-670, tombstone, 1937, wood, center front round dial, upper cloth grill w/vertical bars, BC, SW, 11 tubes, AC........**$150.00**

37-675, console, 1937, wood, upper front round automatic tuning dial, lower cloth grill w/cut-outs, 5 knobs, 6 feet, BC, SW, 12 tubes, AC..**$200.00**

37-690, console, 1937, wood, inner automatic tuning dial, grill cut-outs, double doors, 3 speakers, BC, SW, 20 tubes, AC **$500.00**

37-2620, console, 1937, wood, upper front round dial, lower cloth grill w/3 vertical bars, BC, SW, LW, 6 tubes................**$125.00**

37-2650, console, 1937, wood, upper front round dial, lower cloth grill w/3 vertical bars, BC, SW, LW, 8 tubes, AC **$135.00**

37-2650, tombstone, 1937, wood, rounded shoulders, center front round dial, upper cloth grill w/cut-outs, 4 knobs, BC, SW, LW, AC **$125.00**

37-2670, console, 1937, wood, upper front round dial, lower cloth grill w/4 vertical bars, BC, SW, LW, 11 tubes, AC.......**$175.00**

37-2670, tombstone, 1937, wood, center front round dial, upper cloth grill w/vertical bars, BC, SW, LW, 11 tubes, AC **$150.00**

38, cathedral, 1930, two-tone wood, center front window dial, upper cloth grill w/cut-outs, 4 knobs, battery **$110.00**

38, console, 1933, wood, lowboy, upper front window dial, lower cloth grill w/cut-outs, 4 knobs, battery **$120.00**

38-1, console, 1938, wood, upper front slanted automatic tuning dial, lower cloth grill w/5 vertical bars, BC, SW, 12 tubes, AC **$190.00**

38-2, console, 1938, wood, upper front slanted automatic tuning dial, lower cloth grill w/cut-outs, BC, SW, 11 tubes, AC **$175.00**

38-3, console, 1938, wood, upper front slanted automatic tuning dial, lower cloth grill w/4 vertical bars, BC, SW, 9 tubes, AC **$150.00**

38-4, console, 1938, wood, upper front slanted automatic tuning dial, lower cloth grill w/4 vertical bars, BC, SW, 8 tubes, AC **$150.00**

38-5, console, 1938, wood, upper front round dial, lower cloth grill w/3 vertical bars, 4 knobs, BC, SW, 8 tubes, AC **$135.00**

38-5, tombstone, 1938, two-tone wood, rounded shoulders, center front round dial, upper cloth grill w/cut-outs, BC, SW, 8 tubes, AC **$125.00**

38-7, chairside, 1938, wood, Deco, top dial & knobs, lower round cloth grill w/horizontal bars, center storage, BC, SW, AC **$125.00**

38-7, console, 1938, wood, upper front slanted automatic tuning dial, lower cloth grill w/vertical bars, BC, SW, 6 tubes, AC **$125.00**

38-7, table, 1938, wood, right front round dial, rounded left side, cloth grill w/Deco cut-outs, BC, SW, AC **$70.00**

38-8, console, 1938, wood, upper front round dial, lower cloth grill w/3 vertical bars, 4 knobs, BC, SW, 6 tubes, AC **$125.00**

38-9, console, 1938, two-tone wood, upper front round dial, lower cloth grill w/cut-outs, 4 knobs, BC, SW, 6 tubes, AC...**$135.00**

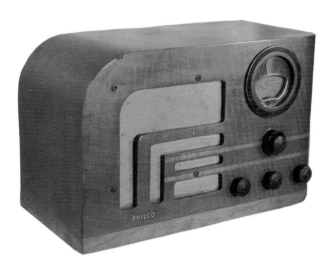

38-9, table, 1938, wood, right front round dial, rounded left side, cloth grill w/Deco cut-outs, 4 knobs, BC, SW, 6 tubes, AC $80.00

38-10, console, 1938, wood, upper front round dial, lower cloth grill w/2 vertical bars, 4 knobs, BC, SW, 5 tubes, AC..**$130.00**

38-10, table, 1938, wood, right front round dial, rounded left side, cloth grill w/Deco cut-outs, 4 knobs, BC, SW, 5 tubes, AC **$100.00**

38-12, table, 1938, wood, 2 versions-one w/left wrap-around grill; one w/left front grill, right dial, BC, 5 tubes, AC/DC $50.00

38-14, table, 1938, plastic, right front dial, left wrap-around cloth grill w/2 horizontal bars, 3 knobs, AC $45.00

38-15, table, 1938, wood, right front dial, left wrap-around grill w/Deco cut-outs, 3 knobs, BC, SW, 5 tubes, AC $50.00

38-22, chairside, 1938, wood, Deco, top dial & knobs, lower front round grill w/horizontal bars, center storage, BC, SW, 6 tubes, AC/DC $125.00

38-22, console, 1938, wood, upper front slanted automatic tuning dial, lower cloth grill w/vertical bars, BC, SW, 6 tubes, AC/DC...$125.00

38-22, table, 1938, wood, right front round dial, left cloth grill w/Deco cut-outs, BC, SW, 6 tubes, AC/DC $75.00

38-23, console, 1938, two-tone wood, 2 styles, upper front round dial, lower grill area, 4 knobs, BC, SW, 6 tubes, AC/DC..........$135.00

38-23, table, 1938, wood, right front round dial, rounded left side, Deco grill cut-outs, 4 knobs, BC, SW, 5 tubes, AC/DC ..$95.00

38-31, console, 1938, wood, upper front slanted slide rule dial, lower grill w/3 vertical bars, pushbuttons, BC, SW, 6 tubes......$130.00

38-33, console, 1938, wood, upper front dial, lower cloth grill w/2 vertical bars, 2 knobs, BC, 5 tubes, battery..................$95.00

38-33, tombstone, 1938, wood, lower front rectangular dial, upper cloth grill w/cut-outs, 2 knobs, BC, 5 tubes, battery $80.00

38-34, console, 1938, wood, upper front dial, lower cloth grill w/2 vertical bars, 2 knobs, BC, 5 tubes, battery..................$95.00

38-34, tombstone, 1938, wood, center front round dial, cloth grill w/cut-outs, 3 knobs, BC, 5 tubes, battery $70.00

38-35, tombstone, 1938, two-tone wood, lower front dial, upper cloth grill w/cut-outs, 2 knobs, battery/AC $80.00

38-38, console, 1938, wood, 2 styles, upper front round dial, lower cloth grill w/bars, BC, SW, 6 tubes, battery $100.00

38-38, table, 1938, wood, right front round dial, rounded left w/Deco grill cut-outs, 4 knobs, BC, SW, battery $50.00

38-39, table, 1938, wood, right front round dial, rounded left w/Deco grill cut-outs, 4 knobs, BC, SW, battery...........$50.00

38-40, table, 1938, wood, Deco, right front round dial, left cloth grill w/ cut-outs, 4 knobs, battery/AC $65.00

38-60, tombstone, 1938, two-tone wood, center front round dial, upper 2-section grill, 4 knobs, BC, SW.......................$120.00

38-62, console, 1938, wood, upper front round dial, lower cloth grill w/3 vertical bars, 3 knobs, BC, 5 tubes, AC $130.00

38-62, table, 1938, two-tone wood, right front round dial, left cloth grill with Deco cut-outs, 3 knobs, BC, 5 tubes, AC........$65.00

38-89, console, 1938, two-tone wood, upper front round dial, lower cloth grill w/cut-outs, 4 knobs, BC, SW, 6 tubes, AC....$135.00

38-89, tombstone, 1938, two-tone wood, center front round dial, cloth grill w/cut-outs, 4 knobs, BC, 6 tubes....$115.00

38-90, table, 1938, wood, Deco, right front round dial, left cloth grill with Deco cut-outs, 4 knobs...................$75.00

38-93, tombstone, 1938, two-tone wood, rounded shoulders, lower front round dial, cloth grill w/cut-outs, 2 knobs, BC, 5 tubes, AC...................................$110.00

38-116, console, 1938, wood, upper front slanted automatic tuning dial, lower cloth grill w/vertical bars, lower right & left front cut-outs, BC, SW, 15 tubes, AC $200.00

38-620, table, 1938, wood, Deco, right front round dial, rounded left w/Deco grill cut-outs, 4 knobs, AC........................$100.00

38-623, console, 1938, wood, upper front round dial, lower cloth grill w/cut-outs, 4 knobs, BC, SW, 6 tubes, battery $110.00

38-623, table, 1938, wood, Deco, right front round dial, rounded left w/Deco grill cut-outs, BC, SW, battery $75.00

38-643, console, 1938, wood, upper front round dial, lower cloth grill w/3 vertical bars, BC, SW, 7 tubes, battery $110.00

38-643, tombstone, 1938, wood, rounded shoulders, center front round dial, upper cloth grill w/cut-outs, 4 knobs, BC, SW, battery $100.00

38-690, console, 1938, wood, upper front slanted automatic tuning dial, lower cloth grill w/cut-outs, right & left front vertical bars, 3 speakers, BC, SW, 20 tubes, AC $400.00

38L, console, 1933, wood, lowboy, upper front window dial, lower cloth grill w/cut-outs, 4 knobs, BC, 5 tubes, battery $125.00

38-TP51 "Transitone," table, 1938, plastic, right front dial, left grill w/horizontal bars, upper pushbuttons, 2 knobs, BC, 5 tubes..$60.00

39-6, table, 1939, walnut w/inlay, right front airplane dial, left cloth grill w/Deco cut-outs, 2 knobs, BC $40.00

39-7, table, 1939, walnut, 2 styles, right front dial, left cloth grill w/bars, pushbuttons, 2 knobs, BC, 5 tubes, AC............$60.00

39-17, console, 1939, wood, upper front dial, large lower cloth grill w/3 vertical bars, 6 pushbuttons, BC, 5 tubes, AC $135.00

39-18, console, 1939, wood, upper front dial, large lower cloth grill w/3 vertical bars, 6 pushbuttons, BC, AC/DC.............$135.00

39-19, console, 1939, wood, upper front dial, large lower cloth grill w/3 vertical bars, 6 pushbuttons, BC, SW, AC $135.00

39-25, console, 1939, wood, upper front slanted slide rule dial, lower cloth grill w/vertical bars, pushbuttons, BC, SW, 5 tubes, AC...$120.00

39-25, table, 1939, wood, slant front, right slide rule dial, left cloth grill w/Deco cut-outs, pushbuttons, BC, SW, 5 tubes, AC...$90.00

39-30, table, 1939, wood, slant front, right slide rule dial, left cloth grill w/Deco cut-outs, pushbuttons, BC, SW, 6 tubes, AC...$90.00

39-31, console, 1939, walnut, 2 styles, upper front slanted slide rule dial, lower cloth grill w/vertical bars, pushbuttons, BC, SW, 6 tubes...$145.00

39-35, console, 1939, wood, upper front slanted slide rule dial, lower cloth grill w/4 vertical bars, pushbuttons, BC, SW, 6 tubes, AC...$145.00

39-36, console, 1939, walnut, upper front slanted slide rule dial, lower cloth grill w/4 vertical bars, pushbuttons, BC, SW, 6 tubes...$135.00

39-40, console, 1939, walnut, upper front slanted slide rule dial, lower cloth grill w/vertical bars, pushbuttons, BC, SW, 8 tubes, AC...$150.00

39-45, console, 1939, walnut, inner dial, pushbuttons, fold-up lid, lower cloth grill w/vertical bars, BC, SW, 9 tubes, AC ..$155.00

39-55, console, 1939, wood, inner slide rule dial, fold-up lid, lower cloth grill w/vertical bars, automatic remote control, BC, SW, 11 tubes, AC...$195.00

39-70, tombstone, 1939, wood, rounded shoulders, lower front square dial, upper cloth grill w/cut-outs, 2 knobs, battery $75.00

39-71, portable, 1939, striped cloth covered, right front dial, left grill area, leather handle, 2 knobs, 4 tubes, battery $25.00

39-72, portable, 1939, striped cloth covered, right front dial, left grill area, handle, 2 knobs, battery $25.00

39-80, table, 1939, wood, lower front dial surrounded by large cloth grill area w/cut-outs, 2 knobs $80.00

39-116, console, 1939, walnut, inner slide rule dial, fold-up lid, lower cloth grill w/vertical bars, automatic remote control, BC, SW, 14 tubes, AC $210.00

39-117, console, 1939, wood, upper front slide rule dial, lower cloth grill w/3 vertical bars, 5 pushbuttons, BC, 5 tubes, AC $130.00

39-117, table, 1939, two-tone wood, upper front slide rule dial, lower cloth grill w/Deco cut-outs, pushbuttons, 5 tubes..$60.00

39-118, console, 1939, wood, upper front slide rule dial, lower cloth grill w/3 vertical bars, 5 pushbuttons, BC, 5 tubes, AC/DC...$130.00

39-119, console, 1939, wood, upper front slide rule dial, lower cloth grill w/3 vertical bars, 5 pushbuttons, BC, SW, 5 tubes, AC $130.00

39-502, table-R/P, 1939, wood, center front square dial, right & left horizontal louvers, 2 knobs, lift top, inner phono, AC $35.00

39-504, portable-R/P, 1939, cloth covered, left front dial, right grill, 2 knobs, handle, lift top, inner phono $30.00

39-6294, table, 1939, wood, right front square dial, left cloth grill w/2 "wavy" cut-outs, 3 knobs...............................$45.00

39-6760, portable, 1939, cloth covered, right front dial, left horizontal louvers, handle, 2 knobs, 5 tubes, AC/DC/battery $30.00

40-42, table-R/P, 1940, wood, right front dial, left grill w/horizontal bars, 2 knobs, open top phono.....................................$30.00

40-74, portable, 1940, striped cloth covered, right front dial, left grill area, handle, 2 knobs, battery $30.00

40-81, portable, 1940, striped cloth covered, right front square dial, left grill area, 2 knobs, handle, battery...................$30.00

40-82, portable, 1940, striped cloth covered, inner right dial, left grill area, fold-down front, 2 knobs, handle, battery $35.00

40-88, portable, 1940, striped cloth covered, right front dial, left grill area, handle, 3 knobs, BC, SW, battery $30.00

40-89, portable, 1940, oblong case, top dial & knobs, front horizontal louvers, aerial built into strap, battery $50.00

40-90, table, 1940, plastic, right front dial, left cloth grill w/2 horizontal bars, 4 tubes, battery $30.00

40-95, table, 1940, wood, upper front slide rule dial, lower cloth grill w/cut-outs, 2 knobs, battery..................................$45.00

40-115, table, 1940, wood, right front dial, left cloth grill w/2 "wavy" horizontal bars, 3 knobs, BC, 6 tubes, AC.........$45.00

40-120, table, 1940, wood, right front square dial, left horizontal louvers, handle, tubular feet, 3 knobs, BC, 6 tubes, AC/DC $50.00

40-124, table, 1940, wood, right front dial, left cloth grill w/Deco cut-outs, 6 pushbuttons, 3 knobs, BC, 6 tubes, AC $60.00

40-125, table, 1940, wood, right front dial, left vertical grill bars, 6 pushbuttons, handle, 3 knobs, BC, 6 tubes, AC/DC $65.00

40-130, table, 1940, wood, upper front slide rule dial, lower cloth grill w/diagonal cut-outs, 4 knobs, BC, 6 tubes, AC $50.00

40-135, table, 1940, wood, upper front slide rule dial, lower cloth grill w/diagonal cut-outs, 6 pushbuttons, 4 knobs, BC, 6 tubes, AC $60.00

40-140, table, 1940, wood, upper front slide rule dial, lower cloth grill w/Deco cut-outs, 4 knobs, BC, SW, 6 tubes, AC....$50.00

40-145, table, 1940, wood, upper front slide rule dial, lower cloth grill w/Deco cut-outs, 6 pushbuttons, 4 knobs, BC, SW, 6 tubes, AC...$60.00

40-150, table, 1940, wood, slant front, right slide rule dial, left cloth grill w/Deco cut-outs, 8 pushbuttons, BC, SW, 7 tubes, AC.......$90.00

40-155, table, 1940, wood, slant front, right slide rule dial, left cloth grill w/Deco cut-outs, 8 pushbuttons, 4 knobs, BC, SW, 8 tubes, AC...$90.00

40-158, console, 1940, wood, upper front dial, lower cloth grill w/vertical bars, 6 pushbuttons, 4 knobs, BC, 6 tubes ..$135.00

40-160, console, 1940, wood, upper front dial, lower cloth grill w/vertical bars, 6 pushbuttons, 4 knobs, BC, 6 tubes, AC $135.00

40-165, console, 1940, wood, upper front dial, lower cloth grill w/vertical bars, 6 pushbuttons, 4 knobs, BC, SW, 6 tubes, AC..**$125.00**

40-170, chairside, 1940, wood, all sides finished, top dial/knobs/6 pushbuttons, cloth grill w/horizontal bars, BC, 6 tubes, AC **$145.00**

40-180, console, 1940, wood, upper front slanted slide rule dial, lower vertical grill bars, 8 pushbuttons, 4 knobs, BC, SW, 7 tubes, AC **$140.00**

40-185, console, 1940, wood, upper front slanted slide rule dial, lower cloth grill w/4 vertical bars, 8 pushbuttons, BC, SW, 8 tubes, AC **$140.00**

40-190, console, 1940, wood, upper front slanted slide rule dial, lower cloth grill w/6 vertical bars, 8 pushbuttons, BC, SW, 8 tubes, AC **$145.00**

40-195, console, 1940, wood, upper front slanted slide rule dial, lower cloth grill w/vertical bars, 8 pushbuttons, thumbwheel knobs, BC, SW, 10 tubes, AC **$160.00**

40-200, console, 1940, wood, inner dial/pushbuttons, fold-up lid, large lower cloth grill w/vertical grill bars, BC, SW, 11 tubes, AC **$175.00**

40-201, console, 1940, wood, inner slide rule dial, pushbuttons, fold-up lid, lower cloth grill w/vertical bars, right & left front cut-outs, BC, SW, AC...**$200.00**

40-205, console, 1940, walnut, inner dial, fold-up lid, lower cloth grill w/vertical bars, automatic remote control, BC, 12 tubes, AC **$200.00**

40-215, console, 1940, walnut, inner dial, fold-up lid, lower cloth grill w/vertical bars, automatic remote control, BC, SW, 12 tubes, AC..**$200.00**

40-216, console, 1940, walnut, inner dial, fold-up lid, lower cloth grill w/vertical bars, automatic remote control, BC, SW, 14 tubes, AC..**$210.00**

40-300, console, 1940, wood, inner slide rule dial, 7 pushbuttons, fold-up lid, large lower vertical grill louvers, BC, SW, 12 tubes, AC..**$175.00**

41-81, portable, 1941, cloth covered, front plastic dial panel with right dial & left horizontal grill bars, 2 knobs, handle, 4 tubes, battery..**$25.00**

41-87, portable, 1941, front plastic dial panel with right dial & left horizontal grill bars, 2 knobs, handle, 5 tubes, AC/DC/battery **$25.00**

41-95, table, 1941, two-tone wood, upper front slanted slide rule dial, lower vertical grill bars, 2 knobs, BC, 5 tubes, battery **$45.00**

41-100, table, 1941, wood, upper front slide rule dial, lower 3 section grill, 6 pushbuttons, 2 knobs, BC, battery..............**$45.00**

40-501, **table-R/P, 1940, two-tone wood, right front dial, left cloth grill w/cut-outs, open top phono, BC, 5 tubes, AC** **$30.00**

40-504, portable-R/P, 1940, cloth covered, left front dial, right grill area, handle, lift top, inner crank phono, battery **$35.00**

40-525, console-R/P, 1940, wood, front dial, pushbuttons, lower cloth grill w/3 vertical bars, lift top, inner phono..........**$120.00**

41-65, console, 1941, wood, upper front slide rule dial, lower cloth grill w/3 vertical bars, 6 pushbuttons, 4 knobs.............**$135.00**

41-220, **table, 1941, wood, right front dial, left cloth grill, handle, feet, 3 knobs, BC, 6 tubes, AC/DC** **$45.00**

41-221, table, 1941, wood, front plastic dial panel with right dial & left horizontal louvers, handle, feet, 3 knobs, BC, SW, 6 tubes, AC/DC **$45.00**

41-225, table, 1941, two-tone wood, right front square dial, left cloth grill, 6 pushbuttons, 3 knobs, BC, 6 tubes, AC/DC **$55.00**

41-226, table, 1941, wood, Deco, front plastic dial panel w/right dial & left horizontal grill bars, fluted left side, 6 upper pushbuttons, 3 knobs, BC, SW, AC **$125.00**

41-230, table, 1941, brown plastic, upper front slanted slide rule dial, lower cloth grill, 4 knobs, BC, 7 tubes, AC............$50.00

41-231, table, 1941, wood, Deco, right front dial, left horizontal louvers, rounded left side, 6 pushbuttons, 3 knobs, BC, SW, 6 tubes, AC/DC $85.00

41-235, table, 1941, wood, upper front slanted slide rule dial, lower cloth grill, plastic trim, 4 knobs, 7 tubes, BC $45.00

41-240, table, 1941, wood, upper front slanted slide rule dial, lower cloth grill w/horizontal bars, 4 knobs, BC, SW, 7 tubes...$50.00

41-245, table, 1941, wood, upper front slanted slide rule dial, lower cloth grill w/horizontal bars, 6 pushbuttons, 4 knobs, BC, SW, 7 tubes...$60.00

41-246, table, 1941, wood, upper front slanted slide rule dial, lower cloth grill w/horizontal bars, 6 pushbuttons, 4 knobs, BC, SW, 7 tubes...$65.00

41-250, table, 1941, wood, Deco, slanted front, inset plastic panel w/slide rule dial/8 pushbuttons/4 knobs, left horizontal grill bars, BC, SW, 8 tubes.................................$100.00

41-255, table, 1941, wood, Deco, slanted front, inset plastic panel w/slide rule dial/8 pushbuttons/4 knobs, left horizontal grill bars, BC, SW, 9 tubes $100.00

41-256, table, 1941, wood, Deco, slanted front, inset plastic panel w/slide rule dial/8 pushbuttons/4 knobs, left horizontal grill bars, BC, SW, 9 tubes...$100.00

41-258, console, 1941, wood, upper front dial, lower cloth grill with 4 vertical bars, BC, 6 tubes, AC $125.00

41-260, console, 1941, wood, upper front slide rule dial, lower cloth grill w/vertical bars, pushbuttons, BC, SW, 7 tubes, AC...$130.00

41-265, console, 1941, wood, upper front slide rule dial, lower grill w/vertical bars, pushbuttons, BC, SW, 7 tubes $125.00

41-280, console, 1941, wood, upper front slanted slide rule dial, lower grill w/vertical bars, 8 pushbuttons, BC, SW, 8 tubes $140.00

41-285, console, 1941, wood, upper front slanted slide rule dial, lower grill w/vertical bars, 8 pushbuttons, 4 knobs, BC, SW, 9 tubes...$135.00

41-287, console, 1941, wood, inner slide rule dial, pushbuttons, fold-up lid, large lower cloth grill w/cut-outs, BC, SW, 9 tubes, AC $150.00

41-290, console, 1941, wood, upper front slanted slide rule dial, lower grill w/wrap-over vertical bars, 8 pushbuttons, 4 knobs, BC, SW, 10 tubes $140.00

41-295, console, 1941, walnut, upper front slanted slide rule dial, lower grill w/vertical bars, 8 pushbuttons, BC, SW, 11 tubes $165.00

41-296, console, 1941, walnut, upper front slanted slide rule dial, lower grill w/vertical bars, 8 pushbuttons, BC, SW, 9 tubes $150.00

41-300, console, 1941, walnut, inner slide rule dial, 8 pushbuttons, fold-up lid, vertical front panels, BC, SW, 12 tubes, AC...$185.00

41-315, console, 1941, walnut, inner slide rule dial, 8 pushbuttons, fold-up lid, lower cloth grill w/vertical bars, BC, SW, 12 tubes $185.00

41-316, console, 1941, wood, inner slide rule dial, 8 pushbuttons, fold-up lid, lower cloth grill w/vertical bars, wireless remote control, BC, SW, 15 tubes...........................$215.00

41-601, table-R/P, 1941, wood, upper front slide rule dial, lower horizontal louvers, lift top, inner phono, BC, 5 tubes, AC $35.00

41-603, table-R/P, 1941, wood, center front square dial, right & left horizontal grill bars, lift top, inner phono $35.00

41-608, console-R/P/Rec, 1941, wood, upper front slide rule dial, tilt-out front, inner phono/recorder, 6 pushbuttons, BC, SW, 9 tubes, AC..$135.00

41-625, console-R/P, 1941, wood, upper front rectangular dial, tilt-out front w/vertical bars, inner phono, BC, SW, 7 tubes, AC...$140.00

41-842, portable, 1941, leatherette, front plastic panel w/right dial & left horizontal grill bars, handle, 2 knobs, 7 tubes, AC/DC/battery $25.00

41-843, portable, 1941, leatherette, inner plastic panel w/right dial & left horizontal grill bars, fold-down front, handle, 7 tubes, AC/DC/battery $35.00

41-844, portable, 1941, inner plastic panel w/right dial & left horizontal grill bars, 2 knobs, tambour door, handle, 7 tubes, AC/DC/battery **$40.00**

41-851, portable, 1941, leatherette, front plastic panel w/right dial & left horizontal grill bars, 3 knobs, BC, SW, 5 tubes, AC/DC/battery **$25.00**

41-854, portable, 1941, leatherette, inner plastic panel w/right dial & left horizontal grill bars, tambour door, handle, BC, SW, 7 tubes, AC/DC/battery **$40.00**

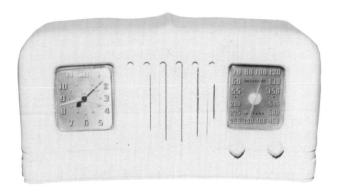

41-KR, table/refrigerator-C, 1941, wood, this set was marketed as a kitchen radio and has an arched base to fit the top of a refrigerator of the era, right front dial, left clock, center vertical grill bars..**$60.00**

42-1-T-96 "Transitone," table, 1942, wood, right front dial w/red pointer, left square cloth grill, 2 knobs..........................**$45.00**

42-100, console, 1942, wood, inner slanted slide rule dial, slide-down lid, lower vertical grill bars, pushbuttons, thumbwheel tuning **$165.00**

42-321, table, 1942, wood, upper front slanted slide rule dial, lower rectangular cloth grill, 2 knobs, feet **$40.00**

42-322, table, 1942, wood, upper front slanted slide rule dial, lower horizontal louvers, 3 knobs, BC, SW **$45.00**

42-327, table, 1942, two-tone wood, upper front slide rule dial, lower cloth grill w/2 horizontal bars, 6 pushbuttons, 3 knobs, BC, SW, AC/DC **$50.00**

42-340, table, 1942, two-tone wood, upper front slanted slide rule dial, lower rectangular cloth grill, 4 knobs, AC **$50.00**

42-345, table, 1942, wood, upper front slide rule dial, lower cloth grill, 6 pushbuttons, 4 knobs, BC, SW, AC....................**$50.00**

42-350, table, 1942, wood, upper front slide rule dial, lower horizontal wrap-around grill bars, 6 pushbuttons, 4 knobs, BC, SW, FM, AC **$75.00**

42-355, table, 1942, walnut, right front slide rule dial, left cloth grill w/horizontal bars, pushbuttons, 4 knobs, BC, SW, FM, 8 tubes, AC **$70.00**

42-380, console, 1942, walnut, upper front slanted slide rule dial, lower vertical bars, 9 pushbuttons, BC, SW, 8 tubes, AC...........**$135.00**

42-390, console, 1942, wood, upper front slanted slide rule dial w/plastic escutcheon, lower vertical grill bars, pushbuttons, 4 knobs, BC, SW, AC..**$145.00**

42-842, portable, 1942, leatherette, upper front plastic panel w/right dial & left horizontal grill bars, handle, 2 knobs...**$35.00**

42-1002, table-R/P, 1942, wood, front slanted slide rule dial, lower horizontal grill bars, 2 knobs, lift top, inner phono, AC ..**$35.00**

42-1003, table-R/P, 1942, wood, front slide rule dial, right & left horizontal wrap-around louvers, lift top, inner phono, AC **$35.00**

42-1005, console-R/P, 1942, wood, upper front slide rule dial, lower tilt-out front w/vertical bars & inner phono, BC, SW.......**$135.00**

42-1008, console-R/P, 1942, wood, upper slanted slide rule dial, lower tilt-out front w/vertical bars & inner phono **$135.00**

42-1013, console-R/P, 1942, walnut, inner dial, pushbuttons, fold-up lid, tilt-out front w/inner phono, BC, SW, FM, AC ...**$200.00**

42-1015, console-R/P, 1942, wood, inner slide rule dial, pushbuttons, fold-up lid, double front doors, tilt-out phono, BC, FM, SW **$200.00**

42-KR3, table, 1942, wood, rounded case, recessed front panel w/right dial & left horizontal louvers, base, 2 knobs **$55.00**

42-KR5, table/refrigerator-C, 1942, wood, this set was marketed as a kitchen radio and has an arched base to fit the top of a refrigerator of the era, rounded sides, recessed front panel w/right dial, left clock & center horizontal grill bars, 2 knobs **$60.00**

42-PT91 "Transitone," table, 1942, plastic, right front dial, right & left horizontal wrap-around louvers, 2 knobs, BC, AC/DC..**$40.00**

42-PT93 "Transitone," table, 1942, walnut w/black, right front dial, left cloth grill, center vertical divider, handle, feet, 2 knobs $50.00

42-PT94 "Transitone," table, 1942, wood, front plastic panel w/right dial & left horizontal grill bars, handle, feet, 2 knobs $50.00

42-PT95 "Transitone," table, 1942, wood, front plastic panel w/right dial & left horizontal grill bars, handle, feet, 2 knobs $50.00

42-PT96 "Transitone," table, 1942, wood, right front dial, left cloth grill, 2 knobs..$40.00

43, cathedral, 1934, wood, center front window dial, upper cloth grill w/cut-outs, 4 knobs, BC, SW, 8 tubes $250.00

43B, cathedral, 1934, wood, center front window dial, upper cloth grill w/cut-outs, 4 knobs, BC, SW, 8 tubes $250.00

44, cathedral, 1934, wood, center front window dial, upper cloth grill w/cut-outs, 4 knobs, 6 tubes, AC $225.00

45, table, 1934, wood, Deco, center front window dial, right & left "butterfly wing" grills, top louvers, 4 knobs, 6 tubes, AC $135.00

45C, table, 1934, wood, Deco, center front window dial, right & left "butterfly wing" grills, top louvers, 4 knobs......$135.00

45L, console, 1934, wood, lowboy, upper front window dial, lower cloth grill w/cut-outs, 4 knobs, BC, SW, 6 tubes, AC...$150.00

46, cathedral, 1931, wood, center front window dial, upper cloth grill w/cut-outs, 3 knobs, 7 tubes, DC............$325.00

46-131, table, 1946, upper front slide rule dial, lower horizontal louvers, 2 knobs, BC, battery $30.00

46-132, table, 1946, wood, upper front slide rule dial, lower cloth grill w/center horizontal bar, 2 knobs, BC, battery.........$25.00

46-142, table, 1946, plastic, upper front slanted slide rule dial, lower horizontal louvers, 2 knobs, BC, battery $30.00

46-200 "Transitone," table, 1946, plastic, right front dial, right & left horizontal wrap-around louvers, 2 knobs, BC, AC/DC..$40.00

46-250 "Transitone," table, 1946, plastic, upper front slide rule dial, lower horizontal louvers, 2 knobs, BC, AC/DC..$40.00

46-350, portable, 1946, wood & leatherette, upper front slide rule dial, lower horizontal grill bars, tambour cover, handle, BC, 6 tubes, AC/DC/battery $45.00

46-420, table, 1946, plastic, step-down top, curved dial & 2 knobs on top of case, lower horizontal wrap-around louvers, BC, 6 tubes, AC/DC $45.00

46-420-I, table, 1946, plastic, step-down top, curved dial & 2 knobs on top of case, lower horizontal wrap-around louvers, BC, 6 tubes, AC/DC $45.00

46-421, table, 1946, walnut, upper front slide rule dial, lower oblong cloth grill, 2 knobs, BC, AC/DC..........................$50.00

46-421-I, table, 1946, ivory, upper front slide rule dial, lower oblong cloth grill, 2 knobs, BC, AC/DC..........................$50.00

46-427, table, 1946, wood, upper front slide rule dial, lower horizontal louvers, 3 knobs, BC, SW, 6 tubes, AC/DC........$45.00

46-480, console, 1946, wood, upper front slanted slide rule dial, lower cloth grill w/vertical bars, 4 knobs, BC, SW, FM, AC $135.00

46-1203, table-R/P, 1946, wood, right front vertical dial, 3 knobs, left horizontal louvers, lift top, inner phono, BC, AC...$40.00

46-1209, console-R/P, 1946, wood, 2 upper front slide rule dials, lower tilt-out phono, pushbuttons, 4 knobs, BC, SW, AC $130.00

46-1213, console-R/P, 1946, wood, inner right slide rule dial, 10 pushbuttons, doors, left fold-out phono, BC, SW, FM, AC $100.00

46-1217, console-R/P, 1946, wood, inner left dial & knobs, fold-up lid, right pull-out phono, lower grill w/cut-outs, AC $150.00

46-1226, console-R/P, 1946, wood, upper front slanted slide rule dial, lower tilt-out phono, 4 knobs, BC, SW, AC $135.00

47, cathedral, 1932, two-tone wood, center front window dial, upper cloth grill w/cut-outs, 4 knobs, battery $120.00

47-204, table, 1947, leatherette, center front plastic panel w/right dial & left horizontal grill bars, 2 knobs, BC, AC/DC......$30.00

47-205, table, 1947, leatherette & plastic, right front dial, left horizontal louvers, 2 knobs, AC/DC $30.00

47-1227, console-R/P, 1947, wood, upper front slanted slide rule dial, lower tilt-out phono, 4 knobs, BC, FM, 9 tubes, AC..........$135.00

47-1230, console-R/P, 1947, wood, upper front slide rule dial, lower tilt-out phono, 4 knobs, pushbuttons, BC, SW, FM, 9 tubes, AC $135.00

48-141, table, 1948, walnut plastic, upper front slide rule dial, lower horizontal louvers, 2 knobs, BC, battery $35.00

48-145, table, 1948, ivory plastic, upper front slide rule dial, lower horizontal louvers, 2 knobs, BC, battery.......................$35.00

48-150, table, 1948, wood, upper front slanted slide rule dial, lower perforated metal grill, 2 knobs, BC, 5 tubes, battery.......$35.00

48-200 "Transitone," table, 1948, walnut plastic, right front dial, right & left horizontal wrap-around louvers, 2 knobs, BC, 5 tubes, AC/DC $40.00

46-1201, table-R/P, 1946, wood, curved front, top slide rule dial, 2 knobs, center cloth grill, lower slide-in record slot, BC, AC $75.00

48-200-I "Transitone," table, 1948, ivory plastic, right front dial, right & left horizontal wrap-around louvers, 2 knobs, BC, 5 tubes, AC/DC $40.00

48-206, table, 1948, leatherette, front plastic panel w/right dial & left horizontal grill bars, rounded corners, 2 knobs, BC, AC/DC...$30.00

48-214 "Transitone," table, 1948, wood, right front dial, left lattice grill, 2 knobs, 5 tubes, BC, AC/DC $35.00
48-225 "Transitone," table, 1948, plastic, right front square dial, left perforated grill, rounded top, 2 knobs, BC, AC/DC..$35.00

48-230 "Transitone," table, 1948, plastic, modernistic dial & grill, rounded top, slanted sides, 2 knobs, BC, AC/DC...$75.00
48-250 "Transitone," table, 1948, walnut plastic, upper front slide rule dial, lower horizontal wrap-around louvers, 2 knobs, 5 tubes, AC/DC $40.00
48-250-I "Transitone," table, 1948, ivory plastic, upper front slide rule dial, lower horizontal wrap-around louvers, 2 knobs, 5 tubes, AC/DC $40.00

48-300 "Transitone," portable, 1948, leatherette, upper front slide rule dial, lower horizontal louvers, 2 knobs, handle, BC, 5 tubes, AC/DC/battery $30.00
48-360, portable, 1948, "alligator," inner slide rule dial, lower horizontal wood louvers, tambour lid, handle, AC, 6 tubes, battery $40.00
48-460, table, 1948, plastic, step-down top, curved dial & 2 knobs on top of case, lower horizontal wrap-around louvers, BC, AC/DC $45.00
48-460-I, table, 1948, ivory plastic, step-down top, curved dial & 2 knobs on top of case, lower horizontal wrap-around louvers, BC, AC/DC $45.00
48-461, table, 1948, wood, upper front slanted slide rule dial, lower recessed cloth grill, 2 knobs, BC, AC/DC $30.00
48-464, table, 1948, brown plastic, upper front slanted slide rule dial, lower horizontal louvers, 4 knobs, BC, SW, 6 tubes, AC/DC $45.00
48-472, table, 1948, walnut plastic, upper front slanted slide rule dial, lower horizontal louvers, 4 knobs, BC, FM, 8 tubes, AC/DC $40.00
48-472-I, table, 1948, ivory plastic, upper front slanted slide rule dial, lower horizontal louvers, 4 knobs, BC, FM, 8 tubes, AC/DC $40.00
48-475, table, 1948, wood, raised top, upper front slanted slide rule dial, lower cloth grill area, 4 knobs, 6 pushbuttons, BC, FM, AC $60.00

48-482, table, 1948, wood, lower front slanted slide rule dial, upper cloth grill, 10 pushbuttons, 4 knobs, BC, SW, FM, 9 tubes, AC...$55.00
48-703, table, 1948, plastic, modernistic dial & grill, rounded top, slanted sides, 2 knobs, BC, AC/DC.............................$75.00
48-1201, table-R/P, 1948, wood, curved front, top slide rule dial, 2 knobs, center cloth grill, lower slide-in record slot, BC, AC...$75.00
48-1253, table-R/P, 1948, walnut, front slide rule dial, 2 knobs, lower horizontal louvers, 3/4 lift top, inner phono, BC, AC $40.00
48-1256, table-R/P, 1948, wood, right front vertical slide rule dial, 3 knobs, horizontal grill bars, lift top, inner phono, BC, 6 tubes, AC $35.00
48-1260, console-R/P, 1948, wood, inner right slide rule dial, inner left slide-in record slot, large lower grill, BC, AC $65.00
48-1262, console-R/P, 1948, two-tone wood, upper front slanted slide rule dial, lower tilt-out phono, 4 knobs, BC, 6 tubes, AC...$110.00
48-1263, console-R/P, 1948, walnut, upper front slanted slide rule dial, lower tilt-out phono, 4 knobs, BC, SW, 8 tubes, AC...$110.00

48-1264, console-R/P, 1948, walnut, upper front slide rule dial, center pull-out phono, lower criss-cross grill, 4 knobs, BC, FM, AC $75.00

48-1266, console-R/P, 1948, wood, inner dial, 4 knobs, 6 pushbuttons, double doors, center pull-out phono, lower criss-cross grill, BC, SW, FM, AC $80.00

48-1270, console-R/P, 1948, wood, inner right slide rule dial, 4 knobs, pushbuttons, door, left pull-out phono, BC, SW, FM, 13 tubes, AC $95.00

48-1274 "Hepplewhite," console-R/P, 1948, mahogany, inner dial & knobs, fold-up lid, front tilt-out front phono, BC, SW, FM, 15 tubes, AC $110.00

48-1276 "Sheraton," console-R/P, 1948, wood, inner slide rule dial, 4 knobs, pushbuttons, fold-up lid, front tilt-out phono, BC, SW, FM, 15 tubes, AC..$125.00

48-1284, console-R/P, 1948, wood, inner right slide rule dial, 4 knobs, door, left pull-out phono, lower grill & storage, BC, SW, AC...$75.00

48-1286, console-R/P, 1948, wood, inner slide rule dial, 4 knobs, lift-up lid, front tilt-out phono, storage, BC, FM, 11 tubes, AC...$95.00

48-1290, console-R/P, 1948, wood, inner right vertical dial, 4 knobs, pushbuttons, door, left pull-out phono, BC, SW, FM, 13 tubes, AC..$100.00

48-1401, table-R/P, 1948, wood & plastic, modern, top right slide rule dial, left arched grill, front slide-in phono, AC.......$125.00

49-100, table, 1949, brown plastic, upper front slide rule dial, lower horizontal louvers, 4 tubes, battery.......................$35.00

49-101, table, 1949, plastic, lower front slide rule dial, upper vertical wrap-over grill bars, 2 knobs, BC............................$35.00

49-472, table, 1949, plastic, upper front slanted slide rule dial, lower horizontal louvers, 4 knobs, BC, FM....................$45.00

49-500 "Transitone," table, 1949, walnut plastic, right front dial, right & left horizontal wrap-around louvers, 2 knobs, BC, 5 tubes, AC/DC $40.00

49-500-I "Transitone," table, 1949, ivory plastic, right front dial, right & left horizontal wrap-around louvers, 2 knobs, BC, 5 tubes, AC/DC $40.00

49-501 "Transitone," table, 1949, brown plastic, modern, right front round dial, left arched perforated grill, 2 knobs, BC, 5 tubes, AC/DC $275.00

49-501-I "Transitone," table, 1949, ivory plastic, modern, right front round dial, left arched perforated grill, 2 knobs, BC, 5 tubes, AC/DC $275.00

49-503 "Transitone," table, 1949, plastic, modernistic dial & grill, rounded top, slanted sides, 2 knobs, BC, AC/DC $75.00

49-504 "Transitone," table, 1949, walnut plastic, upper front slide rule dial, lower horizontal louvers, 2 knobs, BC, 5 tubes, AC/DC $40.00

49-504-I "Transitone," table, 1949, ivory plastic, upper front slide rule dial, lower horizontal louvers, 2 knobs, BC, 5 tubes, AC/DC $40.00

49-505 "Transitone," table, 1949, plastic, center slide rule dial, curved-in checkerboard front, 2 knobs, BC, AC/DC...$50.00

49-506 "Transitone," table, 1949, wood, right dial/center decorative "wedge" over plastic checkered grill, 2 knobs, 5 tubes $45.00

49-601, portable, 1949, plastic, lower front slide rule dial, upper horizontal grill bars, 2 knobs, handle, BC, battery.........$35.00

49-602 "Transitone," portable, 1949, plastic, lower front slide rule dial, upper horizontal louvers, handle, 2 knobs, BC, 4 tubes, AC/DC/battery $35.00

49-603, table/easel style, 1949, leather & plastic, folds open, tiny window dial, 2 thumbwheel knobs, BC, 5 tubes AC/DC $55.00

49-605, portable, 1949, plastic, upper front slide rule dial, large lower grill area, handle, BC, 6 tubes, AC/DC/battery $50.00

49-607, portable, 1949, "alligator," upper front slide rule dial, lower horizontal wooden grill bars, handle, 2 knobs, BC, AC/DC/battery $55.00

49-900-E, table, 1949, ebony plastic, step-down top, curved dial & 2 knobs on top of case, lower horizontal wrap-around louvers, BC, 6 tubes, AC/DC $50.00

49-900-I, table, 1949, ivory plastic, step-down top, curved dial & 2 knobs on top of case, lower horizontal wrap-around louvers, BC, 6 tubes, AC/DC $50.00

49-901, table, 1949, plastic, modern, large right ribbed knob doubles as both station selector and on/off/volume control, left raised grill w/circular cut-outs, BC, 5 tubes, AC/DC $95.00

49-902, table, 1949, plastic, right front dial, right & left horizontal grill bars, 2 knobs, BC, AC/DC $40.00

49-904, table, 1949, plastic, large right slide rule dial on see-through plastic, left grill, 4 knobs, BC, SW, 6 tubes, AC/DC $40.00

49-905, table, 1949, plastic, angled front design, right dial, left horizontal louvers, 3 knobs, BC, FM, AC/DC $35.00

49-906, table, 1949, plastic, upper front slide rule dial, lower horizontal grill bars, 4 knobs, BC, FM, AC/DC..........$35.00

49-909, table, 1949, wood, center front slide rule dial, large upper woven grill, 4 knobs, BC, FM, 9 tubes, AC $35.00

49-1101, console, 1949, mahogany, upper front dial, large lower cloth grill w/3 vertical bars, BC, FM, 9 tubes, AC $75.00

49-1401, table-R/P, 1949, wood & plastic, modern, top right slide rule dial, left arched grill, front slide-in phono, AC.......$125.00

49-1405, table-R/P, 1949, wood, right front square dial, left horizontal louvers, 3 knobs, lift top, inner phono, BC, AC ...$35.00

49-1600, console-R/P, 1949, wood, upper front slide rule dial, 4 knobs, center fold-out phono, lower criss-cross grill, BC, AC $60.00

49-1602, console-R/P, 1949, wood, upper front slanted slide rule dial, 4 knobs, front tilt-out phono, BC, AC $75.00

49-1604, console-R/P, 1949, wood, upper front slide rule dial, center pull-out phono, lower grill area, record storage, AC/DC..$70.00

49-1606, console-R/P, 1949, wood, upper front slide rule dial, 4 knobs, center fold-out phono, lower grill, storage, BC, AC $70.00

49-1613, console-R/P, 1949, wood, inner right slide rule dial, lower storage, door, left fold-out phono, BC, FM, AC....$80.00

49-1615, console-R/P, 1949, wood, inner left slide rule dial, push-buttons, 5 knobs, door, right fold-out phono, lower grill, BC, FM, AC $85.00

49B, cathedral, 1934, two-tone wood, center front window dial, 3 section cloth grill, 4 knobs, BC, SW, DC $200.00

49H, console, 1934, wood, lowboy, upper front window dial, lower cloth grill w/cut-outs, 4 knobs, BC, SW, DC $130.00

49X, console, 1934, wood, upper front window dial, lower cloth grill w/vertical bars, 4 knobs, BC, SW, DC $130.00

50, cathedral, 1931, wood, center front window dial, upper cloth grill w/cut-outs, 3 knobs, battery................................$150.00

50-520 "Transitone," table, 1950, brown plastic, lower front slide rule dial, upper horizontal louvers, 2 knobs, feet, BC, AC/DC $30.00

50-520-I "Transitone," table, 1950, ivory plastic, lower front slide rule dial, upper horizontal louvers, 2 knobs, feet, BC, AC/DC $30.00

50-522 "Transitone," table, 1950, brown plastic, lower front slide rule dial, upper horizontal louvers, 2 knobs, BC, AC/DC ..$35.00

50-522-I "Transitone," table, 1950, ivory plastic, lower front slide rule dial, upper horizontal louvers, 2 knobs, BC, AC/DC ..$35.00

50-524, table, 1950, mahogany, lower front slide rule dial, large upper grill area, 2 knobs, BC, AC/DC..........................$30.00

50-526 "Transitone," table, 1950, maroon plastic, lower front slide rule dial, large upper half-round lattice grill, 2 knobs, BC, AC/DC $45.00

50-527 "Transitone," table-C, 1950, brown plastic, top left thumbwheel dial, left front clock panel overlaps horizontal wrap-around grill bars, BC, AC...................................$45.00

50-527-I "Transitone," table-C, 1950, ivory plastic, top left thumbwheel dial, left front clock panel overlaps horizontal wrap-around grill bars, BC, AC...................................$45.00

50-620 "Transitone," portable, 1950, plastic, lower front slide rule dial, upper horizontal louvers, handle, 2 knobs, BC, AC/DC/battery $35.00

50-621, portable, 1950, plastic, lower front slide rule dial, upper horizontal louvers, handle, 2 knobs, BC, AC/DC/battery $35.00

50-920, table, 1950, brown plastic, top slanted half-round dial, lower horizontal wrap-around louvers, 2 knobs, AC/DC...........$50.00

50-921, table, 1950, ivory plastic, half-round dial on case top, front horizontal louvers, 2 knobs, BC, AC/DC $45.00

50-922, table, 1950, maroon plastic, half-round dial on case top, front horizontal louvers, 2 knobs, BC, AC/DC $45.00

50-925, table, 1950, plastic, diagonal front design, right dial, left grill bars, 3 knobs, BC, FM, AC/DC..............................$30.00

50-926, table, 1950, wood & leatherette, right front dial, left grill area, 3 knobs, BC, FM, AC/DC $25.00

50-1421, table-R/P, 1950, plastic, top right dial, 3 knobs, left lift top, inner phono, front vertical bars, BC, AC.................$65.00

50-1422, table-R/P, 1950, plastic, top right dial, 3 knobs, left lift top, inner phono, front vertical bars, BC, AC.................$65.00

50-1423, table-R/P, 1950, wood, right front dial, left horizontal louvers, 3 knobs, lift top, inner phono, BC, AC $40.00

50-1720, console-R/P, 1950, wood, upper front slide rule dial, 4 knobs, center fold-down phono door, lower grill, BC, FM, AC $65.00

50-1721, console-R/P, 1950, wood, upper front slide rule dial, 4 knobs, center fold-down phono door, lower grill, BC, FM, AC.........$65.00

50-1723, console-R/P, 1950, wood, upper front slide rule dial, center left pull-out phono/right storage area, lower grill, BC, FM, AC $70.00

50-1724, console-R/P, 1950, wood, inner right slide rule dial, 4 knobs, left phono, double front doors, BC, FM, AC.......$70.00

50-1726, console-R/P, 1950, wood, inner right slide rule dial/lower storage, door, left pull-out phono, BC, FM, AC $80.00

50-1727, console-R/P, 1950, wood, inner left slide rule dial, pushbuttons, 5 knobs, door, right pull-out phono, BC, FM, AC $80.00

51-530 "Transitone," table, 1951, plastic, lower front slide rule dial, upper horizontal louvers, 2 knobs, BC, AC/DC......**$30.00**

51-532 "Transitone," table, 1951, plastic, lower front slide rule dial, large upper half-round lattice grill, 2 knobs, BC **$45.00**

51-537 "Transitone," table-C, 1951, plastic, top left thumbwheel dial, left front alarm clock panel overlaps horizontal wrap-around grill bars, BC, AC......................................**$45.00**

51-538 "Transitone," table-C, 1951, plastic, top left thumbwheel dial, left front alarm clock panel overlaps horizontal wrap-around grill bars, BC **$45.00**

51-631, portable, 1951, plastic, upper front slide rule dial, wrap-over vertical bars, right & left side knobs, metal handle, BC, AC/DC/battery **$35.00**

51-930, table, 1951, plastic, raised top w/half-round dial, lower horizontal wrap-around louvers, 2 knobs, BC, AC/DC ..**$50.00**

51-934, table, 1951, plastic, upper front slanted slide rule dial, lower horizontal louvers, 3 knobs, AM, FM, AC/DC **$35.00**

51-1330, table-R/P, 1951, plastic, lower front slide rule dial, upper horizontal louvers, 2 knobs, lift top, inner phono, BC, AC..**$40.00**

51-1730, console-R/P, 1951, wood, upper front slide rule dial, center fold-down phono door, lower grill, 4 knobs.........**$60.00**

51-1732, console-R/P, 1951, wood, inner right slide rule dial, 4 knobs, pull-out phono, left storage, double doors, lower grill, BC, FM, AC **$60.00**

51-1733, console-R/P, 1951, wood, inner right slide rule dial, 4 knobs, pull-out phono, left storage, double doors, lower grill, BC, FM, AC **$60.00**

51B, cathedral, 1932, wood, center front window dial, upper 3-section cloth grill, scrolled base, 3 knobs, 5 tubes **$250.00**

52, cathedral, 1932, wood, center front window dial w/escutcheon, upper cloth grill w/cut-outs, 3 knobs **$250.00**

52-540 "Transitone," table, 1952, plastic, lower front slide rule dial, upper horizontal grill bars, 2 knobs, BC **$30.00**

52-541 "Transitone," table, 1952, plastic, lower front slide rule dial, upper horizontal grill bars, 2 knobs, BC **$30.00**

52-542 "Transitone," table, 1952, plastic, lower front slide rule dial, large upper half-round grill w/horizontal bars, 2 knobs, BC **$35.00**

52-542-I "Transitone," table, 1952, plastic, lower front slide rule dial, upper half-round grill w/horizontal bars, 2 knobs, BC **$35.00**

52-544 "Transitone," table-C, 1952, plastic, raised left top w/thumbwheel dial, lower left front clock panel overlaps horizontal wrap-around grill bars, BC, AC **$45.00**

52-544-I "Transitone," table-C, 1952, plastic, raised left top w/thumbwheel dial, lower left front clock panel overlaps horizontal wrap-around grill bars, BC, AC **$45.00**

52-548 "Transitone," table, 1952, plastic, modern, lower front slide rule dial, large center raised grill area w/vertical bars, feet, 2 knobs, BC..**$75.00**

52-643, portable, 1952, plastic, lower front slide rule dial, upper lattice grill, flex handle, 2 knobs, BC, AC/DC/battery **$30.00**

52-942, table, 1952, plastic, large half-round dial on case top, front horizontal louvers, 2 knobs, BC, AC/DC **$45.00**

52-944, table, 1952, plastic, upper front slanted slide rule dial, lower horizontal louvers, 3 knobs, BC, FM, AC/DC **$30.00**

52-1340, table-R/P, 1952, plastic, lower front slide rule dial, upper lattice grill, 2 knobs, lift top, inner phono, BC, AC **$40.00**

52C, table, 1932, wood, rectangular case, right front window dial, left cloth grill w/cut-outs, 3 knobs, 5 tubes, AC..............**$60.00**

52L, console, 1932, wood, lowboy, upper front window dial, lower cloth grill w/cut-outs, 4 knobs, AC **$135.00**

53-559 "Transitone," table, 1953, plastic, right front square dial panel overlaps horizontal grill bars, 2 knobs, 2 band, 5 tubes, AC/DC **$20.00**

53-560 "Transitone," table, 1953, plastic, right front square dial panel overlaps horizontal grill bars, 2 knobs, BC, AC/DC ..**$25.00**

53-561 "Transitone," table, 1953, plastic, large right front round dial, left horizontal grill bars, 2 knobs, feet **$35.00**

53-562 "Transitone," table, 1953, plastic, right front dial, left horizontal grill bars, 2 knobs, BC, SW, AC/DC....................**$30.00**

53-563 "Transitone," table, 1953, plastic, modern, right front slide rule dial, raised left checkered grill, 2 knobs, AC/DC **$50.00**

53-564 "Transitone," table, 1953, plastic, right front dial w/center stylized "P," left horizontal grill bars, feet, 2 knobs **$35.00**

53-566 "Transitone," table, 1953, plastic, modern, lower front slide rule dial, large center raised grill area w/vertical bars, feet, 2 knobs, BC, AC/DC..**$75.00**

53-656, portable, 1953, plastic, lower front slide rule dial, upper lattice grill, handle, right side knob, BC, SW, AC/DC/battery **$30.00**

53-658, portable, 1953, leather, lower front slide rule dial w/fold-down cover, upper horizontal grill bars, handle, 2 knobs, AC/DC/battery **$30.00**

53-701 "Transitone," table-C, 1953, plastic, right front square dial, left alarm clock, center lattice grill area, BC, AC....**$30.00**

53-702 "Transitone," table-C, 1953, plastic, step-down top, right front round dial overlaps horizontal grill bars, left square clock, 2 band, AC **$30.00**

53-706, lamp/radio/clock, 1953, wood, tall rectangular case, lower front dial, center grill, upper alarm clock, AC...$95.00

53-804, table-C, 1953, plastic, right front round dial, left alarm clock, center checkered grill, 2 band, AC **$30.00**

53-958, table, 1953, wood, right & left front vertical dials, center cloth grill, 3 knobs, BC, FM, AC/DC **$35.00**

53-960, table, 1953, wood, right front recessed 9-band vertical slide rule dial, left grill area, 5 knobs, AC **$50.00**

53-1750, end table-R/P, 1953, wood, drop-leaf, top dial, 2 front knobs, lower pull-out phono drawer, 2 band, AC **$90.00**

53-1754, console-R/P, 1953, wood, inner front slide rule dial, 4 knobs, lower phono, storage, double doors, 2 band, AC...**$50.00**

54, table, 1933, walnut w/inlay, right front dial, center cloth grill w/cut-outs, top louvers, 2 knobs, BC, 5 tubes, AC/DC ..**$75.00**

54S, table, 1934, two-tone wood, "owl-eye" front design, right dial, center cloth grill w/cut-outs, top louvers, 2 knobs, 5 tubes, AC/DC **$75.00**

57C, table, 1933, wood, right front dial, center cloth grill w/cut-outs, top louvers, 2 knobs, BC, AC **$65.00**

59C, table, 1936, walnut w/inlay, right front dial, center cloth grill w/cut-outs, top louvers, 2 knobs, BC, AC.....................**$65.00**

59S, table, 1934, two-tone wood, "owl-eye" front design, right dial, center cloth grill w/cut-outs, top louvers, 2 knobs, AC...**$75.00**

60, cathedral/various styles, 1936, wood, center front window dial w/escutcheon, upper cloth grill w/cut-outs, 4 knobs $140.00

60, console, c1935, wood, upper front window dial with escutcheon, lower cloth grill w/cut-outs, 4 knobs **$130.00**

60, tombstone, 1934, wood, center front round window dial, upper cloth grill w/Deco cut-outs, 4 knobs............................**$125.00**

60B, cathedral/various styles, 1935, wood, center front window dial, upper cloth grill with cut-outs, 4 knobs, BC, SW, 5 tubes, AC **$130.00**

60B, tombstone, 1934, wood, center front round window dial, upper cloth grill w/Deco cut-outs, 4 knobs, BC, 5 tubes..........**$125.00**

60L, console, 1933, wood, lowboy, upper front window dial, lower cloth grill w/cut-outs, 4 knobs, BC, 5 tubes, AC **$130.00**

65, console, 1930, wood, lowboy, upper front window dial, lower cloth grill w/"oyster-shell" cut-out, AC **$135.00**

65, table, 1929, metal, low rectangular case, center front window dial w/escutcheon, 4 knobs, AC **$125.00**

66, tombstone, 1933, two-tone wood, center front window dial, shield-shaped cloth grill w/center vertical bars, 4 knobs...**$100.00**

66B, tombstone, 1935, wood, center front round window dial, upper cloth grill w/Deco cut-outs, 4 knobs, BC, SW, 5 tubes, AC **$110.00**

69, table, two-tone wood, "owl-eye" front design, right dial, center cloth grill w/cut-outs, top louvers, 2 knobs **$75.00**

70, cathedral, 1931, walnut, center front window dial, upper cloth grill w/cut-outs, fluted columns, 7 tubes, AC **$300.00**

70 "Lazyboy," chairside, 1931, cabinet designed by Norman Bel Geddes, top recessed controls, front grill area, 7 tubes..**$150.00**

70, console, 1931, walnut, lowboy, upper front window dial, **lower cloth grill w/cut-outs, stretcher base, 4 knobs, 7 tubes, AC** **$160.00**

70, console-R/P, 1931, walnut, lowboy, upper front window dial, lower cloth grill w/cut-outs, lift top, inner phono, 7 tubes, AC **$150.00**

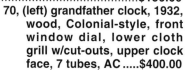

70, (left) grandfather clock, 1932, **wood, Colonial-style, front window dial, lower cloth grill w/cut-outs, upper clock face, 7 tubes, AC** **$400.00**

70B, cathedral, 1931, wood, center front window dial, upper cloth grill w/cut-outs, fluted columns, 7 tubes........**$300.00**

70B, tombstone, 1938, two-tone wood, rounded shoulders, center front square dial, upper cloth grill w/cut-outs, 2 knobs **$100.00**

70L, console, 1931, wood, lowboy, upper front window dial, lower cloth grill w/shield-shaped cut-out, 7 tubes, AC **$140.00**

71, cathedral, 1932, two-tone wood, center front window dial, upper cloth grill w/cut-outs, 4 knobs, AC.......**$250.00**

71 "Lazyboy," chairside, 1932, cabinet designed by Norman Bel Geddes, top controls, front grill area, 7 tubes........**$150.00**

71B, cathedral, 1932, wood, center front window dial w/es-cutcheon, upper cloth grill w/ cut-outs, 7 tubes, AC...**$250.00**

71H, console, 1932, wood, lowboy, upper front window dial, lower cloth grill w/cut-outs, 6 legs, 7 tubes, AC **$140.00**

71L, console, 1932, wood, lowboy, upper front window dial, lower cloth grill w/shield-shaped cut-out, 4 knobs, 7 tubes, AC ..**$140.00**

71T "Traveler," portable, striped case, right front dial, left grill area, handle, 2 knobs, BC, battery **$25.00**

77, console, 1930, wood, lowboy, upper front window dial, lower cloth grill w/vertical bars, 4 knobs, 7 tubes, AC...........**$140.00**

80 "Junior," cathedral, 1933, two-tone wood, center front window dial, upper cloth grill w/cut-outs, 2 knobs, AC **$125.00**

80B, cathedral, 1932, two-tone wood, center front window dial, upper cloth grill w/cut-outs, 2 knobs, 4 tubes, AC **$125.00**

81 "Junior," cathedral, 1933, wood, center front window dial, upper cloth grill with cut-outs, 3 knobs **$125.00**

81B, cathedral, 1933, two-tone wood, center front window dial, upper cloth grill w/cut-outs, 3 knobs, AC **$125.00**

84, cathedral, 1936, two-tone wood, center front dial, upper cloth grill with Deco cut-outs, 2 knobs **$130.00**

84B, cathedral/various styles, 1934, two-tone wood, lower front **dial, upper cloth grill w/cut-outs, 2 knobs, 4 tubes, AC..$140.00**

85, console, wood, highboy, inner window dial w/escutcheon, upper round cloth grill w/cut-outs, small right & left doors, large double front doors, drawer, 8 tubes, AC............**$150.00**

86 "Junior," cathedral, two-tone wood, center front window dial, upper cloth grill w/cut-outs, AC...................................**$130.00**

86, console, 1929, wood, upper front window dial w/escutcheon, lower round cloth grill w/cut-outs, lift top, 8 tubes, AC ..**$150.00**

89, cathedral/various styles, 1934, two-tone wood, center front dial, **upper cloth grill with cut-outs, 4 knobs, BC, SW, AC $175.00**

89B, cathedral/various styles, 1936, two-tone wood, center front dial, upper cloth grill with cut-outs, 4 knobs, BC, 6 tubes, AC **$175.00**

89F, console, 1935, wood, upper front window dial, lower cloth grill w/cut-outs, 4 knobs, BC, 6 tubes **$125.00**

89L, console, 1935, wood, lowboy, upper front window dial, lower cloth grill w/cut-outs, 4 knobs, BC, 6 tubes, AC **$140.00**

90, cathedral, 1931, wood, center front window dial, upper cloth grill w/cut-outs, fluted columns, 4 knobs, 9 tubes, AC ..**$400.00**

90, console, 1931, walnut, lowboy, inner front window dial, cloth grill w/cut-outs, 4 knobs, double doors, stretcher base, 9 tubes, AC **$150.00**

90B, cathedral, 1931, wood, center front window dial, upper cloth grill w/cut-outs, fluted columns, 9 tubes, AC **$400.00**

90H, console, 1931, wood, lowboy, inner front window dial, cloth grill w/cut-outs, double front doors, 9 tubes, AC..........**$150.00**

90X, console, wood, upper front window dial, lower inclined grill area, BC, 9 tubes, AC **$160.00**

91, cathedral, 1934, two-tone wood, center front window dial, upper cloth grill w/cut-outs, 4 knobs, 9 tubes **$275.00**

91L, console, 1932, wood, lowboy, upper front window dial, lower cloth grill w/cut-outs, 4 knobs, 9 tubes, AC **$160.00**

91X, console, 1933, wood, upper front window dial w/escutcheon, lower inclined grill area, 4 knobs, 9 tubes, AC **$175.00**

93B, tombstone, 1937, two-tone wood, rounded shoulders, lower front round dial, upper cloth grill w/vertical bars, 2 knobs **$125.00**

95, console, 1930, wood, highboy, inner front window dial, tapestry grill, sliding doors, side fleur-de-lis cut-outs, 9 tubes, AC **$295.00**

96, console, 1930, wood, lowboy, upper front window dial w/escutcheon, lower cloth grill w/vertical bars, AC......**$140.00**

96H, console, 1930, wood, upper front window dial, lower cloth grill w/cut-outs, stretcher base, 9 tubes **$150.00**

112, console, 1931, wood, lowboy, designed by Norman Bel Geddes, recessed front panel w/upper window dial & lower cloth grill w/cut-outs, 11 tubes, AC......................................**$150.00**

112X, console, wood, upper front window dial w/escutcheon, lower inclined grill area, 11 tubes, AC **$175.00**

116, tombstone, 1935, wood, center front oval dial, upper cloth grill w/cut-outs, 4 knobs, BC, SW, 10 tubes **$135.00**

116B, tombstone, 1936, wood, center front oval dial, upper cloth grill w/cut-outs, 4 knobs, BC, SW, AC **$135.00**

116X, console, 1936, walnut, upper front oval dial, lower cloth grill w/vertical bars, right & left cut-outs, BC, SW, 11 tubes, AC...........**$250.00**

116PX, console-R/P, 1935, wood, front oval dial, lower cloth grill w/cut-outs, right & left cut-outs, lift top, inner phono, BC, SW, AC **$250.00**

118, cathedral, 1934, two-tone wood, center front window dial, upper cloth grill w/cut-outs, 4 knobs **$300.00**

118, tombstone, two-tone wood, shouldered, center front dial, upper cloth grill w/cut-outs, 4 knobs **$135.00**

118B, cathedral, 1934, two-tone wood, center front window dial, upper 3-section cloth grill, 4 knobs, BC, 8 tubes, AC..**$300.00**

118H, console, 1935, wood, upper front window dial, lower cloth grill w/cut-outs, 4 knobs, BC, SW, 8 tubes, AC **$150.00**

118MX, console, 1935, wood, upper front window dial, lower cloth grill w/2 vertical bars, 4 knobs, BC, SW, 8 tubes, AC..**$150.00**

118RX, chairside/remote speaker, 1935, wood, chairside unit w/top dial, separate speaker w/Deco grill cut-outs, BC, SW, 8 tubes, AC..**$200.00**

118X, console, 1935, wood, upper front window dial, lower cloth grill w/3 vertical bars, 4 knobs, BC, SW, 8 tubes, AC ...**$150.00**

144, cathedral, 1934, wood, center front window dial, 3-section cloth grill, 4 knobs, BC, SW, 6 tubes, AC **$225.00**

144B, cathedral, 1934, wood, center front window dial, 3-section cloth grill, 4 knobs, BC, SW, 6 tubes, AC **$225.00**

144H, console, 1935, wood, upper front window dial, lower cloth grill w/cut-outs, 4 knobs, BC, SW, 6 tubes, AC **$140.00**

144X, console, 1935, wood, upper front window dial, lower cloth grill w/3 vertical bars, 4 knobs, BC, SW, 6 tubes, AC..**$140.00**

200X, console, 1934, wood, upper front window dial, lower cloth grill w/center bars, right & left cut-outs, 4 knobs, BC, 10 tubes, AC **$165.00**

212, console-R/P, 1931, wood, lowboy, designed by Norman Bel Geddes, front window dial, lower cloth grill w/cut-outs, lift top, inner phono, 11 tubes, AC.......................................**$150.00**

270, grandfather clock, wood, Colonial-style, front window dial, lower cloth grill w/cut-outs, upper clock face, AC **$350.00**

280 Jr., mantle clock, table-N, 1932, wood, Colonial mantle clock-style, lower knobs, upper clock face, top finials **$275.00**

296, console-R/P, 1930, wood, lowboy, front window dial, lower cloth grill w/vertical bars, lift top, inner phono, AC.......**$165.00**

370 "Lazyboy," chairside, 1931, designed by Norman Bel Geddes, top recessed controls, front grill area, AC **$175.00**

500X, console-R/P, 1935, wood, front window dial, lower inclined grill w/2 vertical bars, lift top, inner phono, BC, SW, 11 tubes, AC **$170.00**

501X, console-R/P, 1935, wood, front window dial, lower inclined grill w/2 vertical bars, lift top, inner phono, BC, SW, 11 tubes, AC **$170.00**

505L, console-R/P, 1935, wood, lowboy, upper front window dial, lower cloth grill w/cut-outs, lift top, inner phono, 6 legs, BC, 5 tubes, AC **$125.00**

511, table, 1928, two-tone Spanish brown metal, rectangular case, center front window dial, 3 knobs, BC, 7 tubes, AC **$95.00**

512, table, 1928, two-tone Mandarin red metal, rectangular case, center front window dial, hand-painted flowers, 3 knobs, BC, 7 tubes, AC **$115.00**

513, table, 1928, two-tone Labrador gray metal, rectangular case, center front window dial, hand-painted flowers, 3 knobs, BC, 7 tubes, AC $115.00

514, table, 1928, two-tone Nile green metal, rectangular case, center front window dial, hand-painted flowers, 3 knobs, BC, 7 tubes, AC $115.00

515 "Impressionistic," table, 1928, gold metal, rectangular case, center front window dial, hand-painted green, red & blue leaves, 3 knobs, BC, 7 tubes, AC $115.00

610, console, 1936, wood, upper front oval dial, lower cloth grill w/cut-outs, fluting, 4 knobs, BC, SW $130.00

610, table, 1936, wood, right front oval dial, rounded left, left cloth grill w/Deco cut-outs, 4 knobs, BC, SW........................$85.00

610, tombstone, 1936, wood, shouldered, center front oval dial, upper cloth grill w/cut-outs, 4 knobs, BC, SW, AC $115.00

620, tombstone, 1934, wood, shouldered, center front oval dial, upper cloth grill w/cut-outs, 4 knobs, BC, SW $115.00

620F, console, 1936, wood, upper front oval dial, lower cloth grill w/cut-outs, 4 knobs, BC, SW....................................$135.00

623, tombstone, 1935, wood, shouldered, center front oval dial, upper cloth grill w/cut-outs, 4 knobs, battery $70.00

623K, console, 1935, wood, upper front oval dial, lower cloth grill w/cut-outs, 4 knobs, BC, SW, battery....................$100.00

624, console, 1935, wood, upper front oval dial, lower cloth grill w/cut-outs, 4 knobs, BC, SW, battery.....................$100.00

625J, console, wood, upper front oval dial, lower cloth grill w/cut-outs, BC, SW, 6 tubes $115.00

625S, console, wood, upper front oval dial, lower cloth grill w/cut-outs, BC, SW, 6 tubes $115.00

630, chairside, 1936, two-tone wood, top oval dial & 4 knobs, front cloth grill w/3 vertical bars, BC, SW, AC $150.00

635B, tombstone, 1935, wood, shouldered, center front oval dial, upper cloth grill w/cut-outs, 4 knobs, BC, SW, 6 tubes $120.00

635PF, console-R/P, wood, upper front oval dial, lower cloth grill w/cut-outs, 4 knobs, lift top, inner phono, BC, SW, 6 tubes, AC...$125.00

635X, console, wood, upper front oval dial, lower cloth grill w/3 vertical bars, 4 knobs, BC, SW, 6 tubes, AC..............$125.00

640, tombstone, 1936, wood, shouldered, center front oval dial, upper cloth grill w/cut-outs, 4 knobs, BC, SW $125.00

640X, console, 1936, wood, upper front oval dial, lower cloth grill w/cut-outs, 4 knobs, BC, SW......................................$135.00

645K, console, 1936, wood, upper front oval dial, lower cloth grill w/cut-outs, 4 knobs, BC, SW, 7 tubes $135.00

650H, console, 1936, wood, lowboy, inner top dial & controls, pop-up lid, front oval grill w/lyre cut-out, BC, SW, 8 tubes, AC $140.00

650MX, console, 1936, wood, inner top dial & controls, lift lid, front cloth grill w/4 vertical bars, BC, SW $150.00

650PX, console-R/P, 1936, two-tone wood, upper front oval dial, lower cloth grill w/vertical bars, 4 knobs, lift top, inner phono, BC, SW..$150.00

650RX, chairside/remote speaker, 1936, wood, chairside table w/top dial & knobs, separate speaker unit w/vertical grill bars, BC, SW...$225.00

650X, console, 1936, two-tone wood, upper front oval dial, lower cloth grill w/3 vertical bars, 4 knobs, BC, SW.............$130.00

655H, console, wood, lowboy, inner top dial & controls, pop-up lid, front oval grill w/lyre cut-out, BC, SW, 8 tubes, AC $140.00

655X, console, wood, upper front oval dial, lower cloth grill w/3 vertical bars, 4 knobs, BC, SW..................................$130.00

655MX, console, wood, inner top dial & controls, lift lid, front cloth grill w/4 vertical bars, BC, SW, 8 tubes $150.00

655PX, console-R/P, wood, upper front oval dial, lower cloth grill w/vertical bars, 4 knobs, lift top, inner phono, BC, SW ..$150.00

660X, console, 1936, two-tone wood, upper front oval dial, lower cloth grill w/3 vertical bars, 4 knobs, BC, SW, 10 tubes ..$140.00

665X, console, wood, upper front oval dial, lower cloth grill w/vertical bars, 4 knobs, BC, SW, 10 tubes..........................$140.00

680X, console, 1935, wood, inner top dial & controls, lift lid, front cloth grill w/vertical bars, right & left front cut-outs, BC, SW, 15 tubes, AC...$175.00

777, table-C, 1962, blue & ivory plastic, lower right front dial knob overlaps horizontal bars, large upper alarm clock face, feet, BC, 5 tubes, AC..$20.00

780, table-C, 1962, ivory or mocha plastic, right front lattice grill area, left alarm clock face with lower dial & on/off/volume knobs, feet, BC, 5 tubes, AC $20.00

782, table-C, 1962, beige/ivory or ivory/aqua plastic, wedge-shaped case, lower right front dial knob, upper alarm clock face, left horizontal grill bars, BC, 5 tubes, AC.............$15.00

783, table-C, 1962, white/pink or white/beige plastic, wedge-shaped case, lower front horizontal dial, upper right alarm clock face, upper left grill area, BC, 5 tubes, AC...........$15.00

784, table-C, 1962, white/aqua or beige/ivory plastic, wedge-shaped case, lower left slide rule dial, large upper lattice grill area, right alarm clock face, pushbuttons, BC, AC........$20.00

785, table-C, 1962, ivory or black plastic, lower front slide rule dial, 2 upper modules—right speaker grill/left alarm clock face, pushbuttons, BC, 5 tubes, AC $25.00

851, table, 1962, ivory plastic, lower right front dial panel overlaps large textured grill area, feet, 2 knobs, BC, 5 tubes, AC...$10.00

852, table, 1962, ivory/mocha or ivory/pink plastic, wedge-shaped case, lower right front dial/lower left front volume knobs overlap large upper grill area w/horizontal bars, BC, 5 tubes, AC/DC $10.00

853, table, 1962, aqua/white or beige/white plastic, wedge-shaped case, right front dial panel, left grill w/horizontal bars, BC, 5 tubes, AC/DC $15.00

855, table, 1962, white/mocha or white/aqua plastic, wedge-shaped case, lower front slide rule dial, large upper 2-section grill area, handle, 2 knobs, BC, 5 tubes, AC/DC $10.00

856, table, 1962, mocha/ivory, charcoal/ivory or aqua/ivory plastic, wedge-shaped case, lower right front slide rule dial, large upper lattice grill area, 2 knobs, BC, 5 tubes, AC/DC ..$20.00

858, table, 1962, black or ivory plastic, lower front slide rule dial, two upper speaker modules, 2 knobs, BC, 5 tubes, AC/DC $25.00

910, table, 1962, ivory/black plastic, right front slide rule dial, left lattice grill area, 2 knobs, FM, 6 tubes, AC...................$10.00

914, table, 1962, aqua/ivory or black/ivory plastic, wedge-shaped case, lower front round dial, upper grill area w/vertical bars, 2 speakers, 2 knobs, AM, FM, AC..................................$15.00

A-801, chairside, 1941, wood, Deco, top vertical slide rule dial, lower open storage, 2 knobs, pushbuttons.................$120.00

B569 "Transitone," table, 1954, plastic, right front half-round dial, left horizontal grill bars, 2 knobs, BC, 5 tubes, AC/DC...$25.00

B570 "Transitone," table, 1954, plastic, right front round dial over horizontal grill bars, arched base, 2 knobs, BC, AC/DC...$30.00

B574 "Multiwave," table, 1954, plastic, right front dial, left horizontal grill bars, 2 knobs, feet, 2 band, AC/DC.............$30.00

B578 "Transitone," "Multiwave," table, plastic, right front dial w/center "P" logo, left horizontal grill bars, feet, 2 knobs..$30.00

B650, portable, 1954, plastic, top thumbwheel knobs, center front grill w/circular cut-outs, fold-back handle, BC, battery ..$30.00

B710 "Transitone," table-C, 1953, plastic, right front dial, left alarm clock, center lattice grill, 5 knobs, BC, AC..........$30.00

B714X, table-C, 1954, plastic, step-down top, right front round dial over horizontal bars, left alarm clock, BC, AC..............$30.00

B-956, table, 1953, plastic, off-center dial w/stylized "P" logo overlaps front lattice grill, 3 knobs, feet, BC, FM.................$35.00

B1349, table-R/P, 1954, plastic, lower front slide rule dial, upper lattice grill, 2 knobs, lift top, inner phono, AC................$45.00

B-1352, table-R/P, 1954, lower front slide rule dial, upper grill, 2 knobs, lift top, inner phono, 2 band, 5 tubes, AC..........$25.00

C580 "Transitone," table, 1955, plastic, right front round dial, lower metal "houndstooth" perforated grill, 2 knobs, BC $30.00

C-660, portable, 1955, plastic, two top thumbwheel knobs, center grill panel w/circular cut-outs, handle, BC, 4 tubes, battery...$30.00

C-663, portable, 1955, plastic, top right dial knob, front vertical grill bars w/center stylized "P" logo, handle, BC, 4 tubes, AC/DC/battery $30.00

C-666, portable/flashlight, 1955, plastic, lower front slide rule dial, upper lattice grill, top flashlight switch, handle, BC, 5 tubes, AC/DC/battery $60.00

C-667, portable/flashlight, 1955, plastic, 2 lower front slide rule dials, upper lattice grill, top flashlight switch, handle, 2 bands, 5 tubes, AC/DC/battery $60.00

D-597, table, 1956, plastic, right front dial, left horizontal bars w/center stylized "P" logo, feet, BC, 5 tubes $25.00

D-665-124, portable, 1956, vanity-case style, inner controls, lift-up mirrored lid, front grill w/center stylized "P" logo, BC, 4 tubes, AC/DC/battery $60.00

D-1345, table-R/P-C, 1957, inner right dial, outer left front clock overlaps perforated grill, lift top, inner phono, handle, BC, 5 tubes, AC $40.00

E-672-124, portable, leather, right front half-round dial, large grill area w/checkered cut-outs, handle, BC, AC/DC/battery $25.00

E-675-124, portable, 1957, leather, right front half-round dial overlaps metal perforated grill, handle, left side on/off/volume knob, BC $25.00

E-810-124, table, 1957, plastic, right front dial over checkered panel, left metal perforated grill, feet, BC, AC/DC.........$20.00

E-812-124, table, 1957, plastic, large right round dial overlaps perforated panel & lower horizontal grill bars, BC, AC/DC $20.00

E-818, table, 1958, center front slide rule dial, twin speakers, lower right "P" logo, 2 knobs, BC, 6 tubes, AC/DC $25.00

E-1370, table-R/P, 1957, right side dial, large front perforated grill w/logo, lift top, inner phono, handle, BC, 5 tubes, AC...$25.00

F238, table-C, plastic, lower right front dial, upper alarm clock, left horizontal grill bars, feet, BC, AC $15.00

F-673-124, portable, 1957, leather case, right front half-round dial, metal perforated grill w/wedge-shaped cut-outs, handle, left side knob, BC $25.00

F675-124, portable, 1957, leather case, right front dial overlaps large center perforated grill, handle, AC/DC/battery $25.00

F752-124, table-C, 1958, plastic, lower right front dial, upper alarm clock, left lattice grill, feet, BC, AC $20.00

F-809, table, 1958, plastic, center front round dial overlaps horizontal wrap-around grill bars, feet, BC, 5 tubes, AC $20.00

F-974, table, 1959, plastic, large center front round dial overlaps lattice grill, 2 knobs, AM, FM, 7 tubes, AC/DC $20.00

G-681-124, portable, 1959, plastic, left front dial, right checkered grill, "Scantenna" handle, right side knob, BC, 4 tubes, AC/DC/battery **$30.00**

G-822 "Deluxe," table, 1959, plastic, lower front off-center dial overlaps vertical grill bars, 2 knobs, BC, 5 tubes, AC/DC **$20.00**

H691-124, portable, plastic, left front leatherette panel w/lower dial, right checkered grill area, rotatable handle, right side knob, BC, AC/DC/battery...**$25.00**

H765-124, table-C, plastic, modern, step-down base contains 2 knobs and lower vertical grill bars, top clock module w/4 pushbuttons, BC, AC...**$75.00**

H836-124, table, plastic, modern, vertically divided front, lower right dial & lower left knob overlap lattice grill area, twin speakers, feet, BC **$20.00**

J775-124, table-C, plastic, modern, step-down base contains 2 knobs and lower vertical grill bars, top clock module w/4 pushbuttons, BC, AC...**$75.00**

L799-124, table-C, 1963, plastic, lower right slide rule dial & upper alarm clock face overlap textured front panel, AM, FM, AC **$20.00**

PT-4 "Transitone," table, 1941, plastic, upper front slide rule dial, lower horizontal wrap-around louvers, 2 knobs, AC/DC...**$40.00**

PT-6, table, 1940, two-tone wood, upper front slide rule dial, lower cloth grill w/3 horizontal bars, 2 knobs, 5 tubes, AC...**$40.00**

PT-7, table, 1942, walnut, upper front slide rule dial, lower horizontal louvers, 2 knobs, 5 tubes, AC/DC........................$40.00

PT-12 "Transitone," table, 1940, two-tone wood, upper front slanted slide rule dial, lower horizontal louvers, 2 knobs...$35.00

PT-25 "Transitone," table, 1939, brown plastic, right front square dial overlaps horizontal louvers, 2 knobs, BC, 5 tubes ..$40.00

PT-26 "Transitone," table, 1940, brown plastic, right front square dial overlaps horizontal louvers, 2 knobs, BC $40.00

PT-27 "Transitone," table, 1939, ivory plastic, right front square dial overlaps horizontal louvers, 2 knobs, BC, AC/DC ..$40.00

PT-33 "Transitone," table, 1940, plastic, right front dial overlaps horizontal bars, handle, 2 knobs $40.00

PT-36 "Transitone," table, 1939, ivory & black plastic, modern, right front dial, horizontal wrap-around grill bars, 2 knobs, BC $90.00

PT-38 "Transitone," table, 1939, walnut, right front dial, left cloth grill w/Deco cut-outs, 2 knobs, BC, SW.......................$45.00

PT-41 "Transitone," table, 1939, walnut, right front dial, left cloth grill w/Deco cut-outs, 2 knobs, BC, SW.......................$45.00

PT-42 "Transitone," table, 1939, two-tone wood, right front square dial, left cloth grill, tapered sides, 2 knobs $45.00

PT-43 "Transitone," table, 1939, wood & plastic, right front dial, left horizontal wrap-around grill bars, handle, 2 knobs, BC, AC $65.00

PT-46 "Transitone," table, 1939, brown plastic, right front dial, left mitered louvers, 6 pushbuttons, 2 knobs, BC..........$65.00

PT-48 "Transitone," table, 1939, ivory plastic, right front dial, left mitered louvers, 6 pushbuttons, 2 knobs, BC...............$65.00

PT-50 "Transitone," table, 1939, maple, right front dial, left cloth grill w/3 horizontal bars, 2 knobs, BC $45.00

PT-61 "Transitone," table, 1940, two-tone wood, Deco, step-down top, right front dial, left horizontal louvers, curved base, BC, AC/DC $115.00

PT-63 "Transitone," portable, 1940, striped cloth covered, right front square dial, left cloth grill, handle, 2 knobs $25.00

PT-66 "Transitone," table, 1939, wood & plastic, right front dial, left grill, base, handle, 6 pushbuttons, 2 knobs, BC $60.00

PT-69 "Transitone," table-C, 1939, wood, trapezoid-shaped, lower right front dial, left cloth grill w/horizontal bars, upper clock, 2 knobs, BC, AC..$85.00

PT-87 "Transitone," portable, 1942, leather & plastic, front plastic dial panel w/right dial & left horizontal grill bars, handle, 2 knobs, 5 tubes, battery $30.00

PT-88 "Transitone," portable, 1942, leather & plastic, inner plastic dial panel w/right dial & left horizontal grill bars, 2 knobs, fold-down front, handle, 5 tubes $35.00

PT-91 "Transitone," table, 1941, plastic, right front dial overlaps horizontal wrap-around louvers, feet, 2 knobs, AC $40.00

PT-93, table, two-tone wood, right front dial, left cloth grill, center vertical divider, feet, handle, 2 knobs $50.00

TH-1 "Transitone," table, 1939, wood, right front gold dial, left cloth grill with horizontal bars, 2 knobs, BC $45.00

PHILHARMONIC
Espey Mfg. Co., Inc.,
528 East 72nd Street, New York, New York

100C, console-R/P, 1948, wood, inner right slide rule dial, 4 knobs, phono, lift top, front criss-cross grill, BC, AC $60.00

100T "Minuet," table-R/P, 1948, wood, upper front slide rule dial, lower horizontal grill bars, 4 knobs, lift top, inner phono, BC, AC ...$35.00

149-C, console-R/P, 1949, wood, inner right dial, left phono, lift top, front criss-cross grill, BC, AC $55.00

249-C, console-R/P, 1949, wood, inner right dial, lift top, left front pull-out phono drawer, lower criss-cross grill, BC, AC ..$60.00

349-C, console-R/P, 1949, wood, inner right slide rule dial, door, left pull-out phono drawer, lower front criss-cross grill, BC, FM, AC $75.00

8712, console-R/P, 1947, wood, inner right slide rule dial, 4 knobs, record storage, door, left lift top, inner phono, BC, 2 SW, AC...$70.00

PHILLIPS 66
Phillips Petroleum Co.,
Bartlesville, Oklahoma

3-12A, portable, 1948, upper front slanted slide rule dial, lower horizontal louvers, handle, 2 knobs, battery..................$35.00

3-20A, table-R/P, 1948, wood, upper front slanted slide rule dial, lower horizontal louvers, 3/4 lift top, inner phono, BC, AC $35.00

3-81A, console-R/P, 1948, wood, inner right slide rule dial, 4 knobs, door, left pull-out phono drawer, BC, SW, FM, 14 tubes, AC..$85.00

PILOT
Pilot Electrical Manufacturing Company,
323 Berry Street, Brooklyn, New York
Pilot Radio & Television Corporation
Pilot Radio and Tube Corporation,
Lawrence, Massachusetts
Pilot Radio Corporation,
37-06 36th Street, Long Island City, New York

The Pilot Electrical Manufacturing Company began business in 1922 making batteries and parts and eventually expanded into the production of radios.

53, tombstone, 1934, wood, center front round dial, upper cloth grill w/cut-outs, 4 knobs, BC, SW, 5 tubes, AC $150.00

63, tombstone, 1934, wood, center front round dial, upper cloth grill w/cut-outs, BC, SW, 6 tubes, AC.........................$125.00

93, table, 1934, walnut w/inlay, center front cloth grill w/cut-outs, BC, SW, 5 tubes, AC/DC...............................$75.00

114, tombstone, 1934, wood, center front round dial, upper cloth grill, BC, SW, AC $120.00

133, table, 1940, wood, right front dial, tuning eye, left horizontal wrap-around louvers, 4 knobs $65.00

193, table, 1936, wood, right front large round dial, left cloth grill w/horizontal bars, 4 knobs, BC, SW, AC $60.00

293, tombstone, 1936, wood, lower front large round dial, upper cloth grill w/vertical bars and center tuning eye, 4 knobs, BC, SW, 7 tubes, AC..$150.00

298, tombstone, 1936, wood, lower front large round dial, upper cloth grill w/vertical bars and center tuning eye, 4 knobs, BC, SW, 7 tubes, DC..$95.00

423, table, 1937, wood, rounded top, lower front large round dial, upper cloth grill w/cut-outs, 4 knobs, BC, SW, 7 tubes, AC/DC...$75.00

B-2, table, 1934, walnut, Deco, right front window dial, center grill cut-outs, 2 knobs, 4 tubes, AC/DC $90.00

B1151 "Lone Ranger," table, 1939, plastic, right front dial w/Lone Ranger & Silver, left horizontal louvers, handle, 2 knobs, 5 tubes $85.00

C-63, console, 1934, wood, upper front round dial, lower cloth grill, 4 knobs, feet, BC, SW, 6 tubes, AC....................$125.00

C-193, console, 1937, wood, upper front large round dial, lower cloth grill w/vertical bars, tuning eye, 4 knobs, BC, SW, 6 tubes, AC..$125.00

C-293, console, 1936, wood, upper front large round dial, lower cloth grill w/center vertical divider, tuning eye, 4 knobs, 7 tubes, BC, SW, AC...$125.00

CG-184, console, 1936, wood, upper front large round dial, lower cloth grill w/center vertical divider, tuning eye, 4 knobs, 7 tubes, BC, SW, AC/DC..$125.00

CX-304, console, 1937, walnut, upper front large round dial, lower cloth grill w/center vertical divider & horizontal bars, tuning eye, 4 knobs, BC, SW, 11 tubes, AC/DC **$135.00**

E-20, table, 1934, burl walnut, Deco, step-down top, right front window dial, center grill cut-outs, 3 knobs, 6 tubes, AC/DC **$90.00**

G-852, table, two-tone wood, right front large round dial, left cloth wrap-around grill, 3 knobs, BC, SW, 5 tubes **$55.00**

L-8, cathedral, 1933, wood, center front half-round dial w/escutcheon, upper cloth grill w/cut-outs, 4 knobs, AC **$260.00**

PG-184, console-R/P, 1938, wood, upper front large round dial, lower cloth grill w/center vertical divider, tuning eye, 4 knobs, lift top, inner phono, BC, SW, 8 tubes, AC/DC **$125.00**

PG-674, console-R/P, 1938, wood, upper front large round dial, lower cloth grill w/center vertical divider, tuning eye, 4 knobs, lift top, inner phono, BC, SW, 7 tubes, AC **$125.00**

RG-184, console-R/P, 1937, wood, inner right round dial, left phono, lift top, lower front grill area, BC, SW, 7 tubes, AC/DC ...**$115.00**

RG-584, console-R/P, 1937, wood, inner right round dial, left phono, lift top, lower front grill area, BC, SW, AC **$115.00**

RG-674, console-R/P, 1937, wood, inner right round dial, left phono, lift top, lower front grill area, BC, SW, AC **$115.00**

T-3, table, wood, upper front slide rule dial, lower horizontal louvers, 3 knobs, BC, SW, 6 tubes **$50.00**

T-301, table, 1941, walnut, upper front slanted slide rule dial, lower cloth grill w/2 horizontal bars, BC, FM, 8 tubes, AC **$50.00**

T-341, table, 1941, walnut, right front slide rule dial, left vertical grill bars, pushbuttons, 8 bands, 10 tubes, AC/DC **$85.00**

T-411-U, table, 1947, wood, center front vertical slide rule dial, right & left grill areas, 4 knobs, BC, SW, AC **$40.00**

T-500U, table, 1947, plastic, large center front dial, right & left horizontal wrap-around grill bars, 3 knobs, BC, SW, 5 tubes, AC/DC **$85.00**

T-511, table, 1946, wood, center front vertical slide rule dial, right & left grill areas, 4 knobs, BC, SW, AC/DC **$40.00**

T-521, table, 1947, wood, lower front slide rule dial, large upper grill area, 4 knobs, BC, FM, AC/DC **$40.00**

T-531AB, table, 1947, wood, lower front slide rule dial, upper horizontal louvers, 4 knobs, BC, 3 SW, FM, AC/DC **$45.00**

T-741, table, 1948, wood, lower front slide rule dial, upper horizontal louvers, 4 knobs, BC, AC/DC **$40.00**

T-1252, table, wood, right front dial, left horizontal wrap-around louvers, handle, 3 knobs, BC, SW, AC/DC **$45.00**

TG-56, tombstone, 1937, wood, lower front large round dial, upper cloth grill w/vertical bars, 4 knobs, BC, SW, battery......**$75.00**

TG-162, table, 1937, wood, right front large round dial, left wrap-around cloth grill w/horizontal bars, 3 knobs, BC, SW, 5 tubes, AC/DC **$50.00**

TG-184, table, 1937, wood, right front large round dial, left cloth grill w/horizontal bars, tuning eye, 4 knobs, BC, SW, 8 tubes, AC/DC **$75.00**

TG-528 "Dragon IV," tombstone, 1937, wood, lower front large 5-band slide rule dial, upper cloth grill w/vertical bars, tuning eye, 6 knobs, BC, SW, 12 tubes, AC **$165.00**

TG-584, table, 1937, wood, right front round dial, left wrap-over cloth grill w/vertical bars, tuning eye, 4 knobs, BC, SW, 8 tubes, AC..**$75.00**

TG-674, table, 1938, wood, right front round dial, left cloth grill w/horizontal bars, tuning eye, 4 knobs, BC, SW, 5 tubes, AC ...**$75.00**

TG-752, table, 1937, wood, right front large round dial, left wrap-around cloth grill w/horizontal bars, 3 knobs, BC, SW, 5 tubes, AC...**$50.00**

TG-5206, tombstone, 1937, wood, lower front large round dial, upper cloth grill w/vertical bars, 4 knobs, BC, SW, battery **$75.00**

TP-32, table-R/P, 1941, walnut, right front slide rule dial, left horizontal wrap-around louvers, 4 knobs, lift top, inner phono, BC, SW, AC...**$30.00**

TP-423, table-R/P, 1937, wood, lower front round dial, upper cloth grill w/center horizontal bar, 4 knobs, lift top, inner phono, 7 tubes, AC/DC **$40.00**

TP-1062, table-R/P, 1941, wood, recessed right front dial, left horizontal wrap-around louvers, 3 knobs, lift top, inner phono, AC $30.00

TX-42, table-R/P, 1941, wood, right front slide rule dial, left criss-cross grill, 4 knobs, lift top, inner phono, AC **$30.00**

UG-184, tombstone, 1938, wood, lower front large round dial, upper cloth grill w/cut-outs and center tuning eye, 4 knobs, BC, SW, 8 tubes, AC/DC...**$145.00**

VG-352, table, 1937, ivory plastic, right front round dial overlaps criss-cross grill area w/center horizontal bar, 3 knobs, BC, SW, 5 tubes, AC/DC..**$60.00**

VX-201, tombstone, 1937, ivory plastic, lower front round dial, upper cloth grill w/vertical bars, 3 knobs, BC, 5 tubes, AC/DC **$175.00**

WG-352, table, 1937, walnut plastic, right front round dial overlaps criss-cross grill area w/center horizontal bar, 3 knobs, BC, SW, 5 tubes, AC/DC..**$60.00**

WX-201, tombstone, 1937, walnut plastic, lower front round dial, upper cloth grill w/vertical bars, 3 knobs, BC, 5 tubes, AC/DC **$175.00**

T-1451, portable, 1939, cloth covered, inner right square dial, left grill area, 2 knobs, fold-in cover, AC/battery......$25.00

X3, table, wood, upper front slanted slide rule dial, lower horizontal louvers, 3 knobs, BC, SW, AC/DC $40.00

X-304 "Challenger," tombstone, 1938, wood, lower front round dial, upper cloth grill w/cut-outs & center tuning eye, 4 knobs, BC, SW, 11 tubes, AC/DC..$150.00

Super Wasp - AC, table, 1928, kit, SW receiver, metal front panel w/two window dials, plug-in coils, AC $375.00

Super Wasp - DC, table, 1928, kit, SW receiver, metal front panel w/two window dials, plug-in coils, DC.........................$375.00

Wasp, table, 1928, kit, SW receiver, metal front panel w/left window dial, 4 knobs, plug-in coils $275.00

PIONEER

578, tombstone, wood w/inlay, lower front round dial, upper cloth grill w/cut-outs, 3 knobs, "Pioneer" nameplate $100.00

PORT-O-MATIC

The Port-O-Matic Corp.,
50 E. 77th St., New York, New York

61-A, portable-R/P, 1941, cloth covered, inner right dial, left round grill area, fold-down front, handle, lift top, inner phono, 6 tubes, AC...$25.00

PORTO BARADIO
Porto Products,
412 North Orleans Street, Chicago, Illinois

PA-510, table-N, 1949, plastic bar/radio, lower front slide rule dial, upper horizontal louvers, side handles, 2 knobs, open top bar, BC, 5 tubes, AC/DC ....$200.00 w/glassware

PB-520, table-N, 1948, plastic bar/radio, lower front slide rule dial, upper horizontal louvers, side handles, 2 knobs, open top bar, BC, 5 tubes, AC/DC ....$200.00 w/glassware

PRECEL
Precel Radio Mfg. Co.,
227 Erie St., Toledo, Ohio

Superfive, table, 1925, wood, tall rectangular case, slanted 3 dial panel, lower storage, 5 tubes, battery $150.00

PREMIER
Premier Crystal Laboratories, Inc.,
63 Park Row, New York, New York

15LW, table, 1946, wood, rounded corners, upper front slide rule dial, lower cloth grill, 2 knobs, BC, AC/DC $35.00

PRIESS
Priess Radio Corporation,
693 Broadway, New York, New York

The Priess Radio Corporation began business in 1924. Beset by financial difficulties, the company was bankrupt by 1927.

PR3, table, 1925, mahogany, low rectangular case, 2 dial front panel, top loop antenna, 5 tubes, battery $195.00

PR4 "Straight 8," table, 1925, wood, low rectangular case, center front dial, top loop antenna, 8 tubes, battery $220.00

Straight Eight, console, 1925, two-tone walnut, inner dial panel and speaker grill w/cut-outs, double front doors, 8 tubes, battery $285.00

Straight Eight, table, 1925, two-tone mahogany w/inlay, low rectangular case, top loop antenna, storage, 8 tubes, battery $230.00

Straight Nine, table, 1926, mahogany, low rectangular case, center front dial, top loop antenna, 9 tubes, battery $245.00

PROMENETTE
The Promenette Radio & Television Corp.
1721 Elmwood Ave., Buffalo, NY

501, table, right front dial, left grill w/horizontal bars, 2 knobs, BC $25.00

601, table, right front dial, left cloth grill w/center horizontal bar, 2 knobs, BC $25.00

PURITAN
Pure Oil Co.,
35 Wacker Drive, Chicago, Illinois

501, table, 1946, plastic, upper front slide rule dial, lower criss-cross grill, 2 knobs, BC, AC/DC $35.00

502X, table, 1946, plastic, upper front slide rule dial, lower criss-cross grill, 2 knobs, BC, AC/DC $35.00

503, table-R/P, 1946, wood, top vertical dial, 3 knobs, front cloth grill, lift top, inner phono, BC, AC $30.00

504, table, 1946, wood, upper front slanted slide rule dial, lower criss-cross grill, 4 knobs, BC, SW, AC $40.00

506, table, 1946, plastic, step-down top, upper front slide rule dial, lower horizontal wrap-around louvers, 3 knobs, BC, AC/DC..$65.00

508, table, 1946, wood, upper front slanted slide rule dial, lower cloth grill, 4 knobs, BC, 2SW, AC $40.00

509, portable, 1947, upper front slanted slide rule dial, lower horizontal grill bars, 2 knobs, handle, BC, AC/DC/battery ..$25.00

515, table, 1947, wood, upper front slanted slide rule dial, lower two-tone cloth grill, 2 knobs, BC, AC/DC......................$35.00

R. K. RADIO LABORATORIES
Chicago, Illinois

S-4233 "Radio Keg," table-N, 1933, looks like keg w/copper hoops, front window dial & knobs, rear grill, AC/DC....$300.00

RADIO VISION

414, tombstone, wood, lower right front dial, left cloth grill w/shield-shaped cut-out, upper panel w/battleships, planes, Statue of Liberty and water that "moves" when radio plays $200.00

RADIOBAR
Radiobar Co. of America,
296 Broadway, New York, New York

200-RBP, console-R/P/Bar, 1940, wood, inner left dial, door, right pull-out phono drawer, upper lighted bar unit with double doors & lift top ....**$1,000.00/with glassware**

508, console/Bar, 1933, wood, lower front dial/knobs/grill, upper bar unit with double doors & lift top ....**$1,200.00/with glassware**

510, console/Bar, 1933, walnut, inner front dial/knobs/grill, doors, upper bar unit with double doors & lift top ....**$1,200.00/with glassware**

528, console/Bar, 1933, wood, Deco, inner front dial/knobs/grill, upper bar unit with double doors & lift top .....**$1,200.00/with glassware**

No #/Philco chassis, console/Bar, 1936, wood, lower front dial, 4 knobs, cloth grill w/cut-outs, upper bar unit w/double doors and lift top ....**$900.00/with glassware**

RADIOETTE
Alamo Electronics Corp.,
San Antonio, Texas

PR-2, portable, 1948, trapezoid shape, front dial, left concentric circular grill bars, handle, 3 knobs, BC, 4 tubes, AC/DC/battery **$40.00**

RADIOLA
Radio Corp. of America,
Home Instrument Division,
Camden, New Jersey

61-1, table, 1947, plastic, upper front slanted slide rule dial, lower horizontal wrap-around louvers, 3 knobs, BC, AC/DC ..**$50.00**

61-5, table, 1947, upper front slanted slide rule dial w/stars, lower horizontal louvers, 3 knobs, BC, SW, AC/DC ..$45.00

61-8, table, 1947, plastic, upper front slanted slide rule dial, lower horizontal wrap-around grill bars, 2 knobs, BC, AC/DC...**$45.00**

61-9, table, 1947, plastic, upper front slanted slide rule dial, lower horizontal wrap-around grill bars, 2 knobs, BC, AC/DC...**$45.00**

61-10 "Postone," table, 1947, plastic, upper front slanted slide rule dial, lower horizontal grill bars, 3 knobs, BC, AC/DC.............**$45.00**

75ZU, table-R/P, 1948, wood, upper front dial, lower horizontal grill bars, 2 knobs, lift top, inner phono, BC, AC............**$30.00**

76ZX11, table, 1948, plastic, upper front slanted slide rule dial, lower horizontal wrap-around grill bars, 2 knobs, BC, AC/DC **$45.00**

76ZX12, table, 1948, plastic, upper front slanted slide rule dial, lower horizontal wrap-around grill bars, 2 knobs, BC, AC/DC **$45.00**

500, table, 1941, walnut plastic, midget, right front dial, left horizontal wrap-around louvers, 2 knobs, BC, 5 tubes, AC/DC **$85.00**

501, table, 1941, ivory plastic, midget, right front dial, left horizontal wrap-around louvers, 2 knobs, BC, 5 tubes, AC/DC **$85.00**

510, table, 1940, mahogany plastic, right front dial, left vertical grill bars, 2 knobs, BC, 5 tubes, AC/DC.............................**$45.00**

511, table, 1940, ivory plastic, right front dial, left vertical grill bars, 2 knobs, BC, 5 tubes, AC/DC.............................**$45.00**

512, table, 1941, wood, right front dial, left cloth grill, flared base, 2 knobs, BC, 5 tubes, AC/DC **$60.00**

513, table, wood, right front dial, left grill w/diagonal bars, 2 knobs, BC, 5 tubes, AC/DC **$50.00**

515, table, 1941, wood, upper front slanted slide rule dial, lower horizontal louvers, 3 knobs, BC, SW, 6 tubes, AC/DC ...**$45.00**

516, table, 1942, plastic, upper front slanted slide rule dial, lower vertical grill bars, handle, 2 knobs, BC, 5 tubes, AC/DC **$45.00**

517, table, 1942, two-tone wood, upper front slanted slide rule dial, lower horizontal louvers, 2 knobs, BC, 5 tubes, AC/DC **$50.00**

520, table, 1942, wood, right front dial, left horizontal grill bars, 2 knobs, BC, 5 tubes, AC/DC **$35.00**

522, table, 1942, wood, upper front slanted slide rule dial, lower horizontal louvers, 2 knobs, BC, 5 tubes, AC/DC.........**$35.00**

526, table, 1942, plastic, upper front slanted slide rule dial, lower vertical grill bars, handle, 2 knobs, BC, SW, 5 tubes, AC/DC **$40.00**

527, table, 1942, wood, upper front slanted slide rule dial, lower vertical grill bars, 2 knobs, BC, SW, 5 tubes, AC/DC **$40.00**

B-50, table, 1940, wood, right front dial, left horizontal grill bars, 2 knobs, BC, 4 tubes, battery **$30.00**

B-52, table, 1940, wood, right front slide rule dial, left horizontal grill bars, 3 knobs, BC, 5 tubes, battery **$30.00**

P-5, portable, 1940, right front dial, left horizontal grill bars, 3 knobs, BC, AC/DC/battery...**$25.00**

R560P, table-R/P, 1942, wood, right front dial, left grill area, 3 knobs, lift top, inner phono, BC, 5 tubes, AC **$30.00**

RAMWAY

R-17, table, wood, low rectangular case, front panel w/3 pointer dials & metal escutcheons, ram's head logo $150.00

RAYENERGY
RayEnergy Radio & Television Corp.,
32 West 22nd Street,
New York, New York

AD, table, 1946, wood, right front dial, left cloth grill w/ cut-outs, 2 knobs, BC, AC/DC **$40.00**

AD4, table, 1946, wood, right front dial, left contrasting horizontal louvers, 2 knobs, BC, AC/DC **$45.00**

SRB-1X, table, 1947, plastic, upper front slide rule dial, lower horizontal louvers, 2 knobs, BC, AC/DC **$45.00**

RCA
Radio Corporation of America,
233 Broadway, New York, New York

RCA was formed in 1919 and soon became one of the largest distributors of radios. The company was one of the pioneers of early radio & broadcasting and began the National Broadcasting Company (NBC) in 1926. As well as being one of the most prolific of radio manufacturers, RCA also made vacuum tubes, Victrolas, marine apparatus, transmitters and other broadcasting equipment. Their mascot, "Nipper," was featured in many company logos listening at the horn for "his master's voice."

1-C-5JE, table-C, plastic, wedge-shaped case, left front slide rule dial & alarm clock face overlap horizontal bars, rear hand-hold, feet, top drowse alarm button, BC, AC ..**$20.00**

1R81, table, 1952, plastic, center front large round dial overlaps horizontal bars, right side knobs, AM, FM, AC **$25.00**

1RA11 "Accent," table, gray plastic, right front round dial overlaps horizontal bars, feet, 2 knobs, AM, 5 tubes, AC/DC **$10.00**

1-RA-20 "Hardy," table, white plastic, right front round dial overlaps horizontal bars, feet, 2 knobs, AM, 5 tubes, AC/DC.........**$10.00**

1-RA-23 "Hardy," table, pink plastic, right front round dial overlaps horizontal bars, feet, 2 knobs, AM, 5 tubes, AC/DC **$10.00**

1-RA-25 "Hardy," table, turquoise plastic, right front round dial overlaps horizontal bars, feet, 2 knobs, AM, 5 tubes, AC/DC ..**$10.00**

1-RA-26 "Hardy," table, beige plastic, right front round dial overlaps horizontal bars, feet, 2 knobs, AM, 5 tubes, AC/DC **$10.00**

1-RA-64, table, plastic, wedge-shaped case, lower front raised panel w/oval dial overlaps horizontal bars, 2 knobs, AM **$25.00**

1-RC-30, table-C, white plastic, wedge-shaped case, lower front slide rule dial, upper right alarm clock, upper left lattice grill, top pushbuttons, feet, AM, FM, 6 tubes, AC **$20.00**

1-RC-31, table-C, white/charcoal plastic, wedge-shaped case, lower front slide rule dial, upper right alarm clock, upper left lattice grill, top pushbuttons, feet, AM, FM, 6 tubes, AC **$20.00**

1-RC-34, table-C, espresso/white plastic, wedge-shaped case, lower front slide rule dial, upper right alarm clock, upper left lattice grill, top pushbuttons, feet, AM, FM, 6 tubes, AC **$20.00**

1X, table, plastic, right front dial, left vertical grill bars, decorative case lines, 2 knobs, BC, 5 tubes, AC/DC **$50.00**

1X2, table, plastic, right front dial, left vertical grill bars, decorative case lines, 2 knobs, BC, 5 tubes, AC/DC **$50.00**

1X51, table, 1952, plastic, upper front half-round dial, lower horizontal grill bars, right side knob, BC, AC/DC.................**$30.00**

1X54, table, 1952, plastic, upper front half-round dial, lower horizontal grill bars, right side knob, BC, AC/DC.................**$30.00**

1X55, table, 1952, plastic, upper front half-round dial, lower horizontal grill bars, right side knob, BC, AC/DC.................**$30.00**

1X56, table, 1952, plastic, upper front half-round dial, lower horizontal grill bars, right side knob, BC, AC/DC.................**$30.00**

1X591, table, 1952, plastic, lower front thin slide rule dial, upper pleated gold grill, right & left side knobs, BC, AC/DC....**$40.00**

1X592, table, 1952, plastic, lower front thin slide rule dial, upper pleated gold grill, right & left side knobs, BC, AC/DC **$40.00**

2B400, portable, 1952, plastic, center front round dial, lower metal perforated grill, fold-down handle, top thumbwheel on/off/volume knob, BC, battery **$35.00**

2B401, portable, 1952, plastic, center front round dial, lower metal perforated grill, fold-down handle, top thumbwheel on/off/volume knob, BC, battery **$35.00**

2BX63, portable, 1953, plastic, upper front slide rule dial, lower horizontal bars, handle, right & left side knobs, BC, AC/DC/battery **$25.00**

2-C-521, table-C, 1953, plastic, right front round dial, left alarm clock, center horizontal bars, 5 knobs, BC, AC **$20.00**

2-S-7, console-R/P, 1953, wood, inner right slide rule dial, 2 knobs, lower pull-out phono, left storage, double doors, lower front grill, BC, AC...**$45.00**

2-S-10, console-R/P, 1953, wood, inner right dial, 5 knobs, upper phono, lower grill, left storage, double doors, BC, FM, 10 tubes, AC..**$60.00**

2US7, table-R/P, 1952, wood, upper front slide rule dial, lower grill, 2 knobs, 3/4 lift top, inner phono, BC, AC..............**$25.00**

2-X-52, table, 1952, plastic, dial on top of case, center front horizontal louvers, 2 knobs, BC, AC/DC **$40.00**

2-X-61, table, 1953, plastic, dial on top of case, center front horizontal louvers, 2 knobs, BC, AC/DC **$40.00**

2-XF-91, table, 1953, plastic, right front FM dial, left AM dial, center horizontal bars, 4 knobs, AM, FM, AC/DC **$35.00**

3-BX-671 "Strato-World," portable, 1954, leather, inner front slide rule dial, flip-up front w/map, telescope antenna, 7 bands, AC/DC/battery **$100.00**

3-RA-30 "Luster," table, antique white plastic, wedge-shaped case, right front dial, left checkered grill area, feet, 2 knobs, AM, 4 tubes, AC **$15.00**

3-RA-31 "Luster," table, charcoal/antique white plastic, wedge-shaped case, right front dial, left checkered grill area, feet, 2 knobs, AM, 4 tubes, AC..$15.00

3-RA-32 "Luster," table, aqua/antique white plastic, wedge-shaped case, right front dial, left checkered grill area, feet, 2 knobs, AM, 4 tubes, AC..$15.00

3-RA-34 "Luster," table, espresso/autumn smoke plastic, wedge-shaped case, right front dial, left checkered grill area, feet, 2 knobs, AM, 4 tubes, AC..$15.00

3-RA-50 "Radiant," table, iceberg white plastic, wedge-shaped case, lower front raised dial panel overlaps horizontal bars, 2 knobs, AM, 4 tubes, AC..$15.00

3-RA-51 "Radiant," table, iceberg white/black pearl plastic, wedge-shaped case, lower front raised dial panel overlaps horizontal bars, 2 knobs, AM, 4 tubes, AC....................$15.00

3-RA-52 "Radiant," table, dark blue/iceberg white plastic, wedge-shaped case, lower front raised dial panel overlaps horizontal bars, 2 knobs, AM, 4 tubes, AC....................$15.00

3-RA-54 "Radiant," table, autumn smoke/espresso plastic, wedge-shaped case, lower front raised dial panel overlaps horizontal bars, 2 knobs, AM, 4 tubes, AC $15.00

3-RA-60 "Splendor," table, mist brown/iceberg white plastic, wedge-shaped case, lower front raised dial panel overlaps horizontal bars, 2 knobs, AM, 4 tubes, AC $15.00

3-RA-61 "Splendor," table, iceberg white/black pearl plastic, wedge-shaped case, lower front raised dial panel overlaps horizontal bars, 2 knobs, AM, 4 tubes, AC $15.00

3-RA-63 "Splendor," table, iceberg white/shrimp plastic, wedge-shaped case, lower front raised dial panel overlaps horizontal bars, 2 knobs, AM, 4 tubes, AC....................................$15.00

3-RA-65 "Splendor," table, dark green/iceberg white plastic, wedge-shaped case, lower front raised dial panel overlaps horizontal bars, 2 knobs, AM, 4 tubes, AC $15.00

3-RB-16 "Squire," table, Sahara plastic, left front vertical slide rule dial, right checkered grill area, 2 knobs, FM, 5 tubes, AC ..$10.00

3-RB-31, table, 1963, black/iceberg white plastic, left front vertical slide rule dial, right checkered grill area, 2 knobs, switch, FM, 5 tubes, AC..$10.00

3-RB-32, table, 1963, academy blue/iceberg white plastic, left front vertical slide rule dial, right checkered grill area, 2 knobs, switch, FM, 5 tubes, AC $10.00

3-RB-34, table, 1963, espresso/iceberg white plastic, left front vertical slide rule dial, right checkered grill area, 2 knobs, switch, FM, 5 tubes, AC $10.00

3-RC-11 "Bulletin," table, black plastic, left front vertical slide rule dial, right checkered grill area, 2 knobs, switch, AM, FM, 6 tubes, AC..$10.00

3-RC-14 "Bulletin," table, espresso plastic, left front vertical slide rule dial, right checkered grill area, 2 knobs, switch, AM, FM, 6 tubes, AC..$10.00

3-RD-40 "Daybreak," table-C, iceberg white plastic, wedge-shaped case, lower front dial panel & upper alarm clock overlap horizontal bars, feet, AM, 4 tubes, AC....................$15.00

3-RD-41 "Daybreak," table-C, iceberg white/black pearl plastic, wedge-shaped case, lower front dial panel & upper alarm clock overlap horizontal bars, feet, AM, 4 tubes, AC.....$15.00

3-RD-43 "Daybreak," table-C, Sahara/shrimp plastic, wedge-shaped case, lower front dial panel & upper alarm clock overlap horizontal bars, feet, AM, 4 tubes, AC....................$15.00

3-RD-45 "Daybreak," table-C, dark green/iceberg white plastic, wedge-shaped case, lower front dial panel & upper alarm clock overlap horizontal bars, feet, AM, 4 tubes, AC.....$15.00

3-RD-50 "Dawnette," table-C, black pearl/iceberg white plastic, wedge-shaped case, lower front dial panel & upper alarm clock overlap horizontal bars, drowse button, feet, AM, 4 tubes, AC..$15.00

3-RD-52 "Dawnette," table-C, iceberg white/starlight blue plastic, wedge-shaped case, lower front dial panel & upper alarm clock overlap horizontal bars, drowse button, feet, AM, 4 tubes, AC..$15.00

3-RD-54 "Dawnette," table-C, autumn smoke/espresso plastic, wedge-shaped case, lower front dial panel & upper alarm clock overlap horizontal bars, drowse button, feet, AM, 4 tubes, AC..$15.00

3-RD-57 "Dawnette," table-C, iceberg white/maple sugar plastic, wedge-shaped case, lower front dial panel & upper alarm clock overlap horizontal bars, drowse button, feet, AM, 4 tubes, AC..$15.00

3-RD-61 "Gloaming," table-C, black pearl/iceberg white plastic, wedge-shaped case, lower front dial panel & upper alarm clock overlap horizontal bars, drowse button, feet, AM, 4 tubes, AC..$15.00

3-RD-65 "Gloaming," table-C, dark green/iceberg white plastic, wedge-shaped case, lower front dial panel & upper alarm clock overlap horizontal bars, drowse button, feet, AM, 4 tubes, AC..$15.00

3-RD-67 "Gloaming," table-C, maple sugar/iceberg white plastic, wedge-shaped case, lower front dial panel & upper alarm clock overlap horizontal bars, drowse button, feet, AM, 4 tubes, AC..$15.00

3-RD-69 "Gloaming," table-C, mist brown/iceberg white plastic, wedge-shaped case, lower front dial panel & upper alarm clock overlap horizontal bars, drowse button, feet, AM, 4 tubes, AC..$15.00

3-RF-91, table, 1952, plastic, center front large round dial over horizontal decorative lines, right & left side knobs, AM, FM ..$45.00

3-X-521, table, 1954, plastic, right front dial, left checkered grill area, left side knob, BC $20.00

3-X-532, table, 1954, plastic, right front dial, left checkered grill area, left side knob, BC $20.00

3-X-535, table, 1954, plastic, right front dial, left checkered grill area, left side knob, BC **$20.00**

4QB, table, 1940, plastic, lower front slanted dial, upper grill area, 2 knobs, BC, SW, 4 tubes, battery **$25.00**

4QB4, table, 1940, plastic, lower front slanted dial, upper grill area, 2 knobs, BC, SW, 4 tubes, battery **$25.00**

4T, cathedral, 1935, wood, center front window dial, cloth grill w/cut-outs, 2 knobs, BC, 4 tubes, AC **$125.00**

4-X, tombstone, 1936, two-tone wood, lower right front dial, upper cloth grill w/3 center bars, 2 knobs, BC, 4 tubes **$70.00**

4-X-3, tombstone, 1936, mahogany finish, lower right front dial, upper cloth grill, 2 knobs, base, BC, 4 tubes, AC **$70.00**

4-X-4, tombstone, 1936, white finish w/contrasting knobs, lower right front dial, upper cloth grill, 2 knobs, BC, 4 tubes, AC **$70.00**

4-X-552, table, 1955, plastic, top right thumbwheel dial, left front horizontal metal grill bars, BC, AC/DC **$45.00**

4-X-648, table, 1956, plastic, lower front slide rule dial, large upper checkered grill area, 2 knobs, BC, 6 tubes **$25.00**

4-Y-511, table-R/P, 1954, plastic, right front round dial overlaps large grill, 3 knobs, lift top, inner 45 phono, BC, 5 tubes, AC **$50.00**

5BT, tombstone, 1936, wood, center front dial, cloth grill w/vertical bars, 2 knobs, 5 tubes, DC **$125.00**

5-BX-41, portable, 1955, plastic, upper front flip-up dial, lower horizontal grill bars, right & left side knobs, BC, 4 tubes, AC/DC/battery **$45.00**

5-C-581, table-C, 1955, lower base with slide rule dial, center front round alarm clock, top knob, BC, 5 tubes, AC **$60.00**

5Q1, tombstone, 1940, wood, center front slide rule dial, upper cloth grill w/2 horizontal bars, 3 knobs, BC, SW, 5 tubes, AC **$75.00**

5Q2, tombstone, 1940, wood, lower front slide rule dial, upper patterned cloth grill, 3 knobs, BC, SW, 5 tubes, AC..........**$75.00**

5Q2X, tombstone, 1940, wood, lower front slide rule dial, upper patterned cloth grill, 3 knobs, BC, SW, 5 tubes, AC/DC **$75.00**

5Q4, table, 1940, wood, right front slide rule dial, left cloth grill w/2 horizontal bars, 3 knobs, BC, SW, 5 tubes, AC............**$50.00**

5Q5, table, 1940, plastic, lower front slanted slide rule dial, upper metal grill, BC, SW, 5 tubes, AC......................**$45.00**

5Q6, table, 1940, plastic, lower front slanted slide rule dial, upper grill area, BC, SW, 5 tubes, AC/DC **$45.00**

5Q8E, table, 1940, brown plastic, lower front slanted slide rule dial, upper grill area, BC, SW, 5 tubes, AC/DC **$45.00**

5Q8F, table, 1940, black plastic, lower front slanted slide rule dial, upper grill area, BC, SW, 5 tubes, AC/DC.....................**$45.00**

5Q8G, table, 1940, ivory plastic, lower front slanted slide rule dial, upper grill area, BC, SW, 5 tubes, AC/DC.....................**$45.00**

5Q8H, table, 1940, maroon plastic, lower front slanted slide rule dial, upper grill area, BC, SW, 5 tubes, AC/DC **$45.00**

5Q12, table, 1940, plastic, lower front slanted slide rule dial, upper grill area, BC, SW, 5 tubes, AC **$45.00**

5Q55, table, 1939, brown plastic, lower front slanted slide rule dial, upper cloth grill, 2 knobs, BC, 2SW, 5 tubes, AC...**$60.00**

5T, (right) tombstone, 1936, wood, center front dial, upper cloth grill w/cut-outs, four knobs, BC, SW, 5 tubes, AC..$125.00

5T1, tombstone, 1936, wood, center front dial, upper cloth grill w/cut-outs, tuning eye, 4 knobs, BC, SW, AC **$125.00**

5T4, table, 1936, wood, right front dial, left cloth grill w/horizontal wrap-around bars............**$70.00**

5U, tombstone-R/P, wood, lower front dial, upper cloth grill w/vertical bars, 4 knobs, lift top, inner phono $95.00

5X, table, 1936, wood, rounded sides, finished front & back, center front dial, top louvers, 3 knobs, BC, SW, AC/DC ...$100.00

5X3, table, 1936, wood, center front dial, top louvers, base, 3 knobs, BC, SW, 5 tubes, AC $80.00

5-X-4, table, 1936, white lacquer/black base/contrasting knobs, center front dial, 3 knobs, BC, SW, AC $60.00

5X5I, table, 1939, ivory finish, right raised dial panel, left horizontal grill bars, 2 knobs, BC, 5 tubes, AC/DC $45.00

5X5W, table, 1939, walnut finish, right raised dial panel, left horizontal grill bars, 2 knobs, BC, 5 tubes, AC/DC.............$45.00

6-BX-6B, portable, 1955, plastic, side dial knob, large front grill area w/horizontal bars, handle, BC, AC/DC/battery $30.00

6-BX-8A, portable, plastic, right side dial knob, left side on/off/volume knob, front checkered grill area w/Nipper logo, fold-down handle, BC, AC/DC/battery $30.00

6-BX-63, portable, 1952, plastic, upper front slide rule dial, lower horizontal grill bars, right & left side knobs, BC, AC/DC/battery ..$25.00

6K2, console, wood, upper front dial, lower cloth grill w/2 vertical bars, 4 knobs, 6 tubes $125.00

6Q1, table, 1940, plastic, lower front slanted slide rule dial, upper grill area, BC, SW, 6 tubes, AC $45.00

6Q4, table, 1940, plastic, lower front slanted slide rule dial, upper grill area, BC, SW, 6 tubes, AC $45.00

6Q4X, table, 1940, plastic, lower front slanted slide rule dial, upper grill area, BC, SW, 6 tubes, AC/DC....................$45.00

6Q7, table, 1940, striped walnut, lower front slide rule dial, upper grill area, BC, SW, 6 tubes, AC $45.00

6Q8, table, 1940, wood, step-down top, lower front slide rule dial, upper grill area, 2 knobs, BC, SW, 5 tubes, AC $45.00

6-RF-9, table, 1956, mahogany, center front large round dial, right & left side knobs, AM, FM, 9 tubes................................$35.00

6-T, tombstone, 1936, wood, center front black dial, upper cloth grill w/cut-outs, 4 knobs, BC, SW, 6 tubes, AC $125.00

6-T-2, tombstone, 1936, wood, center front black dial, upper cloth grill w/cut-outs, 4 knobs, BC, SW, 6 tubes $125.00

6T10, tombstone, 1936, black lacquer/chrome frame, center front dial, upper cloth grill w/center vertical chrome bar, 4 knobs, BC, SW...$475.00

6X2, table, 1942, plastic, right front dial, left vertical grill bars, 2 knobs $40.00

6-X-5A, table, 1956, plastic, right front dial knob overlaps large lattice grill, left Nipper logo, feet, BC, 5 tubes, AC/DC ..$15.00

6-X-5B, table, 1956, plastic, right front dial knob overlaps large lattice grill, left Nipper logo, feet, BC, 5 tubes, AC/DC ..**$15.00**

6-X-7, table, 1956, plastic, right front dial knob over checkered grill area, upper left Nipper logo, feet, BC, AC/DC **$20.00**

6-XD-5A, table, 1956, plastic, lower front dial, large upper lattice grill w/center Nipper logo, 2 knobs, BC, 5 tubes, AC/DC............**$25.00**

6-XF-9, table, 1956, plastic, center front dial panel, right & left checkered grills, feet, 4 knobs, AM, FM **$35.00**

7-BX-5F, portable, 1955, plastic, right & left side knobs, front lattice grill area w/Nipper logo, fold-down handle, BC **$30.00**

7-BX-6E, portable, 1956, plastic, right front dial knob overlaps lattice grill area w/Nipper logo, top rotatable antenna bar, handle, AC/DC/battery **$30.00**

7-BX-6L, portable, 1956, plastic, right front dial knob & left volume knob overlap lattice grill area w/Nipper logo, top rotatable antenna bar, handle, AC/DC/battery **$30.00**

7-BX-8J "Globe Trotter," portable, 1957, plastic, upper front slide rule dial, lower horizontal grill bars, handle, top rotatable antenna bar, BC, AC/DC/battery **$25.00**

7-BX-9H "Yachtsman," portable, plastic, upper front slide rule dial, lower horizontal grill bars, handle, top rotatable antenna bar, 2 knobs, AC/DC/battery **$25.00**

7-BX-10 "Stratoworld," portable, 1954, leather case, inner slide rule dial, flip-up front w/map, telescoping antenna, BC, SW, AC/DC/battery **$100.00**

7-HFR-1, console-R/P/Rec, 1957, wood, upper left front dial, lower pull-out phono, inner top right reel-to-reel recorder, BC, FM, AC **$55.00**

7-K, console, 1936, wood, upper front dial, lower cloth grill w/3 vertical bars, 4 knobs, BC, SW, 7 tubes, AC..............**$125.00**

7K1, console, 1937, wood, upper front dial, lower cloth grill w/3 vertical bars, tuning eye, 4 knobs, BC, SW **$135.00**

7Q4, table, 1940, wood, upper front slanted slide rule dial, large lower grill area, 3 knobs, BC, SW, 7 tubes, AC............**$45.00**

7Q4X, table, 1940, wood, upper front slanted slide rule dial, large lower grill area, 3 knobs, BC, SW, 7 tubes, AC............**$45.00**

7QB, table, 1941, wood, right front slide rule dial, left grill w/2 horizontal wrap-around bars, 4 knobs, BC, SW, 7 tubes, AC/DC..**$50.00**

7QBK, console, 1941, wood, upper front slide rule dial, lower cloth grill w/center vertical bars, 4 knobs, BC, SW, 7 tubes, AC/DC..**$115.00**

7T, tombstone, 1936, wood, center front rectangular dial, upper cloth grill w/cut-outs, BC, SW, 7 tubes, AC **$110.00**

7T1, tombstone, 1936, wood, center front rectangular dial, upper cloth grill w/vertical bars, tuning eye, 4 knobs **$145.00**

7U, console-R/P, 1936, wood, front rectangular dial, lower cloth grill w/cut-outs, tuning eye, 4 knobs, lift top, inner phono, BC, SW, 7 tubes, AC..**$135.00**

8B41 "Jewel Box," portable, 1949, black plastic, inner round dial, grill bars, flip-open lid, handle, BC, 4 tubes, battery......**$45.00**

8B42 "Jewel Box," portable, 1949, brown plastic, inner round dial, grill bars, flip-open lid, handle, BC, 4 tubes, battery **$45.00**

8B43 "Jewel Box," portable, 1949, red plastic, inner round dial, grill bars, flip-open lid, handle, BC, 4 tubes, battery......**$50.00**

8B46 "Jewel Box," portable, 1949, ivory plastic, inner round dial, grill bars, flip-open lid, handle, BC, 4 tubes, battery......**$45.00**

8BX5, portable, 1948, "snakeskin" & plastic, front round dial overlaps horizontal bars, handle, right side knob, BC, AC/DC/battery **$35.00**

8BX6 "Globe Trotter," portable, 1948, aluminum & plastic, upper front slide rule dial, lower horizontal grill bars, thumb-wheel knobs, handle, BC, AC/DC/battery......**$40.00**

8BX6E, portable, 1956, plastic, right front dial knob/left volume knob overlap horizontal grill bars, top rotatable antenna bar, handle, BC, AC/DC/battery **$30.00**

8BX6L, portable, 1956, plastic, right front dial knob/left volume knob overlap horizontal grill bars, top rotatable antenna bar, handle, BC, AC/DC/battery **$30.00**

8BX54, portable, 1948, front round dial overlaps horizontal grill bars, handle, right side knob, BC, AC/DC/battery **$35.00**

8BX55, portable, 1948, front round dial overlaps horizontal grill bars, handle, right side knob, BC, AC/DC/battery **$35.00**

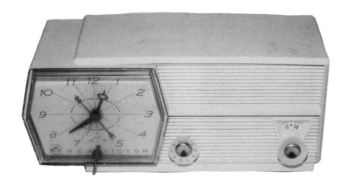

8C5L, table-C, plastic, step-down top, lower right front window dial over horizontal bars, left alarm clock, BC, AC **$25.00**

8F43, table, 1950, wood, upper front slanted slide rule dial, lower horizontal louvers, 2 knobs, BC, battery.......................**$35.00**

8K, console, 1936, wood, upper front rectangular dial, lower cloth grill w/cut-outs, tuning eye, 4 knobs, BC, SW, 8 tubes, AC **$150.00**

8Q1, tombstone, 1940, wood, lower front slide rule dial, upper cloth grill, tuning eye, BC, SW, 8 tubes, AC/DC............**$75.00**

8Q2, table, 1940, wood, lower front slide rule dial, upper cloth grill, tuning eye, 2 knobs, BC, SW, 8 tubes, AC....................**$75.00**

8Q4, table, 1940, wood, center front slide rule dial, curved right & left cloth grills w/horizontal wrap-around bars, 4 knobs, BC, SW, 8 tubes, AC/DC...**$85.00**

8QB, tombstone, 1940, wood, upper front slide rule dial, lower cloth grill w/center horizontal divider, 4 knobs, BC, SW, 8 tubes, AC/DC **$60.00**

8QBK, console, 1940, wood, upper front slide rule dial, lower cloth grill w/3 vertical bars, 4 knobs, BC, SW, 8 tubes, AC/DC..**$125.00**

8QU5C, table-R/P, 1940, wood, lower front slide rule dial, upper cloth grill area, tuning eye, lift top, inner phono, BC, SW, 8 tubes, AC..**$40.00**

8QU5M, table-R/P, 1940, wood, lower front slide rule dial, upper cloth grill area, tuning eye, lift top, inner phono, BC, SW, 8 tubes, AC..**$40.00**

8R71, table, 1949, plastic, recessed dial on top of case, large front cloth grill area, 4 knobs, BC, FM, AC **$45.00**

8-RF-13, console on legs, 1958, wood, front slide rule dial overlaps cloth grill w/horizontal bars, long legs, BC, FM, 13 tubes, AC **$40.00**

8T, tombstone, 1936, wood, lower front rectangular dial, upper cloth grill w/cut-outs, tuning eye, 4 knobs, BC, SW, 8 tubes, AC **$165.00**

8U, console-R/P, 1936, wood, upper front rectangular dial, lower cloth grill w/3 vertical bars, tuning eye, 4 knobs, lift top, inner phono, BC, SW, 8 tubes, AC.....................................**$135.00**

8V7, console-R/P, 1949, wood, inner right dial & knobs, left phono, 2 lift tops, lower front horizontal grill bars, BC, AC **$70.00**

8V90, console-R/P, 1949, wood, inner right vertical slide rule dial, 4 knobs, left phono, double doors, lower criss-cross grill, BC, FM, AC **$65.00**

8V111, console-R/P, 1949, wood, right tilt-out slide rule dial, 4 knobs, left fold-down phono, BC, FM, AC **$80.00**

8V151, console-R/P, 1949, wood, right tilt-out dial, 8 pushbuttons, left fold-down phono, BC, SW, FM, 15 tubes, AC **$100.00**

8X8J, table, plastic, lower front slide rule dial, upper 2-section lattice grill w/twin speakers, feet, 2 knobs, BC $20.00

8X8N, table, plastic, lower front slide rule dial, upper 2-section lattice grill w/twin speakers, feet, 2 knobs, BC **$20.00**

8X53, table, 1948, wood, upper front slanted slide rule dial, lower horizontal grill openings, 2 knobs, BC, 5 tubes, AC/DC...**$40.00**

8X71, table, 1949, maroon plastic, upper front dotted slide rule dial overlaps horizontal grill bars, 3 knobs, AM, FM, AC/DC **$40.00**

8X72, table, 1949, ivory plastic, upper front dotted slide rule dial overlaps horizontal grill bars, 3 knobs, AM, FM, AC/DC..**$40.00**

8X521, table, 1948, maroon plastic, round dial on case top, front horizontal louvers, right side knob, BC, 5 tubes, AC/DC **$55.00**

8X522, table, 1948, ivory plastic, round dial on case top, front horizontal louvers, right side knob, BC, 5 tubes, AC/DC **$55.00**

8-X-541, table, 1949, maroon plastic, center front round dial knob overlaps horizontal grill bars, decorative brass pointer/top strip, BC, 5 tubes, AC/DC.........................$35.00

8-X-542, table, 1949, ivory plastic, center front round dial knob overlaps horizontal grill bars, decorative brass pointer/top strip, BC, 5 tubes, AC/DC...............................$35.00

8-X-547, table, 1949, white plastic, center front round dial knob overlaps horizontal grill bars, decorative brass pointer/top strip, BC, 5 tubes, AC/DC...............................$35.00

9K3, console, 1936, wood, upper front dial, lower cloth grill w/center divider, tuning eye, 5 knobs, BC, SW, 9 tubes, AC..$130.00

9Q1, table, 1940, wood, top recessed slide rule dial, front grill area, 3 knobs, BC, SW, 9 tubes, AC $45.00

9Q4, table, 1940, wood, top recessed slide rule dial, front grill area, 3 knobs, BC, SW, 9 tubes, AC $45.00

9QK, console, 1940, wood, top recessed slide rule dial, front cloth grill w/2 vertical bars, 3 knobs, BC, SW, 9 tubes, AC..$130.00

9SX1 "Little Nipper," table, 1939, walnut plastic w/ivory knobs, Deco, right front round dial, left horizontal louvers, BC, SW, 5 tubes, AC/DC...$150.00

9SX2 "Little Nipper," table, 1939, walnut/ivory plastic w/walnut knobs, Deco, right front round dial, left horizontal louvers, BC, SW, 5 tubes, AC/DC..$200.00

9SX3 "Little Nipper," table, 1939, ivory plastic w/red knobs, Deco, right front round dial, left horizontal louvers, BC, SW, 5 tubes, AC/DC $200.00

9SX4 "Little Nipper," table, 1939, red/ivory plastic w/red knobs, Deco, right front round dial, left horizontal louvers, BC, SW, 5 tubes, AC/DC $300.00

9SX5 "Little Nipper," table, 1939, black/marble plastic w/jet knobs, Deco, right front round dial, left horizontal louvers, BC, SW, 5 tubes, AC/DC...$350.00

9SX6 "Little Nipper," table, 1939, blue/onyx plastic w/blue knobs, Deco, right front round dial, left horizontal louvers, BC, SW, 5 tubes, AC/DC.....................................$350.00

9SX7 "Little Nipper," table, 1939, onyx plastic w/maroon knobs, Deco, right front round dial, left horizontal louvers, BC, SW, 5 tubes, AC/DC $350.00

8X681, table, 1949, maroon plastic, center front large round dial w/inner grill, thumbwheel knobs, BC, SW, 6 tubes, AC/DC $45.00

8X682, table, 1949, ivory plastic, center front large round dial w/inner grill, thumbwheel knobs, BC, SW, 6 tubes, AC/DC $45.00

9BX5, portable, 1948, leatherette & plastic, center front round dial overlaps perforated grill area, handle, BC, AC/DC/battery $40.00

9BX56, portable, 1949, plastic, upper front dial, lower textured panel, wire stand, right & left side knobs, BC, AC/DC/battery $40.00

9K, console, 1936, wood, upper front dial, lower cloth grill w/horizontal & vertical bars, tuning eye, 5 knobs, BC, SW, 9 tubes, AC $130.00

9K2, console, 1936, wood, upper front dial, lower cloth grill w/horizontal & vertical bars, tuning eye, 5 knobs, BC, SW, 9 tubes, AC $150.00

9SX8 "Little Nipper," table, 1939, marble plastic w/jet knobs, Deco, right front round dial, left horizontal louvers, BC, SW, 5 tubes, AC/DC...$400.00

9T, tombstone, 1935, wood, lower front dial, upper cloth grill w/vertical bars, tuning eye, 5 knobs, BC, SW, 9 tubes, AC ..**$165.00**

9TX, table, 1939, Catalin, right front dial knob, left horizontal wrap-around louvers, BC ....**$700.00+**

9TX3, table, 1939, two-tone wood, right front dial knob, left horizontal wrap-around louvers, BC **$45.00**

9TX21, table, 1939, walnut plastic w/tan knobs, right front dial, left horizontal grill bars, 2 knobs, BC, 5 tubes, AC/DC........**$45.00**

9TX22, table, 1939, ivory plastic, right front dial, left horizontal grill bars, 2 knobs, BC, 5 tubes, AC/DC...............................**$45.00**

9TX23 "Little Nipper," table, 1939, wood, Deco, right front dial w/thermometer-type tuning, left grill area, 2 knobs, BC, 5 tubes, AC/DC **$75.00**

9TX31 "Little Nipper," table, 1939, walnut plastic w/tan knobs, right front dial, left horizontal wrap-around grill bars, 2 knobs, BC, 5 tubes, AC/DC **$50.00**

9TX32 "Little Nipper," table, 1939, ivory plastic, right front dial, left horizontal wrap-around grill bars, 2 knobs, BC, 5 tubes, AC/DC..**$50.00**

9TX33 "Little Nipper," table, 1939, wood, Deco, right front vertical "V" dial, left grill area, 2 knobs, BC, 5 tubes, AC/DC **$75.00**

9TX50, table, 1939, wood, off center front dial panel w/thermometer-type tuning overlaps horizontal grill bars, handle, 2 knobs, BC, 5 tubes, AC/DC **$55.00**

9U, console-R/P, 1936, wood, center front dial, lower cloth grill w/horizontal & vertical bars, tuning eye, lift top, inner phono, BC, SW, AC **$145.00**

9W101, console-R/P, 1949, wood, inner right slide rule dial, 4 knobs, inner left pull-out phono drawer, storage, doors, lower grill, BC, FM, AC **$70.00**

9W103, console-R/P, 1949, wood, inner right slide rule dial, 4 knobs, inner left pull-out phono drawer, storage, doors, lower grill, BC, FM, AC..**$75.00**

9W106, console-R/P, 1950, wood, inner right slide rule dial, 3 knobs, left pull-out phono drawer, lower grill & storage, doors, BC, FM, AC **$85.00**

9X11, table, 1939, Catalin, right front dial, left cloth grill with "W" cut-out, 2 right side knobs, BC, 4 tubes, AC/DC ....**$700.00+**

9X12, table, 1939, Catalin, right front dial, left cloth grill with "W" cut-out, 2 right side knobs, BC, 4 tubes, AC/DC ....**$700.00+**

9X13, table, 1939, Catalin, right front dial, left cloth grill with "W" cut-out, 2 right side knobs, BC, 4 tubes, AC/DC ....**$700.00+**

9X14, table, 1939, Catalin, right front dial, left cloth grill with "W" cut-out, 2 right side knobs, BC, 4 tubes, AC/DC ....**$700.00+**

9-X-561, table, 1950, plastic, lower front narrow slide rule dial, upper concentric circular grill bars, right & left side knobs, BC, AC/DC....**$40.00**

9-X-562, table, 1950, plastic, lower front narrow slide rule dial, upper concentric circular grill bars, right & left side knobs, BC, AC/DC **$40.00**

9X571, table, 1950, plastic, lower front narrow slide rule dial, upper "bull-horn" louvers, right & left side knobs, BC, AC/DC **$55.00**

9X572, table, 1949, plastic, lower front narrow slide rule dial, upper "bull-horn" louvers, right & left side knobs, BC, AC **$55.00**

9-X-641, table, 1950, plastic, upper front slanted slide rule dial, lower horizontal grill bars, 2 knobs, BC, AC/DC........**$40.00**

9-X-642, table, 1950, plastic, upper front slanted slide rule dial, lower horizontal grill bars, 2 knobs, BC, AC/DC **$40.00**

9X652, table, 1950, plastic, upper front slanted slide rule dial, lower horizontal louvers, 3 knobs, BC, SW, AC/DC **$40.00**

9-Y-7, table-R/P, 1949, wood, upper front slide rule dial, lower horizontal grill bars, 2 knobs, 3/4 lift top, inner phono, BC, AC **$30.00**

9Y51, table-R/P, 1950, plastic, upper front slide rule dial, lower horizontal grill bars, side knobs, 3/4 lift top, inner phono, BC, AC **$50.00**

9Y510, table-R/P, 1951, plastic, upper front slide rule dial, lower horizontal grill bars, side knobs, 3/4 lift top, inner phono, BC, AC **$50.00**

10K, console, 1936, wood, upper front dial, lower cloth grill w/cut-outs, tuning eye, 5 knobs, BC, SW, 10 tubes, AC **$145.00**

10Q1, tombstone, 1940, wood, lower front slide rule dial, upper cloth grill w/vertical wrap-over bars, 4 knobs, BC, SW, 10 tubes, AC...**$110.00**

10T, tombstone, 1936, wood, center front dial, upper cloth grill w/2 vertical bars, tuning eye, 5 knobs, BC, SW, LW, 10 tubes, AC **$185.00**

10T11, tombstone, 1937, black lacquer w/chrome supports, center front dial, upper cloth grill w/2 vertical bars, tuning eye, 5 knobs, BC, SW, AC $475.00

10X "**Little Nipper,**" table, 1940, plastic, upper front slide rule dial, lower horizontal grill bars, 2 knobs, BC, 5 tubes, AC/DC...$40.00

11X1, table, 1940, plastic, upper front slide rule dial, lower horizontal grill bars, 2 knobs, BC, 5 tubes, AC/DC.............$40.00

12Q4, tombstone, 1940, wood, upper front curved slide rule dial, lower cloth grill w/vertical bars, 5 knobs, BC, SW, 12 tubes, AC/DC..$115.00

12QK, console, 1940, wood, upper front curved slide rule dial, lower cloth grill w/center vertical bars, 5 knobs, BC, SW, 12 tubes, AC/DC $175.00

12X, table, 1942, brown plastic, upper front slide rule dial, lower horizontal grill bars, 2 knobs, BC, 5 tubes, AC/DC........$40.00

12X2, table, 1942, antique ivory plastic, upper front slide rule dial, lower horizontal grill bars, 2 knobs, BC, 5 tubes, AC/DC..$40.00

13K, console, 1936, wood, upper front dial, lower cloth grill w/center vertical bars, tuning eye, 5 knobs, AM, 3SW, 13 tubes...$215.00

14AX, table, 1941, walnut plastic, upper front slide rule dial, lower horizontal grill bars, 2 knobs, BC, SW, 5 tubes, AC/DC ..$40.00

14AX2, table, 1941, ivory plastic, upper front slide rule dial, lower horizontal grill bars, 2 knobs, BC, SW, 5 tubes, AC/DC ..$40.00

14BK, console, 1940, wood, upper front dial, lower cloth grill w/3 vertical bars, BC, 4 tubes, battery $70.00

14BT1, table, 1940, plastic, right front dial, left vertical grill bars, 3 knobs, BC, 4 tubes, battery $30.00

14BT2, table, 1940, wood, right front slide rule dial, left horizontal louvers, 3 knobs, BC 4 tubes, battery $30.00

14X, table, 1941, walnut plastic, upper front slanted slide rule dial, lower horizontal louvers, 2 knobs, BC, SW, 5 tubes, AC/DC $45.00

14X2, table, 1941, ivory plastic, upper front slanted slide rule dial, lower horizontal louvers, 2 knobs, BC, SW, 5 tubes, AC/DC..........$45.00

15BP-1 "**Pick-Me-Up,**" table, 1940, walnut plastic, right front dial, left vertical grill bars, optional carrying case, BC, 5 tubes, AC/DC/battery $45.00

15BP-2 "**Pick-Me-Up,**" portable, 1940, cloth covered, right front dial, left grill area, handle, BC, 5 tubes, AC/DC/battery ..$25.00

15BP-4, portable, 1940, leatherette, right front dial, left grill area, handle, BC, 5 tubes, AC/DC/battery..............................$25.00

15BP-6, table, 1940, wood, right front dial, left horizontal grill bars, handle, optional carrying case, BC, 5 tubes, AC/DC/battery.......$35.00

15BT, table, 1940, wood, right front slide rule dial overlaps horizontal bars, 4 knobs, BC, SW, 5 tubes, battery.............$30.00

15K, console, 1936, wood, upper front dial, lower cloth grill w/center vertical divider, tuning eye, 5 knobs, 15 tubes, BC, SW, AC $250.00

15X, table, 1940, mahogany plastic, upper front slanted dial w/red dot pointer, lower horizontal louvers, 3 knobs, BC, 6 tubes, AC/DC $40.00

16K, console, 1940, wood, upper front slide rule dial, lower cloth grill w/3 vertical bars, pushbuttons, 4 knobs, BC, SW, 6 tubes, AC..$125.00

16T3, table, 1940, wood, right front slide rule dial panel overlaps horizontal bars, 5 pushbuttons, 4 knobs, BC, SW, 6 tubes, AC...$50.00

16T4, table, 1940, wood, right front slide rule dial, left curved grill w/horizontal bars, 5 pushbuttons, 4 knobs, BC, SW, 6 tubes, AC $85.00

16X1, table, 1941, mahogany plastic, upper front slanted dial, lower horizontal grill bars, 3 knobs, BC, 6 tubes, AC/DC...$40.00

16X2, table, 1941, ivory plastic, upper front slanted dial, lower horizontal grill bars, 3 knobs, BC, 6 tubes, AC/DC.......$40.00

16X3, table, 1941, wood, upper front slanted dial, lower horizontal louvers, 3 knobs, BC, 6 tubes, AC/DC $50.00

16X4, table, 1941, two-tone wood, upper front dial, lower grill area, pushbuttons, 3 knobs, BC, AC $50.00

16X11, table, 1940, plastic, upper front slanted slide rule dial, lower horizontal grill bars, 3 knobs, BC, 5 tubes, AC/DC..$35.00

16X13, table, 1940, wood, upper front slanted slide rule dial, lower horizontal louvers, 3 knobs, BC, SW, 5 tubes, AC/DC $45.00

16X14, table, 1940, wood, upper front slanted slide rule dial, lower horizontal grill bars, pushbuttons, 3 knobs, BC, 5 tubes, AC/DC $50.00

17K, console, 1940, wood, upper front oblong slide rule dial, lower cloth grill w/vertical bars, pushbuttons, BC, SW, 7 tubes, AC......$120.00

18T, table, 1940, wood, upper front slanted slide rule dial, lower cloth grill, 6 pushbuttons, 4 knobs, BC, 2SW, 8 tubes, AC $50.00

19K, console, 1940, walnut, upper front oblong slide rule dial, lower vertical grill bars, 6 pushbuttons, 4 knobs, BC, 2SW, 9 tubes, AC...$135.00

16T2, table, 1940, wood, right front slide rule dial over horizontal bars, 4 knobs, BC, SW, 6 tubes, AC $45.00

24BT-1, table, 1940, plastic, right front dial, left vertical grill bars, 2 knobs, BC, 4 tubes, battery $30.00

24BT-2, table, 1940, wood, right front dial overlaps horizontal bars, 2 knobs, BC, 4 tubes, battery $25.00

25BK, console, 1940, wood, upper front slide rule dial, lower cloth grill w/vertical bars, 4 knobs, BC, SW, 5 tubes, battery...$70.00

25BP "Pick-Me-Up," portable, 1941, two-tone leatherette, right front dial, left horizontal louvers, handle, 5 tubes, AC/DC/battery $30.00

25BT-2, table, 1942, wood, right front slide rule dial, left horizontal grill bars, 3 knobs, BC, 5 tubes, battery $30.00

25BT-3, table, 1940, wood, right front slide rule dial, left vertical grill bars, 4 knobs, BC, SW, 5 tubes, battery.................$30.00

25X, table, 1942, wood, right front dial overlaps horizontal bars, 2 knobs, BC, 5 tubes, AC/DC..$40.00

26X1, table, 1941, plastic, upper front slanted slide rule dial, lower horizontal louvers, 3 knobs, BC, SW, 6 tubes, AC $40.00

26X3, table, 1941, upper front slanted slide rule dial, lower horizontal louvers, 3 knobs, BC, SW, 6 tubes, AC/DC........$40.00

26X4, table, 1941, wood, upper front slanted slide rule dial, lower horizontal louvers, pushbuttons, 3 knobs, BC, SW, 6 tubes, AC/DC $50.00

27K, console, 1942, wood, upper front slide rule dial, lower cloth grill w/center vertical bar, pushbuttons, BC, SW, 7 tubes, AC $120.00

28 "Carryette," table, 1933, wood, rectangular case, front window dial, center 3-section cloth grill, 4 knobs $95.00

28C "Colonial," table, 1933, wood, chest-type, front window dial, center 3-section cloth grill, rounded top, side handles, 5 tubes, AC...$95.00

28D, table, 1933, wood, rounded front w/tambour doors, inner window dial, cloth grill w/cut-outs, 3 knobs, 5 tubes, AC $145.00

28E "Sheraton," table, 1933, wood, front window dial, center cloth grill w/cut-outs, 3 knobs, fluted columns, 5 tubes, AC $80.00

28T, table, 1941, wood, upper front slanted slide rule dial, lower cloth grill, 6 pushbuttons, 4 knobs, BC, 2SW, 8 tubes, AC $50.00

28X, table, 1941, wood, upper front slanted slide rule dial, lower horizontal louvers, 4 knobs, BC, SW, 8 tubes, AC/DC ..$50.00

28X5, table, 1941, wood, upper front slanted slide rule dial, lower horizontal louvers, 5 pushbuttons, 4 knobs, BC, SW, 8 tubes, AC/DC..$50.00

29K, console, 1941, wood, upper front slanted slide rule dial, lower vertical grill bars, pushbuttons, BC, SW, 9 tubes, AC $150.00

29K2, console, 1941, wood, raised top, upper front slanted slide rule dial, lower vertical grill bars, pushbuttons, 4 knobs, BC, 2SW, 9 tubes, AC..$195.00

34X, table, 1942, wood, upper front slanted slide rule dial, lower horizontal grill bars, 2 knobs, 5 tubes, AC/DC..............$40.00

35X, table, 1942, wood, upper front slanted slide rule dial, lower horizontal grill bars, 2 knobs, 5 tubes, AC/DC $40.00

36X, table, 1941, wood, upper front slanted slide rule dial, lower horizontal wrap-around louvers, 3 knobs, BC, 6 tubes, AC/DC...$40.00

40X30 "Little Nipper," table, 1939, walnut plastic, right front dial, left horizontal wrap-around louvers, 2 knobs, BC, 5 tubes, AC/DC $50.00

40X31 "Little Nipper," table, 1939, ivory plastic, right front dial, left horizontal wrap-around louvers, 2 knobs, BC, 5 tubes, AC/DC $50.00

40X50 "Modern Blonde," table, 1939, wood, right front dial, left 3-section cloth grill, handle, 2 knobs, feet, BC, 5 tubes, AC/DC $45.00

40X52, table, 1939, ivory finish, right front dial, left horizontal louvers, handle, 2 knobs, BC, 5 tubes, AC/DC $50.00

40X53 "La Siesta," table, 1939, wood, painted w/Mexican scene, right front dial, left cloth grill, handle, 2 knobs, BC, 5 tubes, AC $650.00

40X54 "Treasure Chest," table, 1939, wood, nautical-type, right front dial, left "ship's wheel" grill, 2 knobs, side rope handles, BC, 5 tubes, AC...$200.00

40X55, table, 1939, wood, right front dial, left grill w/horizontal bars, handle, 2 knobs, BC, 5 tubes, AC/DC $45.00

40X56 "1939 World's Fair," table, 1939, Repwood, Trylon & Perisphere pressed into front, right dial, left cloth grill, handle, 2 knobs, BC, 5 tubes, AC $900.00

40X57 "San Francisco Expo," table, 1939, Repwood, Golden Gate Bridge pressed into front, right dial, left grill, handle, 2 knobs, BC, 5 tubes, AC $750.00

45-E, side table/bookcase, 1940, maple finish wood, upper front vertical slide rule dial, right & left horizontal bars, lower 2-shelf book case, 2 knobs, BC, 5 tubes, AC/DC.............$55.00

45-EM, side table/bookcase, 1940, mahogany finish wood, upper front vertical slide rule dial, right & left horizontal bars, lower 2-shelf book case, 2 knobs, BC, 5 tubes, AC/DC.........$55.00

45-EW, side table/bookcase, 1940, walnut finish wood, upper front vertical slide rule dial, right & left horizontal bars, lower 2-shelf book case, 2 knobs, BC, 5 tubes, AC/DC.........$55.00

45-W-10, console-R/P, 1951, wood, inner right pull-out drawer w/slide rule dial & phono, 5 knobs, left storage, BC, FM, AC $65.00

45X1, table, 1940, brown plastic, right front dial, left horizontal wrap-around louvers, 2 knobs, BC, 5 tubes, AC/DC $45.00

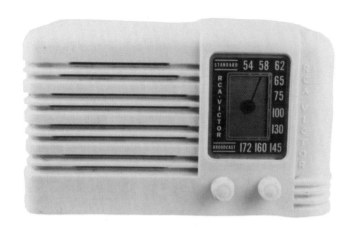

45X2, table, 1940, ivory plastic, right front dial, left horizontal wrap-around louvers, 2 knobs, BC, 5 tubes, AC/DC ..$45.00

45X3, table, 1940, wood, right front dial, left grill area, 2 knobs, BC, 5 tubes, AC/DC $40.00

45X4, table, 1940, wood, right front dial, left horizontal grill bars, 2 knobs, BC, 5 tubes, AC/DC..............................$45.00

45X5, table, 1940 walnut plastic, right front dial, left horizontal wrap-around grill bars, 2 knobs, BC, 5 tubes, AC/DC ...$50.00

45X6, table, 1940 ivory plastic, right front dial, left horizontal wrap-around grill bars, 2 knobs, BC, 5 tubes, AC/DC $50.00

45X11, table, 1940, brown plastic, right front dial, left vertical grill bars, 2 knobs, BC, 5 tubes, AC/DC...............................$50.00

45X12, table, 1940, ivory plastic, right front dial, left vertical grill bars, 2 knobs, BC, 5 tubes, AC/DC...............................$50.00

45X13, table, 1940, two-tone wood, right front dial, left horizontal louvers, 2 knobs, BC, 5 tubes, AC/DC $45.00

45X16, table, 1940, two-tone wood, right front dial, left horizontal louvers, 2 knobs, BC, 5 tubes, AC/DC $45.00

45X17, table, 1940, wood, right front dial, left vertical grill bars, 2 knobs, BC, 5 tubes, AC/DC...............................$45.00

45X111, table, 1940, mahogany plastic, right front dial, left vertical grill bars, 2 knobs, BC, 5 tubes, AC/DC $45.00

45X112, table, 1940, ivory plastic, right front dial, left vertical grill bars, 2 knobs, BC, 5 tubes, AC/DC $45.00

45X113, table, 1940, wood, right front dial, left horizontal louvers, 2 knobs, BC, 5 tubes, AC/DC $45.00

46X1, table, 1940, mahogany plastic, right front dial, left vertical grill bars, 2 knobs, BC, 5 tubes, AC/DC $40.00

46X2, table, 1940, ivory plastic, right front dial, left vertical grill bars, 2 knobs, BC, 5 tubes, AC/DC..............................$40.00

46X3, table, 1939, two-tone wood, right front dial, left horizontal louvers, 2 knobs, BC, 5 tubes, AC/DC $45.00

46X11, table, 1940, mahogany plastic, right front dial, left vertical grill bars, 3 knobs, BC, SW, 5 tubes, AC/DC $50.00

46X12, table, 1939, ivory plastic, right front dial, left vertical grill bars, 3 knobs, BC, SW, 5 tubes, AC/DC $50.00

46X13, table, 1940, wood, right front dial, left square grill area, 3 knobs, BC, SW, 5 tubes, AC/DC...............................$45.00

46X21, table, 1940, walnut plastic, right front dial, left vertical grill bars, 3 knobs, BC, 5 tubes, AC/DC............................$45.00

46X23, table, 1940, wood, right front airplane dial, left horizontal louvers, 3 knobs, BC, SW, AC/DC $45.00

46X24, table, 1940, walnut, right front dial, left grill area, pushbuttons, 3 knobs, BC, SW, AC/DC....................................$55.00

54B1, portable, 1946, inner round dial, perforated grill, thumbwheel knob, flip open lid, handle, BC, battery $50.00

54B2, portable, 1946, inner round dial, perforated grill, thumbwheel knob, flip open lid, handle, BC, battery $50.00

54B5, portable, 1947, plastic, left front round dial, right horizontal wrap-around louvers, top thumbwheel knob, handle, BC, battery $45.00

55F, table, 1946, wood, right front slide rule dial, left horizontal louvers, 3 knobs, BC, battery $30.00

55U, table-R/P, 1946, wood, upper front slide rule dial, lower horizontal louvers, 2 knobs, lift top, inner phono, BC, AC ...$30.00

55X, table, 1942, wood, center front dial, right & left grills w/horizontal louvers, 2 knobs, BC, 5 tubes, AC/DC...............$55.00

56X, table, 1946, plastic, upper front dial w/red dot pointer, lower horizontal louvers, 3 knobs, BC, AC/DC $35.00

56X2, table, 1946, plastic, upper front dial w/red dot pointer, lower horizontal louvers, 3 knobs, BC, AC/DC $35.00

56X3, table, 1946, two-tone wood, upper front slanted slide rule dial, lower horizontal louvers, 3 knobs, BC, AC/DC $40.00

56X5 "The 12,000 Miler," table, 1946, wood, upper front slanted slide rule dial, lower horizontal louvers, 3 knobs, BC, SW, 6 tubes..$50.00

56X10, table, 1946, plastic, upper front slanted slide rule dial, lower horizontal louvers, 3 knobs, BC, SW, AC/DC $40.00

56X11, table, plastic, upper front slanted slide rule dial, lower horizontal louvers, 3 knobs, BC, SW, AC $40.00

58AV, console-R/P, 1946, wood, inner right slide rule dial, 4 knobs, 6 pushbuttons, left phono, lift top, BC, SW $50.00

59AV1, console-R/P, 1946, wood, inner right slide rule dial, 6 knobs, 6 pushbuttons, door, left pull-out phono, BC, 2 SW, AC $75.00

61-8, table, 1948, brown plastic, upper front slanted slide rule dial, lower horizontal wrap-around louvers, 2 knobs, BC, 5 tubes, AC/DC $45.00

61-9, table, 1948, ivory plastic, upper front slanted slide rule dial, lower horizontal wrap-around louvers, 2 knobs, BC, 5 tubes, AC/DC $45.00

64F3, table, 1946, wood, burl graining, upper front slanted slide rule dial, lower horizontal louvers, 2 knobs, BC, battery **$35.00**

65AU, table-R/P, 1947, wood, upper front slide rule dial, lower horizontal louvers, 2 knobs, lift top, inner phono, BC, AC....**$40.00**

65BR9, portable, 1947, center front round dial, lower horizontal grill bars, handle, BC, 5 tubes, AC/battery **$45.00**

65F, table, 1948, wood, right front slide rule dial, left horizontal louvers, 3 knobs, BC, battery **$30.00**

65U, table-R/P, 1947, wood, upper front slide rule dial, lower horizontal louvers, 2 knobs, lift top, inner phono, BC, AC ...**$35.00**

65X1, table, 1948, plastic, upper front slanted slide rule dial, lower horizontal louvers, 2 knobs, BC, 5 tubes, AC/DC $35.00

65X2, table, 1946, plastic, upper front slanted slide rule dial, lower horizontal louvers, 2 knobs, BC, 5 tubes, AC/DC..........**$35.00**

66BX "Globe Trotter," portable, 1947, aluminum/plastic, upper front flip-up dial lid, lower horizontal grill bars, 2 knobs, handle, BC, AC/DC/battery **$40.00**

66X1, table, 1946, walnut plastic, upper front curved slide rule dial, lower cloth grill, rear hand-hold, 3 knobs, BC, SW, AC/DC ...$50.00

66X2, table, 1948, plastic, upper front curved slide rule dial, lower cloth grill, rear hand-hold, 3 knobs, BC, SW, AC/DC **$50.00**

66X3, table, 1946, two-tone wood, upper front curved slide rule dial, lower "zebra" cloth grill, 3 knobs, BC, SW, AC/DC....**$55.00**

66X7, table, 1946, dark blue Catalin, upper front curved slide rule dial, lower horizontal grill bars, 3 knobs, BC, SW, AC ..**$500.00+**

66X8, table, 1946, maroon Catalin, upper front curved slide rule dial, lower horizontal grill bars, 3 knobs, BC, SW, AC ....**$500.00+**

66X9, table, 1946, green swirl Catalin, upper front curved slide rule dial, lower horizontal grill bars, 3 knobs, BC, SW, AC ....**$500.00+**

66X11, table, 1947, brown plastic, upper front slanted slide rule dial, lower concentric rectangular grill cut-outs, 3 knobs, BC, 6 tubes, AC/DC **$40.00**

66X12, table, 1947, ivory plastic, upper front slanted slide rule dial, lower concentric rectangular grill cut-outs, 3 knobs, BC, 6 tubes, AC/DC $40.00

66X13, table, 1948, wood, upper front slanted slide rule dial, lower horizontal louvers, brass trim, 3 knobs, BC, 6 tubes, AC/DC...**$40.00**

66X14, table, 1948, blonde, upper front slanted slide rule dial, lower horizontal louvers, brass trim, 3 knobs, BC, 6 tubes, AC/DC...**$40.00**

66X15, table, 1948, mahogany, upper front slanted slide rule dial, lower horizontal louvers, brass trim, 3 knobs, BC, 6 tubes, AC/DC...**$40.00**

67AV1, console-R/P, 1946, wood, dial & 4 knobs in right tilt-out drawer, left lift top, inner phono, BC, SW, AC **$75.00**

68R1, table, 1947, brown plastic, lower front slide rule dial, upper vertical grill bars, 4 knobs, BC, FM, 8 tubes, AC..........**$40.00**

68R2, table, 1947, ivory plastic, lower front slide rule dial, upper vertical grill bars, 4 knobs, BC, FM, 8 tubes, AC...........**$40.00**

68R3, table, 1946, wood, lower front slide rule dial, large upper grill area, 4 knobs, BC, FM, 8 tubes, AC **$40.00**

68R4, table, 1946, wood, lower front slide rule dial, upper vertical grill bars, 4 knobs, BC, FM, 8 tubes, AC **$40.00**

75X11, table, 1948, maroon plastic & brass, right front dial, left cloth grill w/vertical bars, 2 knobs, BC, 5 tubes, AC/DC $55.00

75X12, table, 1948, ivory plastic & brass, right front dial, left cloth grill w/vertical bars, 2 knobs, BC, 5 tubes, AC/DC **$55.00**

75X14, table, 1948, mahogany plastic & brass, right front dial, left cloth grill w/vertical bars, 2 knobs, BC, 5 tubes, AC/DC **$55.00**

75X15, table, 1948, walnut plastic & brass, right front dial, left cloth grill w/vertical bars, 2 knobs, BC, 5 tubes, AC/DC..........**$55.00**

75X16, table, 1948, blonde plastic & brass, right front dial, left cloth grill w/vertical bars, 2 knobs, BC, 5 tubes, AC/DC..........**$55.00**

75X17, table, 1948, lacquered cabinet w/oriental designs, right front dial, left vertical grill bars, brass trim, BC, AC **$125.00**

75X18, table, 1948, lacquered cabinet w/oriental designs, right front dial, left vertical grill bars, brass trim, BC, AC **$125.00**

75ZU, table-R/P, 1949, upper front dial, lower horizontal grill bars, 2 knobs, lift top, inner phono, BC, 5 tubes, AC **$25.00**

76ZX11, table, 1948, walnut plastic, upper front slanted slide rule dial, lower horizontal wrap-around bars, 2 knobs, BC, 6 tubes, AC/DC **$45.00**

76ZX12, table, 1948, ivory plastic, upper front slanted slide rule dial, lower horizontal wrap-around bars, 2 knobs, BC, 6 tubes, AC/DC **$45.00**

77U, table-R/P, 1948, wood, upper front slide rule dial, lower horizontal louvers, 2 knobs, lift top, inner phono, BC, 6 tubes, AC..**$35.00**

77V1, console-R/P, 1948, wood, inner right slide rule dial, 3 knobs, left phono, lift top, BC, 7 tubes, AC....................**$65.00**

77V2, console-R/P, 1948, wood, right front tilt-out slide rule dial, 4 knobs, left lift top, inner phono, BC, SW, 7 tubes, AC ...**$65.00**

79-10, tombstone, wood, lower front round dial, upper cloth grill w/vertical bars, tuning eye, 5 knobs **$145.00**

84BT, tombstone, 1937, wood, rounded top, lower front dial, cloth grill w/cut-outs, 2 knobs, BC, battery **$80.00**

85E, chairside, 1937, walnut finish, Deco, top square dial & knobs, front grill w/horizontal bars, storage, 5 tubes, AC **$150.00**

85T, table, 1936, wood, right front square dial, left cloth grill w/2 horizontal bars, 3 knobs, 5 tubes, AC **$40.00**

85-T-1, table, 1936, wood, right front dial, left wrap-around cloth grill w/2 horizontal bars, 3 knobs, BC, SW, AC **$40.00**

86T, table, 1937, wood, Deco, right front dial, rounded left side, left cloth grill w/center horizontal bar, 3 knobs, BC, SW, AC **$60.00**

86T1, table, 1937, wood, right front dial, left cloth grill w/horizontal bars, 3 knobs, BC, SW, AC **$50.00**

86T2, table, 1937, two-tone wood, right front slide rule dial, rounded left side, left cloth grill w/curved cut-out, 3 knobs **$75.00**

86T3, tombstone, 1938, wood, center front slide rule dial w/plastic escutcheon, upper cloth grill w/vertical bars, 3 knobs..**$100.00**

86T6, table, 1938, wood, right front slide rule dial, rounded left side, left cloth grill w/curved cut-out, pushbuttons, 3 knobs, BC, SW, 6 tubes, AC...**$75.00**

87K-1, console, 1938, wood, upper front slanted slide rule dial, lower cloth grill w/vertical bars, pushbuttons, tuning eye, BC, SW, 7 tubes $145.00

87K-2, console, 1938, wood, upper front slide rule dial, lower cloth grill w/vertical bars, pushbuttons, tuning eye, BC, SW, 7 tubes $145.00

87T, table, 1937, wood, right front dial, left wrap-around cloth grill w/center horizontal bars, 3 knobs, BC, SW, AC $50.00

87T1, table, 1938, wood, right front slide rule dial, left wrap-around cloth grill w/cut-outs, tuning eye, 3 knobs, BC, SW, 6 tubes..$75.00

87T-2, table, 1938, wood, lower front slide rule dial, upper cloth grill, tuning eye, 6 pushbuttons, 2 knobs, BC, SW $80.00

94BK, console, 1938, wood, upper front dial, lower cloth grill w/center vertical bar, 2 knobs, BC, 4 tubes, battery......$80.00

94BK1, console, 1938, wood, upper front dial, lower cloth grill w/center vertical bar, 2 knobs, BC, 4 tubes, battery......$80.00

94BK2, console, 1938, wood, upper front slide rule dial, lower cloth grill w/center vertical bar, pushbuttons, 2 knobs, BC, SW, 4 tubes, battery $80.00

94BP1, portable, 1939, right front square dial, left grill area, handle, 2 knobs, 4 tubes, battery $30.00

94BP4-B, portable, 1939, "buffalo" covering, right front dial, left grill area, handle, 2 knobs, BC, 4 tubes, battery $30.00

94BP4-C, portable, 1939, "cowhide" covering, right front dial, left grill area, handle, 2 knobs, BC, 4 tubes, battery $30.00

94BP4-R, portable, 1939, "rawhide" covering, right front dial, left grill area, handle, 2 knobs, BC, 4 tubes, battery $30.00

94BP61, portable, 1940, dark brown, small right front dial, left grill area, handle, 2 knobs, BC, 4 tubes, battery $25.00

94BP62, portable, 1940, tan, small right front dial, left grill area, handle, 2 knobs, BC, 4 tubes, battery $25.00

94BP64, portable, 1940, light brown, small right front dial, left grill area, handle, 2 knobs, BC, 4 tubes, battery $25.00

94BP66, portable, 1940, gray, small right front dial, left grill area, handle, 2 knobs, BC, 4 tubes, battery $25.00

94BP80, portable, 1940, brown leather, small right front dial, left grill area, handle, 2 knobs, BC, 4 tubes, battery $25.00

94BP81, portable, 1940, black leather, small right front dial, left grill area, handle, 2 knobs, BC, 4 tubes, battery $25.00

94BT, tombstone, 1938, wood, lower front airplane dial, upper cloth grill w/center horizontal divider, BC, 4 tubes, battery $55.00

94BT1, tombstone, 1938, wood, lower front airplane dial, upper cloth grill w/2 splayed bars, 2 knobs, BC, 4 tubes, battery........$55.00

94BT2, table, 1939, two-tone wood, right front slide rule dial, left cloth grill w/cut-outs, pushbuttons, 2 knobs, BC, SW, 4 tubes, battery $35.00

94BT6, tombstone, 1938, wood, lower front airplane dial, upper cloth grill w/center horizontal divider, 2 knobs, BC, 4 tubes, battery $55.00

94BT61, tombstone, 1938, wood, lower front airplane dial, upper cloth grill w/2 splayed bars, 2 knobs, BC, 4 tubes, battery..$50.00

94X, table, 1938, wood, lower front round dial, upper cloth grill w/horizontal bars, BC, 4 tubes, AC/DC $50.00

95T, table, 1938, wood, large center front dial, right & left grills w/horizontal wrap-around bars, 2 knobs, BC, 5 tubes, AC $50.00

95T5, table, 1938, wood, lower front slide rule dial, upper cloth grill w/vertical bars, 6 pushbuttons, 2 knobs, BC, 5 tubes, AC $60.00

95T5LW, table, 1938, wood, lower front slide rule dial, upper cloth grill w/vertical bars, 6 pushbuttons, 2 knobs, 5 tubes, AC $60.00

95X, table, 1938, wood, lower front dial, upper cloth grill w/vertical bars, 2 knobs, BC, 5 tubes, AC/DC $60.00

95X1, table, 1938, wood, lower front dial, upper cloth grill w/center horizontal bars, top pushbuttons, 2 knobs, BC, 5 tubes, AC/DC $70.00

95X6, table, 1938, wood, lower front dial, upper cloth grill w/vertical bars, 2 knobs, BC, 5 tubes, AC/DC $50.00

95X11, table, 1938, wood, lower front dial, upper cloth grill w/center horizontal bars, top pushbuttons, 2 knobs, BC, 5 tubes, AC/DC $70.00

95XLW, table, 1938, wood, lower front dial, upper cloth grill w/vertical bars, 2 knobs, BC, SW, 5 tubes, AC/DC...............$50.00

96BK6, console, 1939, wood, upper front slide rule dial, lower cloth grill w/center vertical divider, pushbuttons, BC, SW, 6 tubes, battery...$75.00

96BT6, table, 1939, two-tone wood, right front slide rule dial, left cloth grill w/cut-outs, pushbuttons, BC, SW, 6 tubes, battery...$45.00

96E, chairside, 1938, wood, Deco, top dial/knobs/pushbuttons, front grill w/vertical center bar, BC, 6 tubes, AC.........$135.00

96E2, chairside, 1939, two-tone wood, half-round, top dial/knobs/pushbuttons, front grill w/vertical bars, BC, SW, 6 tubes, AC..$175.00

96K, console, 1938, wood, upper front slide rule dial, lower grill w/center vertical bar, 6 pushbuttons, BC, SW, 6 tubes, AC $135.00

96K2, console, 1938, wood, upper front slide rule dial, lower grill w/center vertical bar, pushbuttons, BC, SW, 6 tubes, AC $135.00

96K5, console, 1939, wood, upper front slide rule dial, lower cloth grill w/center vertical divider, pushbuttons, BC, SW, 6 tubes, AC $135.00

96K6, console, 1939, wood, upper front slide rule dial, lower cloth grill w/center vertical bar, 6 pushbuttons, BC, SW, 6 tubes, AC $145.00

96T, table, 1938, wood, lower front slide rule dial, upper cloth grill w/vertical bars, pushbuttons, 2 knobs, BC, 6 tubes, AC ..$65.00

96T1, table, 1938, two-tone wood, lower front slide rule dial, upper vertical grill bars, pushbuttons, 2 knobs, BC, 6 tubes, AC..$75.00

96T2, table, 1938, wood, lower front slide rule dial, upper cloth grill w/vertical bars, 6 pushbuttons, 2 knobs, BC, SW, 6 tubes, AC..$55.00

96T3, table, 1938, wood, lower front slide rule dial, upper cloth grill w/horizontal bars, 6 pushbuttons, 2 knobs, BC, SW, 6 tubes, AC $55.00

96T4, table, 1939, wood, lower front slide rule dial, uppe cloth grill w/2 horizontal chrome bars, 5 pushbuttons, knobs, BC, SW, 6 tubes, AC/DC..............................$80.0(

96T5, **table, 1939, wood, lower front slide rule dial, upper cloth grill w/2 horizontal bars, 5 pushbuttons, 2 knobs, BC, SW, 6 tubes, AC/DC** **$80.00**

96T6, table, 1939, wood, lower front slide rule dial, large upper grill area, 5 pushbuttons, 2 knobs, BC, SW, 6 tubes, AC/DC **$50.00**

96T7, table, 1939, wood, lower front slide rule dial, upper cloth grill w/2 horizontal bars, pushbuttons, 2 knobs, BC, SW, 6 tubes, AC...**$80.00**

96X1, table, 1939, walnut plastic, Deco, step-down top, right front dial, curved left w/horizontal wrap-around louvers, 3 knobs, BC, SW, 6 tubes, AC/DC..**$175.00**

96X2, **table, 1939, black plastic, Deco, step-down top, right front dial, curved left w/horizontal wrap-around louvers, 3 knobs, BC, SW, 6 tubes, AC/DC** **$175.00**

96X3, table, 1939, walnut/ivory plastic, Deco, step-down top, right front dial, curved left w/horizontal wrap-around louvers, 3 knobs, BC, SW, 6 tubes, AC/DC **$175.00**

96X4, table, 1939, ivory plastic, Deco, step-down top, right front dial, curved left w/horizontal wrap-around louvers, 3 knobs, BC, SW, 6 tubes, AC/DC..**$175.00**

96X11, table, 1939, walnut plastic, Deco, step-down top, right front dial, curved left w/horizontal wrap-around louvers, pushbuttons, 3 knobs, BC, SW, 6 tubes, AC/DC **$175.00**

96X12, table, 1939, black plastic, Deco, step-down top, right front dial, curved left w/horizontal wrap-around louvers, pushbuttons, 3 knobs, BC, SW, 6 tubes, AC/DC **$175.00**

96X13, table, 1939, walnut/ivory plastic, Deco, step-down top, right front dial, curved left w/horizontal wrap-around louvers, pushbuttons, 3 knobs, BC, SW, 6 tubes, AC/DC **$175.00**

96X14, table, 1939, ivory plastic, Deco, step-down top, right front dial, curved left w/horizontal wrap-around louvers, pushbuttons, 3 knobs, BC, SW, 6 tubes, AC/DC **$175.00**

97E, chairside, 1938, wood, top dial/knobs/pushbuttons/tuning eye, front grill w/horizontal bars, BC, SW, 7 tubes, AC **$135.00**

97K, console, 1939, wood, upper front slide rule dial, lower cloth grill w/vertical bars, tuning eye, pushbuttons, BC, SW, 7 tubes, AC.......**$145.00**

97K2, console, 1939, wood, upper front slide rule dial, lower cloth grill w/vertical bars, pushbuttons, BC, SW, 7 tubes, AC **$130.00**

97KG, console, 1938, wood, upper front slanted slide rule dial, lower cloth grill w/vertical bars, tuning eye, pushbuttons, BC, SW, 7 tubes, AC..**$140.00**

97T, table, 1938, wood, lower front slide rule dial, upper cloth grill w/wrap-over vertical bars, tuning eye, pushbuttons, BC, SW, 7 tubes, AC...**$65.00**

97T2, table, 1939, wood, lower front slide rule dial, large upper grill area, pushbuttons, BC, SW, 7 tubes, AC **$65.00**

97X, table, 1938, wood, lower front slide rule dial, upper cloth grill w/vertical bars, pushbuttons, 2 knobs, BC, 7 tubes, AC/DC...........**$60.00**

97Y, console, 1938, wood, upper front slide rule dial, lower cloth grill w/center vertical divider, pushbuttons, BC, SW, 7 tubes, AC/DC **$130.00**

98EY, chairside, 1938, wood, top dial/knobs/pushbuttons, front cloth grill w/horizontal bars, BC, SW, 8 tubes, AC/DC..**$125.00**

98K, console, 1938, wood, upper front dial, lower cloth grill w/center vertical bar, tuning eye, 8 pushbuttons, BC, SW, 8 tubes, AC ..**$140.00**

98K2, console, 1939, wood, upper front slide rule dial, lower cloth grill w/vertical bars, tuning eye, pushbuttons, BC, 2SW, 8 tubes, AC **$135.00**

98T, table, 1939, wood, lower front slide rule dial, upper cloth grill w/horizontal bars, pushbuttons, BC, SW, 8 tubes, AC ..**$55.00**

98T2, table, 1938, wood, lower front slide rule dial, upper cloth grill w/horizontal bars, tuning eye, pushbuttons, 2 knobs, BC, SW, 8 tubes, AC/DC...**$70.00**

98X, table, 1938, wood, lower front slide rule dial, upper cloth grill w/wrap-over vertical bars, tuning eye, pushbuttons, BC, SW, 8 tubes, AC/DC **$75.00**

98YG, console, 1938, wood, upper front slanted slide rule dial, lower cloth grill w/vertical bars, tuning eye, pushbuttons, BC, SW, 8 tubes, AC/DC...**$140.00**

99K, console, 1938, wood, upper front curved dial, lower cloth grill w/vertical bars, 8 pushbuttons, BC, SW, 9 tubes, AC ..**$145.00**

99T, table, 1938, wood, lower front slide rule dial, upper cloth grill w/vertical bars, tuning eye, 8 pushbuttons, BC, SW, 9 tubes, AC **$75.00**

100, **cathedral, 1933, wood, center front dial, cloth grill w/cutouts, side moldings, BC, AC** **$175.00**

102, table, 1934, metal, right front dial, center cloth grill w/Deco cut-outs, left volume knob, BC, AC/DC........$80.00

103, tombstone, 1934, wood, lower front round dial, upper cloth grill w/vertical cut-outs, decorative fluting, AC $85.00

110, cathedral, 1933, wood, front window dial, upper cloth grill w/cut-outs, side moldings, 4 knobs, BC, AC...$225.00

110K "Presidential," console, 1940, wood, upper front oblong slide rule dial, lower vertical grill bars, 6 pushbuttons, 4 knobs, BC, 3SW, 10 tubes, AC **$200.00**
110K2, console, 1941, wood, upper front oblong slide rule dial, lower vertical grill bars, pushbuttons, 4 knobs, BC, SW, 10 tubes, AC..**$150.00**
111, table, 1934, inlaid walnut, right front window dial, center cloth grill w/scalloped cut-outs, 4 knobs, BC, SW, AC.........**$100.00**
111K, console, 1941, wood, upper front oblong slide rule dial, lower cloth grill w/vertical bars, pushbuttons, 4 knobs, BC, 3SW, 11 tubes, AC..**$150.00**

114, table, 1934, two-tone wood, right front dial, center 3-section cloth grill, 2 knobs, BC, SW, AC $75.00
117, tombstone, 1934, wood, rounded shoulders, lower front round dial, upper cloth grill w/vertical bars, 4 knobs, BC, SW, 5 tubes, AC..**$115.00**

118, tombstone, 1934, wood, center front round dial, upper cloth grill w/vertical bars, BC, SW, 5 tubes, AC $125.00
119, tombstone, 1935, wood, arched top, lower front round dial, cloth grill w/vertical bars, 4 knobs, AC **$100.00**
120, cathedral, 1933, wood, front window dial, upper cloth grill w/cut-outs, side & top moldings, 4 knobs, BC, AC **$225.00**

121, cathedral, 1933, wood, lower front round dial, cloth grill w/cut-outs, side & top moldings, 4 knobs, BC, SW, AC..**$240.00**

125, tombstone, 1934, wood, arched top, front round airplane dial, upper 4-section cloth grill, fluting, 4 knobs, BC, SW, AC **$115.00**

128, tombstone, 1934, wood, shouldered, rounded top, center front round dial, upper cloth grill w/cut-outs, 5 knobs, BC, 2SW, 6 tubes, AC...**$250.00**

140, tombstone, 1933, wood, scalloped shoulders, lower front round airplane dial, upper cloth grill w/cut-outs, 4 knobs, BC, SW, AC..**$300.00**

142-B, cathedral, 1933, wood, front window dial, upper cloth grill w/cut-outs, side & top moldings, 4 knobs, BC, battery...**$125.00**

143, tombstone, 1933, wood, shouldered, rounded top, round airplane dial, upper cloth grill w/vertical bars, 5 knobs, BC, 3SW, 8 tubes, AC...**$280.00**

211, console, 1934, wood, lowboy, upper front round dial, lower cloth grill w/cut-outs, BC, SW, 5 tubes, AC **$135.00**

211K, console, 1941, wood, upper front slanted slide rule dial, lower vertical grill bars, pushbuttons, 2 speakers, BC, 3SW, 11 tubes, AC **$165.00**

214, console, 1935, wood, upper front round dial, lower cloth grill w/cut-outs, 4 knobs, 5 tubes, AC...............................**$125.00**

220, console, 1933, wood, lowboy, upper front round dial, lower cloth grill w/cut-outs, 4 knobs, 6 legs, BC, AC............**$150.00**

221, console, 1934, wood, lowboy, upper front round dial, lower cloth grill w/cut-outs, BC, SW, 6 tubes, AC **$135.00**

224, console, 1934, wood, lowboy, upper front round dial, lower cloth grill w/cut-outs, 6 legs, BC, SW, 6 tubes, AC......**$150.00**

225, console, 1935, wood, upper front round dial, lower cloth grill w/cut-outs, 4 knobs, BC, SW, AC...............................**$150.00**

240 "All-Wave," console, 1933, wood, lowboy, upper front round dial, lower cloth grill w/cut-outs, 6 legs, BC, SW, AC ..**$150.00**

242, console, 1934, wood, lowboy, upper front round dial, lower cloth grill w/cut-outs, 6 legs, BC, SW, AC **$155.00**

260, console, 1933, wood, lowboy, upper front window dial, lower cloth grill w/cut-outs, 6 legs, BC, 10 tubes, AC **$160.00**

262, console, 1934, wood, lowboy, upper front round dial, lower grill w/cut-outs, 6 legs, BC, SW, 10 tubes, AC **$160.00**

280, console, 1933, wood, lowboy, upper front window dial, lower cloth grill w/cut-outs, 6 legs, BC, 12 tubes, AC **$175.00**

281, console, 1934, wood, lowboy, inner round dial, lower cloth grill w/cut-outs, double doors, 6 legs, BC, SW, 12 tubes, AC..**$195.00**

300 "Duo," table-R/P, 1933, wood, front dial and cloth grill w/cut-outs, lift top, inner phono, BC, AC **$100.00**

301 "Duo," table-R/P, 1934, wood, upright style, lower front round dial, upper grill, lift top, inner phono, BC, SW, AC **$100.00**

310 "Duo," console-R/P, 1933, wood, highboy, front window dial, cloth grill w/cut-outs, stretcher base, BC, SW, AC **$130.00**

340 "All Wave Duo," console-R/P, 1934, wood, lowboy, center front round dial, lower cloth grill w/cut-outs, 6 legs, 8 tubes, AC **$150.00**

341, console-R/P, 1934, wood, lowboy, center front round dial, lower cloth grill w/lyre cut-out, lift top, inner phono, BC, SW, 8 tubes, AC..**$150.00**

381, console-R/P/Rec, 1934, wood, lowboy, inner front round dial, doors, right & left side storage, lift top, inner phono, BC, SW, 12 tubes, AC..**$225.00**

610V2, console-R/P, 1948, wood, inner right slide rule dial, 4 knobs, 6 pushbuttons, door, left pull-down phono, lower grill, BC, FM, 10 tubes, AC **$70.00**

612V3, console-R/P, 1947, wood, pull-down front door w/inner slide rule dial/6 knobs/8 pushbuttons/top phono, BC, SW, FM, AC..**$100.00**

710V2, console-R/P, 1948, wood, right tilt-out slide rule dial/4 knobs, left pull-out phono drawer, lower grill, BC, FM, 10 tubes, AC..**$70.00**

16, table, 1951, plastic, right front dial, left diagonal grill bars, stylized "S" logo, 3 knobs, BC, AC/DC **$30.00**

18, table, 1951, plastic, right front dial, left diagonal grill bars, stylized "S" logo, 3 knobs, BC, FM, AC **$30.00**

24, table, 1929, metal, low rectangular case, front off-center window dial, 2 knobs, switch, battery................................**$60.00**

25, console, 1929, wood, lowboy, inner front window dial & knobs, fold-down front, lower cloth grill w/cut-outs, lift top, battery...**$80.00**

26, console, 1929, wood, lowboy, inner front dial & knobs, upper speaker grill w/cut-outs, double doors, lower battery storage, battery **$80.00**

33, table-R/P, 1950, leatherette, inner right dial, 3 knobs, phono, lift top, handle, BC, AC **$15.00**

58, console-R/P, 1930, walnut, lowboy, inner front window dial, lower cloth grill w/cut-outs, double doors, lift top, inner phono, 8 tubes, AC..**$135.00**

60, console-R/P, 1930, wood, lowboy, inner front window dial, lower cloth grill w/cut-outs, double doors, lift top, inner phono, 9 tubes, AC..**$150.00**

64, console-R/P, 1950, wood, right front tilt-out slide rule dial, inner left phono, lower storage, doors, BC, FM, AC......**$70.00**

72, table-R/Rec, 1951, suitcase-style, inner left dial, right disc recorder, lift top, handle, BC, 5 tubes, AC....................**$20.00**

117, console, wood, upper front window dial w/escutcheon, lower cloth grill w/cut-outs, stretcher base **$150.00**

210, portable, 1950, plastic, right side dial knob, front vertical wrap-over grill bars, handle, BC, battery **$35.00**

215, portable, 1950, plastic, right front dial over horizontal grill bars, flex handle, 2 knobs, BC, AC/DC/battery **$35.00**

225, portable, 1950, "alligator," upper front slide rule dial, lower grill area, handle, 2 knobs, BC, AC/DC/battery **$30.00**

640, table, plastic, small upper front dial, large lower horizontal louvers, 2 thumbwheel knobs, BC................................**$60.00**

1017, table, 1952, wood, center front half-round dial w/inner pointer overlaps large cloth grill, 4 knobs, feet, BC, AC........**$30.00**

1032, table-R/P, 1952, plastic, right front round dial, left vertical grill bars, open top phono, BC, AC................................**$40.00**

1053, console-R/P, 1952, wood, upper front dial, center pull-out phono drawer, lower grill, 3 knobs, BC, AC...................**$40.00**

1055, console-R/P, 1952, wood, upper front dial, center pull-out phono drawer, lower grill, 3 knobs, BC, FM, AC **$40.00**

1260, console-R/P, 1931, walnut, lowboy, center front window dial, lower cloth grill w/cut-outs, lift top, inner phono, AC **$125.00**

1290, cathedral, 1931, wood, lower front window dial, upper cloth grill w/cut-outs, fluted columns, 4 knobs, 6 tubes, battery.......**$125.00**

1292, console, 1931, wood, lowboy, upper front window dial, lower cloth grill w/cut-outs, stretcher base, 6 tubes, battery **$85.00**

1330, console-R/P, 1931, walnut, lowboy, center front window dial, lower cloth grill w/cut-outs, lift top, inner phono, 7 tubes, AC...........**$120.00**

1403, cathedral, 1931, wood, lower front window dial, upper cloth grill w/cut-outs, fluted columns, 3 knobs......................**$235.00**

1561, table, 1940, wood, right front slide rule dial, left cloth grill w/cut-outs, pushbuttons, 4 knobs, 6 tubes, AC **$45.00**

1580, console, wood, lowboy, upper front quarter-round dial, lower cloth grill w/cut-outs, 5 knobs, 7 tubes...............**$145.00**

1582, cathedral, two-tone wood, lower front quarter-round dial, upper cloth grill w/cut-outs, 5 knobs, 7 tubes **$225.00**

1589, cathedral, 1932, burl walnut, lower front quarter-round dial, upper cloth grill w/cut-outs, 5 knobs, 7 tubes **$225.00**

1631, console, 1931, wood, lowboy, upper front quarter round dial, lower cloth grill w/cut-outs, 6 legs, 5 knobs, 9 tubes, AC...**$150.00**

1641, console, 1932, walnut, upper front quarter round dial, large lower grill w/cut-outs, 5 knobs, 2 speakers, BC, SW, 12 tubes, AC...**$175.00**

1650, console, 1935, wood, lowboy, upper front quarter-round dial, lower cloth grill w/cut-outs, 6 legs **$150.00**

1660, cathedral, wood, lower front window dial w/escutcheon, upper cloth grill w/cut-outs, 3 knobs, 5 tubes **$160.00**

1670, console, wood, lowboy, upper front quarter-round dial, lower cloth grill w/cut-outs, 6 legs, AC........................**$140.00**

1705, table, wood, Deco, lower right front dial, center cloth grill w/cut-outs, 4 knobs (2 front, 2 rear), BC, SW, AC.......$75.00

1720, console, wood, lowboy, upper front window dial w/escutcheon, lower cloth grill w/cut-outs, 3 knobs, BC, 10 tubes, AC...**$140.00**

1743, tombstone, two-tone wood, lower front round dial, upper cloth grill w/cut-outs, 3 knobs, 5 tubes $100.00

1745, tombstone, wood, double step-down top, center front round dial, upper cloth grill w/cut-outs, 5 knobs, 6 tubes **$150.00**
1800, cathedral, two-tone wood, center front window dial, upper cloth grill w/cut-outs, 2 knobs, AC **$150.00**

1905, tombstone, wood, lower front round dial w/escutcheon, upper cloth grill w/cut-outs, 5 knobs, 9 tubes **$100.00**

1806, console, wood, upper front dial, lower cloth grill w/cut-outs, 5 knobs, BC, SW $135.00
1822, console, 1935, wood, Deco, upper front dial, lower cloth grill w/curled cut-outs, 5 knobs, 14 tubes, AC **$185.00**
1835, console, 1935, wood, upper front round dial, lower cloth grill w/cut-outs, 5 knobs, BC, SW, 9 tubes, AC.................**$135.00**

1906, tombstone, wood, lower front round dial, upper cloth grill with cut-outs, 4 knobs, 6 tubes, AC $140.00
1911, console, 1936, wood, upper front round dial, lower cloth grill w/vertical bars, BC, SW, 6 tubes, AC **$120.00**

1850, tombstone, 1935, wood, Deco, double step-down top, center front round dial, upper cloth grill w/cut-outs, 5 knobs, 9 tubes, battery $100.00
1851, console, 1935, wood, upper front round dial, lower cloth grill w/cut-outs, 4 knobs, BC, SW, 6 tubes, battery **$90.00**
1852, tombstone, 1935, walnut, Deco, curved shoulders, center front dial, upper cloth grill w/cut-outs, 3 knobs, 6 tubes, battery...**$75.00**

1921, tombstone, wood, shouldered, center front round dial, upper cloth grill w/bars, 4 knobs, 6 tubes, battery ..$125.00
1938, tombstone, 1936, wood, lower front round dial, upper cloth grill w/cut-outs, 4 knobs, BC, SW, 6 tubes, AC **$110.00**
1945, console, 1936, walnut, upper front round dial, lower cloth grill w/cut-outs, tuning eye, BC, SW, 9 tubes, AC **$140.00**
1954, tombstone, wood, lower front round dial, upper cloth grill w/cut-outs, 4 knobs, BC, SW, 6 tubes **$110.00**
1955, tombstone, 1936, wood, step-down top, lower front round dial, upper cloth grill w/3 vertical bars, 5 knobs, BC, SW **$120.00**
1972, console, wood, upper front round dial, lower cloth grill w/3 splayed bars, BC, SW, 8 tubes **$130.00**

1993, console, wood, upper front round dial, lower cloth grill w/3 splayed bars, 5 knobs, BC, SW, battery $85.00
2001, table, 1950, brown metal, right front round dial knob overlaps criss-cross grill, lower left knob, BC, AC/DC..........$65.00
2002, table, 1950, ivory metal, right front round dial knob overlaps criss-cross grill, lower left knob, BC, AC/DC $65.00
2003, table, 1953, brown plastic, upper front slide rule dial, lower checkered grill, feet, 2 knobs, BC, AC/DC $25.00

2004, table, 1953, ivory plastic, upper front slide rule dial, lower checkered grill, feet, 2 knobs, BC, AC/DC $25.00
2005, table, 1953, red plastic, upper front slide rule dial, lower checkered grill, feet, 2 knobs, BC, AC/DC $30.00
2006, table, 1953, green plastic, upper front slide rule dial, lower checkered grill, feet, 2 knobs, BC, AC/DC $30.00
2007, table-C, 1953, plastic, center front round dial, right checkered grill, left alarm clock, BC, AC.................................$25.00
2021, table, plastic, right front round dial, large left grill area w/vertical bars, 3 knobs, AM, FM..$15.00

2022, table, 1953, plastic, right front dial, left diagonal grill bars, stylized "S" logo, 3 knobs, BC, SW, AC/DC $30.00
2028, table, 1953, wood, front half-round metal dial over large grill area, 2 knobs, BC, battery......................................$25.00
2041, table-R/P, 1953, leatherette, right front round dial, 3 knobs, 3/4 lift top, inner phono, handle, BC, AC $25.00
2056, console-R/P, 1953, wood, upper front slide rule dial, 2 knobs, center pull-out phono drawer, lower grill, storage, BC, AC $60.00
2061, console-R/P, 1953, wood, inner right front slide rule dial, 2 knobs, pull-out phono, left storage, double doors, lower grill, BC, AC $60.00
2225, portable, 1953, "alligator," right front half-round dial overlaps lattice grill, handle, 2 knobs, BC, AC/DC/battery ..$30.00
2411, table, wood, right front rectangular dial, left cloth grill w/fluted vertical bars, 4 knobs, DC $45.00
2761, table, wood, lower front slide rule dial, upper cloth grill w/3 vertical bars, 5 pushbuttons, 5 knobs, 6 tubes $60.00
3001, table, 1954, brown plastic, upper front thumbwheel dial, "V" shaped grill w/cloth & checkered panels, BC, 4 tubes, AC $35.00
3002, table, 1954, ivory plastic, upper front thumbwheel dial, "V" shaped grill w/cloth & checkered panels, BC, 4 tubes, AC $35.00

3004, table, 1954, plastic, right front dial, left horizontal grill bars, 2 knobs, feet, BC, 5 tubes, AC/DC...................$20.00
3032, table-R/P, 1953, plastic, right front round dial, left vertical grill bars, 3 knobs, open top phono, BC, AC $40.00
3040, table-R/P, 1953, plastic, front half-round dial w/inner louvers, 2 knobs, 3/4 lift top, inner phono, BC, AC $40.00
3040A, table-R/P, 1955, plastic, front half-round dial w/inner louvers, 2 knobs, 3/4 lift top, inner phono, BC, 5 tubes, AC...........$40.00
3045, table-R/P, 1953, wood, large front metal half-round dial over cloth grill, 2 knobs, lift top, inner phono, BC, AC $30.00
3068, console-R/P, 1955, wood, right front tilt-out slide rule dial, 3 knobs, left pull-down phono door, lower grill, BC, FM, 8 tubes, AC ...$55.00
3210, portable, 1953, plastic, center front round dial overlaps lower horizontal wrap-around bars, fold-down handle, top thumbwheel knob, BC, battery $25.00
3217, portable, 1954, plastic, center front round dial overlaps upper horizontal grill bars, fold-down handle, top thumbwheel knob, BC, AC/DC/battery $25.00
3351 "Commentator," table, 1940, plastic, Deco, left front "candy cane" dial, wrap-over vertical grill bars, 4 pushbuttons, 2 knobs, BC, 5 tubes $85.00
3451, table, plastic, Deco, left front "candy cane" dial, wrap-over vertical grill bars, 4 pushbuttons, 2 knobs, BC, 5 tubes..$85.00
3461, table, plastic, Deco, left front "candy cane" dial, wrap-over vertical grill bars, 4 pushbuttons, 2 knobs, BC $85.00

3561, table, plastic, Deco, left front "candy cane" dial, wrap-over vertical grill bars, 4 pushbuttons, 2 knobs, BC **$85.00**

4032, table-R/P, 1955, plastic, center front half-round dial, 3 knobs, open top phono, BC, AC.....................**$40.00**

4035, table-C, blue plastic, right front vertical slide rule dial, round alarm clock face, left grill w/horizontal bars, feet, BC, 5 tubes, AC **$10.00**

4036, table-C, ivory plastic, right front vertical slide rule dial, round alarm clock face, left grill w/horizontal bars, feet, BC, 5 tubes, AC **$10.00**

4037, table-C, beige plastic, right front vertical slide rule dial, round alarm clock face, left grill w/horizontal bars, feet, BC, 5 tubes, AC **$10.00**

4038, table-C, pink plastic, right front vertical slide rule dial, round alarm clock face, left grill w/horizontal bars, feet, BC, 5 tubes, AC **$10.00**

4068A, console-R/P, 1955, wood, inner right slide rule dial, 3 knobs, left fold-down phono door, lower grill, BC, FM, 10 tubes, AC.....................**$65.00**

4200, table, 1955, plastic, right front trapezoid dial, left horizontal grill bars, 3 knobs, feet, BC, FM, 8 tubes, AC **$20.00**

4204, table, maroon plastic, recessed front with right dial and left cloth grill, 3 knobs, AM/FM **$35.00**

4206, table, ivory plastic, recessed front with right dial and left cloth grill, 3 knobs, AM/FM **$35.00**

4210, portable, 1955, plastic, center front round dial overlaps lower horizontal wrap-around grill bars, top thumbwheel knob, handle, BC, 4 tubes, battery **$25.00**

4212, portable, 1955, right front round dial knob, left lattice grill w/Silvertone logo, BC, 4 tubes, battery **$40.00**

4225, portable, 1955, cloth covered, lower front dial, upper grill area, handle, BC, 5 tubes, AC/DC/battery **$30.00**

4414, table, 1936, plastic, right front round dial knob, left cloth grill w/wrap-over vertical bars, BC, AC............$90.00

4418, table, 1937, wood, center front round dial, top speaker grill, 3 knobs, BC, SW, 4 tubes, battery **$40.00**

4464, tombstone, 1936, two-tone wood, lower front round dial, upper cloth grill w/cut-outs, 4 knobs, 6 tubes, AC **$120.00**

4485, console, 1937, wood, upper front round dial, lower cloth grill w/vertical bars, tuning eye, BC, SW, 8 tubes, AC **$130.00**

4486, console, 1937, wood, upper front round dial, lower cloth grill w/vertical bars, tuning eye, BC, SW, 10 tubes, AC **$130.00**

4487, console, 1937, wood, upper front round self-tuning dial, lower cloth grill w/cut-outs, BC, SW, 11 tubes, AC......**$160.00**

4500, table, 1936, plastic, right front round dial knob, left cloth grill w/vertical wrap-over bars, BC, AC **$90.00**

4500A, table, 1936, plastic, right front round dial knob, left cloth grill w/vertical wrap-over bars, 5 tubes $90.00

4522, tombstone, wood, lower front round dial w/globe, upper cloth grill with cut-outs, 3 knobs, 6 tubes.....................**$100.00**

4563, table, wood, rounded left, right front round dial, left cloth grill w/Deco cut-outs, 4 knobs, 6 tubes **$60.00**

4565, table, wood, off-center round dial w/tuning eye, right & left cloth grills w/cut-outs, 5 knobs, BC, SW $65.00

4612, table, 1939, wood, right front dial, left cloth grill with 2 vertical bars, 4 knobs, battery **$30.00**

4619, tombstone, 1939, walnut w/maple inlays, center front dial, upper cloth grill w/bars, 6 tubes, battery.......................**$80.00**

4652, console, 1939, wood, upper front dial, lower cloth grill w/3 vertical bars, fluted columns, battery.............................**$95.00**

4660, table, 1937, two-tone wood, left front dial, right grill w/cut-outs, tuning eye, 3 knobs, 6 tubes, AC.........................**$60.00**

4663, upright table, 1938, wood, center front dial, curved top w/vertical grill bars, tuning eye, 4 knobs, BC, SW, 6 tubes, AC **$90.00**

4664, table, 1937, wood, right front dial, left cloth grill w/Deco cut-outs, tuning eye, 4 knobs, AC **$55.00**

4665, tombstone, 1938, wood, center front slanted slide rule dial, upper cloth grill w/3 vertical bars, tuning eye, 4 knobs, BC, SW, 8 tubes, AC..**$90.00**

4666, table, 1938, wood, upper front rolling slide rule dial, center automatic tuning, side grill bars, BC, SW, 10 tubes, AC ..**$100.00**

4668, table-R/P, 1938, wood, right front dial, left cloth grill w/vertical bars, fluted columns, lift top, inner phono, AC **$40.00**

4685, console, 1938, wood, upper front slide rule dial, lower cloth grill w/vertical bars, tuning eye, BC, SW, 8 tubes, AC ..**$120.00**

4686, console, 1938, wood, upper front slide rule dial, automatic tuning, lower cloth grill w/vertical bars, tuning eye, BC, SW, 10 tubes, AC..**$150.00**

4688, console, 1938, wood, upper front slide rule dial, lower cloth grill w/vertical bars, pushbuttons, tuning eye, BC, SW, 14 tubes, AC...**$185.00**

4763, table, wood, off-center raised dial panel, left cloth grill w/cut-outs, tuning eye, 4 knobs, BC, SW, 6 tubes ...$65.00

5016, table, 1956, mahogany, right front plastic half-round dial, left cloth grill, 3 knobs, BC, 6 tubes **$20.00**

5017, table, 1956, blonde oak, right front plastic half-round dial, left cloth grill, 3 knobs, BC, 6 tubes **$20.00**

5227, portable, 1955, leatherette, inner slide rule dial, flip-up front w/map, telescope antenna, BC, 2SW, LW, 5 tubes, AC/DC/battery **$50.00**

6000, table, plastic, lower right front dial overlaps upper horizontal grill bars, feet, BC, AC/DC $10.00

6002, table, 1946, metal, midget, small upper right front dial, horizontal louvers, 2 knobs, BC, 4 tubes, AC/DC................**$65.00**

6012, table, 1947, plastic, lower front slide rule dial, upper vertical grill bars, pushbuttons, 2 knobs, handle, BC, AC/DC **$45.00**

6016, table, 1947, plastic, right front square dial, vertical grill bars on front/side/top, handle, 3 knobs, BC, AC/DC **$60.00**

6018, table-C, 1956, plastic, step-down top, right front round dial, left alarm clock, side louvers, BC, 4 tubes, AC **$30.00**

6020, table-C, 1956, brown plastic, trapezoid shape, lower front slide rule dial, large upper clock face, 5 knobs, AC **$25.00**

6021, table-C, 1956, ivory plastic, trapezoid shape, lower front slide rule dial, large upper clock face, 5 knobs, AC......**$25.00**

6042, table, 1939, two-tone wood, right front dial, left oval grill w/center decorative bar, 2 knobs, battery **$35.00**

6050, table, 1947, wood, right front round dial, left cloth grill w/3 horizontal bars, 3 knobs, BC, AC/DC.................$45.00

6051, table, 1947, two-tone wood, lower right front dial, left & upper cloth grill areas w/cut-outs, 2 knobs, battery **$35.00**

6052, tombstone, 1939, walnut w/inlay, shouldered, lower front dial, upper cloth grill w/cut-outs, pushbuttons, 2 knobs, 6 tubes, battery...**$65.00**

6057A, console-R/P, 1956, wood, upper front slide rule dial, center pull-out phono drawer, storage, 2 knobs..................**$65.00**

6064, console, 1939, wood, upper front slanted dial, lower cloth grill w/3 vertical bars, 4 knobs, 6 tubes, battery **$85.00**

6068, console, 1939, walnut, upper front slanted slide rule dial, lower cloth grill w/2 vertical bars, BC, SW, 7 tubes, battery **$85.00**

6071, table-R/P, 1947, wood, right front round dial, left cloth grill w/3 horizontal bars, 3 knobs, lift top, inner phono, BC, AC...**$30.00**

6072, table-R/P, 1947, wood, lower front slide rule dial, upper oblong cloth grill w/3 horizontal bars, 2 knobs, lift top, inner phono, BC, AC **$30.00**

6093, console, 1946, wood, upper front slide rule dial, lower cloth grill w/bars, pushbuttons, 4 knobs, BC, SW, AC **$110.00**

6100, console-R/P, 1946, wood, upper front slanted dial, center pull-out phono drawer, lower cloth grill, 4 knobs, BC, AC **$100.00**

6105, console-R/P, 1946, wood, upper front slanted slide rule dial, center pull-out phono drawer, lower grill, pushbuttons, 4 knobs, BC, SW, AC **$100.00**

6111, console-R/P, 1946, wood, inner right slide rule dial, pushbuttons, 4 knobs, fold-down door, left pull-out phono drawer, lower grill, BC, SW, AC **$85.00**

6111A, console-R/P, 1947, wood, inner right slide rule dial, 4 knobs, 8 pushbuttons, fold-down door, left pull-out phono drawer, lower grill, BC, SW, AC **$85.00**

6122, table, two-tone wood, right front slide rule dial, left cloth grill w/cut-outs, tuning eye, 6 pushbuttons, 4 knobs, BC, SW, 7 tubes...**$75.00**

6177-A, table, plastic, Deco, right front round dial knob, rounded left w/horizontal wrap-around louvers, BC, 5 tubes, AC/DC **$120.00**

6178-A, table, plastic, Deco, right front round dial knob, rounded left w/horizontal wrap-around louvers, BC, 5 tubes, AC/DC **$120.00**

6192, console, wood, upper front slanted slide rule dial, lower cloth grill w/3 vertical bars, tuning eye, 8 pushbuttons, 4 knobs, BC, SW, AC **$145.00**

6200A, table, 1946, plastic, lower front slide rule dial, large upper cloth grill, 2 knobs, BC, battery.....................................**$30.00**

6216A, **portable, gray plastic, upper left front dial area, right horizontal wrap-around bars, handle, 2 knobs, BC..$25.00**

6217, **portable, maroon plastic, upper left front dial area, right horizontal wrap-around bars, handle, 2 knobs, BC..$25.00**

6218, portable, green plastic, upper left front dial area, right horizontal wrap-around bars, handle, 2 knobs, BC **$25.00**

6220A, table, 1946, wood, lower front slide rule dial, upper cloth grill w/cut-outs, 2 knobs, BC, battery **$25.00**

6230A, table, 1947, wood, lower front slide rule dial, upper cloth grill w/scrolled sides, 2 knobs, BC, 3SW, battery **$45.00**

6327, table, wood, upper front slanted slide rule dial, lower cloth grill w/crossed cut-outs, 5 pushbuttons, 2 knobs, 6 tubes **$65.00**

6372, table, 1940, wood, right front vertical slide rule dial, left cloth grill, handle, 2 knobs, battery **$35.00**

6402, table, plastic, midget, small right front dial over horizontal wrap-around louvers, 2 knobs **$75.00**

6425, table, wood, lower front slide rule dial, upper horizontal louvers, pushbuttons, tuning eye, BC, SW.........................**$65.00**

6437, console, 1940, wood, upper front slanted slide rule dial, lower cloth grill w/crossed cut-outs, pushbuttons, 12 tubes, BC, SW, AC...**$160.00**

6491-A, end table, wood, round end table on 4 legged base, inner dial & 4 knobs, double front doors **$185.00**

6821, portable, cloth covered, right front dial, left metal perforated grill, handle, 2 knobs, BC, AC/DC/battery **$35.00**

7006, **table, 1967, brown plastic, step-down top, front off-center dial, left cloth grill area, 2 knobs, BC, AC/DC......$20.00**

7007, **table, 1967, ivory plastic, step-down top, front off-center dial, left cloth grill area, 2 knobs, BC, AC/DC...............$20.00**

7014, **table, plastic, lower front slide rule dial, large upper lattice grill area w/center "V" logo, 2 speakers, 2 knobs, BC, AC $20.00**

7020, **table, Deco, left front "candy cane" dial, wrap-over vertical grill bars, 2 knobs, BC $85.00**

7021, table, 1947, plastic, lower front slide rule dial, large upper grill, 4 pushbuttons, 4 knobs, BC, AC/DC **$45.00**

7022, table, 1946, Deco, left front "candy cane" dial, wrap-over vertical grill bars, 2 knobs, BC **$85.00**

7024, table, Deco, left front "candy cane" dial, wrap-over vertical grill bars, 2 knobs, BC **$85.00**

7025, table, 1947, plastic, Deco, left front "candy cane" dial, wrap-over vertical grill bars, 2 knobs, 4 pushbuttons, BC **$85.00**

7031A, table, two-tone wood, upper front slanted slide rule dial, lower cloth grill w/2 horizontal bars, 4 knobs................**$50.00**

7036A, table, wood, upper front slanted slide rule dial, lower cloth grill w/horizontal bars, 5 pushbuttons, 3 knobs **$60.00**

7038, table, 1941, wood, lower front slide rule dial, upper cloth grill w/horizontal bars, 6 pushbuttons, 4 knobs, BC, SW **$60.00**

7039, table, 1941, wood, Deco, lower front slide rule dial, upper cloth grill w/horizontal bars, 8 pushbuttons, 2 knobs, BC, SW...**$85.00**

7054, table, 1947, wood, lower front slide rule dial, upper grill area, 4 pushbuttons, 4 knobs, BC, AC/DC....................**$35.00**

7070, table-R/P, 1947, plastic, right front dial, left vertical louvers, 2 knobs, curved left side, open top phono, BC, AC..**$40.00**

7085, table-R/P/Rec, 1947, wood, inner right vertical slide rule dial, 4 knobs, phono/recorder, lift top, front horizontal grill bars, BC, AC **$25.00**

7086, table-R/P/Rec, 1947, wood, inner right vertical slide rule dial, 4 knobs, phono/recorder, lift top, front horizontal grill bars, BC, AC **$25.00**

7090, console, 1947, wood, upper front slanted dial, lower cloth grill w/2 vertical bars, 4 pushbuttons, 4 knobs, BC, SW, AC/DC **$95.00**

7100, console-R/P, 1947, wood, inner right slide rule dial, 4 knobs, left phono, lift top, front cloth grill w/cut-outs, BC, AC **$95.00**

7102, console-R/P/Rec, 1947, wood, inner right slide rule dial, 4 knobs, left phono/recorder, lift top, front criss-cross grill, BC, AC **$60.00**

7103, console-R/P/Rec, 1947, wood, inner right slide rule dial, 4 knobs, left phono/recorder, lift top, front criss-cross grill, BC, AC **$60.00**

7104, table, wood, upper front slanted slide rule dial, lower cloth grill w/2 vertical bars, 3 knobs, battery **$30.00**

7108, table, wood, upper front slide rule dial, lower horizontal grill bars, 4 knobs, battery..**$30.00**

7111, console-R/P, 1947, wood, inner right slide rule dial/4 knobs/lower storage, door, left lift top, inner phono, BC, 2SW, AC **$70.00**

7115, console-R/P, 1947, wood, upper front slanted slide rule dial, center pull-out phono drawer, lower grill, 4 knobs, BC, FM, AC...**$90.00**

7116, console-R/P, 1947, wood, right tilt-out slide rule dial & knobs, inner phono, lower front grill, BC, FM, AC **$75.00**

7166, portable, 1946, inner right dial, upper horizontal grill bars, flip-up lid, handle, BC, AC/DC/battery **$35.00**

7204, table, 1957, brown plastic, 2 right front slide rule dials, left cloth grill, 3 knobs, AM/FM **$25.00**

7206, table, 1957, ivory plastic, 2 front right slide rule dials, left cloth grill, 3 knobs, AM/FM **$25.00**

7210, table-R/P, 1948, wood, lower front slide rule dial, upper cloth grill w/crossed bars, 2 knobs, lift top, inner phono, side crank, BC, battery **$35.00**

7222, portable, 1957, upper front slide rule dial, large lower grill area, handle, BC, 5 tubes, AC/DC/battery **$20.00**

7226, table, 1948, wood, lower front slanted slide rule dial, upper cloth grill, 2 knobs, BC, AC/DC/battery **$45.00**

7244, table-R/P, wood, right front dial, left cloth grill w/2 horizontal bars, lift top, inner phono, BC, AC **$35.00**

8000, table, 1948, upper right front dial, lower perforated wrap-under grill, 2 knobs, flared base, BC, AC/DC **$45.00**

8003, table, 1949, blue metal, midget, small upper right front dial, horizontal louvers, 2 knobs, BC, AC/DC $75.00

8004, table, 1949, ivory metal, midget, small upper right front dial, horizontal louvers, 2 knobs, BC, AC/DC $75.00

8005, table, 1948, plastic, upper front slide rule dial, lower aluminum grill, 2 knobs, BC, AC/DC $35.00

8010, table-C, 1948, plastic, slide rule dial lights through lower front grill, upper clock face, 5 knobs, BC, AC $60.00

8020, table, 1948, plastic, upper front slide rule dial, lower perforated metal grill, 4 knobs, BC, FM, AC/DC....................$35.00

8021, table, 1949, plastic, upper front slide rule dial, lower perforated metal grill, 4 knobs, AM, FM, AC/DC $35.00

8024, table, 1949, plastic, lower front slide rule dial, upper vertical grill bars, 2 knobs, AM, FM, AC.....................................$30.00

8041, table-R/P, 1958, top raised slide rule dial, wrap-over front grill, 3 knobs, lift top, inner phono, handle, BC, 5 tubes, AC $35.00

8050, table, 1948, two-tone wood, lower front slide rule dial, upper cloth grill w/cut-outs, 2 knobs, BC, AC/DC $30.00

8051, table, 1948, two-tone wood, lower front slide rule dial, upper cloth grill w/cut-out, 2 knobs, BC, AC/DC......................$30.00

8052, table, 1949, wood, lower front slide rule dial, upper cloth grill, raised pushbuttons, 4 knobs, BC, AC/DC..............$40.00

8055B, console-R/P, 1959, wood, left dial & 5 knobs, right lift top, inner phono, large front grill area, legs, BC, FM, 10 tubes, AC.....$40.00

8057, console-R/P, 1958, wood, inner left dial/right 4 speed phono, lift top, large front grill area, legs, BC, 6 tubes, AC........$40.00

8073, table-R/P, 1950, plastic, right front round dial knob, left vertical grill bars, open top phono, BC, AC $35.00

8080, table-R/P, 1948, plastic, upper front slide rule dial, lower grill area, 4 knobs, lift top, inner phono, BC, AC $40.00

8086A, table-R/P/Rec, 1949, inner vertical slide rule dial/4 knobs/phono/recorder, lift top, front horizontal grill bars, BC, AC $25.00

8090, console, 1948, wood, upper front slanted slide rule dial, lower cloth grill w/2 vertical bars, 4 knobs, BC, AC/DC ..$60.00

8100, console-R/P, 1948, wood, inner right slide rule dial/4 knobs/left phono, lift top, front cloth grill, BC, 5 tubes, AC/DC $50.00

8101C, console-R/P, 1949, wood, inner right vertical slide rule dial/left phono, lift top, front criss-cross grill, BC, AC $50.00

8103, console-R/Rec, 1949, wood, inner right vertical slide rule dial/4 knobs/left recorder, lift top, front criss-cross grill, BC, AC $50.00

8105A, console-R/P, 1948, wood, inner right vertical dial/4 knobs/pushbuttons/left phono, lift top, front cloth grill, BC, SW, AC $65.00

8108A, console-R/P, 1949, wood, right front tilt-out slide rule dial, 4 knobs, left pull-out phono drawer, lower criss-cross grill, BC, FM, AC $65.00

8115B, console-R/P, 1949, wood, right front tilt-out slide rule dial, 4 knobs, pushbuttons, left pull-out phono drawer, lower grill area, BC, FM, AC $60.00

8200, table, 1949, plastic, upper front slide rule dial, lower metal perforated grill, 2 knobs, BC, battery............................$25.00

8210, table-R/P, 1949, wood, inner left vertical dial/2 knobs, phono, lift top, front cloth grill w/cut-outs, crank phono, BC, battery $35.00

8230, table, 1949, wood, lower front slide rule dial, upper criss-cross grill, 2 knobs, BC, 3SW, AC/DC/battery...............$40.00

8270A, portable, 1949, plastic & metal, inner slide rule dial, 2 thumbwheel knobs, flip-up top, lower front grill area, BC, AC/DC/battery $30.00

9000, table, 1949, plastic, diagonally divided front w/right dial knob & graduated vertical wrap-over grill bars, BC, AC/DC $45.00

9001, table, 1949, plastic, diagonally divided front w/right dial knob & graduated vertical wrap-over grill bars, BC, AC/DC $45.00

9002, table, 1959, brown plastic, modern, lower right front dial knob overlaps upper recessed horizontal bars, feet, BC, AC/DC $30.00

9003, table, 1959, ivory plastic, modern, lower right front dial knob overlaps upper recessed horizontal bars, feet, BC, AC/DC...$30.00

9005, table, 1949, mahogany plastic, upper front V-shaped slide rule dial, lower vertical grill bars, 2 knobs, BC, AC/DC..$30.00

9006, table, 1949, white plastic, upper front V-shaped slide rule dial, lower vertical grill bars, 2 knobs, BC, AC/DC **$30.00**

9012, table, 1959, plastic, right front vertical slide rule dial, large center grill area, 4 knobs, BC, 6 tubes, AC/DC **$20.00**

9022, table, 1949, plastic, right front square dial, wrap-around vertical grill bars, 3 knobs, BC, FM, AC.............................**$40.00**

9028, table-C, 1959, plastic, lower front dial, upper alarm clock, right & left grill areas, feet, BC, 6 tubes, AC..................**$15.00**

9049, console-R/P, 1959, wood, inner dial & 4 speed phono, lift top, large front grill area, legs, BC, FM, 12 tubes, AC...**$40.00**

9054, table, 1949, wood, right front vertical slide rule dial over criss-cross grill, 4 knobs, multi-band, AC **$35.00**

9061, console-R/P, 1959, wood, controls under top "piano-lid" cover, lower right front pull-out phono, legs, BC, FM, 15 tubes, AC..**$40.00**

9073B, table-R/P, 1950, plastic, right front round dial knob, left vertical grill bars, open top phono, BC, AC **$35.00**

9082, table-R/P, 1950, wood, center front dial over large grill area, 4 knobs, lift top, inner phono, BC, AC **$25.00**

9105, console-R/P, 1950, wood, upper front dial w/right & left cut-outs, 3 knobs, center pull-out phono drawer, lower grill area, BC, FM, AC **$50.00**

9201, table, 1959, plastic, wedge-shaped case, right vertical FM dial, left vertical AM dial, large center cloth grill, 2 speakers, 4 knobs, AM, FM, 6 tubes, AC **$25.00**

9260, portable, 1948, plastic, lower right front dial, upper vertical metal wrap-over grill bars, fold-down handle, 2 knobs, BC, AC/DC/battery **$35.00**

9270, portable, 1950, leatherette, upper front slide rule dial, lower grill area, handle, 2 knobs, BC, AC/DC/battery **$20.00**

9280, portable, 1950, "alligator," luggage-style, upper front slide rule dial, lower grill area, handle, 2 knobs, BC, AC/DC/battery ..**$20.00**

Neutrodyne, table, 1924, wood, low rectangular case, 3 dial black front panel, lift top, 5 tubes, battery **$120.00**

R1261, table, two-tone wood, front off-center slide rule dial, right & left cloth grill areas w/bars, 5 pushbuttons, 4 knobs, BC, SW $60.00

———————————————————————

SIMPLEX
Simplex Radio Co., Sandusky, Ohio

H, cathedral, 1930, wood, center front window dial, upper round cloth grill w/cut-outs, 2 knobs **$160.00**

N, cathedral, 1932, two-tone wood, center front window dial, upper cloth grill w/cut-outs, 5 tubes, 3 knobs **$160.00**

NT, console, 1936, wood, upper front oval black dial, lower cloth grill w/3 vertical bars, tuning eye, 4 knobs, BC, SW, 10 tubes, AC **$150.00**

NT, tombstone, 1936, wood, center front oval dial, upper cloth grill w/horizontal bars, tuning eye, 4 knobs, BC, SW, 10 tubes, AC $110.00

P, tombstone, 1932, two-tone wood, lower front window dial, upper cloth grill w/lyre cut-out, 3 knobs, BC, SW, 5 tubes, AC **$150.00**

Q, cathedral, 1932, two-tone wood, center front window dial, upper cloth grill w/cut-outs, 3 knobs, 5 tubes **$200.00**

RF, table, 1925, wood, low rectangular case, 2 dial front panel, 4 tubes, battery...**$135.00**

RS5, table, 1925, mahogany, low rectangular case, 3 dial front panel, 5 tubes, battery..**$110.00**

R1181, table, 1940, wood, lower front slide rule dial, upper 3-section cloth grill, 6 pushbuttons, 2 knobs, BC, SW..$55.00

RX, table, 1925, wood, square case, 2 dial front panel, 4 tubes, battery **$110.00**

SR8, table, 1925, mahogany, low rectangular case, slanted 3 dial front panel, 5 tubes, battery **$120.00**

SIMPLON
Industrial Electronic Corp.,
505 Court Street, Brooklyn, New York

CA-5, table-R/P, 1947, upper front slanted dial, lower grill, 2 knobs, handle, 3/4 lift-top, inner phono, BC, AC **$20.00**

WVV2, table, 1947, wood, upper front slanted slide rule dial, lower cloth grill w/4 horizontal bars, 2 knobs, BC, AC/DC **$40.00**

SKY KNIGHT
Butler Bros.,
Randolph & Canal Streets, Chicago, Illinois

CB-500-P, table, 1947, wood, right front square dial, left 3-section cloth grill, 2 knobs, BC, battery **$30.00**

SKYROVER
Butler Bros.,
Randolph & Canal Streets, Chicago, Illinois

22B5, console, wood, upper front round airplane dial, lower cloth grill w/cut-outs, 4 knobs, BC, SW, 12 tubes, AC **$160.00**

9022-N, table, 1946, plastic, upper front slanted slide rule dial, lower horizontal louvers w/3 vertical bars, 3 knobs, BC, AC $35.00

C-10, cathedral, wood, lower front window dial w/escutcheon, upper cloth grill w/cut-outs, 3 knobs **$200.00**

N5-RD-250, table, 1946, plastic, upper front slanted slide rule dial, lower horizontal louvers w/ 3 vertical bars, 3 knobs, BC, AC/DC **$40.00**

N5-RD295, table, 1947, plastic, right front square dial, left vertical grill bars, decorative case lines, 2 knobs, BC, AC/DC ..**$50.00**

SMOKERETTE
Porto Products, Inc.

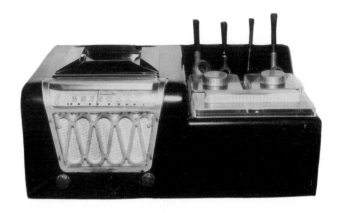

SR-600W "Smokerette," table-N, 1947, plastic, combination radio/pipe rack/humidors/ashtray, left front slide rule dial, lower cloth grill w/plastic cut-outs, 2 knobs, AC....$200.00

SONIC
Sonic Industries, Inc.,
19 Wilbur Street, Lynbrook, New York

415, table-R/P, 1958, plastic, inner right front dial, 3 speed record player, lift top, handle, BC, 5 tubes, AC **$15.00**

465, table-R/P, 1958, center front dial overlaps horizontal grill bars, 3/4 lift top, inner phono, handle, BC, 5 tubes, AC...........**$20.00**

SONORA
Sonora Radio & Television Corp.,
325 North Hoyne Avenue, Chicago, Illinois

100, table, 1948, plastic, upper front curved slide rule dial, lower horizontal louvers, 2 knobs, BC, AC/DC **$35.00**

101, portable, 1948, plastic, lower front slide rule dial, upper curved horizontal louvers, handle, 2 knobs, BC, battery **$30.00**

102, portable, 1949, plastic, lower front slide rule dial, upper curved horizontal louvers, handle, 2 knobs, BC, AC/DC/battery **$30.00**

102B, portable, 1949, plastic, lower front slide rule dial, upper curved horizontal louvers, handle, 2 knobs, BC, AC/DC/battery **$30.00**

171, table, 1950, plastic, lower front slide rule dial, upper horizontal grill bars, 2 knobs, BC, AC/DC **$35.00**

306, table-R/P, 1950, wood, center front dial, right & left criss-cross grill areas, 4 knobs, lift top, inner phono, BC, AC **$30.00**

379, table, 1954, plastic, large front dial with decorative lines, 2 knobs, BC, 6 tubes, AC/DC...**$20.00**

401, console-R/P, 1948, wood, small cabinet, upper front square dial, 4 knobs, lower storage, lift top, inner phono, BC, AC..**$55.00**

538, portable, 1957, plastic, 2 upper front thumbwheel knobs, large lower perforated grill w/"V," handle, BC, 4 tubes, AC/DC/battery **$30.00**

568, table, 1957, wood, lower front slide rule dial, large upper cloth grill, 2 knobs, BC, 6 tubes, AC/DC **$25.00**

652, table, plastic, right front dial, left grill panel w/decorative lines & circular cut-outs, 2 knobs, BC, AC/DC......................**$20.00**

C-22, table, 1938, plastic, right front slide rule dial over horizontal bars, left lattice grill, 2 knobs, BC, AC **$50.00**

D-12, table, 1938, wood, right front slide rule dial, rounded left w/horizontal louvers, 4 knobs, BC, SW, 6 tubes, AC/DC...........**$60.00**

D-800, table, 1926, wood, low rectangular case, two front window dials w/thumbwheel tuning, lift top, battery..................**$150.00**

DDA-14, table, 1938, wood, right front slide rule dial, left horizontal grill bars, 4 pushbuttons, 3 knobs, 6 tubes, AC/DC ..**$55.00**

FA-55, table, 1938, wood, right front slide rule dial, left horizontal wrap-around louvers, pushbuttons, 4 knobs, BC, SW, 7 tubes, AC...**$55.00**

GA-66, table, 1938, wood, center front slide rule dial, right & left horizontal wrap-around louvers, pushbuttons, 4 knobs, BC, SW, 9 tubes, AC...**$60.00**

GA-88, console, 1938, wood, upper front slide rule dial, lower cloth grill w/2 vertical bars, pushbuttons, 4 knobs, BC, SW, 9 tubes, AC...**$115.00**

KF, table, 1941, two-tone plastic, small case, top right dial knob, front vertical grill bars, BC, 4 tubes **$60.00**

KG-132 "Brownie," portable, 1941, brown plastic, left side knobs, front round grill, handle, BC, 4 tubes, battery................**$40.00**

KL-185, console-R/P/Rec, 1942, wood, inner right slide rule dial/pushbuttons/knobs, left phono/recorder, lift top, front grill, 9 tubes, AC..**$100.00**

KM "Coronet," table, 1941, Catalin, right front square dial, left horizontal grill bars, handle, 2 knobs, BC, 5 tubes, AC/DC ....**$800.00+**

KM-450, table, wood, right front square dial, left angled grill w/horizontal bars, 2 knobs, BC, 5 tubes, AC/DC **$50.00**

KNF-99, table-R/P, 1940, walnut, right front square dial, left cloth grill w/horizontal & vertical bars, 3 knobs, lift top, inner phono, BC, 5 tubes, AC...**$25.00**

KNF-148, table-R/P, 1941, walnut, right front square dial, left lattice grill, 3 knobs, lift top, inner phono, 5 tubes, AC **$30.00**

KT "Cameo," table, 1941, plastic, right front airplane dial, left horizontal louvers, 2 knobs, BC, 5 tubes, AC/DC..............**$40.00**

KT-87 "Cameo," table, 1941, tan/brown plastic, right front dial, left horizontal louvers, 2 knobs, BC, 5 tubes, AC/DC....**$40.00**

KT-89 "Cameo," table, 1941, ivory plastic, right front dial, left horizontal louvers, 2 knobs, BC, 5 tubes, AC/DC...............**$40.00**

KY-94, console, 1940, walnut, upper front slanted slide rule dial, lower cloth grill w/horizontal & vertical bars, pushbuttons, BC, SW, 7 tubes, AC **$115.00**

KZ-111, table, 1940, wood, right front dial, left cloth grill w/vertical bars, 2 knobs, battery...**$30.00**

LD-93, table, 1941, walnut, right front square dial, left horizontal louvers, 3 knobs, BC, SW, 5 tubes, AC/DC **$40.00**

LKS-180, table, 1942, walnut, right front airplane dial, raised left grill area w/horizontal cut-outs, 3 knobs, BC, 6 tubes, AC/DC **$50.00**

LLS-179, table, 1942, walnut, right front dial, left cloth grill w/horizontal & vertical bars, 2 knobs, BC, 6 tubes, AC/DC **$45.00**

LM "Stratoliner," table, 1942, plastic, upper front slanted slide rule dial, lower horizontal grill bars, 2 knobs, BC, 5 tubes, AC/DC **$35.00**

LQ "Clipper," table, 1942, plastic, lower front slide rule dial, upper horizontal grill bars, 2 knobs, BC, 5 tubes, AC/DC **$35.00**

LR-147 "Triple Play," portable, 1941, leatherette, lower front slide rule dial, upper horizontal grill bars, handle, 3 knobs, BC, AC/DC/battery **$35.00**

LTF-465, table-R/P, 1942, walnut, right front square dial, left horizontal louvers, 3 knobs, lift top, inner phono, BC, 5 tubes, AC...**$25.00**

LV-186, console-R/P, 1942, wood, upper front slanted dial, center pull-out phono, lower grill area, 4 knobs, 7 tubes, AC **$100.00**

P-100 "Teeny-Weeny," table, 1938, plastic, midget, right front dial, left grill w/2 horizontal bars, 2 knobs, BC, 4 tubes, AC/DC **$75.00**

PL-29 "Playboy," portable, 1939, striped cloth covered square case, front dial & grill, handle, battery **$35.00**

PS-102, table, 1938, plastic, midget, right front dial, left vertical grill bars, 2 knobs, BC, 5 tubes, AC/DC **$75.00**

RBU-175, table, 1946, plastic, upper front slanted slide rule dial, lower horizontal louvers, 2 knobs, BC, AC/DC.............**$40.00**

RBU-176, table, 1946, plastic, upper front slanted slide rule dial, lower horizontal louvers, 2 knobs, BC, AC/DC..$40.00

RBU-177, table, 1946, plastic, upper front slanted slide rule dial, lower horizontal louvers, 2 knobs, BC, AC/DC.............**$40.00**

RBU-207, table, wood, upper front slanted slide rule dial, lower horizontal grill bars, 2 knobs, BC $35.00

RCU-208, table, 1946, wood, right front square dial, curved left side w/vertical louvers, 3 knobs, BC, AC/DC **$60.00**

RDU-209, table, 1946, two-tone wood, upper front slide rule dial, lower horizontal louvers, 3 knobs, BC, AC/DC **$45.00**

RET-210, table, 1947, wood, right front square dial, left cloth grill, 4 knobs, BC, SW, AC **$40.00**

RGMF-230, table-R/P, 1947, wood, right front dial, left horizontal grill bars, 2 knobs, lift top, inner phono, BC, AC...........**$25.00**

RKRU-215, table-R/P, 1946, wood, upper front dial, lower grill, lift top, inner phono, BC, AC/DC **$25.00**

RMR-219, console-R/P, 1947, wood, inner right dial/4 knobs/pushbuttons, left phono, lift top, front grill w/vertical bars, BC, SW, AC **$80.00**

RQU-222, table, 1946, plastic, upper front curved slide rule dial, lower 2-section grill w/horizontal louvers, 3 knobs, BC, AC/DC **$50.00**

RX-223, table, 1947, wood, right front square dial w/plastic escutcheon, left cloth grill w/bars, 2 knobs, BC, battery...**$35.00**

TH-46, table, 1940, wood, right front vertical slide rule dial, left cloth grill, battery **$25.00**

TK-44, table, 1939, walnut w/gold band overlay, right front dial, left horizontal grill bars, 2 knobs, AC **$45.00**

TN-45, table, 1939, wood, right dial panel over large wrap-around front grill, 2 knobs, BC, AC/DC **$50.00**

TNE-60, table-R/P, 1939, wood, lower front square dial, right & left wrap-over cloth grills, 2 knobs, lift top, inner phono, AC **$30.00**

TSA-105 "Cosmo," table, 1939, plastic, right front half-round dial, left horizontal louvers, "Air Magnet" antenna, AC/DC ...**$45.00**

TT-52, table, 1939, walnut, center front slide rule dial, upper wrap-over cloth grill, pushbuttons, 2 knobs, AC **$60.00**

TT-128, table, 1940, wood, right front slide rule dial, rounded left w/horizontal wrap-around grill bars, pushbuttons, 2 knobs, 5 tubes, AC...**$55.00**

TV-48, table, 1939, plastic, small case, center front round dial knob, right & left vertical grill bars, AC/DC **$60.00**

TW-49, table, 1939, plastic, Deco, large round dial knob on right top of case, left horizontal wrap-around grill bars, right front pushbuttons, 5 tubes, AC/DC...................................**$125.00+**

TZ-56, console, 1939, wood, upper front slanted slide rule dial, lower cloth grill w/vertical bars, pushbuttons, 4 knobs, BC, SW, AC...**$125.00**

WAU-243, table, 1939, plastic, Deco, large round dial knob on right top of case, left horizontal wrap-around grill bars, right front pushbuttons, 5 tubes, AC/DC...........................**$125.00+**

WBRU-239, table-R/P, 1948, wood, right front dial, 4 knobs, left grill, lift top, inner phono, BC, AC **$30.00**

WCU-246, radio/lamp, 1948, plastic, controls right & left sides of case, top grill bars, front lamp switch, BC, AC/DC **$70.00**

WDU-233, portable, 1947, two-tone, upper front slide rule dial, lower perforated grill, handle, 2 knobs, BC, 4 tubes, AC/DC/battery **$40.00**

WDU-249, portable, 1948, mottled case w/plastic accents, upper front slide rule dial, lower perforated grill, handle, 2 knobs, BC, AC/DC/battery **$40.00**

WEU-262, table, 1948, plastic, right front dial, left cloth grill, decorative case lines, 4 knobs, BC, FM, AC/DC..................**$50.00**

WGFU-241, table-R/P, 1947, plastic, right front round dial knob, left vertical grill bars, 2 knobs, open top phono, BC, AC **$45.00**

WGFU-242, table-R/P, 1947, plastic, right front round dial knob, left vertical grill bars, 2 knobs, open top phono, BC, AC **$45.00**

WJU-252, table, 1948, plastic, midget, top right dial knob, top left on/off/volume knob, front/back/top grill bars, BC, AC/DC **$90.00**

WKRU-254A, console-R/P, 1948, wood, inner right dial/4 knobs, left phono, lift top, front grill, BC, FM, AC **$60.00**

WLRU-219A, console-R/P, 1948, wood, inner right half-round dial/4 knobs, left phono, lift top, front grill w/vertical columns, BC, FM, AC **$75.00**

YB-299, table, 1950, plastic, right front half-round dial, left horizontal louvers, 2 knobs, BC, AC/DC **$45.00**

SOUND, INC.

Sound, Inc.,
221 East Cullerton Street, Chicago, Illinois

5R2, table, 1947, two-tone, upper right front dial, center horizontal grill bars, 2 pointer knobs, BC, AC/DC **$40.00**

SPARTON

Sparks-Withington Company,
Jackson, Michigan

The Sparks-Withington Company began to manufacture radios in 1926. In the 1930's, their introduction of Deco-styled mirrored radios, along with other Deco cabinet designs by Walter Dorwin Teague, helped make the Sparton line one of the most sought after by collectors of Deco radios. The company produced one of the most expensive-to-own radios in today's collecting world — the 1936 Nocturne, a Deco, 46" round mirrored console which currently sells for over $25,000.

4-6, tombstone, wood, lower front round airplane dial, upper cloth grill w/cut-outs, 5 knobs..**$135.00**

4AW17, table, 1948, plastic, raised top, upper front slanted slide rule dial, lower vertical grill bars, 2 knobs, BC, battery..**$30.00**

4AW17-A, table, 1948, plastic, raised top, upper front slanted slide rule dial, lower vertical grill bars, 2 knobs, BC, battery **$30.00**

5, cathedral, 1931, wood, lower front window dial, upper round cloth grill w/cut-outs, 2 knobs, 5 tubes, AC **$225.00**

5AI16, table, 1947, plastic, raised top, upper front slanted slide rule dial, lower vertical grill bars, 2 knobs, BC, AC/DC $45.00

5AM26-PS, table-R/P, 1946, wood, upper front slide rule dial, lower grill area, 2 knobs, lift top, inner phono, BC, AC ..**$30.00**

5AW06, table, 1946, plastic, upper front slide rule dial, lower horizontal wrap-around louvers, 2 knobs, BC, AC/DC **$45.00**

6-66A, table, 1948, leatherette, right front rectangular dial, left cloth grill, 3 knobs, BC, SW, AC/DC............................**$25.00**

6A66, table, 1948, metal, right front rectangular dial, left round grill area, 3 knobs..$40.00

6AM06, portable, 1948, leatherette, inner right dial, 2 knobs, left grill area, fold-down front, handle, BC, AC/DC/battery **$30.00**

6AW26PA, table-R/P, 1947, wood, inner right slide rule dial/4 knobs, left phono, lift top, front grill area, BC, SW, AC..**$25.00**

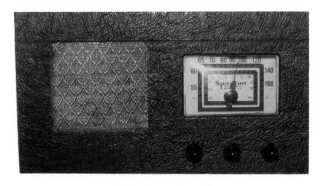

6CL66, table, 1948, leatherette, right front rectangular dial, left cloth grill, 3 knobs $25.00

7-46, console-R/P, 1946, wood, upper front slide rule dial, lower cloth grill w/2 vertical bars, tilt-out phono, 4 knobs, AC $100.00

7AM46, console, 1946, wood, upper front slide rule dial, lower cloth grill w/2 vertical bars, 4 knobs, BC, SW, AC.......$100.00

9, console, 1931, wood, lowboy, front window dial, lower cloth grill w/cut-outs, 2 knobs, 5 tubes, AC................................$125.00

10, tombstone, 1931, wood, shouldered, lower front half-round dial, upper cloth grill w/cut-outs, 3 knobs, 7 tubes, AC........$125.00

10AM76-PA, console-R/P, 1947, wood, inner right slide rule dial, door, left pull-out phono, lower horizontal louvers, BC, SW, FM $90.00

10BW76PA, console-R/P, 1947, wood, inner right slide rule dial/4 knobs, door, left pull-out phono drawer, lower cloth grill w/vertical bars, BC, SW, FM, AC $85.00

14, console, 1932, wood, lowboy, front half-round dial, lower cloth grill w/cut-outs, 3 knobs, 6 legs, 8 tubes, AC $125.00

15, console, 1931, wood, lowboy, front half-round dial, lower cloth grill w/cut-outs, decorative front carvings, 7 tubes, AC ..$150.00

18, console, 1932, wood, lowboy, upper front half-round dial, lower cloth grill w/vertical bars, 4 knobs, 10 tubes, AC $130.00

20, console-R/P, 1932, wood, lowboy, center front half-round dial, lower cloth grill w/cut-outs, lift top, inner phono, AC....$140.00

25, console, 1931, wood, upper front half-round dial, lower cloth grill w/cut-outs, 3 knobs, 10 tubes, AC $140.00

27, console, 1932, wood, inner half-round dial, lower cloth grill w/cut-outs, double front doors, 13 tubes $150.00

28 "Triolian," console, 1932, wood, inner dial & knobs, double front doors, front & side cut-outs, 13 tubes, AC $175.00

53, table, 1934, wood, front round dial, center grill w/cut-outs, 2 knobs, BC, SW, 5 tubes, AC/DC.................................$75.00

57, table, 1934, walnut w/inlay, front round dial, center grill w/cut-outs, 2 knobs, BC, SW, 5 tubes, AC/DC $75.00

62, table, 1926, wood, low rectangular case, center front window dial w/escutcheon, 3 knobs, AC $125.00

65, tombstone, 1934, wood, lower front round airplane dial, upper cloth grill w/cut-outs, 5 knobs, BC, SW, 6 tubes, AC...$125.00

67, tombstone, 1934, two-tone wood, center front round airplane dial, upper cloth grill w/cut-outs, 4 knobs, BC, SW, 6 tubes, AC $125.00

68, console, 1934, wood, lowboy, upper front round airplane dial, lower cloth grill w/cut-outs, 4 knobs, BC, SW, 6 tubes, AC $125.00

69, table, 1928, two-tone wood, low rectangular case, center front window dial w/escutcheon, 3 knobs, lift top..$100.00

72, console, 1933, wood, lowboy, upper front half-round dial, lower cloth grill w/cut-outs, 6 legs, 7 tubes, AC...........$130.00

74, console, 1933, wood, upper front half-round dial, lower cloth grill w/cut-outs, 4 knobs, BC, SW, 9 tubes, AC...........$130.00

75A, tombstone, 1933, wood, lower front half-round dial, upper cloth grill w/cut-outs, 5 knobs, BC, SW, 8 tubes, AC...$130.00

80, console, 1934, wood, upper front round dial, lower cloth grill w/cut-outs, 4 knobs, BC, SW, 8 tubes, AC.................$125.00

83, console, 1934, wood w/inlay, upper front round airplane dial, lower cloth grill with cut-outs, feet, BC, SW, 8 tubes, AC............$130.00

89-A, console, 1928, wood, inner window dial, lower cloth grill w/cut-outs, 3 knobs, double doors, 9 tubes, AC.........$185.00

100, table, 1948, plastic, upper front slide rule dial, lower horizontal wrap-around louvers, 2 knobs, BC, AC/DC $45.00

104, console, 1934, wood, upper front round airplane dial, lower cloth grill with cut-outs, 4 knobs, BC, SW, 10 tubes, AC...........$150.00

132, table, 1950, plastic, oblong case, right front half-round dial, metal perforated grill, 2 knobs, BC, AC/DC...................$60.00

134 "Triolian," console, 1934, walnut, lowboy, inner front dial, lower cloth grill w/cut-outs, 5 knobs, double doors, BC, SW, 13 tubes, AC..$175.00

141A, table, 1950, wood, lower front slanted slide rule dial, large upper grill area, 4 knobs, AM, FM, AC $30.00

141XX, table, 1951, wood, lower front plastic panel w/slide rule dial, large upper grill area, 4 knobs, AM, FM, AC...........$50.00

152, portable, 1950, plastic, inner dial, lower checkered grill, 2 thumbwheel knobs, flip-up front, handle, BC, AC/DC/battery $35.00

232, table, 1953, plastic, oblong case, right front half-round dial, center woven grill area, 2 knobs, BC, AC/DC $60.00

301 "Equasonne," console, 1929, carved wood, highboy, inner dial & knobs, double front doors, lower back panel, AC $650.00

309, portable, 1953, plastic covered, left front dial, center lattice grill, handle, BC, AC/AC/battery $35.00

345, table, 1953, left front round dial, center concentric circular louvers over perforated grill, BC, AC/DC......................$30.00

409-GL, table, 1938, blue mirror glass, 7 sided Deco case, right front dial, left round grill, 2 black feet, 5 tubes, AC/DC..$2,000.00+

410 "Junior," upright table, 1930, wood, arched top, lower front window dial, upper round cloth grill w/cut-outs, finials, feet $250.00

500 "Cloisonne," table, 1939, Catalin, enamel & chrome, Deco, right front slide rule dial, left round cloth grill w/horizontal bars, 2 knobs, AC/DC.....................$2,000.00+

500-C "Cloisonne," table, 1939, Catalin, enamel & chrome, Deco, right front slide rule dial, left round cloth grill w/horizontal bars, 2 knobs, 5 tubes, AC/DC ....$2,000.00+

500-DG, table, 1939, wood w/inlay, step-down sides, right front dial, left vertical grill bars, 2 knobs, 5 tubes, AC/DC $45.00

506 "Bluebird," table, 1936, round blue or peach mirror glass w/chrome accents, Deco, round front dial, feet, 3 knobs, BC, SW, AC ....$3,000.00+

506, table, 1935, wood, center front round airplane dial over cloth grill w/cut-outs, BC, SW, 5 tubes, AC $75.00

516, tombstone, 1935, wood, shouldered, center front round dial, upper cloth grill w/vertical bars, 4 knobs, BC, SW, 5 tubes, AC $110.00

537, upright table, 1936, wood, large center front round dial, top grill, 4 knobs, BC, SW, 5 tubes, AC...............................$85.00

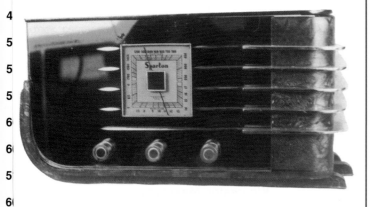

A 557, table, 1936, blue or peach mirror glass, Deco, front square dial, horizontal chrome fins wrap-around right side, black or brown base, 3 knobs, BC, SW, 5 tubes, AC/DC..$2,000.00+

558, table, 1937, blue or peach mirror glass, Deco, front square dial, horizontal chrome fins wrap-around right side, black or brown base, 4 knobs, BC, SW, 5 tubes, AC/DC ....$2,000.00+

567, console, 1936, wood, upper front round dial, lower cloth grlll with cut-outs, BC, SW, 5 tubes, AC...........................$125.00

570-M, table, 1936, wood, right front slide rule dial, raised left grill w/vertical bars, 4 pushbuttons, 3 knobs, BC, SW, AC/DC $70.00

577, console, 1936, wood, upper front round dial, lower cloth grill w/center vertical bars, BC, SW, 5 tubes, AC..............$120.00

589, console, 1930, wood, carved cabinet w/side lion's head decorations, inner dial/3 knobs, double front doors, upper grill area w/ornate cut-outs & pillars $950.00

616, tombstone, 1935, wood, Deco, lower front airplane dial, upper cloth grill w/cut-outs, 4 knobs, BC, SW, 6 tubes, AC $150.00

617, tombstone, 1936, wood, center front round dial, upper cloth grill w/horizontal bars, 4 knobs, BC, SW, 6 tubes, AC..$150.00

637, tombstone, 1937, wood, lower front round dial, upper cloth grill w/4 horizontal bars, 4 knobs $150.00

666, console, 1935, wood, upper front dial, lower cloth grill w/vertical bars, 4 knobs, BC, SW, 6 tubes, AC....................$115.00

STEWART-WARNER
Stewart-Warner Corp.,
1826 Diversey Parkway, Chicago, Illinois

01-5D9, table-R/P, 1939, wood, right front dial, left cloth grill w/horizontal bars, 2 knobs, lift top, inner phono, AC **$35.00**

01-5H7, console, 1939, walnut, upper front slide rule dial, lower cloth grill w/2 vertical bars, pushbuttons, BC, SW, AC **$135.00**

01-6A7, console, 1939, wood, upper front slanted slide rule dial, lower cloth grill w/3 vertical bars, pushbuttons, 4 knobs, BC, SW, AC **$150.00**

01-6B9, console-R/P, 1939, walnut, upper front slide rule dial, lower vertical grill bars, pushbuttons, AC **$150.00**

01-8A7, console, 1939, wood, upper front slide rule dial, lower cloth grill w/vertical bars, pushbuttons, BC, SW, AC...**$150.00**

01-8B7, console, 1940, wood, upper front slide rule dial, lower cloth grill with vertical bars, 8 pushbuttons, 8 tubes **$150.00**

01-611, table, 1939, wood, right front dial, raised left horizontal louvers, pushbuttons, 4 knobs, AC..........................**$60.00**

01-817, console, 1939, wood, upper front slide rule dial, lower cloth grill w/2 vertical bars, pushbuttons, 2 band, 8 tubes, AC **$160.00**

02-411, portable, 1939, striped cloth covered, right front dial, left grill, handle, 2 knobs, battery **$25.00**

03-5C1, table, 1939, two-tone wood, right front dial, left horizontal louvers, 2 knobs, AC/DC **$40.00**

03-5E1, upright table, 1939, plastic, center front airplane dial, upper horizontal louvers, 7 pushbuttons, 2 knobs, 5 tubes, AC/DC **$110.00**

03-5K3 "The Magician," table, 1939, plastic, streamlined, right front dial knob, rounded left w/horizontal wrap-around louvers, AC...**$85.00**

07-5B, table, 1939, plastic, Deco, right front dial, left round grill w/"wavy" cut-outs, 7 tubes, AC/DC **$225.00**

07-5B3Q "Dionne Quints," table-N, 1939, plastic, Deco, decals of quints, right front dial, left round grill w/"wavy" cut-outs, 7 tubes, AC/DC **$1,000.00**

07-5R3, table, 1940, ivory plastic, streamlined, right front slide rule dial, rounded left w/horizontal wrap-around louvers, 2 knobs, 5 tubes **$75.00**

07-51H, table, 1940, plastic, streamlined, right front dial, rounded left w/horizontal wrap-around louvers, 2 knobs, BC **$85.00**

07-55BK, bed, 1939, wood, bed made by Jiranek, waterfall headboard w/built-in radio, large dial knob, grill cut-outs, BC, AC/DC...**$250.00**

07-512 "Campus," table, 1939, plastic, streamlined, right front dial, rounded left w/horizontal wrap-around louvers, optional school letters or initials, 2 knobs, BC, 5 tubes, AC/DC...**$85.00**

07-513 "Gulliver's Travels," table-N, 1939, plastic, streamlined, decals of Gulliver's Travels, right front dial, rounded left w/horizontal wrap-around louvers, 2 knobs, AC..........**$625.00**

07-513Q "Dionne Quints," table-N, 1938, plastic, streamlined, decal of quints, right front dial, rounded left w/horizontal wrap-around louvers, 2 knobs, AC/DC **$1,000.00**

07-514, table, 1939, two-tone wood, Deco, right front dial, left horizontal wrap-around louvers, AC/DC **$65.00**

07-516 "Fireside," chairside, 1939, wood, slanted front dial, horizontal louvers, lower magazine shelf, 4 legs, AC/DC..**$100.00**

4B4, table, 1940, two-tone wood, center front slide rule dial, right & left grills w/horizontal bars, 2 knobs, battery **$45.00**

4C1, table, 1940, wood, right front dial, left cloth grill w/cut-outs, 2 knobs, 4 tubes, battery **$30.00**

4D1, table, 1940, two-tone wood, right front dial, left cloth grill w/cut-outs & vertical bars, 2 knobs..............................**$45.00**

5R7, table, 1940, walnut, center front slide rule dial, right & left grills w/vertical bars, 2 knobs, 5 tubes, AC/DC **$60.00**

5V9, table-R/P, 1941, wood, right front dial, left cloth grill w/horizontal bars, lift top, inner phono, AC **$30.00**

6T8, table-R/P, 1940, inner right dial, left grill, 4 knobs, fold-down front, lift top, inner phono, handle, BC, AC **$30.00**

6U2GA, portable, 1942, upper front slanted slide rule dial, lower grill area, handle, 3 knobs, 6 tubes, AC/DC/battery **$30.00**

9B7, console, 1940, wood, upper front slide rule dial, lower cloth grill w/vertical center divider & bars, pushbuttons, 4 knobs, BC, SW, 9 tubes, AC **$125.00**

13-5U, table, 1939, two-tone wood, right front dial, rounded left grill w/cut-outs, 2 knobs **$45.00**

50, console, 1932, wood, lowboy, upper front dial, lower cloth grill w/cut-outs, 6 legs, BC, SW, 11 tubes.........................**$160.00**

51, console, 1932, wood, lowboy, inner dial/knobs, double doors, lower cloth grill w/cut-outs, 5 legs, BC, SW, 11 tubes ..**$165.00**

51T56, table, 1948, wood, upper front slanted slide rule dial, large lower grill area, 2 knobs, BC, AC/DC **$30.00**

51T136, table, 1947, wood, upper front slanted slide rule dial, large lower cloth grill, 2 knobs, BC, AC/DC...................**$30.00**

61T16, table, 1946, upper front slanted slide rule dial, lower cloth grill, 3 knobs, BC, AC/DC **$35.00**

61T26, table, 1946, plastic, upper front slide rule dial, lower horizontal louvers, 3 knobs, BC...**$35.00**

62T36, table, 1946, Catalin, upper front slanted slide rule dial, lower inset horizontal louvers, 3 knobs, BC, SW **$700.00**

62TC16, table, 1946, wood, right front slide rule dial, left wrap-around cloth grill w/horizontal bars, 6 pushbuttons, 4 knobs **$65.00**

62TC18, table, 1946, wood, right front slide rule dial, left cloth wrap-around grill w/horizontal bars, pushbuttons, 4 knobs..**$65.00**

72CR26, console-R/P, 1947, wood, inner right slide rule dial/4 knobs/6 pushbuttons, door, left pull-out phono drawer, BC, SW, AC...**$75.00**

91-511, table, 1938, walnut, right front slide rule dial, left horizontal louvers, pushbuttons, 2 knobs **$50.00**

91-512, table, 1938, wood, right front slide rule dial, left wrap-around horizontal louvers, 4 pushbuttons, 2 knobs, 5 tubes, AC **$50.00**

91-513, table, 1938, wood, triangular case, front slide rule dial, 4 pushbuttons, cloth grills w/cut-outs on all four sides, 5 tubes, AC **$185.00**

91-514, table, 1938, black & ivory, Deco, right front slide rule dial, left vertical grill bars, pushbuttons, 2 knobs, AC **$75.00**

91-531, upright table, 1938, walnut, center front dial, upper cloth grill w/vertical bars, pushbuttons, BC, SW, 5 tubes, AC ..**$75.00**

91-536, chairside, 1938, wood, half-round, top dial/pushbuttons/knobs, front grill w/horizontal bars, BC, SW, 5 tubes, AC..**$150.00**

91-537, console, 1938, wood, upper front dial, lower cloth grill w/center vertical bar, pushbuttons, 2 knobs, 5 tubes, AC..**$125.00**

91-617, console, 1938, wood, upper front dial, lower cloth grill w/center divider, pushbuttons, 4 knobs, BC, SW, 6 tubes, AC..**$125.00**

91-621, table, 1938, wood, right front dial, left horizontal wrap-around louvers, tuning eye, pushbuttons, BC, SW, 6 tubes, AC **$75.00**

91-627, console, 1938, wood, upper front dial, lower cloth grill w/horizontal bars, tuning eye, pushbuttons, 6 tubes, AC...**$130.00**

91-817, console, 1938, wood, upper front horizontal dial, lower cloth grill w/center vertical divider, base, tuning eye, pushbuttons, 3 knobs, BC, SW, 8 tubes, AC **$165.00**

91-1117, console, 1938, wood, upper front dial, lower horizontal grill bars, tuning eye, pushbuttons, 4 knobs, BC, SW, 11 tubes, AC **$155.00**

95-514, table, two-tone wood, Deco, upper right front slide rule dial, left cloth grill w/vertical bars, 4 pushbuttons, 2 knobs **$115.00**

97-521, table, 1938, walnut, right front slide rule dial, left horizontal louvers, pushbuttons, 2 knobs................................**$50.00**

97-562, table, 1939, plastic, Deco, right front dial, left round grill w/"wavy" cut-outs, 5 tubes, AC/DC **$225.00**

300, table, 1925, wood, low rectangular case, front panel w/3 half-round dials, 5 tubes, battery **$95.00**

303, table, wood, rectangular case, slanted black 3 dial front panel, lift top, 5 tubes **$130.00**

305 "Aeromaster," table, 1925, wood, rectangular case, slanted 3 dial front panel, 5 tubes, battery **$130.00**

310, console, 1925, wood, inner panel w/3 half-round dials, fold-down front, upper cloth grill w/cut-outs, lower storage, battery...**$185.00**

325, table, 1925, wood, low rectangular case, metal front panel w/3 half-round pointer dials, lift top, battery.................**$115.00**

350, table, 1926, wood, high rectangular case, center front dial w/escutcheon, lower cloth grill w/cut-outs, 3 knobs, battery...**$150.00**

355, console, 1926, wood, upper front dial w/escutcheon, center cloth grill w/cut-outs, lower storage, battery **$175.00**

360, console, 1926, wood, inner dial w/escutcheon, fold-down front, upper left cloth grill w/cut-outs, storage, battery...**$185.00**

385, table, 1927, wood, low rectangular case, center front dial, 6 tubes, battery...**$95.00**

520, console, 1927, wood, lowboy, upper front window dial, lower round metal grill w/dancing girl cut-outs, 3 knobs, 6 tubes..**$300.00**

801, table, 1928, metal, low rectangular case, center front dial, 2 knobs, switch, 6 tubes, AC **$85.00**

802, table, 1928, metal, low rectangular case w/top built-in speaker, center front dial, 2 knobs, switch, 6 tubes, AC **$125.00**

900, console, 1929, walnut, lowboy, upper front window dial w/escutcheon, lower round cloth grill w/cut-outs, AC ..**$135.00**

900AC, table, 1929, metal, low rectangular case, center front window dial, lift-off top, 3 knobs, AC **$85.00**

1101, table, 1933, wood, rounded top, center front window dial, right & left cloth grills w/cut-outs, 3 knobs, 10 tubes, AC..........**$85.00**

1102, console, 1933, wood, lowboy, upper front window dial, lower cloth grill w/cut-outs, 3 knobs, 10 tubes **$130.00**

1104, side table, 1933, wood, Duncan Phyfe-style, inner window dial, right & left cloth grills w/cut-outs, fold-down front, 10 tubes, AC.......**$135.00**

1105, console, 1933, wood, small French commode-style case, inner window dial, fold-down front, 2 lower drawers, 10 tubes, AC........**$135.00**

1106, console/bookcase, 1933, wood, shouldered top, inner window dial, double doors, upper & lower bookshelves, 10 tubes, AC **$225.00**

1111, table, 1933, walnut, front dial, center grill w/figural cut-out, fluted metal wrap-over bands, 2 knobs, 6 tubes, AC...**$180.00**

1116, table-N, 1933, red leatherette, looks like stack of 3 books, inner dial and "S/W" cut-out, fold-open front, 2 knobs, 6 tubes **$225.00**

1117, table-N, 1933, green leatherette, looks like stack of 3 books, inner dial and "S/W" cut-out, fold-open front, 2 knobs, 6 tubes......**$225.00**

1118, table-N, 1933, brown leather, looks like stack of 3 books, inner dial and "S/W" cut-out, fold-open front, 2 knobs, 6 tubes...**$225.00**

1119, table, 1933, jade green enamel, front dial, center grill w/figural cut-out, fluted silver metal wrap-over bands, 2 knobs, 6 tubes, AC...**$230.00**

1152, side table, 1933, wood, Duncan Phyfe-style, inner dial & cloth grill w/cut-outs, fold-down front, 6 tubes, AC **$110.00**

1153, side table, 1933, wood, Duncan Phyfe-style, inner window dial, right & left cloth grills w/cut-outs, fold-down front, 6 tubes, AC...**$135.00**

1154, console, 1933, wood, small French commode-style case, inner window dial, fold-down front, 2 lower drawers, 6 tubes, AC...**$135.00**

1155, table, 1933, wood, front dial, center cloth grill w/cut-outs, fluted side panels, 6 tubes, AC......................................**$65.00**

1262 "Stuart," tombstone, 1934, wood, lower front quarter-round dial, upper cloth grill w/cut-outs, 4 knobs, 7 tubes, AC ..**$150.00**

1264, console, 1934, wood, lowboy, upper front quarter-round dial, lower cloth grill, 6 legs, BC, SW, AC...................**$140.00**

1265, console, 1934, wood, lowboy, upper front quarter-round dial, lower cloth grill w/cut-outs, 6 legs, BC, SW, 7 tubes, AC...**$140.00**

1421, table, 1936, two-tone wood, center front round dial, upper right cloth grill w/cut-outs, 2 knobs, 5 tubes **$70.00**

1883, chairside, 1937, walnut, half-round case, top dial under glass, front cloth grill w 3/horizontal bars, 6 tubes, AC/DC..**$185.00**

3041, table, 1937, rectangular case lays down or stands up, slide rule dial, wrap-around grill w/cut-outs, 5 tubes..............**$75.00**

9000-B, table, 1947, wood, upper front slanted slide rule dial, lower horizontal louvers, 3 knobs, BC, SW, AC/DC **$55.00**

9001-E, end table, 1946, wood, drop leaf-style, inner slide rule dial, 4 knobs, pushbuttons, fold-down front, BC, SW, AC....**$125.00**

9001-F, end table, 1946, wood, inner slide rule dial, pushbuttons, 4 knobs, fold-down front, lower 4-legged base...........**$135.00**

9002-A, table, 1948, plastic, upper front curved slide rule dial, large lower grill area, 3 knobs, BC, AC/DC **$40.00**

9002-B, table, 1948, plastic, upper front slanted slide rule dial, lower horizontal louvers, 3 knobs, BC **$40.00**

9007-F, portable, 1946, luggage-style, inner right dial, left grill, 3 knobs, fold down front, handle, BC, AC/DC/battery **$25.00**

9150-D, console-R/P, 1950, wood, right front tilt-out dial & knobs, left pull-down phono door, lower storage & grill **$110.00**

9151-A, table, 1950, plastic, right front raised see-through dial overlaps checkered grill, 2 knobs, AM, FM, AC/DC **$35.00**

9152-A, table, 1950, plastic, right round dial over vertical front grill bars, 2 knobs, feet, BC, AC/DC...................................**$30.00**

9152-B, table, 1950, plastic, right round dial over vertical front grill bars, 2 knobs, feet, BC, AC/DC...................................**$30.00**

9153-A, table, 1950, plastic, lower right front dial knob, large upper perforated metal grill, BC, AC/DC/battery **$35.00**

9154-C, console-R/P, 1951, wood, upper front dial, center pull-out phono drawer, lower grill, 3 knobs, BC, AC..................**$50.00**

9160-AU, table, 1952, plastic, right front round dial, left lattice grill, 2 knobs, BC, AC/DC **$30.00**

9162, table-C, 1952, plastic, left front half-round dial over alarm clock, upper horizontal bars, lower right circular cut-outs, feet, BC, AC..$30.00

9165-A, table, 1953, plastic, right front half-round dial over dotted grill area, 2 knobs, feet, BC **$25.00**

9170-B "Gadabout," portable, 1954, plastic, top dial & volume knobs, 2-section front lattice grill, fold-down handle, BC, AC/DC/battery **$30.00**

9170-D "Gadabout," portable, 1954, plastic, top dial & volume knobs, 2-section front lattice grill, fold-down handle, BC, AC/DC/battery **$30.00**

9178-C, table-R/P, 1955, wood, right side dial knob, large front grill area, lift top, inner phono, BC, AC **$25.00**

9180-H, table, 1954, plastic, right front raised round dial, left recessed lattice grill, 2 knobs, BC **$30.00**

A6-1Q "Dionne Quints," table-N, 1938, plastic, decals of Dionne quints, top thumbwheel knobs, wrap-over vertical bars **$1,000.00**

1401, tombstone, 1935, two-tone wood, 2 lower front windows w/escutcheon, upper cloth grill w/cut-outs, 2 knobs, AC $140.00

A51T3 "Air Pal," table, 1947, plastic, upper front slide rule dial, lower vertical grill bars, 2 large top knobs, BC, AC/DC..**$100.00**

A61CR3, console, 1948, wood, upper front recessed slanted dial, center pull-out phono drawer, lower grill, 3 knobs, BC, AC **$50.00**

A61P1, portable, 1948, leatherette, inner right dial, left vertical grill bars, 3 knobs, fold-down front, handle, BC, AC/DC/battery **$40.00**

A72T3, table, 1948, wood, upper front slanted slide rule dial, lower criss-cross grill, 3 knobs, AM, FM, AC/DC..........**$35.00**

A92CR6, console-R/P, 1947, wood, inner right slide rule dial/4 knobs/6 pushbuttons, door, left pull-out phono drawer, lower criss-cross grill, BC, FM, AC...**$75.00**

B51T2 "Air Pal," table, 1949, plastic, upper front slanted slide rule dial, lower grill area w/"X," 2 thumbwheel knobs on case top, BC, AC/DC **$75.00**

B61T1, table, 1949, plastic, upper front slide rule dial, left wraparound horizontal louvers, 3 knobs, BC, AC/DC **$40.00**

B72CR1, console-R/P, 1948, wood, upper front wrap-over slide rule dial, center front pull-out phono drawer, lower grill area, 4 knobs, BC, FM, AC...**$60.00**

B92CR1, console-R/P, 1949, wood, inner right recessed dial/3 knobs, door, left lift top, inner phono, lower front criss-cross grill, BC, FM, AC **$55.00**

C51T1, table, 1948, plastic, right front half-round dial, left horizontal wrap-around louvers, 2 knobs, BC, AC/DC **$55.00**

C51T2, table, 1948, plastic, right front half-round dial, left horizontal wrap-around louvers, 2 knobs, BC, AC/DC **$55.00**

R-104, chairside, wood, front half-round dial, lower right & left side cloth grills w/cut-outs, right & left side handle **$185.00**

R-109-A, cathedral, 1932, wood, center front window dial, upper cloth grill w/cut-outs, fluted columns, 3 knobs, 6 tubes, AC **$215.00**

R-110-A, tombstone, two-tone wood, center front window dial w/escutcheon, upper cloth grill w/cut-outs, 4 knobs..**$160.00**

R-110-AT, table, 1933, wood, center front window dial w/escutcheon, right & left cloth grills w/cut-outs, 2 speakers, 4 knobs, 10 tubes **$100.00**

R-116-AH, table, 1933, wood, right front dial & volume windows, left cloth grill w/horizontal bars, 2 knobs, AC..**$70.00**

R-172-A, table, wood, right front round black dial, left front & side cloth grills w/vertical bars, 4 knobs, BC, SW **$55.00**

R-192 "Good Companion," table, 1936, Deco, round case design with base, upper front half round dial, center circular grill area, 4 tubes..**$400.00**

R-1235A, tombstone, 1935, wood, lower front dial & knobs, upper cloth grill w/aluminum cut-outs, top fluting..................**$215.00**

R-1262A, tombstone, two-tone wood, step-down sides, lower front quarter-round dial, upper cloth grill w/cut-outs, 4 knobs, AC **$235.00**

R-1301-A, tombstone, wood, rounded/step-down top, lower front round dial, upper cloth grill w/cut-outs, 4 knobs **$160.00**

R-1361-A, tombstone, 1934, two-tone wood, center front round dial, upper cloth grill w/cut-outs, 4 knobs ...$160.00

R-1725-A, console, wood, upper front round black dial, lower cloth grill w/3 bars, 4 knobs, BC, SW $135.00

R-3043-A, table, wood, rectangular case lays down or stands up, slide rule dial, cloth grill w/bars, 2 knobs $75.00

STRATOVOX
Grossman Music Co.,
210 Prospect Street, Cleveland, Ohio

579-1-58A, table, 1946, wood, upper front slanted slide rule dial, lower cloth grill w/2 horizontal bars, 2 knobs, BC, AC/DC $40.00

STROMBERG-CARLSON
Stromberg-Carlson Company,
100 Carlson Road, Rochester, New York

Stromberg-Carlson was formed in 1894 for the production of telephone equipment. The company began to make radio parts and by 1923 was producing complete radios. Stromberg-Carlson was well-known for its commitment to quality and their products are often called the "Rolls Royce" of radios.

1-A, table, 1924, wood, low rectangular case, 3 dial black Bakelite front panel, 5 tubes, battery $175.00

1-B, table, 1924, wood, low rectangular case, 3 dial black Bakelite front panel, lift top, 5 tubes, battery..........$175.00

2, console, 1924, wood, inner three dial panel, fold-down front, lower storage, 5 tubes, battery $250.00

19, console, 1931, wood, lowboy, upper front window dial, lower cloth grill w/cut-outs, 9 tubes, AC $165.00

20, console, 1931, wood, highboy, upper front window dial, lower cloth grill w/cut-outs, stretcher base, 9 tubes, AC $170.00

22, console, 1931, walnut, lowboy, inner window dial, lower cloth grill w/cut-outs, double doors, carved legs, 10 tubes, AC..$190.00

24, console-R/P, 1932, wood, lowboy, inner window dial, lower cloth grill w/cut-outs, double doors, lift top, inner phono, 6 legs, 10 tubes, AC $190.00

25, console, 1931, wood, lowboy, upper front window dial, lower cloth grill w/cut-outs, stretcher base, 8 tubes, AC $150.00

27, console, 1931, walnut, highboy, inner window dial, lower cloth grill w/vertical bars, double doors, 6 legs, AC $185.00

37, console, 1932, walnut finish, lowboy, upper front window dial, lower cloth grill w/cut-outs, 3 knobs, AC.....................$150.00

38, console, 1932, wood, lowboy, upper front window dial, lower cloth grill w/cut-outs, bowed legs, 9 tubes, AC............$170.00

39, console, 1932, wood, lowboy, inner window dial, lower cloth grill w/circular cut-outs, double doors, stretcher base, 10 tubes, AC..$180.00

40, console, 1932, walnut, inner window dial, lower cloth grill w/cut-outs, 3 knobs, double doors, AC......................$165.00

41, console-R/P, 1932, wood, lowboy, inner window dial, lower cloth grill w/cut-outs, double doors, lift top, inner phono, 6 legs, 9 tubes, AC $175.00

49, console, 1933, wood, lowboy, inner window dial, lower cloth grill w/circular cut-outs, double doors, 11 tubes, AC ...$200.00

51, console-R/P, 1933, wood, lowboy, inner window dial, lower cloth grill w/cut-outs, double doors, lift top, inner phono, 6 legs, 11 tubes, AC $200.00

52, console, 1933, wood, lowboy, inner window dial, lower cloth grill w/cut-outs, double doors, carved legs, 4 knobs, 12 tubes, AC $200.00

54, console-R/P, 1933, wood, lowboy, inner window dial, lower cloth grill w/cut-outs, double doors, lift top, inner phono, 6 legs, 12 tubes, AC $200.00

55 "**Te-lek-tor-et,**" table/remote speaker, 1933, wood, chest-type table set w/inner dial & knobs, separate speaker case, 8 tubes, AC..$275.00

56, console, 1933, wood, Deco, hinged front door hides knobs & dial, lower cloth grill w/Deco cut-outs, 8 tubes, AC $225.00

56-R, console, 1933, wood, Deco, removable tuning mechanism for remote control, hinged front door hides knobs & dial, lower cloth grill w/Deco cut-outs, 8 tubes, AC $250.00

58-L, console, 1935, wood, upper front octagonal airplane dial, lower cloth grill w/cut-outs, 3 knobs, BC, SW, 6 tubes, AC..$135.00

58-T, tombstone, 1935, wood, lower front octagonal dial, upper cloth grill w/vertical bars, 3 knobs, BC, SW, AC.........$145.00

58-W, console, 1935, wood, upper front octagonal airplane dial, lower cloth grill w/cut-outs, 3 knobs, BC, SW, 6 tubes, AC $135.00

60-H "**Treasure,**" console, 1934, walnut finish, highboy, inner window dial, lower cloth grill w/vertical bars, double sliding doors, 6 legs, BC, SW, 7 tubes, AC $175.00

60-L "**Treasure,**" console, 1934, walnut, upper front window dial, lower cloth grill w/vertical bars, 4 knobs, BC, SW, 7 tubes, AC..$130.00

60-M, console, 1935, wood, lowboy, upper front dial, lower cloth grill w/cut-outs, 6 legs, BC, SW, AC $145.00

60-PR "**Treasure,**" console-R/P, 1935, walnut, inner front window dial & phono, double doors, lower cloth grill w/vertical bars, BC, SW, 7 tubes, AC...$160.00

60-T "**Treasure,**" tombstone, two-tone wood, center front window dial, upper cloth grill w/2 horizontal bars and cut-outs, 4 knobs, BC, SW, 7 tubes, AC $135.00

61-H, table, 1935, wood, Deco, front off-center octagonal dial, right & left cloth grills w/cut-outs, 3 knobs, AC **$75.00**

61-L, console, 1936, wood, upper front octagonal airplane dial, lower cloth grill w/cut-outs, 3 knobs, BC, SW, 6 tubes, AC **$140.00**

61-N, console, 1936, wood, upper front octagonal dial, lower cloth grill w/cut-outs, feet **$140.00**

61-T, tombstone, 1935, wood, lower front octagonal dial, upper cloth grill w/vertical bars, 3 knobs, BC, SW, AC **$135.00**

61-U, tombstone, 1935, wood, step-down top, lower front octagonal airplane dial, upper 5-section cloth grill, 3 knobs..$140.00

61-W, console, 1935, wood, upper front octagonal airplane dial, lower cloth grill w/cut-outs, 3 knobs, BC, SW, 6 tubes, AC **$140.00**

61-Y, table, 1936, wood, off center octagonal airplane dial, right & left cloth grill areas w/bars, AC/DC...............................**$60.00**

61-Z, console, 1936, wood, upper front octagonal airplane dial, lower cloth grill w/cut-outs, AC/DC **$150.00**

62, console, 1935, walnut, upper front octagonal dial, lower cloth grill w/cut-outs, 5 knobs, BC, SW, 8 tubes, AC **$160.00**

63, console, 1935, wood, upper front octagonal dial, lower cloth grill w/cut-outs, feet, 5 knobs, BC, SW, 8 tubes, AC ...**$160.00**

64, console, 1934, wood, Deco, upper front dial, lower cloth grill w/cut-outs, 5 knobs, feet, 8 tubes, AC.........................**$160.00**

65 "Te-lek-tor-et," table/remote speaker, 1935, wood, chest-type table set w/inner dial & knobs, separate speaker case, BC, 9 tubes, AC...**$275.00**

68, console, 1934, wood, Deco, upper front octagonal airplane dial, lower cloth grill w/cut-outs, tuning eye, 4 knobs, BC, SW, 10 tubes, AC..**$190.00**

68R, console, 1935, wood, lowboy, inner dial & knobs, double front doors, 6 legs, stretcher base, BC, SW, AC **$150.00**

70, console, 1935, wood, lowboy, inner dial & knobs, double front doors, lower cloth grill w/cut-outs, 2 speakers, 6 legs, BC, SW, 13 tubes, AC..**$225.00**

72, console-R/P, 1935, wood, inner dial & phono, double front doors, lower vertical grill bars, 2 speakers, 6 feet, BC, SW, 13 tubes, AC..**$225.00**

74, console-R/P, 1935, wood, inner dial & phono, double front doors, lower vertical grill bars, 2 speakers, 6 feet, BC, SW, 16 tubes, AC..**$300.00**

80, console, 1936, wood, upper front octagonal airplane dial, lower cloth grill w/vertical bars, 6 feet, 9 tubes, AC.....**$170.00**

82, console, 1935, walnut, upper front octagonal airplane dial, lower cloth grill w/cut-outs, tuning eye, 4 knobs, BC, SW, 10 tubes, AC..**$185.00**

83, console, 1935, walnut, upper front octagonal airplane dial, lower cloth grill w/cut-outs, tuning eye, 4 knobs, BC, SW, 11 tubes, AC..**$185.00**

84, console, 1935, wood, upper front octagonal airplane dial, lower cloth grill w/cut-outs, tuning eye, 6 feet, BC, SW, 12 tubes, AC..**$200.00**

115, console, 1936, wood, upper front octagonal dial, lower cloth grill w/cut-outs, BC, SW, 7 tubes, battery **$110.00**

125-H, table, 1936, two-tone wood, right front octagonal dial, left cloth grill w/vertical bars, BC, SW, AC **$60.00**

130-H, table, 1936, wood, front off-center octagonal dial, left cloth grill w/crossed bars, BC, SW, AC.................................**$60.00**

130-J "Treasure Chest," table, 1937, wood, Deco, step-down top, right front octagonal dial, left vertical grill bars, 4 knobs, BC, SW ..**$110.00**

130-L, console, 1936, wood, upper front octagonal dial, lower cloth grill w/2 vertical bars, BC, SW, 7 tubes, AC........**$135.00**

130-M, console, 1936, wood, upper front octagonal dial, lower cloth grill w/vertical bars, BC, SW, 8 tubes, AC...........**$140.00**

130-R, table, 1936, two-tone wood, Deco, front off-center octagonal dial, left grill, 4 knobs, BC, SW, AC **$85.00**

130-U, tombstone, 1936, wood, lower front octagonal dial, upper cloth grill w/horizontal bars, 4 knobs, BC, SW, 7 tubes, AC..**$135.00**

140-H, table, 1936, wood, rectangular case, front octagonal dial, left horizontal louvers, 4 knobs, BC, SW, AC **$75.00**

140-L, console, 1936, wood, upper front octagonal dial, lower cloth grill w/vertical bars, tuning eye, 4 knobs, BC, SW, 9 tubes, AC **$160.00**

140-M, console, 1937, wood, upper front octagonal dial, center cloth grill w/horizontal bars, tuning eye, 4 knobs, feet ..**$185.00**

140-P, console, 1936, wood, front octagonal dial, lower cloth grill w/vertical bars, tuning eye, feet, 9 tubes **$175.00**

145-L, console, 1936, wood, upper front dial, lower cloth grill w/cut-outs, feet, BC, SW, 10 tubes, AC **$180.00**

145-SP, console-R/P, 1937, wood, front dial w/escutcheon, lower cloth grill w/center vertical bars, tuning eye, 5 knobs, inner phono **$170.00**

150-L, console, 1936, wood, upper front dial, lower cloth grill, 5 knobs, feet, BC, SW, 12 tubes, AC **$200.00**

160-L, console, 1936, wood, upper front dial, lower "U"-shaped cloth grill, feet, BC, SW, 14 tubes, AC.......................**$225.00**

225-H, table, 1937, wood, right front octagonal dial, left cloth grill w/floral cut-outs, 4 knobs, BC, SW, AC $85.00

228-H, table, 1937, wood, right front octagonal dial, left cloth grill w/vertical bars, 4 knobs, BC, SW, AC **$75.00**

228-L, console, 1937, wood, upper front octagonal dial, lower cloth grill w/vertical bars, 4 knobs, BC, SW, 6 tubes, AC **$135.00**

1210-H "Courier," table, 1948, two-tone wood, 3 right front dials, left cloth criss-cross grill, 4 knobs, BC, 2FM $45.00

1210PLM, console-R/P, 1948, wood, 3 inner right dials/4 knobs, door, left pull-out phono drawer, lower criss-cross grill, BC, 2FM, 11 tubes, AC **$110.00**

1220-PL, console-R/P, 1948, wood, inner right slide rule dial, left phono, lift top, lower front criss-cross grill, BC, SW, AC ..$60.00

1235-PLM, console-R/P, 1948, wood, inner right slide rule dial/pushbuttons/knobs, door, left pull-out phono drawer, BC, 2SW, 2FM, 16 tubes, AC..**$125.00**

1400, table, 1949, plastic, raised top, upper front slide rule dial, lower horizontal wrap-around louvers, BC, AC/DC **$50.00**

1407PFM, console-R/P, 1949, wood, inner right slide rule dial, left pull-out phono drawer, lower storage & grill, double front doors, BC, FM, AC **$95.00**

1409PGM, console-R/P, 1949, wood, inner right slide rule dial, door, left pull-out phono drawer, BC, FM, 14 tubes, AC...........**$110.00**

1500, table, 1951, plastic, raised top, upper front slide rule dial, lower horizontal wrap-around louvers, 2 knobs, BC, AC/DC **$50.00**

1500-HR "Dynatomic," table, maroon plastic, raised top, upper front curved slide rule dial, lower horizontal wrap-around louvers, 2 knobs, AC **$50.00**

1507, console-R/P, 1951, wood, inner right slide rule dial/4 knobs, door, left pull-out phono drawer, lower criss-cross grill, BC, FM, AC **$80.00**

1608, console-R/P, 1951, wood, inner right slide rule dial/5 knobs, left phono, lower storage & grill, double doors, BC, AC...**$60.00**

AWP-8, portable, 1956, inner slide rule dial, fold-up front w/world map, handle, 8 band, 6 tubes, AC/DC/battery............**$100.00**

C-1, table-C, 1951, plastic, right front dial, left alarm clock, center checkered panel, BC, AC **$40.00**

C-3, table-C, 1955, plastic, right side dial knob, left front clock, right circular louvers, BC, 5 tubes, AC **$35.00**

C-5 Deluxe, table-C, 1955, plastic, right side dial knob, left front alarm clock, right perforated grill area, BC, 5 tubes, AC **$25.00**

EP-2, portable, 1955, top dial and on/off/volume knobs, front grill w/decorative "V," rounded sides, handle, BC, 4 tubes, AC/DC/battery **$40.00**

FR-711M, console-R/P, 1958, wood, inner right dial, left phono, lift top, large front grill, legs, BC, FM, 11 tubes, AC **$40.00**

SR-407, table, 1957, center front slide rule dial, 4 knobs, 4 push-buttons, high fidelity, AM, FM, 12 tubes, AC **$25.00**

T-4, table, 1955, plastic, right side dial & volume knobs, front brick-like grill panel, BC, 5 tubes, AC/DC **$35.00**

SUPREME (LIPAN)
Aim Industries,
41 Union Square, New York, New York

750, table-R/P, 1949, leatherette, inner right dial, 4 knobs, phono, lift top, BC, 5 tubes, AC **$15.00**

SYLVANIA
Sylvania Electric Products (Colonial Radio & TV),
254 Rand Street, Buffalo, New York

FR-506 "Jupiter," console-R/P, 1957, wood, inner dial/knobs/phono, lower front grill panels, feet, AM, FM, AC **$70.00**

5T13, table, 1961, plastic, wedge-shaped case, center front round dial overlaps vertical bars, left grill area, 2 knobs, BC **$25.00**

430L, portable, 1952, leatherette, center front panel w/round dial overlaps cloth grill, handle, 2 knobs, BC, AC/DC/battery **$25.00**

433YE, portable, 1955, top dial & on/off/volume knobs, large front checkered grill area, handle, BC, AC/DC/battery **$25.00**

510B, table, 1950, plastic, raised top area, right front round dial overlaps horizontal louvers, 2 knobs, BC, AC/DC $30.00

511B, table, 1952, plastic, right front round dial, bowed front panel with checkered grill, BC, AC/DC.................................$20.00

519, table, plastic, right side dial knob, left side on/off/volume knob, front horizontal grill bars, BC $20.00

540MA "Tune-Riser," table-C, 1951, plastic, upper right front slide rule dial, right & left horizontal grill bars, center alarm clock, 4 knobs, BC, AC..$35.00

542GR, table-C, 1952, plastic, lower front slide rule dial, large upper alarm clock face, side horizontal bars, BC, AC ...$30.00

1102, table, 1957, plastic, right side dial knob, left side on/off/volume knob & switch, front lattice grill, BC, AC/DC $25.00

2108, table-C, 1959, plastic, right side round dial knob, left front alarm clock, right horizontal bars, BC, 4 tubes, AC.......$15.00

2109TU, table-C, 1959, plastic, lower right front round dial knob overlaps horizontal wrap-around louvers, left alarm clock, BC, 5 tubes, AC...$20.00

2302H, table-C, 1957, plastic, lower center front slide rule dial, upper alarm clock w/day-date, side knob, BC, 5 tubes, AC...$25.00

3303TA, portable, 1957, leather, center front round compass over grill, right & left side knobs, strap, BC, 4 tubes, AC/DC/battery..$45.00

4501, table-R/P, 1958, two-tone, top dial, wrap-over front grill, 3 knobs, lift top, inner phono, handle, BC, 6 tubes, AC....$20.00

AK17, table-C, 1963, plastic, right front see-through panel w/inner vertical slide rule dial & alarm clock, left lattice grill area, BC...$20.00

Z5T17, table, plastic, center front dial panel overlaps checkered grill area w/upper right logo, feet, 2 knobs, AM...$25.00

SYMPHONY

200, table/lamp/planter, 1948, lamp radio w/trapezoid-shaped case, right front dial, left trapezoid-shaped grill, 2 top plant pots, BC, AC/DC $125.00

200L-R, table/lamp/planter, 1948, lamp radio w/trapezoid-shaped case, right front dial, left trapezoid-shaped grill, 2 top plant pots, BC, AC/DC $125.00

250, portable, 1949, upper right front dial, left volume knob, lower round grill w/vertical bars, handle, BC, battery..............$40.00

260 "Hollywood," table-N, 1948, striped grasscloth w/painted palm trees, left front dial panel, handle, battery $150.00

348, portable, 1948, leatherette, inner right half-round dial, left round grill w/horizontal bars, 2 knobs, flip-up front, AC/DC/battery $40.00

401, cathedral, two-tone wood, lower front round airplane dial, upper cloth grill w/cut-outs, 3 knobs $225.00

TECH-MASTER

538, table, two-tone wood, upper front slanted slide rule dial, lower horizontal wrap-around grill bars, 3 knobs, BC...$40.00

TELE KING

**Tele King Corp.,
601 West 26th Street, New York, New York**

RK41, table, 1953, plastic, right front round dial overlaps raised checkered grill panel, 2 knobs, BC, AC/DC..................$35.00

RK51A, table, 1953, plastic, right front round dial overlaps raised checkered grill panel, 2 knobs, BC, 5 tubes, AC/DC $35.00

RKP-53-A, portable, 1954, plastic, right side dial knob, large front checkered grill area, handle, BC, AC/DC/battery $30.00

TELE-TONE

**Tele-tone Radio Corp.,
609 West 51st Street, New York, New York**

100, table, 1946, wood, lower front slide rule dial, upper horizontal grill bars, 2 knobs, 5 tubes, BC $40.00

109, table, 1946, plastic, lower front slide rule dial, upper grill w/circular cut-outs, 2 knobs, BC, AC/DC......................$45.00

111, table, 1948, wood, slanted lower front w/slide rule dial, upper patterned grill, 2 knobs, BC, AC/DC $35.00

117, table, 1946, wood, slanted front w/lower slide rule dial, upper grill w/circular cut-outs, 2 knobs, BC $35.00

117A, table, 1946, wood, slanted front w/lower slide rule dial, upper grill w/circular cut-outs, 2 knobs, BC, AC/DC $35.00

D-91(
D941,
D-101
D-101
D104(
D1117
D124(
D-161
D1644
E-5
F-6
F-6
F-6
G-4
G-4
G-4
G-4
G-5
G-5
G-5
G-5
G-5

D2483, table, 1954, plastic, lower front slide rule dial, upper grill area, right side knob, BC, SW, 6 tubes, AC/DC **$35.00**

D2556A, table-R/P, 1955, wood, right side dial knob, large front grill area, lift top, inner phono, BC, 6 tubes, AC **$25.00**

D2560A, table-R/P, 1955, two-tone leatherette, center front round dial, 2 knobs, lift top, inner phono, handle, BC, 5 tubes, AC **$25.00**

D2582A, table, 1955, plastic, right front half-round dial, horizontal grill bars, 2 knobs, feet, BC, 4 tubes, AC/DC **$20.00**

D-2610, table, 1946, plastic, large center front square dial, right & left side horizontal louvers, 2 knobs.............$75.00

D2612, table, 1946, plastic, upper front slanted slide rule dial, lower criss-cross metal grill w/crossed bars, 3 knobs, BC, AC/DC **$35.00**

D2613, table, 1947, plastic, upper front slanted slide rule dial, lower criss-cross grill w/crossed bars, 3 knobs, BC, SW, AC/DC **$35.00**

D2615 "Stratoscope," table, plastic, upper right front slide rule dial, left vertical grill bars, center vertical divider, 6 pushbuttons, right side knob, base, BC **$85.00**

D2616, table, 1946, plastic, upper front slanted slide rule dial, lower curved louvers, 2 knobs, 6 pushbuttons, BC, AC/DC **$50.00**

D-2616B, table, 1948, plastic, upper front slanted slide rule dial, lower curved louvers, 2 knobs, 6 pushbuttons, BC, AC/DC **$50.00**

D-2619, table, 1947, wood, lower front slanted slide rule dial, large upper grill area, 2 knobs, BC, AC/DC.................**$35.00**

D2620, table, 1946, two-tone wood, upper front slanted slide rule dial, lower cloth grill with 2 horizontal bars, 2 knobs, BC, AC/DC **$50.00**

D-2621, table, 1946, two-tone wood, upper front slanted slide rule dial, lower cloth grill w/cutouts, 2 knobs, BC, battery **$40.00**

D-2622, table, 1947, wood, rounded corners, upper front slanted slide rule dial, large lower cloth grill, 2 knobs, BC, AC/DC **$45.00**

D2623, table, 1947, wood, upper front slide rule dial over large cloth grill area, 4 knobs, BC, AC **$40.00**

D2624, table, 1946, wood, upper front slanted slide rule dial, lower metal criss-cross grill, 3 knobs, BC, SW, AC/DC............**$40.00**

D2626, table, 1948, wood, upper front slanted slide rule dial, lower criss-cross grill, 4 knobs, BC, SW, AC.................**$40.00**

D2630, table, 1946, plastic, upper front slanted slide rule dial, lower cloth grill, 3 knobs, BC, SW, AC/DC **$35.00**

D-2634, table, 1947, wood, lower front see-through slide rule dial over large cloth grill area, 3 knobs, BC, AC **$35.00**

D2637A, table, 1956, plastic, center front recessed round dial over horizontal bars, 2 knobs, BC, 6 tubes, AC/DC **$25.00**

D2640, table-R/P, 1948, wood, lower front slanted slide rule dial, upper criss-cross grill, 2 knobs, lift top, inner phono, BC, AC...**$25.00**

D2642, table-R/P, 1947, wood, upper front slide rule dial, lower grill w/3 vertical bars, 2 knobs, lift top, inner phono, BC, AC **$30.00**

D2644, table, 1947, wood, upper front slanted slide rule dial, lower criss-cross grill, 2 knobs, BC, battery **$30.00**

D2645, table-R/P, 1946, wood, top right vertical slide rule dial, 4 knobs, front cloth grill, lift top, inner phono, BC, SW, AC ..**$30.00**

D2661, table, 1946, plastic, large center front square dial, right & left side horizontal louvers, 2 knobs, BC, battery **$75.00**

D2663, table, 1947, wood, upper front slanted slide rule dial, lower cloth grill w/center horizontal bar, 2 knobs, BC, battery **$30.00**

D2665, table, 1947, center front dial, right & left cloth grills, chrome accents, 2 knobs, BC, battery **$50.00**

D-2692, table, 1948, wood, upper front slanted slide rule dial, lower horizontal grill bars, 2 knobs, BC, AC/DC............**$30.00**

D-2709, table, 1947, plastic, right front dial, left lattice grill, base, 2 knobs, BC, AC/DC **$45.00**

D2710, table, 1947, plastic, upper front slanted slide rule dial, large lower grill area, 2 knobs, BC, AC/DC **$40.00**

D2718, table, 1947, plastic, upper front slide rule dial, lower horizontal wrap-around louvers, 3 knobs, BC, SW, AC/DC..**$45.00**

D2718B, table, 1947, plastic, upper front slide rule dial, lower horizontal wrap-around louvers, 3 knobs, BC, SW, 7 tubes, AC/DC **$45.00**

D-2743, table-R/P, 1947, wood, right front dial, left horizontal louvers, 3 knobs, open top phono, BC, AC **$20.00**

D2748, table-R/P, 1947, wood, lower front slide rule dial, upper horizontal louvers, 4 knobs, lift top, inner phono, BC, AC.....**$25.00**

D2806, table, 1948, plastic, right front round dial overlaps lower horizontal louvers, 2 knobs, BC, AC/DC **$35.00**

D2807, table, 1948, plastic, right front round dial overlaps lower horizontal louvers, 2 knobs, BC, AC/DC **$35.00**

D2810, table, 1948, plastic, upper front slanted slide rule dial, lower cloth grill, 2 knobs, BC, AC/DC...........................**$40.00**

D2815, table, 1948, plastic, upper front slanted slide rule dial, lower curved louvers, 2 knobs, pushbuttons, BC, AC/DC..$50.00

D2819, table, 1948, plastic, upper front slide rule dial, lower horizontal wrap-around louvers, 4 knobs, BC, FM, AC **$45.00**

D2819E, table, 1948, plastic, upper front slide rule dial, lower horizontal wrap-around louvers, 4 knobs, BC, FM, AC **$45.00**

D2836A, table, 1958, plastic, upper right front AM dial/upper left front FM dial over large grill area w/center horizontal bar, AM, FM, 8 tubes, AC **$20.00**

D-2851, table-R/P, 1948, wood, upper front slanted slide rule dial, lower grill, 4 knobs, lift top, inner phono, BC, AC **$30.00**

D2857A, table, 1958, plastic, right side dial knob, horizontal front louvers w/center vertical divider & crest, feet, BC, 5 tubes, AC/DC...**$20.00**

D2907, table, 1949, plastic, right front round dial overlaps raised center lattice grill area, 2 knobs, BC, AC/DC **$30.00**

D2910, table, 1949, plastic, upper front slanted slide rule dial, large lower grill area, 2 knobs, BC, AC/DC **$40.00**

D2919, table, 1949, plastic, lower front slide rule dial, upper lattice grill, horizontal decorative bands, 4 knobs, BC, FM, AC/DC...**$45.00**

D2923, table, wood, upper front slide rule dial overlaps large grill area, 4 knobs, BC, SW, 6 tubes, AC **$40.00**

D2963, table, 1949, plastic, upper front slanted slide rule dial, large lower grill area, 2 knobs, BC, battery **$30.00**

D3120A, portable, 1953, plastic, upper front slide rule dial, left front horizontal bars, right & left side knobs, handle, BC, AC/DC/battery **$30.00**

D3210A, portable, 1953, plastic, right side dial knob, left side on/off/volume knob, front & rear horizontal bars, handle, BC, AC/DC/battery **$35.00**

D3265A, portable, 1952, leatherette & plastic, upper front round dial, handle, 2 knobs, BC, AC/DC/battery **$30.00**

D3300, portable, 1953, plastic, large center front round dial over horizontal bars, fold-down handle, left side knob, BC, battery **$30.00**

D3490, portable, 1955, plastic, large center front round dial over lower horizontal grill bars, fold-down handle, BC, 4 tubes, battery **$30.00**

D3600A, portable, 1957, plastic, left thumbwheel dial knob, right thumbwheel on/off/volume knob, lower front grill, fold-down handle, BC, 4 tubes, battery.......................................**$35.00**

D3615, portable, 1947, leatherette, upper right front half-round dial, center lattice grill area, handle, BC, AC/DC/battery **$35.00**

D3619, portable, 1946, luggage-style, upper front slide rule dial, lower grill area, 2 top knobs, handle, BC, AC/DC/battery.............**$30.00**

D3630, portable, 1947, luggage-style, inner right dial overlaps horizontal louvers, 2 knobs, fold-down front, handle, BC, AC/DC/battery **$35.00**

D-3720, portable, 1947, leatherette, small lower right front round dial overlaps woven grill area, handle, BC, AC/DC/battery **$25.00**

D-3721, portable, 1948, leatherette, lower front slide rule dial, plastic grill w/horizontal bars, handle, 2 knobs, BC, AC/DC/battery **$25.00**

D3722, portable, 1948, leatherette, plastic front panel, right dial overlaps horizontal louvers, handle, 2 knobs, BC, AC/DC/battery **$30.00**

D3780A, portable, 1957, leather, upper right round dial knob, front grill cut-outs, right side thumbwheel on/off/volume knob, handle, BC, 4 tubes, battery................................**$25.00**

D3784A, portable, 1957, leather, upper right round dial knob, front grill cut-outs, right side thumbwheel on/off/volume knob, handle, BC, 4 tubes, AC/DC/battery.................................**$25.00**

D3789A, portable, 1957, leather, right side dial knob, left side on/off/volume knob, front grill cut-outs, handle, BC, AC/DC/battery **$25.00**

D3809, portable, 1948, plastic, small upper front slide rule dial, lower recessed horizontal louvers, handle, 2 knobs, BC, battery **$30.00**

D-3810, portable, 1948, plastic, small upper front slide rule dial, lower recessed horizontal louvers, handle, 2 knobs, BC, AC/DC/battery **$30.00**

D3811, portable, 1948, inner right dial, upper grill bars, radio plays when flip-up lid opens, BC, AC/DC/battery **$35.00**

D3840, portable, 1948, leatherette, inner right dial, left vertical grill bars, 3 knobs, fold-down front, handle, BC, AC/DC/battery **$35.00**

D3910, portable, 1949, plastic, lower right front dial, upper horizontal grill bars, handle, 2 knobs, BC, AC/DC/battery...**$25.00**

DC2154, table, plastic, upper right front dial panel, large lattice grill area w/logo, feet, BC **$10.00**

DC2980A, table, 1959, plastic, right front round dial, left lattice grill, BC, 4 tubes, AC/DC...**$15.00**

DC2989A, table-C, 1959, plastic, wedge-shaped, upper right front dial, left alarm clock, center horizontal bars, feet, BC, 6 tubes, AC **$15.00**

DC3800, portable, 1959, plastic, right & left side knobs, front perforated grill, handle, BC, 4 tubes, AC/DC/battery..........**$20.00**

DC5987A, table-R/P, 1959, right front dial, upper random-patterned perforated grill, handle, lift top, inner phono, BC, 6 tubes, AC..**$25.00**

TUSKA
The C.D. Tuska Co.,
Hartford, Connecticut

222, table, 1922, wood, low rectangular case, 2 dial black front panel, battery..**$450.00**

224, table, 1922, wood, low rectangular case, 2 dial black front panel, 1 tube, battery...**$350.00**

225—Single Panel, table, 1923, mahogany, low rectangular case, 2 dial black Bakelite single panel, 3 tubes, battery...**$400.00**

225—Double Panel, table, 1923, mahogany, low rectangular case, 2 dial black Bakelite double panel, 3 tubes, battery **$600.00**

228 "Superdyne," table, 1924, wood, low rectangular case, 2 dial black front panel, 4 tubes, battery **$225.00**

301 "Junior," table, 1925, wood, low rectangular case, 3 dial front panel, 3 tubes, battery **$235.00**

305 "Superdyne," table, 1925, wood, low rectangular case, black front panel w/2 window dials, 4 tubes, battery $195.00

401, table, wood, low rectangular case, black front panel w/3 gold half-round pointer dials...**$250.00**

20TH CENTURY
Electronic Devices Corp.,
601 West 26th Street, New York, New York

100X, table, wood, right front square black dial, left cloth grill w/vertical bars, 3 knobs, BC, SW, AC/DC **$35.00**
101, table, 1947, wood, right front square black dial, left criss-cross grill, 3 knobs, BC, SW, AC/DC.............................**$40.00**

U. S. RADIO

9-A, tombstone, 1932, wood, center front quarter-round dial, upper cloth grill w/cut-outs, 4 knobs, 9 tubes **$150.00**
3040, console, 1933, wood, lowboy, upper front window dial, lower cloth grill w/cut-outs, 6 legs, 5 tubes.................**$125.00**
3074, console, 1933, wood, lowboy, upper front dial, lower cloth grill w/cut-outs, 6 legs, 7 tubes **$125.00**
3084, cathedral, 1933, wood, center front window dial, upper cloth grill w/cut-outs, 3 knobs, 5 tubes, battery **$125.00**
3086, cathedral, 1933, wood, lower front window dial, upper cloth grill w/cut-outs, 3 knobs, 5 tubes, battery **$125.00**
3092, table, 1933, wood w/inlay, front dial, center cloth grill w/cut-outs, BC, 5 tubes, AC/DC...**$75.00**

ULTRADYNE
Regal Electronics Corp.,
20 West 20th Street, New York, New York

L-43, table, 1946, wood, right front black dial, left cloth grill w/"V" cut-out, 2 knobs, 4 tubes, AC/DC...................$40.00

L-46, table, 1946, wood, right front half-round dial, left cloth grill w/curved bars, 2 knobs, BC, AC/DC **$40.00**

ULTRATONE
Audio Industries,
Michigan City, Indiana

355, table-R/P, 1956, right side dial knob, large front grill area, handle, lift top, inner phono, BC, 5 tubes, AC **$20.00**

UNITED UTILITIES

1021TB, table, plastic, upper front slanted slide rule dial, lower woven grill area, 3 knobs, BC $35.00

UNITONE
Union Electronics Corp.,
38-01 Queens Boulevard,
Long Island City, New York

88, table, 1946, wood, upper front slanted slide rule dial, lower cloth grill w/2 horizontal bars, 2 knobs, BC, SW, AC/DC **$40.00**

UNIVERSAL
Universal Battery Co.,
Chicago, Illinois

72A6, tombstone, 1935, wood, lower front round dial, upper cloth grill with cut-outs, battery...**$60.00**
73A6, console, 1935, wood, upper front round dial, lower cloth grill with cut-outs, battery...**$80.00**
7222, console, 1935, wood, upper front round dial, lower cloth grill with cut-outs, battery **$80.00**
7232, tombstone, 1935, wood, lower front round dial, upper cloth grill with cut-outs, battery **$60.00**

VAL-KEEN

572, table, 1946, wood, upper right front slide rule dial, lower & left cloth grill areas w/horizontal bars, 3 knobs, AC $40.00

VAN CAMP

**Van Camp Hardware & Iron Co.,
401 West Maryland Street,
Indianapolis, Indiana**

576-1-6A, table, 1946, wood, upper front slide rule dial, lower cloth grill w/vertical bars, 3 knobs, BC, AC/DC $55.00

VIKING

**Viking Radio Laboratories,
433 N. LaSalle St.,
Chicago, Illinois**

5-A, table, wood, low rectangular case, 3 dial front panel, 5 tubes, battery $115.00
5-A, console, wood, inner three dial panel, fold-down front, upper speaker grill, lower storage, 5 tubes, battery..............$185.00
599, table, 1926, two-tone cardboard & leatherette, large center front dial, lift back, 5 tubes $165.00

VIZ

**Molded Insulation Co.,
335 East Price Street,
Philadelphia, Pennsylvania**

RS-1, table, 1947, plastic, right front round dial, left horizontal wrap-around louvers, BC, AC/DC $60.00

VOGUE

**Sheridan Electronics Corp.,
2850 South Michigan Avenue,
Chicago, Illinois**

2554R, table, 1946, plastic, right front half-round dial, left horizontal wrap-around louvers, 2 knobs, handle, BC, AC/DC $45.00

WAGNER

72AE-184, table, two-tone wood, right front dial, left cloth grill w/horizontal bars, tuning eye, 4 knobs, 5 tubes, AC..$65.00

WARE

**Ware Radio Corporation,
529-549 West 42nd Street, New York, New York**

B1 "Bantam," cathedral, 1931, two-tone wood, right front dial, upper cloth grill w/cut-outs, fluted columns, finials, 7 tubes.......$275.00

L, table, 1925, wood, low rectangular case, 3 dial black front panel, lift top $110.00
T, table, 1924, mahogany, high rectangular case, slanted 2 dial panel with 3 exposed tubes, battery..........................$275.00
TU, console, 1926, wood, inner panel w/3 exposed tubes, lift top, inner front speaker grill, double doors, battery $325.00
W, table, 1924, walnut, low rectangular case, 3 dial front panel, 5 tubes, battery...$125.00
WU, console, 1925, wood, inner slanted 3 dial panel, upper speaker grill, double doors, battery $175.00
X, table, 1925, walnut, low rectangular case, 3 dial front panel, meter, 5 tubes, battery $120.00

WATTERSON

**Watterson Radio Mfg. Co.,
2700 Swiss Avenue, Dallas, Texas**

4581, table, 1946, wood, right front square dial overlaps horizontal grill bars, 2 knobs, BC, AC/DC **$35.00**
4582, table, 1946, wood, right front square dial, left cloth grill w/horizontal bars, 2 knobs, BC, battery.......................**$25.00**
4782, table, 1947, two-tone wood, right front dial, left cloth grill w/cut-outs, 2 knobs, BC, battery **$35.00**
4790, table, 1947, two-tone wood, right front dial, left cloth grill w/horizontal bars, 3 knobs, BC, AC/DC **$35.00**
4800, table, 1948, wood, front oblong slide rule dial over large grill area, 4 knobs, BC, FM, AC/DC **$30.00**
ARC-4591A, table-R/P, 1947, wood, top right vertical slide rule dial, 4 knobs, front horizontal louvers, lift top, inner phono, BC, AC..**$25.00**
RC-4581, table-R/P, 1947, wood, right front square dial, left horizontal grill bars, 3 knobs, lift top, inner phono, BC, AC ..**$25.00**

WECCO
William E. Cheever Co., Providence, Rhode Island

Junior, table, wood, crystal set, 1 dial black front panel **$150.00**

WELLS
Wells Mfg. Co., Fond du Lac, Wisconsin

24, table, 1925, wood, low rectangular case, black front panel w/center dial, 4 tubes, battery **$130.00**

WESTERN COIL & ELECTRICAL
Western Coil & Electrical Co., 313 Fifth St., Racine, Wisconsin

WC-5B "Radiodyne," table, 1925, wood, low rectangular case, 3 dial front panel, 4 tubes, battery **$125.00**
WC-11 "Radiodyne," console, 1925, wood, inner three dial panel, lower speaker grill, fold-back top, double front doors, 4 tubes, battery...**$175.00**
WC-11B "Radiodyne," table, 1925, wood, high rectangular case, 3 dial front panel, 4 tubes, battery **$140.00**
WC-12 "Radiodyne," console, 1925, wood, inner three dial panel, lower speaker grill, fold-back top, double front doors, 6 tubes, battery...**$200.00**

WC-12B "Radiodyne," table, 1925, wood, high rectangular case, 3 dial front panel, 6 tubes, battery **$160.00**
WC-15-JR "Radiodyne," table, 1926, wood, slanted 2 dial front panel, open top w/5 exposed tubes, side knob, battery **$200.00**

WESTERN ELECTRIC

Western Electric began business in 1872 making the Bell Telephone equipment. In the early 1920s, the company began radio production — at first only for commercial interests.

4B, table, 1923, wood, low rectangular case, 2 dial black front panel, battery...**$550.00**
4C, table, c1924, wood, low rectangular case, 2 dial front panel, battery **$600.00**
4D, table, c1924, wood, low rectangular case, 2 dial front panel, battery **$475.00**
7A, table/amp, wood, amplifier, black Bakelite front panel with 3 exposed tubes **$325.00**

WESTINGHOUSE
Westinghouse Electric Corp., Home Radio Division., Sunbury, Pennsylvania

The Westinghouse company sold its line of radios through RCA until 1930. The company is well-known for its slogan: "You Can Be Sure If It's Westinghouse."

Aeriola Jr., table, 1922, wood, crystal set, square case, lift top, inner control panel, storage..**$295.00**
Aeriola Sr., table, 1922, wood, square case, inner 1 dial panel w/1 exposed tube, lift top, battery..............................**$175.00**
H-103, table, 1946, wood, curved top, recessed front, lower slide rule dial, upper horizontal louvers, 4 knobs, BC, 2SW...**$55.00**

H-104, table, 1946, wood, curved top, recessed front, lower slide rule dial, upper horizontal louvers, 6 pushbuttons, 4 knobs, BC, 2SW, AC **$65.00**
H-117, console-R/P, 1947, wood, upper slide rule dial, 4 knobs, 6 pushbuttons, inner pull-out phono, double doors, BC, SW, 14 tubes, FM, AC **$110.00**
H-119, console-R/P, 1947, wood, inner left slide rule dial/4 knobs/6 pushbuttons, door, left pull-out phono drawer, BC, SW, FM, 14 tubes, AC...**$110.00**
H-122, table-R/P, 1946, front plastic radio unit detaches from wood phono case, radio case has top dial/lower horizontal louvers/4 knobs, BC, AC/DC **$75.00**
H-124 "Little Jewel"/"Refrigerator," portable, 1945, dark green plastic w/metal center panel, upper front dial, lower cloth grill w/vertical bars, fold-down handle, 2 knobs, BC, AC/DC **$95.00**

H-125 "Little Jewel"/"Refrigerator," (left) portable, 1945, light green plastic w/metal center panel, upper front dial, lower cloth grill w/vertical bars, fold-down handle, 2 knobs, BC, AC/DC $95.00

H-126 "Little Jewel"/ "Refrigerator," portable, 1945, ivory plastic w/metal center panel, upper front dial, lower cloth grill w/vertical bars, fold-down handle, 2 knobs, BC, AC/DC..............$95.00

H-127 "Little Jewel"/"Refrigerator," portable, 1945, burgundy plastic w/metal center panel, upper front dial, lower cloth grill w/vertical bars, fold-down handle, 2 knobs, BC, AC/DC..................$95.00

H-130, table, 1946, wood, top recessed slide rule dial, lower front cloth grill, 4 knobs, AC/DC $45.00

H-133, table, 1947, two-tone wood, upper front slanted slide rule dial, lower cloth grill, 3 knobs, BC, battery $35.00

H-138, console-R/P, 1946, wood, front slide rule dial w/upper horizontal louvers, lower cloth grill w/2 vertical bars, 4 knobs, 6 pushbuttons, BC, SW, AC $100.00

H-142, table, 1948, wood, upper front slanted slide rule dial, lower grill area, top fluting, 5 knobs, BC, 4SW, 9 tubes, AC ...**$65.00**

H-147, table, 1948, plastic, right front dial panel overlaps large cloth grill area, 2 knobs, BC, AC/DC $40.00

H-148, portable, 1947, small upper right front dial over large criss-cross grill area, 2 knobs, handle, BC, AC/DC/battery ...$25.00

H-157, table, 1948, wood, lower front slide rule dial, large upper recessed cloth grill, 2 knobs, BC, AC/DC $30.00

H-161, table, 1948, wood, right front curved dial over large cloth grill, 4 knobs, AM, FM, 8 tubes, AC $45.00

H-165, portable, 1948, inner dial, upper horizontal grill bars, 4 knobs, fold-down front, handle, BC, 5 tubes, AC/DC/battery........$25.00

H-166, console-R/P, 1948, wood, inner left slide rule dial/4 knobs, door, right pull-out phono drawer, lower grill, BC, FM, 12 tubes, AC..$95.00

H-168, console-R/P, 1948, wood, inner right curved dial/4 knobs, left phono, lift top, front grill cut-outs, BC, FM, 8 tubes, AC $65.00

H-168A, console-R/P, 1948, wood, inner right curved dial/4 knobs, left phono, lift top, front grill cut-outs, BC, FM, 8 tubes, AC $65.00

H-169, console-R/P, 1948, wood, inner left slide rule dial/4 knobs, door, right pull-out phono drawer, BC, 2SW, FM, 14 tubes, AC ..$125.00

H-171, console-R/P, 1948, front plastic radio unit detaches from wood console cabinet, radio case has top slide rule dial/lower horizontal louvers/4 knobs, console cabinet has lift top/inner phono, BC, AC $145.00

H-178, table, 1948, two-tone wood, upper front slanted slide rule dial, lower cloth grill, 3 knobs, BC, battery $30.00

H-182, table, 1949, plastic, upper front slanted slide rule dial, lower cloth grill, decorative case lines, 3 knobs, AM, FM, 6 tubes, AC/DC $35.00

H-183A, console-R/P, 1948, wood, inner right dial/4 knobs, door, left pull-out phono drawer, lower grill & storage, BC, AC $75.00

H-185, portable, 1949, plastic, upper front slide rule dial, lower horizontal grill bars, handle, 2 knobs, BC, 4 tubes, AC/DC/battery $30.00

H-186, console-R/P, 1949, wood, inner right slide rule dial/pushbuttons/4 knobs, door, left pull-out phono drawer, lower front grill, BC, FM, 12 tubes, AC $85.00

H-188, table, 1948, plastic, Oriental design, right front dial, left cloth grill w/cut-outs, 2 knobs, BC, 5 tubes, AC/DC $70.00

H-190, console-R/P, 1949, wood, upper front slide rule dial, 4 knobs, center pull-out phono drawer, lower grill, BC, FM, 8 tubes, AC...$65.00

H-191, console-R/P, 1949, wood, inner right slide rule dial/4 knobs, left pull-out phono drawer, double doors, BC, FM, 8 tubes, AC...$70.00

H-191A, console-R/P, 1949, wood, inner right slide rule dial/4 knobs, left pull-out phono drawer, double doors, BC, FM, 8 tubes, AC...$70.00

H-195, portable, 1949, leatherette, upper front slide rule dial, lower cloth grill, handle, 2 knobs, BC, 4 tubes, AC/DC/battery...$30.00

H-198, table, 1949, wood, lower front slide rule dial, large upper cloth grill, 2 knobs, AM, FM, AC $25.00

H-202, table, 1948, plastic, upper front slanted slide rule dial, large lower grill area, decorative case lines, 3 knobs, BC, FM $40.00

H-203, console-R/P, 1949, wood, inner right slide rule dial, door, left pull-out phono drawer, lower grill & open storage, BC, FM, 8 tubes, AC $70.00

H-204, table, 1948, plastic, upper front slanted slide rule dial, lower cloth grill w/Oriental cut-outs, decorative case lines, 3 knobs, BC, SW..$45.00

H-204A, table, 1948, plastic, upper front slanted slide rule dial, lower cloth grill w/Oriental cut-outs, decorative case lines, 3 knobs, BC, SW $45.00

H-210, portable, 1949, plastic, right front vertical slide rule dial, wrap-around horizontal louvers, handle, 2 knobs, BC, 5 tubes, AC/DC $45.00

H-211, portable, 1949, plastic, right front vertical slide rule dial, wrap-around horizontal louvers, handle, 2 knobs, BC, 5 tubes, AC/DC $45.00

H-214A, console-R/P, 1949, wood, upper front slide rule dial, 2 knobs, center pull-out phono drawer, lower grill, right & left storage, BC, 6 tubes, AC...$50.00

H301T5, table, 1950, plastic, lower front slide rule dial, large upper grill area, 2 knobs, BC, AC/DC............................$25.00

H-302P5, portable, 1950, leatherette, luggage-style, upper front slide rule dial, lower grill, handle, 2 knobs, BC, AC/DC/battery ...$30.00

H303P4, portable, 1950, plastic, upper front slide rule dial, lower horizontal louvers, handle, 2 knobs, BC, AC/DC/battery........$35.00

H-307T7, table, 1950, plastic, lower front slide rule dial, upper horizontal louvers, 2 knobs, AM, FM, AC/DC $35.00

H-309P5, portable, 1950, plastic, upper front slide rule dial, lower horizontal louvers, handle, 2 knobs, BC, AC/DC/battery ..$30.00

H-311T5, table, 1950, plastic, lower front slide rule dial, upper vertical wrap-over grill bars, 2 knobs, BC, AC/DC..............$40.00

H-312P4, portable, 1950, plastic, upper front slide rule dial, lower contrasting grill, handle, 2 knobs, BC, AC/DC/battery...$35.00

H-316C7, console-R/P, 1950, wood, inner left slide rule dial & 2 knobs over large grill area, right pull-out phono drawer, double doors, BC, FM, AC $55.00

H318T5, table, 1950, plastic, slanted front design, right round dial over perforated grill, 2 knobs, BC, AC/DC $30.00

H-321T5, table, 1950, plastic, lower front slide rule dial, upper cloth grill w/geometric plastic cut-outs, 2 knobs, BC...$40.00

H-324T7U, table, 1950, plastic, lower front slide rule dial, upper horizontal louvers, 2 knobs, AM, FM, AC/DC...............$35.00

H-333P4U, portable, 1952, plastic, upper front slide rule dial, lower lattice grill, 2 top thumbwheel knobs, handle, BC, AC/DC/battery $35.00

H-334T7UR, table, 1951, plastic, large center front curved dial overlaps grill area, 2 knobs, BC, AC/DC $40.00

H-336T5U, table, 1951, plastic, slanted front design, right round dial over perforated grill, 2 knobs, BC, AC/DC $30.00

H-341T5U, table, 1951, plastic, large right front round dial with inner pointer over woven grill, 2 knobs, BC, AC/DC......$35.00

H-343P5U, portable, 1951, plastic, large center front round dial w/inner perforated grill, 2 thumbwheel knobs, fold-back handle, BC, AC/DC/battery $55.00

H-350T7, table, 1951, plastic, large center front curved dial overlaps grill area, 2 knobs, AM, FM, AC/DC $40.00

H-354C7, console-R/P, 1952, wood, upper front curved dial overlaps grill area, lower pull-out phono, right & left storage, BC, FM, AC $75.00

H-355T5, table-C, 1952, maroon plastic, right front thumbwheel dial, left alarm clock, center grill w/horizontal divider, BC, AC..$40.00

H-356T5, table-C, 1952, ivory plastic, right front thumbwheel dial, left alarm clock, center grill w/horizontal divider, BC, AC........$40.00

H-357C10, console-R/P, 1952, wood, inner left curved dial/lower grill, right pull-out phono, storage, double front doors, BC, FM, AC $80.00

H-357T5, table-C, 1952, brown plastic, right front thumbwheel dial, left alarm clock, center grill w/horizontal divider, BC, AC $40.00

H-359T5, table, 1953, plastic, large center front half-round dial w/inner textured grill, 2 knobs, BC, AC/DC $30.00

H-361T6, table, 1952, plastic, large right front round dial with inner pointer over cloth grill, 2 knobs, BC, AC/DC $30.00

H-365T5, table, 1952, brown plastic, right front round dial, left recessed "tic/tac/toe" grill, 2 knobs, BC $30.00

H-366T5, table, 1952, ivory plastic, right front round dial, left recessed "tic/tac/toe" grill, 2 knobs, BC $30.00

H-370T7, table, 1953, black plastic, large center front round dial w/inner pointer, 2 knobs, AM, FM..................................$35.00

H-371T7, table, 1953, brown plastic, large center front round dial w/inner pointer, 2 knobs, AM, FM..................................$35.00

H-374T5, table-C, 1952, plastic, right front thumbwheel dial knob, left alarm clock, center lattice grill, BC, AC $30.00

H-378T5, table, 1953, plastic, large right front round dial knob overlaps lower horizontal bars, feet, BC, AC/DC $20.00

H-379T5, table, 1953, plastic, large right front round dial knob overlaps lower horizontal bars, feet, BC, AC/DC $20.00

H-381T5, table, 1953, plastic, large right front round dial knob overlaps lower horizontal bars, feet, BC, AC/DC $20.00

H-382T5, table, 1953, brown plastic, right front half-round dial over horizontal bars, 2 knobs, BC $20.00

H-383T5, table, 1953, ivory plastic, right front half-round dial over horizontal bars, 2 knobs, BC $20.00

H-388T5, table-C, 1953, plastic, right front dial, left alarm clock, center "woven" panel, 4 knobs, BC, AC $25.00

H-393T6, table, 1953, plastic, large center front half-round dial w/inner textured grill, 2 knobs, BC, AC/DC $35.00

H-397T5, table-C, maroon plastic, small tombstone style, center front slide rule dial, upper alarm clock, lower grill, BC, AC $45.00

H-398T5, table-C, ivory plastic, small tombstone-style, center front slide rule dial, upper alarm clock, lower grill, BC, AC $45.00

H-409P4, portable, 1954, plastic, upper front thumbwheel dial, large lower lattice grill w/"W" logo, handle, BC, battery ..$30.00

H-417T5, table, 1954, maroon plastic, center front round dial over large lattice grill, wire stand, left side knob, BC, AC......$35.00

H-418T5, table, 1954, ivory plastic, center front round dial over large lattice grill, wire stand, left side knob, BC, AC $35.00

H-434T5, table, 1955, black plastic, lower front raised slide rule dial, upper horizontal bars w/center divider, 2 knobs, BC, AC/DC $25.00

H-435T5, table, 1955, ivory plastic, lower front raised slide rule dial, upper horizontal bars w/center divider, 2 knobs, BC, AC/DC $25.00

H-435T5A, table, 1955, ivory plastic, lower front raised slide rule dial, upper horizontal bars w/center divider, 2 knobs, BC, AC/DC $25.00

H-436T5, table, 1955, maroon plastic, lower front raised slide rule dial, upper horizontal bars w/center divider, 2 knobs, BC, AC/DC $25.00

H-437T5, table, 1955, tan plastic, lower front raised slide rule dial, upper horizontal bars w/center divider, 2 knobs, BC, AC/DC $25.00

H-437T5A, table, 1955, tan plastic, lower front raised slide rule dial, upper horizontal bars w/center divider, 2 knobs, BC, AC/DC $25.00

H-438T5, table, 1955, green plastic, lower front raised slide rule dial, upper horizontal bars w/center divider, 2 knobs, BC, AC/DC $25.00

H-438T5A, table, 1955, green plastic, lower front raised slide rule dial, upper horizontal bars w/center divider, 2 knobs, BC, AC/DC $25.00

H-440T5, table, 1955, grey plastic, lower front raised slide rule dial, upper horizontal bars w/center divider, 2 knobs, BC, AC/DC $25.00

H-447T4, table, 1955, brown plastic, right front dial, lower horizontal grill bars, lower left knob, feet, BC $25.00

H-448T4, table, 1955, grey plastic, right front dial, lower horizontal grill bars, lower left knob, feet, BC $25.00

H-449T4, table, 1955, aqua plastic, right front dial, lower horizontal grill bars, lower left knob, feet, BC $25.00

H-471T5, table-C, 1955, grey plastic, step-down top, right front dial knob over checkered grill area, left alarm clock, BC, AC $30.00

H-472T5, table-C, 1955, ivory plastic, step-down top, right front dial knob over checkered grill area, left alarm clock, BC, AC $30.00

H-473T5, table-C, 1955, rose plastic, step-down top, right front dial knob over checkered grill area, left alarm clock, BC, AC ..$30.00

H-474T5, table-C, 1955, green plastic, step-down top, right front dial knob over checkered grill area, left alarm clock, BC, AC $30.00

H-482PR5, table-R/P, 1955, lower front slide rule dial, large upper grill w/"W" logo, right side knob, handle, lift top, inner phono, BC, 5 tubes, AC..$25.00

H-486T5, table-C, 1955, ivory plastic, lower front slide rule dial, large upper alarm clock face, metal bezel & knobs, BC, AC..$30.00

H-487T5, table-C, 1955, maroon plastic, lower front slide rule dial, large upper alarm clock face, metal bezel & knobs, BC, AC **$30.00**

H-488T5, table-C, 1955, black plastic, lower front slide rule dial, large upper alarm clock face, metal bezel & knobs, BC, AC $30.00

H-489T5, table-C, 1955, grey plastic, lower front slide rule dial, large upper alarm clock face, metal bezel & knobs, BC, AC......**$30.00**

H-499T5A, table, 1955, black plastic, right front dial knob over plaid metal perforated grill, BC, AC/DC **$30.00**

H-500T5A, table, 1955, red plastic, right front dial knob over plaid metal perforated grill, BC, AC/DC **$30.00**

H-501T5A, table, 1955, brown plastic, right front dial knob over plaid metal perforated grill, BC, AC/DC **$30.00**

H-502T5A, table, 1955, green plastic, right front dial knob over plaid metal perforated grill, BC, AC/DC **$30.00**

H-503T5A, table, 1955, light grey plastic, right front dial knob over plaid metal perforated grill, BC, AC/DC **$30.00**

H-536T6, table, 1956, plastic, lower front slide rule dial, upper horizontal grill bars, 2 knobs, BC, 6 tubes, AC/DC **$30.00**

H-537P4, portable, 1957, grey plastic, top dial knob, front metal perforated grill, handle, feet, BC, AC/DC/battery **$35.00**

H-557P4, portable, 1957, two-tone green plastic, top dial, front metal grill, feet, handle, BC, AC/DC/battery **$35.00**

H-558P4, portable, 1957, white & sand plastic, top dial, front metal grill, handle, feet, BC, AC/DC/battery $35.00

H-559P4, portable, 1957, grey & black plastic, top dial, front metal grill, handle, feet, BC, AC/DC/battery **$35.00**

H-562P4, portable, 1957, plastic, upper right front dial, lower perforated grill, top thumbwheel knobs, side strap, BC, battery **$25.00**

H-574T4, table, 1956, black plastic, raised right front panel w/round dial knob, left criss-cross grill, feet, BC...........**$25.00**

H-575T4, table, 1956, ivory plastic, raised right front panel w/round dial knob, left criss-cross grill, feet, BC...........**$25.00**

H-576T4, table, 1956, pink plastic, raised right front panel w/round dial knob, left criss-cross grill, feet, BC **$25.00**

H-577T4, table, 1956, red plastic, raised right front panel w/round dial knob, left criss-cross grill, feet, BC **$25.00**

H-627, table, plastic, right front round dial knob over large grill area, BC $15.00

H-627T6U, table, 1951, plastic, lower front slide rule dial, upper cloth grill w/geometric plastic cut-outs, 2 knobs, BC, AC/DC **$40.00**

H-632T5A, table, plastic, lower front slide rule dial, large upper grill area w/horizontal & vertical bars, 2 knobs, BC, AC/DC $15.00

H-636T6, table, 1958, ivory/white plastic, lower front slide rule dial, large upper grill area w/horizontal & vertical bars, 2 knobs, feet, BC, AC/DC...**$15.00**

H-637T6, table, 1958, coral/white plastic, lower front slide rule dial, large upper grill area w/horizontal & vertical bars, 2 knobs, feet, BC, AC/DC...**$15.00**

H-666P5, portable, 1959, upper right front round dial, lower lattice grill, telescope antenna, handle, BC, 5 tubes, AC/DC/battery...**$20.00**

H-678T4, table-C, 1959, plastic, right side round dial knob, large front alarm clock, feet, BC, 4 tubes, AC **$15.00**

H-681T5, table, 1959, plastic, wedge-shaped case, lower right front round dial knob, horizontal bars, left side knob, BC, 5 tubes, AC/DC **$15.00**

H-704T5, table, chestnut brown/white plastic, wedge-shaped case, right front round dial knob, large left grill area w/horizontal bars, twin speakers, BC, AC $15.00

H-705T5, table, turquoise/white plastic, wedge-shaped case, right front round dial knob, large left grill area w/horizontal bars, twin speakers, BC, AC $15.00

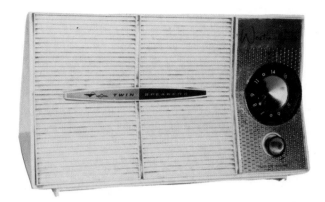

H-706T5, table, ivory/white plastic, wedge-shaped case, right front round dial knob, large left grill area w/horizontal bars, twin speakers, BC, AC.......................................$15.00

H-742TA, table, 1956, aqua plastic, raised right front panel w/round dial knob, left criss-cross grill, feet, BC............$25.00

H-743TA, table, 1956, shadow white plastic, raised right front panel w/round dial knob, left criss-cross grill, feet, BC ..$25.00

H-744TA, table, 1956, carnation pink plastic, raised right front panel w/round dial knob, left criss-cross grill, feet, BC ..$25.00

H-816L5, table-C, white plastic, right front dial knob, large left alarm clock area w/oversize numerals, feet, BC, AC $15.00

HR102BN, console-R/P, 1958, wood, inner right round dial, 6 knobs, left phono, lift top, large front grill, BC, FM, 11 tubes, AC...$45.00

RC (RA/DA), table, 1922, wood, 2 boxes—receiver & amp, black front panels, 1 dial, 3 tubes, lift top, battery.................$235.00

WR-5, console, 1930, walnut, upper front window dial, lower cloth grill w/cut-outs, 3 knobs, 9 tubes, AC.........................$130.00

WR-7, console-R/P, 1930, walnut, lowboy, inner front window dial, lower cloth grill w/cut-outs, double front doors, lift top, inner phono, 9 tubes, AC...$150.00

WR-8 "Columaire," grandfather clock, 1931, wood, Deco, right side dial/knobs/switch, upper front clock face, top speaker, 9 tubes, AC...$250.00

WR-8-R "Columaire," grandfather clock, 1931, wood, Deco, right side dial/knobs/switch, upper front clock face, top speaker, remote control, 9 tubes, AC.............................$275.00

WR-10A "Columette," tombstone, 1931, two-tone walnut, lower front window dial, upper 3-section cloth grill, 3 knobs, 8 tubes, AC $95.00

WR-10-AH, console, 1931, wood, inner window dial, lower cloth grill w/cut-outs, 3 knobs, sliding doors, 8 tubes, AC....$150.00

WR-10-AL, console, 1931, walnut, lower front window dial, upper 3-section cloth grill, 3 knobs, 8 tubes, AC $135.00

WR-12 "Columaire, Jr.," console, wood, grandfather clock-shaped cabinet without the clock face, Deco, center front window dial, top speaker, 3 knobs, 8 tubes, AC $200.00

WR-12C "Columaire, Jr.," grandfather clock, 1931, wood, Deco, center front window dial, upper clock face, top speaker, 3 knobs, AC...$250.00

WR-12X3, table, 1941, wood, upper front slanted slide rule dial, lower horizontal louvers, 2 knobs, 5 tubes, AC/DC $40.00

WR-12X4, table, 1941, wood, upper right front dial, left horizontal louvers, 5 pushbuttons, 2 knobs, 5 tubes, AC/DC.........$45.00

WR-12X7, table, 1941, wood, right front slide rule dial, left cloth grill, 6 pushbuttons, 4 knobs, BC, SW, 5 tubes, AC/DC..........$45.00

WR-12X8, table, 1942, plastic, upper front slanted slide rule dial, lower horizontal grill bars, 2 knobs, 5 tubes, AC/DC $35.00

WR-12X10, table, 1942, plastic, upper front slanted slide rule dial, lower horizontal grill bars, 3 knobs, 6 tubes, AC/DC $35.00

WR-12X12, table, 1942, plastic, upper front slanted slide rule dial, lower horizontal grill bars, 3 knobs, BC, SW, 6 tubes, AC/DC...$35.00

WR-12X14, table, 1942, wood, upper front slanted slide rule dial, lower horizontal louvers, 6 pushbuttons, 3 knobs, 6 tubes, AC/DC $45.00

WR-12X15, table, 1942, wood, right front slide rule dial, left horizontal louvers, 5 pushbuttons, 3 knobs, BC, SW, 6 tubes, AC/DC $45.00

WR-12X16, table, 1941, wood, upper front slanted slide rule dial, lower horizontal louvers, 5 pushbuttons, 4 knobs, BC, SW, 8 tubes, AC/DC $50.00

WR-13, console-R/P, 1931, wood, lower front window dial, upper 3-section cloth grill, 3 knobs, lift top, inner phono, 8 tubes, AC......$120.00

WR-14, cathedral, 1931, two-tone wood, lower front window dial, upper 3-section cloth grill, 3 knobs, 4 tubes ..$125.00

WR-15, grandfather clock, 1931, wood, Deco, center front window dial, upper gold clock face, top speaker, 3 knobs, 9 tubes, AC $250.00

WR-20, table, 1934, wood, front dial, center cloth grill with cut-outs, 2 knobs, decorative case lines, BC, AC $60.00

WR-21, table, 1934, wood, front dial, center cloth grill with horizontal bars, 2 knobs, BC, SW, 5 tubes, AC $60.00

WR-22, tombstone, 1934, wood, center front window dial, upper cloth grill w/Deco cut-outs, BC, SW, 5 tubes, AC........$100.00

WR-23, tombstone, 1934, wood, lower front quarter-round dial, upper vertical grill bars, 4 knobs, BC, SW, 7 tubes, AC $130.00

WR-24, console, 1934, wood, upper front quarter-round dial, lower cloth grill w/3 vertical bars, 4 knobs, BC, SW, 7 tubes, AC $130.00

WR-27, table, 1934, wood, front dial, center cloth grill with cut-outs, 2 knobs, BC, 4 tubes, AC $65.00

WR-28, tombstone, 1934, wood, center front round dial, upper cloth grill w/cut-outs, 4 knobs, BC, SW, 6 tubes, AC...$125.00

WR-29, console, 1934, wood, upper front round dial, lower cloth grill w/cut-outs, 4 knobs, BC, SW, 6 tubes, AC $150.00

WR-30, console, 1934, wood, upper front quarter-round dial, lower cloth grill w/cut-outs, decorative medallions, 4 knobs, BC, SW, 10 tubes, AC..$175.00

WR-42X1, table-R/P, 1941, wood, right front dial, left grill area, 3 knobs, lift top, inner phono, 5 tubes, AC $25.00

WR-42X7, console-R/P, 1942, walnut, upper front slanted dial, 4 knobs, center pull-out phono drawer, lower grill, BC, SW, AC........$115.00

WR-62K1 "Carryette," portable, 1941, striped cloth covered, right front dial, left grill, 3 knobs, handle, BC, AC/DC/battery ..$35.00

WR-62K2 "Carryette," portable, 1941, leatherette, inner right dial, left grill, 3 knobs, fold-down front, handle, AC/DC/battery...$35.00

WR-100, tombstone, 1935, wood, lower front round dial, upper cloth grill w/cut-outs, BC, 5 tubes, AC $100.00

WR-101, table, 1935, wood, lower front dial, upper cloth grill w/cut-outs, 4 knobs, BC, SW, AC...................................$60.00

WR-102, table, 1936, wood, right front dial, left cloth grill, 3 knobs, BC, 5 tubes, AC/DC $40.00

WR-103, table, 1936, wood, right front oval dial, left 3-section cloth grill, 3 knobs, BC, 6 tubes, AC/DC.......................$50.00

WR-120, table, 1937, plastic, right front dial, left grill area, 3 knobs, BC, SW, 6 tubes, AC $45.00

WR-152, table, 1939, wood, right front dial, left cloth grill w/center horizontal bars, 2 knobs, BC, 6 tubes, AC/DC $45.00

WR-154, table, 1939, wood, right front dial, left wrap-around cloth grill w/horizontal bars, BC, 6 tubes, AC/DC.................$50.00

WR-162, table, 1939, wood, right front slide rule dial, left wrap-around cloth grill w/horizontal bars, tuning eye, BC, SW, 8 tubes, AC/DC $60.00

WR-165M, table, 1939, wood, right front round dial, left horizontal wrap-around louvers, BC, 5 tubes, AC......................$50.00

WR-166A, table, 1939, plastic, right front round dial, left & right horizontal wrap-around bars, 2 knobs, BC, AC $50.00

WR-168, table, 1939, wood, right front slide rule dial, left cloth grill w/2 horizontal bars, 2 knobs, BC, AC/DC $50.00

WR-169, table, 1939, wood, right front slide rule dial, left cloth grill w/vertical bars, 5 pushbuttons, 2 knobs, BC, 5 tubes, AC/DC $60.00

WR-170, table, 1939, two-tone walnut, right front slide rule dial, left wrap-around cloth grill w/horizontal bars, 6 pushbuttons, 2 knobs, BC, SW, 5 tubes, AC/DC $65.00

WR-172, table, 1939, wood, right front slide rule dial, left wrap-around cloth grill w/horizontal metal bars, pushbuttons, 4 knobs, BC, SW, 6 tubes, AC/DC $65.00

WR-182, table, 1940, two-tone walnut, right front dial, left grill area, 3 knobs, BC, SW, 5 tubes, AC/DC.....................$50.00

WR-186, table, two-tone wood, right front slide rule dial, left vertical grill bars, 6 pushbuttons, 4 knobs, AC $65.00

WR-201, tombstone, 1935, wood, lower front round dial, upper cloth grill w/cut-outs, BC, SW, 5 tubes, AC $95.00

WR-203, tombstone, 1935, wood, lower front round dial, upper cloth grill w/cut-outs, 4 knobs, BC, SW, 6 tubes, AC...$125.00

WR-204, tombstone, 1935, wood, lower front round dial, upper cloth grill w/cut-outs, 4 knobs, BC, SW, 7 tubes, AC...$135.00

WR-205, tombstone, 1935, wood, lower front round dial, upper cloth grill w/cut-outs, 4 knobs, BC, SW, 8 tubes, AC...$135.00

WR-207 "Trumpter," table, 1935, wood, front off-center round black & white dial, left grill area, 4 knobs, BC, SW, 5 tubes, AC $40.00

WR-208 "Jubileer," table, 1935, wood, front off-center round black & white dial, left grill area, 4 knobs, BC, SW, 5 tubes, AC $40.00

WR-209, table, 1936, wood, right front oval dial, left cloth grill w/horizontal bars, 3 knobs, BC, SW, AC $50.00

WR-210, table, 1936, wood, right front oval dial, left cloth grill w/center horizontal bar, 3 knobs, BC, SW, 5 tubes, AC ..$50.00

WR-211, table, 1936, wood, right front oval dial, left cloth horseshoe-shaped grill w/center horizontal bar, 4 knobs, BC, SW, AC $55.00

WR-212, table, 1936, wood, right front round dial, left cloth grill w/vertical bars, tuning eye, 4 knobs, BC, SW, AC $65.00

WR-214, tombstone, 1936, wood, lower front oval dial, upper cloth grill w/cut-outs and center tuning eye, 4 knobs, BC, SW, 10 tubes, AC..$150.00

WR-217, table, 1937, wood, right front oval dial, left cloth horseshoe-shaped grill w/cut-outs, BC, SW, 5 tubes, AC $55.00

WR-222, table, 1937, wood, large right front dial, left cloth grill w/cut-outs, 4 knobs, BC, SW, AC................................$50.00

WR-224, table, 1937, wood, large right front dial, left cloth grill w/horizontal bars, 4 knobs, BC, SW, AC $40.00

WR-228, table, 1937, walnut, right front dial, left wrap-around grill w/vertical bars, tuning eye, 4 knobs, BC, SW, 8 tubes, AC $55.00

WR-256, table, 1939, wood, right front dial, left wrap-around cloth grill w/horizontal bars, 5 tubes, AC..............................$50.00

WR-258, table, 1938, wood, lower front slide rule dial, upper cloth grill w/horizontal bars, 6 pushbuttons, 2 knobs, AC...**$60.00**

WR-262, table, 1939, wood, right front slide rule dial, left wrap-around cloth grill w/horizontal bars, tuning eye, pushbuttons, BC, SW, 6 tubes, AC.....................................$60.00

WR-264, table, 1939, wood, lower front slide rule dial, upper cloth grill w/vertical bars, tuning eye, pushbuttons, BC, SW, 7 tubes, AC...$65.00

WR-270, table, 1939, wood, right front slide rule dial, left wrap-around cloth grill w/horizontal bars, 6 pushbuttons, 2 knobs, 5 tubes, AC..$60.00

WR-272, table, 1939, wood, right front slide rule dial, left wrap-around cloth grill w/horizontal metal bars, pushbuttons, 4 knobs, BC, SW, 6 tubes, AC **$65.00**

WR-274, table, 1939, wood, right front slide rule dial, left wrap-around horizontal grill bars, tuning eye, pushbuttons, 4 knobs, BC, SW, 7 tubes, AC....................................$70.00

WR-288, table, 1940, wood, right front slide rule dial, left horizontal grill bars, 5 pushbuttons, 4 knobs, BC, SW, AC.......$60.00

WR-290, table, 1941, wood, upper front slanted slide rule dial, lower grill area, 6 pushbuttons, 4 knobs, BC, SW, 8 tubes, AC...$50.00

WR-303, console, 1935, wood, upper front round dial, lower cloth grill w/cut-outs, 4 knobs, BC, SW, 6 tubes, AC...........$135.00

WR-304, console, 1935, wood, upper front round dial, lower cloth grill w/cut-outs, 4 knobs, BC, SW, 7 tubes, AC..........$135.00

WR-305, console, 1935, wood, upper front round dial, lower cloth grill w/cut-outs, 4 knobs, BC, SW, 8 tubes, AC..........$140.00

WR-306, console, 1935, wood, upper front round dial, lower cloth grill w/cut-outs, 4 knobs, BC, SW, 10 tubes, AC.........$150.00

WR-311, console, 1936, wood, upper front round dial, lower cloth grill w/center vertical bars, 4 knobs, BC, SW, AC.......$130.00

WR-312, console, 1936, wood, upper front round dial, lower cloth grill w/vertical bars & cut-outs, tuning eye, 4 knobs, BC, SW, 8 tubes, AC...$150.00

WR-314, console, 1936, wood, upper front oval dial, lower cloth grill w/2 vertical bars, tuning eye, 4 knobs, BC, SW, 10 tubes, AC..$150.00

WR-315, console, 1936, wood, upper front oval dial, lower cloth grill w/center vertical divider, tuning eye, BC, SW, 12 tubes, AC..$165.00

WR-316, console, 1936, wood, upper front round dial, lower cloth grill w/vertical bars & cut-outs, BC, SW, AC/DC.........$130.00

WR-326, console, 1937, walnut, upper front dial, lower cloth grill w/center vertical bar, tuning eye, BC, SW, 7 tubes, AC..$145.00

WR-328, console, 1937, wood, upper front dial, lower cloth grill w/2 vertical bars, tuning eye, BC, SW, 8 tubes, AC....$145.00

WR-334, console, 1937, wood, upper front half-round dial, lower cloth grill w/center vertical bar, BC, SW, 12 tubes, AC..$175.00

WR-336, console, 1937, wood, upper front half-round dial w/automatic tuning, lower cloth grill w/center vertical bar, BC, SW, 12 tubes, AC...$180.00

WR-338, chairside, 1939, wood, slanted front dial, lower grill area, tuning eye, 4 knobs, BC, SW, 7 tubes, AC.................$160.00

WR-342, console, 1939, wood, upper front half-round dial w/automatic tuning, lower cloth grill w/center vertical bars, tuning eye, BC, SW, 8 tubes, AC...$150.00

WR-366, console, 1939, wood, upper front slide rule dial, lower cloth grill w/vertical bars, tuning eye, pushbuttons, 4 knobs, BC, SW, 8 tubes, AC...$140.00

WR-368, console, 1938, wood, upper front slide rule dial, lower cloth grill w/vertical bars, tuning eye, pushbuttons, 4 knobs, BC, SW, 10 tubes, AC..$165.00

WR-370, console, 1939, wood, upper front slide rule dial, lower cloth grill w/splayed bars, tuning eye, pushbuttons, 4 knobs, BC, SW, 12 tubes, AC..$165.00

WR-372, console, 1939, wood, upper front slide rule dial, lower cloth grill w/vertical bars, 6 pushbuttons, 4 knobs, BC, SW, 6 tubes, AC...$130.00

WR-373, console, 1939, wood, upper front slide rule dial, lower cloth grill w/center vertical bars, tuning eye, pushbuttons, 4 knobs, BC, SW, 7 tubes, AC.....................................$130.00

WR-373-Y, console, 1939, wood, upper front slide rule dial, lower cloth grill w/center vertical bars, tuning eye, pushbuttons, 4 knobs, BC, SW, 7 tubes, AC/DC................................$130.00

WR-374, console, 1939, wood, upper front slide rule dial, lower cloth grill w/center vertical bars, pushbuttons, 4 knobs, BC, SW, 8 tubes, AC...$140.00

WR-388, console, 1940, wood, upper front slide rule dial, lower cloth grill w/bars, 6 pushbuttons, 4 knobs, BC, SW, 9 tubes, AC $140.00

WR-468, table-R/P, 1939, two-tone wood, right front dial, left cloth grill w/horizontal bars, 2 knobs, lift top, inner phono, 5 tubes, AC $30.00

WR-470, table-R/P, 1939, wood, right front slide rule dial, left wrap-around cloth grill w/horizontal bars, pushbuttons, 3 knobs, lift top, inner phono, 5 tubes, AC $40.00

WR-472, table-R/P, 1939, wood, left front dial, right cloth grill w/horizontal bars, 3 knobs, lift top, inner phono, BC, AC $35.00

WR-473, console-R/P, 1939, wood, inner right dial/knobs, left phono, lift top, front cloth grill w/center vertical bars, BC, SW, 7 tubes, AC..$100.00

WR-474, console-R/P, 1939, wood, inner right dial/knobs, left phono, lift top, front cloth grill w/4 vertical bars, BC, SW, 8 tubes, AC..$100.00

WR-478, table-R/P, 1948, two-tone wood, right front dial, left grill, 3 knobs, lift top, inner phono, BC, 5 tubes, AC.............$30.00

WR-480, table-R/P, 1940, wood, right front slide rule dial, left cloth grill w/center horizontal bars, pushbuttons, 3 knobs, lift top, inner phono, AC **$35.00**

WR-602, tombstone, 1935, wood, center front round dial, upper cloth grill w/cut-outs, BC, SW, battery **$80.00**

WR-603, tombstone, 1936, wood, lower front round dial, upper 3-section cloth grill, 4 knobs, BC, 4 tubes, battery **$80.00**

WR-605, tombstone, 1936, wood, center front round dial, upper 3-section cloth grill, 4 knobs, BC, SW, 6 tubes, battery....**$80.00**

WR-606, console, 1936, wood, upper front round dial, lower cloth grill w/center vertical bars, 4 knobs, 4 tubes, battery **$75.00**

WR-608, console, 1936, wood, upper front round dial, lower cloth grill w/center vertical bars, 4 knobs, BC, SW, 6 tubes, battery **$75.00**

WR-675 "Carryette," portable, 1939, cloth covered, right front slide rule dial, left grill area, 2 knobs, handle, battery **$30.00**

WR-675A "Carryette," portable, 1939, cloth covered, right front slide rule dial, left grill area, 2 knobs, handle, battery ...**$30.00**

WR-678 "Carryette," portable, 1940, brown & white cloth covered, upper front dial, lower grill area, handle, 2 knobs, AC/DC/battery **$30.00**

WR-679 "Carryette," portable, 1940, two-tone leatherette, upper front dial, lower grill area, handle, 2 knobs, AC/DC/battery **$30.00**

WR-682, portable, 1941, inner horizontal chrome bars, right window dial, left cloth grill, flip-open front, BC, battery **$55.00**

WILCOX-GAY
Wilcox-Gay Corp., Charlotte, Michigan

5A6-75, tombstone, 1935, wood, center front round airplane dial, upper cloth grill w/cut-outs, 4 knobs, 6 tubes, battery. ..**$80.00**

A-17, table, 1936, circular case w/ebony finish, Deco, center front dial, decorative vertical bars, feet, 4 knobs, BC, SW, AC/DC **$550.00**

A-32, table, 1937, two-tone wood, upper front slide rule dial, center automatic tuning, right & left grill areas, AC **$60.00**

A-37, console, 1937, wood, upper front slide rule dial & telephone dial, lower cloth grill, 5 knobs, 6 tubes, AC.................**$165.00**

A-51, table, 1938, plastic, right front dial, left round cloth grill w/wrap-around horizontal bars, 2 knobs, BC, 4 tubes, AC/DC **$50.00**

A-52, table, 1938, walnut, right front slide rule dial, left cloth grill w/Deco cut-outs, BC, 5 tubes, AC...............................**$55.00**

A-53 "Thin Man," table, 1939, plastic, thin case can stand, lie or hang, front dial, cloth grill with bars, decorative case lines, 2 knobs, AC **$50.00**

A-54, table, 1939, walnut, right front slide rule dial, left horizontal wrap-around louvers, pushbuttons, BC, SW, 7 tubes, AC...........**$60.00**

A-55, console, 1939, walnut, upper front slide rule dial, lower horizontal grill bars, pushbuttons, BC, SW, 7 tubes, AC ...**$130.00**

A-58, table, 1940, wood, right front slide rule dial, left cloth grill with cut-outs, 4 tubes **$45.00**

A-69, console-R/P, 1939, walnut, inner dial/knobs/phono, lift top, front grill, lower record storage, AC...........................**$150.00**

A-111, console-R/P, 1941, wood, inner left slide rule dial, lower storage, right grill w/horizontal bars, lift top, inner phono, BC, FM, 9 tubes, AC **$135.00**

TXF-67, console-R/P, 1940, wood, inner right dial/knobs, left phono, lift top, lower front grill area, BC, SW, AC **$130.00**

WILMAK
Wilmak Corp., RR 3, Benton Harbor, Michigan

W-446 "Denchum," table, 1947, wood, top plastic handle w/built-in thumbwheel dials, side louvers, BC, AC/DC **$70.00**

WINGS

540, table, two-tone wood, right front dial, center cloth grill w/slanted cut-outs, base, 2 knobs, BC, AC/DC.........$75.00

01006, table, 1938, wood, large right front dial, left cloth grill w/Deco cut-outs, 6 pushbuttons, 3 knobs, BC, SW, 5 tubes, AC/DC $75.00

WOOLAROC
Phillips Petroleum Co.,
Bartlesville, Oklahoma

3-1A, table, 1946, plastic, streamline, upper front slanted slide rule dial, lower horizontal louvers wrap around left side, 3 knobs, BC, AC/DC $65.00

3-2A, table, 1946, plastic, streamline, upper front slanted slide rule dial, lower horizontal louvers wrap around left side, 3 knobs, BC, AC/DC.....................................$65.00

3-3A, table, 1946, wood, upper front slanted slide rule dial, lower cloth grill, 4 knobs, BC, 2SW, AC $50.00

3-5A, table, 1947, two-tone plastic, right front square dial, left horizontal grill bars, handle, 2 knobs, BC, AC/DC...............$65.00

3-6A/5, table, 1947, wood, upper front slanted slide rule dial, large lower cloth grill, 2 knobs, BC, AC/DC $35.00

3-9A, table, 1946, ivory plastic, upper front slide rule dial, lower criss-cross grill, 2 knobs, feet, BC, AC/DC $45.00

3-10A, table, 1946, plastic, upper front slide rule dial, lower criss-cross grill, 2 knobs, feet, BC, AC/DC $45.00

3-11A, table, 1946, wood, upper front slanted slide rule dial, lower criss-cross grill, 4 knobs, BC, SW, AC $35.00

3-12A/3, portable, 1947, leatherette, upper front slanted slide rule dial, lower metal grill, 2 knobs, handle, BC, AC/DC/battery $25.00

3-15A, table, 1948, metal, right front dial, left graduated horizontal louvers, 2 knobs, BC, AC/DC $60.00

3-17A, table, 1948, plastic, upper front slide rule dial, lower horizontal louvers, 2 knobs, BC, AC/DC $45.00

3-20A, table-R/P, 1947, wood, upper front slanted slide rule dial, lower horizontal louvers, 4 knobs, lift top, inner phono, BC, AC $35.00

3-29A, table-R/P, 1946, wood, top right vertical slide rule dial, 3 knobs, right front grill, left lift top, inner phono, BC, AC ..$25.00

3-70A, console-R/P, 1948, wood, inner right slide rule dial/4 knobs, door, left pull out phono drawer, lower front grill, BC, SW, AC..$85.00

3-71A, console-R/P, 1948, wood, inner right slide rule dial/4 knobs, door, left pull-out phono drawer, lower front grill, BC, FM, AC $85.00

WORKRITE
The Workrite Manufacturing Co.,
1806 East 30th Street,
Cleveland, Ohio

Workrite began business manufacturing automobile equipment. Following WW I, they began to produce radio parts and by 1924 were producing complete radio sets. Due to increasing competition, by 1929 the company was out of business.

17, table, 1927, two-tone wood, low rectangular case, slanted front panel w/center window dial, 2 knobs, 6 tubes, battery $90.00

18, table, 1928, two-tone wood, low rectangular case, slanted front panel w/center window dial, 2 knobs, AC...........$110.00

38, table, 1928, wood, rectangular case, center front window dial w/escutcheon, 2 knobs, 9 tubes, AC $130.00

Air Master, table, 1924, wood, high rectangular case, slanted 3 dial front panel, 5 tubes, battery $120.00

Aristocrat, console, 1924, mahogany, inner slanted 3 dial panel, fold-down front, inner left speaker, inner right storage, battery..$235.00

Chum, table, 1924, wood, high rectangular case, slanted 2 dial front panel w/3 exposed tubes, battery $225.00

Radio King, table, 1924, mahogany, tall case, lower front slanted 3 dial panel, upper enclosed speaker w/grill cut-outs, 5 tubes, battery $210.00

WURLITZER LYRIC
Rudolph Wurlitzer Mfg. Co.,
North Tonawanda, New York

408, console, two-tone wood, upper front window dial, lower cloth grill w/cut-outs, feet, BC, SW.....................................$120.00

470-B, tombstone, wood, center front round dial, upper cloth grill w/cut-outs, vertical fluting, 4 knobs, BC, SW, 7 tubes $110.00

470-W, console, wood, upper front round dial, lower cloth grill w/cut-outs, vertical fluting, BC, SW $120.00

C-4-LI, table, 1934, wood, right front dial, center grill w/horizontal louvers, 2 knobs, 2 band, 4 tubes $55.00

M-4-L, table, 1934, wood, right front dial, left horizontal wrap-around louvers, 4 tubes..$55.00

M-4-LI, table, 1934, two-tone wood, right front dial, left horizontal wrap-around louvers, 4 tubes.....................................$60.00

SA-5-L, tombstone, 1934, wood, shouldered, center front window dial, upper cloth grill w/cut-outs, 3 knobs, 5 tubes.......$120.00

SA-46, console, 1934, wood, lowboy, upper front window dial, lower cloth grill with cut-outs, 4 tubes.........................$120.00

SA-99, console, 1934, wood, lowboy, upper front window dial, lower cloth grill with cut-outs, 6 legs, 9 tubes $145.00

SA-120, console, 1934, wood, lowboy, upper front half-round dial, lower cloth grill w/cut-outs, 6 legs, 12 tubes $180.00

SA-133, console, 1934, wood, upper front quarter-round dial, lower cloth grill with cut-outs, 13 tubes.......................$200.00

SU-5 "Duncan Phyfe," side table, 1934, wood, Duncan Phyfe style, inner dial & knobs, fold-down front, 5 tubes, AC/DC $150.00

SU-5 "Queen Ann," side table, 1934, wood, Queen Ann style, inner dial & knobs, fold-down front, 5 tubes, AC/DC ...$150.00

SW-88, tombstone, 1934, two-tone wood, step-down top, center front window dial, upper horizontal grill bars, 4 knobs, BC, SW, 8 tubes..$100.00

SW-89, console, 1934, wood, upper front window dial, lower cloth grill w/cut-outs, 6 legs, 4 knobs, 8 tubes $135.00

ZANEY-GILL
Zaney-Gill Corp.,
Los Angeles, California

2445 "Music Box," cathedral, 1930, wood, center front window dial, upper cloth grill w/cut-outs, small fluted columns, 3 knobs, 6 tubes $225.00

Clarion, cathedral, 1930, mahogany, lower front dial w/ornate bronze-finished escutcheon, upper round grill, AC $250.00

Legionair, cathedral, 1930, mahogany, peaked top, Deco, center front dial, upper grill w/"sun-burst" cut-outs, AC $265.00

ZENITH
Zenith Radio Corporation,
Chicago, Illinois

The Zenith company began as Chicago Radio Labs in 1918 and the name "Zenith" came from the station call letters of its founders — 9ZN. Commander Eugene McDonald built Zenith into one of the most successful and prolific of radio manufacturers. Some of the most sought after Zenith sets today are the black dial sets of the 1930's.

3-R, table, 1923, wood, low rectangular case, 1 dial front panel, 4 tubes, battery..$375.00

4-B-131, tombstone, 1937, walnut, lower front round dial, upper cloth grill w/cut-outs, decorative fluting, BC, 4 tubes, battery..$130.00

4-B-132, table, 1937, wood, cube-shaped, step-down sides, front round dial, top grill, BC, 4 tubes, battery $100.00

4-B-231, table, 1937, wood, lower front black dial, upper cloth grill w/vertical bars, BC, 4 tubes, battery.............................$55.00

4-B-313, table, 1939, plastic, right front dial, rounded left w/horizontal wrap-around grill bars, 2 knobs, BC, 4 tubes, battery $75.00

4-B-314, table, 1939, plastic, right front dial, rounded left w/horizontal wrap-around grill bars, 5 pushbuttons, 2 knobs, BC, 4 tubes, battery..$85.00

4-B-317, table, 1939, wood, right front dial, rounded left wrap-around grill w/vertical glass bars, pushbuttons, 2 knobs, BC, 4 tubes, battery..$125.00

4-B-355, console, 1939, wood, upper front slanted dial, lower cloth grill w/vertical bars, BC, 4 tubes, battery $85.00

4-B-422, table, 1940, plastic, right front dial, rounded left w/horizontal wrap-around grill bars, 2 knobs, BC, 4 tubes, battery..$75.00

4-B-437, table, 1940, walnut, right front dial, left wrap-around grill w/horizontal bars, 2 knobs, BC, 4 tubes, battery...........$40.00

4-B-466, console, 1940, wood, upper front dial, lower cloth grill w/vertical bars, BC, 4 tubes, battery..............................$85.00

4-B-515, table, 1941, plastic, right front dial, rounded/raised left w/horizontal wrap-around louvers, 2 knobs, BC, 4 tubes, battery $110.00

4-B-535, table, 1941, walnut, right front dial, left wrap-around grill w/horizontal bars, 2 knobs, BC, 4 tubes, battery...........$40.00

4-B-536, table, 1941, wood, right front dial, left cloth grill w/cut-outs, 2 knobs, BC, 4 tubes, battery $45.00

4-B-639, table, 1942, wood, right front black dial, left cloth grill w/crossed bars, 2 knobs, BC, 4 tubes, battery $45.00

4-F-227, table, 1937, wood, lower front black dial, upper cloth grill w/vertical bars, BC, 4 tubes, battery..........................$55.00

4-G-800, portable, 1948, plastic, inner left dial, large lattice grill area, flip-up front, handle, BC, AC/DC/battery $35.00

4-G-800Z, portable, 1948, plastic, inner left dial, large lattice grill area, flip-up front, handle, BC, AC/DC/battery $35.00

4-J-40, portable, plastic, top dial & on/off/volume knobs, front round perforated grill area w/center crest, handle, BC, AC/battery $35.00

4-K-016, table, 1946, mottled plastic, front inverted V-shaped dial & louvers, 2 knobs, handle, BC, 4 tubes, battery $40.00

4-K-035, table, 1946, walnut veneer, right front black dial, left cloth grill w/horizontal bars, 2 knobs, BC, 4 tubes, battery..$45.00

4-K-035G, table, 1946, limed walnut, right front black dial, left cloth grill w/horizontal bars, 2 knobs, BC, 4 tubes, battery..$45.00

5-S-128, table, 1937, wood, cube-shaped, center front round black dial, top grill cut-outs, 4 knobs, BC, SW, 5 tubes, AC $140.00

5-S-150, console, 1937, wood, upper front round black dial, lower cloth grill w/vertical bars, 4 knobs, BC, SW, 5 tubes, AC $150.00

5-S-151, console, 1936, wood, upper front round black dial, lower cloth grill w/vertical bar, BC, SW, 5 tubes, AC $175.00

5-S-161, console, 1937, wood, upper front round black dial, lower cloth grill w/vertical bars, BC, SW, 5 tubes, AC...........$160.00

5-S-218, table, 1937, wood, front off-center round black dial, left grill cut-outs, feet, 3 knobs, BC, SW, 5 tubes, AC $140.00

5-S-220, table, 1937, wood, large center front round black dial, feet, 3 knobs, BC, SW, 5 tubes, AC $150.00

5-S-220Y, table, 1937, ebony finish, large center round black dial, feet, 3 knobs, BC, SW, 5 tubes, AC $175.00

5-S-228, tombstone, 1937, wood, lower front round black dial, upper cloth grill w/cut-outs, feet, 3 knobs, BC, SW, 5 tubes, AC $150.00

5-S-228W, tombstone, 1937, bone white, lower front round black dial, upper cloth grill w/cut-outs, feet, 3 knobs, BC, SW, 5 tubes, AC...$150.00

5-S-237, chairside, 1938, wood, Deco, step-down top w/round dial & knobs, front vertical grill bars, lower shelf, BC, SW, 5 tubes, AC $150.00

5-S-237W, chairside, 1938, bone white, Deco, step-down top w/round dial & knobs, front vertical grill bars, lower shelf, BC, SW, 5 tubes, AC...$150.00

5-S-237Y, chairside, 1938, ebony, Deco, step-down top w/round dial & knobs, front vertical grill bars, lower shelf, BC, SW, 5 tubes, AC $160.00

5-S-250, console, 1937, wood, upper front round black dial, lower cloth grill w/vertical bars, BC, SW, 5 tubes, AC $125.00

5-S-252, console, 1937, wood, upper front round black dial, lower cloth grill w/vertical bars, 3 knobs, BC, SW, 5 tubes, AC .$130.00

5-S-319, table, 1937, wood, front oblong gold dial, left wrap-around cloth grill w/horizontal bars, 5 pushbuttons, 4 knobs, BC, SW, 5 tubes, AC...$100.00

5-S-320, table, 1939, wood, front oblong gold dial, left horizontal wrap-around grill bars, 5 pushbuttons, 4 knobs, BC, SW, 5 tubes, AC $100.00

5-S-327, tombstone, 1938, wood, lower front oblong gold dial, upper cloth grill w/horizontal bars, pushbuttons, 4 knobs, BC, SW, 5 tubes, AC...$175.00

5-S-338, chairside, 1939, wood, top dial/knobs/pushbuttons, front grill, lower open storage, BC, SW, 5 tubes, AC $150.00

5-S-339M, chairside, 1939, wood, top dial/knobs/pushbuttons, front grill, lower open storage, BC, SW, 5 tubes, AC ..$150.00

5-X-230, tombstone, 1939, wood, lower front round black dial, upper cloth grill w/cut-outs, 4 knobs, BC, SW, 5 tubes, battery...$130.00

5-X-248, chairside, 1939, wood, half-round, top round black dial & 4 knobs, front grill, BC, SW, 5 tubes, battery $110.00

5-X-274, console, 1939, wood, upper front round black dial, lower cloth grill w/vertical bars, BC, SW, 5 tubes, battery.....$115.00

6-A-40 "Transoceanic," portable, black leatherette, inner multi-band dial, lattice grill, fold-up front, handle....................$80.00

6-B-129, tombstone, 1936, wood, lower front black dial, upper cloth grill w/cut-outs and scalloped top edge, BC, SW, 6 tubes, battery...$150.00

6-B-164, console, 1937, wood, upper front black dial, lower cloth grill w/vertical bars, BC, SW, 6 tubes, battery $145.00

6-B-321, table, 1939, wood, front round dial, left wrap-around grill, pushbuttons, 4 knobs, BC, SW, 6 tubes, battery..........$60.00

6-D-014, table, 1946, swirl plastic, front inverted V-shaped dial & louvers, handle, 2 knobs, BC, 6 tubes, AC/DC $50.00

6-D-014W, table, 1946, white plastic, front inverted V-shaped dial & louvers, handle, 2 knobs, BC, 6 tubes, AC/DC $50.00

6-D-014Y, table, 1946, black plastic, front inverted V-shaped dial & louvers, handle, 2 knobs, BC, 6 tubes, AC/DC $50.00

6-D-015 "Consoltone," table, 1946, walnut plastic, right front quarter-round dial, right & left concentric quarter-round louvers, metal center strip, handle, BC, 6 tubes, AC/DC ...$65.00

6-D-015W "Consoltone," table, 1946, ivory plastic, right front quarter-round dial, right & left concentric quarter-round louvers, metal center strip, handle, BC, 6 tubes, AC/DC ...$65.00

6-D-015Y "Consoltone," table, 1946, black plastic, right front quarter-round dial, right & left concentric quarter-round louvers, metal center strip, handle, BC, 6 tubes, AC/DC ...$65.00

6-D-029, table, 1946, walnut, front inverted V-shaped black dial, lower cloth grill, 2 knobs, BC, 6 tubes, AC/DC $50.00

6-D-029G, table, 1946, lime walnut, front inverted V-shaped black dial, lower cloth grill, 2 knobs, BC, 6 tubes, AC/DC $50.00

6-D-030, table, 1946, walnut, right front quarter-round black dial, right & left cloth grill areas, metal center strip, BC, 6 tubes, AC/DC $55.00

6-D-030E, table, 1946, mahogany, right front quarter-round black dial, right & left cloth grill areas, metal center strip, BC, 6 tubes, AC/DC $55.00

6-D-116, table, 1936, wood, right front round black dial, left cloth grill w/horizontal bars, 3 knobs, BC, SW, 6 tubes, AC ..$65.00

6-D-117, table, 1936, wood, right front round black dial, left cloth grill w/horizontal bars, 3 knobs, BC, SW, 6 tubes, AC..$75.00

6-D-118, table, 1936, wood, right front round black dial, left cloth grill w/vertical bars, 6 tubes, AC $55.00

6-D-219, table, 1937, wood, rounded right top, right front round dial, left cloth grill w/horizontal bars, 3 knobs, BC, SW, 6 tubes, AC/DC $65.00

6-D-219W, table, 1937, bone white, rounded right top, right front round dial, left cloth grill w/horizontal bars, 3 knobs, BC, SW, 6 tubes, AC/DC $65.00

6-D-219Y, table, 1937, ebony, rounded right top, right front round dial, left cloth grill w/horizontal bars, 3 knobs, BC, SW, 6 tubes, AC/DC $65.00

6-D-221, table, 1937, wood, right front round black dial, left cloth grill w/cut-outs, feet, 3 knobs, BC, SW, 6 tubes, AC/DC..$65.00

6-D-311, table, 1938, plastic, Deco, right front half-round dial, left horizontal wrap-around louvers, "Z" knob, BC, 6 tubes, AC $150.00

6-D-312, table, 1938, plastic, right front dial, rounded/raised left w/horizontal wrap-around louvers, pushbuttons, 2 knobs, BC, 6 tubes, AC/DC $150.00

6-D-315, table, 1938, plastic, Deco, right front half-round dial, left horizontal wrap-around louvers, handle, "Z" knob, BC, 6 tubes...$160.00

6-D-316, table, 1938, wood, right front dial, left cloth grill w/horizontal bars, pushbuttons, 2 knobs, BC, 6 tubes, AC/DC......$60.00

6-D-317, table, 1938, wood, right front dial, rounded left wrap-around grill w/vertical glass bars, pushbuttons, 2 knobs, 6 tubes, AC/DC $250.00

6-D-326, table, 1938, wood, miniature child's console, upper front half-round dial, lower cloth grill w/center vertical bar, "Z" knob, BC, 6 tubes, AC..$200.00

6-D-336, chairside, 1938, wood, top dial & knobs, slanted grill w/horizontal bars, legs, BC, 6 tubes, AC $110.00

6-D-337, chairside, 1938, wood, top dial/knobs/pushbuttons, front grill, lower open storage, BC, 6 tubes, AC/DC $115.00

6-D-410, table, 1939, brown plastic, right front dial, left vertical wrap-over grill bars, BC, 6 tubes, AC/DC $75.00

6-D-411, table, 1939, plastic, right front dial, left vertical wrap-over grill bars, BC, 6 tubes, AC/DC $75.00

6-D-413, table, 1939, brown plastic, front off-center dial, left vertical wrap-over grill bars, 5 pushbuttons, 6 tubes, AC/DC $85.00

6-D-414, table, 1939, plastic, front off-center dial, left vertical wrap-over grill bars, 5 pushbuttons, 6 tubes, AC/DC $85.00

6-D-425, table, 1939, wood, right front dial, left cloth grill w/vertical bars, BC, 6 tubes, AC/DC $50.00

6-D-426, table, 1939, wood, right front dial, left cloth grill w/vertical spiral bars, pushbuttons, BC, 6 tubes, AC/DC $70.00

6-D-427, table, 1939, wood, right front dial, left cloth grill w/horizontal bars, pushbuttons, BC, 6 tubes, AC/DC $65.00

6-D-446, chairside, 1940, wood, top dial/knobs/pushbuttons, front grill, right & left storage, BC, 6 tubes, AC/DC $125.00

6-D-455, bookcase, 1940, wood, inner dial/knobs/grill, fold-down front, 2 lower shelves, BC, 6 tubes, AC/DC $200.00

6-D-510, table, 1941, brown plastic, right front black dial over horizontal wrap-around grill bars, handle, 2 knobs, 6 tubes, AC/DC $45.00

6-D-510W, table, 1941, ivory plastic, right front black dial over horizontal wrap-around grill bars, handle, 2 knobs, 6 tubes, AC/DC.......$45.00

6-D-516, table, 1940, plastic, right front black dial over horizontal wrap-around grill bars, handle, 2 knobs, 6 tubes $45.00

6-D-520, table, 1941, two-tone walnut plastic, right front black dial over wrap-around lattice grill, handle, 2 knobs, BC, 6 tubes, AC/DC $45.00

6-D-520W, table, 1941, plastic, right front black dial over wrap-around lattice grill, handle, 2 knobs, BC, 6 tubes, AC/DC $45.00

6-D-525, table, 1941, walnut, right front black dial, left raised horizontal grill bars, 2 "Z" knobs, BC, 6 tubes, AC/DC $70.00

6-D-526, table, 1941, walnut, "waterfall" front, right dial, left vertical grill bars, BC, 6 tubes, AC/DC $65.00

6-D-538, table, 1941, wood, right front black dial, left horizontal & vertical grill cut-outs, decorative case lines, 2 knobs, BC, 6 tubes, AC/DC $65.00

6-D-612, table, 1942, brown plastic, right front recessed black dial, horizontal wrap-around grill bars, handle, 2 knobs, BC, 6 tubes, AC/DC $45.00

6-D-612W, table, 1942, white plastic, right front recessed black dial, horizontal wrap-around grill bars, handle, 2 knobs, BC, 6 tubes, AC/DC...................................$45.00

6-D-614 "Consoltone," table, 1942, plastic, front black "boomerang" dial w/inner concentric circular louvers, handle, 2 knobs, BC, 6 tubes, AC/DC.......................................$55.00

6-D-614W "Consoltone," table, 1942, black & white plastic, front black "boomerang" dial w/inner concentric circular louvers, handle, 2 knobs, BC, 6 tubes, AC/DC $65.00

6-D-615 "Consoltone," table, 1942, plastic, front "boomerang" dial w/inner curved grill bars, 4 pushbuttons, handle, 2 knobs, BC, 6 tubes, AC/DC $65.00

6-D-615W "Consoltone," table, 1942, white plastic, front "boomerang" dial w/inner curved grill bars, 4 pushbuttons, handle, 2 knobs, BC, 6 tubes, AC/DC $65.00

6-D-620, table, 1942, plastic, front black "boomerang" dial w/inner concentric circular louvers, handle, 2 knobs, BC, SW, 6 tubes, AC/DC $55.00

6-D-620W, table, 1942, black & white plastic, front black "boomerang" dial w/inner concentric circular louvers, handle, 2 knobs, BC, SW, 6 tubes, AC/DC $65.00

6-D-628, table, 1942, wood, right front black dial, left cloth grill w/cut-outs, 2 knobs, BC, 6 tubes, AC/DC $50.00

6-D-629, table, 1942, wood, front black "boomerang" dial, lower cloth grill w/cut-outs, 2 knobs, BC, 6 tubes, AC/DC $45.00

6-D-630, table, 1942, wood, front black "boomerang" dial, center round cloth grill w/cut-outs, 4 pushbuttons, 2 knobs, BC, 6 tubes, AC/DC $55.00

6-D-644, table, 1942, wood, front black "boomerang" dial, center cloth grill w/cut-outs, 2 knobs, BC, SW, 6 tubes, AC/DC...$45.00

6-D-815, table, 1949, plastic, front round dial w/numbers on clear plastic over large metal grill area, flex handle, 2 knobs, BC, 6 tubes, AC/DC $30.00

6-D-2615, table, 1942, wood, arched top, front black "bomerang" dial, lower cloth grill w/vertical bars, 4 pushbuttons, 2 knobs, BC, 6 tubes...$60.00

6-G-001Y "Universal," portable, 1946, black leatherette, inner right quarter-round dial, right & left concentric quarter-round louvers, metal center strip, flip up lid, handle, 2 knobs, BC, 6 tubes, AC/DC/battery $40.00

6-G-001YX "Universal," portable, 1946, black leatherette, inner right quarter-round dial, right & left concentric quarter-round louvers, metal center strip, flip up lid, handle, 2 knobs, BC, 6 tubes, AC/DC/battery $40.00

6-G-004Y "Universal," portable, 1947, black leatherette, inner right quarter-round dial, right & left concentric quarter-round louvers, metal center strip, flip up lid, handle, 2 knobs, BC, SW, 6 tubes, AC/DC/battery..$40.00

6-G-005TZ1 "Transoceanic," portable, black leatherette, inner black dial, right & left grill areas, fold-up front w/"Z" logo, handle, 6 tubes, AC/DC/battery..$80.00

6-G-038, table, 1948, wood, right front black dial, left criss-cross grill, pushbuttons, 2 knobs, telescoping antenna, BC, 2SW, 6 tubes, AC/DC/battery **$50.00**

6-G-560, console, 1941, wood, upper front black dial, lower cloth grill w/center vertical bar, BC, 6 tubes, AC/DC/battery ..**$130.00**

6-G-601D, portable, 1942, blue/gray cloth covered, inner right black dial, left grill w/sailboat, 2 knobs, fold-down front, handle, BC, 6 tubes, AC/DC/battery..........................$55.00

6-G-601L, portable, 1942, leather, inner wood panel w/right black dial & left grill w/sailboat, 2 knobs, fold-down front, handle, BC, 6 tubes, AC/DC/battery **$65.00**

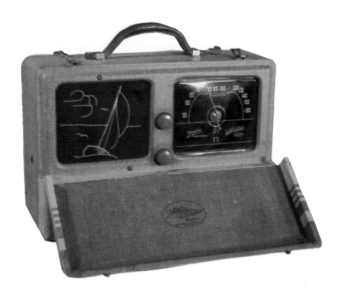

6-G-601M, portable, 1941, brown cloth covered, inner right black dial, left grill w/sailboat, 2 knobs, fold-down front, handle, BC, 6 tubes, AC/DC/battery..........................$55.00

6-G-601MH, portable, 1941, brown/ivory, inner right black dial, left grill w/sailboat, 2 knobs, fold-down front, handle, BC, 6 tubes, AC/DC/battery **$55.00**

6-G-601ML, portable, 1942, brown "alligator," inner right black dial, left grill w/sailboat, 2 knobs, fold-down front, handle, BC, 6 tubes, AC/DC/battery **$65.00**

6-G-601Y, portable, 1948, leatherette, inner right quarter-round dial, right & left concentric quarter-round louvers, metal center strip, flip up lid, handle, 2 knobs, 6 tubes **$40.00**

6-G-638, table, 1942, wood, right front black dial, left cloth grill w/cut-outs, pushbuttons, 2 knobs, BC, SW, 6 tubes, AC/DC/battery **$60.00**

6-G-660, console, 1942, wood, upper front slanted black dial, lower cloth grill w/vertical bars, pushbuttons, 2 knobs, BC, SW, 6 tubes, AC/DC/battery......................................**$150.00**

6-G-801, portable, 1949, plastic, inner dial/grill/knobs, fold-open front doors, flex handle, pull-up antenna, 2 knobs, BC, 6 tubes, AC/DC/battery **$45.00**

6-J-230, tombstone, 1937, wood, lower front round black dial, upper cloth grill w/cut-outs, 4 knobs, BC, SW, 6 tubes, battery/AC **$160.00**

6-J-257, console, 1937, wood, upper front round black dial, lower cloth grill w/center vertical divider, 4 knobs, BC, SW, 6 tubes, battery/AC **$165.00**

6-J-322, table, 1939, wood, step-down top, right front dial, rounded left grill w/horizontal bars, pushbuttons, 4 knobs, BC, SW, 6 tubes, battery/AC...**$85.00**

6-J-357, console, 1939, wood, front round black dial, lower cloth grill w/vertical bars, pushbuttons, BC, SW, 6 tubes, battery/AC **$185.00**

6-J-436, tombstone, 1940, wood, lower front round black dial, upper wrap-over grill w/vertical bars, pushbuttons, BC, SW, 6 tubes, battery/AC..**$135.00**

6-J-463, console, 1940, wood, upper front round black dial, lower cloth grill w/vertical bars, pushbuttons, BC, SW, 6 tubes, battery/AC **$185.00**

6-L-03, table-C, 1953, plastic, step-down top, right front dial/left alarm clock overlap center horizontal bars w/crest, feet, 5 knobs, BC...**$35.00**

6-P-416, table, 1940, brown plastic, right front dial, left vertical wrap-over grill bars, BC, 6 tubes, AC **$65.00**

6-P-417, table, 1940, plastic, right front dial, left vertical wrap-over grill bars, BC, 6 tubes, AC **$65.00**

6-P-418, table, 1940, brown plastic, right front dial, left horizontal wrap-around louvers, pushbuttons, handle, BC, 6 tubes, AC **$60.00**

6-P-419, table, 1940, plastic, right front dial, left horizontal wrap-around louvers, pushbuttons, handle, BC, 6 tubes, AC..**$60.00**

6-P-429, table, 1940, wood, right front dial, left wrap-around cloth grill w/horizontal bars, pushbuttons, BC, 6 tubes, AC ...**$65.00**

6-P-430, table, 1940, step-down top, right front dial, rounded left w/horizontal wrap-around louvers, pushbuttons, BC, 6 tubes, AC **$100.00**

6-R-060, console, 1946, walnut, upper front slanted black dial, large lower cloth grill w/3 vertical bars, BC, 6 tubes, AC **$130.00**

6-R-084, table-R/P, 1947, wood, front black "boomerang" dial, cloth grill, lift top, inner phono, feet, BC, 6 tubes, AC....**$40.00**

6-R-087, console-R/P, 1946, walnut, upper front black dial, 2 knobs, center pull-out phono, lower cloth grill, BC, 6 tubes, AC ..**$110.00**

6-R-480, table-R/P, 1940, wood, right front dial, left cloth grill w/cut-outs, feet, open top phono, BC, 6 tubes, AC **$40.00**

6-R-481, table-R/P, 1940, wood, right front dial, rounded left w/grill cut-outs, lift top, inner phono, BC, 6 tubes, AC............**$100.00**

6-R-583, table-R/P, 1941, walnut, right front black dial, left grill, 3 knobs, lift top, inner phono, BC, 6 tubes, AC **$35.00**

6-R-631, table, 1941, wood, front black "boomerang" dial, lower cloth grill w/cut-outs, pushbuttons, 2 knobs, BC, 6 tubes, AC ...**$75.00**

6-R-683, table-R/P, 1942, wood, right front black dial, left cloth grill w/2 vertical bars, 4 knobs, lift top, inner phono, BC, 6 tubes, AC..**$40.00**

6-R-684, table-R/P, 1942, wood, right front black dial, left cloth grill w/vertical bars, 4 knobs, lift top, inner phono, BC, 6 tubes, AC **$40.00**

6-R-687, console-R/P, 1942, walnut, inner right black dial/left phono, lift top, front cloth grill w/lyre cut-out, BC, 6 tubes, AC..**$150.00**

6-R-687R, console-R/P, 1942, mahogany, inner right black dial/left phono, lift top, front cloth grill w/lyre cut-out, BC, 6 tubes, AC..**$150.00**

6-R-688 "Modern," console-R/P, 1942, blonde, inner right black dial/left phono, lift top, front cloth grill w/cut-outs, feet, BC, 6 tubes, AC..**$130.00**

6-R-886, table-R/P, 1948, wood, front round dial/louvers, 2 knobs, fold-back cover, inner phono, BC, 6 tubes, AC.............**$40.00**

6-S-27, tombstone, 1935, wood, lower front round black dial, upper cloth grill w/cut-outs & scalloped top edge, 4 knobs, BC, SW, 6 tubes, AC...**$225.00**

6-S-52, console, 1935, wood, upper front round black dial, lower cloth grill w/cut-outs, 4 knobs, BC, SW, 6 tubes, AC...**$225.00**

6-S-128, tombstone, 1936, wood, lower front black dial, upper cloth grill w/horizontal bars, BC, SW, 6 tubes, AC ..$225.00

6-S-137 "Zephyr," tombstone, 1936, wood, lower front black dial, upper cloth grill w/horizontal wrap-around louvers, BC, SW, 6 tubes, AC...**$225.00**

6-S-147 "Zephyr," chairside, 1936, wood, Deco, top dial & knobs, lower horizontal wrap-around louvers, BC, SW, 6 tubes, AC...**$160.00**

6-S-152, console, 1936, wood, upper front black dial, lower cloth grill w/3 vertical bars, BC, SW, 6 tubes, AC...............**$195.00**

6-S-157 "Zephyr," console, 1936, wood, upper front black dial, lower horizontal wrap-around louvers, BC, SW, 6 tubes, AC **$200.00**

6-S-203, chairside-R/P, 1937, wood, top round dial, lift top, inner phono, lower record storage, BC, SW, 6 tubes, AC....**$145.00**

6-S-203W, chairside-R/P, 1937, bone white, top round dial, lift top, inner phono, lower record storage, BC, SW, 6 tubes, AC **$145.00**

6-S-222, table, 1937, wood, cube-shaped, center front round black dial, top grill w/cut-outs, 4 knobs, BC, SW, 6 tubes, AC **$140.00**

6-S-223, table, 1937, wood, right front round black dial, left cloth grill w/cut-outs, feet, 4 knobs, BC, SW, 6 tubes, AC ...**$130.00**

6-S-229, tombstone, 1937, wood, lower front round black dial, upper cloth grill w/cut-outs, 4 knobs, BC, SW, 6 tubes, AC **$160.00**

6-S-238, chairside, 1938, wood, half-round, top dial & knobs, front grill w/vertical bars, BC, SW, 6 tubes, AC **$185.00**

6-S-239, chairside, 1937, wood, step-down top w/round black dial & 4 knobs, lower open storage, BC, SW, 6 tubes, AC **$140.00**

6-S-241, chairside/bar, 1937, wood, top round dial & 4 knobs, front cloth grill w/vertical bars, storage & bar area, BC, SW, 6 tubes, AC...**$160.00**

6-S-241W, chairside/bar, 1937, bone white, top round dial & 4 knobs, front cloth grill w/vertical bars, storage & bar area, BC, SW, 6 tubes, AC..**$160.00**

6-S-249, chairside, 1938, wood, half-round, top dial & knobs, lower front horizontal wrap-around louvers, BC, SW, 6 tubes, AC **$190.00**

6-S-254, console, 1937, wood, upper front black triangular dial, lower cloth grill w/vertical bars, BC, SW, 6 tubes, AC ..**$225.00**

6-S-254H, console, 1937, wood, upper front black triangular dial, lower cloth grill w/vertical bars, BC, SW, 6 tubes, AC ..**$225.00**

6-S-254W, console, 1937, bone white, upper front black triangular dial, lower cloth grill w/vertical bars, BC, SW, 6 tubes, AC........**$225.00**

6-S-254Y, console, 1937, ebony, upper front black triangular dial, lower cloth grill w/vertical bars, BC, SW, 6 tubes, AC ..**$230.00**

6-S-256, console, 1937, wood, upper front black triangular dial, lower recessed cloth grill w/center vertical divider, 4 knobs, BC, SW, 6 tubes, AC...**$235.00**

6-S-275, console, 1938, wood, upper front round black dial, lower cloth grill w/vertical bars, BC, SW, 6 tubes, AC...........**$225.00**

6-S-301, chairside-R/P, 1939, wood, top dial & knobs, lift top, inner phono, rounded front w/horizontal wrap-around louvers, BC, SW, 6 tubes, AC...**$185.00**

6-S-305, console-R/P, 1938, wood, inner left dial/pushbuttons, right phono, lift top, front cloth grill w/center vertical bar, 6 tubes...**$160.00**

6-S-321, table, 1937, wood, right front dial, left wrap-around cloth grill w/center horizontal bars, pushbuttons, 4 knobs, BC, SW, 6 tubes, AC..**$75.00**

6-S-322, table, 1939, wood, step-down top, right front dial, left wrap-around cloth grill w/horizontal bars, pushbuttons, 4 knobs, BC, SW, 6 tubes, AC **$90.00**

6-S-330, tombstone, 1938, wood, lower front round black dial, upper cloth grill w/cut-outs, pushbuttons, BC, SW, 6 tubes, AC **$170.00**

6-S-340, chairside, 1939, wood, half-round, top dial/knobs/push-buttons, wrap-around vertical grill bars, BC, SW, 6 tubes, AC **$195.00**

6-S-341, chairside, 1938, wood, Deco, half-round, top dial & knobs, lower front horizontal wrap-around louvers, BC, SW, 6 tubes, AC...**$210.00**

6-S-361, console, 1939, wood, upper front round black dial, lower cloth grill w/vertical bars, pushbuttons, BC, SW, 6 tubes, AC..**$215.00**

6-S-362, console, 1939, wood, upper front round black dial, lower cloth grill w/vertical bars, pushbuttons, BC, SW, 6 tubes, AC..**$215.00**

6-S-439, table, 1940, wood, front black slide rule dial, left wrap-around cloth grill w/horizontal bars, pushbuttons, BC, SW, 6 tubes..**$100.00**

6-S-469, console, 1940, wood, upper front slide rule dial, lower cloth grill w/vertical bars, pushbuttons, BC, SW, 6 tubes, AC..**$140.00**

6-S-511, table, 1941, brown plastic, right front dial, left horizontal wrap-around grill bars, pushbuttons, handle, BC, SW, 6 tubes, AC..**$55.00**

6-S-511W, table, 1941, ivory plastic, right front dial, left horizontal wrap-around grill bars, pushbuttons, handle, BC, SW, 6 tubes, AC..**$55.00**

6-S-527, table, 1941, wood, right front dial, left horizontal grill bars, pushbuttons, 3 knobs, BC, SW, 6 tubes, AC........**$60.00**

6-S-528, table, 1941, wood, right front black dial, left cloth grill w/vertical bars, pushbuttons, 3 knobs, BC, SW, 6 tubes, AC **$75.00**

6-S-532, table, 1941, wood, large front black dial, wrap-around grill, pushbuttons, 2 knobs, BC, SW, 6 tubes, AC **$75.00**

6-S-546, chairside, 1941, wood, top black dial/knobs/pushbuttons, front cloth grill, casters, BC, SW, 6 tubes, AC..$135.00

6-S-556, console, 1941, wood, upper front black dial, lower cloth grill w/vertical bars, pushbuttons, BC, SW, 6 tubes, AC **$175.00**

6-S-580, table-R/P, 1941, wood, right front black dial, left vertical grill bars, pushbuttons, lift top, inner phono, BC, SW, 6 tubes, AC **$65.00**

6-S-632, table, 1942, wood, front black dial, left wrap-around cloth grill w/horizontal bars, pushbuttons, 2 knobs, BC, SW, 6 tubes, AC..**$55.00**

6-S-646, chairside, 1942, walnut, top black dial/knobs/pushbuttons, front cloth grill w/cut-outs, BC, SW, 6 tubes, AC **$145.00**

6-S-646R, chairside, 1942, mahogany, top black dial/knobs/pushbuttons, front cloth grill w/cut-outs, BC, SW, 6 tubes, AC **$145.00**

6-S-656, console, 1942, wood, upper front black dial, lower cloth grill w/vertical bars, pushbuttons, 2 knobs, BC, SW, 6 tubes, AC **$145.00**

6-S-892, table, wood, front black dial, left wrap-around cloth grill w/2 horizontal bars, pushbuttons, 2 knobs, BC, SW, 6 tubes..**$65.00**

6-V-27, tombstone, 1935, wood, lower front round black dial, upper cloth grill w/cut-outs & scalloped top edge, 4 knobs, BC, SW, 6 tubes, battery..**$150.00**

6-V-62, console, 1936, wood, upper front round black dial, lower cloth grill w/cut-outs, 4 knobs, BC, SW, 6 tubes, battery..........**$150.00**

7-D-126, table, 1936, wood, cube-shaped, center front round black dial, top grill cut-outs, 4 knobs, BC, SW, 7 tubes, AC/DC **$140.00**

7-D-127, tombstone, 1937, wood, lower front round black dial, upper cloth grill w/horizontal bars, 4 knobs, BC, SW, 7 tubes, AC/DC **$145.00**

7-D-138 "Zephyr," tombstone, 1936, wood, lower front round black dial, upper cloth grill w/horizontal wrap-around louvers, BC, SW, 7 tubes, AC/DC **$185.00**

7-D-148 "Zephyr," chairside, 1936, wood, top dial & knobs, sliding glass cover, front horizontal wrap-around louvers, BC, SW, 7 tubes, AC **$160.00**

7-D-168 "Zephyr," console, 1936, wood, upper front round black dial, lower horizontal wrap-around louvers, BC, SW, 7 tubes, AC/DC **$200.00**

7-D-203, chairside-R/P, 1937, wood, top round black dial, lift top, inner phono, lower grill & record storage, BC, SW, 7 tubes, AC/DC **$140.00**

7-D-203W, chairside-R/P, 1938, bone white, top round dial, lift top, inner phono, lower grill & record storage, BC, SW, 7 tubes, AC/DC **$140.00**

7-D-222, table, 1937, wood, cube-shaped, center front round black dial, top grill cut-outs, 4 knobs, BC, SW, 7 tubes, AC/DC **$135.00**

7-D-223, table, 1937, wood, right front round black dial, left cloth grill w/cut-outs, feet, 4 knobs, BC, SW, 7 tubes, AC/DC **$100.00**

7-D-229, tombstone, 1937, wood, lower front round black dial, upper cloth grill w/cut-outs, 4 knobs, BC, SW, 7 tubes, AC/DC..**$160.00**

7-D-239, chairside, 1937, wood, step-down top w/round black dial & 4 knobs, lower open storage, BC, SW, 7 tubes, AC/DC **$140.00**

7-D-241, chairside/bar, 1937, wood, top round dial & 4 knobs, front cloth grill w/vertical bars, storage & bar area, BC, SW, 7 tubes, AC/DC **$160.00**

7-D-241W, chairside/bar, 1937, bone white, top round dial & 4 knobs, front cloth grill w/vertical bars, storage & bar area, BC, SW, 7 tubes, AC/DC..**$160.00**

7-D-243, chairside, 1937, wood, Deco, step-down top w/dial, large front horizontal wrap-around louvers, BC, SW, 7 tubes, AC/DC **$160.00**

7-D-253, console, 1937, wood, upper front round black dial, lower cloth grill w/vertical bars, BC, SW, 7 tubes, AC/DC **$195.00**

7-G-605 "Transoceanic," portable, 1941, leatherette, inner black dial, left grill w/airplane or sailboat, fold-down front, handle, 6 bands, 7 tubes, AC/DC/battery................................**$175.00**

7-H-820, table, 1948, plastic, center front round concentric circular louvers and dial, 3 knobs, BC, FM, AC/DC **$45.00**

7-H-822, table, 1949, plastic, diagonally divided front w/left black dial & right perforated grill area w/crest, 3 knobs, BC, FM, AC/DC **$30.00**

7-H-918, table, 1949, plastic, center front round dial w/inner perforated grill, 2 knobs, FM, AC/DC....................................**$30.00**

7-H-920, table, 1949, plastic, center front round concentric circular louvers and dial, 3 knobs, BC, FM, AC/DC **$45.00**

7-H-921, table, 1949, plastic, diagonally divided front w/left black dial & right perforated grill area w/crest, 3 knobs, AM, FM, AC/DC **$30.00**

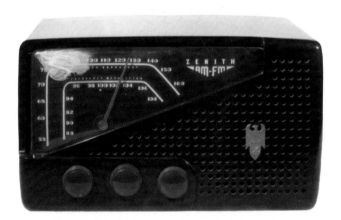

7-H-921Z, table, 1949, plastic, diagonally divided front w/left black dial & right perforated grill area w/crest, 3 knobs, AM, FM, AC/DC $30.00

7-H-922, table, 1950, plastic, diagonally divided front w/left black dial & right perforated grill area w/crest, flex handle, 3 knobs, AM, FM, AC/DC..**$30.00**

7-J-232 "Walton's," tombstone, 1937, wood, large case, lower front black "robot" dial, upper 2-section cloth grill, 4 knobs, BC, SW, 7 tubes, AC/battery **$550.00**

7-J-259, console, 1937, wood, upper front black "robot" dial, lower cloth grill w/center vertical bars, BC, SW, 7 tubes, battery/AC **$250.00**

7-J-328, table, 1939, wood, front black "robot" dial, left wrap-around cloth grill w/horizontal bars, pushbuttons, BC, SW, 7 tubes, battery/AC..**$95.00**

7-J-368, console, 1939, wood, upper front black "robot" dial, large lower horizontal wrap-around louvers, pushbuttons, BC, SW, 7 tubes, battery/AC **$275.00**

7-R-070, table-R/P, 1948, front plastic "automobile" grill w/dial & volume knobs, lift top, inner phono, BC, AC.................**$50.00**

7-R-887, console-R/P, 1949, wood, upper front slanted black dial, pushbuttons, center fold-down phono door, lower grill, BC, 7 tubes, AC..**$115.00**

7-S-28, tombstone, 1936, wood, lower front round black dial, upper cloth grill w/cut-outs, 4 knobs, BC, SW, 7 tubes, AC **$195.00**

7-S-53, console, 1936, wood, upper front round black dial, lower cloth grill w/vertical bars, 4 knobs, BC, SW, 7 tubes, AC..........**$225.00**

7-S-232 "Walton's," tombstone, 1937, wood, large case, lower front black "robot" dial, upper 2-section cloth grill, 4 knobs, BC, SW, 7 tubes, AC **$700.00**

7-S-240, chairside, 1938, wood, Deco, top black "robot" dial & knobs, front cloth grill w/vertical bars, storage, BC, 2SW, 7 tubes, AC **$225.00**

7-S-240W, chairside, 1937, bone white, Deco, top black "robot" dial & knobs, front cloth grill w/vertical bars, storage, BC, 2SW, 7 tubes, AC **$225.00**

7-S-242, chairside, 1937, wood, Deco, top "robot" dial & knobs, large horizontal wrap-around louvers, BC, SW, 7 tubes, AC ...**$250.00**

7-S-242W, chairside, 1937, ebony finish, Deco, top "robot" dial & knobs, large horizontal wrap-around louvers, BC, SW, 7 tubes, AC **$250.00**

7-S-258, console, 1937, wood, upper front black "robot" dial, lower cloth grill w/vertical bars, tuning eye, BC, SW, 7 tubes, AC **$275.00**

7-S-258W, console, 1937, bone white, upper front black "robot" dial, lower cloth grill w/vertical bars, tuning eye, BC, SW, 7 tubes, AC **$275.00**

7-S-260, console, 1937, wood, upper front black "robot" dial, lower cloth grill w/vertical bars, BC, SW, 7 tubes, AC..........**$275.00**

7-S-260Y, console, 1937, ebony finish, upper front black "robot" dial, lower cloth grill w/vertical bars, BC, SW, 7 tubes, AC **$275.00**

7-S-261, console/bookcase, 1937, wood, upper front black "robot" dial, lower cloth grill w/cut-outs, right & left side book shelves, BC, SW, 7 tubes, AC **$450.00**

7-S-323, table, 1939, wood, front round black dial, left wrap-around cloth grill w/horizontal bars, pushbuttons, BC, SW, 7 tubes, AC **$75.00**

7-S-342, chairside, 1939, wood, top black dial/knobs/pushbuttons, front grill w/vertical bars, right & left side shelves, BC, SW, 7 tubes, AC **$140.00**

7-S-343, chairside, 1939, wood, top black dial/knobs/pushbuttons, front scalloped cloth grill w/cut-outs, feet, BC, SW, 7 tubes, AC **$145.00**

7-S-363, console, 1939, wood, upper front round black dial, lower cloth grill w/vertical bars, pushbuttons, tuning eye, BC, SW, 7 tubes, AC **$200.00**

7-S-364, console, 1939, wood, upper front slanted round black dial, lower cloth grill w/vertical bars, pushbuttons, BC, SW, 7 tubes, AC..**$185.00**

7-S-366, console, 1939, wood, ornate cabinet w/carvings, upper front round black dial, lower grill area, pushbuttons, BC, SW, 7 tubes, AC **$250.00**

7-S-432, table, 1939, wood, right front dial, rounded left w/horizontal wrap-around bars, pushbuttons, BC, SW, 7 tubes, AC **$85.00**

7-S-433, table, 1939, wood, lower front slide rule dial, upper cloth grill w/horizontal bars, pushbuttons, BC, SW, 7 tubes, AC **$90.00**

7-S-434, table, 1939, wood, lower front slide rule dial, upper half-round cloth grill w/cut-outs, pushbuttons, columns, BC, SW, 7 tubes, AC..**$125.00**

7-S-449, chairside, 1939, wood, top dial/knobs/pushbuttons, front grill w/curved vertical bars, BC, SW, 7 tubes, AC **$150.00**

7-S-453, table, 1939, wood, front round black dial, left wrap-around cloth grill w/horizontal bars, pushbuttons, BC, SW, 7 tubes **$135.00**

7-S-458, console, 1939, wood, upper front slide rule dial, lower cloth grill w/vertical bars, pushbuttons, BC, SW, 7 tubes, AC..**$160.00**

7-S-461, console, 1939, wood, upper front slide rule dial, lower cloth grill w/vertical bars, pushbuttons, BC, SW, 7 tubes, AC..**$175.00**

7-S-462, console/bookcase, 1939, wood, upper front slide rule dial, lower vertical grill bars, pushbuttons, 2 drawers, right & left shelves, BC, SW, 7 tubes, AC.............................**$250.00**

7-S-529, table, 1941, wood, front black dial, left wrap-around cloth grill w/horizontal bars, pushbuttons, 2 knobs, BC, SW, 7 tubes, AC..$85.00

7-S-530, table, 1941, wood, right front black dial, left grill w/vertical bars, pushbuttons, BC, SW, 7 tubes, AC................**$85.00**

7-S-547, chairside, 1941, wood, top black dial/knobs/pushbuttons, front grill area, casters, BC, SW, 7 tubes, AC **$160.00**

7-S-557, console, 1941, wood, upper front black dial, lower cloth grill w/vertical bars, pushbuttons, BC, SW, 7 tubes, AC........**$200.00**

7-S-558, console, 1941, wood, upper front black dial, lower cloth grill w/vertical bars, pushbuttons, BC, SW, 7 tubes, AC........**$225.00**

7-S-581, chairside-R/P, 1941, wood, top dial/knobs/pushbuttons, lift top, inner phono, front horizontal grill bars, BC, SW, 7 tubes, AC **$160.00**

7-S-582, console-R/P, 1941, wood, upper front black dial, center phono, lower vertical grill bars, pushbuttons, BC, SW, 7 tubes, AC..**$175.00**

7-S-585, console-R/P, 1941, wood, step-down top, upper front black dial, center phono, lower vertical grill bars, pushbuttons, BC, SW, 7 tubes, AC....................................**$190.00**

7-S-598, console-R/P, 1941, wood, inner right dial/knobs/pushbuttons, inner left phono, double doors, lower front grill, BC, SW, 7 tubes, AC..**$135.00**

7-S-633, table, 1942, wood, front black dial, left wrap-around cloth grill w/horizontal bars, pushbuttons, 2 knobs, BC, SW, 7 tubes, AC..**$85.00**

7-S-634, table, 1942, wood, right front black dial, left cloth grill w/vertical spiral bars, pushbuttons, 2 knobs, BC, SW, 7 tubes, AC..**$85.00**

7-S-634R, table, 1942, wood, right front black dial, left cloth grill w/vertical spiral bars, pushbuttons, 2 knobs, BC, SW, 7 tubes, AC..**$85.00**

7-S-635, table, 1942, wood, front black dial, left wrap-around cloth grill w/horizontal bars, pushbuttons, 2 knobs, BC, SW, 7 tubes, AC..**$75.00**

7-S-657, console, 1942, wood, upper front slanted black dial, lower cloth grill w/vertical bars, pushbuttons, 2 knobs, BC, SW, 7 tubes, AC..**$145.00**

7-S-681 "Westchester," chairside-R/P, 1941, wood, top black dial/knobs/pushbuttons, front pull-out phono unit, BC, SW, 7 tubes, AC..**$120.00**

7-S-682 "Beverly," console-R/P, 1942, wood, upper front black dial, center pull-out phono, lower cloth grill w/vertical bars, pushbuttons, 2 knobs, BC, SW, 7 tubes, AC..............**$140.00**

7-S-685 "Carleton," console-R/P, 1942, wood, inner right black dial/pushbuttons/knobs, door, left lift top, inner phono, front vertical grill bars, BC, SW, 7 tubes, AC......................**$120.00**

7-X-075, console-R/P, 1946, wood, upper front black dial, center pull-out phono, lower cloth grill, BC, 7 tubes, battery **$80.00**

8-A-02, console, 1940, wood, upper front round black dial, lower cloth grill w/horizontal bars, pushbuttons, BC, SW, 8 tubes $200.00

8-D-363, console, 1939, wood, upper front round black dial, lower cloth grill w/vertical bars, pushbuttons, tuning eye, BC, SW, 8 tubes, AC/DC **$210.00**

8-D-510, table, plastic, right front black dial w/white pointer over horizontal wrap-around grill bars, handle, 2 knobs........**$45.00**

8-G-005 "Transoceanic," portable, 1946, black leatherette, inner dial & grill, fold-up front, telescoping antenna, handle, 6 bands, 8 tubes, AC/DC/battery.....................................**$80.00**

8-G-005Y "Transoceanic," portable, 1946, black leatherette, inner dial & grill, fold-up front, telescoping antenna, handle, 6 bands, 8 tubes, AC/DC/battery.....................................**$80.00**

8-G-005YT "Transoceanic," portable, 1946, black leatherette, inner dial & grill, fold-up front, telescoping antenna, handle, 6 bands, 8 tubes, AC/DC/battery.....................................**$80.00**

8-G-005YTZ1 "Transoceanic," portable, 1949, black leatherette, inner dial & grill, fold-up front, telescoping antenna, handle, 6 bands, 8 tubes, AC/DC/battery.....................................**$80.00**

8-H-023, table, 1946, plastic, large front half-round dial w/inner concentric semi-circular louvers, 2 knobs, BC, FM, AC/DC **$45.00**

8-H-034, table, 1946, wood, front curved black dial, lower cloth grill area, feet, 2 knobs, BC, 2FM, AC/DC.....................**$50.00**

8-H-061, console, 1946, wood, upper front slanted black dial, lower cloth grill w/vertical bars, pushbuttons, 2 knobs, BC, FM, 8 tubes, AC **$135.00**

8-H-832, table, 1948, wood, lower front black dial w/brass & plastic escutcheon, upper cloth grill, 3 knobs, 6 pushbuttons, BC, 2FM, AC...**$50.00**

8-S-129, tombstone, 1936, wood, lower front black dial, upper cloth grill w/vertical bars, BC, SW, 8 tubes, AC..........**$195.00**

8-S-154, console, 1936, wood, step-down top, upper front black dial, lower cloth grill w/vertical bars, BC, SW, 8 tubes, AC **$225.00**

8-S-443, table, 1940, wood, step-down top, right front round black dial, left vertical wrap-over bars, pushbuttons, BC, SW, 8 tubes, AC **$125.00**

8-S-451, chairside, 1940, wood, top round black dial/knobs/pushbuttons, front grill w/cut-outs, BC, SW, 8 tubes, AC....**$145.00**

8-S-463, console, 1939, wood, upper front round black dial, lower cloth grill w/vertical bars, pushbuttons, BC, SW, 8 tubes, AC **$225.00**

8-S-531, table, 1941, wood, step-down top, right front round black dial, left vertical grill bars, pushbuttons, BC, SW, 8 tubes, AC **$125.00**

8-S-548, chairside, 1941, wood, top round black dial/knobs/pushbuttons, front cloth grill w/cut-outs, BC, SW, 8 tubes, AC **$150.00**

8-S-563, console, 1941, wood, upper front round black dial, lower cloth grill w/horizontal bars, pushbuttons, BC, SW, 8 tubes, AC **$200.00**

8-S-563X, console, 1942, wood, upper front round black dial, lower cloth grill w/vertical bars, pushbuttons, BC, SW, 8 tubes, AC..$200.00

8-S-647, chairside, 1942, wood, top black dial/knobs/pushbuttons, front cloth grill w/center vertical divider, 3 bands, 8 tubes, AC **$175.00**

8-S-661, console, 1942, wood, upper front black dial, lower cloth grill w/center vertical bar, pushbuttons, BC, SW, 8 tubes, AC **$140.00**

8-T-01C "Universal," portable, black leatherette, inner right quarter-round dial, right & left concentric quarter-round louvers, metal center strip, flip up lid, handle, 2 knobs, BC, 8 tubes, AC/DC/battery **$40.00**

9-H-079, console-R/P, 1946, wood, large black dial & knobs on top of case, center pull-down phono door, lower grill, BC, 2FM, AC **$125.00**

9-H-081, console-R/P, 1946, wood, large black dial & knobs on top of case, center pull-down phono door, lower grill, BC, 2FM, AC **$130.00**

9-H-088R, console-R/P, 1946, wood, right front tilt-out black dial, left pull-out phono, lower criss-cross grill, BC, FM, 9 tubes, AC **$100.00**

9-H-881, console-R/P, 1948, wood, dial & knobs on top of case, center pull-out phono, lower criss-cross grill, BC, 2FM, 9 tubes, AC **$85.00**

9-H-984LP, console-R/P, 1949, wood, dial & knobs on top of case, center fold-down phono door, lower criss-cross grill, BC, FM, AC **$85.00**

9-H-995, console-R/P, 1949, wood, right front tilt-out black dial, left fold-down phono door, BC, FM, 9 tubes, AC **$80.00**

9-S-30, tombstone, 1936, wood, lower front round black dial, upper cloth grill w/cut-outs, 4 knobs, BC, SW, 9 tubes, AC **$195.00**

9-S-54, console, 1936, wood, upper front round black dial, lower cloth grill w/cut-outs, 4 knobs, BC, SW, 9 tubes, AC...**$225.00**

9-S-55, console, 1936, wood, shouldered, upper front round black dial, lower cloth grill w/cut-outs, 4 knobs, BC, SW, 9 tubes, AC ..**$240.00**

9-S-204, console-R/P, 1937, wood, upper front black "robot" dial, lower cloth grill w/center vertical bars, inner phono, BC, SW, 9 tubes, AC **$275.00**

9-S-232 "Walton's," tombstone, 1937, wood, large case, lower front black "robot" dial, upper 2-section cloth grill, 4 knobs, BC, SW, 9 tubes, AC....................................**$900.00**

9-S-242, chairside, 1937, wood, step-down top w/"robot" dial, large horizontal wrap-around louvers, BC, SW, 9 tubes, AC **$275.00**

9-S-242Y, chairside, 1937, ebony finish, step-down top w/"robot" dial, large horizontal wrap-around louvers, BC, SW, 9 tubes, AC ..**$275.00**

9-S-244, chairside, 1937, wood, top "robot" dial, front cloth grill with vertical bars, BC, SW, 9 tubes, AC **$250.00**

9-S-262, console, 1937, wood, upper front black "robot" dial, lower cloth grill w/2 vertical bars, tuning eye, BC, SW, 9 tubes, AC **$275.00**

9-S-263, console, 1937, wood, upper front black "robot" dial, lower cloth grill w/vertical bars, tuning eye, BC, SW, 9 tubes, AC **$255.00**

9-S-264, console, 1937, wood, low cabinet, upper front black "robot" dial, lower cloth grill w/vertical bars, tuning eye, BC, SW, 9 tubes, AC..**$260.00**

9-S-319, table, 1938, wood, front oblong gold dial, left wrap-around cloth grill w/horizontal bars, pushbuttons, 4 knobs, BC, SW, 9 tubes **$100.00**

9-S-324, table, 1939, wood, front black "robot" dial, left wrap-around cloth grill w/horizontal bars, pushbuttons, BC, SW, 9 tubes, AC **$175.00**

9-S-344, chairside, 1939, wood, top "robot" dial/knobs/pushbuttons, lower horizontal wrap-around louvers, BC, SW, 9 tubes, AC **$245.00**

9-S-365, console, 1939, wood, upper front black "robot" dial, lower cloth grill w/vertical bars, pushbuttons, BC, SW, 9 tubes, AC..**$260.00**

9-S-367, console, 1938, wood, upper front round black "robot" dial, lower horizontal wrap-around louvers, pushbuttons, BC, SW, 9 tubes, AC **$275.00**

9-S-369, console, 1939, wood, step-down top, upper front black "robot" dial, lower cloth grill w/vertical bars, pushbuttons, BC, SW, 9 tubes, AC **$295.00**

10, console, 1931, wood, lowboy, upper front dial, lower cloth grill w/cut-outs, 8 tubes **$165.00**

10-A-3R, console, wood, upper front round black dial, lower cloth grill w/center cut-outs, pushbuttons, BS, SW, 10 tubes, AC **$250.00**

10-H-551, chairside, 1941, wood, top round black dial/pushbuttons/ knobs, front grill w/vertical bars, AM, FM, SW, 10 tubes, AC..............**$275.00**

10-H-562, console, 1941, wood, spinet piano-style, upper front slanted round black dial, lower cloth grill w/"lyre" cut-out, pushbuttons, spindles, BC, SW, 10 tubes, AC **$350.00**

10-H-571, console, 1941, wood, spinet piano-style, upper front slanted round black dial, lower cloth grill w/"lyre" cut-out, pushbuttons, spindles, BC, SW, FM, 10 tubes, AC.....**$350.00**

10-H-573, console, 1941, wood, upper front slanted round black dial, lower cloth grill w/cut-outs, pushbuttons, BC, FM, SW, 10 tubes, AC..**$230.00**

10-S-130, tombstone, 1936, wood, lower front black dial, upper cloth grill w/cut-outs, BC, SW, 10 tubes, AC **$215.00**

10-S-147 "Zephyr," chairside, 1936, wood, top black dial & knobs, large lower horizontal wrap-around louvers, BC, SW, 10 tubes, AC...**$215.00**

10-S-153, console, 1936, wood, upper front black dial, lower cloth grill w/splayed bars, BC, SW, 10 tubes, AC **$230.00**

10-S-155, console, 1936, wood, upper front black dial, lower cloth grill w/vertical bars, BC, SW, 10 tubes, AC **$225.00**

10-S-156, console, 1936, wood, upper front black dial, lower cloth grill w/vertical bars, BC, SW, 10 tubes, AC **$220.00**

10-S-157 "Zephyr," console, 1936, wood, upper front black dial, large lower horizontal wrap-around grill bars, tuning eye, BC, SW, 10 tubes, AC..**$250.00**

10-S-160, console, 1936, wood, upper front black dial, lower cloth grill w/center vertical bar, BC, SW, 10 tubes, AC **$250.00**

10-S-443, table, 1940, wood, step-down top, right front round black dial, left vertical wrap-over grill bars, pushbuttons, BC, SW, 10 tubes, AC...**$125.00**

10-S-452, chairside, 1940, wood, half-round, top black dial/knobs/pushbuttons, lower horizontal wrap-around grill bars, BC, SW, 10 tubes, AC.....................................**$275.00**

10-S-464, console, 1940, wood, upper front round black dial, lower cloth grill w/horizontal bars, pushbuttons, BC, SW, 10 tubes, AC..**$235.00**

10-S-470, console, 1940, wood, upper front round black dial, lower concave grill area, pushbuttons, BC, SW, 10 tubes, AC ..**$250.00**

10-S-491, console-R/P, 1940, wood, upper front black dial, center pull-out phono, lower horizontal wrap-around louvers, pushbuttons, BC, SW, 10 tubes, AC **$220.00**

10-S-531, table, 1941, wood, step-down top, right front round black dial, left vertical grill bars, pushbuttons, BC, SW, 10 tubes, AC **$125.00**

10-S-549, chairside, 1940, walnut, top round black dial/knobs/pushbuttons, front cloth grill w/cut-outs, storage, BC, SW, 10 tubes, AC **$225.00**

10-S-566, console, 1941, wood, upper front round black dial, lower cloth grill w/vertical bars, pushbuttons, BC, SW, 10 tubes, AC...**$245.00**

10-S-567, console, 1941, wood, upper front round black dial, lower vertical grill bars, pushbuttons, BC, SW, 10 tubes, AC..**$245.00**

10-S-568, console, 1941, wood, upper front round black dial, lower vertical grill bars, pushbuttons, BC, SW, 10 tubes, AC..**$225.00**

10-S-589, console-R/P, 1941, wood, upper front round black dial, center pull-out phono, lower horizontal wrap-around louvers, pushbuttons, BC, SW, 10 tubes, AC **$230.00**

10-S-599, console-R/P, 1941, wood, inner right black dial, inner left phono, double doors, lower vertical grill bars, BC, SW, 10 tubes, AC...**$175.00**

10-S-669, console, 1939, wood, upper front black dial, lower cloth grill w/vertical bars, pushbuttons, BC, SW, 10 tubes, AC **$175.00**

10-S-690 "Wilshire," console-R/P, 1942, wood, inner right black dial, door, left pull-out phono, lower vertical grill bars, BC, SW, 10 tubes, AC...**$145.00**

11, console, 1931, wood, lowboy, upper front window dial, lower cloth grill w/cut-outs, stretcher base, 8 tubes **$150.00**

11, table, 1927, walnut, rectangular case, slanted front panel w/center thumbwheel dial, battery.............................**$150.00**

11-E, table, 1927, wood, rectangular case, slanted front panel w/center thumbwheel dial, AC.................................**$150.00**

11-S-474, console, 1940, wood, upper front round black dial, lower cloth grill w/vertical bars, pushbuttons, BC, SW, 11 tubes, AC **$250.00**

12, console, 1931, wood, highboy, inner front dial, double doors, arched stretcher base, 8 tubes **$150.00**

12, table, 1927, mahogany, rectangular case, slanted front panel w/off-center dial, 6 tubes, battery $120.00

12-A-57, console, 1936, wood, upper front round black dial, lower cloth grill w/cut-outs, 4 knobs, BC, SW, 12 tubes, AC..$300.00

12-A-58, console, 1936, wood, upper front round black dial, lower cloth grill w/"torch" cut-out, 2 speakers, 4 knobs, BC, SW, 12 tubes, AC..$375.00

12-H-090, console-R/P, 1946, wood, right front tilt-out dial/push-buttons/knobs, left fold-down phono door, lower cloth grill w/vertical bars, BC, SW, FM, 12 tubes, AC................$120.00

12-H-092R, console-R/P, 1946, mahogany, right front tilt-out black dial/pushbuttons/knobs, left fold-down phono door, lower cloth grill w/cut-outs, BC, SW, 2FM, 12 tubes, AC $120.00

12-H-093R, chairside-R/P, 1946, wood, top dial/push-buttons/knobs, front pull-out phono, side cloth grill w/cut-outs, BC, FM, SW, 12 tubes, AC....................................$130.00

12-H-094E, console-R/P, 1946, bleached mahogany, right front tilt-out dial/pushbuttons/knobs, left pull-out phono, lower criss-cross grill, BC, SW, FM, 12 tubes, AC...............$120.00

12-H-650 "Lenox," chairside, 1942, wood, top black dial/pushbuttons/knobs, front cloth grill w/vertical bars, BC, SW, 12 tubes, AC..$140.00

12-H-670 "Newport," console, 1941, wood, upper front slanted black dial, lower cloth grill w/vertical bars, pushbuttons, BC, SW, FM, 12 tubes, AC..$190.00

12-H-679, console-R/P, 1941, wood, inner dial/knobs/phono, double front doors, lower cloth grill, BC, SW, FM, 12 tubes, AC..$150.00

12-H-689 "Kenwood," console-R/P, 1942, wood, upper front black dial, center pull-out phono drawer, lower cloth grill w/vertical bars, pushbuttons, storage, BC, SW, 12 tubes, AC $150.00

12-H-691 "Chatham," chairside, 1942, wood, top dial/pushbuttons/knobs, front pull-out phono drawer, side criss-cross grill, BC, FM, SW, 12 tubes, AC.........................$135.00

12-H-695 "Williamsburg," console-R/P, 1942, wood, inner right black dial, door, left lift top, inner phono, lower front cloth grill, storage, BC, SW, 12 tubes, AC $150.00

12-H-696 "Georgetown," console-R/P, 1942, wood, inner right black dial, door, left lift top, inner phono, lower front cloth grill, storage, BC, SW, 12 tubes, AC $150.00

12-S-205, console-R/P, 1937, wood, inner "robot" dial & phono, lift top, front cloth grill w/horizontal & vertical bars, storage, BC, SW, 12 tubes, AC..$300.00

12-S-232 "Walton's," tombstone, 1937, wood, large case, lower front black "robot" dial, upper 2-section cloth grill, 4 knobs, BC, SW, 12 tubes, AC...$1,200.00

12-S-245, chairside, 1937, wood, recessed center top w/black "robot" dial, side cloth grill w/horizontal bars, BC, SW, 12 tubes, AC..$275.00

12-S-265, console, 1937, wood, upper front black "robot" dial, lower cloth grill w/center vertical bar, BC, SW, 12 tubes, AC..$300.00

12-S-266, console, 1937, wood, upper front black "robot" dial, lower arched cloth grill w/cut-outs, BC, SW, 12 tubes, AC $300.00

12-S-267, console, 1937, wood, upper front black "robot" dial, lower cloth grill w/vertical bars, BC, SW, 12 tubes, AC $310.00

12-S-268, console, 1937, wood, wide cabinet, upper front black "robot" dial, lower cloth grill w/horizontal & vertical bars, BC, SW, 12 tubes, AC $350.00

12-S-345, chairside, 1939, wood, top black "robot" dial & pushbuttons, front circular cloth grill w/horizontal bars, BC, SW, 12 tubes, AC..$295.00

12-S-370, console, 1939, wood, upper front black "robot" dial, lower grill w/horizontal bars, pushbuttons, BC, SW, 12 tubes, AC $395.00

12-S-371, console, 1939, wood, half-round, upper front black "robot" dial, lower cloth grill w/vertical bars, pushbuttons, BC, SW, 12 tubes, AC...$395.00

12-S-445, table, 1940, wood, step-down top, right front "robot" dial, left vertical wrap-over grill bars, pushbuttons, BC, SW, 12 tubes, AC...$195.00

12-S-453, chairside, 1945, wood, top "robot" dial/pushbuttons/knobs, bowed front grill, storage, feet, BC, SW, 12 tubes, AC ...$200.00

12-S-471, console, 1940, wood, upper front black "robot" dial, lower grill w/center vertical panel w/cut-outs, pushbuttons, BC, SW, 12 tubes, AC...$300.00

12-S-550, chairside, 1941, wood, top "robot" dial/pushbuttons/knobs, front cloth grill w/center vertical divider, feet, BC, SW, 12 tubes, AC...$200.00

12-S-568, console, 1940, wood, step-down top, upper front "robot" dial, lower cloth grill w/vertical bars, pushbuttons, BC, SW, 12 tubes, AC..$325.00

12-S-569, console, 1940, wood, upper front slanted "robot" dial, lower vertical grill bars, pushbuttons, BC, SW, 12 tubes, AC $325.00

12-U-158, console, 1936, wood, upper front round black dial, lower cloth grill w/vertical bars, BC, SW, 12 tubes, AC $295.00

12-U-159, console, 1936, wood, upper front round black dial, lower cloth grill w/center vertical panel w/cut-outs, BC, SW, 12 tubes, AC $250.00

14-H-789, console-R/P, 1948, wood, right front tilt-out dial/pushbuttons/knobs, left fold-down phono door, lower grill, BC, SW, 2FM, AC...$120.00

15-S-372, console, 1939, wood, upper front black "robot" dial, lower cloth grill w/center vertical bars, pushbuttons, BC, SW, 15 tubes, AC...$650.00

15-S-373, console, 1939, wood, upper front black "robot" dial, lower horizontal wrap-around louvers, pushbuttons, BC, SW, 15 tubes, AC...$675.00

15-U-246, chairside, 1938, wood, recessed center top w/black "robot" dial & knobs, side cloth grill w/horizontal bars, BC, SW, 15 tubes, AC..$450.00

15-U-269, console, 1937, wood, upper front black "robot" dial, lower cloth grill w/horizontal & vertical bars, BC, SW, 15 tubes, AC..$695.00

16-A-61 "Stratosphere," console, 1936, wood, upper front round black dial, lower concave grill area, 2 speakers, BC, SW, 16 tubes, AC...$4,000.00

16-A-63 "Stratosphere," console, 1936, wood, ornate cabinet, inner black dial, double front doors, lower concave grill area, 2 speakers, BC, SW, 16 tubes, AC $5,500.00

17E, console, 1927, wood, looks like spinet piano, slanted front w/dial & escutcheon, 6 tubes, AC..............................**$175.00**

27, table, 1927, wood, rectangular case, slanted panel w/2 pointer dials, right/left eliminator storage, AC.......$225.00

33-X, table, 1928, wood, rectangular case, slanted thumbwheel dial w/escutcheon, decorative rosettes, AC................**$160.00**

35-PX, console, 1928, wood, highboy, inner thumbwheel dial, upper cloth grill w/cut-outs, double doors, AC............**$175.00**

40-A, console-R/P, 1929, wood, massive ornate carved cabinet, upper front dial, lower grill cut-outs, pushbuttons, AC..**$850.00**

52, console, 1929, wood, lowboy, upper front dial w/escutcheon, lower cloth grill w/cut-outs, pushbuttons, 9 tubes, AC..**$275.00**

54, console, 1929, wood, lowboy, upper front dial w/escutcheon, lower cloth grill w/cut-outs, pushbuttons, 9 tubes, AC..**$325.00**

55, console, 1929, wood, lowboy, ornate case, upper front dial w/escutcheon, lower cloth grill w/cut-outs, pushbuttons, remote control, 9 tubes, AC........................**$325.00**

61, console, 1930, wood, lowboy, upper front dial, lower cloth grill w/cut-outs, 9 tubes, AC.............................**$275.00**

64, console, 1930, wood, lowboy, upper front dial, lower cloth grill w/cut-outs, inner pushbuttons, 9 tubes, AC.................**$350.00**

67, console, 1930, wood, massive ornate lowboy, upper front dial, lower cloth grill w/cut-outs, inner pushbuttons, 9 tubes, AC............**$400.00**

210 "Zenette," cathedral, 1932, wood, lower front window dial, upper scalloped cloth grill w/cut-outs, 3 knobs, 7 tubes..**$275.00**

210-5 "Zenette," cathedral, 1932, wood, lower front window dial, upper scalloped cloth grill w/cut-outs, 4 knobs, BC, LW, 7 tubes..**$275.00**

215 "Zenette," cathedral, 1932, wood, center front window dial, upper scalloped cloth grill w/cut-outs, fluted columns, 4 knobs...$275.00

220, console, 1932, wood, lowboy, upper front window dial, lower cloth grill w/cut-outs, 3 knobs, 7 tubes, AC.................**$150.00**

230 "Zenette," tombstone, 1930, wood, peaked top, center front window dial, upper cloth grill w/cut-outs, 4 knobs, 8 tubes, AC..$220.00

240, console, 1932, wood, lowboy, upper front window dial, lower cloth grill w/cut-outs, 6 legs, 8 tubes, AC...................**$160.00**

245, console, 1932, wood, lowboy, upper front window dial, lower cloth grill w/cut-outs, inner pushbuttons, 4 knobs, 6 legs, 8 tubes, AC...**$235.00**

250, cathedral, 1932, wood, center front window dial, upper scalloped cloth grill w/cut-outs, 5 knobs, BC, SW, 9 tubes, AC $295.00

260, console, 1932, wood, upper front window dial, lower cloth grill w/cut-outs, 6 legs, BC, SW, 9 tubes, AC..............**$175.00**

270, console-R/P, 1932, wood, lowboy, front window dial, lower cloth grill w/cut-outs, lift top, inner phono, 7 tubes, AC..**$160.00**

288, tombstone, 1934, two-tone wood, Deco, center front window dial, upper cloth grill w/cut-outs, 6 knobs, BC, SW, 8 tubes, AC **$175.00**

293, console, 1933, wood, lowboy, upper front window dial, lower cloth grill w/cut-outs, 6 legs, BC, SW, 7 tubes, AC......**$160.00**

672, console, 1930, wood, massive ornate lowboy, upper front dial, lower cloth grill w/cut-outs, inner pushbuttons, 9 tubes, AC **$400.00**

701, table, 1933, wood w/inlay, right front dial, center cloth grill w/cut-outs, side fluting, 2 knobs, 5 tubes, AC/DC **$100.00**

705, table, 1933, wood, flared base, right front window dial, center cloth grill w/cut-outs, side fluting, 2 knobs, 6 tubes, AC ..**$115.00**

706, table, 1933, wood, right front window dial, center cloth grill w/horizontal bars, 2 knobs, 6 tubes, AC **$75.00**

707, table, 1933, wood w/inlay, right front window dial, center cloth grill w/cut-outs, 2 knobs, 6 tubes, AC **$115.00**

711, table, 1933, wood, flared base, right front window dial, center cloth grill w/cut-outs, 2 knobs, 6 tubes, AC **$115.00**

715, tombstone, 1933, wood, shouldered, center front window dial, upper cloth grill w/cut-outs, 4 knobs, AC **$240.00**

755, console, 1933, wood, lowboy, upper front window dial, lower cloth grill w/cut-outs, 6 legs, 8 tubes, AC **$175.00**

760, console, 1933, wood, upper front dial w/escutcheon, lower cloth grill w/scrolled cut-outs, 6 feet, 9 tubes, AC.......**$210.00**

765, console, 1933, wood, inner dial, lower cloth grill w/scrolled cut-outs, double sliding doors, 6 legs, 9 tubes **$250.00**

801, table, 1934, wood, step-down top, right front dial, center cloth grill w/cut-outs, 2 knobs, 5 tubes, AC **$100.00**

805, cathedral, 1934, two-tone wood, center front window dial, upper cloth grill w/cut-outs, 4 knobs, BC, SW, 5 tubes, AC...**$225.00**

807, tombstone, 1933, wood, lower front round dial, upper cloth grill with cut-outs, 4 knobs, BC, SW, 5 tubes, AC **$165.00**

808, tombstone, 1934, wood, lower front round dial, upper cloth grill w/vertical bars, 4 knobs, BC, SW, 6 tubes, AC.....**$165.00**

809, tombstone, 1934, wood, front round dial, upper cloth grill w/Deco chrome cut-outs, 4 knobs, BC, SW, 6 tubes, AC.............**$275.00**

827, table, 1934, wood, right front window dial, center cloth grill w/vertical chrome bars, 4 knobs, BC, SW, 7 tubes, AC..**$145.00**

829, tombstone, 1934, wood, lower front round dial, upper cloth grill w/chrome cut-outs, BC, SW, 7 tubes, AC............**$275.00**

845, console, 1934, wood, upper front window dial, lower cloth grill w/cut-outs, 4 knobs, BC, SW, 5 tubes, AC **$140.00**

847, console, 1934, wood, upper front window dial, lower cloth grill w/cut-outs, 4 knobs, BC, SW, 5 tubes, AC **$140.00**

850, console, 1934, wood, upper front round dial, lower cloth grill w/cut-outs, BC, SW, 5 tubes, AC **$150.00**

860, console, 1934, wood, upper front round airplane dial, lower cloth grill w/cut-outs, 6 legs, BC, SW, 6 tubes, AC......**$150.00**

861, console, 1934, wood, upper front round dial, lower cloth grill w/cut-outs, BC, SW, 6 tubes, AC **$160.00**

970, console, 1934, wood, upper front round dial, lower cloth grill with scrolled cut-outs, 6 legs, 9 tubes, AC **$180.00**

975, console, 1934, wood, upper front round dial, lower cloth grill w/cut-outs, sliding doors, 6 legs, 9 tubes, AC **$180.00**

1000-Z "Stratosphere," console, 1934, wood, upper front round black dial, lower concave grill, 3 speakers, BC, SW, 25 tubes, AC ....**$7,000.00+**

1103, console, 1939, wood, upper front round black dial, lower curved grill area w/center vertical divider, pushbuttons, BC, SW, 10 tubes, AC **$225.00**

1117, tombstone, 1935, wood, lower front round dial, upper cloth grill with cut-outs, BC, SW, 6 tubes, AC **$150.00**

5808, console, 1940, wood, upper front round black dial, lower curved grill w/vertical bars, pushbuttons, BC, SW, 8 tubes **$235.00**

A-400 "Holiday," portable, plastic, right & left side knobs, large front wrap-over grill w/crest, handle, BC, AC/DC/battery **$35.00**

A-402 "Sea Shore," portable, 1957, plastic, upper front dial, lower checkered grill area w/crest, handle, BC, AC/DC/battery...**$25.00**

A-404L "Carousel," portable, leather, right & left side knobs, front grill area w/crest, handle, BC, AC/DC/battery **$30.00**

A-504 "Sun Valley," portable, plastic, upper front dial, lower checkered grill area w/crest, handle, BC, AC/DC/battery.........**$25.00**

A-508B, table, plastic, lower right front dial over large lattice grill area w/center crest, feet, BC.............................**$25.00**

A-513G, table, 1958, plastic, right & left side knobs, large front oval checkered grill area w/center crest, BC, AC/DC **$25.00**

A-513R, table, 1958, plastic, right & left side knobs, large front oval checkered grill area w/center crest, BC, AC/DC..**$25.00**

A-519Y, table-C, 1958, plastic, center front dial/right clock face over large checkered grill w/crest, feet, BC, 5 tubes, AC.........**$20.00**

A-600 "Transoceanic," portable, 1957, black leatherette, inner multi-band slide rule dial, left lattice grill, fold-up front, telescope antenna, handle, BC, SW **$80.00**

A-600L "Transoceanic," portable, 1957, leatherette, inner multi-band slide rule dial, left lattice grill, fold-up front, telescope antenna, handle, BC, SW **$125.00**

B-400L, portable, plastic, right & left side knobs, large front metal perforated wrap-over grill w/crest, handle, BC ..**$30.00**

B-513V, table, 1959, plastic, lower right dial, large front oval grill w/vertical bars & center crest, BC, AC/DC **$15.00**

B-514F, table-C, 1959, plastic, right front oval dial/left oval clock over large checkered grill area w/center crest, BC, 5 tubes, AC...**$20.00**

B-600 "Transoceanic," portable, leatherette, inner multi-band slide rule dial, left lattice grill, fold-up front, telescope antenna, handle..............................**$80.00**

B-615F, table, 1959, plastic, lower right dial knob, large front oval grill w/vertical bars & center logo, left side knob, feet, BC, 6 tubes, AC/DC **$15.00**

B-728C, table-C, 1959, plastic, lower front slide rule dial, upper center clock face, right & left grill areas, 4 knobs, AM, FM, 7 tubes, AC/DC **$20.00**

C-730, table, 1955, wood, lower front slide rule dial, large upper plastic woven grill area, 2 knobs, AM, FM **$25.00**

F-508B, table, 1961, plastic, upper right front dial knob overlaps lower vertical bars, feet, BC, AC/DC **$15.00**

G-500 "Transoceanic," portable, 1950, leatherette, inner black dial, fold-up front w/crest, telescope antenna, BC, 5SW, AC/DC/battery **$80.00**

G-503, portable, 1950, leatherette, flip-over dial w/crest, inner metal grill & 2 knobs, handle, BC, AC/DC/battery **$45.00**

G-503Y, portable, 1950, leatherette, flip-over dial w/crest, inner metal grill & 2 knobs, handle, BC, AC/DC/battery $45.00

G-510Y, table, 1950, plastic, right front round dial over large metal criss-cross grill, feet, 2 knobs, BC $30.00

G-511, table, 1950, plastic, right front round dial over large metal criss-cross grill, flex handle, 2 knobs, BC......$35.00

G-516, table-C, 1950, plastic, right front round metal dial/left round alarm clock over perforated grill w/center crest, 5 knobs, BC, AC $40.00
G-516W, table-C, 1950, plastic, right front round metal dial/left round alarm clock over perforated grill w/center crest, 5 knobs, BC, AC $40.00

G-600 "Transoceanic," portable, leatherette, inner black dial, fold-up front w/crest, telescope antenna, BC, SW, AC/DC/battery...$80.00

G-615, table, 1950, plastic, center front round metal dial over metal criss-cross grill, flex handle, 2 knobs, BC, AC/DC..........$35.00
G-660, table-R/P, 1950, plastic, front square dial w/inner perforated grill, 4 knobs, lift top, inner phono, BC, AC..............$45.00
G-723, table, 1950, plastic, diagonally divided front w/left dial & right perforated grill area w/crest, 3 knobs, AM, FM, AC/DC...$30.00
G-724, table, 1950, plastic, diagonally divided front w/left dial & right perforated grill area w/crest, flex handle, 4 knobs, AM, FM, AC/DC $30.00
G-725, table, 1950, plastic, center front round dial w/crest, flex handle, 3 knobs, BC, FM, AC/DC $40.00

G-730, table, wood, lower front slide rule dial, large upper grill area, 2 knobs, AM, FM, AC $25.00
G-882, console-R/P, 1950, wood, inner right dial & knobs, lower storage, doors, left pull-out phono, lower grill, BC, FM, AC $70.00
H-401, portable, 1952, plastic, center front round dial w/inner perforations, handle, 2 knobs, BC, AC/DC/battery $35.00

H-500 "Transoceanic," portable, 1951, black leatherette, inner dial, left lattice grill area, fold-back front, handle, BC, SW, AC/DC/battery $80.00

H-503X, portable, 1951, leatherette, inner round dial w/crest & inner grill area, 2 knobs, fold-back front, handle, AC/DC/battery $45.00
H-511 "Consoltone," table, 1951, plastic, oblong case, right front half-round dial, center horizontal metal strip, feet, 2 knobs, BC, AC/DC $40.00
H-511W "Consoltone," table, 1951, plastic, oblong case, right front half-round dial, center horizontal metal strip, feet, 2 knobs, BC, AC/DC...$40.00
H-615, table, 1951, plastic, center front square dial w/inner metal criss-cross grill, flex handle, 2 knobs, BC, AC/DC $40.00
H-615W, table, 1951, plastic, center front square dial w/inner metal criss-cross grill, flex handle, 2 knobs, BC, AC/DC..........$40.00

H-615Z, table, 1952, plastic, center front square dial w/inner metal criss-cross grill, feet, 2 knobs, BC, AC/DC.....$40.00
H-615Z1, table, 1952, plastic, center front square dial w/inner metal criss-cross grill, flex handle, 2 knobs, BC, AC/DC $40.00
H-661R, table-R/P, 1951, leatherette, center front round dial overlaps large grill area, 4 knobs, lift top, inner phono, BC, 6 tubes, AC...$30.00

H-664, table-R/P, 1951, plastic, front raised round metal dial w/inner perforated grill, 2 knobs, lift top, inner phono, BC, AC.....$75.00
H-723, table, 1951, plastic, off-center round dial, criss-cross grill w/crest, feet, 3 knobs, BC, FM, AC/DC $30.00
H-723Z, table, 1951, plastic, off-center round dial, criss-cross grill w/crest, feet, 3 knobs, BC, FM, AC/DC $30.00
H-724, table, 1951, plastic, off-center round dial, criss-cross grill w/crest, flex handle, feet, BC, FM, AC/DC $30.00
H-724Z1, table, 1952, plastic, off-center round dial, cloth grill w/crest, flex handle, feet, BC, FM, AC/DC $30.00
H-724Z2, table, 1952, plastic, off-center round dial, cloth grill w/crest, flex handle, right side knob, BC, FM, AC/DC...$30.00

H-725, table, 1951, plastic, center front round dial w/inner perforated grill, flex handle, 2 knobs, BC, FM, AC/DC...$40.00
H-845 "Super Interlude," table, 1964, wood, left front vertical slide rule dial, large grill area w/vertical bars and center crest, AM, FM..$15.00
H-880R, console-R/P, 1951, wood, inner right dial w/crest, door, left pull-out phono, lower grill area, BC, FM, AC $75.00
H-880RZ, console-R/P, 1950, wood, inner right dial w/crest, lower storage, doors, left pull-out phono, lower grill, BC, FM, AC........$75.00
HF-660F, table-R/P, 1959, left front dial, large grill area, lift top, inner phono, handle, BC, 6 tubes, AC $15.00
HF-772R, console-R/P, 1957, wood, inner right slide rule dial/4 knobs, left phono, lift top, large front grill area, BC, 7 tubes, AC $40.00
HF-1286RD, console-R/P, 1958, wood, inner left slide rule dial/5 knobs/pull-out phono, door, right criss-cross grill, BC, FM, 11 tubes, AC $50.00
J-402, portable, 1952, plastic, top left dial knob, top right on/off/volume knob, front circular perforated grill w/center crest, handle, 2 knobs, BC, AC/DC/battery $35.00
J-420T, table, 1952, plastic, oblong case, right front half-round dial, center horizontal metal strip, 2 knobs, feet, BC, SW, battery........$40.00
J-506 "Pacemaker," table, 1964, plastic, upper right front dial knob overlaps lower vertical bars, feet, BC, AC/DC......$10.00
J-508B, table, plastic, upper right front dial knob overlaps lower vertical bars, feet, BC, AC/DC $10.00

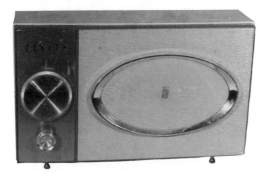

J-512W "Executive," table, 1964, plastic, left front dial knob, large right metal perforated grill area w/metal oval & center crest, feet, BC, AC/DC $15.00

J-514, table-C, 1952, plastic, oblong case, right front dial, left alarm clock, center horizontal bars, 5 knobs, BC, AM **$40.00**
J-615, table, 1952, plastic, center front half-round dial w/inner circular grill louvers & crest, feet, flex handle, 2 knobs, BC.....**$45.00**
J-616, table-C, 1952, plastic, oblong case, right front dial, left alarm clock, center horizontal bars w/crest, 5 knobs, BC, 6 tubes, AC **$40.00**
J-733, table-C, 1952, plastic, left front square dial & right square clock face overlap textured grill w/center crest, feet, 6 knobs, AC **$30.00**

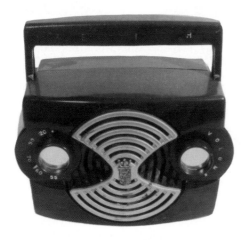

K-412R, portable, 1953, plastic, front "owl-eye" knobs, center concentric circular louvers w/crest, handle, BC $50.00

K-412Y, portable, 1953, plastic, front "owl-eye" knobs, center concentric circular louvers w/crest, handle, BC $50.00

K-508 "Emblem," table, 1964, plastic, large right front dial, left textured grill area, feet, BC, AC/DC **$10.00**

K-510W, table, 1952, plastic, center front round dial w/inner perforations, 2 knobs, BC, AC/DC $40.00

K-518, table-C, 1952, plastic, oblong case, right front dial, left alarm clock, center horizontal bars w/crest, feet, BC, AC...$40.00

K-526, table, 1953, plastic, center front round dial w/inner lattice grill & crest, flex handle, 3 knobs, BC $35.00
K-615B, table, 1963, plastic, wedge-shaped case, lower front slanted slide rule dial, large upper grill area w/vertical bars & center crest, BC...**$20.00**

K-615C, table, 1963, plastic, wedge-shaped case, lower front slanted slide rule dial, large upper grill area w/vertical bars & center crest, BC.................................$20.00

K-622, table-C, 1953, plastic, step-down top, right front dial/left alarm clock overlap center horizontal bars w/crest, 2 knobs, BC $35.00

K-666R, table-R/P, 1953, plastic, step-down front w/lower half-round metal dial, 3 knobs, lift top, inner phono, BC, AC ..$40.00

K-725, table, 1953, plastic, large center front round metal dial w/inner perforated grill & crest, flex handle, 2 knobs, BC, FM, AC/DC $40.00

K-777R, console-R/P, 1953, wood, inner right slide rule dial, 3 knobs, left pull-out phono, fold-down front, lower grill area, BC, AC $50.00

L, cathedral, 1931, two-tone wood, lower front window dial, upper cloth grill w/cut-outs, 3 knobs, 5 tubes $200.00

L-406R, portable, 1953, plastic, top dial & on/off/volume knobs, front round perforated grill w/center crest, handle, BC, SW, AC/DC/battery $35.00

L-507, portable, 1954, leatherette, inner dial, flip up front w/world map, handle, BC, 2SW, AC/DC/battery.......................$50.00

L-509 "Sovereign," table, 1964, plastic, left front dial knob over-laps large textured grill area, BC, AC/DC.....................$15.00

L-513 "Reminder," table-C, 1964, plastic, left front dial knob, right & left horizontal bars, center alarm clock, BC, AC...$15.00

L-515, table, plastic, oblong case, right front dial, left alarm clock, center horizontal grill bars, feet, 5 knobs, BC...$40.00

L-515W, table, plastic, oblong case, right front dial, left alarm clock, center horizontal grill bars, feet, 5 knobs, BC...$40.00

L-516B "Sandman," table-C, 1964, plastic, right front dial, left alarm clock, center grill area w/crest, BC, AC $20.00

L-518, table-C, 1953, plastic, oblong case, right front dial, left alarm clock, center horizontal louvers w/crest, 2 knobs, BC, AC $40.00

L-520R, table-C, 1954, plastic, step-down top, right front dial & left alarm clock overlap horizontal grill bars w/center crest, feet, BC......$30.00

L-566, table-R/P, 1954, plastic, step-down front w/lower half-round metal dial, lift top, inner phono, BC, 5 tubes, AC $40.00

L-622, table-C, 1953, plastic, step-down top, right front dial & left alarm clock overlap horizontal grill bars w/center crest, feet, BC, AC $35.00

L-721, table, 1954, plastic, diagonally divided front w/left black dial & right perforated grill area w/crest, 3 knobs, AM, FM, AC/DC $30.00
L-846, chairside-R/P, 1954, wood, top dial & knobs, front louvered pull-out phono drawer, legs, BC, FM, AC $50.00
L-880, console-R/P, 1954, wood, inner right dial/knobs/lower storage, doors, left pull-out phono, lower grill, BC, FM, 8 tubes, AC...$70.00

LH "Zenette," cathedral, 1931, two-tone wood, lower front window dial, upper scalloped cloth grill w/cut-outs, 3 knobs, 7 tubes $275.00
LP "Zenette," cathedral, 1931, two-tone wood, lower front window dial, upper cloth grill w/cut-outs, 3 knobs, 5 tubes $200.00
M-505, portable, 1953, plastic, top round dial knob, front gold metal grill w/center logo, handle, right & left side knobs, AC/DC/battery..$40.00

M510-R, table, 1955, plastic, oblong case, right front round dial overlaps large checkered grill area, fold-down handle, 2 knobs, BC, AC/DC $40.00

R-510G, table, 1955, plastic, oblong case, right front round dial overlaps large checkered grill area, fold-down handle, 2 knobs, BC, AC/DC..$40.00

R-510R, table, 1955, plastic, oblong case, right front round dial overlaps large checkered grill area, fold-down handle, 2 knobs, BC, AC/DC $40.00

R-510Y, table, 1955, plastic, oblong case, right front round dial overlaps large checkered grill area, fold-down handle, 2 knobs, BC, AC/DC $40.00
R-510Z1, table, 1955, plastic, oblong case, right front round dial overlaps large checkered grill area, fold-down handle, 2 knobs, BC, AC/DC..$40.00
R-511F, table, 1955, plastic, right front half-round dial, center checkered grill w/crest, fold-down handle, feet, 2 knobs, BC, AC/DC $40.00

R-511R, table, 1955, plastic, right front half-round dial, center checkered grill w/crest, fold-down handle, feet, 2 knobs, BC, AC/DC..$40.00

R-511V, table, 1955, plastic, right front half-round dial, center checkered grill w/crest, fold-down handle, feet, 2 knobs, BC, AC/DC **$40.00**

Super-Zenith X, console, 1924, wood, front panel w/2 pointer dials, upper built-in speaker w/grill, lower battery storage, battery **$275.00**

R-600 "Transoceanic," portable, 1954, black leatherette, inner slide rule dial, left lattice grill area, fold-back front, handle, BC, SW, AC/DC/battery **$80.00**

T-402, portable, plastic, right front dial, center horizontal grill bars, fold-back handle, rear crest, BC......................**$45.00**

R-615F, table, plastic, upper front half-round dial, inner circular louvers w/center crest, handle, feet, 2 knobs, BC **$40.00**
R-615G, table, plastic, upper front half-round dial, inner circular louvers w/center crest, handle, feet, 2 knobs, BC **$40.00**
S-829, tombstone, 1934, wood, raised top, lower front round dial over Deco chrome grill cut-outs, 4 knobs, 7 tubes **$295.00**
SF-177E, console-R/P, 1959, wood, modern, inner left dial & knobs, lower pull-out phono, door, right grill area, stretcher base, BC, 7 tubes, AC...**$50.00**
Super-Zenith VII, table, 1924, mahogany, low rectangular case, front panel w/2 pointer dials, right & left storage compartments, 6 tubes, battery..**$200.00**
Super-Zenith VIII, console, 1924, mahogany, model "Super-Zenith VII" on legs, right & left storage compartments, 6 tubes, battery...**$250.00**
Super-Zenith IX, console, 1924, model "Super-Zenith VII" on legs w/built-in speaker & battery storage, 6 tubes, battery **$275.00**

T-521G, table-C, plastic, right front dial, left alarm clock, center lattice grill w/inner perforations, feet, 6 knobs, BC, AC..**$25.00**
T-545, table-R/P, 1955, plastic, large front square dial w/inner perforations, 4 knobs, lift top, inner phono, BC, 5 tubes, AC...**$40.00**
T-600 "Transoceanic," portable, 1953, black leatherette, inner multi-band slide rule dial, left lattice grill area, fold-up front, telescope antenna, handle **$80.00**
T-825, table, 1955, plastic, large center front round metal dial w/inner perforations, handle, 2 knobs, BC, FM **$40.00**
U-723, table, plastic, off-center round dial over checkered grill w/crest, feet, 3 knobs, BC, FM **$35.00**
WH, console, 1931, wood, lowboy, upper front window dial, lower cloth grill w/cut-outs, stretcher base, 3 knobs, AC **$135.00**
X-306, table, plastic, right front round dial overlaps large textured grill area, 2 knobs, switch, feet, FM, AC........................**$10.00**
Y-506L, portable, 1957, leather case w/front lattice grill & crest, side knobs, handle, BC, 5 tubes, AC/DC/battery **$30.00**

Y-513, table, plastic, right & left side knobs, large front oval checkered grill area w/center crest, fold-down handle, BC, AC/DC $30.00

Y-723, table, 1956, plastic, off-center round dial over checkered grill w/crest, handle, side knob, AM, FM $35.00

Y-724, table, 1956, plastic, off-center round dial over checkered grill w/crest, handle, side knob, AM, FM $35.00

Y-825, table, 1956, plastic, large center front round dial w/inner metal perforated grill, 2 knobs, handle, AM, FM, AC/DC $35.00

Z-316W, table, plastic, right front dial overlaps large textured grill area, feet, AM, FM...$10.00

Z-550G, table-R/P, 1957, left side dial, large front grill w/crest, 2 knobs, lift top, inner phono, handle, BC, 5 tubes, AC...$20.00

Z-615F, table, plastic, center front oval dial overlaps horizontal grill bars, feet, 2 knobs, BC, AC/DC $20.00

Z-733, table-C, 1956, plastic, step-down top, left front dial/right alarm clock over large textured grill w/center crest, AM, FM, AC $35.00

ZEPHYR
Zephyr Radio Co.,
13139 Hamilton Avenue, Detroit, Michigan

35Y12, console, 1937, walnut, upper front large round dial, lower cloth grill w/vertical bars, tuning eye, 4 knobs, BC, SW, 10 tubes...$195.00

41X6, table, 1937, walnut w/inlay, right front dial, left grill, 3 knobs, base, 5 tubes..$55.00

Radio Periodicals

Antique Radio Classified (published monthly)
by John V. Terrey
P.O. Box 2-V32
Carlisle, MA 01741

Transistor Network (published monthly)
by Marty & Sue Bunis
RR 1, Box 36
Bradford, NH 03221

Radio Clubs

The following is a list of antique radio clubs throughout the country. They are always happy to supply potential members with information about their activities and publications. The two clubs listed first are national organizations; the rest are regional.

Antique Wireless Association
P.O. Box E
Breesport, NY 14816

Antique Radio Club of America
William Dawson
300 Washington Trails
Washington, PA 15301

Alabama Historical Radio Society
4721 Overwood Circle
Birmingham, AL 35222

Antique Radio Club of Illinois
Carolyn Knipfel
RR3, 200 Langham
Morton, IL 61550

Antique Radio Club of Schenectady
Jack Nelson
915 Sherman Street
Schenectady, NY 12303

Antique Radio Collectors Club of Ft. Smith, Arkansas
Wanda Conatser
7917 Hermitage Drive
Ft. Smith, AR 72903

Antique Radio Collectors & Historians of Greater St. Louis
Gloria Juedemann
262 Churchill Ln.
Ballwin, MO 63011

Antique Radio Collectors of Ohio
Stan Kleen
200 Castle Dr.
Dayton, OH 45429

Arkansas Antique Radio Club
Tom Burgess
P.O. Box 9769
Little Rock, AR 72219

Arizona Antique Radio Club
Treasurer
8311 E. Via de Sereno
Scottsdale, AZ 85258

Belleville Area Antique Radio Club
Charles Haynes
219 W. Spring
Marissa, IL 62257

Buckeye Antique Radio and Phonograph Club
Steve Dando
4572 Mark Trail
Copley, OH 44321

California Historical Radio Society
P.O. Box 31659
San Francisco, CA 94131

North Valley Chapter, CHRS
Norm Braithwaite
P.O. Box 992443
Redding, CA 96099

Carolina Antique Radio Society
Carl Shirley
824 Fairwood Road
Columbia, SC 29209

Central New York/Northern PA Antique Radio Club
Mark Gilbert
711 Elm Street
Groton, NY 13073

Cincinnati Antique Radio Collectors
Tom Ducro
6805 Palmetto
Cincinnati, OH 45227

Colorado Radio Collectors
Larry Weide
5270 E. Nassau Circle
Englewood, CO 80110

Connecticut Area Antique Radio Collectors
Walt Buffinton
500 Tobacco Street
Lebanon, CT 06249

Delaware Valley Historic Radio Club
P.O. Box 624
Lansdale, PA 19446

Florida Antique Wireless Group
Paul Currie
Box 738
Chuluota, FL 32766

Greater Boston Antique Radio Collectors
Richard Foster
12 Shawmut Avenue
Cochituate, MA 01778

Greater New York Vintage Wireless Association
Bob Scheps
12 Garrity Avenue
Ronkonkoma, NY 11779

Hawaii Chapter/ARCA
Leonard Chung
95-2044 Waikalani Pl. C-401
Mililani, HI 96789

Houston Vintage Radio Association
P.O. Box 31276
Houston, TX 77231-1276

Hudson Valley Antique Radio and Phonograph Society
John Gramm
P.O. Box 1, Rt 207
Campbell Hall, NY 10916

Hudson Valley Vintage Radio Club
Al Weiner
507 Violet Ave.
Hyde Park, NY 12538

Indiana Historical Radio Society
725 College Way
Carmel, IN 46032

Kentucky Chapter/ARCA
Robert Dickerson
1907 Lynn Lea Road
Louisville, KY 40216-2836

Louisiana & Mississippi Gulf Coast Area
F. V. Bernauer
1503 Admiral Nelson Dr.
Slidell, LA 70461

Michigan Antique Radio Club
Jim Clark
P.O. Box 585
Okemos, MI 48864

Mid-America Antique Radio Club
Stephen Phipps
10201 W. 52nd Ter.
Shawnee Mission, KS 66203

Mid-Atlantic Antique Radio Club
Lloyd Kendall
1312 Deep Run Ln.
Reston, VA 22090

Middle Tennessee Old Radio Club
Grant Manning
Rt 2, Box 127A
Smithville, TN 37166

Mid-South Antique Radio Collectors
Ron Ramirez
811 Maple Street
Providence, KY 42450-1857

Mississippi Historical Radio & Broadcasting Society
Randy Guttery
2412 C Street
Meridian, MS 39301

Music City Vintage Radio and Phonograph Society
Wade Jessen, WSM Radio
2644 McGavock Pike
Nashville, TN 37214

Nebraska Antique Radio Collectors Club
Steve Morton
905 West First
North Platte, NE 69101

New England Antique Radio Club
P.O. Box 474
Pelham, NH 03076

New Jersey Antique Radio Club
Kathleen Flanagan
92 Joysan Terrace
Freehold, NJ 07728

Niagara Frontier Wireless Association
Gary Parzy
135 Autumnwood
Cheektowaga, NY 14227

Northland Antique Radio Club
P.O. Box 18362
Minneapolis, MN 55418

Northwest Vintage Radio Society
P.O. Box 82379
Portland, OR 97282-0379

Oklahoma Vintage Radio Collectors Club
P.O. Box 72-1197
Oklahoma City, OK 73172

Pittsburgh Antique Radio Society
Richard Harris, Jr.
407 Woodside Road
Pittsburgh, PA 15221

Puget Sound Antique Radio Association
P.O. Box 125
Snohomish, WA 98291-0125

Rhode Island Antique Radio Enthusiasts
Len Arzoomanian
61 Columbus Avenue
North Providence, RI 02911

Sacramento Historical Radio Society
P.O. Box 162612
Sacramento, CA 95816-9998

E. H. Scott Historical Society, Inc.
John Meredith
P.O. Box 1070
Niceville, FL 32588-1070

Society for the Preservation of Antique Radio Knowledge
Harold Parshall
2673 So. Dixie Drive
Dayton, OH 45409

Society of Wireless Pioneers, Inc.
Paul Dane
146 Coleen Street
Livermore, CA 94550

Southeastern Antique Radio Society
Charles Pierce
4380 E. Brookhaven Dr.
Atlanta, GA 30319

Southern California Antique Radio Society
C. Alan Smith
6368 Charing Street
San Diego, CA 92117

Southern Vintage Wireless Association
Bill Moore
3049 Box Canyon Road
Huntsville, AL 35803

South Florida Antique Radio Collectors
Victor Marett
3201 N. W. 18 Street
Miami, FL 33125

Vintage Radio & Phonograph Society
Larry Lamia
P.O. Box 165345
Irving, TX 75016

Vintage Radio Unique Society
Jerryl Sears
312 Auburndale Street
Winston-Salem, NC 27104

Western Wisconsin Antique Radio Collectors Club
Dave Wiggert
1611 Redfield Street
La Crosse, WI 54601

West Virginia Chapter, ARCA
Geoff Bourne
405-8th Avenue
St. Albans, WV 25177

Xtal Set Society
Phil Anderson
789 N. 1500 Rd.
Lawrence, KS 66049-9194

collector's guide to

NOVELTY RADIOS

Marty Bunis and Robert F. Breed
Bunis and Breed have collaborated to produce this exciting guide to novelty radios of all shapes and sizes. Color photos of over 600 radios will help you spot these finds — even the ones you didn't realize were radios!

#3881•8½x11•224 pages•PB•$18.95

Marty and Sue Bunis
The relatively new field of transistor radios is comprehensively covered in this guide by well-known radio authors Marty and Sue Bunis. Over 2,000 transistor radios are listed with complete descriptions and current values.

#3730•5½x8½•256 pages•PB•$15.95

COLLECTOR BOOKS
A Division of Schroeder Publishing Co., Inc.

P.O. Box 3009 • Paducah, KY 42002-3009

Schroeder's ANTIQUES Price Guide

. . . is the #1 best-selling antiques & collectibles value guide on the market today, and here's why . . .

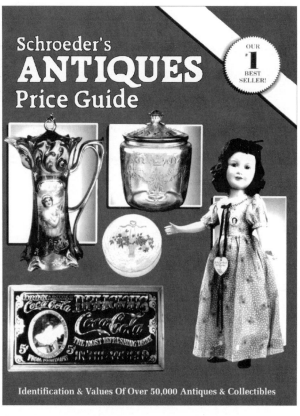

8½ x 11, 608 Pages, $12.95

• More than 300 advisors, well-known dealers, and top-notch collectors work together with our editors to bring you accurate information regarding pricing and identification.

• More than 45,000 items in almost 500 categories are listed along with hundreds of sharp original photos that illustrate not only the rare and unusual, but the common, popular collectibles as well.

• Each large close-up shot shows important details clearly. Every subject is represented with histories and background information, a feature not found in any of our competitors' publications.

• Our editors keep abreast of newly developing trends, often adding several new categories a year as the need arises.

If it merits the interest of today's collector, you'll find it in *Schroeder's*. And you can feel confident that the information we publish is up to date and accurate. Our advisors thoroughly check each category to spot inconsistencies, listings that may not be entirely reflective of market dealings, and lines too vague to be of merit. Only the best of the lot remains for publication.

Without doubt, you'll find
SCHROEDER'S ANTIQUES PRICE GUIDE
the only one to buy for
reliable information and values.

COLLECTOR BOOKS
A Division of Schroeder Publishing Co., Inc.